The Empire Stops Here

The Empire Stops Here

A Journey along the Frontiers
of the Roman World

PHILIP PARKER

JONATHAN CAPE
LONDON

To Tania and Livia

Published by Jonathan Cape 2009

2 4 6 8 10 9 7 5 3

First published in Great Britain in 2009 by
Jonathan Cape
Random House
20 Vauxhall Bridge Road
London SW1V 2SA
www.rbooks.co.uk

Addresses for companies within The Random House Group Limited can be found at:
www.randomhouse.co.uk/offices.htm

The Random House Group Limited Reg. No. 954009
www.randomhouse.co.uk

A CIP catalogue record for this book is available from the British Library

ISBN 9780224077880

The Random House Group Limited supports The Forest Stewardship Council (FSC),
the leading international forest certification organisation. All our titles that are printed
on Greenpeace approved FSC certified paper carry the FSC logo.
Our paper procurement policy can be found at
www.rbooks.co.uk/environment

Typeset by Palimpsest Book Production Ltd,
Grangemouth, Stirlingshire

Printed and bound in Great Britain by
Clays Ltd, St Ives plc

Contents

The Roman Empire to AD 211

Roman Empire to 100 BC
Added to Empire by AD 14
Added to Empire by AD 96
Added to Empire by AD 211
Client kingdoms
Borders, AD 211
Legionary base

Part of Moesia Inferior, 106–118

Frisia, Roman-held, 12 BC–AD 28

Raetian Wall

Antonine Wall annexed, 138–161

Hadrian's Wall

Fossatum Africae

1 Banat, Roman-held, 106–118

Caspian Sea

Euphrates

Tigris

PARTHIA *(temporary annexation under Trajan)*

ARMENIA

OSRHOENE

MESO-POTAMIA

Antioch

SYRIA COELE

CILICIA

SYRIA PHOENICE

Tyre

SYRIA PALAESTINA

ARABIA

CAPPADOCIA

PONTUS

GALATIA

LYCIA & PAMPHYLIA

CYPRUS

AEGYPTUS

Nile

Alexandria

BOSPORAN KINGDOM

Black Sea

ASIA

Ephesus

CRETE

CYRENE

MOESIA INFERIOR

DACIA

MOESIA SUPERIOR

THRACIA

Byzantium

MACEDONIA

EPIRUS

ACHAEA

PANNONIA INFERIOR

DALMATIA

SICILIA

Mediterranean Sea

Leptis Magna

PANNONIA SUPERIOR

NORICUM

RAETIA

GERMANIA INFERIOR

GERMANIA SUPERIOR

Danube

Augusta Treverorum

Rhine

BELGICA

ALPES

ITALIA

Rome

Carthage

AFRICA

NUMIDIA

LUGDUNENSIS

AQUITANIA

NARBONENSIS

TARRACONENSIS

Tarraco

MAURETANIA CAESARIENSIS

BRITANNIA

Atlantic Ocean

LUSITANIA

BAETICA

MAURETANIA TINGITANA

INTRODUCTION

limes – frontier   *limites* – the frontiers

An invisible thread connects Carlisle and the Lowlands of Scotland with Hungary, Syria, southern Egypt, Libya and Morocco. A traveller can journey from Newcastle to Cologne, Budapest, Amman and Rabat without once crossing beyond the bounds of this line. This bond is not some Euro-enthusiast's vision of the future, but a common history as frontier regions of the Roman Empire. It is here, at the limits of its territory, that such an empire can speak to us most directly and most poignantly. It is here, along the vast length of its frontier, that I have chosen to investigate the complex entity that was Rome. I have concentrated deliberately on the edge of the Roman world, on the lands that promised victory, booty and glory and yet so often left the bitter taste of compromise or defeat instead. Here, unique societies developed, distinct from that of the mother-city, but which were still intimately influenced by the central authorities' determination of their laws, minting of their money and stationing of their garrisons to ensure internal security and fend off depredations from outsiders.

Rome is familiar and at the same time alien. Its history and heritage loom large in European and European-influenced cultures. But for all Rome's size, longevity and an impressive array of gods, poets, emperors and soldiers, our understanding of it is at best fragmentary. Hadrian's Wall, Julius Caesar, Antony and Cleopatra, Claudius, Attila the Hun: all these have entered our shared culture. Yet how exactly do those familiar characters fit into the vast canvas of Roman time and space? What evidence survives to bring them out of the shadows of myth into a historical world that is the lineal ancestor of our own? How did Rome come to conquer such an enormous territory, and where and why did its expansion halt and fold in upon itself to leave a joint legacy for the citizens of more than thirty modern countries? What is that legacy and how powerfully does it survive, both physically and cultur-ally? These are the questions this book seeks to answer.

If the Roman Empire had survived until today, it would constitute the seventh-largest country in the world, at some 6.5 million square kilometres approaching the area of Australia or Brazil. At their height, Rome's frontiers stretched approximately 10,000 kilometres, almost double the distance from London to New York. The span of time that Roman history covers is just as enormous: more than 2,000 years separate the city's traditional foundation date of 753 BC from the fall of Constantinople, its second capital, in AD 1453 (and the loss of its very last territories within a decade of that).

Rome had humble beginnings; the account of its foundation by Romulus marks the establishment of a small settlement occupying just one of the city's seven hills.[1] For four centuries thereafter, the future superpower struggled for its very survival in the face of invasions from neighbouring Latin tribes,[2] who were just as eager as the Romans for plunder and land into which they could expand. Yet by 200 BC, Roman legions had crushed the armies of their most dangerous opponent, the Carthaginian general Hannibal, and carried their eagle standards throughout the western Mediterranean. By the time of Julius Caesar, Roman forces had broken Gaul and in 55 BC crossed the English Channel to give the Britons a bloody nose.[3] Rome's rise was by now irresistible. The pace did not slacken, and one by one the neighbouring kingdoms fell into its grasp. By around AD 117, under the emperors Vespasian, Domitian and Trajan, yet another string of territories had been subdued: parts of modern Switzerland and Germany; Dacia; Armenia and Mesopotamia. As the legions advanced and more and more territory fell under Roman dominion, there was almost no concept of a frontier. The Roman emperors claimed the whole world as theirs by right. Certain parts of it they did not occupy merely because it was not profitable to do so.

In one sense, the Roman Empire had a series of 'frontiers', each one established at the time of a conquest and then rendered redundant when the line of control moved forward, a process that began at the very start of the city of Rome's existence and carried on until the furthest extent of the Empire's control, then going by stages into reverse until Rome itself fell in 476.

Rome's first frontier was the *pomerium*, by tradition the line that Romulus marked out with a plough as he demarcated the area that would belong to his new foundation. That Rome would long have trouble along its frontiers was tragically foretold by the action of his brother Remus, who leapt over the perimeter in a fit of jealousy that the new city was not being established on a site chosen by him, and was promptly murdered by Romulus. The *pomerium* was marked out by boundary stones – the oldest of which date from the 1st century AD. This boundary, and there-fore the ceremonial area of the city into which serving generals and foreign sovereigns could not enter, and within which the dead could not be interred, was extended several times, by the dictator Sulla in 80 BC,[4] for instance, as well as under the emperors Claudius (AD 41–54) and Vespasian (69–79), expansions often intended to mirror (and magnify) a real enlargement of the Empire.[5]

Yet ultimately the pace of expansion slackened, the emperors grew wary of the ambitions of successful generals, and advance legionary camps became permanent garrisons. Static defences were constructed to mark the edge of the Empire and to keep a watchful eye on the unsubdued tribes and kingdoms beyond. Instead of new provinces to be subdued, the lands beyond the frontier – known indifferently as *barbaricum* – became the domain of barbarian tribes and the source of occasional terrifying and devastating incursions into imperial territory. This turning away from an automatic assumption that the Empire would expand unceasingly had begun even under Augustus, who according to Tacitus advised his heir (Tiberius) to 'keep the empire within its boundaries'.[6] This did not, however, stop the imperially favoured poet Virgil from including the formula 'To the Romans I set no boundaries in space or time' in his great epic *The Aeneid*.[7] Perhaps it was the disas-trous defeat by the Germans at the Battle of Teutoberger Wald in AD 9 – which caused the loss of three legions – that soured Augustus's early enthusiasm for territorial aggrandisement. In any case, the acqui-sitions under his successors were on a lesser scale, save for an attempted grab of the whole of Mesopotamia by Trajan.

Exactly what the Romans meant by the word *limes* (or *limites* in the plural) becomes a much more germane point once those frontiers solidified. It is the term generally used by modern historians (and archae-ologists) to denote the boundaries of the Empire and, more specifically, those that were actively defended by a series of fixed fortifications or a network of fortified cities. In truth, its earliest use seems to have referred to a military road, normally employed either as an avenue of penetra-tion into new territory or as a means by which to safeguard rapid communications just behind the frontier. Only in the 1st to 3rd centuries AD does the word come to refer to the general land frontier of the Empire, though not in the modern sense of lines on a map that separ-ate sharply delineated areas of political control. In the later Empire, from the 4th century, its meaning changed once more to denote a fron-tier area, rather than the frontier itself, and the territory commanded by a *dux*, a late-Roman category of military officer.[8] What it never seems

The Later Roman Empire, 284–565

Territory lost before reign of Diocletian
Empire under Diocletian, 284–307
Provinces under Diocletian
Territory evacuated by Diocletian

Tigris
Euphrates

Antioch
Tyre
Nile
Syene

Black Sea

Byzantium
(Constantinople)
Ephesus
Alexandria

Danube

Mediterranean Sea

Leptis Magna

Colonia Agrippinensis (Cologne)
Mogontiacum (Mainz)
Augusta Treverorum (Trier)
Rhine
Londinium
Lutetia

Aquileia
Rome
Massilia

Carthage

Tarraco

Corduba

Tingis

Atlantic Ocean

—— Empire at the accession of Justinian, 527

–– –– Conquests under Justinian, to 565

to have referred to is the system of fortifications itself, precisely the usage that most modern historians have, for convenience, taken up.

The influence of the frontier stretched both ways, beyond the Empire and backwards into its interior. The Romans maintained outposts and fortresses in areas that would conventionally be regarded as 'beyond' the Empire (as, for example, at Divitia-Deutz in modern Cologne) and they arrogated to themselves the right to operate in *barbaricum* whenever they felt it in their interests to do so. Only with the Persian Empire, the most politically and militarily potent of Rome's neighbours, were treaties made that actually delimited the frontier and laid down regulations about contacts along it and where fortifications might be permitted to be built by each side.[9] Even if they did not, strictly speaking, lie directly upon the boundary itself, the principal cities in those provinces situated along the *limes* were strongly influenced by their proximity to the frontier. The legions that provided the Empire's principal military strike forces were often garrisoned some way back from the frontier itself, allowing them to move to wherever they were needed, rather than watching impotently as barbarian forces bypassed the frontier positions themselves.

Because of the Romans' own rather elastic notion of what a 'frontier' actually was, I have chosen to look at the history of the Roman frontier provinces, rather than the actual line of the border, whatever that might be determined to be. This allows a certain amount of flexibility regarding the actual date of the frontiers to be examined. In general I have chosen the maximum extension of the Empire, wherever it reached in any particular area, as long as the occupation was more than ephemeral. In North Africa, this includes the advancement of the *limes* towards the desert fringes under Septimius Severus (193–211), whilst in Britain it permits an examination of the occupation of the Scottish Lowlands under Antoninus Pius (138–61) and the building of the Antonine Wall, more than 150 kilometres north of the 'traditional' border along Hadrian's Wall. At the same time, it excludes treatment of the conquests by Trajan of the 'provinces' of Assyria and Mesopotamia in 115–17, on the grounds that they revolted and broke away from the Empire almost as soon as the Emperor returned from his campaigning there.

The question of exactly why the Roman frontiers ended up where they did, and whether there was a self-conscious policy on the part of Roman leaders towards them, has taxed historians almost ever since.[10] The apparent predilection for river frontiers where they were practicable seems to be one factor, for in Europe the *limes* came to occupy the line of the Rhine and the Danube, along much of their length. The campaigns in Germany under Augustus up until the Teutoberger Wald debacle may well have been aimed at extending the Empire's border to run along the Elbe. In the east the Euphrates, and to a lesser extent the Tigris, formed a similar role in demarcating the frontier with the Persian Empire. Although not ideal defensive positions, rivers did form barriers that could only be crossed at certain favourable locations (unless, as was the case in 405–6 with the Rhine, the river actually froze, permitting barbarians to cross over in uncontrollable numbers). They also acted as convenient arteries for trade, a vital advantage in an era when land transportation was costly and slow, and the need to supply large numbers of troops stationed in fixed positions made the rivers or their near vicinity obvious places to build forts to house them.[11]

In North Africa, and indeed in Britain, there was no such obvious river line, and in the case of the former it was the desert that formed a barrier into which the Romans did not, on the whole, cross. Oasis positions such as Bu Ngem and Ghadames in Libya or Castellum Dimmidi in Algeria were garrisoned, but here local conditions permitted the stationing of troops, and there was the added advantage that dominating the water sources meant that the routes along which local tribes could penetrate without risking severe hardship from thirst were already controlled by the Romans. To proceed any further would have meant difficulties in supplying their own forces and, in the case of permanent occupation, would have left an unfriendly environmental belt behind the frontier, which could not undergo the type of economic development or support the building of the network of towns that characterised most Roman provinces.

In Britain, the Highland zone posed a similar – if less daunting – ecological barrier to advancement. Although there would have been a certain logic in occupying the whole of the island of Britain, it was something the Romans came close to, but never quite achieved.[12] Once the resources available to the governors diminished, it never seemed worth the trouble to risk the security of the province to the south in an effort to absorb such mountainous regions that promised little in the way of plunder or produce.

That things were not always so simple is indicated by the case of Germany, where, as early as the reign of Vespasian, the Romans began to creep forward from the lines of the Danube and the Rhine, in part to find positions that would plug the hole where those two rivers do not quite meet in the north-east of modern Switzerland. Yet the final advance of just thirty kilometres under Antoninus Pius left an impressively straight 100-kilometre-long stretch of frontier, but one far removed from the original river line. Here, too, the environment may have played a part, for the heavily forested areas of the German interior offered little in the way of obvious economic benefit and had no tradition of urban culture such as even the hilltop *oppida* (fortified settlements) of Celtic Gaul had presented to Julius Caesar. In the absence of any central authority, the conquest of the German tribes was a will-o'-the-wisp. Once one leader had been beaten, his followers simply melted away into the forests, only for a new war chieftain to emerge elsewhere.

A debate has raged amongst historians since the 1970s as to whether the Romans in fact had a 'Grand Strategy' towards the question of expansion and how best to defend their frontiers. Sparked by Edward Luttwak's *The Grand Strategy of the Roman Empire* (published in 1976), discussion has centred on his thesis that there was a self-conscious and deliberate change of stance after the early phase of expansion. According to Luttwak, this developed into a middle situation of 'forward defence' whereby a maximum of resources was stationed at the frontier. This was then modified, under the uncontainable pressure of barbarians pushing against the borders, to a strategy of 'defence in depth' in which the rigidity of a fixed line held against all-comers was replaced by a deep network of positions extending far back into the frontier, where the intruders would become entangled and finally retreat.[13]

Yet to search for consistency in policy over such a vast period of time is probably fruitless. Doubtless individual emperors understood something of the nature of the challenges facing the Empire and deliberately initiated policies to address them. Thus, it is clear that Hadrian adopted a more defensive stance than his predecessors and did order the building of a set of fixed barriers. He also travelled far more extensively than previous rulers and so, presumably, gained more of an understanding of the real situation on the imperial frontiers than an emperor such as Tiberius, who rarely strayed from the environs of Rome when in power.

However, the Romans lacked the intelligence resources to predict the routes and strengths of the waves of barbarians that crashed against the frontiers from the later 2nd century.[14] Responses to these tended to be reactive and localised. Once a problem had arisen, it had to be solved, but it was rarely foreseen, with a solution devised to head it off. Whilst the rulers of the Roman Empire may well, therefore, have been constantly reassessing their options in the light of events, this hardly amounts to a 'Grand Strategy'. Major initiatives such as the conquest of Britain by Claudius in AD 43 scarcely amount to a strategy at all, conditioned more by the need to demonstrate military prowess and acquire glory than by any desire to promote the security or well-being of the Empire – in fact, Caligula's annexation of a large stretch of North Africa in AD 40 seems to have been prompted by a fit of pique at the dress sense of his cousin, King Ptolemy of Mauretania.[15]

Hadrian ordered the building of his eponymous wall across northern Britain in the early part of the 2nd century AD, and though it was perhaps intended to control movement rather than act as a solid barrier, the fortified Wall has since become an apt symbol of the increasing defensiveness of Rome. In Germany, too, watchtowers were reinforced at this time with more permanent and forbidding obstacles. And then, as if the very fear of retreat had summoned up its own genie, the pace of barbarian pressure against the frontiers increased. The catalogue of barbarian invasions grows ever more dense in the 3rd century, although it is hard to determine which, for example, of the ten recorded incursions between 253 and 298 gravely threatened the security of the Empire.[16] A series of civil wars and a revolving-door procession of short-lived rulers also seriously undermined it, and it was doubtless this weakness that contributed to the Romans' increasing inability to see off the barbarians. Decius was killed in battle against the Goths in 251 – the first emperor to die in combat against an enemy – and in 263 the Romans withdrew from a province in Europe for the first time, when they abandoned the Agri Decumates (part of modern Germany and Switzerland). Dacia (modern Romania) was similarly evacuated soon afterwards, and it was only under Aurelian in the 270s that a sense of equilibrium was restored. The historian Ammianus Marcellinus described the threatening barbarian invasions of this period as 'like a river which had burst its barriers'.[17] The barbarians did not go away, pressed from behind by yet more distant tribes, and in the end the *limes* proved untenable.

At the conclusion of the 3rd century, chastened by its close call in the turmoil of the preceding half-century, the Empire reinvented itself. Although some of his predecessors had undertaken reforms dictated by the desperate necessity of pressing crises, Diocletian (284–305) implemented more wholesale changes. Everything from the central administration to the army, the taxation systems and the long-standing organisation of provinces was modified, resulting, on balance, in a more centralised structure, with more resources immediately available to the Emperor to help him impose his will. In contrast, the government of the early Empire had been largely a matter of the *amici* ('friends') of the Emperor operating in a largely informal system with relatively few bureaucrats, who were in any case principally imperial slaves or freedmen.[18]

Although the process was not entirely straightforward – few of the 'simple' notions about the Roman Empire ever are – Diocletian broadly speaking doubled the number of provinces that the Empire had previously possessed. Thus Britain, which had beforehand been divided into two provinces, Britannia Inferior and Superior,[19] now had four provinces: Britannia Prima, Britannia Secunda, Maxima Caesariensis and Flavia Caesariensis. The resources available to the governors of each of these four provinces, most particularly the local garrison, were thus divided and diminished, so the danger of an overmighty governor recruiting a few of his neighbours and assembling a force that might overthrow the Emperor himself – an occurrence that had become disturbingly commonplace in the 3rd century – was largely removed. The number of bureaucrats necessary to service all these new governors was multiplied by the grouping of several provinces into a diocese, each supervised by a vicar. Thus the Diocese of Africa, which included modern Tunisia, much of Algeria and parts of Libya, comprised the provinces of Zeugitana, Byzacena, Mauretania Caesariensis, Numidia and Tripolitania. In turn, the dioceses were grouped together into praetorian prefectures (generally one for Gaul, including Spain and Britain; one for Italy, including most of North Africa; one for Illyricum, essentially much of the Balkans; and one for the remainder of the Eastern Empire).[20] For the sake of simplicity, I have largely ignored these new provincial boundaries and titles from the reforms of Diocletian, and my chapter divisions reflect earlier usage.

The office of prefect, which had previously designated the supreme army officer of the Empire, was now shorn of its military responsibilities and instead the praetorian prefect became a sort of bureaucratic supremo and, until the later 5th century, theoretically the most important person in the Empire after the Emperor himself. Despite this great increase in administrative personnel, the Empire still had relatively few officials compared to a modern state, and never aspired to the provision of services such as universal education or health-care. Even in the judicial field, much later Roman legislation – such as the setting of tariffs payable by litigants – had as much to do with rationing access to justice through the establishment of financial barriers as with any notion of equity for all.[21]

Even the government of the Later Roman Empire, with its uniformed corps of officials able to extend the reach of the authorities to an extent that had been inconceivable earlier, was not an efficient beast. Policies and laws determined at the centre were often watered down to the point of ineffectiveness by the time they reached the provinces, and even resorting to officials who lay outside the normal structures, such as the *agentes in rebus* – who acted almost as a secret police service in the Later Empire – only marginally increased the Emperor's ability to know what was actually going on in the vast territory over which he ruled. At the frontiers, this problem was magnified by distance; even employing the comparatively speedy journey times permitted by transit along the rivers, it could take a minimum of eleven days to get from southern Germany (near Ulm) to Sirmium (in modern Serbia),[22] while imperial rulings issued in Milan in the 4th century took somewhere between two and ten weeks to travel just as far as Rome. The lag between order and implementation could sometimes have near-comic effects. In AD 40 the Emperor Caligula sent a letter to Publius Petronius, then governor of Syria, ordering him to commit suicide; fortunately it took more than three months to reach him, and by the time it did, the governor already had in his hands another letter that informed him of Caligula's assassination in January 41. Under such circumstances it was extremely difficult, and ultimately pointless, to try to micromanage the border provinces.

The frontier, as established by the time of Trajan, links important places whose Roman provenance can only be guessed at in their current guise – Colonia Agrippinensis (Cologne), which hosted the Roman Rhine fleet; Mogontiacum (Mainz); Vindobona (Vienna), where the Emperor Marcus Aurelius died; Aquincum (Budapest), with its twin military and civilian amphitheatres; Naissus (Niš), which was so comprehensively destroyed by Attila the Hun that a Roman army had to camp outside its walls in a field filled with human bones; and Singidunum (Belgrade), which began life as a legionary camp; and other more brooding ruins, such as Volubilis (in Morocco), Leptis Magna (in Libya) and Petra (in Jordan). After the fall of the Empire, these cities and provinces went their separate ways, but all had shared the rule of Rome for centuries. Their common heritage cries out for recognition.

Roman emperors did not have the luxury, as we have, of looking at the extent of their empire and the course of the *limes* on precisely drawn maps, with towns and forts carefully marked out by neat squares and circles. The Romans were inveterate surveyors, carefully dividing out the land on which they intended to establish cities into neat squares. Yet the skills of the *agrimensores*, the men who performed this task (and equally, the division of the countryside around the towns, establishing the boundaries between segments with stones), were not put to similar use in mapping the Empire. The Romans, when they put their minds to cartography, thought in terms of 'Itineraries', or depictions of routes, showing the distances between stages on a journey rather than a topographically accurate representation of the terrain. The most famous of these, known as the Peutinger Table (or Tabula Peuteringiana),[23] is a medieval copy of a probably late-4th- or early-5th-century original. It is made up of a roll around 7 metres long and 34 centimetres wide, depicting more than 110,000 kilometres of roads, and showing 6,000 marked distances between towns, fort and *mutationes* (stations of the *cursus publicus* or public post).

More than 500 locations are decorated with miniature depictions of towns or other places of interest, which, in the case of the major cities of the Roman world, such as Rome, Constantinople and Antioch (Antakya), are quite elaborate. With its muted colours and stretched-out representation of the Roman provinces, the Peutinger Table forms an attractive mainstay of museums the entire length and breadth of the frontier. That it was not unique is indicated by another source, the *Antonine Itinerary*, a purely written (as opposed to visual) set of routes throughout the Empire, probably dating from the early 3rd century, which may have been prepared for use by the Emperor Caracalla himself.

The Peutinger Table has in particular provided an invaluable treasure trove of information for archaeologists and historians seeking to establish the names (and sometimes the locations) of Roman sites that are not otherwise attested in literary sources. Another equally useful resource (if not, strictly speaking, a map or an itinerary) is the *Notitia Dignitatum*, a list of principal office-holders, both civil and military, in the eastern and western portions of the Empire, together with the junior officials they supervised or the troops they commanded. It has a complex history: probably drawn up around 395, after which its eastern and western portions were then kept up to date haphazardly, with the western section being revised until about 408.[24] As well as information on the deployment of the late-Roman army – if the *Notitia* can be believed to portray this accurately, rather than promote a bureaucratic theory that was not reflected in reality – it also contains priceless indications of the names of garrison stations in the early 5th century. Information contained in it (and in more localised sources) assisted historians and archaeologists in determining the correct names of the forts along Hadrian's Wall, where the names were either not recorded at all by contemporary writers or were referred to in an ambiguous fashion.

By the time of the *Notitia*, the Empire had changed dramatically from the beast it had been at the time of Augustus, the first emperor. The reforms of Diocletian in the late 3rd century had been followed by an equally portentous transformation under Constantine I, who by the Edict of Milan in 313 decreed the toleration of Christianity in the Empire.[25] The urban topography of the Empire now began to shift, with rich benefactors, where they still existed, giving money for the construction of churches rather than temples or theatres, and the bishops emerging as powerful alternative power bases in the cities. Over time, the politics of the Christian Church, and struggles over who was to command obedience within it, began to overshadow power plays over the army and the central administration itself.

For all its success in weathering storms that would have destroyed any lesser state, the Roman Empire's frontiers began to leak badly in the 4th century, and by the early 5th century barbarian groups had come to be established permanently within what had formerly been the borders, many of them as *foederati* claiming a treaty relationship that permitted their otherwise troubling transgression. From the end of the 4th century the Empire's survival was further compromised by its division into eastern and western portions, in theory still part of one unit, but in practice pretty much looking after their respective interests. The last Roman emperors in the West fought vainly to stabilise the situation, with resources progressively compromised by each loss of territory and the destruction of previously productive cities. Once the Vandals became established in North Africa in 429 and the precious grain supply that its provinces had provided to Italy was lost, the game was nearly up. The Western Empire staggered on for nearly fifty years until what was in effect a military *coup d'état* by the Germanic majority in the army over-threw the last emperor in 476. Yet the Eastern Empire survived, and under Justinian (527–65) even managed to reconquer many of the lost provinces in the West, before these ephemeral successes were in turn swept away by another series of crises and invasions as the Lombards, the Avars and then – inspired by the new religion of Islam – the Arabs rolled back the tide of the Byzantine advance.

Although Byzantium[26] – the term by which historians generally refer to the Eastern Empire after the late 5th century – recovered, and indeed flourished once more, only portions of the old *limes*, in eastern Anatolia and along the Danube, remained. In general, where the Roman history of an area had not ended earlier – through its conquest by Germanic or Slav invaders – I have taken the Arab invasions of the 7th century as the point beyond which I will not trace its history. In travelling along the frontier all the way from Bowness-on-Solway in the north of England to Volubilis in Morocco, I have encountered more than five centuries of Roman history, in some twenty-one modern countries, covering a range of climatic variations from a snowstorm in Switzerland to a sandstorm at forty-five degrees Centigrade in Egypt's Dakhleh Oasis, and have covered more than 20,000 kilometres on the ground. Through all this astonishing variation, the staggering fact is that the Roman Empire and its *limes* endured for centuries, where many modern states have barely held on to their conquests for decades. Along the frontier a vibrant and unique culture grew up, which has bequeathed to us many towns and cities that still thrive today and, even where they do not, a legacy of some of the most beautiful and inspiring ruins in the world. In this sense Rome, and more especially its frontiers, are truly eternal.

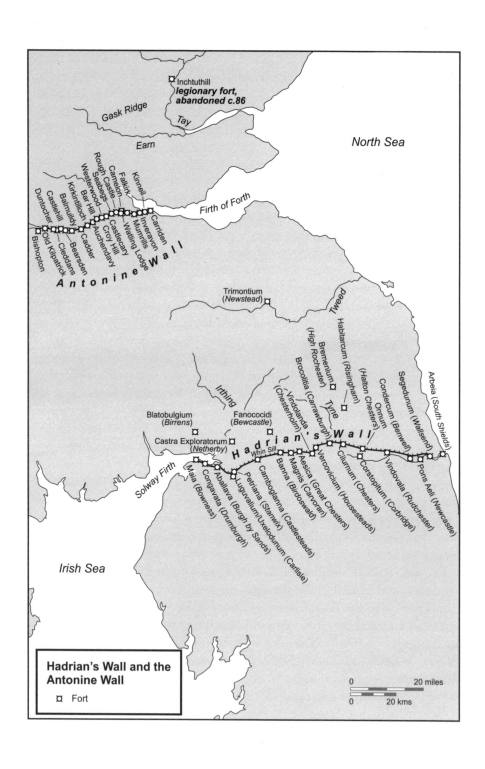

Inchtuthill
legionary fort, abandoned c.86

Gask Ridge

Tay

Earn

North Sea

Kinneil
Rough Castle
Camelon
Westerwood
Seabegs
Falkirk
Castlecary
Croy Hill
Auchendavy
Bar Hill
Kirkintilloch
Balmuildy
Cadder
Castlehill
Bearsden
Cleddans
Duntocher
Old Kilpatrick
Bishopton

Inveravon
Mumrills
Watling Lodge
Carriden

Firth of Forth

A n t o n i n e   W a l l

Irish Sea

Trimontium
(Newstead)

Tweed

Habitancum *(Risingham)*
Bremenium *(High Rochester)*
Brocolitia *(Carrawburgh)*
Vindolanda *(Chesterholm)*
Onnum *(Halton Chesters)*
Condercum *(Benwell)*
Segedunum *(Wallsend)*
Arbeia *(South Shields)*

Blatobulgium *(Birrens)*

Fanococidi *(Bewcastle)*

Irthing

Castra Exploratorum *(Netherby)*

Whin Sill

H a d r i a n ' s   W a l l

Solway Firth

Maia *(Bowness)*
Congavata *(Drumburgh)*
Aballava *(Burgh by Sands)*
Luguvallium/Uxelodunum *(Carlisle)*
Petriana *(Stanwix)*
Camboglanna *(Castlesteads)*
Banna *(Birdoswald)*
Magnis *(Carvoran)*
Aesica *(Great Chesters)*
Vercovicium *(Housesteads)*
Cilurnum *(Chesters)*
Corstopitum *(Corbridge)*
Vindovala *(Rudchester)*
Pons Aeli *(Newcastle)*

Tyne

**Hadrian's Wall and the
Antonine Wall**

¤ Fort

| 0 | 20 miles |
| 0 | 20 kms |

CHAPTER I

Britannia

The hard road goes on and on – and the wind sings through your helmet-plume – past altars to Legions and Generals forgotten, and broken statues of Gods and Heroes, and thousands of graves where the mountain foxes and hares peep at you . . . Just when you think you are at the world's end, you see a smoke from East to West as far as the eye can turn, and then, under it, also as far as the eye can stretch, houses and temples, shops and theatres, barracks and granaries, trickling along like dice behind – always behind – one long, low, rising and falling, and hiding and showing line of towers. And that is the Wall!
Rudyard Kipling, *Puck of Pook's Hill*[1]

In truth it seems more like an ending than a beginning, the estuary of the Solway Firth wide and tranquil, the sun bouncing off the lazily drifting water, giving a rare sparkle and hint of the Mediterranean in this northern clime. The broad beach is backed by a thick strip of grass and a clump of swaying trees, its mud-water trails winding aimlessly towards a small headland. Across the water, in Scotland, four factory chimneys break the otherwise picture-pretty panorama of fields punctuated by a few low houses. This enticing, if unexceptional, landscape marks the beginning of Hadrian's Wall, one of the defining achievements of Roman military engineering.

For sure, Roman defence works of one kind or another continued on westwards and snaked round the coast of Cumbria to reach Lancashire,[2] but it is here that the Wall, as conceived and ordered by Hadrian, reached its westernmost point. It has impressed scholars, travellers and tourists for centuries, and its magnificent state of preservation – at least in its central section, striking straight and unyielding across crags and low ground alike – has served to awe, but has at the same time bedevilled our understanding of the nature of the Roman frontier. For it is tempting to think that such a linear barrier was intended as a definitive line to be held at all costs against potential invaders, who, suitably cowed, would lurk on their 'barbarian' side of the line, never to be admitted to the Roman 'civilised' side. Unfortunately, both the historical development of the Wall and its engineering give the lie to this oversimplified view. In fact the Wall most probably served as a mix of imperial propaganda – which, in view of its fame close to 2,000 years later, must be judged a success – and a means of economic control.[3]

The answer to exactly how the frontier came to be here lies in the nature of the Roman conquest of Britain. The island had first come into the sights of Rome in 55 BC, when Julius Caesar, flush from having subjugated the best part of Gaul in a freelance campaign that brought him enormous glory and caused not inconsiderable chagrin to his senatorial adversaries, decided that a sally across the 'Ocean' that traditionally marked the end of the world might add a little something to his already sky-high reputation. Although he returned in 54 BC and won a series of encounters with the rather disunited Britons, a revolt in Gaul the next year diverted his attention, after which the greater call of power politics on the central Roman stage meant that he never returned to the frankly rather peripheral island. Yet he may well have made some kind of treaty arrangement with British chiefs, and the expectation really must have been that his successes were a preliminary to the organisation in short order of Britain as a properly constituted Roman province.[4]

It took almost a hundred years for Claudius to despatch Roman arms back across the Channel and to begin the conquest of Britain in earnest. His motivation may have been the desire to win an easy victory, for his elevation to the throne had followed the murder of his nephew Caligula, and he was put forward by the praetorians, the elite imperial bodyguard, as much as a candidate who would not punish them for their involvement in the murder of his predecessor as for any perceived fitness for the job. Indeed, it was precisely his reputation as something between a drooling idiot and an academic stuck in an ivory tower that attracted them; Claudius would, they thought, be a pliable and malleable emperor, easily shaped by the interests of the faction that had promoted him.

Claudius, who was in fact nobody's fool and had feigned idiocy as a ploy to prevent his volatile nephew from having him assassinated, was badly in need of some martial achievements to bolster his position. Landing somewhere in Kent (probably at Rutupiae,[5] modern Richborough), in the summer of AD 43, his forces[6] rapidly secured the south-east, and the Emperor himself was able to make a brief cameo appearance to bask in some of the glory.

Over the next four decades, Roman control pushed inexorably northwards and westwards, weathering on the way a revolt by Boudicca's

Iceni in the early 60s, which nearly brought the whole enterprise of Britannia to a premature end.[7] Finally, by around 74, direct Roman control reached to the edge of modern Scotland. Four years later a new governor of Britannia arrived, who has, thanks to the biography written by his son-in-law Tacitus, become the most famous of them all.

Gnaeus Julius Agricola, who had previous experience in Britain,[8] was to serve an unusually long stint in the post.[9] He conducted a series of six campaigns, which projected Roman power ever further northwards, and looked set to establish the whole island of Britain as Roman territory. The campaigns can only really be followed by seeking to identify the marching camps which the Roman army built each evening as they campaigned, for the information provided by Tacitus is frustratingly imprecise and too vague to determine the exact lines of advance.

It seems, however, that by 80 the Romans had reached the estuary of the Tay, and forts were established along the line of the Forth–Clyde isthmus, the most obvious stopping point short of occupation of the Highlands. Finally, in 83, the Caledonians, the principal tribal group in the area, were pressured into standing and fighting a pitched battle, almost always a serious misjudgement on the part of Rome's barbarian enemies.

The location of this battle at 'Mons Graupius' is uncertain, but may have been somewhere north of Aberdeen.[10] The Caledonians, led by Calgacus, were roundly defeated; Agricola lured them off the high ground they had occupied by weakening his centre, which the disorganised tribesmen then rushed to envelop, leaving them vulnerable to a rout by fresh cavalry regiments that the Roman general had held in reserve. The victory had, unusually, been achieved almost entirely by auxiliary regiments; the elite legionaries had not been engaged. At any rate, some 10,000 Caledonians are said to have died, for the loss of just 360 Romans. Tacitus puts a moving and rather philosophical speech into the mouth of Calgacus after the battle. The Romans, he said, had 'made a desert and called it peace',[11] a taunt which the defeated have levelled at the victors throughout history, but which has always availed them little.

The Romans now settled in for a permanent occupation of Scotland.[12] Although Agricola was withdrawn, most probably in 84, a legionary fortress was built at Inchtuthil, on the Tay, about 25 kilometres to the north of Perth. It was probably destined to be the home of the XX Valeria Victrix legion, but a sudden change of plan altered the destiny both of the fortress and of the whole of Scotland. Some time after 86,[13] the order came to evacuate Inchtuthil, probably prompted by a crisis on the Danube, which called for fresh troops to be transferred there; the fortress was not even completed yet, for no *praetorium* (commander's house) or bathhouse has been located. When the legionaries left, they buried a huge quantity of nails – some one million in all – in an enormous pit, not wanting to cart such a weight of ironwork back south with them, but also wanting to deny the Caledonians the use of such a precious resource, which might be remanufactured into weaponry.[14]

The Romans were now left with insufficient forces to hold down the Highlands of Scotland, and the advance positions were abandoned. A line of towers that had occupied the Gask Ridge, blocking incursions through the surrounding glens, was also evacuated in the early 90s. None of these positions had really constituted a linear frontier; rather they were points from which further advances could be made, and now that any movement forward was not in prospect, the search began for a more sustainable set of strong-points further south. Tacitus sniffily notes that the complete conquest of Britain had in effect been achieved and then allowed to slip away.[15]

The exact stages by which this gradual retreat took place are obscure, but by the end of it, early in the reign of Trajan (98–117), most of the Roman conquests north of the Solway–Tyne isthmus had been abandoned, save for a series of forts, such as Trimontium (Newstead), which acted as outposts in territory that was presumably still notionally allied to the Romans and over which some level of supervision had to be exercised. Trajan's need for troops to carry out his own wars against the Dacians in 101–2 and in 105–6 then ensured that there would be no easy return to the north of Scotland.[16]

A Roman military road, which had been constructed during the governorship of Agricola, ran from Lugovalium, the fort at modern Carlisle in the west, to Corstopitum (Corbridge) almost at the eastern end of the isthmus. This road, which is known to historians by its name in medieval times, the Stanegate (or 'Stone Road'), now in effect became the northern frontier of Britannia. A series of other forts lay along the line,[17] built during the reign of Vespasian, Titus or Domitian,[18] sited around a day's march (or about 20 kilometres) from each other.

These posts did not form a comprehensive frontier system such as Hadrian was about to implement, but instead sat along a route that permitted easy movement of troops and rapid reinforcement. With a concentration of force not far removed from the recently evacuated territories, this enabled the Roman army to turn rapidly from a defensive posture to an offensive one, should imperial policy come to dictate it again.

In 117, Trajan died. He was succeeded by Hadrian, who had received a letter announcing his adoption by the Emperor just a day earlier, thereby making him the heir apparent. There was a great deal of gossip, possibly well founded, that Trajan had not in fact initiated the move, and that it had been concocted by a clique centred around his wife Plotina (who was rumoured to be rather too fond of the young general). In 122, Hadrian visited Britain. It was not an expedition that was widely noted by Roman historians, with only the *Historia Augusta* unambiguously reporting that 'he made for Britain, where he set many things right'.[19] There seems to have been some kind of disturbance in the province at the start of his reign and Hadrian now perhaps came to the far-flung north-west of the Empire to see for himself.[20]

Hadrian's Wall

For such a grand and showy feat of engineering, Hadrian's Wall receives curiously little notice in the sources of the time. Again, it is only the *Historia Augusta* that remarks that Hadrian 'was the first to construct a wall eighty miles in length, which was to separate barbarians and Romans'.[21] Exactly why the Emperor ordered the building of such a permanent barrier is unclear. That he was, as far as the limits of the Empire were concerned, conservative is clear, tending to preserve and reinforce what he already held, rather than hunt for new territories with rash campaigning beyond the frontiers.[22]

He had a few years previously ordered the transformation of the border area between Germania Superior and Raetia, where the gap between the Rhine and Danube rivers left an awkward and vulnerable salient. A palisade of oak posts was erected, running for hundreds of kilometres, symbolically and clearly marking the line of the frontier; the barbarians could make no mistake, or trade on any uncertainty, about where the line went.[23] Beyond that barrier, they would be trespassing on Roman territory.

In northern England, Hadrian went for an altogether more ambitious scheme. Just why Britannia ended up with a stone (or, in parts, turf) wall, when Germania had to make do with a ditch and a wooden barrier, and Raetia only got a stone wall some six decades later,[24] is not obvious. The reason may be as prosaic as the comparative scarcity of sufficient wood in northern Britannia to build a barrier similar to the one in Germania, or it could have been that the shorter stretch of frontier to be covered along the Solway–Tyne isthmus permitted a much grander and – at least for those able to see or hear of it – more prestigious structure to be attempted. Given that Hadrian was not particularly popular to begin with, since his legitimacy was suspect and his reign began with a purge of senators suspected of opposing his accession,[25] the creation of such a striking monument would have been an extremely useful symbol of his power.

The VI Victrix legion was sent north to begin work on the project. For the first 45 Roman miles,[26] the Wall was built in stone, and from the River Irthing to the Solway Firth (another 31 Roman miles) it was constructed out of turf, a decision that may have indicated that stone was less readily available along the western portion of the Wall's route. Initially, too, the plan for the eastern stone section was that it should be 3.1 metres in width and approximately 4 metres in height. The Turf Wall needed to be wider (at around 6.2 metres) to ensure its stability, and was probably just less than 4 metres high. Every (Roman) mile, a miniature fort, or 'milecastle', would be placed and in between each of these there would be two turrets. In front of the Wall, a ditch would be placed as an additional obstacle, varying in length depending on the terrain, though in some places along the Wall this feature was absent.

In the central section, the Wall incorporates the dramatic volcanic outcrop of the Whin Sill, and in general occupies vantage points offering reasonable visibility to the north. Where it does not (as in the region around Great Chesters), the planners did nothing to deviate the Wall to a more convenient route, preferring the geometric simplicity of a straight line to the more mundane advantages of being able to sight intruders before they actually arrived.

The purpose of Hadrian's Wall was almost certainly to exercise a high degree of control over the movements of those entering and leaving the Roman province; the Wall is provided with gateways at regular intervals, with travellers not having to travel more than a kilometre along the Wall at any one point to reach one,[27] not a sensible provision if it had been seen as a purely military barrier. The gates, presumably, mark the points at which those carrying goods for sale into the Roman province would have paid their tolls.

Moreover, the Wall was not intended as a platform from which to fight. Its width – around 10 Roman feet at most – would barely have permitted two armed soldiers to pass one another, and so would have made a most impracticable defensive position. In addition, at whatever point intruders might attack, it would take time for even small units to make their way from the nearest milecastle or turret; and then, should the enemy somehow not already have passed over the Wall, the confined fighting space available would mean that the Roman soliders would not be able to bring their full force to bear. That is, unless the barbarians should choose to attack at one of the forts along the Wall, a most unlikely tactic for those intent merely on quick plundering raids to the south.

The history of the Wall's construction is complex. Building probably commenced north of the existing Stanegate fort at Corstopitum (Corbridge), and one team of legionaries built eastwards towards Pons Aeli (Newcastle), while another worked their way west to the point where the Turf Wall began.[28] Although the Wall was originally planned to sit on a foundation of around 3 metres, only in the section from Newcastle to the North Tyne (known as the Broad Wall) was this actually achieved. Between that point and the Irthing, although the foundations had already been laid, the Wall was actually built to a narrower gauge of 2.4 metres (the Narrow Wall).

Initially, the only troops along the Wall line were stationed at the mile-castles and fortlets, with reinforcements, if needed, having to be summoned from the Stanegate forts to the rear. Before the construction of the barrier was completed, however, there was yet another change of plan and a decision was taken to construct new forts along the Wall itself, with a distance of around 10–14 kilometres between each of them. Eleven in all were attached to the Wall structure,[29] normally with one-third of the fort (and three gates) projecting out into *barbaricum*, an arrangement which again suggests that Roman military planners thought in terms of issuing out of the forts to face the enemy, rather than having to defend those three vulnerable gates against attack.

The Stanegate forts were rendered redundant by these new Wall forts, and were for the most part abandoned, or turned over to civilian use. The system was completed by the digging of another ditch to the rear of the Wall, known to modern archaeology as the Vallum, which may have marked out the limit of the *territorium*, the district under the direct control of the military. 'Outpost' forts were also built north of the Wall line, at Blatobulgium (Birrens) and Fanococidi (Bewcastle), an indication that, whatever the beguiling simplicity of regarding Hadrian's Wall as a fixed and rigid barrier, the Romans had no intention whatsoever of abdicating all control or freedom of manoeuvre in the territory immediately to the north of it.

Inscriptions discovered on the Wall show that the building was undertaken by detachments from all three of Britannia's legions: II Augusta, which came up from Isca (Caerleon) in Wales; XX Valeria Victrix from Deva (Chester); and VI Victrix, which was based at Eboracum (York).[30] The first season of building probably took place in 122,[31] the year of Hadrian's visit, although there would not have been time to make a great deal of progress. By 124, large sections of the Stone Wall were complete and probably all of the Turf Wall.[32] It was possibly then that the decision to bring the forts up to the line of the Wall was taken. The forts themselves, though, were still being built in the 130s, with Magnis (Carvoran) probably not being completed until 136/7. Apart from the inevitable repairs and minor improvements conducted during the life of the Wall, the final changes to the original scheme took place with the rebuilding in stone of part of the turf section late in the reign of Hadrian, and the completion of the same work in the section from milecastle 54 to Bowness around 160, under Antoninus Pius.

The effort required to complete all these works was staggering; including various outpost stations, twenty forts had to be built, together with 100 milecastles and around 200 turrets. The total amount of material required seems to have been in the region of one million cubic metres for the Stone Wall and about four-fifths of that amount for the Turf Wall.[33] When the Wall scholar Collingwood Bruce enlisted the services of Robert Rawlinson, a friendly engineer, to determine the costs of the material used, he based it on a figure of 10,000 men needed to build the Wall and dig the ditch and taking 240 days. The cost, in the mid-19th century, came out at an estimated £1,021,000, barely enough in the early 21st century to purchase a three-bedroom flat in a fashionable part of central London.[34]

The visitor hoping for visible relics of the Wall in its westernmost reaches will be disappointed, as none of the original line is to be seen in place and almost all the stones have long gone. Somewhere in the current main street of Bowness stood the fort of Maia, utterly vanished now, though the point where its internal roadways intersected stands conveniently on the site of the King's Arms pub. The nearby church of Saint Michael, however, does at least incorporate some Roman masonry within it, and these probably represent the last remains of the most westerly fort along the Wall.

Past Drumburgh, which once housed the fort of Congavata, the line of the Wall passes through Burgh-by-Sands, where Aballava stood. Here, again at the church of Saint Michael (who, as a rather militaristic archangel, is an appropriate consumer of recycled Roman army material), some Roman masonry can be seen, patches of red sandstone, presumably cannibalised from the fort and Wall. The rather imposing square tower of the church incorporates arrow slits, for this was long contested territory between England and Scotland, and the need for such defensive installations overrode any ecclesiastical admonitions to love one's neighbour.

The next fort to the east lay on a site that has prospered more since

Roman times. Indeed, Carlisle, or Luguvalium, as it was known, is one of only two main urban centres along the Wall (the other being Pons Aeli/Newcastle at the eastern extremity). A delightful cathedral city, its population of 70,000 hardly competes with other metropolises elsewhere along the Roman frontier, but it is nonetheless a stark contrast to the rural stretches along which the Wall traces its course in this westerly region. An earlier Flavian fort (called Uxelodunum) was built here, probably around 72, but it was later demolished and a new building constructed upon the mound on which now soar up the medieval battlements of Carlisle Castle. This Roman fort was still standing, at least in part, more than two centuries after the province fell from the Empire's grasp in 410, for there is a record of the Northumbrian holy man and bishop, Saint Cuthbert, visiting the place in 685.[35]

It was not just at Luguvalium that the Wall remained substantially intact at the time. The 8th-century monk Bede makes mention of it in his *Ecclesiastical History*, implying that stretches of it may still have existed on the easternmost part of its course, close to his monastery at Jarrow. Bede, though, mistakenly attributes the construction of the Wall to Septimius Severus rather than Hadrian.[36] For those living in an era in which northern England was only just emerging from the chaotic and impoverished world of the first two post-Roman centuries, the remains of the Wall must have seemed an almost impossible achievement. Nowadays, in contrast, apart from a few stones built into the structure of Carlisle Castle, it is only possible to get a real sense of the Roman achievement on the western part of the Wall at Carlisle's Tullie House Museum.

The troops that garrisoned the Wall represented the Roman military machine at the peak of its military effectiveness. In early imperial times, the Roman army overwhelmingly consisted of an annual levy of farmers who exchanged their sickles for swords each year, hoping to return home for harvest time. It was men such as these who had subdued the other peoples of the Italian peninsula, defeated Hannibal and begun the acquisition of Rome's Spanish and Balkan provinces. By the start of the 1st century BC, however, the length of time the soldiers were needed had stretched from months into years, and the civil wars of the middle of that century led to the raising of armies hugely in excess of the legion or two that had been traditional. It also led to increasing professionalisation of the army as the soldiers, and particularly the centurions (the senior NCOs), fought in campaign after campaign and came to form the backbone of a seasoned and effective fighting force.

When Augustus emerged triumphant as sole ruler of the Empire, having seen off Mark Antony and his Egyptian ally Cleopatra at the Battle of Actium in 31 BC, he commanded around eighty legions, possibly in excess of 400,000 men. The expectation, at least of those who held to the republican way of doing things, might have been that he dismiss the vast majority of these and then raise fresh troops whenever the exigencies of future campaigning should demand it. Augustus did dispense with more than half of the force – it was simply too expensive to keep them in uniform – but he retained twenty-eight permanent legions, Rome's first full standing army. The number would vary slightly over the coming centuries: three legions lost against the Germans in AD 9, a clutch cashiered in AD 70 for disloyalty,[37] two raised in Italy in 165 to act as a strategic reserve and a further three for Septimius Severus's expedition against the Parthians in the 190s. The total, however, did not vary dramatically until the shape of the whole army was modified whole-sale in the late 3rd century under external pressures with which the old system could not cope.

By the time of Hadrian, the organisation of the legions was also set out on a more formal basis than it had been in the initial years of the Empire. Every legion was numbered – although confusingly, there were often several sharing the same designation – and each had a nickname that identified it more securely, such as the V 'Alaudae' ('the larks') or, more martially, the XII 'Fulminata' ('the lightning-throwers'). Each legion was essentially an infantry force, made up of ten cohorts of 480 men, each in turn subdivided into six 'centuries' of eighty men,[38] reinforced by a small cavalry force of 120, which together with specialists and officers made a total complement of something over 5,000 soldiers.[39]

All of the men had to be Roman citizens on enlistment, and they were commanded by a legionary legate, always from the senatorial elite,[40] often an ambitious politician with at least one prior military posting. He was assisted by a subordinate tribune, normally only in his twenties but again of senatorial rank, for whom this would be his first military experience. The effective third in command was the *praefectus castrorum* (prefect of the camp), normally a long-serving senior centurion, and then beneath him five junior tribunes, the *tribuni angusticlavii*, recruited from the equestrian class (the next step down socially from the senatorial order), who were – though very much subordinate to the senatorial tribune – likely to be older than him.

The nearest legionaries to the Wall, apart from building parties or at times when active campaigning was going on, were based well back at the fortress in Eboracum (York). They were supported by a roughly equal number of auxiliaries, and it was these who made up the garrison of

Hadrian's Wall. The Romans had long recruited foreign allies to their armies, allies whose fighting styles were often well adapted to the conditions of particular terrains or campaigns. The organisation of these forces was once again regularised under Augustus. They still formed a non-citizen force, but three different types of unit were established. The cohort (*cohors*) was entirely composed of infantry and was either quingenary (480 men) or milliary (800 men). The cavalry were divided into *alae* ('wings'), each either quingenary (512 men) or milliary (768).[41] Further variation was provided by mixed units of cavalry and infantry, termed *cohortes equitatae*. Within these basic designations there was a great deal of flexibility, and units of slingsmen, archers and even, in the East, of camel-borne soldiers are recorded.[42]

Both legionaries and auxiliaries had to sign up for twenty-five years of service – the term had been twenty years early in the imperial period, but was soon extended.[43] Legionaries received a bonus on their retirement, which in AD 5 was set at some 12,000 sesterces, a sum equal to more than twelve years' salary.[44] Instead of a cash payment, the auxiliaries were awarded Roman citizenship on completing their term of service, a privilege that they could pass onto their descendants (although sons actually born during their time of service were excluded, so that they in turn would be forced to join the army if they wanted to enjoy the privilege of Roman citizenship).[45] On being discharged they were given a diploma, inscribed on leaves of bronze, which proved their right to citizenship, a copy of which was supposed to be deposited in Rome. Scores of these diplomas have been found, although representing only a fraction of those originally issued, and the fact that they also list the units and provinces from which the troops were being discharged makes them an invaluable resource for tracking the movements of auxiliary units around the Empire.

The strength of the garrison on the Wall obviously varied somewhat depending on military contingencies. After the principal Roman line of defence was pushed northwards in the 140s to the Antonine Wall on the Forth–Clyde isthmus, it dropped to virtually zero. When Hadrian's Wall was completed in about 138, however, the garrisons of the forts and milecastles represented up to 8,000 men.[46] By the 3rd century, under Septimius Severus, this number was probably somewhat lower, although by then the troops had to man a greatly reduced number of turrets and milecastles, many of which had been decommissioned. From this time, there was more stability in the units garrisoning each defensive position, and many of those attested in residence at the start of the 3rd century probably remained in place until the last years of Roman rule in Britain.

The next-door fort to Luguvalium was around 12 kilometres to the east. Petriana, now in the village of Stanwix, housed the biggest and most prestigious unit of all along the entire British frontier, the *Ala Petriana milliaria*, a 1,000-strong cavalry regiment, one of few such double-strength units anywhere in the Empire.[47] To accommodate this number of soldiers, Petriana, whose remains lie beneath yet another church of Saint Michael, was itself the largest fort on the Wall.

The terrain around it is open, ideally suited to operations by cavalry units, and, equally, more vulnerable to large-scale incursions from across the frontier than the broken-up, undulating and craggy sections further to the east. It has also, sadly, militated against the survival of much of the Wall, for the robbing of stones was considerably easier in this area, where the settlements in which they could be reused were much closer at hand.

It is only after a nearly 20-kilometre hike from Stanwix east to Hare Hill that the first extant section of the Wall appears, up a pleasant tree-shaded rise and behind a fine beech hedge. It is also, by chance, the highest section on the whole north-British frontier. Rising up in the shape of an omega truncated at one side, this chunk gives some sense of the scale on which the entire Wall would originally have appeared. Yet it seems strangely domesticated in this tranquil setting, a secret that has integrated itself into the landscape, hidden far away from its military purpose. The facing stones that concealed the rubble core are not the original ones, having been replaced by others found here and there along the Wall by restorationists in the 19th century, enthusiasts who were rather keener on the effect than the authenticity of their work, and who additionally re-erected the upper courses of the Hare Hill section, which had long since fallen into ruin.

The Wall, indeed, has long attracted the interest of antiquarians, being one of the structures that first sparked off real interest in Britain's Roman heritage in the 16th century. Hare Hill was remarked upon by one of the most notable of them all, William Hutton, who in 1802 noted, 'I viewed this relick with admiration. I saw no part higher . . . Near this place the Wall is five feet high.'[48]

From Hare Hill it is less than a kilometre east to the first surviving turret at Banks – denominated as 52a, according to the generally accepted numbering system[49] – set beside a little lay-by off the main road. Wings of the Wall head off from either side of the small square turret, recon-structed to around a metre in height, but the main feature of interest is a huge chunk of masonry preserved in the place where it fell when the turret collapsed. The building was occupied at least until the 3rd century, when cutbacks and rationalisations meant that many of the turrets were abandoned.

A few hundred metres away, in a rolling pasture at Pike Hill, lie the ruins of a Roman signal station. Only the fractured remains of the original survive, for it was damaged when the modern road was built in the 1870s, but the view – the reason for which the station was sited here so close to other military buildings – is tremendous. The signal station in fact pre-dated the Wall, and was awkwardly bonded with it, but the vantage point, towards the foothills of the Cheviots to the north, and as far as the northern reaches of the Lake District to the south, made its preservation worthwhile. Inside the ruined structure a platform that led to the upper storeys of the tower can just be made out, a reminder that many of the buildings along the Wall originally rose to far above the level that can be seen today.

For those walking east along the Wall's line, the way here continues to be mercifully flat, past the remains of Lea Hill turret and through an attractive (and cooling) wood from which the grassed-over V-shape of the Vallum can clearly be seen striking across the landscape – a welcome reminder (as the Wall itself here is almost wholly missing) that this is still the course of the frontier. Just beyond this section, between Wall Burn and High House Farm, a rare section of the Turf Wall can be seen, a continuous bumpy ridge that looks as though a burial mound had been seized, stretched and elongated for several hundred metres.

This whole western section of the Wall, which stretched initially from the River Irthing to Bowness – and which was rebuilt in stone in two stages, in the late 130s and then around 160 – lay largely on a foundation of turf, although in places (such as around milecastle 72) this was replaced by cobblestones. The specified size of the turves – according to the military manual of Vegetius[50] – was 18 Roman inches by 12 by 6, although it is hard to tell if the legionary builders on the northern frontier kept to this standard, as insufficient evidence survives to gauge the measurements accurately. Most of the Turf Wall seems to have been destroyed when it was rebuilt in stone, explaining the slightness of the remains that can be seen today.

From this stretch at High House Farm, the way continues northeastwards across flat farmland for a short distance until the walls of the Birdoswald estate come into view. The Romans chose to site the fort of Banna here, to the north of the Irthing gorge, providing a platform from which to strike northwards, rather than the purely defensive location that would have meant constructing the camp to the south of the river. Originally built in timber (probably around 125), it was replaced by a stone fort around 138,[51] and seems to have been in use right until the end of Roman Britain (and quite possibly beyond). The place may well be the Amboglanna of the *Notitia Dignitatum* (which gives as its garrison the *Cohors I Aelia Dacorum*, originally from Dacia in modern Romania).

Birdoswald is the first of the forts along the Wall that survives in anything like its original state, neither robbed wholesale for its stones, nor completely obliterated by the expansion of the urban settlements around it (as at Carlisle), and it displays many of the features of classic early imperial military architecture. Roman forts of this period were normally constructed using a 'playing-card' design – in a rectangular shape, with the corners rounded. In general they had four gates, one at each of the cardinal points, while the strength of the surrounding ditches and earthworks (and whether the wall or internal buildings of the fort were of turf or stone) depended very much on the topography, the materials available, the perceived threat from outsiders and the length of time that the site was occupied.

Defence was not the primary concern in choosing the site because, just as the Wall itself was not intended as a fighting platform, so the legions or auxiliary cohorts were not expected – save in the most unfavourable circumstances – to have to defend themselves from within their forts. The early Roman army was an aggressive strike force and the forts were instead bases from which to dominate land already held and launch invasions to acquire further territory or mount punitive raids on those tribes that might dare to disturb the *pax Romana*.

The placement of the gates and the internal buildings of the fort very much mirrored those of a Roman marching camp; every evening on campaign the troops were expected to construct a temporary fortification, whose design both promoted military discipline and provided some level of protection in the case of unexpected attack. The camps and forts were laid out along two spinal roads; the *via principalis* ran from the gateways at the longer end of the fort, and was joined at right angles by the *via praetoria* at the point where it touched the main headquarters building of the fort, the *principia*.

The *principia* itself was normally composed of a colonnaded courtyard, around which were arrayed offices, and behind which lay a cross-hall or basilica to which the garrison could be summoned for important meetings or ceremonies, and in which may have been displayed statues of the imperial family. At the far wall of the cross-hall normally lay the *aedes*, or temple of the standards, where the unit's symbols and flags were kept, together with its most sacred image, the *aquila* or eagle, whose loss was the worst disgrace that a legion could endure.

Close to the *principia* was situated the *praetorium*, the accommodation for the legate (the commander of a legion) or the prefect in charge of an auxiliary unit. Often a luxurious affair, sometimes with hypocausts to provide under-floor heating, this was a far cry from the provision for the rest of the soldiers. The soldiers' accommodation at least in infantry units, was based upon the eight-man *contubernium* structure. The smallest tactical unit in the army on the march, was a *contubernium* traditionally housed in a single tent (of canvas or leather). In the more permanent fortifications, a pair of rooms was provided for eight men, one of these probably being set aside for the storage of equipment and the other for living and sleeping. At the end of a row of such blocks, a slightly larger unit was normally destined for the use of the centurion or one of the other senior non-commissioned officers.

Apart from the barracks blocks, which often took up most of the area inside the fort, other important buildings included the *valetudinarium* or hospital, for military units were one of the few places where men with less-than-elite status might have access to proper medical care; the *horrea* or granaries, where the unit's supplies were kept; and the bathhouse, an important social amenity which, apart from its undoubted hygienic purpose, acted as a meeting place for the soldiers and helped mitigate the numbing boredom of garrison life.

Much of the middle area of Birdoswald is unexcavated, and so most of these internal structures are visible only through slight contours and bumps.[52] The only significant remains, apart from the gates and the walls, which can be seen above ground are the granaries, built at the start of the 3rd century,[53] following a period of some forty years when the fort had lain abandoned after the move of the frontier line northwards to the Antonine Wall.[54] The bulk of the external curtain wall of Birdoswald, however, still stands, save for the northern section, whose stones were robbed to build a bastle or fortified farmhouse in the 14th century during a time when the Borders, the territory disputed between England and Scotland, were dominated by families of reivers, cattle-raiding clans whose hatred of each other was matched only by a mutual enmity for outsiders.

The fort actually butts against the Wall, although before the Stone Wall replaced the turf construction in about 138, it had projected beyond it. The gates are in reasonable condition, particularly the main west gate or *porta principalis sinistra*, which was originally a double-entrance flanked by two side-towers that may have risen to two storeys. In the 3rd century, this was rebuilt using stonework of a very high quality that was inserted into the more mundane masonry construction of the adjoining wall. Its smooth working, still visible today, seems to come from another structure and is unlike anything found elsewhere on Hadrian's Wall. It is even possible that it was taken from an unknown imperial monument in the vicinity.[55] By the mid-3rd century the southern end of this double-gateway was blocked up, in general taken to be a sign of diminished security or at least lessened confidence, for it made the fort easier to defend, an indication that the garrison now felt this was something it might actually be called upon to do.

There are a large number of inscriptions from the 3rd century, one recording building work on the east gate in 219, but little evidence of trouble from the tribes to the north, and the garrison may even have been removed in the late 3rd century to man new forts on the south coast of England.[56] An inscription from that time records that the commander's residence at the fort needed to be rebuilt as it had 'fallen into ruin'[57] and was covered in earth. Presumably the residence had fallen into disrepair during a period of abandonment, unless military discipline had become so lax as to permit such neglect while a garrison was actually in station.

A small section of wall within the fort marks evidence that the training of the soldiers was taken seriously at Banna. It is the remains of the southern part of a basilical hall, but not one intended for meetings or religious worship. Instead, this was a place for exercise and drill. Such a *basilica exercitaria* is mentioned by Vegetius, who writes that it was intended to allow the troops (presumably infantry) to train when conditions outside were wet or windy.[58] As the country around Hadrian's Wall has more than its fair share of inclement weather, this hall presumably saw extensive use, under the supervision of a centurion who would deploy a wooden vine stick (or *vitis*) to encourage idling or recalcitrant soldiers.

By the 4th century troops had been at Banna for almost 300 years. Now, however, conditions in Britain, which had escaped much of the turmoil that afflicted Rome's mainland European (and particularly her Danubian) frontiers, took a turn for the worse. In 360, the Picts and Scots attacked from the north, and the general Lupicinus[59] was sent to deal with them. But it was not enough; for seven years later a 'barbarian conspiracy'[60] broke out and Britain was attacked simultaneously, in the north by the Picts and from the south by seaborne barbarian raiders. Nectaridus, a senior officer in command of the coastal defences,[61] was killed, and Fullofaudes, a *dux*,[62] was captured by the invaders. The Emperor, Valentinian I, was galvanised into drastic action and despatched his trusted general Theodosius to regain the British provinces. After landing in the spring of 368 at Rutupiae (Richborough) in Kent, he marched on London, rallied the legionary garrisons and then secured the southern part of England, before proceeding north to flush out any remaining bands of raiders who had tarried unduly about the securing of their plunder.[63]

Around the middle of the 4th century, the northern of the two granary buildings at Banna collapsed and was not repaired. In its stead a timber hall was built at the start of the 5th century, which was later replaced by a more substantial wooden long-hall, whose outline is marked out today by wooden poles in the ground. At one end a hearth was built. It all seems more reminiscent of the halls of early medieval kings, or of the Dark Age potentates of the *Beowulf* saga, than anything normally found in a classical Roman fort.

The troops who garrisoned Banna in the last years of its life would have belonged to units referred to collectively as *limitanei*. Until the 3rd century, the principal division in the Roman army had been between the legionaries and the auxiliaries, but during the later Empire this distinction blurred, particularly after 212 when the award of citizenship to all free males meant that the main motive for service in the auxiliaries (the gaining of citizen status after twenty-five years) vanished. The main division now came to be between the *comitatenses*, or field armies – which had their origin in the units that the beleaguered emperors of the second half of the 3rd century gathered about themselves to stave off barbarian invasions or the depredations of rivals to their throne – and the *limitanei*, or border troops, who were assigned to garrison duty on the frontiers.[64]

The army had long been changing to adapt to the very real challenges the Empire faced, and units of around 1,000 men (as opposed to the 5,000 of the traditional legions) began to be more common, whilst from the 3rd century new formations known as *numeri*, which were drawn from particular ethnic groups and did not conform to the normal Roman command structure, appeared in increasing numbers. Units detached from a legion, known as 'vexillations', now tended to serve for long periods apart from their parent unit, whereas previously they had only really done so if needed for a particular campaign.

The command structures of the army also changed. While before the 3rd century the legionary commander, the *legatus legionis*, had normally been a senator progressing upwards on the career ladder for the nobility known as the *cursus honorum*, and which might lead as its next stage to a junior governorship, from around 260 the senatorial legates were replaced by officers of equestrian rank.[65] The next step down in the Roman social hierarchy, this class was originally composed of members of families not very dissimilar to those of the senatorial aristocracy, but less ambitious or able in the quest for power. The property qualification for membership of the equestrian class was also lower, a mere 400,000 sesterces under the early Empire, as opposed to the 1,000,000 sesterces for the senatorial order.[66]

The 3rd century saw other changes in the shape of the army. In the 260s, Gallienus established a mobile cavalry force, a necessary expedient for an emperor who faced the falling away of the western provinces, chaos in the east and significant barbarian threats on all fronts. Exactly whether these new units survived into the 4th century or whether the change was reinvented under Diocletian (284–305) is unclear,[67] but alongside his administrative changes, the new emperor also reformed the army, raising some elite legions (most notably the Ioviani and Herculiani) and a number of lower-strength legionary units, which appear to have had only around 1,000 men.

By 305, the thirty-three legions that had existed under Septimius Severus had been increased to sixty-seven, whilst the number of auxiliary units was correspondingly multiplied.[68] The size of the army was doubtless augmented, probably to the maximum level it ever reached, but what that total was remains unclear. The 6th-century bureaucrat and historian John Lydus gives a worryingly precise number of 389,704 under Diocletian, whilst Agathias, writing a little later, says that the army's strength had been 645,000 in the 4th century.[69]

Under Constantine (306–37) the process went a step further, with the field army of *comitatenses* being increased in size and becoming the most important element in the army. He abolished the old praetorian guard and replaced it with units of *protectores* and *scholae*, which owed a personal loyalty to the Emperor. The historian Zosimus accused Constantine of having ruined the Empire by withdrawing troops from the frontiers, where they had formed a strong barrier, and stationing them in provinces further to the interior that did not need protection.[70] Yet in truth, the larger field army was able to move more quickly to address threats against the frontier, which could come with little warning and at almost any point. Now that the Empire was on the defensive, it was actually better served by a more lightly held perimeter, so that forces to the rear could move more rapidly to plug any breaches of the frontier.

A short stroll to the east down a country lane from Banna lies the first really substantial section of Wall, around half a kilometre long. First, by Harrow Scar, is a section of consolidated Wall, which then leads on to the tranquil shaded haven of Willowford Brook, where a confusing assembly of ruins marks several phases of the abutment of a Roman bridge crossing. The erosion of parts of it in Roman times, and the subsequent shifting of the river's course, has left it looking beached and most unbridge-like in a grassy meadow. Just beyond, set against the barn wall of Willowford Farm, is the unlikely setting of one of the 'centurial stones', markers placed into the walls by the various legionary gangs to signify the completion of each section. This one was erected by the century of Gellius Philippus, which, presumably, was responsible for the nearby section of Wall that strikes down in a lovely line stretching along the river, and which was in part reused for the building of local stone farmhouses and outbuildings.

A kilometre or so away at Poltross Burn (milecastle 48), the Roman ruins are set right against the line of the railway, whose construction caused their partial destruction. Nonetheless, they are some of the most intact along the western sectors of Hadrian's Wall, built on a slight downward slope, which must have been the cause of much cursing by the tired auxiliary troopers on watch as they trudged up and down towards it. The solid southern gate entrance, which survives well, and the bulky thickness of the remaining walls show that even these relatively minor milecastle installations could give good protection to their garrison – in this case the barrack buildings in the interior indicate about sixty-four men – in times of need. Later on, when the true history of the frontier was long forgotten, this ruin became known in folk tradition as the stables of King Arthur.

A nearby stretch of the path features an advert by 'Jefficus', a local Roman re-enactor who has appended a reproduction legionary shield on a shed as publicity for his services, while later on the frontier cuts through a small patch of garden completely filled with an assortment of gnomes (although no legionary gnomes at all were visible – all off on campaign, no doubt). Besides Tipalt Burn, a couple of kilometres to the east, the path touches Thirlwall Castle, a romantic medieval shell, a fortified manor house built in the 14th-century by the local de Thirlwall family and almost entirely composed of masonry acquired from the Roman Wall.

The fort of Magnis lies just a little further on, a few hundred metres south of the line of the Wall. The first military building here was probably erected around 90 under Domitian, but nothing of it, or the subsequent Hadrianic fort, can be seen. It serves as the site, however, of the Roman Army Museum, which details the life of the garrison, the First Cohort of Hamian Archers (from modern Homs, in Syria) who called Magnis their home from around 136–7[71] to at least 163. An inscription to the goddess 'Syria', which was found there, is an unmistakable sign of the eclectic mix of religions that could be found amongst troops who were posted to the frontier from a great variety of provinces throughout the Empire (and who for at least several generations, if their units' posting should last that long, would have conserved the traditions of their homeland).

That the names of the Wall forts such as Magnis are known (or have been deduced) is due to a variety of sources, not all of them literary. The most striking of these are the Rudge Cup and the Amiens Skillet. The cup, found in 1725, is a bronze drinking vessel, which contains an inscription moulded into it detailing the names of five of the forts along Hadrian's Wall, and a stylised representation of the battlements of the Wall itself. Its exact date is unclear, but it may well show the forts along the Wall during the latter part of the reign of Hadrian.[72] Unfortunately, the craftsman seems to have corrupted some of the names, or at least shortened them in order to squash the letters into the confined space available. They therefore do not agree with those on the Amiens Skillet, a Roman cooking pan found in France in 1949, on which are inscribed the names of six forts. A further cooking pan, found in 2003 in Staffordshire, adds another fort at Drumburgh (or Congavata), near the far west of the Wall, which is not represented on either of the previous two vessels.[73] All of these pieces were most likely made as souvenirs for former members of the garrison, and though their accuracy cannot be guaranteed, they must have been made for soldiers who had first-hand experience of the Wall and its forts, and so can be presumed to bear some close approximation to the reality.

The literary sources include the *Antonine Itinerary*, which details more than 200 routes across the Empire, amongst them one showing part of the Wall's system at the time of Caracalla (211–17), which includes the outpost forts at Blatobulgium (Birrens) and Netherby (Castra Exploratorum). The *Ravenna Cosmography*, composed in the early 8th century, and intended to include all the towns and roads of the known world, incorporates details on Britain, and thus the Wall.[74] Finally, the *Notitia Dignitatum*, although a very late source, and which may include elements of the Wall garrison that had already been withdrawn, adds some important elements to the mix. It does, however, miss out forts that are incontrovertibly known to have existed, such as Maia (Bowness). The reconciliation of all these sources is fraught with difficulty, but in general the names of the main forts are now agreed by archaeologists and historians, although always able to be thrown out of kilter by a new discovery on the ground.[75]

From Magnis, the Wall enters its hilly central stretch. For the modern-day walker the way can be punishing, with constant rises and falls, beginning here with the 'Nine Nicks of Thirlwall', but as the Wall snakes up and down, and the higher ground gives enhanced visibility of its course further to the east, the views are truly mesmerising and the restored Wall at some points almost rises up to head height. The crags that punctuate the route from here to Corstopitum (Corbridge) are of whinstone, a dark, hard stone that resisted weathering over the geological ages and thus left exposed outcrops, the spines of which Hadrian and his surveyors used to form the backbone of the Wall.

At Walltown Gap, the crags are dramatically interrupted by a lone Roman turret that keeps watch, providing one of the most spectacular panoramas along the Wall. After this the way leads, via a succession of ascents and descents, past a section of unconsolidated wall, whose weathered and collapsed masonry shows the fate the rest of the Wall would have endured, had it not been for a succession of restorations. The route continues through a small and pleasantly shaded wood, at the entrance to which stands part of the structure of an old gate, an ancient Roman milestone clearly built into it.

Aesica (or Great Chesters), the next fort, lay just about 3 Roman miles east of Magnis, a closer interval than might be expected, and the construction of the fort over the foundations of the preceding milecastle 43 shows that it was something of an afterthought, built to guard the Caw Gap. It is quite modest in area, at about 1.2 hectares and, from an inscription to Hadrian that includes a title (*pater patriae* or 'father of the country')[76] which he took only in 128, must date to after that period. Much of its perimeter is intact, delineating the fort boundaries, although on one side a modern farm has subsumed part of Aesica's interior and encroached upon the walls. The west gate still survives relatively well, its 3rd-century level almost a metre higher than the original Hadrianic part of the structure, showing how the ground rose with successive years of occupation on the fort site.

The interior is mostly empty, pocked by bumps here and there marking unexcavated interior buildings, and patrolled only by the odd tourist and a lazily sprawling cat. In the centre of the site the remains of the strongroom which sat beneath the *aedes* in the *principia* can be made out, very overgrown and neglected. In one corner of the fort a solitary altar stands, much eroded, with its inscription wholly illegible. But upon it passing travellers have set coins, a pile of latter-day votive offerings, which are themselves weathering in the rain and wind, the bronze ones already having acquired a deceptively aged patina of green. The most ancient, however, far from being an original Roman relic, is just twenty years old.

Outside the fort a complex series of ditches (not just the normal single line) gave extra security to Aesica, but its lack of a fresh-water spring, which necessitated the piping of water from some 10 kilometres away, did not make it the most ideal location to site a garrison. Beyond, the Wall proceeds along a series of boot-breaking crags, always taking advantage of the high ground, past Cawfield Crags – chilly in winter and searingly exposed in the summer – where milecastle 42's south gate is preserved to an impressive height of 1.8 metres (almost the highest on the Wall), to the equally vertiginous Peel Crags. At times the view, with the Wall undulating as the landscape rises and falls, creates an almost hypnotic effect, drawing the visitor physically into the past.

Between these peaks and the next set of hills, Highshield Crags, the high ground is interrupted by Sycamore Gap, named for the extremely old tree that spreads its branches here, and which was immortalised by a scene in Kevin Costner's *Robin Hood: Prince of Thieves*. The Wall here is almost all original, up to seven courses high, and not reconstructed, as it mostly is elsewhere in this dramatic section of its line. The next break in the crags, at Milking Gap, opens the way to a wonderfully preserved fort (and one of the few in private hands), Vindolanda. It was also the scene of one of the most spectacular finds and feats of preservation in the annals of Roman archaeology.

Set a couple of kilometres south of the Wall, Vindolanda was one of the Stanegate forts, and did not form part of the defences of Hadrian's Wall proper. A timber fort was constructed here around AD 80[77] although it was rebuilt and enlarged in about 92 and then reconstructed in stone around 124.[78] A new fort was then built on the site in the 220s, which remained in use until the 4th century. As well as the military buildings, the site contains the best-excavated *vicus* (or civilian settlement associated with an auxiliary fort) to be found on the whole of Hadrian's Wall, including a small Romano-Celtic temple (featuring a grotto to a nymph, artfully provided with mood music by the site owners), a military bath-house and a *mansio* (or inn) for officially sanctioned travellers.

The interior buildings of the fort largely date from the 3rd-century phase of Vindolanda, when it was garrisoned by the Fourth Cohort of Gauls. It contained, as well as the regular structures, a series of round huts, an odd feature that has caused much archaeological head-scratching.[79] The foundations of the *principia* of the first stone fort are visible, as well as those of the cross-hall of the 3rd-century incarnation, and the *praetorium*, which was still in use and being restored as late as 370. A set of timber buildings that lay alongside the *via principalis* and probably formed part of the *praetorium* was the site of the find of the first (and the majority) of the so-called Vindolanda Tablets.

These tablets, on thin leaves of wood only a few millimetres thick, were inscribed in ink and seem to have formed a cheap and relatively ephemeral means of record-keeping and the sending of personal letters that were not expected to end up in an official archive. At Vindolanda, the majority of those found seem to have been discarded in some kind of a clear-out, and some show evidence of having been deliberately – but unsuccessfully – burnt.[80]

The survival of the tablets is due mainly to northern England's inclement climate: the waterlogging of the ground into which the tablets had been secreted created an oxygen-poor environment in which the wood did not (as would otherwise have been expected) rot away. The contents of the tablets provide a wealth of incidental detail about military life, the most extensive set of correspondence being that of Flavius Cerealis, who was prefect of the Ninth Cohort of Batavians around 100. A later period, from about 105 to 120, has yielded evidence from the tablets of a new garrison, the First Cohort of Tungrians.

Whatever the information to be gleaned from the stocklists and accounts of garrison duties in which the tablets abound, it is the more personal revelations that are most touching. One tablet huffily complains about the local Britons and their low-down fighting tactics, referring to them by the extremely derogatory term *brittunculi*, which translates approximately as 'filthy little Britons'.[81] Another soldier writing home asks to be sent a quantity of socks and two pairs of underpants, as presumably the military issue was not sufficiently warm in the northern climes, which made frozen toes an unpleasantly real winter hazard.[82]

Flavius Cerealis corresponded with a wide range of fellow-officers in the province. Amongst those to whom he wrote was Aelius Brocchus, another equestrian prefect, whose wife Claudia Severa exchanged letters with Cerealis's own wife Sulpicia Lepidina. By this stage, it was not unusual for the officers in auxiliary units to have their wives and families stationed with them, a privilege that was denied to the troopers, who were not, until the late 2nd century, allowed to make legal marriages.

In one of the most poignant of all the tablets, Claudia Severa writes to Sulpicia Lepidina, inviting her to attend her birthday party on 11 September.[83] It is one of the few surviving letters from antiquity written by one woman to another in very probably her own hand. These are astonishing shafts of light illuminating the otherwise hidden world of day-to-day friendships, of the mundane life of a far-flung garrison. They are all the more precious for the ephemeral nature of their contents, which would not have been judged worthy of preserving in any more permanent form.

After Highshield Crags, weary legs are rewarded by the only section of Hadrian's Wall where it is officially permitted actually to walk along the Wall itself. Through a small wood, marching over the original (but consolidated stones), it is possible for a brief few minutes to visualise oneself as a Roman auxiliary peering over to the north and barbarian territory, wondering when, if ever, an assault might come.

The next fort is but a few hundred metres away, and is preceded by the dramatic span of the arch of milecastle 37's gateway, through which it might be imagined wheeled traffic trundled to and fro as the economic life of the frontier – at least in the early days of the Wall – remained untrammelled by its presence. Unfortunately, this particular gate actually collapsed almost as soon as it was built, since the foundations were inadequate, and so the attractive opening in the Wall visible today existed for only a very short time before the (presumably rather embarrassed) engineers blocked it up, only to reopen a much smaller version in the 3rd century.

Up a slight slope, the eastern wall of Vercovicium, or Housesteads, comes into view. Its name has been tentatively translated (from a Celtic root) as meaning 'hilly place'[84] – a choice, given the local terrain, as unimaginative as it is accurate. Built as part of the Hadrianic decision to move the forts up to the Wall, its early garrison was probably the *Cohors I Tungrorum milliaria*, a double-strength (1,000-man) infantry regiment from what is now Belgium. The fort was abandoned after just two decades, when the frontier moved forward into Scotland, but repairs to the fort (especially to part of the north wall) took place in the late 2nd century, following its recommissioning. Further restoration occurred in about 200 under Septimius Severus, another emperor who gave the northernmost frontier of his realm some personal attention. Occupation here appears to have continued at least until the later 4th century, when a small bathhouse was placed inside the fort to replace an earlier, external complex.

Exactly when Housesteads was abandoned is unclear, but if it remained garrisoned at the end of that century, it would have experienced the last of the attempts by the central political authority in Rome to address its security, initiated by Stilicho, the part-Vandal military commander in the early 5th century.[85]

The barracks in the interior of Housesteads preserve in stone some sense of how the later Roman army deployed its diminishing resources to face new threats from tribes besetting the British frontier. In place of the neat rows of barracks seen earlier, rows of separate 'chalets' were built, in clusters of six, with a larger house at the end, presumably for a senior NCO. The Housesteads *praetorium*, the commander's house in the central range, retains some sense of the more prosperous and secure times, with its impressively large-scale construction, in which the hypocaust tiles of the 4th-century baths are visible alongside the villa's private kitchens.

Next to the *principia*, a strikingly large set of *horrea* is visible, its size showing the difficulty of providing sufficient grain to feed 1,000 hungry soldiers throughout the year. Nearby, the fort's latrines are the best preserved in Roman Britain, with a set of five individual seats surviving, but no partitions in between, for the Roman sense of privacy was not that of the modern age, and modesty did not demand that such bodily functions be regarded as a private act. A large water tank sat close by, for there was no aqueduct to deliver a suitable water supply to flush away the results hygienically.

The walls of Housesteads survive in reasonably good order, patrolled now by large groups of summer tourists peering quizzically north across the border or trying in vain to pronounce *valetudinarium* ('hospital'). As Housesteads did not project north of the wall, as did the other forts, only one of its gates pointed towards 'hostile' territory and the others were not blocked up early, as happened elsewhere. The south gate's basic structure, with two arched entrances and stone piers at the front and back, is clear, with the wear caused to the sill at the front by centuries of use quite obvious. The west gate is, however, even better preserved, its massive blocks of masonry rising above head height, showing just how imposing the basic elements of Roman military architecture could be.

Outside the south gate a *vicus* rose up, as around many of the forts along the Wall. The buildings that clustered around the protection of the Wall included a mix of residential houses, commercial establishments (most notably an inn) and, to minister to the inhabitants' spiritual needs, a variety of temples, including one to the oriental god Mithras and another to a Celtic-Roman hybrid, Mars Thinscus. In one house, set a little further from the fort wall, evidence of an ancient crime was uncovered, for beneath the clay floor were found two skeletons, one of them with part of a knife still embedded in its ribs, evidently victims of a murder, which was then covered up.

The museum at Housesteads contains a good representative collection of the various artefacts found on or near the site, but perhaps its finest piece is a carving of three hooded deities (or *cuculli*), their arms folded within cloaks, staring out with almost identical expressions. These hooded cloaks, of a type called *byrus britannicus*, were a well-known export from the province of Britannia. Strabo, in the 1st century BC, had remarked that the island was renowned for its exports of 'corn, cattle, gold, silver, iron, hides, slaves and dogs' – not, save for the metals, the stuff to set the economic world of the Empire alight.[86]

It is an open question, indeed, whether the occupation of Britain was actually profitable. Here, though, as elsewhere along the frontier, the presence of so many soldiers who were actually paid in (and therefore liable to spend) cash accelerated the development of a monetary economy, and encouraged the development of economic structures slightly different from those elsewhere in the province. Yet, with the exception of Luguvalium and Pons Aeli, no large urban centres developed along the line of the Wall, and there are few examples in this area of the large rural villas that are found elsewhere in Britain. Moreover, once the Wall garrisons were withdrawn, certainly at the start of the 5th century, the economic *raison d'être* of the civilian communities that had grown up around them disappeared, and much of the region would have relapsed into the state of subsistence farming in which the Romans had found it in Hadrian's day.

Around 6 kilometres east along the Wall line from Housesteads lies the fort of Carrawburgh (or Brocolitia). Reaching it on foot involves the negotiation of Sewingshield Crags, one of the Wall country's most pictur-esque and leg-shattering stretches, compensated for by the views north over the enticing blue water of Broomlew Lough. All that remains of the fort itself is a rather unprepossessing grassy mound fenced off and overshadowed by the next-door car park. Home to a cohort of Batavians (*Cohors I Batavorum*) from the 3rd century,[87] its earlier garrison is not definitely established, although the fort was certainly constructed as part of the second wave of Wall defences in the late 120s or early 130s.

Carrawburgh's Latin name, Brocolitia, probably derives from a local Celtic term and may mean 'covered in heather'[88] or, more romantically, 'the place of the badgers'. It also boasts two of the most important reli-gious sites on the wall. Down in a shallow dip around from the fort site itself lie the remains of a *mithraeum*, a temple to Mithras. Probably constructed in the early 3rd century, at a time when such cults were gaining increasing vogue in the Empire, and especially amongst its soldiers, the temple was uncovered in 1949. Lacking a roof and much of its enclosing wall, it is hard to comprehend that this sacred space – now open to the elements – was intended to mimic a cold, dark cave, a place of mystery and awe, from which initiates might be reborn into the light. Originally an ante-chapel screened off the central cult space, which was flanked by stone benches to the side of today's reconstructed concrete pillars, and had a set of altars at the other end. If modern impressions are accurate, all the sculptures would have been painted in colours that stood out in sharp relief against the temple's darkness.

Mithraism has been classified – by modern scholars, not by the Romans – amongst a set of beliefs known as 'mystery cults'. What these cults, which included the worship of Jupiter Dolichenus (who originated in Doliche, near Gaziantep in modern Turkey) and Isis (an Egyptian import), had in common was a closed membership and a reservoir of sacred knowledge, which must not be revealed to the non-initiate. They existed in parallel with mainstream Roman religion, and belonging to one of them did not mean abstinence or exclusion from official rites; there was no 'Great Persecution' of Mithraists, at least not until Christianity achieved official recognition in the 4th century and, with its insistence on exclusive adherence, undermined the position of ambitious pagans.

There has been much speculation about the origin of Mithraism.[89] There is a deceptively obvious connection to be made with the Persian god Mitra, who is attested at least as early as the 5th century BC, and who may have been the god of contracts or oaths (his name means 'contract' or 'treaty'). His popularity in the areas influenced by Persia is evidenced by the royal dynasty of Pontus in modern Turkey, no fewer than six of whom were named Mithridates ('gift of Mithras') between the 3rd and 1st centuries BC. He was part of a religious system that included a personification of supreme good, Ahura Mazda, and of evil, Ahriman, who were engaged in an eternal struggle for mastery. This dualist belief had a long lifespan in the Middle East, influencing a variety of Christian heresies (and the not-quite Christian Manichaeism) and surviving into modern times in the guise of Zoroastrianism. There is, however, no concrete evidence that the Persian Mitra-cult evolved directly into Roman Mithraism, which emerged seemingly fully formed around the start of the 1st century AD. Conscious echoes or borrowings there may have been – something similar happened with the new cult of Serapis in Egypt, which combined Greek and Egyptian elements – but the Roman army was hardly likely to tolerate what was practically the state religion of its greatest adversary, Persia.

Mithraic temples are found throughout the Empire, from Egypt to the Rhine provinces. In Britannia, as well as the Brocolitia Mithraeum, and that at Housesteads, another was found at Rudchester (on the eastern sector of the Wall). This cult seems to have found its greatest number of devotees in the army. Entry was strictly confined to men, and the limited size of its congregations – most mithraea probably had space for a congregation of only a score or so – may have given it something of the flavour of a secret military confraternity. Backing of the cult extended quite high up the military hierarchy, however: Marcus Valerius Maximianus, one of Marcus Aurelius's leading generals, dedicated an altar to Mithras at Apulum in Dacia while still a legionary legate, and a further two at Lambaesis in Numidia.[90]

The temples themselves were generally very small – one of the largest, in Rome, is still only about 23 metres long[91] – and in the cities they were often incorporated into private buildings. The ideal *mithraeum*, however, was a subterranean cave, a reference to Mithras as the 'rock-born god', in which guise he is depicted on one of the Carrawburgh altars, his head wreathed in a halo of sunburst, his muscle-bound torso emerging fully formed from the blank rock below. The temples were decorated with statues of a variety of other deities, most commonly Cautopates and Cautes, Mithras's divine attendants, the former holding a flaming torch held downwards to represent sunset and the autumn equinox, and the latter directing his torch upwards, symbolizing sunrise, the spring equinox and rebirth.

The most important depictions, however, related to the mystical narrative of the life of Mithras himself. These included his birth from the rock, a date that Mithraists celebrated on 25 December, which was then identified as the winter solstice. The popularity of this festival of *Sol Invictus* ('the Unconquered Sun') – a name often used by devotees to refer to Mithras – may well have played a role in the early Christians' adoption of it as the birthday of their own saviour. The central drama of Mithraism, though, was the bull-slaying, an event dramatically depicted in temples throughout the Empire: Mithras forces the beast to the ground, pushing it down with his left knee, grasping the animal's struggling head in his left hand, ready to plunge a dagger into its throat with his right. From this death and the sacrifice of the bull's blood, the Mithraists believed, would come rebirth: both literal, in the renewal of the cycle of growth each year, and metaphorical, in guaranteeing the survival of the universe and heavenly salvation.

The *mithraeum* is often adorned with references to the number seven, which seems to have been regarded as sacred, or at least auspicious. Symbols abound of the zodiac and the seven planets – which in the classical world were enumerated as the Sun, the Moon, Mercury, Venus, Mars, Jupiter and Saturn. Many temples were built with seven steps leading down into the sanctuary, and Mithras was sometimes depicted as having seven stars on his cloak.

The importance of seven extended into the organisation of the cult itself, for there were seven graded levels of initiates, although we only have their names from a letter of the Christian writer, Saint Jerome. At the lowest level came the Raven, followed by the Bridegroom, Soldier, Lion, Persian, Sun-Runner and, at the top of the hierarchy, the Father (*Pater*), who seems to have been the congregational leader of each *mithraeum*. What role the others played, and how progression from one rank to another was achieved, is unclear and it seems that, except perhaps informally, there was no system for linking the various temples into groups of more than just one congregation. It was a fatal weakness, and although Mithraists do not seem to have had any conscious ambitions for universality, when they came up against Christianity – a religion that did possess this drive – there was no internal organisation to defend the cult. By the 4th century, coin series at *mithraea* came to an end, statues were carefully concealed or buried, altars overturned. Jerome related with some relish that the urban prefect, one Gracchus, had broken up and caused to be burnt 'all the monstrous images' at a *mithraeum* in Rome.[92] The Brocolitia temple, like so many others, was abandoned and forgotten.

Equally forsaken at Brocolitia was the nearby shrine to a water-nymph, the spring at 'Coventina's Well', which was located a few hundred metres from the *mithraeum*, across a mud-spattered, boggy field. Today there is no evidence of the devotion accorded to this local deity. Indeed, the spring itself dried up in Victorian times as a consequence of lead-mining in the vicinity. In the 2nd and early 3rd centuries, however, believers deposited hundreds of coins and inscribed altars, the dedicators most commonly coming from the Lower Rhine and Netherlands. A stone relief from Brocolitia depicts Coventina bare-chested, a light flowing veil-like garment covering her lower half, looking for all the world like a prototype mermaid. This was a landscape in which the religious options open to the soldiers were far more varied than the official pantheon might suggest.

A couple of kilometres further on, as the Wall itself becomes more sparse, its spectacular stride through the central crags now done, it passes through 'Limestone Corner', which, apart from being the most northerly tip of the Wall, marks the point where even the Roman engineers gave up trying to drive the ditch north of the wall through the solid rock. The end of their endeavours is marked by massive chunks of limestone lying scattered about, already sliced away by the masons, but simply left in place after the decision to give up the ditch over this stretch. That such monumental pieces of rock were broken away without the use of explosives is a sober reflection on the monomania and sheer back-breaking effort that was involved in the construction of such an amazingly ambitious project as the Wall.

Around 3 kilometres further on, the fort of Cilurnum (or Chesters) lies in an attractive position astride the North Tyne River. Across a rather busy and noisy road, a curiously humpbacked modern bridge leads down, via a fenced approach that hems in any straying tourists, to the abutment of the Roman bridge. Down in a dip, it all seems at first a confusing mass of masonry, which resolves itself on inspection into one bridge pier and a tower, with the abutment itself – in the shape of a sundial or radial sun-pattern – lying beneath. Nearby an almost complete column lies prostrate, with a little knob on the side, rather like a bollard. Up the slope caused by the excavators' digging lies a display area for a whole array of miscellaneous fragments, looking rather like a huge jigsaw puzzle abandoned in frustration by the archaeologists.

There were in fact two bridges on the site, the first one (which preceded this more massive structure) being built around 122, at the time the Wall and fort were constructed.[93] It seems that the walkway across the bridge was around 3 metres wide, the same width as the Wall itself at this point, so that it in effect acted as a continuation of the Wall across the river. The second bridge was intended to act as a roadway for wheeled traffic and dates from the early 3rd century, although it is not clear at what point it fell into disuse.

The fort of Cilurnum lies on the other side of the river, and access would have been gained to it in Roman times across the bridge. Its Latin name is associated with a Celtic root, which may mean 'cauldron',[94] a possible reference to the swirling eddy in the river just by the site of the bridge. It was a cavalry fort, variously housing the *Cohors I Augusta* and *Ala II Asturum*. The remains of the walls, gates, *principia* and bathhouse date largely from the Hadrianic phase of Cilurnum, whilst the commander's house and many of the barracks are from the later phase of occupation of the site during the 3rd century. The site seems strangely fragmented, the protective fences and gates around the various internal fort buildings breaking it up and making it difficult to take in as an organic whole. It is an attractive setting, however, set in the lush fields of the Clayton estate, with trees liberally sprinkled outside the perimeter of the fort itself and a gentle slope down to the cooling balm of the Tyne.

The north gate, which projected beyond the line of the Wall, would originally have been 10 metres high, though now less than a metre remains, only fragments of its flanking tower being intact. One side of the gate seems to have been blocked soon after it was built, and indications from the other fort gates point to the unblocked part of this double-entrance being the sole passageway into Cilurnum from beyond the Wall. The west gate, which also projected beyond the Wall, is rather better preserved, and the thresholds and pivot-holes of the original can still be seen. It was from the northern guardpost here that a water tank (fed by an external aqueduct) channelled water to the other parts of the fort, as it represents the highest point on the site.

In the north-east of the fort lie the remains of the barracks, an impressive array of rectangular stone blocks, though the symmetry is rather broken up by the third of the triple barrack blocks, which was later subdivided, possibly to create 'chalets' similar to those of the last phase of Housesteads fort. The *principia* also remains in good shape (although of course mostly only in outline and just a couple of stone-courses high). It is even possible to make out, off the cross-hall leading from the main courtyard, the range of rooms in which the administrative grind of legionary life – all the rosters, stocktaking and details of the soldiers' pay and deductions – would have been worked out and archived. In one corner of the next-door *praetorium*, a small hypocaust indicates that the prefect of the *ala* had his own bath-suite and so did not have to slum it by taking the waters with his troopers.

Outside the east gate, where the Wall met the fort – a section of it survives just a metre or two away – a gentle slope leads down to the river. Sited close by was the soldiers' bath complex. Its position outside the fort meant there was less risk of fire, which might be caused by the furnaces necessary to keep the warm and hot rooms of the baths at a suitable temperature, but such a location – which it shares with many military baths along the frontier in Britannia and elsewhere – had the disadvantage of leaving the soldiers at risk of a surprise attack. The baths seem large for an auxiliary camp, and were reconstructed several times over the years, meaning that the exact shape and purpose of some of the rooms is unclear (and the walls, though still in fair shape, have deteriorated over the years since their initial excavation in 1884–5).

A large rectangular area at the northern end of the bath complex is obviously the *apodyterium* or changing room. The row of seven niches in the west wall here is sometimes interpreted by the overly pragmatic as lockers for the soldiers to place their clothes and valuables in as they bathed. But there are no holes where doors might have been fixed; besides, there would be room only for seven troopers to store their valuables at once, leading to queues or unseemly rows. Instead it is likely that the niches originally contained statues for the seven gods of the week.[95] The baths were provided with all of the normal facilities of *frigidarium* (cold room) – not, presumably a popular choice in the English winter – *tepidarium* (warm room) and *caldarium* (hot room) so that the soldiers could replicate the bathing rituals being enjoyed by their comrades across the Empire, from here to Durostorum on the Danube and Lambaesis in the North African desert.

The Chesters museum is a real old-style relic, containing a mass of stonework crowded together in a manner that is deliberately reminiscent of the customary style of display in the 19th century. Including material found at nearby forts, it is a treasure house in which to browse and take relief from the visual overload of the Wall and from ice-cream-wielding visitors. Its finest piece is a statue of Juno Regina, the consort of Jupiter Dolichenus, who played a central role in a mystery cult imported from Cappadocia in Asia Minor that was popular with the military. There is also a wealth of altar dedications, including some in honour of emperors such as Numerian (283–4) whose reigns were so fleeting as to scarcely have bothered the scorers.

The beginning of the process that would ultimately lead to the public stewardship of the Wall and its scientific study and conservation began in 1796, when Nathaniel Clayton bought the estate on which the Roman fort of Chesters lay. Although Roman studies took a step backwards when he ordered the razing of much of 'this eyesore', as he called the fort – which was then clearly visible to a much greater extent than it is today – he passed on the land to his son in 1832, leaving him a collection of Roman sculpture and monuments that had been preserved from demolition. From 1843 John Clayton began to excavate at Chesters, and assiduously bought up any section of land containing Roman remains that came up for sale. By 1890 he owned no fewer than five of the Wall forts, and had excavated parts of Housesteads, too, and so to him is owed directly the preservation of some of the most splendid Roman monuments in northern Europe.

The Wall as it can be seen today also owes a great deal to John Clayton, for he ordered his workmen to reconstruct large sections of it, using surviving facing stones to build a drystone wall infilled with rubble up to a level of about seven courses, and topped with turf to prevent erosion. Without Clayton there would be no stone barrier snaking its way through the low hills and crags of the central sections of the frontier. In a sense, therefore, he stands alongside Hadrian himself as the 'builder' of the Wall.

Further eastwards there are still sections of Wall surviving, though nothing like the continuous runs of the hilly country in the west. The pathway along the Wall line leads for the most part through fields populated by nothing more threatening than overcurious sheep, soon reaching Brunton turret, just a kilometre from Chesters. Here, a nice section of Wall brackets the remains of one of the watchtowers, complete up to ten courses or so, hidden in a dip beside a row of trees. A further kilometre beyond, in open fields at Planetrees, is one of the most surprising and revealing survivals of the Wall. It is the point at which it changes from being the Narrow Wall, which has been its form in all the stretches west of here, to the Broad Wall, which was the architects' original conception for the whole, though possibly in this case the widening of the Wall is the result of building work around 205 rather than the modifications of the 120s.[96] It is possible to see exactly the point where the change was made, as the stones of the broader foundation, which have hitherto projected outside the curtain of the Wall, disappear underneath it at a rather awkward, but fascinating join.

A few kilometres to the east lie the remains of the Wall fort of Onnum. Unexcavated, and marked by just a few bumps in the ground, it is a convenient point to deviate away from the Wall, back to the line of the Stanegate forts and to one of the best-preserved Roman monuments in the north of England. This area was probably first occupied by the Romans around 79 during Agricola's governorship. They built an early fort around a kilometre from the present one to act as a supply base for the push northwards against the Caledonians. By the mid-80s, however, the new base had been built at Corstopitum, around three kilometres south of the future line of Hadrian's Wall. Today it lies in a neat rectangular enclosure that creates the deceptive impression that the fort was an isolated affair, for the civilian settlement and other diverse buildings that grew up around the military base have either not been dug up or have, over the years, been backfilled by the excavators.

The new fort was destroyed by fire around 105[97] and a replacement built with timber internal buildings. When the Wall was constructed in the 120s, Corstopitum was not initially abandoned, but when the decision was later taken to construct new forts along the line of the Wall, it must have suffered at least a reduction in its garrison, if not outright withdrawal. Corbridge lies in a strategic position close to Dere Street, the main road that led north into Scotland, and so when Antoninus Pius ordered the frontier moved northwards around 139, it actually prospered anew, in contrast to the posts on Hadrian's Wall. A new stone fort was constructed; an inscribed dedication stone of the time records the name of the then governor, Quintus Lollius Urbicus, who was responsible for the work.

By 163 at the latest, however, the Antonine frontier had been abandoned and Hadrian's Wall reoccupied, leading to another reversal of fortune, as Corstopitum again ceased to be a military post; its ramparts may have been thrown down and the site opened up for civilian occupation. For the next century or so it prospered modestly as a regular town, although one exposed to the vagaries of frontier life – it may have been burnt around 180 in a barbarian incursion to which the historian Cassius Dio makes vague reference.[98] Little is known of the subsequent history of the site, although it certainly seems to have been occupied until the later 4th century. How long, if at all, it survived the final Roman evacuation of Britannia is obscure.

The main street of Corstopitum is something of a palimpsest, the surface of the east end much higher, indicating its 4th century level, while towards the centre of the site, where excavation has cleared away most of the subsequent rebuildings, its 1st-century level is almost a metre lower. Interestingly, the 3rd-century reconstruction of parts of the fort contained a large amount of reused sculpture and architectural fragments, indicating that the Romans of the time were much less precious than modern sensibility would allow about putting antique stonework to use, when the practical demands of the time dictated it. To the north side of the road lies a pair of enormous *horrea*. Stone vents that are still visible on the lower level allowed the circulation of air, which prevented the corn from going mouldy, while the top, which presents the appearance of a great stone platform, still retains some of its flagged paving stones. The granaries date from 180, and thus supplied the town once it had been given over to civilian use, but, whether for reasons of bureaucratic impediments or sheer lack of funds is unclear, it took well into the 3rd century to complete them.[99]

Just to the east of the granaries lies a house fronted by the remains of a monumental fountain. Only the basin survives, but it was originally flanked by two statues of winged Victories, with a building dedication by the XX Valeria Victrix legion. Such a showy public fountain or *nymphaeum* was once an essential statement of civic pride in cities throughout the Empire, and Corstopitum was not to be outdone.

One of the most curious areas in the interior of the fort, known as 'Site 11', was at first interpreted by the excavators as a forum. The grassy rectangular area flanked by ranges of buildings does, indeed, initially give this impression, but equally persuasive arguments have been made for its having been a military depot or a storehouse.[100] The history of the occupation of the flanking buildings, however, gives eloquent testimony to the decline of Corstopitum during its later years, for whereas in the 3rd century most of the rooms in both building ranges were being occupied, by the mid-4th century just three rooms were still being used.

The eastern compound of the site, to the south of the main street (the *decumanus*), is more of a jumble of stones, containing a variety of residential complexes, the remains of an old barracks and the former *principia* of the fort, as well as workshops and temples. In the *principia* was found, among the ruins of the temple of the standards, an altar dedicated to 'Imperial Discipline' by the II Augusta legion, which still retained traces of the original red paint used to highlight the lettering. Such dedications to abstract martial virtues – and other edifying concepts such as *Concordia* ('Concord') and *Pax* ('Peace') – were an important part of imperial propaganda. Indeed, it is hard not to suspect that dedications to *Pax* proliferated most in times when war threatened, and those to *Disciplina* multiplied when there had been outbreaks of mutinous behaviour in the ranks of the army.

East of Corstopitum the landscape begins to grow more urban. At Heddon-on-the Wall (some 16 kilometres along the Wall line from Corbridge) and Denton Hall, a stretch of Wall in a field and the remains of a turret can be seen, while on the outskirts of Newcastle the remains of a Mithraic temple poke through in an incongruous suburban setting at Benwell. Newcastle itself, or Pons Aeli, had the signal honour – given to no other installation on the Wall – of being named after Hadrian himself (whose full name was Publius Aelius Hadrianus). Of the fort itself, which guarded a key crossing over the Tyne, nothing survives, Roman Newcastle (and the neighbouring forts) instead being encapsulated within the walls of the Great North Museum.[101]

East of Pons Aeli, the Wall, mostly invisible, wends its way through the industrial landscape of the Tyne's journey towards the sea. Segedunum fort at Wallsend lies squeezed beside the Swan Hunter shipyard, whilst coal-mining in the area since the 18th century further damaged the site, leaving relatively few pieces of original masonry intact. The towers and cranes of the shipyard look over the Roman ruins, and small cruise boats meander by, blaring out music that breaks the calm and reverie of a summer's evening. What it lacks in the grandeur of the surviving remains, though, Segedunum makes up with the imagination with which it has been displayed. A great glass tower gives an eagle's-eye-view over the site, clearly displaying the outline of the fort and the way in which it – and most other typical Roman military bases – were organised, a panorama for which no amount of fort plans on paper can make up. A rebuilt military bathhouse (not on the site of the original) also gives a taste of what the real thing would have been like, when fully decorated and provided with its various pools, mosaics and frescoes, a sensation far removed from that which the bare, but original, stones elsewhere provoke.

The fort housed the Fourth Cohort of Lingones in the 3rd and 4th centuries, a part-mounted unit, and excavations of what is left of the cavalry barracks (marked on the site by stone outlines) revealed that far from there being separate stable blocks in Roman cavalry forts, as had been supposed, the men lived with their horses in the same blocks, the animals being housed in neighbouring cubicles.[102] A little way beyond the fort's car park a 30-metre section of Wall has been reconstructed, with (possibly anomalous) crenellations, fronted by pits inset with wooden spikes, a Roman anti-personnel trap that must have been horribly effective against incautious marauders. Beside it is a low stretch of Wall foundation, the last along the frontier, and almost the final vestige of Hadrian's great project.

Not quite the last, however, for eventually the stretch from Wallsend to the coast some 10 kilometres away, which it had not initially been deemed necessary to defend, was fortified, a decision that was then reversed – taken, presumably, to prevent hostile forces from the north slipping across the Tyne at a point where it was only lightly guarded. At South Shields, just south of the mouth of the Tyne, lies Arbeia, originally constructed in the 2nd century as a regular auxiliary fort, and now surrounded by low, neat terraces, a world away from the sparse rural settings of the remains at Housesteads or Chesters. It has been speculated that the name derives from an Aramaic term for 'Arab', an etymology reinforced to some extent by the presence in the 4th century of a *numerus Barcariorum Tigrisiensium* (a number of Tigris boatmen) as its garrison.[103] Another ancient immigrant to Tyneside is commemorated in Arbeia's museum, where the tombstone of Regina, a native Briton (from the Catuvellauni tribe) is on display. Originally a slave, she was freed by her master, Barates, who came from far-off Palmyra in modern Syria. His tomb, astonishingly, also survived and is in the museum at Corbridge.

Not much remains of the actual wall of the fort at Arbeia, but its western gateway has been reconstructed in its entirety, giving a rare chance in Britain – the habit is much more common along the German sections of the frontier – to see how impressive the Roman monuments must have been in their heyday. Whether it should have been built with crenellations or whether the towers had roofs is the subject of endless debate,[104] but its sheer imposing presence is a reminder that what we now see as jumbles of stone and fragments of defences were once part of complete, towering buildings and continuous, dominating sections of wall. The gateway, too, gives a splendid view over the site, and in particular over the series of *horrea* that were built over the northern third of

Arbeia at the start of the 3rd century. The fort was also extended at this time and, over the course of a decade, more and more granaries were built, so that from 205/8 (when fourteen were built) to about 220, the total reached an astonishing twenty-four grain stores. It was only at the end of the 3rd century that many of these were converted back into use as barracks.

The reason behind this proliferation of granaries was Rome's last serious strike northwards into the Highlands of Scotland. Since the border had been pulled back to Hadrian's Wall in 169, the frontier had been fairly quiet.[105] Following the civil war that brought Septimius Severus to the throne in 193, and which also involved Clodius Albinus (the then governor of Britain) in a failed attempt to become Emperor, a decision was taken to cut Britannia in two – a fate also meted out to Syria, where Septimius's other rival, Pescennius Niger, had been governor. The southern part of Britain became Britannia Superior, with its governor based in London, whilst the north, including Hadrian's Wall, fell to Britannia Inferior, with its capital (and sole legion) at Eboracum (York).[106]

It seems that the northern tribes were keen observers of the Romans' troubles and, when Albinus withdrew part of the garrison for his ill-fated march through Gaul,[107] a confederacy in the Lowlands, known as the Maetae, started to cause trouble. It was only in 207 that the frontier line was restored once more and in a position to take any further punishment the Maetae might want to throw at it. The Emperor, however, was not content, and in 208 Septimius arrived in Britain in person, accompanied by his senior officials and his two sons, Caracalla and Geta. The latter, the younger son, was left in London to administer, with suitable guidance, the province from the rear, whilst Septimius and Caracalla marched north to deal out suitable retribution to the recalcitrant Maetae.

The army seems to have moved rapidly to the Forth–Clyde isthmus and then used Carpow in Fife as a springboard to launch a series of operations further north. Septimius's campaign is said to have taken him almost to the extremities of the island and, wherever he did reach, no Roman force would ever again operate so far north.[108] The Maetae were temporarily cowed, and the Emperor felt sanguine enough to allow the issue of coins with the legend *Victoriae Britannicae*.[109] Yet in summer 210 they once again rose up in revolt, this time in alliance with the Caledonians. Septimius was now too ill to join his legions on their march north and appointed Caracalla to lead the troops instead. The old Emperor's death at Eboracum in February 211, however, brought a rapid end to the campaign. Although the legionaries were still present in Scotland (at Carpow) in 212, Caracalla seems to have done a deal with the Maetae to allow his and Geta's return home to Rome, a necessary move to forestall any attempts at usurpation.

As he lay dying, Septimius had given his two sons a piece of advice, culled from long experience of revolt and government: 'Pay the army, love each other, and forget all else.'[110] Caracalla and Geta stopped their ears to his middle counsel, for they loathed each other, and within months had turned the imperial palace at Rome into a virtual war zone, divided between the contesting parties. Caracalla, the eldest, although less popular with the army, proved the more ruthless, and in December the same year he had his brother murdered at a meeting ostensibly called to effect a reconciliation between them.[111]

The Antonine Wall

Hadrian's Wall almost became the greatest white elephant in Roman military history when the Emperor died barely a decade after its completion. His successor, Antoninus Pius, who was Hadrian's adoptive son (even though just ten years younger),[112] gained a reputation as a peace-loving scholarly type. In stark contrast to Hadrian, he rarely left the confines of Rome or his villas on its outskirts.

It was perhaps, therefore, his desire to gain a reasonably cheap victory that lay behind his decision to move the frontier forward again, this time to the shorter line of the Forth–Clyde isthmus. Interestingly, he made a similar advance in Germany, where he pushed the *limes* in Germania Superior eastward by 30 kilometres; all a case of a few cautious steps forward, which might reap a rich harvest in glorious proclamations. The move 160 kilometres or so north of the line of Hadrian's Wall probably took place within months of Pius's accession in July 138.[113] It seems to have been a great success, meeting no serious resistance, and the Emperor, well satisfied, awarded himself the title *imperator*, normally bestowed only on victorious generals (but, after the very early days of the Empire, the exclusive prerogative of the emperors themselves).

Hadrian's Wall was now abandoned, the Vallum filled in and the garrisons moved to new positions further north. Here, along the Forth–Clyde isthmus, a new wall was constructed, this time entirely of turf. It was just 60 kilometres long, barely half the length of its southern predecessor, and so in many ways was a more defensible proposition. It probably stood around 3 metres in height, on a base of stone about 15 Roman feet (approximately 4.5 metres) in width.[114] Whether there were any plans to relay the Antonine Wall in stone at a later point is unknown, and its subsequent early abandonment meant that it remained for ever a turf construction. Like Hadrian's Wall, it was provided with a ditch, around 4 metres deep, but the Vallum dug behind the southern barrier was not replicated in the Antonine scheme. Just like Hadrian's Wall, it was provided with forts, and these, like their southern counterparts, became subject to a change of plan that left much greater levels of force actually stationed along the Wall line. Whilst initially it seems that the Antonine Wall was only to have six forts, with fortlets (similar to the milecastles on Hadrian's Wall) every Roman mile (or 1.6 kilometres), the number of forts was greatly increased during the actual building process, leading to a dense network with one sited every 3.2 kilometres.

The forts were generally placed against the line of the Wall, and did not project from it, in another variance from the early plan of Hadrian's Wall. They thus had only one gate facing into 'enemy' territory. Like the southern wall, the garrison was composed of a mixture of units, mostly auxiliaries, but with a distinct lack of cavalry, unlike Hadrian's Wall.[115] The construction gangs, as ever drawn from the legions stationed in the province at the time, came from the II Augusta, VI Victrix and XX Valeria Victrix legions, and seem to have worked in blocks of 4 Roman miles (or 6 kilometres) in the western half, with a slightly different division in the east.[116]

From Old Kilpatrick at the far west of the line to Carriden at the eastern end, the legionary working parties placed a distance slab at the end of each section they completed. Whereas plain inscriptions were deemed sufficient on Hadrian's Wall, for the Antonine Wall much more elaborate carvings were set into the fabric of the wall. In one, the goddess Victory awards the legion a laurel wreath in token of its achievement, whilst in the most elaborate, found in the east at Bridgeness, a priest makes a sacrifice of a bull, pig and sheep, the suovetaurilia that was normally offered at the start of a military campaign, and which might be evidence that the building of the Wall started from the east and went westwards.[117] As a final component of the defensive system, the legionaries built the Military Way, a road sited to ensure effective communications and rapid movement between the various military installations, and which ran right the way along the frontier, at a distance of 15–40 metres behind the rampart.

Although less easy to trace along the ground than Hadrian's Wall, a reasonable number of the forts and some stretches of the Antonine Wall can be visited today, though the comparatively fragile nature of the material used to build the Wall and the flatter terrain on which it was built have meant that there are none of the spectacular stretches of stone-clad hills which have made Hadrian's Wall the more famous and visited of the two Roman walls in Britain. Beginning at the western extremity, little of the Antonine Wall is visible until Bearsden, which housed the fourth fort along the line in the revised scheme, less than 10 kilometres to the east of Glasgow. A short section of the Wall base is exposed in New Kilpatrick cemetery, but of more interest, the military baths at Bearsden are the Antonine frontier's first major surviving relic. The fort itself is now entombed beneath the housing estate whose low blocks surround the baths on three sides, the fourth bordered by a minor, but busy road. The bath complex is almost complete, and the various rooms stand to a reasonable height, as much as seven courses in places.[118] They include a *laconicum*, a small room whose very name suggests it was a super-heated or sauna room in which lingering for very long was not advised. Hedged about, its survival seems a lucky accident, when so much of the Wall has simply vanished.

About 10 kilometres east, into the central section of the Wall and already practically halfway across the frontier, Bar Hill sits high on a rise above the B802 road, almost entirely hidden behind a screen of trees that blocks off views of the slope where the fort lies. Unlike most of the forts and fortlets on the Wall, the garrison here is known, being made up of the *Cohors I Baetasiorum*, followed by the *Cohors I Hamiorum*, a unit of archers from Syria,[119] who presumably must have found the wet and cold climate distinctly uncomfortable. Faint remains of the *principia* are visible on the slopes, together with a bathhouse that was, unusually, built within the perimeter of the fort. It was a small complex, as befitted such an isolated outpost.

At Seabegs, 4–5 kilometres to the east, a fine section of the Wall rampart and ditch can be seen at the edge of a small wood that obscured it until the overgrown section was cleared away. The ditch strikes in a dramatic V-shape, towered over by the grass hump of the mound, giving a sense, for the first time on the Antonine frontier, of a formidable barrier. Its grassed-over remains also provide a pleasant park-like atmosphere and, even in the impending gloom of mid-autumn, is more populated by the cries of children enjoying a post-picnic play than by the echoes of legionaries cutting out and laying endless sections of turf.

The next fort along the line, a couple of kilometres away at Rough Castle, is perhaps the most spectacular setting along the whole Antonine Wall. Both Wall and ditch here survive in excellent condition, with the tiny fort of Rough Castle itself – barely 0.4 hectares – sitting in a very ruined state on a promontory overlooking the undulating site. Through the turf and the grass, odd pieces of stonework poke through, and to the east of the site parts of an annexe can be discerned in a low mound and vestigial ditch. It is a very up-and-down outpost, with ditch, rampart and mounds in a beautiful wooded setting, but within it a hidden danger lurks, at least for intruders in ancient times. North-west of the ditch, opposite the castle itself, ten rows of pits were uncovered, each of which would have been booby-trapped with wooden spikes and then covered with vegetation. The wounds caused to any unsuspecting intruders would have been horrendous. With grim military humour, the Roman army referred to these silent watchdogs as *lilia* ('lilies').

Three kilometres to the east, on the outskirts of modern Falkirk, a busy town and the largest in the Edinburgh–Glasgow corridor apart from those cities themselves, lies another finely preserved portion of the Wall. Set beside a busy road, a thin strip of a park shaded by a straggly line of trees conceals a section of ditch that has survived to almost its full depth, some 5 metres deep, making a walk along the rampart edge above a precarious business. The latter has not survived quite so well, and had the 3-metre-high lip which it originally formed at the edge of the ditch remained, it would have been possible to gain a truly accurate impression of quite how difficult the scramble down ditch and up rampart would have been, to all but the truly determined. Yet even so, peering down at the ditch bottom, part choked by autumn leaves that render the whole thing a riot of golden orange, one realises why the Caledonians made little serious effort to penetrate the Wall whilst it was still in commission.

At the eastern stretch of the Antonine Wall again little is visible, although the ditch has often remained where the Wall itself has been obliterated. The final relic (apart from the remains of the fort at Cramond, which was not strictly on the Wall line) is at Kinneil, near Bo'ness, where a milefortlet, the only one to have been excavated, sits in an open area screened by a small wood from the rest of the park in which it lies. The fort only really survives at its north-east corner, where the stone base of the rampart has resisted the ravages of time. Elsewhere a couple of the gates have been marked out with posts, while very indistinctly the line of the Wall ditch can be made out. For the most part, however, it seems a forgotten place, ignored even by the procession of dog-walkers sheltering beneath the trees from an unwelcome shower.

The abandonment of the Antonine Wall remains something of a mystery.[120] The consensus of opinion seems to be that it was around 161 that the withdrawal began.[121] Building works were undertaken on Hadrian's Wall at about this time, which would be consistent with a recommissioning of its defences.[122] That the process of withdrawal was not a simple one is indicated by a coin found at Old Kilpatrick dated 164–9 and some pottery at Castlecary, which would also support a similar date for occupation. Yet the Romans had always held outpost forts beyond Hadrian's Wall, such as those at Birrens and Newstead, and it is expecting too much in the way of a smooth transition for them not to have held onto at least some positions of the Antonine Wall as long as they found it convenient.[123]

Exactly why the pull-back took place is obscure. There had been little obvious strategic reason for the occupation of the Scottish Lowlands in the first place, and equally little compelling motive for drawing back from it. Antoninus Pius's successor, Marcus Aurelius, had despatched Calpurnius Agricola as the new governor to Britannia in 161, as some kind of war seemed to threaten. Perhaps this rising tension on the frontier led to his recommending a retreat, which might have been viewed as temporary, as the best way of easing pressure. After Antoninus Pius's death in 161, there would have been no emotional reason for a reoccupation of his Wall line, and Marcus Aurelius had other preoccupations, becoming embroiled in a decade-long war against the Sarmatians on the Danube.[124] Once back on Hadrian's Wall, the Roman army units were to stay, for the most part, for the rest of the life of the Roman province.

The Saxon Shore

The 3rd century was a time of growing uncertainty for the Empire. The western provinces, which had known a high level of security and prosperity for 200 years, began to feel the danger of external invasion, which had been absent for generations. Towns, and particularly those in highly urbanised Gaul, began to acquire walls, often enclosing only a reduced area, with their circuit excluding areas that were still populated – but from which, into the safety of the defences, the people would in due course remove themselves. The walls were bulky, thick affairs, often with rounded projecting towers from which crossfire could be rained down on the heads of assailants. They were platforms from which to defend, and a far cry from the relatively modest stone ramparts of the earlier legionary fortresses. Britain was not immune to this development, and in the 3rd century a new frontier opened up far to the south of Hadrian's Wall, as barbarian raiders – far from trying to breach the land defences – took to boats and conducted plundering raids aimed at the comparatively easy pickings to be had along the southern and eastern coasts of Britannia.

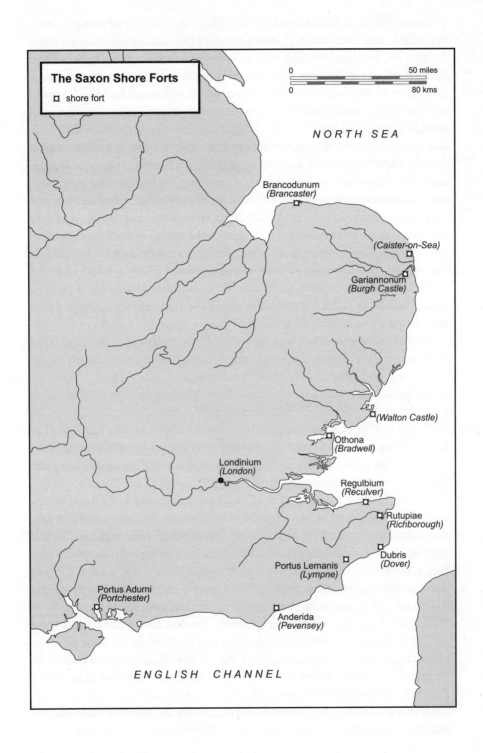

The Saxon Shore Forts

¤ shore fort

0   50 miles
0   80 kms

NORTH SEA

Brancodunum
(Brancaster)

(Caister-on-Sea)

Gariannonum
(Burgh Castle)

(Walton Castle)

Othona
(Bradwell)

Londinium
(London)

Regulbium
(Reculver)

Rutupiae
(Richborough)

Dubris
(Dover)

Portus Lemanis
(Lympne)

Portus Adurni
(Portchester)

Anderida
(Pevensey)

ENGLISH CHANNEL

The defence of Britain's south coast had long devolved to the *Classis Britannica*, the British fleet, with its principal stations at Gesoriacum (Boulogne) and Dubris (Dover), and smaller supply bases at ports like Fishbourne. Most evidence of this fleet comes in the 2nd century, such as an altar located at Lemanis (Lympne) set up by Lucius Aufidius Pantera, prefect of the fleet.[125] In the 3rd century, however, the number of coin hoards buried in south-east England seems to increase, often a sign of insecurity, as the owners stashed them in troubled times, hoping to return (but, by definition, never did, enabling their discovery by modern archae-ologists). There is some evidence of destruction by burning in sites in the south such as London and Colchester,[126] although whether this was caused by hostile action or by accident is hard to determine. It seems that the *Classis Britannica* was failing to hold back the raiders; indeed, it may almost have ceased to operate, as the last mentions of it come in the 250s.[127] The historians Eutropius and Aurelius Victor relate that the whole area of northern Gaul had become infiltrated by nests of pirates, who must have caused grave difficulties for the authorities both there and across the Channel in Britannia.[128]

The Roman response was to build a new chain of defences that stretched from roughly the Solent in the south-west to the Wash in the north-east, and which has become known as the 'Saxon Shore'. Whether this came as the result of a single decision by one emperor (or governor) is doubtful, for, although erosion has caused difficulty in dating certain sites (the one at Walton disappeared beneath the waves as the coastline retreated in the 17th century), the architectural style of the individual forts does seem to indicate a spread of more than half a century between the dates of their construction.[129]

The earliest of these forts was most probably that at Caister, which may even have been begun as early as 200, whilst the latest, at Pevensey, was still being worked on in the 290s.[130] What is certain, however, is that the defence of this area was dramatically illuminated in 286 when Britannia broke away from the Empire. From the early 280s Gaul had been suffering the depredations of a group of rebels known as the Bagaudae. The nature of their revolt is unclear, and whether they were merely a bunch of brigands, a proto-nationalist insurrection or a local self-help militia that got out of control has been widely debated.[131] The rebels kept the central state at bay for several decades, particularly in Armorica (modern Brittany), and so they were probably more than just a bunch of ill-disciplined bandits.

In 284, Maximian was appointed co-Emperor by Diocletian, in a move that foreshadowed the system of four cooperating emperors that would be known as the Tetrarchy.[132] As part of this reorganisation, Carausius was promoted to admiral with a special brief to deal with the problem of the pirates still plaguing the narrow straits between Britannia and Gaul. Eutropius dismisses him as 'a man of the lowest birth',[133] although this was an assertion that he was able to make at the safe distance of almost a century. He further alleges that Carausius got into the habit of allowing the barbarians to pillage the coast of Britannia Superior with impunity and only moved to intercept them when they were on their way back home, their ships laden with plunder – which of course the admiral then sequestered for his own personal enrichment.

Whether he was actually engaged in such nefarious activity, came under suspicion for another reason or acted entirely on his own initiative, by 286 or early 287 Carausius had raised the standard of revolt and declared himself Emperor. He thus began a tradition of British breakaway emperors, which would persist right up until the end of the Roman occupation. Maximian was now faced with a serious crisis. His early attempts to deal with the problem were distinctly unsuccessful, and seem to have ended up in 288–9 with the destruction of those elements of the fleet that he still commanded.[134] Carausius remained secure in this possession both of Britannia and of the northern shores of Gaul, including the former *Classis Britannica* base at Gesoriacum.

He apparently ruled his new domain with some discretion, actually increasing the bullion content of the coins, rather than introducing a debasement that would have indicated economic distress.[135] He joined in the imperial propaganda game with great panache, issuing coins with the legends *Pax Auggg* ('the peace of the three Augusti') and incorporating busts of Diocletian and Maximian, thereby hinting visually that he was actually a legitimate member of the college of emperors, rather than a rank usurper, as the other two regarded him to be. He even pinched elements of the official imperial nomenclature, renaming himself Marcus Aurelius Mausaeus Carausius.[136] Diocletian and Maximian were not mollified, and when the Tetrarchy reached its full form in 293, with the appointments of two junior emperors or Caesars, one of them, Constantius I (who became Maximian's deputy), was given the brief of sorting out Carausius once and for all. In the autumn of the same year, however, half of Constantius's job was done for him, when Allectus, who had been Carausius's chief financial minister, assassinated his master and took over as British Emperor himself.[137]

It took until 296 for Constantius to assemble a fleet powerful enough to attempt a crossing of the English Channel.[138] The force was divided into two squadrons, one of which assembled at the mouth of the Seine under Constantius himself, while the other gathered at Gesoriacum, led by his praetorian prefect, Asclepiodotus.[139] Constantius's force was delayed by bad weather, so it was the army of Asclepiodotus that encountered such units as Allectus had been able to cobble together, possibly somewhere in the region of Silchester in Hampshire.[140] Allectus's army was roundly beaten and he himself died on the battlefield. The retreating remnants of his force, which included a large contingent of Franks, decided to make the best of their deteriorating fortunes by heading for London and the good prospect of plunder there, before melting away as best they could. Constantius, however, had finally arrived and reached London just in time to intercept them, thereby getting the restoration of imperial rule in Britain off to a very good start.[141]

By the 360s, matters had deteriorated dramatically, and in 367 the great 'barbarian conspiracy' referred to by Ammianus broke out, combining raids across the line of Hadrian's Wall with seaborne assaults on vulnerable sections of the coastline. By the early 5th century the south coast came under the jurisdiction of the count of the *Litus Saxonicum* (or Saxon Shore), who commanded troops at Dubris (Dover), Lemanis (Lympne), Brancodunum (Brancaster), Regulbium (Reculver), Rutupiae (Richborough) and Anderida (Pevensey), all places that contain fortifications now regarded as part of the 'Saxon Shore' system. Portus Adurni (Portchester), which is included in modern historians' lists, seems to have been abandoned by 369.[142] Whether the name 'Saxon Shore' refers to an area settled by Saxon federates (or allies) or whether, indeed, the name is a convention and the sites are no more than fortified ports, not intended to guard against any specific threat, is also debated.[143] Whatever the original purpose, or the reason for its naming, the end result was that the North Sea and Channel coastlines of southern England, which had not hitherto been heavily defended, were hedged around, by the late 3rd century, with a substantial set of fortifications.

Although their construction spanned more than fifty years, to the modern eye the Saxon Shore forts share a superficial similarity of appearance: bulky walls, which have survived the test of time far better than most of the earlier installations in the British Isles (with the obvious exception of Hadrian's Wall); bonding courses of brick (or tile) and stone, alternating to give a striated effect as the red bricks stand out against the duller stone of the facing and, where exposed, the rubble core; and in most cases large, rounded, projecting towers that prefigure the classic architecture of the early medieval castle (and which on occasion were co-opted to form part of such baronial fortifications). The quantity of material needed to construct the Saxon Shore defences was vast; it has been calculated that for Pevensey alone – albeit one of the larger forts – it amounted to around 1,600 boatloads of building materials.[144]

Today many of these forts do not sit along the coastline, being beached instead some distance inland (or, in the case of Walton, actually under the water). It is therefore hard to gain a sense of the original topography of the land as the Romans would have experienced it. At Brancaster in Norfolk, the most northerly of the forts generally ascribed to the Saxon Shore, the island that blocks off egress from the creek on which the fort sits was simply not there in Roman times.[145] Similarly, the complex series of channels and waterways near Great Yarmouth on which Burgh Castle and Caister-on-Sea forts sit was already being affected by the contrary forces of erosion and silting during Roman times, so that the coastline at Caister-on-Sea actually lay 2 kilometres to the east of its present position.

South of Burgh Castle and Caister-on-Sea, the approaches to the Essex coast were watched over by the now-vanished Walton Castle and Othona (or Bradwell). The Kent and Sussex shorelines were guarded by what are perhaps the most famous – and visually striking – set of castles at Regulbium (Reculver), Rutupiae (Richborough), Dubris (Dover), Anderitum (Pevensey) and Portus Adurni (Portchester). Regulbium, which in ancient times sat alongside the Wantsum Channel that made the Isle of Thanet a true island, was probably one of the earliest of the forts. Although half of it has been washed away, its architecture is more reminiscent of traditional auxiliary-fort construction than its near-neighbour Rutupiae. An inscription attributed the construction of part of the *principia* of the fort to the time of Rufinus, probably the man who was governor between 225 and 230, so the start of building works at Regulbium must have been not too long before that. Its nearly square form, without apparent bastions, now hosts the dramatic silhouette of the ruined 12th-century church of Saint Egbert, its own rectangular towers seeming to offer the protection that Regulbium's robbed walls lack.

Garrisoned by the *Cohors I Baetasiorum* in the 3rd century, the fort may have been abandoned after the time of Carausius[146] and then reoccupied in the 4th. There is little evidence of its being used in the early 5th century, however, and it, and the neighbouring port, had probably lain abandoned for more than a century before Saxons chose it as the site of a church in 669.[147]

Only around 15 kilometres south of Regulbium lies the fort of Rutupiae. There was much less ease of access in ancient times, when the Wantsum Channel meant that to travel between the two forts demanded a boat journey or land trip all the way south-westwards towards Durovernum (Canterbury) and then back eastwards to Rutupiae, which then sat on a small coastal island, and not, as today, 4 kilometres inland. The pleasant walk through fields and along the River Stour to Richborough brings the fort into view at its most attractive, the elongated stretch of its southern wall rising to 8 metres in height, cut off where its south-western tower would have been, looking like a great stone boat with its angular prow pointed away from the sea. These walls, undoubtedly the most impressive feature of the site, come from its late 3rd-century phase, but Rutupiae has a much longer history, which is in a way a microcosm of that of the province of Britannia itself.

The ditch that fronts the wall at a distance of 20 metres or so, cutting a swathe through the verdant green of the field around, comes from the very earliest Roman occupation, for Richborough is believed to have been the main landing place of the invasion force under Aulus Plautius in AD 43,[148] and an earth rampart would have been built around the site at that time. The ditch, however, was soon filled in, and for the next four decades Rutupiae experienced a more humdrum existence as a rear supply base for the gradual Roman advance across the whole island.

Another curious feature lies in the eastern half of the fort, looking like a great cruciform mound, raised a metre or more and covered in grass. Far from being some precocious evidence of early Christianity in the province, this is the remains of the base of a triumphal arch, which was erected around 85. The centre of the site was raised and an enormous monument, probably around 25 metres high[149] and possibly topped with a bronze statue, was constructed. Exactly what shape it took – and whether it was built to celebrate the victory at Mons Graupius in 83, which might have been said to mark the final 'conquest' of the island – is unknown, but it was clad in white Carrara marble imported all the way from Italy, the only building in Roman Britain known to have received such a prestigious treatment.[150] When completed, it must have been visible over a great distance and would have formed a hugely impressive gateway to the province.

The town that grew up around the monument – and whose streets lie buried in the surrounding fields – prospered and the remains of a stone *mansio* or inn, complete with small hypocaust, can be seen in the interior of the fort. However, times changed and in the middle of the 3rd century a new earth fort was built on the site, a token that Kent needed defending in a way that for almost two centuries had not been necessary. The monument itself suffered the indignity of being converted into a watchtower, and the interior of what would become the Saxon

Shore fort was scored with a system of huge triple ditches, which even when partly filled in and grassed over are extremely unkind on the ankle and would have amply broken up the momentum of any concerted charge that an enemy might have cared to launch.

This phase was comparatively short-lived, and some time around 280 the remains of the monument were pulled down and the whole site was cleared. Debris from the demolition was incorporated into a new set of walls, which are those that can be seen so dramatically today. With its huge towers and massive 3-metre-thick walls, the Saxon Shore fort of Rutupiae must have been every bit as impressive a statement of Roman might as the monument had been, but the province was clearly living on reduced means. Only wooden internal structures have been found, presumably of the barracks of the II Augusta legion, the garrison listed for the fort in the *Notitia Dignitatum*.

However, the port continued to be a principal gateway for arrivals to the province, and for high dignitaries whenever Britannia attracted the attention of the central authorities. It was at Rutupiae in 368 that Theodosius landed on his mission to restore order following the barbarian conspiracy of the previous year, but by this time the end was nearly in sight for the Saxon Shore system. In the late 4th or early 5th century a Christian church (of timber) was erected within the fort precinct (its hexagonal stone font can still be seen), but it was about the last structure to be built there under the Romans. By the time Saint Wilfrid visited the area in 687, he went ashore instead at Sandwich, possibly indicating that Rutupiae's harbour had by now silted up.[151] It was not wholly abandoned, for eventually a late-Saxon church was built there, the indistinct remains of which can still be seen alongside the much more dramatic relics of the Roman fort.

The shortest journey across the English Channel between Gaul and Britannia was guarded by the Roman port and fort at Dubris (modern Dover), which was situated close to the medieval Dover castle. It was almost certainly occupied at a very early stage, possibly shortly after the Claudian invasion of 43, and in the 2nd century it became a principal base for the British fleet, the *Classis Britannica*, with a new fort built about 130.[152] Parts of the fort's wall and one of its gates have been unearthed, as well as some internal buildings, but more substantial remains have been found of the Saxon Shore fort, which was constructed around 270. With its wall of tufa and chalk, it lay a little north-east of the by-now-demolished naval fort. Beside it, and possibly preceding it by a few decades, was the building now known as the 'Painted House', which was in turn destroyed to make way for the Saxon Shore defences and in which were discovered, during the 1970s, the most extensive set of Roman wall paintings to be found north of the Alps.

In the grounds of Dover Castle lies the last of Dubris's monuments to survive, the Roman lighthouse, a most unlikely bell tower to the 11th-century church of Saint Mary in Castro (which itself incorporated a great deal of robbed Roman stonework). Although somewhat modified (with the top 5 metres or so being totally rebuilt), a sense can still be gained of the lighthouse's unique octagonal structure (resolving itself into a rectangle in the internal chambers), which tapered to the top where a fire would have been kept burning to guide mariners into the harbour and safety.

About 20 kilometres south-west along the coast from Dubris lay Portus Lemanis (Lympne) on the edge of Romney Marsh, and after this, a further 60 kilometres further on, the Saxon Shore's next major installation was at Anderitum (Pevensey). It is one of the later forts in the system, and was still under construction at the end of the 3rd century. Its massive walls are punctuated by eleven U-shaped towers that still rise for the most part to about 8 metres in height, crowning a hillock that is now several kilometres inland, but to which, in antiquity, a navigable channel existed. Inside the walls a huge grassy oval is surrounded only by the stumps of walls a metre or two high, but halfway along the north wall a deep archaeological trench sunk in the 1930s shows how much lower the ground was during the 3rd century.

A walk around the perimeter, negotiating both a sleepy country lane and the far-less-tranquil avenue of the A27, which bounds the fort on the north, shows the walls off to their true and dramatic height. They are built with the typical late-Roman *opus mixtum* technique, with layers of stonework alternating with bands of coloured tiles and bricks that lent stability to the structure. In places, where these bands do not entirely meet each other, evidence can be seen in the mismatch of the separate working groups of soldiers who constructed the different sections of wall.

Anderitum provides possible evidence for the process by which the garrisons of Britain were evacuated to the Continent, for a unit attested in the *Notitia Dignitatum* with the name of the fort is later listed as being stationed near Paris [153] At each successive crisis of the 4th century, and with each successive British usurper, more and more forts like this one must have been left with only skeleton defence forces, if any at all. The survival of the fort's defences into the 5th century, however, is indicated by a reference in the *Anglo-Saxon Chronicle* under 491, which records the siege by Aelle and Cissa of a force of Britons within a place named

'Andreadsceaster', which must surely be Anderitum. In one sense they were the very last defenders of the Saxon Shore, but, once Aelle had captured the place, they were slaughtered to the last man.'[154]

Even afterwards, the walls stood firm, since a medieval keep, whose first incarnation was built shortly after the Norman conquest of England in 1066,[155] is in places bonded with the stonework of the Roman fort. Anderitum, at some 4 hectares in area, was too large for the Normans to defend and the eastern part of the interior was sectioned off with a wall and ditch. That those defending Pevensey prior to the Norman invasion were the very folk against whose forefathers the Romans had built the 'Saxon Shore' forts in the first place is a rich historical irony, but not one that their king, Harold, who died a few weeks later at the Battle of Hastings, had much leisure to contemplate.

Forming the final link in the chain, Portus Adurni (modern Portchester), 120 kilometres to the west of Anderitum, sits on a low spit of land that projects out into Portsmouth Harbour. Contrary to the case at many of the other forts, the topography here has changed little since Roman times. It must have been an attractive place to be garrisoned, its narrow beach giving spectacular views to the other side of the harbour, with a cooling breeze in summer. The Roman fort's walls survive intact (but reduced in width) almost around the whole circuit. It is a rare pleasure to be able to walk the entire perimeter, gazing up at original Roman masonry all the way, although many of the bastions and some of the gates are missing (at least in their original form). Along the east and south side a water-filled moat, crossed by a modern bridge, harbours a mass of small crabs, which together with the open grassed-over area of the fort's interior attracts large numbers of late-summer visitors, and gives it the air of a tranquil country park, which just happens to have one of Britain's most stunning Roman remains within its bounds.

Enclosing just short of 4 hectares, and lacking internal structures apart from the 12th-century keep built in one corner and the Church of Saint Mary in the north-west (of similar vintage), the interior magnifies the sense of the sheer space and size of the fort. Amidst the ball-playing, kite-flying and picnicking it now hosts, the central area gives an unrivalled vantage point for a look at the whole of an almost intact fort wall. Unusually, the gates (which survive in the Landgate and Watergate, respectively to the east and west of the fort) do not possess projecting towers, with the Watergate – whose central arch retains its original Roman masonry and which was not reconstructed in medieval times – showing this particularly clearly.

The fort seems to have been built in the late 280s or 290s.[156] It was still in use until at least the 350s, with some evidence of rebuilding in the 340s, possibly in association with a visit by Emperor Constans to Britannia in 342.[157] There are very few coins datable after 367, even though a military garrison is listed in the *Notitia*,[158] revealing at best a very light military presence at Portus Adurni in the later 4th century. The next finds at Portchester are of Saxon huts dating from the 5th century, an indication that the life of Roman Britannia and of the Saxon Shore frontier was by that time at an end.

There had certainly still been a Roman army in the province in the second decade of the 5th century, for at that point yet another series of usurpers was raised up by it, the last of whom, Constantine III, was instrumental in the final collapse of Roman authority on the island. With Gaul seemingly lost after a large force of barbarians crossed the Rhine late in 405,[159] Britain was left to its own devices. The army there adopted the tried and tested method of electing its own emperor. It took them several times to get it right, for usurpers named Marcus and Gratian were elevated and murdered in rapid succession, before the poisoned chalice was passed to Constantine, who may have had no better recommendation for the job than his illustrious-sounding name. Constantine III (as he now became) lost no time in assembling the remnants of the army and in 407 or 408 crossed over to Gaul, intending to rescue the province from the barbarians and then either overthrow Honorius or come to some agreement with him over sharing out the rapidly diminishing imperial pie.

The local authorities in Britain were faced with the unpalatable truth that their one last hope, Constantine III, had promptly marched off with the remains of the army supposed to defend them. According to the historian Zosimus, by 410 they had ejected the remaining representatives of Roman authority and begun to govern themselves. Although the coherence of Zosimus's narrative has been disputed,[160] and it has even been suggested that instead of Britannia he was referring to a unilateral declaration of independence by Bruttium in southern Italy, it remains clear that the central government was in no position to reassert its authority in Britain. Northern Gaul was henceforth held by the Romans only intermittently, if at all, and the reduced resources of the Empire were simply not up to launching an expedition to bring Britain back into the fold, and certainly not to supporting a sufficiently strong garrison to maintain order there. With the horizons of the Roman government in Ravenna increasingly those of a regional and not a Europe-wide power, the process of Britain's slipping the Roman leash was probably more extended than Zosimus implies, but the result was nonetheless the same. Constantine himself fared little better than the province he had abandoned. In 411, weakened by a revolt by his own lieutenant, Gerontius, in Spain, he surrendered and was promptly executed.

In many British town and cities, the population diminished, as the economic sophistication and long-distance trade necessary to support large-scale settlement dwindled away. Layers of 'dark-earth' are found within the former urban grids, suggesting to some that there was now agricultural production going on actually within the towns.[161]

Britain did not, however, fall totally outside the cultural sphere, or knowledge, of Rome. In 429 Bishop Germanus of Auxerre visited the island at the request of the British episcopate,[162] who were concerned to staunch the spread of the Pelagian heresy, which taught that mankind had not been irrevocably tainted by original sin when Adam was expelled from the Garden of Eden, and thus, to a great extent, an individual's own actions were responsible for his salvation or damnation. Germanus found there an urban elite still carrying on their lives in a familiar way and encountered officials with recognisably Roman titles, such as a *vir tribunicia potestatis* ('a man of tribunician authority')[163] He also discovered Christian communities (although no bishops).[164] However, the shadow that would finally blot out this post-Roman landscape was already spreading. Germanus was said to have helped the Britons defeat a Saxon war band by simply chanting 'Alleluia', at which their adversaries, believing that the sky was about to fall down upon them, fled.[165]

Once Constantine III had removed the last of the Roman army from Britain in 407–8, the Britons were thrown back on their own resources and these proved pitifully inadequate. In a previous century it might have been expected that one or other emperor might eventually have reincorporated Britannia, but by the second quarter of the 5th century the Empire was struggling even to retain Gaul and Spain in the face of barbarian inroads on a scale it had never before experienced. According to a Gallic chronicler, Britain was 'devastated by an incursion of Saxons',[166] and the 'Groans of the Britons', an appeal to the patrician Aëtius, the Roman military supremo of the moment in 446,[167] went unanswered. Procopius, writing in the 6th century, observes that Britain from this time remained under the rule of 'tyrants'.[168] It is probably petty warlords such as these 'tyrants' that underlie the later legends of Vortigern – who by tradition invited the Saxon brothers Hengist and Horsa to Kent, thereby unleashing a demon he could not control – and Arthur, to whom legend ascribes a last-ditch and ultimately fruitless defence against the newcomers.

What is abundantly clear is that, deprived of a central authority that could fund an effective army and maintain the forts, the Britons found themselves militarily, as well as politically, fragmented. As the defensive systems of Hadrian's Wall and the Saxon Shore effectively ceased to exist, increasing numbers of barbarians breached both frontiers. They came to settle, and over a short time irrevocably changed the societies they invaded, bringing Roman Britannia to an end and starting the slow process by which England, Wales and Scotland would in due course emerge.

The *limes* in Germania Inferior and Germania Superior

Zuider Zee

Ems

0   50 miles
0   80 kms

Katwijk
Matilo *(Leiden)*
Albaniana *(Alphen)*
Utrecht
Rijn
Noviomagus Batavorum *(Nijmegen)*
Waal
Vetera *(Xanten)*
Lippe
Weser

GERMANIA INFERIOR

Maas

Novaesium *(Neuss)*
Rhine
Colonia Agrippinensis/Ara Ubiorum *(Köln)*
Bonna *(Bonn)*

Butzbach

Rigomagus *(Remagen)*
Saalburg
Sentiacum *(Sinzig)*
Confluentes *(Koblenz)*

BELGICA

Wiesbaden
Bingen
Mogontiacum *(Mainz)*
Worms
Eulbach
Odenwald-Neckar Limes
Würzberg
Osterburken
Jagsthausen

Meuse

Moselle

GERMANIA SUPERIOR

Antonine Limes
Mainhardt
Murrhardt
Welzheim
Köngen
Lorch
Schirenhof

Argentorate *(Strasbourg)*

Neckar

Rhine

Danube

Arae Flaviae *(Rottweil)*

RAETIA

Iller

Lake Constance
Konstanz
Pfyn
Basilia *(Basel)*
Turicum *(Zürich)*

**The *limes* in Germania Inferior
and Germania Superior**

Roman Empire, c.160–260
Roman Empire after 260
– – – Frontier of Empire, c.15 BC–AD 60
Germany Limes palisade
⌑ Roman fort

CHAPTER 2

Germania

The peaks of the Alps seemed to collapse upon one another and so send up three columns of fire; the sky in many places seemed ablaze and numerous comets appeared at one and the same time; spears seemed to dart from the north and to fall in the direction of the Roman camps; bees formed their combs about the altars in the camps; a statue of Victory that was in the province of Germany and faced the enemy's territory turned about to face Italy . . .

Cassius Dio, *Roman History*, on omens associated with the German victory against the Romans at Teutoberger Wald.[1]

Germania Inferior

Just like the site of the fort of Maia in the far north of Britannia, Katwijk seems an unlikely spot for the start of a frontier, this time that of Rome's long land border through Europe, a frontier that will stretch for several thousand kilometres through river, plain, mountain and forest, down the great Rhine and Danube rivers, before it touches the Black Sea coast amidst a spider's web of delta waterways far off in Moesia Inferior (in modern Romania). Here on the North Sea coast of the Netherlands, the fort of Lugdunum lay as the first post along this immense string of defensive installations. It was a fortified naval base, which, as well as playing a role in the Rhine fleet, had the task of supervising a section of the North Sea that was particularly vulnerable to raids by the Frisians and Chauci, barbarians who had acquired a naval capability.

Katwijk has, however, long since totally disappeared, finally sinking beneath the waves early in the 17th century, having, most fortuitously, been sketched by the cartographer Abraham Ortelius in the 1580s. Its precise location is unknown and the pretty, unassuming beach resort, with its rows of small grass-tufted dunes, bears only two clues to its past. The first is a bus stop named Brittenburg, which was long the local name for the vanished Lugdunum fort, as though the local transportation company possesses arcane knowledge denied to the archaeologists. More obvious is the large white lighthouse that is Katwijk's most notable landmark.

It may not have been the first lighthouse in the area, for in AD 40 Caligula notoriously took a fancy to finishing off what Julius Caesar had left uncompleted ninety-five years before in his abortive invasion of Britain. Having raised two new legions for the purpose (the XV and XXII Primigenia), Caligula marched north to the coast opposite the island. Once there, he either lost his nerve or there was the threat of a mutiny, resulting in him ordering his soldiers up and down the beach to collect seashells instead. These most unmartial proceedings were accompanied by the erection of a lighthouse that would have guided the invasion fleet on its way. One tradition has it that it was at Lugdunum that this was built, the predecessor of that which stands on the shoreline today.[2]

The two provinces of Germania Inferior and Superior experienced some of the defining crises of the Roman Empire. It was here that the Romans' expansive urge met its first serious check for centuries in the catastrophic defeat by the German tribes in AD 9 at Teutoberger Wald; and here, in 405–6 that the most notorious breach of the Empire's frontiers took place, as barbarians flooded through into Gaul and Spain. In the intervening period, the border stayed largely put on the Rhine, save at the southern end in Germania Superior, where the gap between the Rhine and the Danube was successively occupied from the time of Domitian to Antoninus Pius, creating an additional triangular salient of land (the Agri Decumates) that was only finally abandoned in the mid-3rd century.[3]

The Romans first reached the line of the Rhine during the time of Julius Caesar. The great Roman general's and politician's impulsive urge to obtain glory through (strictly unauthorised) expansion in Gaul brought him across the river twice, in 55 BC and 53 BC.[4] There is, however, little archaeological evidence of the camps he established whilst campaigning there, and he had more than enough to deal with when the great Gaulish revolt led by Vercingetorix broke out in 53 BC than to embark on further trans-Rhenish adventures.

Apart from the integration of the territories on the west bank, and particularly those of the Treveri (around Trier) and the Ubii (in the vicinity of Cologne), the line of the Rhine is largely where matters lay until 16 BC.[5] In that year the Sugambri destroyed a legion under Marcus Lollius, causing Augustus[6] to reassess his policy towards the Rhineland and the Danube in general. It was at about this time that the forts of Vetera (Xanten) and Mogontiacum (Mainz) were first established, together with Novaesium (Neuss), each of which received a garrison of two legions.

A series of campaigns over the next two decades seem to have aimed at securing a buffer zone in western Germany and then pushing this gradually forward. By 9 BC Roman armies under Drusus had reached the Elbe, and the following year a successful campaign by Tiberius may have led the unwary to believe that the whole of Germany was on the point of becoming a Roman province. Whether it was Augustus's intention to engage in a permanent occupation of the territory between the Rhine and the Elbe has, however, been obscured by the disastrous Roman reverse that occurred at Teutoberger Wald in AD 9 and led to the evacuation of the area.[7]

Combining intelligence and ruthless ambition, Augustus had, in the space of two decades, made the transition from a widely underestimated nineteen-year-old to the feared (and respected) master of the Roman world.[8] In addition to extending his own personal powers, he expanded the physical bounds of the Roman state enormously. He could hardly not do so, for his possession of a large (twenty-eight-legion-strong) army meant that he had to find employment for it, and military success was also necessary to avoid unfavourable comparisons with his adoptive father, Julius Caesar. As well as the acquisition of Egypt, which had come with the defeat of Cleopatra, Augustus sent expeditions to Ethiopia and Arabia.[9] In Spain he finished off the resistance of the Cantabrian tribes in the north-west by about 19 BC, and strengthened Rome's grip on North Africa. In the Alps he extended Roman control in modern Switzerland and the mountain passes that led into southern Germany and Noricum (Austria), while in the Balkans he sponsored campaigns into Illyricum, which began to establish a permanent Roman presence north of their existing holdings in Macedonia.[10]

Around AD 7, Publius Quinctilius Varus took command of the enterprise that was Roman Germany. Married to the daughter of Augustus's great friend and lieutenant Marcus Agrippa, Varus had advanced quickly, from a consulate in 13 BC to governorships in Judaea and Syria. In neither had he excelled, and he seems to have been more a capable bureaucrat than an imaginative military commander. Yet Germany was supposed to have been subdued, so perhaps it was assumed that Varus could get on safely with the more mundane business of organising it as a civilian province. Sadly, that was not to be. The Germans were already restive, and Arminius, an aristocrat of the Cherusci tribe who had served in the Roman army and gained citizenship, managed to form a broad coalition of the German tribal nobility opposed to further Roman encroachment. He lulled Varus into a false sense of security by feigning favourable intent and lured him deep into Teutoberg Forest.[11]

There, in September of AD 9, Varus and his three legions (the XVII, XVIII and XIX) were ambushed by the Germans at the Kalkriese Hill near modern Osnabrück. Constricted into a narrow space, the Romans were unable to deploy effectively into battle order and, after a bitter struggle were overwhelmed.[12] Exactly how long the Roman resistance went on during the battle is unclear, but it seems that Varus and his senior officers, sensing that their position was hopeless, committed suicide, leaving the centurions to fight on as best they could. As many as 20,000 Roman soldiers died and, more wounding to Roman pride, the eagle symbols of the three legions fell into tribal hands. The effect of the disaster was electric. Roman positions east of the Rhine were swept away, while Augustus, distraught, was said by Suetonius to have wandered in a dishevelled state about his palace for hours after hearing the news, crying out, 'Quintili Vare, legiones redde' ('Quinctilius Varus, give me back my legions').[13]

The task of revenging the legions was given to Germanicus, the grandson of Augustus's wife, Livia (and also, as it happened, of Mark Antony). In a series of campaigns from AD 15 to 16 he achieved mixed results, although he recovered one of the eagles from the Bructeri in AD 15. By the time he was recalled in AD 16, the Romans were back in their positions in the forts along the Rhine, and it was here that the frontier coalesced.

The Rhine frontier then seems to have remained relatively quiescent, apart from the further abandonment of territory in the modern Netherlands north of the Rhine in AD 28 following a Frisian revolt[14] and raids by the Chauci in AD 47, which caused damage in the same sector. Some time between 85 and 90, the area west of the Rhine was officially organised into two provinces – up until then it had been under direct military administration. The two new regions, Germania Inferior (or Lower Germany) to the north and Germania Superior (or Upper Germany) in the south, had their mutual border between Bonna (Bonn) and Confluentes (Koblenz). Germania Inferior had its capital at Ara Ubiorum (Cologne), while the governor of Superior had his seat at Mogontiacum (Mainz), an arrangement that was to last for two centuries. The frontier in Germania Inferior would remain the Rhine, but in Germania Superior the border gradually moved forward to the north and east, with an increasingly sophisticated series of defensive works to compensate for the lack of a riverine barrier.

Under Domitian a series of wooden watchtowers were built along a military road designed to supervise the upper German frontier, while in the reign of Hadrian this was supplemented by a wooden palisade erected on the side of the road facing the Germans. In the 2nd century, the wooden towers were replaced by stone versions and a ditch and rampart were constructed. In the Agri Decumates, meanwhile, the Romans gradually moved forward from initial positions around Vindonissa (Windisch) to push into the Swabian forest and up to the River Neckar, reaching their most advanced position under Antoninus Pius in around 160.

There was a scare late in 88, when Antonius Saturninus, the governor of Germania Superior, revolted against Domitian and enlisted the help of the Chatti, but his barbarian allies failed to come to his aid when loyalist troops arrived to put the revolt down. Domitian promptly ordered the abolition of double legionary camps, because the presence of such large concentrations of troops on one spot clearly offered too great a temptation to any generals who harboured treacherous designs.

The German frontier suffered few further shocks during the early 2nd century, apart from raids by the Chatti in Upper Germany and a seaborne assault by the Chauci on the Channel coast of Gaul.[15] In the early 3rd century, however, the appearance of larger tribal confederations amongst the free Germans began to threaten the tranquillity of the *limes*. The Alamanns, who emerged to the south, opposite Germania Superior, are first attested in 213,[16] while the Franks who raided Germania Inferior in 257 began to settle alongside the Rhine in the northern sector.

The process by which these new groups coalesced from pre-existing formations is unclear, but the very presence of the Roman frontier must have played a part. For with an insuperable barrier blocking any further migration westward or southward, and increasing pressure to their rear from other barbarian groups moving towards the Empire, those who reached the frontier had little choice but to establish an uneasy symbiosis with the Romans. Their elites would have recognised the undoubted advantages offered both by some level of cooperation with the Empire, which might manifest itself in subsidies or actual service in the army, and by occasional raiding acros the frontier that might result in the acquisition of more immediately tangible benefits. In one sense, of course, the establishment of the tribal confederacies actually aided the Romans, for it meant there were fewer players on the barbarian side with whom they had to deal, and treaties could be made with more powerful rulers who actually stood some chance of making them stick.

Pressure by the Alamanns resulted in the abandonment of positions across the Danube in Raetia, and in the loss of the Agri Decumates some time after 250. The threat became so grave that the Emperor Gallienus was forced to come to Gaul in person in 257 to deal with them. Thus began the tradition of an imperial presence on the Rhine frontier, which would, in some shape or form, survive for around a century until the reign of Julian. By then the frontier had become permeable indeed, and

Julian campaigned against the Alamanns as far west as Senones (Sens), where he was besieged by them in the winter of 356.[17] In the north, a Frankish invasion of 275–6 marked the beginning of a process by which the Roman population was pushed inexorably out of the lands occupied in ancient times by the Batavi. By the end of the 3rd century, the squeeze in the north was total and the area of the modern Netherlands west of the Rhine had largely been abandoned to the Franks.

The last really successful attempts to reinforce the Rhine frontier took place in the 4th century under Constantine I and Valentinian I, both of whom ordered the building of fortifications on the 'barbarian' side of the river. Although the Goths under Alaric – who had traversed the whole of the Balkans, creating havoc both economically and politically – placed the Empire under very great pressure in the late 4th and early 5th centuries, the Rhine frontier itself held until 405. Then, on the last day of the year, a great horde of Alans, Vandals and Sueves poured across the river near Mogontiacum (Mainz), brushing aside the Franks who were manning the river defences in notional alliance with the Romans.[18] Pausing briefly to sack that city, they marauded west towards Augusta Treverorum (Trier) and then took a turn south-westwards, leaving a trail of devastation as far as the Pyrenees. The Alamanns, meanwhile, crossed the frontier near Argentorate (Strasbourg), spreading destruction and despair in equal measure along that sector.

As the situation deteriorated in the 4th and 5th centuries, the Empire came increasingly to rely on *foederati* ('federates') whose obligations were less onerous, still involving military service in exchange for land, but generally fighting under their own war chiefs and thus retaining a higher degree of autonomy.[19] Some historians believe that they actually received a fixed share (*sors*) of the land on which they settled, others that this *hospitalitas* that was imposed on their Roman hosts only extended to a percentage of the income or tax revenue of the estates on which they were foisted.[20] Whichever is the case, over time the temporary billeting of these barbarian federates became indistinguishable from ownership and contributed to the formation of the new Germanic kingdoms that emerged in western and southern Europe in the later 5th and 6th centuries.

Well before the deposition in 476 of Romulus Augustulus, the last Roman Emperor in the West, the frontier on the Rhine had ceased to have any meaning. The Romans did exercise intermittent control over parts of Gaul and fragments of Germania Superior, but it was very much a patchwork, dependent on the resistive qualities of particular strong-holds and on local conditions and treaties. In central Gaul the Roman general Syagrius, whose forces must have been largely composed of barbarian federates, managed to hold out for ten years after the 'fall' of Rome, being finally defeated by the Frankish King Clovis in 486 at Soissons.[21] In the southern Gallic provinces a heavily Romanised aristocracy remained loyal to the central government until the 470s, their faithfulness flying in the face both of reality and prudence. Yet they were just breakwaters, and the flood that had overwhelmed the *limes* itself some decades before soon submerged even these hold-outs.

A 10-kilometre drive south-east from Katwijk across flat terrain riven with dykes and waterways lies Leiden, which in Roman times housed the small fort of Matilo, and which is situated at the confluence of the Oude and Nieuwe Rijn (the Old and New Rhine, the manifestations of the great river in the Netherlands). A pretty town of 100,000, criss-crossed by canals lined with tall gabled 17th-century houses, Leiden preserves its Roman past only in the collection of local finds in the museum: principally the graves and altars that would have lined the streets outside the town and a few telltale signs of the Roman military presence, such as cavalry helmets and tile stamps.[22]

More important than these paltry remnants is Matilo's position at the head of one of the most astonishing Roman engineering works in the north-western provinces, the *Fossa Corbulonis*, or 'Ditch of Corbulo'. Domitius Corbulo was sent by Claudius in AD 47 to deal with a serious outbreak of piracy amongst the Chauci that was troubling the Lower Rhine frontier, and to reimpose Roman authority over Frisia, which imperial forces had evacuated in 28.[23] After defeating Gannascus, the Chaucian leader, Corbulo set to building a fort in the territory of the Frisians, but was ordered back to the Roman side of the Rhine by Claudius before he could make the settlement permanent. Once there, and perhaps to compensate himself for the opportunities of glory that he had missed, he set his men to digging a canal between the Rhine and the Meuse that would enable ships to reach the Meuse estuary, thus avoiding the long trip up the Rhine to Katwijk.

The other end of the canal stands 15 kilometres to the south-west, near modern Voorburg, not far from The Hague. Here, from around AD 120, the small settlement that had grown up was reconstructed in stone and renamed Forum Hadriani in honour of the then ruling Emperor. It served as the capital for the district inhabited by the Cananefates, one of the leading tribes of western Holland, who were later involved in the great Batavian revolt of 69–70.[24] The west wall of the town ended on the banks of what is now the Vliet Canal, which in all probability was in antiquity the *Fossa Corbulonis* itself. On it, river boats ply slowly up and down, while along its banks small groups lazily take advantage of the summer sun, cycling, walking and lounging, perhaps totally unaware of the canal's original military purpose. On a nearby side-branch a party of schoolboy rowers makes steadier progress along the narrower waterway, its grassy banks dotted with low-hanging willows, while beyond, a small estate of pretty housing gives a clearer indication of the place's Roman heritage, with street names such as Agrippinastraat, Hadriansstraat and, in memory of the great engineer-soldier himself, Corbulokade.

Where the Aar River joined the Oude Rijn at Alphen aan de Rijn, around 12 kilometres east of Leiden and the remains of Matilo, stood the small auxiliary fort of Albaniana, which seems to have been built around 41, possibly in association with Claudius's preparations for his invasion of Britain.[25] Part of one of the gateways has been excavated, but more striking for those on the hunt for echoes of Rome is the Archeon, one of Europe's few archaeological theme parks, which occupies a site not far from that of ancient Albaniana. On a lakeside setting, amidst twisting and winding tracks, the unwary visitor in search of a Roman legionary can find himself trailing alongside a Bronze Age Frisian leading long-horned cattle to pasture, or walking past a virtuoso display of medieval weaving.

The Romans are fully represented by a bath-complex and an open palaestra (gymnasium) area, where, cheered on by a latter-day legionary in impeccably reproduced *lorica segmentata*,[26] an office party of Dutch pharmaceutical workers on an incentive day out practise archery, striking a target some 5 metres off with a worrying level of accuracy. Next door a reproduction amphitheatre, suitably miniature for a provincial backwater such as Albaniana (with seating for just a thousand or so), hosts fake (but oddly compelling) gladiatorial fights. As a trident-wielding *retiarius*[27] falls to the ground, his body prone against the sandy floor of the arena, the crowd of visitors bays for his opponent to finish him off. If ten minutes of athletic mimicry can invoke such a thirst for the gladiatorial sport, no wonder a regular diet of such spectacles instilled a deep-seated taste for such bloody pursuits throughout the Empire.

For those desiring a quieter, more reflective moment, or perhaps expiation for their guilty enjoyment of the gladiator's demise, a Gallo-Roman temple to the goddess Nehalennia, much worshipped in northern Germania Inferior, provides the opportunity. A blue-robed priestess offers the tourists a chance to make their very own burnt offering of fruit and to invoke Nehalennia's good wishes for their future ventures. As an experience it may lack objective authenticity, but in bringing flesh to the bones of what, on many sites, are but bare stones, it makes the point that – for all their distance in time, and in their modes of thought – the Romans were, after all, just human beings.

Ninety kilometres to the east, and almost at the border with modern Germany, Noviomagus, which became the chief administrative town for the Batavi under Roman rule, was occupied early by the armies of Augustus. The Romans took the pre-existing Batavian *oppidum* around 12–9 BC as part of Drusus's campaign to expand Roman control in the area. A legionary base was constructed on a steep plateau a couple of kilometres east of the modern city centre of Nijmegen, but was not finished, and both this and a civil settlement to the west seem to have been destroyed in AD 70 during the Batavian revolt. A new legionary fortress was built between the two older sites for the X Gemina legion, which occupied it from 71. This camp remained in use until about 175, and several of the gates and the *principia* have been explored, though stone-robbing in the Middle Ages erased most traces of the remaining internal buildings.[28] A civil settlement, meanwhile, grew up to the west of the modern town, close to the banks of the Waal River. Although generally referred to as Noviomagus Batavorum, it also bore the name Batavodurum, and there is some confusion as to whether there were in fact twin settlements rather than a single town. It received imperial patronage in 104, when Trajan had it renamed Ulpia Noviomagus Batavorum, thereby awarding it a title that reflected his own family name.

Modern travellers leaving Nijmegen to the east are greeted by a solitary statue of the Emperor, sword in hand, which presides over a ragged band of hitch-hikers hoping for a lift into Germany. More prosaically, this is also the way to the Huneberg Hill, the promontory on top of which the area's first Augustan camp was built, and where a Roman-era necropolis has been found. From around 260, however, when Frankish tribes began to occupy the area in some force, both of these sites were abandoned, and the remaining population clustered together in a more central position on top of the Valkhof Hill; for in the flattish Netherlands, any high ground was regarded as an advantageous place to site a defensive stronghold.

The Valkhof Hill is one of the few places in modern Nijmegen where the transportation mode of choice is not the bicycle, and the pedestrian is king. It seems that it was still retained by the Roman central author-ities into the 300s and was refortified under Constantine I and then again by Valentinian I towards the end of the century.[29] The park that now occupies it again housed a fortress in the 9th century and its stones were ransacked once more in 1796, during the Napoleonic occupation of the Netherlands when most of the structures there were dismantled. The nearby remains of the apse of the Church of Saint Martin, probably dating originally from Carolingian times and then rebuilt by Frederick Barbarossa in the 12th century, have, however, resisted all these vagaries. High up on the shell of the second storey, two Roman columns are embedded in the wall, a stray fragment of what must once have been a prosperous settlement.

The Romans early on recognised the strategic significance of the point where, in ancient times, the Lippe probably entered the Rhine – though their confluence has moved further south over time – and built a double legionary fortress here as early as 12 BC. This camp, known as Vetera I, was the first of a series intended to assist infiltration up the Lippe deep into free Germany and, as the reverse side of the coin, to defend against any German attacks that might strike the Roman territories on the Lower Rhine and the less well-fortified hinterland province of Gallia Belgica. It sits some 50 kilometres south-east of Nijmegen, just outside the modern German town of Xanten, whose attractive historic centre is dominated by the soaring spire of the Gothic Cathedral of Saint Victor, which, though begun in 1263, took nearly three centuries to complete. The church lies on the site of the shrine that gave the town its modern name, which is a corruption of *Ad Sanctos* ('at the place of the saints'), for it is supposed to represent the last resting place of Saint Victor, one of the martyrs of the 'Theban legion'.

A tradition grew up in early medieval times that an entire legion, which had been recruited in the Thebaid in Egypt, had converted to Christianity and, once drafted to Europe in 286, refused to sacrifice to the Emperor. For this insolent behaviour, it was to a man put to death at Agaunum (Saint-Maurice in modern Switzerland). The veracity of the legend is uncertain, and it seems unlikely that an entire military unit of around 6,000 men could have been executed without provoking a storm of commentary in the contemporary literary sources, but there really was a legion that embarked from Egypt at about the time, so the story may contain a germ of truth.[30]

In 1933, two graves were found beneath the Cathedral, of men in their thirties who had been killed violently. The burial was dated to around 360, and was thus about eighty years after the time of the Theban legion, so the skeletons may well represent some unknown early Christian martyrs to whom the legend became attached.[31] Whatever the reality, members of the Theban legion were venerated the length of the Rhine, particularly in Cologne and Xanten, with Saint Victor becoming the latter's very own military saint.

When it became apparent that a Roman push east, deep beyond the Rhine, was to be abandoned or postponed indefinitely, the garrison at

Vetera – made up from AD 43 of the V Alaudae and the XV Primigenia legions – settled in for a long stay. Unfortunately for them, their fate was to be very different. The year AD 69 started out as a bad one for the Roman Empire – its subsequent nickname as the 'Year of the Four Emperors' is a good indication of the chaos – and was to turn into an even worse one for the German provinces, threatening for a time to overturn the whole edifice of Roman control, both there and in Gaul.

The crisis had its roots in the final years of the reign of Nero, the last ruling member of the Julio-Claudian dynasty. The latter part of his reign had degenerated into a tedious round of licentiousness, conspiracy and unbridled revenge. Although a revolt in 68 by Julius Vindex, the legate of Gallia Lugdunensis, was put down by a force of Rhineland legions, the tide of power had begun to ebb and the Emperor lost his nerve. He committed suicide on 9 June, dying as flamboyantly as he lived with the bon mots 'What an artist the world loses in me'[32] upon his lips.

His successor Galba, already over seventy at the time of his accession, was soon afterwards murdered in the Forum by the praetorian guard, who had really been rather fond of Nero and nursed a grudge against the man who had supplanted him. The same day, 15 January 69, they declared Otho, who had been governor of Lusitania (in modern Portugal) under Nero, their new Emperor, a move countered by the Rhine army who sought to elevate their own commander, Vitellius, to the throne. Having scavenged imperial power from the corpse of Galba in such an unseemly fashion, neither of the two 'emperors' was to enjoy it for very long. This complex power struggle ended with the triumph of a third military strongman, Vespasian, who from 67 had been entrusted with the task of putting down a serious Jewish revolt in Judaea.[33]

Unfortunately, for Germania things were even more complicated. In a desperate bid to scrabble together reinforcements, Vitellius had ordered the conscription of extra auxiliary troops amongst the Batavians in Lower Germany. Under their leader Julius Civilis, who had backed Galba in the multifaceted civil war, the Batavians refused, declared themselves for Vespasian and set to besieging the pro-Vitellian legion that was based at Vetera (Xanten).[34]

What began as a ploy in a piece of imperial power politics soon took on the colours of a native revolt. For Civilis was a member of the traditional Batavian royal family, and local resentment at the heavy exactions on his people caused by the levies needed to fight the three-way civil war had fuelled nostalgia for the days when the Batavians were independent. Exactly what Civilis hoped to achieve is hard to determine, for much of the evidence for the revolt comes from Tacitus's *Historia*,[35] and it is sometimes hard to disentangle what are commonplace literary themes (such as the barbarian thirsting to throw off the yoke of Roman oppression) from actual motives or events.

What is indisputable is that in March, when the legionaries at Vetera tried to evacuate, they were slaughtered almost to a man by the Batavians. Civilis should now by rights have called off his men, for Vitellius was dead and Vespasian the unchallenged Emperor. Instead he made contact with Julius Classicus, a noble from Augusta Treverorum (Trier) who had been a Vitellian cavalry commander, and with Julius Tutor, who had been Vitellius's commander of the Rhine garrisons. Classicus declared himself Emperor of an independent Gaul and, with the aid of several Rhine legions that defected to him (including IV Macedonica and XXII Primigenia), finally captured Vetera and swept down the Rhine destroying fortresses as far south as Vindonissa (Windisch), which was spared, however, as the insurgents thought its garrison was sympathetic to them.

In the aftermath of these successes, the legate of one of the defeated legions[36] was captured and sent northwards as a present for Veleda, a prophetess of the Bructeri, whose supernatural sight was said to have foretold the Batavian victory. On the way the luckless legate was killed by his captors, and so, when Civilis captured the flagship of the Roman Rhine fleet some time later, it was rowed back and sent to Veleda as compensation for her loss. In the aftermath of the fall of Vetera, Civilis, who had at the start of the revolt sworn to cut neither his hair nor his beard until the Romans had been swept from the Batavians' land – and who therefore probably cut rather an alarming figure with a long, flowing red mane – symbolically cut short his locks, in a potent gesture that suggested there was nothing further to fear from their defeated adversaries.

By spring 70, however, the Romans were on the counter-attack, ably led by Petillius Cerealis,[37] who arrived at Mogontiacum (Mainz) in May. The disloyal I and XVI legions were defeated (and let off with a lecture), Julius Classicus and Julius Tutor fled back to the Batavian heartland, and those Gauls who had thought of joining the revolt were chastened back into cautious compliance with Roman rule. Mopping-up operations took some time, with bitter fighting south of the 'Island of the Batavians' across the Waal. Tacitus's account breaks off just at the point where Civilis is negotiating his surrender on a half-ruined bridge across the river, so it is unclear exactly what fate befell the Batavian leader.[38] If he really fell into the hands of the Romans, it was unlikely to have been a kind one, for his leadership of the revolt had led to the death of at least one legionary legate and the destruction of a swathe of forts. Their reconstruction took years, and the whole affair led to abandonment of the practice by which auxiliary regiments could serve in the province where they were raised; henceforth Batavian units would be drafted elsewhere,[39] far from the theatre in which Civilis had been able to use them to cause such mayhem.

The legionary camp at Vetera was not reconstructed; instead a new fort was built about 1.5 kilometres to the east, close to the Rhine (into which it would eventually collapse during the Middle Ages, rendering excavation practically impossible). This new site housed only a single legion, first the VI Victrix and then the XXX Ulpia, which was stationed there from around 125 until the time of Diocletian. Some way to the north-west of this a civilian settlement, known as Civitas Cugernorum, had grown up before the Batavian revolt. This was refounded under Trajan in about AD 100 under the name Colonia Ulpia Traiana. The new settlement may have been properly speaking a *colonia*, for the settlement of retired veterans of the legion.[40]

Colonia Ulpia Traiana is a little way out of the centre of modern Xanten. A deep ditch leads into a park, in which, on the day of our visit, a Celtic music festival was taking place, with strains of very un-Roman music wafting over the breeze, as though the Batavians and a bunch of their Gallic allies were about to make another attempt on Vetera. Through a crowd of incongruously tartan-clad spectators, the entrance to the archaeological site lay just beyond.

Ulpia Traiana is spectacular in a restrained sort of way, for it is the most complete reconstruction of a Roman city wall to be found anywhere. It emphatically does not pretend to be the original – although it runs along the line of the old perimeter – but its unbroken run of crenellated walls and the imposing bulk of its reconstructed gateways give some authentic sense of quite how imposing Roman urban defence works would have seemed to anyone tempted to have a crack at storming them.

Inside, the latter-day *colonia* is a mix of tree-lined paths striking straight (in true Roman town-planning fashion) between neat, verdant patches of lawn. Interspersed between them are those elements of Ulpia Traiana's major buildings that have been excavated and conserved. As many as 10,000 people lived here, crammed together in the 73-hectare site, which would have made it twice as crowded as modern Hong Kong or Singapore.[41] Despite the relatively advanced sewage systems possessed by Roman towns, the general conditions must have been incredibly unsanitary and the urban centres needed constant replenishment from the countryside to keep their populations stable.[42]

Although Ulpia Traiana possessed a major harbour and base for the Rhine fleet (the *Classis Germanica*), today only a column stump remains of the vast quays that carried vital trade up and down the river. Coastal and riverine communities such as this enjoyed privileged access to a cheaper and wider range of goods, as land transport was extremely expensive – for some non-luxury goods, prohibitively so – and therefore wherever possible merchants would transport their wares as far as they could by water.[43]

The most impressive of the city's reconstructed buildings is the amphitheatre, which had seating for about 10,000 (and so capable of holding the entire population of the town) around its enormous oval. The tiers of seats have been restored for modern spectacles, but standing in the centre of the sand-strewn arena, the entrance gates seem a long way off and the 3-metre internal wall dauntingly high. It inspires a moment of panic that escape might not be possible – just as it was not, without a potentially fatal encounter, for the gladiators who fought in it almost two millennia ago.

The second-largest temple in the colony was the Harbour Temple.[44] To which god it was dedicated is unknown, but its reconstruction is extremely striking. Most of the columns on the temple podium have been left as stumps, with only four restored to their complete height and topped with a portion of the architrave cut off at a 45-degree angle, making it look as if it has been sliced away deliberately and methodically by some very angry deity.

Apart from this, most of the rest of the site slumbers in peace. A reconstructed bathhouse and an unrestored bathing complex just outside the city walls under a large, modern glass protective cover are reflections of the level of amenities that inhabitants in such an important centre could expect, but in times of insecurity on the frontier the economies of the towns were simply not up to supporting them. Ulpia Traiana was still occupied in the 4th century; it was refortified under Constantius I, but by then it no longer seems to have housed a significant civilian population and had become a purely military station. Like all else in the area, it was swept away under Frankish pressure by the 5th century. That it survived as a significant centre of some sort is indicated by its appearance in the *Nibelungenlied*, a medieval Germanic epic (that almost certainly has even earlier oral antecedents) in which the exploits of Siegfried, a prince from a noble family based in Xanten, include the slaying of a dragon in order to win the hand of the princess Kriemhild of Worms.

From Vetera, the Rhine proceeds in a generally south-eastern direction, the modern landscape becoming more populated and visibly prosperous as it goes, this being one of the economic powerhouses of Germany. After around 35 kilometres the river reaches Neuss, which in Roman times was Novaesium, a Roman legionary fortress from about 12 BC until AD 92, when its garrison, the VI Victrix, was transferred to Vetera, and the camp was thenceforth home only to auxiliary units. It

was held as late as 359, when Julian reconstructed it, and in 378 one of the last Roman expeditions to venture beyond the Rhine into German territory crossed here.

It is only 35 kilometres from Neuss to Cologne, a major metropolis both of modern Germany and of the Rhineland frontier of the Roman Empire. Now a city of one million people, at the centre of an urban sprawl that houses many times this number and spreads its concrete fingers almost back as far as Neuss, Cologne began its history as the *oppidum* of the Germanic Ubii people, who are first attested at the time of Caesar's conquest of Gaul. Having favoured the Romans, and as a consequence in some danger from their fellow-Germans across the Rhine, the Ubii were resettled on the Roman side of the Rhine by Marcus Agrippa in 38 BC.[45] There they founded the town that would ultimately become modern Cologne. In an interestingly toadying example of street planning, the grid of the new city was laid out in such a way that the east–west axis was diverted a few degrees in order to line up with the direction of the sun on 23 September, the birthday of Augustus. The Emperor, no doubt, would spare a brief smile for this piece of topographic flattery on the part of some of his northernmost subjects. Perhaps in gratitude, around 9 BC the town was allowed to build an altar (*ara*) to honour Rome and Augustus, and because of this became known as Ara Ubiorum.

Although initially only a forward base for the conquest of the rest of Germany, after the Varan disaster of AD 9, the town became the chief centre of the securely pacified area that would later become Germania Inferior. The legionary camp that was built nearby had housed two legions, probably the XVII and XIX, both of which perished in the Battle of Teutoberger Wald.[46] To replace the lost units, the I Germanica and the XX Valeria Victrix were drafted in, but during the reign of Tiberius both were transferred away (to Bonna and Novaesium), and Ara Ubiorum became a purely civilian settlement. In AD 50 it was raised to the status of *colonia* in honour of the marriage of the Emperor Claudius to Agrippina, after whom it received the new name of Colonia Claudia Ara Agrippinensium (or Colonia Agrippinensis for short), from which its modern name derives.

As the capital of Germania Inferior, and hence the seat of the governor, Colonia Agrippinensis was furnished with all the prestige buildings to be expected of a leading Roman provincial centre. Most of them, however, were submerged beneath the modern city, including the walls that it received at the time of its re-establishment as a *colonia*.[47] These were only brought back to light in many areas through the damage done by bombing during the Second World War, destruction that yielded a very small silver lining in permitting the archaeological investigation of ancient strata of the city that had long been inaccessible.

Although it lacked a military garrison, Colonia Agrippinensis experienced a relatively tranquil existence until the mid-3rd century. The only real exception was its central role in the revolt of Aulus Vitellius, as it was here that he was declared Emperor in 69. As he processed through the streets, Vitellius is said to have carried the sword of Julius Caesar, which had been deposited in one of the city's temples.[48] The city experienced the rather more successful making of a new emperor, in 98, when Trajan, who was then governor of Germania Superior, happened to be staying in Colonia Agrippinensis when he received the news that Nerva was dead and that he was now ruler. Fittingly, that news was brought to him by Hadrian, who would in turn – though under rather more controversial circumstances – accede to the throne on Trajan's demise.

During the second half of the 3rd century, however, this part of the Rhine frontier began to suffer severely from Alamannic raids. The response of the central government was strong, if ultimately ineffective. In 257, Gallienus, who had hitherto been more than occupied in stemming a rising tide of barbarian incursions on the Danube, moved to base himself at Augusta Treverorum (Trier), using Colonia Agrippinensis as a forward position from which to strike back at the Alamanns. At this point, a series of appalling disasters struck. Gallienus's elder son, Valerian II, who had been elevated to the rank of Caesar, died; and, when a revolt broke out on the Danube,[49] Gallienus was left with no choice but to appoint his younger son Saloninus to the same rank and leave the inexperienced young man in charge of Colonia Agrippinensis. Meanwhile, Gallienus's father Valerian was captured after a serious defeat by the Persians on the Empire's eastern frontier in 260,[50] and, to make matters even worse, the Alamanns overran the Agri Decumates, while the Iuthungi, not to be left out, poured across the Danube.

Gallienus struggled to deal just with the Iuthungi, who penetrated as far as Rome, before finally being beaten near Milan in the summer of 260. The fear that their raid spread across Italy, which had not known fighting against foreign invaders on its soil for centuries – though it had had more than its fair share of campaigning in a variety of civil wars – led directly to the building by Aurelian, his successor, of a new set of walls around Rome for the first time since Severus (one of the early kings of Rome) in the 6th century BC.

When Gallienus left Saloninus in Colonia Agrippinensis, he had entrusted his safety to the guardianship of a senior official, the Frank Silvanus. Unfortunately, tension developed between Silvanus and Marcus Postumus, the governor of Germania Inferior,[51] and when a quarrel broke out in summer 260 over the distribution of spoils from a successful encounter with a Frankish raiding party, the soldiers mutinied and proclaimed Postumus as Emperor.[52] Gallienus was unable to provide any assistance to his son, and Saloninus and Silvanus were both murdered by the city garrison, their corpses thrown over the ramparts and the gates opened to Postumus.

The newly proclaimed Emperor rapidly secured control of Gallia Belgica, and then over a matter of months extended his rule over Germania Inferior. The rest of Gaul, together with Britain and Spain, and for a time even Raetia, also defected to him.[53] Apart from the personality clash with Silvanus, the revolt may be seen as an example of local self-help, for Gallienus was patently unable to come to the aid of the western provinces, whilst Postumus had shown himself at least modestly successful in holding back Frankish raids (though not the Alamannic ones that engulfed the Agri Decumates).

Having consolidated his position in the west, Postumus made no move to march on Rome, leading to a stand-off in which he remained firmly ensconced in his 'Gallic Empire', while Gallienus controlled the Italian peninsula and the Balkans. It is unclear whether Postumus was intent on the establishment of a permanent breakaway empire, or if he regarded himself in some sense as an (unrecognised) colleague of Gallienus in the imperial office – or, indeed, whether he had designs on absorbing the rest of the Empire, should the opportunity ever present itself. Given that he was based in Gaul, he had neither sought nor received senatorial approval and the constitutional legitimacy that it might bestow. Yet no one much seems to have been bothered by this, and it is clear that in an age of crisis the Roman state was being forced to adapt by whatever means it could to ensure its survival.

Postumus kept the Franks at bay on the Rhine, even though he could do nothing much about the Alamanni in the Agri Decumates. He retained an administration very much along Roman lines, complete with a local senate and representatives who mirrored in their titles those employed by the official imperial regime.[54] Having beaten back an attempt by Gallienus in 264–5 to secure southern Gaul, his regime was sufficiently self-confident that in late 268 he was able to celebrate his *decennalia*, the commencement of his tenth year on the throne, something no 'legitimate' emperor had succeeded in doing for over thirty years.[55]

The next year, Laelianus, who was probably Postumus's governor in Germania Superior,[56] revolted. The uprising was put down, but when Postumus refused his troops permission to pillage Mogontiacum (Mainz), the disgruntled soldiers murdered him. The Gallic Empire did not collapse immediately upon its founder's demise. The central Roman Empire was still too weak, and Claudius II Gothicus and Aurelian too preoccupied, first in the Balkans fighting the Goths, and then in dealing with the revolt of Queen Zenobia of Palmyra in the east, to reabsorb the western separatist empire. Victorinus, who had been head of Postumus's praetorian guard, was proclaimed Emperor by the troops in Trier,[57] but he lasted just two years before his own murder and replacement by Tetricus, who had previously been governor of Aquitania.

By now, the Gallic Empire was seriously weakened, and it was further undermined when Hispania restored its allegiance to the Rome-based Emperor. Once Aurelian had defeated Zenobia in the east, it was only a matter of time before he turned his attention to the reconquest of Gaul.

In early summer 274 Aurelian crossed the Alps and on the Catalaunian Fields, near Châlons, the two armies met. It was, by strange historical coincidence, precisely the same area where, 177 years later, Attila the Hun would suffer his first major defeat.[58] Tetricus was taken prisoner during the course of the fighting and his men panicked and fled, resulting in the predictable slaughter that was inflicted on retreating armies in ancient times. One version of the events has it that Tetricus so despaired of coming out victorious, and was in any case so tired of dealing with troops ever on the point of mutiny, that he had been in secret negotiations with Aurelian before the battle.[59] It is unlikely, however, that his capture was prearranged, for it failed to avert the large-scale loss of life that such a deal would have been expected to broker.[60]

Tetricus certainly did receive merciful treatment at Aurelian's hands. Far from being executed (or left to the mercy of the victorious army, which was tantamount to a death sentence), he was packed off to be the administrator of Lucania, a relatively unimportant district in southern Italy. Aurelian had now achieved the reintegration of the Roman Empire, something that had seemed impossible just a decade before.[61]

Colonia Agrippinensis, too, was by this time back under the authority of the Emperor at Rome. But it was a changed world now, and increasingly rulers had to base themselves in the provinces if they were to have any hope at all of dealing with the multifaceted problems that they could never seem to solve definitively and certainly could not cope with from the safe, but isolating, distance of Rome. Constantine I established himself in Colonia Agrippinensis around 310, when he also engaged in some important refortification works. The city saw a further attempted usurpation in the troubled years after the revolt of Magnentius, who had succeeded in bringing the whole of Gaul to his side and was only defeated in a close-run battle by Constantius II at Mursa (Osijek) in Moesia in 351.

In August 355, Constantius's infantry commander in Gaul, Silvanus, revolted and was proclaimed Emperor by his troops in Colonia Agrippinensis; he had been a former supporter of Magnentius, and had defected at a crucial moment in the Mursa battle, so his double treachery was all the more surprising.[62] Although Silvanus was dealt with inside a month – his supporters were suborned by Constantius's envoy Ursicinus and the usurper dragged from the church within which he had taken refuge, and then murdered – it was clear that the Rhineland provinces could not be left to their own devices. Constantius, in desperate need of a deputy whom he could trust to shore up the imperial position there, turned to his young cousin Julian, one of the last surviving male members of Constantine I's family (most of the others had been killed in a purge probably instigated by one or other of Constantine's sons immediately upon his death in 337, with the aim of eliminating potential rivals).[63]

Constantius had previously entrusted the position of Caesar in the East to Julian's older brother Gallus, but he had proved difficult to manage and was executed for possible treasonous designs in 354. The Emperor consequently tried to restrain his young cousin on a tight leash, and Julian was therefore sent to Gaul in 356 with only a few hundred troops under his command.[64] Colonia Agrippinensis had in the meantime fallen to the Salian Franks, who were busily extending the area under their control from their heartland at the mouth of the Rhine. It took ten months before it could be retaken, and so Julian was probably involved in the campaign that ended in its recapture.[65] He became increasingly assertive and his military senior officers, who believed they had been appointed to act as the inexperienced Caesar's minders, grew disenchanted. They intimated to Constantius that Julian might even be aiming to replace his cousin as the senior Emperor. When Julian came under siege in Sens by a group of Franks in winter 356, the cavalry commander Marcellus made no move to relieve him, and as a result Constantius sacked him at Julian's request.

Henceforth, the young Caesar was given far more leeway in ruling his own affairs in Gaul, and his victories against the Franks and Alamanns over a two-year period of campaigning show the success of this policy. In a later account of his time in Gaul,[66] Julian celebrates his triumph in recovering Colonia Agrippinensis, and proclaims that after this Roman ships were once more able to sail down the Rhine, a vital prerequisite of establishing security in the province. In 356 and 357, Julian engaged in a series of small-scale campaigns against the Franks that recovered many of the smaller towns which had fallen to them and generally restored the security of the countryside.

The next year, a coordinated campaign, which was supposed to have dealt with the Alamanni in conjunction with a thrust from Augusta Raurica (Kaiseraugst) in the south by Constantius's infantry commander Barbatio, faltered when the southern arm got the timing wrong and did not link up with Julian's force. Instead, Julian launched an attack on Chnodomarius, the Alamannic king near Argentorate (Strasbourg). He was probably seriously outnumbered (Ammianus says he had 13,000 men to Chnodomarius's 35,000),[67] but Roman discipline told, and when their battle line failed to buckle under the weight of uncoordinated Alamannic attacks, their adversaries turned tail and fled to the river, where huge numbers drowned, while many of the rest were picked off by Roman arrows and javelins. Chnodomarius, who made a last stand on a nearby hill, was captured and despatched to Constantius's court in Milan.[68]

Flushed with success, Julian defeated several minor Alamannic kings ensconced near Mogontiacum (Mainz) and rooted out a band of Franks who were in possession of two abandoned Roman forts on the Meuse. Over the next two years, he managed to reduce the taxation burden on the Gauls – in the face of dogged resistance from his praetorian prefect Florentius, who felt that a higher tax rate would yield more revenue, Julian implemented the simpler policy of actually collecting more efficiently the tax that was owing.[69] He also mounted two more expeditions against the Alamanns across the Rhine, which in places reached the former line of the *limes* under Antoninus Pius, positions that had been abandoned almost a century earlier.

Julian's victorious career in Gaul, and the security he had brought to the frontier regions, would end with his proclamation as Emperor by his troops in Paris in February 360. The rest of his career was to be bound up in the East, and his fame in subsequent centuries has owed more to his attempt – which failed because of his early death – to restore paganism as the official religion of the Roman Empire.[70]

Although Julian had succeeded in reconquering Colonia Agrippinensis from the Franks, the same group again laid waste to the city in 388, and barely seventy years later, in 455, one of their sub-groups, the Ripuarians, retook it. By now, there was almost no Roman army to speak of anywhere on the Rhine, so there was absolutely no prospect of reclaiming it for the Empire. Colonia Agrippinensis became the Ripuarian capital, which it remained until 507, when Sigebert was defeated by Clovis, the Salian Frankish king, after which the city formed part of the Merovingian and then the Carolingian Frankish kingdoms.

Modern Cologne houses the Römisch-Germanisches Museum, one of Europe's premier collections of Roman archaeological remains, which

lies roughly in the north-west corner of the former Roman city. Its masterpiece is the Dionysus mosaic, which is preserved in its original position,
its vast 7 x 10.5-metre canvas probably saved by the fire that destroyed
the roof of the building in which it originally lay, possibly during one of
the Frankish sackings of the city in 355 or 388.[71] It is composed of more
than one million individual tesserae and is a work of the highest order.
Its central panel depicts a youthful Dionysus leaning louchely on a satyr,
with an empty wine cup at his feet. Around this, other panels show
maenads and satyrs dancing ecstatically, while the outer register of panels
portrays a medley of edible animals, including peacocks and ducks.

Amidst a wealth of other survivals of Roman Colonia Agrippinensis,
two stand out. The central arch of the city's north gate has been reconstructed in the museum, made up of thirteen heavy slabs of limestone;
through here, traffic coming in from Novaesium (Neuss) to the north
would have entered directly onto the *cardo maximus*, which today forms
Cologne's Hohe Straße. The fragment of inscription on the arch, which
reads 'Galliena', is most likely a reference to Gallienus, and so probably
dates it to the 250s, before the usurpation of Postumus brought the city
into the territory of the Gallic Empire.

At the museum's entrance stands one of the most spectacular and showy
items, the reconstruction of the mausoleum of Poblicius, a veteran of the
V Alaudae legion, which was based in Vetera. It is a huge multi-storey
affair on which the dead man is depicted flanked by his family, standing
between the columns of a 4-metre-high temple portico, which forms the
mausoleum's centrepiece. Dressed in a toga, and bearing a scroll, Poblicius
himself has a sanguine, almost resigned, expression about him. The inscription at the base of the monument is finished off with the initials 'H.M.H.';
the presumed additional (but missing) letters 'N.S.' would make it stand
for *Hoc Monumentum Heredem Non Sequitur* ('This monument is not to fall
to the lot of my heir). In other words, Poblicius's sons and successors are
to keep their hands off his tomb and not pull it down to replace it with
one of their own. Evidently filial piety could only be ensured beyond the
grave by the threat of legal sanctions implicit in this formula.[72]

Another of the highlights of the museum is its collection of Roman
glassware, the majority of it discovered in one or other of the extensive
Roman-era cemeteries that lined the roads out of the ancient city. Most
of it is well made but plain, in a variety of colours and shapes; the finest
examples, however, are delicately incised with coloured paintwork. One
piece, in particular, stands out: the Achilles Goblet, found by chance in
the grounds of a student hostel in 1991. In vibrant colours, the myth of
Achilles is recounted. The hero has been hidden by his mother Thetis and

dressed as a girl to avoid being sent to the war against Troy, but is revealed when, unlike his female companions, he does not run away at the sound of a war trumpet, instead seizing a spear to face down the intruder.

A few hundred metres south of the museum, tucked beneath the modern Rathaus, a rather anonymous-looking square-shaped structure with iron grilles marks the entrance to one of Cologne's most important archaeological relics. It is the *praetorium*, the remains of the Roman governor's palace, and it was probably here or hereabouts that Vitellius was proclaimed Emperor in 69, and that Postumus later had his headquarters. It served all this time as the capital of Germania Inferior and houses a complex series of remains, which represent several stages of building throughout the long centuries of its use. Underground, the light that illuminates the shattered walls ranges from yellow to metallic blue, giving the disorienting effect that the past is refracted as it passes through the various phases of the *praetorium*.

The first stone building on this site, surviving in two parallel walls 4 metres apart, comes from a time before Colonia Agrippinensis and probably represents the headquarters building for Germanicus, who resided here in AD 13–17, using it as a base for his campaigns across the Rhine into Free Germany.[73] It was probably here that his daughter Agrippina was born in AD 15, for whom, after her marriage to Claudius in 50, the city would be renamed. Another structure is clear in the semi-darkness, with two apses and a water basin that come from a phase in the mid-2nd century. The building was then adapted yet again in the later 3rd century, when a galleried hall was created. One of the tile stamps found here can be deciphered to reveal the name 'Didius Julianus', who was governor of Germania Inferior in the early 180s and who, for a brief few months in 193, would become Emperor (having effectively bought the imperial office from the praetorian guards in an auction).[74] A final phase of the building, an octagonal structure, is also clearly discernible amongst the jumbled walls of the various levels. This was built some time in the mid-to late 4th century, although whether it can be ascribed to Julian's stay in the city is unclear.[75]

The building was rediscovered as long ago as 1570, when the foundations for the old Rathaus were dug, and in 1630 a stone was found with the inscription 'Praetorium', resulting in its identification as a Roman governor's palace. Leading off from the main building, a passage that is traversable for a few hundred metres in dark and claustrophobic gloom is in fact a Roman-era sewer. Not a place to linger long, and certainly not in reflecting on its original use, for there are far more edifying Roman remains to be found nearby, beneath the Dom, the cathedral of Cologne.

The soaring Gothic towers of the church, whose current building was begun in 1248, are one of Germany's most famous landmarks. It remained unfinished, however, for more than 400 years, before a fit of antiquarian interest in Germany's medieval heritage and a goodly dose of civic pride caused its completion in the mid-19th century, very much in the spirit of the plans that had been conceived seven centuries earlier.

The cathedral had been a place of Christian worship for 700 years even before that, and so lies on top of one of Germany's earliest attested churches. The city's first recorded bishop, Maternus, attended the synod called by Constantine I in Rome in 313 to adjudicate on the Donatist schism that was afflicting North Africa,[76] but there must have been a Christian community in Colonia Agrippinensis at least a little before this. Beneath the medieval cathedral, an underground world of remains overlies the presumed site of this earliest basilica. Massive blocks mark the foundation stones of the 13th-century church, while scattered around lie walls from its 8th-century predecessor (the Alter Dom or 'Old Cathedral'). The whole is a maze of walls, blocks and rubble, lying silent save for the occasional guided tour, and unknown to the vast majority content to view the huge edifice above.

The very first phase of the building is represented by the remains of a Roman hypocaust, which came from a 1st-century structure, which was, a couple of centuries later, enlarged by the addition of a long atrium, at which point the building could have served as the meeting house for Cologne's Christians – indeed, this may have been the determining factor in the selection of this site for the city's first major Christian construction. The building had an octagonal basin, which may have served as a baptismal font for the community. In the 5th or 6th century the land next to this building was being used as a cemetery, possibly by the Frankish community, which by then occupied the city. Archaeologists currently believe that there was not in fact a temple of Mercury below the deepest level of Christian occupation,[77] a variance from the tradition of siting churches on ancient pagan cult sites.

The cathedral hides yet another secret, for in the treasury a section of the city's north wall protrudes, a massive bulk some 7 metres high and 20 metres long. Although the remains of this wall then disappear under the north transept of the Dom, it is possible in Cologne, unlike in most cities of Roman origin, to follow much of the line of the wall and still see fair sections of it intact. The original circuit, constructed at the time of the *colonia*'s foundation in the mid-1st century, was around 4 kilometres in length and punctuated by nine gates, three to the west, three on the Rhine side of the city, two in the south and only one to the north (which is the one that has been reconstructed in the museum).[78] The outer and inner walls, which rose to almost 8 metres in height, were constructed of small ashlar stone, with a mixture of rubble and tiles forming a supporting core.

To follow the line of the walls today involves a walk of roughly three hours and is one of the most extraordinary experiences that the Roman frontier can offer. It seems, walking along main roads, on alleys between apartment blocks and through squares crowded with traffic, that the city truly is a palimpsest on which the modern version has been inscribed over an incomplete erasure of the ancient. The circuit begins in the most unlikely of settings, an underground car park. A massive section of masonry sits in a quiet corner, just metres away from rows of neatly parked Audis and Volkswagens, the faint smell of petrol fumes the only distraction from the surprise of the place.

Back above ground the remains of the eastern arch of the north gate to the city lie in a small park to the west of the Dom. It survived the dismantling of much of the gate in 1106, as it was then built into the cathedral provost's house, and was moved here from its original position a little to the west in 1971. It seems very precariously perched now, almost skeletal, and totally drowned out by the to-and-fro rush of tourists in search of postcards and ice cream or dashing to catch that last train from the main station just a few hundred metres away.

Westwards on Komedienstraße, which begins unpromisingly with a parade of kebab shops and other cheap snack stalls, a small section of the wall lies, matter of fact in the middle of the pavement, only around a metre tall, but providing a very convenient perch for a pair of local teenagers to lounge and catch a leisurely coffee. Where the road hits a busy junction with the side Nord-Süd-Fahrt stands the most visible tower on this stretch of the wall, known as the Lysolphturm, the outline of its shell complete to over a metre in height, but looking rather beleaguered as the traffic whizzes by its ancient form.

A couple of hundred metres further west, not far from Cologne's history museum, stands the Römerbrunnen or 'Roman Fountain', built in 1915 to commemorate the city's Roman heritage. It was badly damaged during the Second World War, and only an image of the Capitoline She-Wolf suckling Romulus and Remus – a reference to Rome's foundation myth – and six portraits and busts of Roman emperors and empresses remain of the original scheme. As a strictly modern evocation of Cologne's Roman past, it has a self-conscious monumentality of which the Romans would have been proud, and is, therefore, in a way as authentic as the remains of the wall itself.

Just where the north wall ends and the west wall begins, the Römerturm looms into view. This angle tower is the best preserved along the wall circuit, and almost three-quarters of its shape juts out from the junction of the north and west walls. It is richly ornamented in rosettes, triangles and lozenges, and, though the battlements at the top are a reconstruction from a rebuilding undertaken in 1898, its present use as a private residence is certainly far less humiliating than its fate in the early 19th century, when it was employed by the Franciscan nuns of the convent of Saint Clara as their communal lavatory.

Just to the south along Saint Apernstraße lies the Saint Helenturm, a romantic ruin entirely overgrown with a layer of creepers and vegetation so that the tower, although its semicircular outline is clearly visible, is scarcely noticed by modern passers-by. Beyond the Ehrentor, which marked one of the city's western gates, reproductions of murals and parts of the Roman road are visible under glass slabs in the foyer of a savings bank, making them seem like a part of some everyday advertising campaign promoting the virtues of an antique lifestyle.

Just further south, where Im Laach Street bends round to meet Marsilstein, the Roman aqueduct came into the city. Until the late 18th century part of it was still visible, a surviving section of the water channel, which was dubbed in the Middle Ages the Marsilisusstein and believed to be the sarcophagus of an (entirely fictional) local hero named Marsilius who had, it was supposed, saved the city when it was under siege by a Roman emperor.

On this western section of the ancient city's perimeter, several sections of wall are clearly visible in the foundations of modern apartment blocks, sitting below hanging baskets or forming the frame of basement windows. In Bobstraße, a section of the wall pokes into a shop that seems to be a hairdressing salon, matter of factly protruding amongst the clients' chairs, whilst a lady who is doing the wall tour with her small son tries to explain to her disbelieving child that this architectural oddity is not some piece of botched building work, but a precious cultural relic almost two millennia old. A little way further south along the western wall, between two sets of apartment blocks behind Mauritiussteinweg, the wall survives in a section around 50 metres long. Partly overgrown, this precious relic is the most extraordinary everyday footpath of the modern residents.

The wall then becomes more fragmentary and its remains more elusive. Just at the point where it curves east to form the south wall, there once stood a gate that formed the exit point for those citizens on their way to the city's hippodrome, a structure attested in sources but as yet unlocated. Along Alte Mauer am Bach – from which the ditch, at least, of the ancient wall can be seen – lies another interval tower, opposite a heavily graffitoed modern wall, with old, broken-down suitcases and a grubby, discarded mattress piled in a heap beside it.

From such indignities, the wall proceeds north-eastwards past the site of the city's main south gate, which lay at one end of the *cardo*. It now turns north for its final stretch alongside the Rhine. Here lies the tower that has become known as the Ubiermonument. Discovered in 1965, and built on massive oak piles composed of wood felled in AD 4,[79] the huge square structure pre-dates the rest of the walls, possibly by decades, and may have served either as a bulwark for a fortification of the *oppidum* Ubiorum, which preceded Colonia Agrippinensis, or even (according to one interpretation) as a mausoleum, which was later adapted for use in the line of the colony's new walls.

A hundred metres north lay the Capitoline temple, later transformed into the Romanesque church of Saint Maria in Kapitol, preserving its origins in its name. Remains of the *capitolium* were found beneath the lovely round church in the early 20th century, and its heart lay more or less directly under the altar of the current building, a clear sign of the Christians' intent in appropriating the sacred spot of the pagans whom they were displacing. Further north, just by the little square today appropriately called Marspforte, there was by tradition a temple to Mars. It was from here that Vitellius took the sword of Julius Caesar, which played a central role in his proclamation as Emperor in 69. In the 16th century, two statues were erected here, one to Mars and the other to his Christian warrior analogue, the Archangel Michael, and, set in a wall nearby, the stone pedestal of the Saint Michael statue can still be seen.

Along the northernmost section of the eastern wall, the Roman harbour once lay, not far from the Drachenpforte, which was long the city's main passage to reach the Rhine. Until the later Roman period, the Rhine reached almost to the city walls, and an island lay between it and the current riverbank. This, however, silted up some time after the 2nd century, leaving the river's course much as it is today. The wall now finally turns west, liberated from main roads, traffic and apartment buildings, and strikes under the cathedral to appear in the Treasury where the walk began.

Many of Cologne's other surviving Roman buildings lurk around or beneath its collection of Romanesque churches. Beneath the massive tower of the church of Saint Georg, just outside the city's southern gates, stood, for example, a post of the *beneficiarii*, the sub-section of the military that was tasked with protecting the road system and ensuring that tolls owed by travellers carrying goods for sale were handed over to the authorities.

West of the church of Saint Gereon, the outline of a Roman atrium that pre-dated the church is marked out in stones. The church itself marks another of the supposed sites of the martyrdom of a member of the Theban legion. A column fragment inside is alleged to be the stone over which the blood of the martyr flowed at his execution. By tradition, no person who attempted to pass by the column harbouring a guilty secret would find it possible to proceed. The conscience of the few modern Cologners visiting the church seems, mercifully, to be completely clear, and no one is left humiliatingly stuck in the porch.

A more surprising remnant of Colonia Agrippinensis is to be found in the busy shopping street of Schildergasse, which lies on the line of the *decumanus maximus*, the main east–west axis of the ancient city. It was here, in 1995, that the remains of the forum were discovered during the demolition of a brewery. The five pedestals and columns that were unearthed at the time were not preserved and were removed. However, one piece at least of the forum can be seen in its original find-spot. It involves an expedition into the basement of the C&A department store. There, to the side of a McDonald's franchise and just beyond women's swimwear, a section of masonry 1.5 metres high is preserved, lodged beneath the stairs besides the ladies' toilets, access to it partly blocked off by the cleaners' trolleys. It is one of the more unusual settings for Roman ruins on the frontier, but at least one can munch on a burger or try on the latest beach fashion whilst admiring the vestiges of Colonia Agrippinensis's civic heart.

Across the railway bridge that leads over the Rhine (looking back from which the most staggering view of the Dom can be snatched), a confusing spaghetti tangle of roads and pathway leads down to the site of Divitia, the bridgehead fort built around 310 by Constantine I to guard the landing place opposite the main city. It was constructed by the XXII legion[80] as part of a programme to establish fortified positions on the east bank of the Rhine, which would secure traffic along the river, discourage any barbarians who might be so disposed from attempting to cross over directly opposite the main cities, and provide a suitable base from which to launch punitive expeditions into German territory.

It is a rather melancholy site now, sandwiched between the concrete blocks of a Lufthansa administrative building and an old people's home, an unmarked and unloved Roman relic. Two of the east-gate towers survive, extant to about 60 centimetres in height. One of the towers is wholly overgrown in nettles, the other sporting a recent graffito. A small section of the south wall lies hidden in an underground garage, while part of the north wall's central tower is marked in the pavement some way off. The camp originally had fourteen towers and two gates, with sixteen rows of barracks inside the walls to house up to a thousand soldiers. The sole ancient depiction of the fort comes from a medal minted in Trier around 315, which shows Constantine standing inside its wall, as though delivering a speech. On it, seven towers can be made out, together with the 400-metre-long Roman bridge across the river. The Emperor would, no doubt, be most displeased at the fate of his handiwork.

Just as today's Cologne sprawls untidily in every direction, threatening to engulf the countryside and suck the neighbouring towns and villages into its ambit, so ancient Colonia Agrippinensis had suburbs and satellite towns. The old cemeteries that spread out for many kilometres outside the city are one sign of this. Many of the funerary monuments are now visible only in museums, divorced through necessity from their original settings. In the suburb of Weiden, around 9 kilometres west of Cologne (a half-hour ride on the U-bahn), one of Colonia's ancient mausolea can, however, still be seen in place. It lies in the garden of a suburban house, a concrete protective chamber built above it, and a sign for the 'Römergrab' (Roman tomb) the only indications that this is anything other than an overly ambitious shed.

Once led downstairs by the householder, the atmosphere changes. A small display of Roman glass, found after the mausoleum was opened in 1843, leads down to further steps. And there the tomb sits, as though time has utterly passed it by. In the centre lies a partly shattered sarcophagus of white marble, a relief carved on it of winged goddesses flanking a medallion with portraits of the deceased and two youthful figures. To the right and left, niches hold busts, presumably of the deceased; a man with a moustache and curly sideburns and, to the left, two women, one with a severe expression and a garment flung over her shoulder, her hair parted in the middle, and the other seemingly by a different artist, her face more crudely delineated.

Either side of the doorway, precise limestone reproductions of wicker armchairs perch. They were probably for funerary feasts in honour of the deceased, and would be used by the women (men generally reclined on couches to take their meals). Coins found in the chamber indicate that it was probably used from the 2nd century to the mid-4th century, housing several generations of the dead of one family. It is a very striking place. Those who were buried here, and their loved ones, thought they would never be forgotten and that their names and memories would be cherished for ever. Yet although their names and identities are utterly erased, the faces – albeit anonymous – of at least three of them really have survived.

Thirty kilometres south-east of Cologne, the former legionary camp at Bonna (Bonn) has undergone some dramatic swings in fortune during its time. Occupied originally by an auxiliary unit in about 10 BC, it became the home of the I Germanica legion in around AD 30,[81] who then built a wooden fortress there, a construction that was upgraded to stone around 83, some time after its destruction in the Batavian revolt. After Colonia Agrippinensis was effectively demilitarised in 50, Bonna became the main garrison point in the area.

The fortress lay in the middle of the old town of the modern city of Bonn, which was from 1945 until 1990 the capital of West Germany (and very briefly of a unified Germany, before the transfer of the capital back to Berlin), but only the street grid and stray finds betray this heritage. The southern edge of the camp's east wall is recorded by a plaque on a tower that now forms part of a beer garden. Further north and between two apartment blocks in a run-down part of town, the tomb of a soldier indicates the *porta principalis sinistra* of the camp, a lonely marker stuck on the edge of a dual carriageway. The Römerstraße seems a very ordinary busy road in a down-at-heel neighbourhood, but it leads on to what was the south gate of the camp, indicated by yet another tombstone, this time set into the wall of a house. Here the deceased was an auxiliary in the V Asturum cohort who reached the rank of signifer, the standard-bearer for the unit, and died aged just thirty, after six years of service. His monument at least survives, but, rather disrespectfully, it has a yellow wheelie-bin parked beside it for the refuse from the neighbouring houses.

Of the interior buildings of the fort and town, even less is intact, though the old auxiliary fort is believed to have been on the site of the Old Rathaus, a baroque affair, finished in sickly-sweet pink and white, which stands near the central market. Bonn's cathedral, the Münster, also, stands on ancient ground, for it was built on top of a 4th-century *cella memoriae* that honoured two further members of the ubiquitous Theban legion, saints Cassius and Florentinus.

Most of Bonn's Roman memories, however, are entombed in the Rheinisches Landesmuseum, a curious structure, which looks as if the architect despaired halfway through and just encased what he had so far achieved within a glass sarcophagus. Its most famous piece is the tomb-stone of Marcus Caelius, which was originally discovered embedded in a monastery wall near Xanten.[82] Caelius was a centurion serving in the XVIII legion and died aged fifty-three during Varus's campaign in AD 9, if not at the final disastrous battle itself.[83] Wherever he perished, Caelius stares out from his monument flanked by two freedmen and heavily adorned with military decorations demonstrating his bravery, including *phalerae*, disk-like medallions, one of which is decorated with the head of Medusa. Around his head he wears the *corona civica*, a wreath of oak leaves and acorns, which was only awarded to soldiers who saved the life of a Roman citizen in the heat of battle.

Rigomagus (modern Remagen), some 20 kilometres to the south-east of Bonn, marks the last major defensive position in Germania Inferior. An auxiliary fort was built here in the 1st century, and it remained in use until the 5th century. Perhaps its most unusual relic is an inscription recording the repair in 218 of the camp sundial by the commander Petronius Athenodorus, who was, presumably, fed up of his men turning up late for parades.

Germania Superior

Just a couple of kilometres down the river from Rigomagus, and a little south of Sentiacum (Sinzig), began the province of Germania Superior. Here, the *limes* starts to take on an altogether different quality, as for roughly two centuries the Rhine (and to the east the Danube) did not form the frontier of the Empire at all. Instead, in a complicated series of moves forward, successive emperors pushed away from the line of the rivers, in effect demilitarising them and carving out new provincial territory in the Agri Decumates, whose occupation provided increased security for major centres such as Mogontiacum (Mainz) and Augusta Raurica (Kaiseraugst in Switzerland).

The result is that the frontier here has a series of *limites*. There is the line of the Rhine and Danube, which marked the border until the late 1st century and would do so again from the later 3rd century. Further east of the Rhine and Danube, the first advanced position reached by the Romans is known as the 'Neckar–Odenwald *limes*', whilst a final forward push under Antoninus Pius (138–61) led to a position known – although only to modern scholars of the frontiers – as the 'Antonine *limes*'.

A narrow area of land on the Upper Rhine between the river and the beginning of the Black Forest had probably been under the control of the Roman military since the reign of Augustus. Gradually more permanent forts were established in this area, the Wetterau, a fertile plain that lies between the river and the Taunus mountains to the north-west. Amongst these was Aquae Mattiacorum (modern Wiesbaden), which was first built in timber under Claudius and re-established by Vespasian after its destruction by the Chatti in around AD 50. Vespasian also promoted the building of roads to enhance communications between Mogontiacum and Augusta Vindelicum (Augsburg) in Raetia, necessitating the moving of some forts to the east bank of the river. Finally, in AD 73–4 a large-scale campaign became necessary, led by Cnaeus Pinarius Clemens, legate of the Upper Germany army, which secured the region around the lower Neckar river, so allowing the Romans to build a road through the Black Forest. At the same time, another road was constructed leading from Vindonissa (Windisch) in the south up to Arae Flaviae (Rottweil), and in the south-east control was extended in Raetia beyond the Danube, with the building of a line of forts, including Günzburg.[84]

A further extension of the line was achieved under Domitian, particularly as a result of a major campaign against the Chatti, who were the dominant tribe in the area of modern Hesse. The actual date for the outbreak of the war is frustratingly vague, but it probably began in summer 82 or the winter of 82–3.[85] The Chatti seem to have been a much more organised group than most of the tribes on the *limes* (with the exception of the Batavians in 69) and are said to have elected their officers, and to have drawn up plans for each day's operations in advance, as well as building proper camps each night on Roman lines.[86] The Roman force that undertook the campaign was very large, possibly 50,000–60,000 men including units from at least five legions,[87] and used Mogontiacum as the main base for the assault. The course of the war is uncertain, but it was clearly prolonged and bitter, and on one occasion the Emperor is recorded as having made his cavalry dismount so that they could chase the Chatti into the otherwise impenetrable forest, which the barbarians employed as a refuge.

Exactly how far Domitian's army advanced is unclear; Frontinus in his *Strategemata* maintains that he moved the *limes* forward '120 miles' (equivalent to about 175 kilometres), and although this may be too far, a significant push north-east towards the Taunus mountains was definitely achieved.[88] The major victories seem to have been won in 83, after which Domitian celebrated a triumph, although fighting actually went on until 85. The new frontier was reinforced with a series of watchtowers and timber forts, running into the Taunus and to the south along the Main and then the Odenwald forest, before linking up with the previously secured border line along the central course of the Neckar river.

It was also under Domitian's rule, probably in the years immediately following the end of the Chattian War, that Germania Inferior and Superior were constituted as regular provinces. The system he established remained more or less unchanged along the northern stretches until the middle of the 3rd century, a lasting achievement for which he is often denied credit amidst the welter of accusations that accompanied his later decline into suspicion and paranoia.[89] Domitian had never been expected to be Emperor; it was his older brother Titus, fresh from a successful military career (including the finishing-off of the Jewish revolt in AD 71), who had initially succeeded to the throne, but his early death in 81 of a fever led to the younger brother's unheralded elevation. Possibly as a result of his comparative inexperience, Domitian tended to stress heavily his own military achievements as Emperor – he awarded himself no fewer than twenty-three imperial salutations, more even than Augustus had achieved – and this may have led him into the prosecution of the war against the Chatti[90] (and one against the Dacians in 88–9).

Further fortification of the area took place under Trajan, but it was with his successor Hadrian in the second quarter of the 2nd century that the new frontier was truly consolidated. Many of the watchtowers were rebuilt in stone, and along the whole length of the frontier a palisade of oak stakes was erected. This was placed in front of the military road that led along the frontier on the barbarian side of the line, acting more as a visible marker and obstacle to small-scale incursions than as a fixed point to defend. Thus, to Hadrian, who in northern Britain laid out the most visible frontier defences on the whole *limes*, is also owed an analogous system in Germania.

Finally, under Antoninus Pius, the forts along the Neckar and Odenwald in the central sector were moved around 30 kilometres forward, creating a stretch of frontier that ran 80 kilometres southwards, which in all that distance deviated by only a matter of metres from a dead-straight line, an astonishing achievement on the part of the Roman surveyors. Under Caracalla the defences of the *limes* were again strengthened by the addition of a steep ditch and an earth rampart behind the palisade, improvements that rendered the barrier of more than symbolic significance. In Raetia, the palisade was replaced by a stone wall studded at intervals with watchtowers, very similar in its basic conception to Hadrian's Wall.

Thirty-five kilometres south down the original river line from Sentiacum, the frontier led past Koblenz, where the confluence of the Rhine and the Mosel gave the town its Latin name, Confluentes, and whose Liebfrauenkirche contains a 15-metre-high section of the fortress built here in Constantinian times (although there had been some form of military encampment since very early in the 1st century AD). This section of the Rhine is studded with fairytale castles perched impossibly high up on crags, the most famous of them the 'Pfalz' (or Burg Pfalzgrafenstein) whose pentagonal keep acted as a tollhouse on the river from the 13th century right up until 1867. The river also flows here through the Rhine Gorge, a picturesque 60-kilometre-long section whose soaring cliffs were cut by the erosive action of the river over many millennia. On the east bank the most famous landmark of all, the rock of the Lorelei, rises up. The Lorelei's striking silhouette and the murmuring sound of the Rhine as it rushes against its base gave rise to the legend of the 'Rhine Maidens', monsters who lured sailors to their death against the rocks, in a German reprise of the Greek myth of the Sirens.

Around 25 kilometres south of Koblenz is Boppard – Bodobriga to the Romans – which was probably occupied by them in the 1st century AD, but became demilitarised when the frontier moved east during Flavian times. Once the frontier returned to the river, however, its position blocking any westwards thrust towards Augusta Treverorum (Trier) rendered it worthy of a new fort as late as Valentinian, under whom the extensive wall that can be seen today was constructed. The Roman castle, which was rectangular with 3-metre-thick towers, has become an organic part of the modern town, in many places determining its grid pattern, at others popping up as an integral part of newer buildings or as surprisingly mundane adjuncts to parking lots or municipal parks.

In the Römerpark, a small area of green away from the town centre, lies the largest surviving section, containing a substantial portion of wall and part of the south tower of the fortress; here the remains were integrated in the 10th century into the precinct of a convent. In the 15th century, a dance-hall or tavern was built over the ruins of the convent; the local teenagers hanging out here are possibly in search of a faint hint of the merriment that once rose up on the remains of the Roman town, but really it is a quiet and sombre place, the 6-metre-high silhouette of the tower faintly threatening. In one corner, markers indicate where more than forty 7th-century Frankish graves were found, including one of a high-status lady wearing a silver finger-ring and carrying spindles and two bronze keys.

The *Notitia Dignitatum* lists the garrison here as the *milites balistarii*,[91] an artillery unit, whose speciality must have come in handy when lobbing projectiles into barbarian territory across the Rhine, but which may have been of limited use in actual field campaigns into unfriendly territory. The remains of the north-east wall of the fort are just discernible, built into the Hotel Römerburg, its pretty exterior studded with the telltale herringbone pattern of Roman stonework. Burggrabe, the street that runs southward from this, marks the eastern wall of the fort, and there, lying between numbers 4 and 6 is, if you please, a whole Roman tower (presumably number 5). It sits, minding its own business, intact almost to its complete height, although partly overgrown with creepers and dead branches; the quiet bourgeois houses to either side with their well-tended gardens seem to do their best to ignore their incongruous neighbour. More sections of the wall lie to the rear of houses further down the street, some of it visible, other parts gated off. The south-east tower at the end of the street sits in a small cark park; its facing is medieval, but the core is fundamentally Roman. The south wall occupies the line of Mergstrasse, where another tower sits squarely in the centre of a back garden. If ever for sale, presumably the house (in estate-agent-speak) would be said to 'benefit from the unique amenity of a 4th-century Roman tower'.

Further evidence of Boppard's Roman past comes in the main church of Saint Severus off the old town's main square, its pretty whitewashed exterior and high towers punctuated by single columns set into the wall. This was the site of a 4th-century bathhouse, although the church also includes part of the city wall in its own north wall. During the 5th century, the baths were converted into an early Christian basilica, which incorporated in its structure an *ambo* – a common feature of the liturgy in early Western Christianity – a key-shaped platform along which the clergy would process to perform certain parts of the service. At the back of the current church, which largely dates from the 13th century, the graves of a couple of Bodobriga's earliest Christians are on display, including one Audicia, whose memorial stone is inscribed with doves and Christograms, unmistakable indications of her religious allegiance.

An afternoon's gentle cruise down the Rhine from Boppard, and just opposite the confluence of the river and the Main, lies Mainz, another city whose subsequent success has done much to bury its antecedents, in this case as the Roman city of Mogontiacum. First occupied during the reign of Augustus, at which time a double legionary camp was constructed, it long formed one of the main Roman bases for campaigns into free Germany, although its military importance was reduced after the reduction of its garrison to a single legion after 89. This came about through the revolt of Lucius Antonius Saturninus,[92] who was either governor of Germania Superior or commander of the army there,[93] after the suppression of which Domitian decreed that henceforth no legionary fortress would hold more than a single legion; the total number of legions garrisoned in Germania Superior was reduced to three. The Emperor also forbade the soldiers to keep more than 1,000 sesterces-worth of their savings in the legionary strong-room, since Saturninus had financed his revolt by plundering the troops' savings stashed in the fortress at Mogontiacum.

From 92 until the mid-3rd century Mogontiacum was defended by the

XXII Primigenia Pia Fidelis legion, but the outline of the camp they inhabited is uncertain beneath the modern city. During this period of Roman advance the town was no longer on the frontier, and from the 1st century Mogontiacum's civilian settlement developed rapidly and it became the capital of the province of Germania Superior. In 235, the town saw a key moment in the beginning of the period of 'military anarchy' that would afflict the empire for most of the rest of the 3rd century, when Alexander Severus and his mother, Julia Mamaea, were murdered there by their own soldiers.[94]

Opposition to Alexander had coalesced around Julius Verus Maximinus,[95] a Thracian of peasant origin who had made good in the army. In March, the soldiers declared him Emperor, and Alexander failed to take decisive action. The army defected, and Alexander and his mother met their fate.[96] Thus commenced a half-century in which it was rare in the extreme for an emperor to die naturally, several being killed (and one captured) by barbarians, but most of them falling in battle against 'usurpers' who in turn became Emperor, or at the hands of their own troops. The effect of these five decades of mayhem was debilitating in the extreme for the Empire, and for a while in the middle of the century it looked as though it might not survive at all.

Once the *limes* to the east of the Rhine had been abandoned around 260, Mogontiacum received a stone wall. It was not of sufficient strength to prevent the city from falling briefly into the hands of the Alamanns in the 350s, only being recovered after Julian's victory over them at Strasbourg in 357. The defence of the Mogontiacum sector of the Rhine was by this time in the hands of the *dux Mogontiacensis*, one of the new breed of regional commanders who supervised the defence of the late-Roman frontiers. With the eruption of the Vandals and their allies across the Rhine late in 405, the position of Mogontiacum became well nigh untenable. It was occupied by Burgundians, as Roman federates, who in 411 proclaimed Jovinus, a Gallic notable, Emperor. The city's last moment as an imperial capital in the fading twilight of Roman rule in the West was pitiably brief. Jovinus had to balance the competing interests of Burgundians, Alans and, most notably, the Visigothic chieftain Athaulf. The Visigoth by 413 found a rapprochement with the official Emperor, Honorius, more convenient, and had Jovinus executed, his head sent as a grizzly present to his new ally.

Of all of this comparatively little now survives, but Mainz has become a city of 200,000, the capital of the German Land of Rhineland-Palatinate. Down towards the river on a grandly laid-out square (the Ernst Ludwig Platz) stands a reconstructed Jupiter column, made using casts of the

2,000 or so pieces of the original that were found embedded in the late-Roman wall. Soaring some 15 metres high, it is a richly decorated affair, made up of five drums atop a double-plinth. The original was erected in honour of Nero in around 60 by the *canabari*, the inhabitants of the civilian settlement around Mogontiacum. The plinths and drums are covered in reliefs of various deities, whose exact identities are uncertain, but which include Jupiter himself, Juno, Mars, Neptune, Apollo, Diana, Hercules and Fortuna. The top would have been surmounted by a bronze statue of Jupiter bearing a thunderbolt. Such columns are a phenomenon mainly of eastern France and the Rhineland,[97] but were erected by a wide range of social groups within that area. They seem to represent an integration of existing localised beliefs with Roman religious forms (as expressed by the range of deities that appear upon them).

The religious world of Rome was not a place of comforting certainties and theological absolutes. The clamour of later Christians for the imposition of orthodoxy was not a position much understood by pagans, who – save for the special position of the mystery cults – did not really have an organised 'church' and confined their acts of zealotry to reactive strikes against overenthusiastic bishops or sullen adherence to traditional practices (such as dancing at funerals), which they saw no good reason to abstain from.

So varied, and in some sense accepting, was the pagan world-view that in many cases local deities were simply absorbed into the Roman pantheon by equating them with the nearest appropriate Latin deity and then worshipping such hybrids as Apollo Grannus (very popular in Gaul), Jupiter Ammon (in Egypt) and Juno Caelestis (in Africa). This syncretism suited Roman purposes very well, for the acceptance of local cult practices meant that a potential source of resentment against imperial rule was removed. Only where native cults were seen as possible sources of political resistance, or practised rites that the Romans regarded as abhorrent, were they suppressed. Druidism in Britain suffered such a fate because of its adherents' involvement in the final resistance to the Roman conquest in Wales, and for their alleged performance of human sacrifices.

On the other side of the square, nestled between a playground and a school, a replica of the arch of Dativius Victor was erected in 1962. It commemorates the giving of an arch and colonnades to the city by a former priest of the imperial cult. Dated from the mid-3rd century, and thus after the collapse of the Roman trans-Rhenish territory in the area, it shows that, even in those increasingly uncertain times, the virtue of municipal benefaction did not die out altogether.

The nearby Mittelrheinisches Landesmuseum houses another of Germany's best collection of Roman artefacts. Amongst its finest pieces are the 'Mainz pedestals', which originally made up the supporting columns of a structure near the *praetorium* of the legionary camp. They may perhaps celebrate the victory of Domitian over the Chatti, and, though provincial in execution, their reliefs show a brutal aspect of imperial power. The faces on the carvings are fuller and less well defined than the more refined depictions on Trajan's Column in Rome.[98] In one, a legionary holds a spear, poised to thrust it into a helpless barbarian. In another, two prisoners are held by chains around their neck. In a third, a figure representing Germania sits and weeps at the victory of Rome. The pedestals exude a striking air of raw power and menace, precisely the sort of image the Empire would want to project across the frontier for the consumption of any restive barbarians.

Mogontiacum possessed one of the comparatively rare temples of Isis to be found in the north-western part of the empire. One of the group of mystery cults – most notably including Mithraism – that came into vogue in the 3rd century, Isis-worship had travelled very far west from its Egyptian homeland by the time it reached the Rhine. Its shaven-headed priests might have been more obvious than most of the leaders of its sister cults, and its temples tended to have a more 'public' aspect than those of Mithras or Attis, but to enter the remains of an Iseum today is still to pass into a world that seems more linked to its oriental roots than to the orderly world of the Capitoline Triad.[99] The Mogontiacum Isis temple, however, now sits in the basement of a modern shopping arcade, hung about with the panoply of Christmas decorations and crowded with Saturday shoppers making that essential last-minute purchase.

It seems to have been built under Vespasian, making it one of the very early examples of the genre in the Empire. The remains themselves represent a sanctuary used over several centuries. An atmospheric cloud of smoke provided by the modern guardians of the site drifts over as an evocation of the sacrifices (mostly of burnt fruit and vegetables) that would have taken place here. There seems to have been some kind of official dedication to Vespasian, and on the ceiling of the dimly lit museum that enfolds the site, a representation of the stars on the precise day of the Emperor's accession (21 December 69) is projected.

Among the discoveries made here were curse tablets, a sign of the darker side of Roman religion.[100] Most often scratched on lead, and often scrawled in almost indecipherable script, they were then buried at sacred locations such as this in the hope that the deity present might grant the writer's darkest wishes. At the Mogontiacum shrine were found, in addition, a series of clay figurines that had been mutilated by sticking pins into them or breaking off limbs, as if summoning up some voodoo magic to inflict unbearable pain on the person in whose image the doll was fashioned.

The scant remains of Mogontiacum's legionary camp lie on a high terrace of a modern development in the district of Kästrich. The estate is called 'Am Römer Tor', and is a surprisingly tasteful setting for the ruins. Not many such housing estates can boast mosaic-style insets in the pavement that celebrate Roman warships and emperors or commemorate a legionary garrison. The tower after which the complex is named formed part of a city gate from the 4th century that in turn used stones from the legionary encampment. The stone skeleton of the gate structure survives on the ground, while the tower itself is more complete, intact to around half a metre. In one place part of a carved stone can be seen inset on its outside face. Set down a few metres below the present surface and ringed with residential blocks, the little archaeological corner also presents a section of the Via Praetoria of the camp, in which, many centuries later, the ruts worn in the gate's pavement by decades of use can still be made out.

The Jakobsberg hill, which lies just behind Mainz's main railway station, formed a strategic gap in the city's defences during the Middle Ages, and in the mid-17th century a quadrangular fortress was constructed there, which remained in military use until the Treaty of Versailles forced its slighting in 1919. It served for centuries as the military headquarters of the Electors of Mainz, one of the college of princes and archbishops responsible for the choice of each successive Holy Roman Emperor, and so it retained the ghost of a memory of Mogontiacum's Roman past.

In one corner of the citadel lies the Drusussteine ('Stone of Drusus'), a Roman funerary monument. It is a huge cylindrical structure, partly hidden by an emerald screen of trees to one side, and resembles faintly one of the Martello towers that dotted the south coast of England to defend against an invasion from Napoleon that never came. The tower once had a conical roof, but stone-quarrying at about the time the citadel was built resulted in the removal of this and the loss of several metres in height.

Its alternative name, Eichelstein (or 'Acorn Stone'), was once thought to be derived from the mutilated state of the monument after it had been robbed of so much of its stone, but may well be a variant on the Latin *aquila* or eagle, from a possible representation of the bird that might have crowned the structure; or even a corruption of *aguila*, a late Latin word that means, more prosaically, 'obelisk'.[101] It has long been associated with Drusus, an extremely popular and able general, who died in 9 BC after a fall from his horse following a successful campaign against the Chatti and Marcomanni. However enticing the notion that the structure is his memorial, it has been found to contain later stonework, complicating the dating process and preventing any firm conclusion as to the monument's true origin and significance.

Further down the citadel hill, nearly at its base, lies a Roman amphitheatre. It was the largest Roman auditorium north of the Alps, with a capacity for some 10,000 spectators, and a stage more than 40 metres wide. Not regularly open and hemmed in by building works, it sits just beside Platform 4 of the Sudbahnhof; indeed, the best views of it are to be had as the trains pull out on their meticulously punctual journeys south towards the cathedral cities of Worms and Speier.

Mogontiacum's final visible relic lies on the south-west edge of town, in the suburb of Mainz-Zahlbach. This is the 'Römersteine', part of the aqueduct that once fed the city and the camp. The remains languish in a field to the side of a tree-fringed footpath. In their eroded and ruined state, they seem more like some straightened-out piece of megalithic stone circle than a testament to Roman hydrographic genius. Originally these stumps would have reached 25 metres in height and marched 9 kilometres from the source of the water right to the edge of Mogontiacum. Their survival, though, when almost all of the city they were built to serve has vanished, seems nothing short of miraculous.

Even more astonishing are the remains of several Roman ships dredged up in the Rhine and on display in the Antiker Schiffahrts Museum in the centre of town. Substantial timber sections of these shallow oar-driven vessels (which date from the early 5th century) survived for more than 1,500 years at the bottom of the river, possibly representing part of one of the very last Roman military contingents in the city. Enough remained to recreate the curved shape of the hull of one of the boats, and a more complete reconstruction using modern timbers allows the eye to run over an almost complete late-Roman warship.

The Roman navy was never, under the Empire, the senior service. Although it had played an important role in Rome's victories against Carthage during the Punic Wars, the last naval battle that really decided the issue of a campaign was the defeat of Mark Antony and Cleopatra by Octavian – soon to take on his more familiar name as Augustus – at Actium in 31 BC. Yet thereafter the navy still played a crucial role in the transportation of armies, in securing lines of communication in the Mediterranean and on the north-western coastlines of the Empire, and, most importantly for the frontier, in patrolling the river-stretches of the boundary between Rome and the barbarians.

The fleet had its own hierarchies, with the navarchs very roughly approximating to centurions in the army and acting as squadron commanders, and trierarchs as the captains of individual ships.[102] The sailors in the various imperial fleets had less prestige than their land-based counterparts; indeed, during the reign of Commodus, one legionary was actually transferred to naval duty as a punishment.[103] They were, on the whole, not citizens (though some freedmen served) and, like members of auxiliary regiments, only received citizenship on discharge from the service, in their case after twenty-six years, one year more than their counterparts in the army.[104]

The greatest Roman naval bases were at Misenum (Porto Miseno) and Ravenna in Italy.[105] All of the river sections of the frontiers had their own provincial fleet (with the exception of the Euphrates in the East, where the nature of the threat from the Persians with their large, well-organised land armies made it redundant).[106] The *Classis Germanica*, the German fleet, is the best attested of all the provincial naval units. It had its origins in the Augustan expansion into Germany, and easier passage for it to the North Sea was the motive for Drusus's excavation of yet another waterway, the *Fossa Drusiana* between the Rhine and the Zuider Zee.[107] Drusus exploited this new route in 12 BC to attack the Frisians, but the naval element in his campaign (even though it managed to circumnavigate Denmark) achieved only relatively modest success. In AD 4, the Rhine fleet again sailed along the north coast of Germany, and met with Tiberius on the Elbe, where it resupplied his army, the furthest point the Roman navy ever reached in Germania.

As the advance into Germany faltered in the second decade of the 1st century, the *Classis Germanica* became stationary, stalled at its main base at Colonia Agrippinensis, from where it provided additional security through its patrols on the river. When the Batavian revolt broke out in 69 and the Romans abandoned the forts on the Lower Rhine, the fleet did little good and was swiftly destroyed, with the humiliating capture of the flagship. Thereafter, apart from a possible role in suppressing the revolt of Saturninus in 89, the fleet did not appear in any high-profile operations.[108]

South of Colonia Agrippinensis there were no permanent bases, and once the *limes* was advanced under Domitian, the Rhine in Germania Superior was not the actual frontier, so a strong naval force would have been redundant. In Germania Inferior, however, the situation was different, and there continued to be naval bases at Novaesium (Neuss), at Vetera (Xanten) and probably at Noviomagus (Nijmegen) and in several stations nearer the Rhine delta, such as Lugdunum (Katwijk) and Forum Hadriani (Voorburg). The last mention of an organised fleet comes in

235, when Alexander Severus used a squadron on the Upper Rhine,[109] and it seems that the naval stations were abandoned by the middle of the century. Some kind of naval arm must still have existed, for patrols are mentioned as late as the 4th century,[110] but it was clearly not on the scale of the early Empire, and the disappearance of the *Classis Germanica* must have contributed at least a little to the general decline in security along the Rhine frontier.

The *Classis Germanica*'s northern flank was patrolled by the *Classis Britannica*, whose mission was to protect the Channel crossings and the security of the British coastline. Further to the east, the Danube, too, was patrolled by the Roman navy, in this case the *Classis Pannonica* for the western section and the *Classis Moesica* for the eastern stretch ending at the Danube delta. These two units seem, and particularly in Moesia, to have carried out their duties virtually to the end of Roman rule there, an unsung but vital element in the military system that secured the safety of the frontier, and thus of the provinces in the interior of the Empire.

Set back from the Rhine and the frontier itself (and 120 kilometres south-west of Mainz), but in virtual symbiosis with these, the city of Augusta Treverorum (Trier) in Gallia Belgica provided an important base and vital centre for the supply of the armies that guarded the river. It became one of the most important administrative centres of the Later Empire and, while all about it seemed in decline, was embellished to become a virtual second Rome in the North. Its preserved monuments are grander than those of anywhere else in Germany and it is one of the few places in northern Europe where it is possible to get some sense of the sheer scale of the Roman cities that once dotted the landscape. In the market square of Trier, surrounded by medieval and faux-Gothic gabled shop-fronts, the 'Rotes Haus', a survival from the 14th century, states, in impeccable Latin, that Trier was founded some 1,300 years before Rome.[111] It is a boastful declaration, and the Celtic antecedents of the town probably do not stretch much further back than the 2nd century BC,[112] but the city still has a fair claim to be amongst the oldest in Germany.

The site lies on the road that led from Lugdunum (Lyons) in the interior of Gaul, at the point where it crossed the Moselle and then proceeded across to the Rhine. The local tribe, the Treveri, allied themselves early on with Julius Caesar during his conquest of Gaul, and in 57 BC sent a force of cavalry that served alongside the Roman army.[113] They subsequently caused the conqueror no end of trouble, rising up in 55 BC under the leadership of Indutiomarus, and again in 51 BC (though they remained sullenly on the sidelines during the great revolt of Vercingetorix).

A fort was probably built here under Augustus, and it was then that the settlement that grew up took the name Augusta Treverorum. When the frontier definitively reached the Rhine under Tiberius, the fort was abandoned, and Treverorum never again acquired a military garrison.

Augusta Treverorum seems to have attained the rank of *colonia* under Claudius.[114] His reign signalled the start of an era of great prosperity for the town, but imperial favour was briefly interrupted when the Treveri failed to support Galba's bid for the throne in 69 and instead joined the adherents of Vitellius. Moreover, Julius Classicus and Julius Tutor, the leading lights in the rebel movement that coalesced around Julius Civilis, were both Treverans. However, the revenge of the loyalist general Petillius Cerealis and his troops when they took the city was surprisingly muted. Thereafter the Treverans remained steadfastly loyal to the Emperor (although not always to the official Emperor), and reaped the rewards of the economic development that followed, with the construction of monumental public buildings, such as amphitheatres and some of the most imposing bath complexes to be found outside Rome itself.

The tranquillity of the city was shattered in the late 2nd century, when it seems to have been besieged by forces loyal to Clodius Albinus, the governor of Britain, in his bid to unseat Septimius Severus as Emperor.[115] It was a token of things to come, for, as the *limes* came under threat from the Alamanns and successive emperors failed to provide for the security of Germania and the Gallic provinces, in 259 Augusta Treverorum threw in its lot with the breakaway Gallic empire of Postumus, and, though not ever the leading city in that venture, it was closely associated with Postumus's successor, Victorinus.[116] Once calm (and the unity of the Empire) was restored, however, Treverorum reaped benefits from the new order of things in a way that its leading citizens cannot have dreamt of.

Under the reorganisation of provinces conducted by Diocletian after his accession in 284, the city became the capital of the new province of Belgica Prima. The new Emperor recognised early on that one of the causes of the military anarchy that had afflicted the Empire for the last half-century was that no one man could possibly attend to all the challenges now facing it on the frontiers. Further, the absence of the Emperor on campaign in one direction might very well invite a usurpation by another army strongman in an opposite part of the Empire, precisely the dismal military merry-go-round that had seemed unstoppable since the death of Caracalla in 217.

In 285, Diocletian appointed Maximian, another army officer, whose origins also lay in Illyria, to be his co-Emperor with the rank of 'Caesar'.

It was not the first time there had been joint emperors; this had initially occurred officially with Marcus Aurelius and Lucius Verus in the mid-2nd century. Indeed, the idea of associating a potential successor with the ruling emperor by rendering him certain imperial powers dated back to the very early years of the Empire; Augustus had given Tiberius tribunician power in AD 4. Diocletian's design was of a wholly different order, though it is not clear whether he conceived it all in one go or developed the plan piecemeal as he went along.[117] For in 286, Maximian was raised to the rank of 'Augustus' alongside Diocletian, and then, in 293, each of the two senior emperors appointed a 'Caesar' to assist them, with Constantius serving under Maximian (who was his father-in-law), while Galerius acted as subordinate to Diocletian.

This new system, known as the Tetrarchy, had a number of advantages. It meant that the four emperors could divide in order to face the diverse enemies who beset the Empire, while remaining united (in theory) in terms of policies. The elimination of one of them by any potential opponents would still leave three members of the tetrarchal group to avenge their colleague, and this, for almost a quarter of a century, acted as a powerful disincentive to revolt. What eventually caused the whole complex structure to come crashing down, though, was the thorny matter of succession and whether, as Diocletian thought, it should be on the basis of merit or whether (as various other male members of the four imperial families considered) family ties and a dynastic principle should be the pre-eminent consideration.

Although the Tetrarchy did not involve a simple geographical division of the Empire, with each Emperor ruling over a given set of provinces, in general Diocletian and Galerius held sway over the east, while Maximian and Constantius looked after the western provinces.[118] Each of the Tetrarchs tended to base themselves in regional capitals, closer to the areas in which action was likely to be necessary. Galerius, for example, spent much of his time in Salonica, while Diocletian favoured Nicomedia in Asia Minor (modern Iznik). Maximian chose Augusta Treverorum as one of his preferred residences (the others being Milan and Aquileia in Italy), and the city thus became an imperial capital, a role that it fulfilled during a golden age which spanned around five decades. In 293, Constantius I, Maximian's Caesar, also made Treverorum his capital, and the city then became the centre of the main mint for the Western Empire.

Constantius's son, Constantine I, arrived in Trier in 306, shortly after he had been proclaimed Emperor by the troops in Britain. He would be based here for the better part of the next decade, presiding over a period of rebuilding in the city intended to create a setting appropriate for an imperial capital. It is from this period that the majority of the city's most notable surviving monuments come. Even when Constantine moved on to greater things, his elder son Crispus was based in Trier, and after Crispus fell from grace (and was executed in 326), it remained an imperial residence, first of Constantine II, and then of his brother Constans. After the usurpation of Magnentius in 350, which the Treverans supported, the city's prosperity tailed off, and Julian did not use it as his capital, basing himself instead mainly in the region around modern Paris.

The lure of the city's strategic location and its amenities, however, led to its restoration to favour under Valentinian I, who moved there in 367 and used it as his main base for the next eight years. His son, Gratian, too, would reside here until his death in 383, providing the city with a late Indian summer and a security that most other cities in northern Gaul would have envied. Amongst the residents of the imperial court in these halcyon days was Decimus Magnus Ausonius, doyen of the late flourishing of Latin literary culture.[119]

Many of Ausonius's poems deal with life at court, even referring to individual works of art; one glorifies a painting in which Gratian was shown slaying a lion, both poem and painting being suitably flattering works of art to soothe a sensitive imperial ego[120] Ausonius paints an almost idyllic picture of Treverorum, of its relative security and wealth, despite its proximity to the Rhine and the barbarian dangers beyond. His most celebrated work, the *Mosella*, describes a journey from Bingium (Bingen) to Treverorum, conjuring up a bucolic image of a countryside in which nothing has changed for centuries and all – both prosperous and peasants – live in a state of almost cloying contentment. Yet the mention by the poet of Sarmatians living near Noviomagus (Nijmegen) reminds us that the settlement of barbarians as *laeti* inside the frontiers – including groups of Franks who had been settled near Trier by Probus (276–82) – was changing the demography of the area in quite dramatic ways.[121]

Ausonius's charmed world came to an abrupt end in 383, when Magnus Maximus, who had been the *comes Brittaniarum* in charge of the forces in Britain, rebelled, was proclaimed Emperor by his troops, crossed over into Gaul and suborned the Rhineland legions. After some minor engagements near modern Paris, Gratian's Frankish general Merobaudes defected and the Emperor was compelled to flee with a small force of loyal cavalry. In August, he was caught at Lugdunum (Lyons) and unceremoniously executed. Maximus set himself up at Treverorum, making no initial moves to unseat Valentinian II and absorb Italy. Ausonius, however, caught up in the winds of a very unwelcome change, made haste for his estates in Burdigala (Bordeaux), where he lived out the last decade of his life in the kind of enforced idleness that only the leisured Roman aristocracy knew how to exploit to the full.

Some time after 395 the seat of the praetorian prefect for the north-western provinces of the Empire was transferred from Treverorum to Arelate (Arles) in the south of Gaul, and the city's importance declined. It may have resisted the onslaught of the Vandals and their allies in 406[122] but it seems to have been sacked by the Franks in 411. The city was still serving as a mint in 414–16 when it coined for Attalus, a puppet Emperor installed by Attila the Hun, and for another usurper, Johannes, in 423. Treverorum was then battered by successive barbarian attacks – one writer refers to it being sacked four times between 400 and 450.[123] By the 480s, it was in the hands of one Arbogast, who bore the title *comes* and may have been in some sense a representative of Roman rule,[124] but soon after-wards it was annexed by Clovis's growing Frankish kingdom.

Approaching the city from the Moselle, Roman travellers would have crossed over into Augusta Treverorum on one of two bridges. The south-ernmost still survives in part, carrying buses and cars thundering across the river on a modern bridge, which sits atop the unmistakably massive bulk of some of the original Roman piers. Five of the seven that bear the bridge's weight are of Roman vintage, their pointed shape upstream moulding the water's flow to act as ice-breakers.[125] From here the road led eastwards, eventually arriving at the west façade of the forum, an area that is comparatively little known, but whose construction (prob-ably in the early 2nd century) marks the beginning of the provision of a truly monumental centre for the city.[126] More substantial are Treverorum's places of public and private entertainment, the baths and the amphitheatre.

On a square of middle-class housing set just east of the river between the busy arteries of Südallee and Friedrich-Wilhelmstraße lie the Barbarathermen, one of the city's two grand sets of imperial baths. Probably built during the first quarter of the 2nd century, they are a very tangible symbol of the Romanisation of the area. The ruins still give some idea of the general layout of a Roman bath complex. To the south lay the *caldarium*, a large, elaborate structure set in a position to receive the maximum amount of sun. Beyond it, just to the north, a smaller, cross-shaped structure, the *tepidarium*, was a luke-warm room, and then at the north, a large rectangular building represents the *frigidarium*, along-side which lay various porticoes and a *palaestra* or exercise yard. Now utterly ruined, the Barbarathermen were in use as late as Frankish times, and in the 12th century the *caldarium* was adapted for use by a local noble family as their palace. As late as the 17th century much of the structure still survived, before it was dismantled by the local Jesuits, who used it to construct a college.

Baths have a good claim to be one of the defining elements in the spread of the 'Roman way' throughout the Empire and spanned the whole spectrum from relatively simple establishments in small villages in modern Syria to the grand, fully fledged examples built in Treverorum. They are referred to as *thermae* or *balnea* – the exact distinction is unclear, though *thermae* may have been more elaborate examples.[127] In the increasingly crowded environment of Roman towns, they acted as a social centre in which to meet one's peers, as well as providing a vital hygienic function in the majority of settlements where the provision of private household water supplies was the privilege of a select few. The baths required vast quantities of water, and would normally need to be supplied by an aqueduct. According to Frontinus, who was *curator aquarum* (the official in charge of Rome's water supply) in 97, no less than 45 per cent of the water coming from the city's aqueducts was used for public purposes, which, on the whole, would have meant for the baths.[128]

As well as these more obvious functions, the baths also provided ample opportunity for local notables to publicise their generous benefactions to their native towns by giving funds for a portico here, the reconstruction of a *caldarium* there, or, perhaps the money to provide the oil needed in the baths or the fuel for the furnaces that heated them – all expenses that would otherwise have to be met out of public funds. Such self-conscious generosity (or euergetism) is memorialised in countless inscriptions on baths – and of course on other buildings – throughout the geographic extent of the Empire.

The experience of a visit to the baths of course varied slightly, depending on the nature of the building and the local climate. However, it seems that mixed bathing was (contrary to the confident assertion of guides in the more conservative modern countries) not uncommon at all; the poet Martial sulkily criticises those women who do not want to bath with him, and makes unkind comments about the appearance of some of them naked.[129] It may, of course, be that certain days or sections in bathing complexes were reserved for women, but this was by no means the universal rule.

There were, of course, more nefarious goings-on at the baths, and Ovid refers to them as places where young lovers might meet unmolested,[130] while certain of the graffiti found at Herculaneum (the neighbour of Pompeii) make unmistakable references to prostitution occurring in the baths. Another perennial problem was, apparently, the theft of clothes, an unavoidable hazard when the customers bathed naked, and to guard against which attendants called *capsarii* could be hired to see to the safe-keeping of possessions. The *capsarii* were of course not always themselves to be trusted, and a specific provision in Justinian's law code deals with dishonest members of the profession.[131]

Having disrobed and left their clothes to the tender mercies of the attendants or to the chance of an unguarded corner, bathers would proceed through the series of bathing rooms, many of them with marble or mosaic flooring and decorated with statues and friezes (whose lavishness depended on the wealth of the establishment), before returning, cleansed, to collect their possessions. Generally speaking, bathers would first be anointed with oil – a service for which there would be an extra charge – followed by visits to the various hot rooms: first the *tepidarium*, then the *caldarium* and, if feeling intrepid, the *sudarium* (or steam room). In hotter climates, the *frigidarium* and various plunge pools would provide relief from the sticky heat outside. At an intermediate point during the visit, bathers would be scraped with a strigil to remove the oil and dirt that had accumulated on their bodies, a process that undoubtedly added a certain amount of pain to the general pleasure of a visit to the baths, should the tips to the ministering slaves not be large enough.

The baths catered for the whole gamut of society, from senators to the most humble, and there are even records of visits by emperors to public establishments (though they no doubt mostly confined their ablutions to the facilities provided for them in the imperial palaces). The most celebrated example comes from the *Historia Augusta*,[132] where Hadrian is said to have caught sight of the veteran of one of his military campaigns rubbing himself against a wall. When the Emperor asked what his former comrade was doing, the ex-soldier said that he was simply too poor to afford to pay for a slave to rub his back. Hadrian instantly ordered that a number of slaves be given to the man, along with money to house them, so that the old soldier would not in future have to suffer such public indignity. On the Emperor's next visit to the baths, he found a large crowd of men massaging their backs against the wall, hoping that they would receive a similar benefaction. Hadrian, however, was not so easily fooled, and simply remarked that they should get together and rub each other's backs, thereby resolving their respective 'problems'.

Just to the east of the city centre, up a quiet street, lies the city's other early relic, the amphitheatre. Probably built in the early 1st century, it is not a free-standing colossus such as the Flavian amphitheatre at Rome or the one at Arles, but instead made use of the slope of the Petrisberg

hill, supplemented by earthworks to create the oval shape required for
the building. The banks of seats that were set into this housed up to
20,000 spectators, a huge number even for a place the size of Treverorum.
Most of the stone structure has now gone, apart from a section of the
southern entrance, and the gates through which the spectators issued
out into the seats (the *vomitoria*). Down below in the cellars lies a scattering of stones and a lot of ground water, creating a dank and very
dark atmosphere, appropriate for a place where cages for condemned
criminals would have been housed. Up above, all is strangely tranquil,
as the grassed-over mounds of the auditorium hold little sense of the
bloody spectacles that once took place here.

Around 400 metres to the west lies the first evidence of the great
building programme of Treverorum's career as a tetrarchic capital, the
Kaiserthermen (or 'imperial baths'). The huge shell of the *caldarium* rears
up as one of the most prominent landmarks of Roman northern Europe,
the massive double-tier of open arches in red brick alternating with
lighter tiles that make it seem almost like a massive aqueduct rather than
a bath building. Everything about the Kaiserthermen is monumental,
and they are indeed the largest baths outside Italy itself (the second-
largest being the Barbarathermen). They originally formed part of the
palace precinct constructed for Constantine I, and in their skeletal state
it requires a great effort to imagine the lavish decoration with which
they must have been adorned. The triple-apsed *caldarium* is the best
surviving building, with the *tepidarium* and *frigidarium* nearby surviving
to a much lower height. Although almost all above is ruined, beneath
the rooms, tunnels and drainage channels that made up the sub-structure
survive almost complete, creating a claustrophobic underworld in whose
maze it is easy to be gripped with a nameless sense of panic.

Astonishingly, the baths seem never to have been completed. Although
begun in the early 4th century, work on them seems to have been incomplete by 316, when Constantine left Treverorum for his new capital at
Constantinople. No traces of the water-pipes that would have been an
absolute necessity in such a structure have been found, and the building
seems to have lain neglected for some time. During the reigns of
Valentinian I and Gratian, however, an extensive programme of remodelling was undertaken, with the *frigidarium* being completely levelled,
leaving the *caldarium* to act as a monumental hall of some kind. Its
exact function is unclear, though it could have acted as a meeting place
for the *curia*, the municipal council. Bizarrely, considering the genesis
of the building, a new, much smaller bathhouse was built just north of
the original site.[133]

The other principal remnant of the Constantinian palace lies a couple of hundred metres to the north, in a pretty park attached to the 18th-century palace of the Electors. The Aula Palatina (or 'Basilika' as it was known for centuries) is one of the most complete Roman buildings anywhere and gives a rare chance to experience the sheer size and interior space of a Roman original, largely uncluttered by subsequent accretions or demolitions. At 67 metres long, about 27 wide and 30 high, its long, rectangular shape, studded with arched windows, with a circular apse at the end, is characteristic of late-Roman audience chambers, the function that it performed in Constantine's palace. Much of the brick-work of the outside walls is not in fact original, for in the 17th century the building of a new bishop's palace resulted in the removal of the east wall and the partial demolition of the south wall. Yet a great deal of this has been restored, while on the west wall the original Roman masonry can be clearly discerned. Having served as a barracks in the 18th century, the Aula Palatina owes its restoration to King Friedrich Wilhelm IV of Prussia, who ordered it rebuilt in its original form and gave it to the Evangelical Protestant community at Trier to serve as their church, a function the venerable building still performs today.[134]

Inside, the austerity of the decoration, with just a simple cross on the far wall of the apse, heightens the grandeur of the space. The windows in the apse were made deliberately smaller, an architectural trick that makes it seem more distant and draws the eye towards the space where the platform on which the Emperor, in full pomp, would have sat to receive visitors.[135] It was all part of the tendency under the Later Roman Empire, particularly accentuated from the time of Constantine, for the distance between sovereign and subject to grow. Whilst there had been a kind of suspension of disbelief until the 2nd century, a fiction that the emperors were really a superior kind of senator and that, at a pinch, the Republic might just be restored, the chaos of the 3rd century brought forward a reformed structure that was more dogmatic, much more bureaucratic and in which the Emperor was set apart as an unapproachable ideal.[136]

As the aura of mystique around them grew, of course, those Emperors who were not strong-minded came to be dominated by their civil servants, largely unaware of what was really going on outside the palace walls, and able to command only that which they comprehended, which was really very little. Honorius, who ruled from 395 to 423, is the classic case of this. From his palace in Ravenna, surrounded by miasmic marshes, which protected the imperial person but from whose security he rarely ventured, Honorius seems to have known little and cared less. One of his favourite pastimes, it seems, was to spend a choice hour feeding his pet chickens. When Rome was sacked by Alaric's Goths in 410 and one of the ministers was deputed to tell the Emperor that Rome had fallen, Honorius was, for a brief moment, shocked, believing that he was being informed instead that one of his beloved fowl had died.[137]

More tangible evidence of Constantine's connection with the city was found in a room beneath Trier's cathedral, the Dom. Medieval legend had long held that the church owed its origins to the donation of a palace by Helena, his mother, upon which the predecessor of the Dom was built in the late 4th century. A section of bricked-up Roman masonry can indeed be seen on the north side of the cathedral today. In 1945–6, however, a room from the palace was discovered, containing thousands of plaster fragments. When reassembled, they proved to be a series of wall paintings (now on display in the Diocesan Museum).

The three most striking paintings seem to be of imperial women, clad in purple robes and richly adorned with jewels and golden diadems. One, veiled, may be Helena herself, the other figure with a diadem possibly his wife Fausta. The third and youngest woman, who wears flowers in her hair and toys with a jewel box, her expression quizzical, as though she holds the key to some kind of mystery, could be Helena the Younger, who became Constantine's daughter-in-law by her marriage to his eldest son, and presumptive heir, Crispus in 322.

It has been suggested that the portraits were painted to commemorate the marriage of Crispus and Helena; if so, their subsequent neglect is easily explicable, for it was a match that ended tragically. In 326, Constantine suddenly summoned Crispus, who had been commanding imperial forces on the eastern front, to the Balkans, and there, at Pola, he was summarily executed. The reasons for this were never made public, but it seems that the young Caesar was accused of an illicit affair with his stepmother Fausta. However, the whole thing seems to have been a malicious plot of Fausta's, and once this was discovered the following year she was shut up in an overheated bath where she slowly choked to death. Constantine is said to have suffered remorse for the rest of his life, knowing that he had unjustly put his own child to death at the behest of his conniving wife, who had almost certainly been jealous of Crispus, the product of her husband's first marriage.

Between the 2nd and 4th centuries, Treverorum possessed a city wall. It was certainly built after the second half of the 2nd century, for it cut through a cemetery of that date,[138] and there is a record in 353 of the Treverans shutting the gates of their city to Decentius, the brother of the usurper Magnentius, so a wall must have been in place then. It was probably around 6 metres high and enclosed some 285 hectares within its circuit. Beyond it a ditch was constructed for extra security. To re-inforce one section, part of the wall of the amphitheatre was incorporated to act as a bulwark for the fortification, which presumably implied the blocking up of at least some of that building's entrances, and possibly its total disuse as a place of public spectacle.

The one significant relic of the wall, and also Trier's poster child of its Roman heritage, is the Porta Nigra ('Black Gate'), which is the ori-ginal northern gate of the city. Its twin, rounded arcaded towers, one of them missing a storey, stand either side of the gate and are connected by a two-storey arcade running above the gate's arches. The ground floors of the twin towers lack windows, however, presumably for defen-sive reasons. Although magnificent and overawing all about it (even the traffic that speeds by, obscuring the efforts of the most assiduous of photographers), the gate was in fact completed rather hurriedly and its finish is rough. The unfaced sandstone then weathered to black over the ages, giving the structure a solemn and austere appearance, which renders it all the more powerful.

The Porta Nigra owes its survival, when all the other gates were dismantled in medieval times, to a hermit named Simeon of Syracuse, who in around 1000 chose the structure as the location of his cell. After he died in 1035, the building was converted into a church, and an apse attached. The remains of several late-medieval religious monuments can still be seen in the interior of the Porta on its first floor. They are what is left of a once-large collection stripped away by Napoleon in 1804, when, after annexing the city, he ordered that the Porta Nigra be restored to its original state, a process that was completed in the 1870s.

It was another piece of misplaced piety that preserved one of the best Roman-era monuments in the vicinity of Trier, the Igelersaüle, standing in the small village of Igel around 8 kilometres south-west of the city. It is in fact the funerary monument of the Secundinii, a rich merchant family who made their money in the cloth trade. A single column surrounded by friezes, it consists of several storeys that soar up to 23 metres. Although weathered, the main scene of the front frieze is quite clear, possibly showing the sons of Lucius Secundinius Securus bidding their father farewell. Another scene shows the transportation of cloth, with bales of the stuff being drawn by mules. More recondite scenes include the rescuing of Andromeda by Hercules, part of a cycle that may be associated with a mystical journey by the soul to heaven.[139] The funerary monument owes its survival to the belief that the figures repre-sented on it were not Secundinius and his wife, but instead Constantius

I and Helena, the parents of Constantine I. As their son had brought Christianity to the Roman Empire, it was therefore perceived as almost sacrilegious to tinker with it, and so the Igel altar survived the ages nearly unscathed.

From Mainz, the pre-Flavian frontier followed the line of the Rhine past Borbetomagus (Worms), down towards the legionary camp at Argentorate (Strasbourg) where the VIII Augusta legion was stationed from AD 70 until at least the 3rd century, while units detached from it may be the ones recorded for the town in the *Notitia Dignitatum* at the start of the 5th century.

The river now enters the hilly territory north of the Alps, and modern Switzerland. There is not a great deal to show in quietly prosperous Basle of its Roman predecessor Basilia. The Roman settlement was established on the Münsterhügel, a promontory above the Rhine on which the modern cathedral sits, and which was also the site chosen by the Celtic Raurici for their *oppidum*, captured by Drusus in 15 BC. Just off the Münsterplatz, under a glass display roof, part of the Celtic wall has been unearthed. It dates from the early 1st century BC, and is constructed using a technique that became known as *murus gallicus*, which involved the building of an earth rampart with a stone or rubble facing reinforced internally by wooden beams. The pile of rubble formed when the wall collapsed can still be seen, close to a section where in medieval times the grave of a small child was set into the ancient wall.

In the nearby museum a fragment of Roman wall lies immured in the basement; after the fall of the *limes* of the Agri Decumates in the 260s, the Münsterhügel was reinforced and fortified as it once again became a link in the frontier defence system on the Upper Rhine. It is from later in this period (374) that the first mention of the name Basilia (or Civitas Basiliensis) comes. By the early 5th century, however, the garrison seems to have abandoned the place, leaving the old *vicus* of the fort to survive unguarded, which then over the centuries developed into a thriving city of more than 150,000.

Just 12 kilometres and a short train ride southwards down the Rhine the *limes* reached Augusta Rauricorum, now in the village of Kaiseraugst, which, not having enjoyed such a glittering existence following the Roman period, has survived in substantially better shape than ancient Basilia. The snow-topped trees and icy fields are a salutary reminder that, though the real barrier of the Alps lies elsewhere, in winter this was still forbidding terrain and campaigning in such weather was an act of desperation or an attempt to spring an unwelcome surprise on the enemy.

An inscription records that Augusta Rauricorum was established around 44 BC as a colony by Lucius Munatius Planus, his aim being to block off any incursions from further east into Caesar's newly conquered provinces in Gaul.[140] It was not until the time of Augustus, however, and the absorption of the central Alps by Tiberius and Drusus in 15 BC, that the town really became important and a building boom ensued. Around AD 40–70 the residential areas were rebuilt in stone, and a rash of public buildings was erected in the 70s, including the theatre, the forum and a large temple. Small army detachments from units based in Vindonissa (Windisch) to the east garrisoned it, and in 73–4 it served as a springboard for Domitian's occupation of the Agri Decumates.[141] After 260, although it lay once more on the frontier, the civilian population appears to have become sparser, and in the 4th century most of the town was abandoned, leaving only the upper section (Kastelen) in occupation. In around 320, the old fort was razed, and a new one built to the north, which took the name Castrum Rauracense. The old colony of Augusta Rauricorum began its descent into ruin, to be rescued only by archaeological investigations that began in Switzerland as early as 1582 under the humanists Andreas Ryff and Basilius Amberbach.[142]

A short walk from the train station, with neat, low modern houses for its neighbours, lies a Roman merchant building, for, although not militarily important (save in exceptional circumstances, such as Domitian's expedition), the town was a prosperous trading centre and derived much of its wealth from the transportation of goods up and down the Rhine. It seems that fulling was carried out in this particular building, and an inn was attached to the complex, for visiting merchants to rest in before selling their wares or pressing on down the road towards Vindonissa. The criss-cross of low stone walls and sequence of rectangular rooms give out little of the secret of the place, and it is the small items such as the cache of five *lares*, or household gods, that carry a real resonance of the past life of Rauricorum.

About five minutes' walk up the gently sloping hill on which the bulk of the town was built lies the Augst museum, with a Roman-style portico out front, its red-tiled roof coldly outlined against a threatening grey sky. Inside, the fine collection features a lovely bronze bust of Minerva, with staring white eyes and a Medusa's-head breastplate, and a consular diptych in ivory, together with a collection of exquisite small votive figurines of a constellation of deities.

The masterpiece is undoubtedly the Kaiseraugst Treasure, a hoard unearthed in the winter of 1961/2 in the late-Roman fortress of Rauracense. It seems to have been buried around 352, and is made up of sixty-eight pieces from an extremely rich table service, largely of silver, together with a large hoard of coins. The mix of coins suggests that the treasure's owner was probably a follower of the usurper Magnentius, but that, in the face of an onslaught of Alamanns who attacked the Magnentian-held fort in 351–2, he buried his portable wealth and was never able to come back to collect it.

The array of pure silver bowls, spoons and large plates is staggering and the story of its discovery a wonderful example of archaeology by accident. During the winter of the discovery the snow lay deep near the fortress walls, and when a mechanical digger tore the hoard out of the ground by chance, it lay unnoticed for some time. When finally the precious pieces were spotted and experts were called in to identify them, many items had already been spirited away. A lovely rectangular silver bowl depicting Ariadne with Dionysus and a group of satyrs was subsequently retrieved from a rubbish pit into which it had been pitched, while a bowl with a portrait of Achilles etched into it was found hidden under the bed of a young boy, who had, no doubt, found an unexpected prize on his way into school that morning.

Just opposite the museum sits the theatre, Switzerland's largest Roman monument, now heavily restored. It was rebuilt on at least three occasions over its three centuries of life, so that little clearly survives from the original structure that was raised in about 70, save some monumental blocks lying deep down beside the refreshments kiosk. Although parts of the stage backdrop can be seen in place, around 110 the theatre was adapted to serve as an amphitheatre for gladiatorial contests rather than the more refined dramas it had hosted hitherto. An oval arena had to be built in place of the hemispherical stage that had preceded it, though most of the seating was kept intact. Around 200, it was restored to its original use and the place became a theatre once more. The seating now seems strangely complete, but this is a function of the theatre's use as a venue for the Pro Augusta Raurica jazz festival rather than any miraculous feat of preservation.

On a small hill opposite the theatre stands the great stone block of the Schönbühl temple, accessed by a flight of modern steps. What survives is actually the base of the 3-metre-high platform of an enormous shrine, part of a complex that included six smaller temples, the outlines of the walls of which can still be seen just south of the massive foundation of the later temple. With nothing surviving on top of the base save the stumps of six pillars, it seems more like an Aztec or other Meso-American construction than a Gallo-Roman shrine. The sanctuary was established around 50–70, just at the time that Augusta Raurica was undergoing its first real building boom, and coins found on the site indicate that it was in use at least until 217.[143] A large hole is evidence of an attempted forced entry into the interior by an overenthusiastic pre-modern excavator, a sign that, even here, plundering of sites was not unknown in the past.

A few hundred metres behind the theatre to the north-east lay the colony's forum. It is now a large, square meadow broken slightly by bumps where the public buildings of the site may lie. As late as 1918 it was still in use for farming, and in that year much of the platform of the monumental temple of Roma and Augustus was torn down. In front of the ruined temple site, there now stands a reconstructed marble altar, with an eagle bearing a thunderbolt. It was the only temple in Augusta Raurica to be built in the purely Italian manner, a rectangular colonnaded affair rather than the square sanctuaries within a walled compound that are more characteristic of the way of temple-building in Celtic-influenced provinces. A wooden framework façade has also been erected; supposed to represent the original, but with nothing behind it but sky, it has the definite air of a Potemkin temple on the Rhine.

At the other end of the forum lies the 1st-century basilica, or law court, nothing now surviving but a few pieces of pillar (as the excavated remains have been covered over), but the nearby *curia* or town hall, where the municipal temple met, has been restored. About five tiers of semicircular rows of seats, where the councillors met, are visible, together with a podium where the *duumvirs*, or two senior magistrates of the city, stood to address the assembly.

Just beyond the *curia* at the foot of a slope (which in turn became the focus of new fortifications in the late 2nd and early 3rd centuries) is a residential area, with a small bathhouse which may have been part of a *mansio*, or inn. The complex is quite small (in contrast to the leviathans of Trier) and so is more easily comprehensible at a casual glance, with the *frigidarium* and the hypocaust for the *caldarium* all still in place. Built in the late 2nd century, it faced onto the street, presumably providing a welcome amenity to local residents and traders.

Steps down beside the baths lead into an underground well-house, in the shaft of which five human skeletons were found together with the remains of a number of dogs. Related finds in the vicinity turned out to be clay moulds used in the counterfeiting of coins,[144] an occupation that became more widespread during the high inflation of the 3rd century when the central mints simply could not (or did not bother to) keep up with the demand for small change. It all adds up to an intriguing and insoluble murder mystery. Down below in the shaft it feels extremely claustrophobic – not a place to linger with the ghosts of the ancient counterfeiters.

From here the way leads back towards the centre of town, along a road fringed by fields that passes by the site of the former central baths south-east of the theatre, now discernible only by the irregular cast of the ground. Built in the mid-1st century AD, and altered and enlarged in the 2nd century, they remained in use until the upper part of the town was abandoned in the 3rd century, but the only remaining portion is a cellar and sewer, which survived because they were filled in with a heap of potsherds around 100. It is possible to follow the sewer, which was intended for drainage from the baths, for about a hundred metres, a passage that provokes a peculiar and alarming sensation as one makes slow, dark progress along a channel for ancient Roman effluent.

On the eastern edge of town, just by the site of a 'Roman zoo' in which modern children have the opportunity to experience ancient breeds of sheep and goats (although most of them seem to be more concerned with impromptu picnic parties at the top of the panorama tower erected nearby), there sit the remains of the eastern gate of Augusta Raurica, lying along a stretch of the town's eastern walls, which have been identified for a length of 500 metres. The gate's projecting round towers, which have been reconstructed to eight or nine layers of the facing bricks, with the rubble core still exposed, were clearly intended as part of a great monumental gateway, but the plans were cut back to something less ambitious several times during its construction. The building seems to have begun around AD 80,[145] but was never in fact completed, an affront to the prestige of the town, which must have been all too visible over the next two centuries.

Perhaps the eye of the citizens was more taken by the massive funerary monument that lies just 50 metres away. Only the stone skeleton of its base now survives, indicating a massive stone cylinder that was 15 metres in diameter, probably topped with a mound of earth on which a statue of the deceased might have stood. It was built around the same time as the east gate, and the human remains, which were cremated on the spot, were probably of a man about thirty-five to forty years in age. He must have been someone of great importance, for it is neither a modest nor a discreet monument, and one that anyone entering or leaving the town in this direction could not fail to have remarked upon.

Moving from the eastern gate to visit the town's second amphitheatre – this time not a conversion – involves a walk beside the modern motorway, a rude awakening from the silence that enfolds most of the ruins. Across the lanes of speeding cars, a small portion of the western wall of Raurica is visible – all that remains, and heavily graffitoed. The amphitheatre, built around 200, and with seating for around 5,000 spectators, was a late addition to the town, but the citizens had been able to enjoy the adapted theatre for blood spectacles, and presumably only when it was turned back over to the dramatic arts was it deemed necessary to acquire a dedicated building. The arena's oval measures about 50 x 30 metres, strewn about with damp leaves, while the slopes upon which the seats once stood are populated by a thin copse of trees. The monumental western entrance survives more intact, with evidence of deep buttresses, which were added in Roman times to halt the slippage of the steep seating slope that has threatened ever since to collapse.

In a valley below, on a stretch of marshy land to one side of the theatre, lies the 'Grienmatt' shrine, a complex of Gallo-Roman temples set on a small plateau. The main one, right in the middle of an open field, is hedged about by an alarming forest of electric fences, clearly erected by a local farmer who is not that keen on visitors to the antiquities. The bold base of a platform survives, surrounded by the vestigial remains of a portico, with two or three columns still in place, and has been variously interpreted as a temple to the healing god Asclepius – in whose honour a number of inscriptions were found – or to the gods of the days of the week.

Back to the centre of town and a short walk north over to the Rhine, in a rather sleepy-looking section of Kaiseraugst (the twin village of Augst), lies the late-Roman fortress of Castrum Rauracense, directly on top of which the medieval settlement grew. It gets several notices in Ammianus Marcellinus (as Rauracum)[146] and is mentioned also in the *Notitia Dignitatum*, for the area was now a lynchpin between the imperial capital at Trier and the Danubian province of Raetia to the east.

Probably built in the early 4th century, it was visited by Julian in 360 and its fortifications may have been strengthened by Valentinian I in 370.[147] At about 3.5 hectares in area, it is the largest of Switzerland's late-Roman forts and housed units of the I Martia legion. The south wall is in fair condition, rising to around 4 metres in height, a section of its facing stones having been neatly restored. Part of the foundation of the south-western round tower is visible and it was close to this point that the Kaiseraugst Treasure was unearthed in 1960. The fort was probably destroyed in about 350, around the time the treasure was buried, but was subsequently rebuilt. Much of the interior of the fort is taken up with the site of a modern primary school, and the neat houses that surround the place and the general air of tranquillity give it more the atmosphere of a village green than a military monument.

Alongside the 'Rhine Baths' that lie in a jumble of ruins a few hundred metres away, a palaeo-Christian church perches just on the banks of the

river. Almost hidden away in trees and under a protective shelter, the
first building here was erected in the 4th century and remained in use
possibly until the 6th century. Inside the apse of the church can just be
made out, and it was here that the local bishops presided up to the 7th
century, when the see was transferred to the up-and-coming settlement
of Basle just down the river.[148] Deprived even of its position as an ecclesiastical centre, Castrum Rauracense went the way of its neighbour
Augusta Raurica and dwindled to become a small village.

Just across the river, hidden amongst a deep screen of trees, lie the
remains of a bridgehead fort built by Valentinian I, who ordered a general
reinforcement of the whole of the Rhine defences right the way from
Basilia to Lake Constance. Lying about 40 kilometres to the east of
Raurica, and set back around 15 kilometres from the Rhine, the legionary
fortress of Vindonissa formed part of this chain of defence. The scenery
of low hills seems to have strayed straight off a chocolate box, the cows
doing their scenic duty even in the face of a light dusting of snow.
Vindonissa, which lies interleaved with the modern town of Brugg, was
sited at the confluence of three rivers, the Aare, Reuss and Limmat, and
dominated a pass over the Jura mountains, as well as blocking off access
southwards to intruders passing beyond the Rhine, so it commanded a
position of huge strategic importance.

The first legionary camp was probably constructed here in about AD
16, and until 45 it was the base for the XIII Gemina legion, who were
replaced by the XXI Rapax some time before 69. Then, following the
civil war of that year, the fort became the home to the XI Claudia.
Deprived of much of its military function once the *limes* advanced forward
around 75, Vindonissa lost its full legionary garrison around 101, but
continued to be the station for elements from the VIII legion based at
Argentorate (Strasbourg). Reoccupied when the frontier moved back to
the Rhine after 260, a smaller fortress, known as Castrum Vindonissense,
retained a garrison into the early 5th century; and, once the Roman army
had abandoned its positions on the Rhine, the continuing role of this
site as a Christian bishopric indicates that some, at least, of its civilian
population stayed put.

A few hundred metres south of the railway station, on a site revealed
when a modern building was demolished, a Roman pottery-manufacturing
area has been unearthed. This comparatively heavy industry lay outside
the main *vicus* of the settlement, enabling it to reach a scale that would
have been unimaginable in a residential district. Little can be made out
of the structures involved, but in one of the excavated trenches, strata
of *terra sigillata* – the high-quality red-glazed ware for which the Rhineland

and parts of Gaul became famous, and which was exported throughout the Roman world – can be seen.[149]

To the extreme south-east of the main settlement lay the amphitheatre, a short way from the main legionary camp. All around are pretty terraces of houses on streets evoking the place's past, with names such as Römerstraße and Arenastraße, and the name indicated on old maps for the site translates as 'place of the bears', a possible folk-memory of the animal displays that may once have taken place here. Intriguingly, though no bones of lions (or other wild beasts) have so far been dug up, archaeologists did find the remains of a camel. The amphitheatre had a capacity of about 5,000 and was rebuilt at the end of the 1st century. The oval of the arena, and the earth banks on which the terraces of seats once stood, are fairly intact and the arena wall itself has been partly reconstructed with a double ring of stones.

The site of the main fort lies on an area known as the Königsfeld, a large open park, in part occupied by a church. The camp perimeter was irregularly shaped, with seven sides rather than the regulation four, in part determined by the difficulty of the terrain, overlooking the river gorge. The few remains to be seen today date from the 3rd-century version of the fort; its monumental west gateway is well preserved in outline, with a triple-entrance, the two at the sides being for pedestrians and the central archway for wheeled traffic. A stone set against one side of the central entrance seems to have been placed there because the road outside branched in two directions, forming a Y-junction, so that carts cutting in to avoid a bottleneck where the roads met must have been forever crashing against the gate and damaging its posts; the stone was to protect the structure and discourage such reckless driving. No other structures are apparent in the camp (though some have been identified by archaeological soundings) apart from the north gate, a smaller affair with square towers and deep rectangular holes set within the stone, which may represent a pre-existing wooden structure that was simply encased within the new building. The gate overlooks the river and a deep cut that was made when the railway was constructed in the 19th century. An earlier stretch of the wall strikes off to the north-east before disappearing into the ravine, much of it lost.

A short way outside the camp, under a protective roof, a 1st-century *mansio* marks the more purely civilian side of life in Vindonissa. It was extended on several occasions, so that it had its own bath-complex, complete with *frigidarium* and a small hypocaust for the warm rooms. In one corner of the complex a water-channel indicates an even earlier bath-house. A few hundred metres from this lies the last major visible relic of

Vindonissa's Roman life, the 'kitchen building'. Accessed through a metal grille at the bottom of a short flight of steps, it sits in the grounds of a primary school, and its entrance feels more like that of a bomb shelter than that of an archaeological site. It may well have formed part of the house of a centurion of the XI Claudia legion, possibly of the *primipilus*, the most senior of all. At one side of it were various inns, and part of the wall of one of these still survives in this subterranean world.

The main body of the ruins comprises the kitchen itself, which was in places built over the walls of the Celtic *oppidum* that existed at Vindonissa before the Roman occupation, and into which part of the Roman level has collapsed. A couple of rooms, quite bare of adornment, survive; in one corner blackening of the brickwork is visible, though whether from the normal sort of accident that might occur in a kitchen or through deliberate destruction is unclear.

Kitchen waste found here indicated a surprisingly high level of imported food being consumed, including oysters, which because of the need to ensure their freshness were a rarity, though a delicacy much in demand amongst Roman gourmands.[150] At the time, however, river transportation was possible all the way from Massilia (Marseilles), so the freshness of the produce in the centurion's kitchen would have been satisfactorily assured. When it was abandoned, the house was stripped and almost nothing left, save items that had been damaged or were considered worthless, such as a few tile stamps and a mortar, which was left behind as it had a hole in it.

Thirty-five kilometres of gentle countryside to the south-east of Windisch, Turicum's Roman past has been totally obscured by its development into the major banking centre of Zurich, but perhaps a precursor of the city's later international financial role was the station of the *beneficiarii*, the military units who collected road tolls, which was situated near here. A fort was also constructed under Valentinian I in the 370s, though abandoned with the rest of the *limes* in the early 5th century. Some thirty minutes by train to the south-east of the city lies a much better-preserved Roman fort, at Pfäffikon.

The landscape here is predominantly of low hills, and it is prime agricultural territory punctuated by crisp-looking villages. Around a kilometre from the centre of Pfäffikon village, set on a low hill at the back of houses, the fort's isolation is accentuated by a blanket of snow, its slopes now home to nothing more martial than a family tobogganing down the hill. Its quadrangular walls were reconstructed early in the 20th century, the dark, smallish bricks making it seem like a rather outmoded office building. Inside, the only hint of an interior structure on the day of our visit was almost totally covered by the snow. It is the outline of a 1st-century *villa rustica*, which occupied the site before the fort was built. Two rooms have been identified along with a hypocaust that sits beneath the fort's south-eastern tower.

Coins found from the reign of Valentinian I suggest that it was under this emperor that the fort was constructed, as part of a building programme to shore up the leaking sieve that the *limes* had become. The site could equally, however, date to the late 3rd or early 4th century and a similar programme by Diocletian, which led to the building of forts at Oberwinterthur, Stein-am-Rhein, Pfyn and Arbon, securing a line leading up to Lake Constance. From there the late-Roman *limes* followed the line of the Iller river, defended by a series of large watchtowers, until it reached the Danube between Lorch and Schirenhof.

The Agri Decumates

North and east of the portions of Switzerland that shelter behind the Rhine, the Agri Decumates – the territory that was occupied as the *limes* advanced from around 74 to 260 – was one of the more ephemeral of Roman conquests, with only Dacia beating it for the brevity of its occupation. According to Tacitus, the area had once been settled by a mixture of Gallic tribes, a fact confirmed by 2nd-century inscriptions that mention the Boii, Mediomatrici and Senones.[151] The exact meaning of the term that came to be applied to this area between the Neckar, Black Forest and Swabian Alps is unclear; it was once believed that it derived from *decuma*, meaning 'tithe', but it is more probable that it comes from a Celtic-term meaning 'ten' and refers to an area comprising ten districts or cantons.

Among the chief towns of the region, which experienced two centuries of prosperity under Roman rule, was Arae Flaviae, whose very name suggests a temple to the Flavian conquerors of this region. Now just outside the modern town of Rottweil, it lies on the banks of the Neckar river. Founded in around AD 73, it owed its existence to a slight realignment of the frontier by Pinarius Clemens, which meant that new forts had to be built to secure a straighter line between the Upper Rhine and the Danube. The town's main Roman remains, the baths, lie almost enclosed by the cemetery to the east of town. They are the biggest in south-western Germany and originally formed part of a legionary camp of the XI Claudia from 75. When this was abandoned after just five years, they were integrated into a smaller cohort camp. The auxiliary troops

who were then stationed at Arae Flaviae thus found themselves in possession of a facility far grander than their numbers (no more than 1,000)
would normally have permitted. Set in a dip a few metres deep and
surrounded by a grassy bank, the bath complex was originally purely
symmetrical, but a part of one wing was lopped off when the camp was
reduced in size (from its original extent of 16 hectares to a mere 5.7).

Just across the river, where the civilian settlement developed, one of
the surprises of the *limes* sits under the church of Saint Pelagius (which,
though much reconstructed, originally dates from the 8th or 9th century).
Down in the basement, behind a barely openable wooden door, is a
section of hypocaust, some 40 metres square, which may have survived
through its later use as living quarters. The pillars of this hypocaust are
particularly tall and so it is possible to walk, or rather to crouch, in this
subterranean interstice. It must, however, have made a very damp
bedroom indeed, with the constant dripping of water creating an atmosphere of foul dankness.

A 50-kilometre drive to the north-east, again along the line of the
Neckar, lies Sumelocenna (modern Rottenburg). The town seems to have
had its origin as part of an imperial estate, for it is known in the earliest
records (in the mid-80s) as the Saltus Sumelocennensis,[152] though it later
became the civilian capital of the region. It had a city wall more than 2
kilometres long built at the end of the 2nd century, of which parts
survive. But the most intriguing relic, over which the local museum has
been built, is probably the largest public latrine to be seen in the Roman
world. Although others can be found along the *limes*, mostly associated
with bathhouses and particularly well preserved in North Africa, none
is as impressive as this. Set around a courtyard, it is provided with individual marble seats, each with its own hole down which urine and faeces
would be deposited. It was very much a public facility, for in performing
this (to modern Western sensibilities, very private) act, the Romans were
surrounded by their fellows. Around the latrine a water channel normally
ran, and the public were provided with sponges, which served in lieu of
the modern predilection for toilet paper. With the remains of impressive pillars set into the middle of the courtyard, this mammoth provision
for a very mundane need seems strangely like a temple.

Behind the latrine a small section of street survives, together with
part of a private villa. Elsewhere, a temple has been located in the area
of the modern gaol, together with two sets of baths. The second of
these sits in the basement of the Eugen Bolz Gymnasium, a school not
far from the museum, and seems to have been built in the mid-2nd to
early 3rd centuries. The area of the ruins is quite small, with a dusty and

neglected air, but from there a fine view can be had of the school library (and, presumably, vice versa), an echo of the ancient habit of siting libraries near bath complexes to cater to those for whom mere pampering of the body was not satisfaction enough.

The Neckar-Odenwald and Antonine Limes

To trace the advances of the *limes* of Germania Superior requires a jump back northwards from the Agri Decumates to the point where (after the time of the Flavian emperors) the *limes* deviated from the line of the Rhine south of Remagen between Hönningen and Rheinbroh. It then proceeded generally south-eastwards, parallel to the river, but around 7 kilometres to the east of its course. It passed into the Taunus mountains, and then around Bad Schwalbach turned east. Soon after this, about 5 kilometres from the modern town of Bad Homburg, stands the Saalburg, one of Germany's most famous Roman forts. That this auxiliary camp should achieve such fame, when it is really no more significant than its fellows to east and west, is in large part due to Kaiser Wilhelm II, who spent a great deal of time in the area as a child, grew fond of the place and, when he ascended to the throne in 1888, ordered that it be reconstructed, a process that was completed in 1907.[153] So fond was he of the Saalburg that, fancying himself, as German Emperor, to be the heir of his Roman counterparts, he had an inscription set above the main gatehouse, which, in impeccable Latin, honoured him as the re-founder of the Saalburg, accompanied by a statue of Antoninus Pius.

Originally an earthwork fort built under Domitian in around 83 as part of his war against the Chatti,[154] it was rebuilt in timber soon afterwards, and sometime between 125 and 139 received a regular garrison of the *Cohors II Raetorum civium romanorum*, a part-mounted auxiliary unit from the neighbouring province to the east. The fort was reconstructed in stone around 139, but seems to have been destroyed during the Alamannic invasion of 233, after which it was briefly restored, only to be abandoned with the rest of the Agri Decumates around 260.

The Saalburg occupies a rectangular ground-plan with rounded corners, each wall punctuated by a gate. With their neat crenellations and perfectly tiled roofs for the towers, the fortifications seem, perhaps, too immaculate – the grey stone and brooding forest around giving a sense that somehow a Roman fort had mated with a Gothic castle and produced this uneasy compromise as offspring. This is perhaps unfair, for everything is meticulously done, and the museum presents an excellent display of finds from the site, including a very large collection of Roman footwear, which was found in waterlogged levels that had preserved the boots' leather. Around the centre of the fort, the *principia* has been reconstructed, including a representation of the Temple of the Standards, complete with legionary flags, although most of the main buildings lie in ruins or still beneath the ground.

Outside to the south-west of the main gate, a *vicus* grew up around the fort, today just a confusing collection of ruined shells. One of these was once an inn, possibly for official visitors, whilst beside it lay the bath-house. Further into the surrounding woods, a Jupiter column has been set up, reconstructed in the 19th century from fragments found nearby, very much along the lines of the one in Mainz. Its particularly fine panel of Hercules wielding an enormous club seems lost in the trees, viewed only by the occasional dog-walker.

Around 200 metres to the north of the Saalburg lies a section of the *limes*: a rather overgrown ditch is backed by an earth rampart some 2 metres high, and in front of this a long, low palisade of wooden stakes has been erected, a small token of a barrier that originally stretched for hundreds of kilometres. Up in the wood-wreathed hills above the Saalburg the *limes* continues, punctuated by the occasional watchtower, one of a string that policed the frontier at surprisingly short intervals. The walk is a pleasant one, shaded by the canopy of the trees from both rain and sunshine. A kilometre or so away, at Fröhlichmannskopf, a small tower, originally of timber, but reconstructed in stone in the mid-1st century after a fire, lies lost in the wood, with only about 20 centimetres of stone poking up above the ground to indicate its plan. The next tower, which is around 500 metres away in the Köpern valley, may originally have been a comparative giant, at three storeys, with the entrance on the middle floor. However, its remains are now only fractionally more complete than those of its neighbour, overgrown with grass and partly concealed by leaves. Here, the *limes* is a very quiet and forgotten place.

From this point the frontier turned north towards Butzbach, then arched round southwards to reach the Main at Hanau, protected by a series of forts on the west bank of that river until it reached Miltenberg. It then cut through the Odenwald, forming two distinct lines, one west of Miltenberg proceeding via Eulbach and Würzberg to reach the Neckar in the south near Köngen, and the other about 30 kilometres to the east, attained during the reign of Antoninus Pius, cutting in a south-easterly direction until it hit the Raetian border near Lorch.

At Eulbach, the unlikely setting of the 'English Garden' of the Counts of Erbach-Erbach's hunting lodge houses some of the best-preserved remains of the pre-Antonine (or Odenwald) *limes* in this section. It was established between 1802 and 1818 by Count Franz I, an inveterate collector of ancient remains and an exponent of the then current fashion of arranging them artfully in a seemingly natural setting. Amongst his other acquisitions was a herd of buffalo, thus providing the nearest connection that the Romans, in a sense, ever made to North America.

The guardian seems rather surprised to see visitors at opening time and surveys me suspiciously as we make our way in search of the Roman castles within. In the slightly muddy maze of pathways, the first sign of Rome is an obelisk, probably a Jupiter stone, placed to the side of the path. Then, beyond a clump of legionary gravestones, the gateway of Eulbach fort lies. It is the east gate of the fort, which housed an irregular unit (or *numerus*) in its 5.5-hectare precinct. It was originally sited to the east of the park, only 80 metres from the *limes*, before the count uprooted it and planted it close to his other antiquities. It only saw military use between 100 and 159, before Antoninus Pius moved the frontier eastwards and the posts on the Odenwald–Neckar *limes* were evacuated. The rest of the fort was subsequently destroyed, so the count's apparent act of vandalism in fact saved this portion, a single gateway rising to a couple of metres. A short distance away sits another, rather more complete gate, from Würzberg fort, though its battlements resemble more the image of a medieval portal than a Roman gateway and seem to have been a later addition. The final piece in the count's collection, beyond the line of the wood's edge, is the remains of a stone watchtower, which was removed from a position south of Eulbach. It is the most complete, placed on a small mound, with a couple of votive altars set inside it for good measure.

The small fort of Würzberg is 3–4 kilometres a little further south, lying alone in the Odenwald. The bathhouse, which is all that remains apart from the gate in the 'English Garden', was built, along with the fort, in the early 140s by a unit from the north of England. The turn-off to the fort is by a car park at the edge of the forest. A few hundred metres within, along a tree-shaded track, lie the Roman remains, but a lorry-load full of rifle-wielding hunters – predominantly dressed in green to blend in with the trees, a few among them wearing a feather in their caps – block the way. Their leader, a belligerent type in late middle age, is aggressive, demanding that we leave the forest at once, for there is a hunt today and access to the Roman ruins is, he insists, forbidden. Appeals to reason fail, and tension mounts. Faced with a dozen or more armed and increasingly irritated men for whom the idea of waiting a quarter of an hour is far too much of an affront to bear, we leave, and Würzberg fort remains elusive. It is, perhaps, the only encounter with genuine 'barbarians' along the whole frontier.

Twenty kilometres to the east, along the line of the *limes* as advanced by Antoninus Pius, the *numerus* fort of Haselburg lies in fields near the village of Reinhardsachsen. Only a small section of tower and wall survives, hemmed in by fields on either side. It was built in around 150, and lies just 60 metres or so from the line of the frontier itself, which can just be made out in a copse of trees to the east. One gate of the wall remains, seemingly pointing into the middle of nowhere in this picturesque but lonely rural setting. A coin of 264/5 was found on the site (an *antonianus* of Gallienus),[155] creating a minor mystery, as it was supposed that the *limes* had been evacuated by this time. But there is no need to suppose that Haselburg was held as an isolated outpost after that point, for Roman troops would continue to have patrolled beyond the new line, engaging in proactive patrols and strikes against any Alamanns who looked foolish or bold enough to penetrate the Rhine, and there was no more natural place to base themselves temporarily than the recently abandoned fort sites.

Not far to the south, the modern town of Walldürn, attractively set in woodlands, lies about 2 kilometres north-west of the point where the *limes* begins a run of 80 kilometres in an almost dead-straight line. It does so with little regard for the terrain it traverses, a testament to the obstinacy (as well as the skill) of the Roman surveyors. There was a fort here, about 30 metres off the main road, but it has almost totally disappeared, marked only by slight undulations in the ground, though down a little incline the military baths have survived in reasonable shape. They were completed in their final form only in 232 – a dedication to the goddess Fortuna provided the date – a bare three decades before the *limes* fell and the Romans abandoned the place for ever. The baths were then destroyed by fire, but whether in an accident or by invading German tribesmen is unknown. The complex is quite small, with just a few stone courses to give the outline of the rooms, but the setting, half-hidden by the higher fields to one side, is pleasantly peaceful.

At Osterburken, around 20 kilometres to the south, an original auxiliary cohort fort that was built around 155 (and garrisoned by a unit from Aquitania) has been totally submerged beneath the modern village. However, under Commodus the auxiliaries were supplemented by a *numerus* and a second fort was built for the newcomers on a slope above the old camp. It is an irregular-shaped trapezium, which employed one wall of the auxiliary fort as its own north-western perimeter. The original fort had in any case been at something of a disadvantage with this high point overlooking its walls, and so the new structure, as well as housing the *numerus*, would have provided additional security for the Aquitanians. As usual, it seems to have been legionaries who were the workhorses of this major building project, and detachments of the VIII Augusta from Argentorate (Strasbourg) were drafted in to erect it.

The west wall of the fort is the best preserved, with a fine view of the roofs of the modern village, but it was in the ditch of the earlier cohort fort that the most interesting finds were dug up (in 1991). Two levels of burning were found, together with pottery and the bones and skulls of two adults showing signs of a violent death. It could be evidence of the final Germanic assault on the place. In the village museum the main items of interest are no fewer than twenty-one altar stones dedicated by *beneficiarii* (customs officers) who had a shrine set up nearby; over successive decades each new head of the station added a new altar. Alongside are the remains of a bathhouse, one of two found at Osterburken (the other lying buried beneath a local bank).

Past the bathhouse of the fort at Jagsthausen, the *limes* now proceeds gently south-east into largely wooded territory. At Pfahldoebel, a section of 200 metres or so of the original earth rampart and ditch survives, hidden deep in the forest. The V-shape of the ditch is clearly visible amongst the fallen leaves and branches; the effect is very much like that of the Antonine Wall in Scotland, hardly surprising given that they both date from the same emperor's programme of works on the frontier. At Gleichen, still deep in the woods, along a kilometre or so of trackway, lies one of the more unusual watchtowers. Its base survives only up to three courses or so, but it is, quite exceptionally, hexagonal, as though the architect had decided in some small way to stand out, or the commander of the unit based there felt he had to be different from the Julii next door. More scientifically based speculation suggests that the six-sided shape gave extra strength, but if so, it is an innovation that was only rarely adopted elsewhere.[156]

Only twenty minutes' drive further south lies the small town of Mainhardt, which housed a fort for the *Cohors I Asturum equitata*, a part-mounted unit from the north-west of Spain. It was transferred here from the Neckar–Odenwald *limes* under Antoninus Pius, but then at the start of the 3rd century was sent to Britain,[157] and its replacement unit in Germany is unknown. The remnants of the fort are very slight, a small stretch lying near the local sports hall, together with a corner tower. The line then disappears into thick undergrowth, although for the truly determined it can be traced further at the base of a tangled hedgerow (and a further section – now invisible – was preserved under the sports field

built by the United States army in 1945). The town is also home to one
of the frontier's best small museums, including some stone reliefs of a
mother goddess suckling a child, which are highly unusual and only found
along this small section of the *limes* and in Gaul. Their kinship with later
representations of the Madonna and baby Jesus is unmistakable.

The next section of *limes* to the south is thickly populated by watchtowers in the woods. At Grab, around 5 kilometres from Mainhardt, one
has been reconstructed in wood, recreating a middle state of the *limes*,
with tower, rampart and ditch, and a wooden palisade in front of it. At
more than 20 metres tall, the tower provides a good Roman's-eye-view
of the wooded *barbaricum* beyond, and shows clearly that to scramble
over the palisade and then through the ditch and over the earth banks
would have created such a commotion that intruders would have been
detected relatively easily, although dealing with them would very much
have depended on the numbers in which they came. It seems that the
proportion of large trees such as oak and fir in the forest declined in
Roman times,[158] so there may have been a deliberate attempt to thin out
the forest canopy to encourage better visibility.

Further south at Heidenbuhl in the Murrhardt forest, a watchtower[159]
lies up a slight slope. The structure was composed of two separate towers,
and the outline of one, really just the stone foundation, can be made
out, and next to it a reconstructed but still-ruinous twin, complete to
around 4 metres on one side and 2 metres on the other. Utterly
surrounded by trees, it bears a most romantic air. The two towers are
less than a metre apart, and it seems that the first stage was destroyed
in a fire, but then rapidly reconstructed without using the shell of the
original. The foundations of this second stage, though, were badly set
– proving that the Romans were on occasions poor engineers – and the
reconstructors therefore chose to use the older watchtower's foundations for their handiwork.

Another series of watchtowers strikes south-east; in one of them a
Roman shoehorn was dug up, providing the first evidence that the
Romans wore shoes that were closed at the back.[160] Finally, the *limes*
emerges from the woods near Welzheim, at the edge of a modern village.
Originally there were two forts, but the western one has disappeared,
while the smaller eastern one (only 1.6 hectares in extent) has in part
survived. Although otherwise not particularly remarkable, the eastern
fort does have one curious feature. It lies east of the line of the *limes*,
with a gap in the frontier palisade enabling communication and access
into 'friendly' territory to the west. The western fort had a cavalry
garrison (the *Ala I Scubulorum*),[161] whilst this one was garrisoned by a

unit of *exploratores* (or scouts), appropriate for such a forward position. It seems that the eastern fort was established first, and then when the *limes* ended up running as straight as it did, the decision was taken not to abandon it.

The remains now lie in an open field, with few structures standing. The south gateway and a section of the south wall have been impressively rebuilt, though, complete with ditch in front, the 10 metres or so to either side of the single entranceway contrasting with the ruinous state of the rest. The internal buildings have gone, but the field is liberally sprinkled with altars and sculptures, including one of Mithras killing the bull. The low line of the remaining walls is cut in places by water-overflow channels, an indication that the site was not chosen carefully enough and suffered from flooding. In confirmation of this, the south-eastern tower shows evidence of having collapsed several times during the life of the fort.

Just about 10 kilometres further to the south-east lies Lorch, most famous for its abbey, Kloster Lorch. The modern town has completely covered the Roman fort that lay here (part of which is buried beneath the church itself). In compensation, a watchtower has been reconstructed nearby on a site that may have been occupied by a smaller fort. It seems a fairly suburban sort of a tower, neat, manicured and utterly unmilitary, but it provides excellent views over the Rems valley. Just beside Lorch lay the Rotenbachtal, a narrow 3-kilometre-long valley, which from the mid-2nd century marked the border between Germania Superior and Raetia to the east. It was a heavily fortified area both on the German and Raetian sides, marking a strategic trade route as well as a provincial boundary. Amongst the trees and the gentle rush of brooks, it all seems a very long way from Germania's northernmost reaches, far away on the shores of the North Sea.

Raetia and Noricum

Roman Empire before c.160 and after c.260

Frontier of Empire, c. 160–c.260

Raetian Wall

German palisade

Roman fort

Map labels

Danube

PANNONIA

Mur

Vindobona (Vienna)

Commagena (Tulln)

Astura

Augustiana (Traismauer)

Ad Iuvense (Zeiselmauer)

Faviana (Mautern)

Ad Iuvense (Ybbs)

Solva

Poetovio

Lauriacum (Enns-Lorch)

Celeia

Ločica

N O R I C U M

Enns

Boiodurum (Passau Instatt)

Lentia (Linz)

Stanacum (Oberrana)

Ovilava (Wels)

Magdalensburg

Castra Batavorum (Passau)

Ad Mauros (Eferding)

Virunum

Sorviodurum (Straubing)

Quintana (Künzing)

Teurnia

Castra Regina (Regensburg)

Iuvavum (Salzburg)

Salzach

Eining

I T A L I A

Isar

Günzenhausen
Icianiacum (Theilenhofen)
Sablonetum (Ellingen)
Burgsalach

Vetoniana (Pfünz)

Raetian Wall

(Aenus) Inn

R A E T I A

Augusta Vindelicum (Augsburg)

Lech

Biriciana (Weissenburg)

Dalkingen

Aalen (Weissenburg)

Rainau-Buch

Böbingen

Schirenhof ⊠ Heidenheim

Danube

Günzburg

GERMANIA SUPERIOR

Scale

50 miles

80 kms

0

CHAPTER 3

Raetia and Noricum

The troops at Batavis, however, held out. Some soldiers of this troop had gone to Italy to fetch the final pay to their comrades, and no one knew that the barbarians had slain them on the way. One day, as Saint Severinus was reading in his cell, he suddenly closed the book and began to sigh greatly and to weep. He ordered the bystanders to run out with haste to the river, which he declared was in that hour besprinkled with human blood, and straightway word was brought that the bodies of the soldiers mentioned above had been brought to land by the current of the river.

Eugippius, *Vita Sancti Severini*, c.20[1]

Raetia

The transalpine sections of southern Raetia, now in southern Germany, first came into the Roman sphere during the campaigns of Augustus and Tiberius in 15 BC, expeditions that would also result in the conquest of the Norican kingdom to the east. It was occupied by peoples of Celtic origin, and the failure of the Romans to annex this area any earlier had left a salient from which raiders or invaders could cut off Roman access to the Balkans or, indeed, threaten the security of the newly acquired territories along the Rhine. The groups who dwelt there were, however, separated into a number of small tribes, often controlling barely more than the valley that they inhabited, and so the chance of a concerted assault south of the Alps was slight. The territory of Vindelicia – around modern Augsburg – which lay in the north and east of Raetia, was conquered by the Romans at about the same time as southern Noricum, and a legion was stationed there, only to be withdrawn in about AD 16–17. The remaining central portion of Raetia was not then formally constituted a province until about AD 50, and thus had no official governor, being administered by the military.

Although many of the forts south of the Danube in the western part

of Raetia were destroyed in the upheavals that surrounded the complex
civil war of 69 and the revolt of Julius Civilis the same year,[2] by the time
of Vespasian they had been rebuilt. A complicated series of moves forward
– in part in connection with the Roman desire to bridge the gap between
the Rhine and the Danube, and in part to fill holes in the defensive
system further east along the Danube – resulted in an extensive building
programme and a shifting about of military units until the mid-2nd
century. The Marcomannic Wars (166–80) caused some damage in the
east and probably led directly to the stationing of a legion, the III Italica,
in the province.

Throughout this time the Raetian *limes* was, as in Germania Superior,
marked out by a wooden palisade. This was replaced in 205–6[3] by the
building of a stone wall, some 3 metres high, studded with interval
towers. Just like Hadrian's Wall, it was not a suitable platform from which
to mount a fixed defence, but it was a potent statement of intent, and
would seriously have hindered small-scale raids whilst obstructing larger-
scale incursions, at least to the extent of facilitating the passing of warning
messages further back into the province, where reinforcements could
then be mustered. By the mid-3rd century, however, serious damage had
been done by the Alamanns and other barbarian raiders, and some positions north of the Danube may have been evacuated, whilst others were
abandoned when the Agri Decumates to the west were lost and the *limes*
was restored to its 1st-century position in Switzerland.

The early 4th century was surprisingly quiet in Raetia, but serious
raids by the Iuthungi in 357–8[4] led to a sharp retort under Valentinian I
and to the refortification of significant parts of the *limes* both on the
Rhine and the Danube. But the withdrawal of troops by Stilicho, probably in 401, to meet the challenge posed by Alaric and his Goths, led to
the stripping of vital Raetian garrisons, after which it is hardly possible
to talk of a consistently held frontier line at all.

Just east of Lorch in Baden-Württemberg, the border between Raetia
and Germania Superior was a provincial border of administrative convenience, and did not mark out any great shift in landscape or culture. A
covering mantle of conifers closes in along the path through the
Rotenbachtal, the voices of those visitors to the park who are more intent
on forest walks than archaeology fade and the distant past begins to feel
ever more present. After a while, across a shallow brook via a small
modern bridge – the wooden piles of whose Roman ancestor remain
elusive in the free-flowing water – the way leads up a gentle wooded
slope. Here at length the beginning of the Raetian wall comes into view.
At this point it is reconstructed, its stones rebuilt in a stepped fashion,

with one small section rising to a metre or so in height and half a metre thick. Largely concealed by the thin forest canopy, it seems almost impossible to believe that this low and weathered wall was part of one of the most ambitious and extensive Roman defensive works in the entire Empire.

Around 20 metres higher up the rise lies a very weathered altar or dedication stone and part of a worn frieze, possibly originally topped by rosettes. It is an altar to Terminus, the god of frontiers and borders. It is a most appropriate place to find a shrine to this ancient deity, whose worship seems to date from the very beginning of Rome. His birthday was celebrated on 23 February each year with the festival of the Terminalia, when sacrifices were made by landowners at the boundaries of their holdings, and an offering of blood was sprinkled on the stones dividing their fields.[5]

On the southern edge of these woods lie the small Roman baths at Schirenhof, their stones greyed and dulled by the weather, the small park in which they are set surrounded by prim suburban housing. Set on a slight hill, their position gives a wonderful view back down across the wooded valley. The complex was much reduced in size in the 3rd century, possibly as a result of the slighter hold that the Romans then exercised along the *limes*. The wall continued until it met the Danube just north of Eining, some 150 kilometres to the east, from where the river line made such a fortification redundant. Between Zimmer and Böbingen an der Rems (around 8 kilometres east of Schirenhof), where the wall takes a slight detour to the north-east, another section of it is visible, really just a few metres long set on a grassy stretch next to the B29 road. In a laudable demonstration of municipal pride, a locally erected sign declares 'World Heritage Site', a reference to the designation by UNESCO of the German *limes* as such in 2005.[6]

A few kilometres north-east lay the fort of Böbingen, situated on a hill above the Rems river. Originally enclosing an area some 145 x 135 metres in area, the fort was constructed in around 150, and was probably occupied until around 260, when many of the positions in this part of Raetia were abandoned. The ancient site has now largely been gobbled up by the car park of a family restaurant, though its gate towers are still intact, surrounded by a vast array of BMWs and Volkswagens. Both towers of the gateway have been partially reconstructed, though the right-hand one is filled with rubble and seems to have been subjected to some recent damage.

Around 30 kilometres to the east of Böbingen, and in turn about 5 kilometres behind the line of the *limes* wall, is the largest fort along this sector of Raetia and certainly the most spectacular in terms of its visible remains.

Built around 160, Aalen also housed the largest cavalry unit in the Western Empire north of the Alps, the *Ala II Flavia milliaria*, a rare double-strength mounted troop of around 1,000 men. It was one of only seven such milliary *alae* in the Empire (if one includes the camel unit stationed near Palmyra in Syria, a truly unique detachment).[7] Its commander would have been the most senior military officer in the province of Raetia until the stationing of the III Italica legion in Augusta Vindelicorum (Augsburg) around a decade later, although just as with the cavalry commander at Stanwix on Hadrian's Wall, there is no evidence of his exercising any general supervisory capacity over the provincial *limes*.

The western half of the fort's former site has been swallowed up by the Johannis Friedhof, a large cemetery thickly shaded with trees. It seems truly a place of sleep and forgetfulness, many of the crosses commemorating local men who died in the two World Wars, some of them simply 'lost in Russia'. Beyond, at the entrance to the archaeological area proper, lies the remains of the *porta principalis sinistra*, excavated in 1962. It is a double-gate with two passages, each around 3 metres wide – substantial enough, in other words, to let two mounted soldiers pass with relative ease. It leads the way into the Limes Museum, the leading German museum devoted to the study of the Roman frontier, which was founded in 1964. It was not the beginning of study into the *limes*, for in Germany (just as in Britain) a fascination for these ruins that could be seen without excavation was a venerable hobby, and scientific study of the frontier began early with the establishment of the Reichslimeskomission in 1892. This undertook many of the first excavations along the *limes*, and was headed up from its foundation until 1903 by Theodor Mommsen, the redoubtable doyen of German historians of the Roman Empire.[8]

The exhibits include fine examples of all the pieces expected to be associated with a significant Roman military presence: a votive table to Jupiter Dolichenus; from Osterburken, a relief to Mithras, another favoured god amongst the military; and a hoard of silver from Hildesheim, a sobering reminder that, for all the presence of this imposing military unit along the central Danube, instability and the threat of barbarian raiding were never wholly absent.

The main surviving structure of the fort is the *principia*, the outlines of whose stones rise a couple of courses in height, including the apse of the Temple of the Standards and the basilical cross-hall, a rather imposing statue of Marcus Aurelius presiding over it all. There are two dedication inscriptions. One of them, dating from 163–4, uniquely refers to the temple as a *capitolium*, a term more appropriate for a town or city forum than a military camp. The second, from the time of Commodus, may mark some rebuilding of the fort. The other buildings are less well defined, and down towards the *porta principalis dextra*, at the opposite end of the camp to the museum entrance, the ruins dwindle into a grassy patch and a few bumps, the remains of excavations during the 1970s. The Roman presence at Aalen, however, did not survive the tidal wave of Alamannic incursions and the general pull-back to more defensible positions that took place around 260.

From Aalen it is only about 15 kilometres north-east to the next cluster of important Roman Raetian remains at Rainau-Buch, the site of an auxiliary cohort fort, possibly of the *Cohors III Thracum*, posted here from the eastern Balkans. The fort itself lies up a slight slope, surrounded by fields and hedgerows. There is no visible evidence of internal structures, and only the remains of the southern gate and part of the wall give any evidence that the Roman army ever occupied the site. The gate is flanked by two square towers reconstructed to half a metre or so in height. On their own, shorn of most of the original structures, and beaten by late autumn rain, they seem somehow beleaguered, still conscious of being in fundamentally unfriendly country.

As was customary, the fort's bathhouse was sited some way from the main building and now lies by the side of an artificial lake in a kind of country park. A surprisingly grand structure for such a place, it seems more appropriate for a small town than a modest military detachment, but may have undergone some expansion in anticipation of a visit by Caracalla to the *limes* in 219–20; and the outline of a large building just by the water's edge, composed of two stepped terraces and interpreted as residential, may well have been erected as accommodation for the Emperor or some senior member of his entourage.

A short way to the north-west in the Mahdholz woods lurks yet another reconstruction of a *limes* watchtower. It rises two storeys up, its wooden bulk bolstered by a core of concrete, providing an excellent view for many kilometres east and west. The real gem, however, waits in the trees behind it. In a quiet clearing, accessed by a few metres of muddy track, is the most impressive section of the Raetian wall along the whole *limes*.

Although heavily reconstructed, it gives a good sense of how the barrier might have looked. A section around 8–10 metres long, it soars to around 3 metres in height and is around a metre thick. The end-piece where the reconstruction finishes exposes the mass of irregular stones that made up the wall's core, looking as though it has been sliced by some enormous cleaver. Running along 166 kilometres of the boundary, it must have been a truly imposing sight, and only the relative sparseness of its remains rob it of its place next to Hadrian's Wall as the most magnificent of Roman defensive works. Beside it are the remains of the original watchtower (an earlier phase of which the modern version represents). Evidence can be made out here for several phases of reconstruction of the stone-built phase of the *limes*, as the outline of a smaller, square tower is superimposed on the remains of an earlier rectangular watchtower.

A couple of kilometres to the east, at Dalkingen, lie the ruins of another cohort fort, in an isolated location off a minor side-road and thence up a muddy track. The remains are of a rectangular building, walls and gates with two levels, one of them marked out by wooden stakes that indicate the internal buildings of an earlier phase. The history of the *limes* fortifications here is relatively complex, for a hedge barrier under Hadrian was then followed by a watchtower, and in turn by a large stone building. In its fourth stage, however, Dalkingen departed from the normal career trajectory of a Raetian fort, since around 213 part of the building was dismantled and replaced by a façade with 3.5-metre-thick walls and a triumphal arch. The strength and depth of the foundations indicate that this was of a very significant height, and it seems that a larger-than-life statue of the Emperor Caracalla was incorporated within it. It was almost certainly built to honour him during his fighting against the German tribes in this area, although the construction of the arch may have been more about flattery of the Emperor than a true representation of the results of the campaign.

Caracalla had crossed the frontier in August 213, accompanied by Gaius Suetrius Sabinus, intent on punishing the Alamanns, who were only then beginning to threaten the borderlands. Having launched the attack, he proceeded back up the Rhine towards Mainz, where he seems to have defeated the Cenni. After a further victory near the Main river, Caracalla had himself declared *imperator* (for the third time) and *Germanicus Maximus*. Contemporary writers who were almost universally negative towards Caracalla complained that he had bought peace from the Germans and that his comparison of himself with earlier martial emperors was shameful. Perhaps they were thinking in purely territorial terms, for it is true that the Emperor did not actually annex any new land, but the salutary lesson he taught the Alamanns, and the strengthening of sections of the *limes* that he ordered, may have restored peace to the frontier for the best part of two decades – a far more effective use of resources than a showy and expensive acquisition of ultimately indefensible territory.

From Dalkingen to Gunzenhausen, a distance of some 120 kilometres, the frontier curved gently to the north-east, pushing almost to its furthest extent into Free German territory. Nothing remains of the small fort that was situated in Gunzenhausen, though in 1897 part of the ramparts and *principia* were unearthed by the town's main church. It seems only to have been around 80 metres square, and so must have housed a relatively small unit. A coin hoard dated to 241–3 is suggestive of destruction along this sector of the frontier at the time, but little more is known of the site's history.

A little way out of the centre of town, on a high rise behind the cemetery, lies further evidence of the Raetian wall. It is a quiet place, populated almost entirely by deer and the odd winter walker following the confusing complex of waymarked trails. Just at the top of the hill rises an obelisk with a base of cut stones. The face on the attached plaque is not that of a Roman emperor, however, but of Bismarck, the key figure in the 19th-century unification of Germany. The 'Bismarckturm' does, though, incorporate some antique remains, as it was constructed with stones from a primitive ring fortification built on this hill by the Alamanni in the 8th century, which probably in turn borrowed stones from the remains of the nearby Roman watchtowers and wall. Bismarck's obelisk may, therefore, partly be composed of third-hand building material, some of it very ancient indeed.

Beyond the Bismarckturm lie the remains of the small Roman watchtower itself, just the outline now surviving, but laid out with an unusual double-room. Around 4.5 x 6 metres in area, it was constructed in the 1st century AD and at the time would have been protected by a wooden palisade. A reconstruction of this has duly been erected nearby, with a metre-deep ditch underneath it, which was filled with stones to stabilise the sharpened wooden stakes. At around 3 metres high, the barrier was bound together with wooden bands and, just like its later stone successor (wings of which can be seen coming off the watchtower), would have provided just enough of an obstacle to frustrate minor incursions and disrupt the course of major ones.

Around 40 kilometres to the south-east, the Roman fort of Icianiacum at Theilenhofen is, like many other forts, largely represented only by its bathhouse, some of whose walls rise to a metre or so in height. It is set in a slight dip, screened by trees. At some 2 kilometres behind the *limes*, the soldiers here, from the *Cohors III Bracaraugustanorum* (originally all the way from Braga in modern Portugal), were at less danger than most of being surprised by barbarians whilst about their ablutions.

A short way along the frontier, where it begins to curve once more down to the south-west, lies the fort at Ellingen, ancient Sablonetum. It was one of the early excavations by the Reichslimeskomission in 1895, but further work was not possible until the early 1980s when a programme to encourage consolidation by farmers of disparate land-holdings made the site once more available for digging.[9] The building inscription found here refers to a reconstruction in 182, at the start of the reign of Commodus, though it was probably originally built in wood under Hadrian and housed a *numerus* whose identity is unknown. Around 80 metres square, the site has had one wall and a 30-metre section of stone rampart extensively reconstructed. A lower section of wall survives and runs to the east, reaching the the remains of an angle tower. It sits on a very flat area, with good visibility over the fertile farmland all around. The fort was probably abandoned some time before 233, during the Alamannic Wars, an evacuation that may have been planned, as no evidence has been found of destruction.

To the south-west of Ellingen and a few kilometres back from the *limes* is the auxiliary fort of Biriciana, now modern Weissenberg. It was established under Domitian around AD 90 after his campaign against the Chatti had pushed the Roman frontier forward into the Rhine–Danube gap. First built in earth, it was reconstructed in stone around 140 and then renovated again, possibly after 179, when this section of the frontier received new attention after the posting of a legion to nearby Augusta Vindelicum (Augsburg). It was very badly damaged during the Alamannic invasions of 233–4 and, although rebuilt after a campaign by Maximinus Thrax to restore the situation, was definitively abandoned later in the 250s when most positions north of the Danube were evacuated. Biriciana is most notable for its reconstructed north gate, from which two rounded towers project outwards, surmounted by an inscription in which the modern councillors of Weissenberg have fancied themselves as *decuriones*,[10] dating their work using the AUC system (from the foundation of the city of Rome), in the absence of contemporary emperors or consuls to use as reference points.[11] A small portion of the protective wall has been faced with a reflective white stone, supposed to represent the finishing that gave the place its name in early medieval times: 'The White Fortress'.

A few kilometres away to the east, beyond the actual line of the *limes* wall (which continued to curve to the south-east), is Burgsalach. There is another reconstructed wooden watchtower here, five minutes' walk off the road beside some woods, but of more interest is the *burgus*, which lies a kilometre away in a small and muddy wood. A massive square fortification, this style of oversized watchtower was uncommon in earlier times, and its occurrence here is echoed with greater prevalence in several other provinces, including in Pannonia at Lussonium[12] and the *centenaria* of the North African desert. Its life was probably short, for it was most likely abandoned at the time when the territory north of the Danube was given up in the mid-3rd century. Probably originally two storeys high, only the lower level now survives in a deep indentation in the ground. The large semicircular curve that formed part of the monumental façade of the building is clearly visible amongst a jumble of ruins. The blockier, denser and more inward-looking style of the *burgus* seems to be an intimation of a more defensive mentality and an awareness set in stone that the frontiers were under severe stress.

The fortress at Vetoniania (modern Pfunz), which lies 30 kilometres to the east of Burgsalach, was built near the River Altmühl, again when the frontier was moved north across the Danube during the reign of Domitian, and its role was to guard a military road that was constructed from Biriciana to Kösching. Around 2.7 hectares in extent, it housed the *Cohors I Breucorum civium Romanorum equitata*, a unit whose designation indicates that all its serving members at a particular point in time had been granted Roman citizenship (which would normally only have come on completion of their twenty-five years' service) for some unspecified act of bravery. Rebuilt in stone under Antoninus Pius, its final destruction seems to have come in 233 during the severe Alamannic incursion of that year. That the onslaught was sudden is indicated by the skeletons of guards found in the southern tower, bereft of their shields, while a prisoner who was being held in a cell in the *principia* died with a chain still shackled around his shinbone.

The whole of the west wall has been reconstructed, its neat crenellations and just-so towers gracing many a poster and book about the *limes*. The interior of the fort, however, is almost entirely given over to cultivation, and a cabbage patch sits over the remains of all the interior buildings. The line of the field goes to within a few centimetres of the east wall, and stones that have been upcast by ploughing seem to indicate that the remains beneath continue to be degraded by this surprising persistence of agriculture inside an important cultural monument. The eastern gate itself has been partly reconstructed and one other angle tower at the north-east pokes up to about a metre in height, with a small section of wall projecting from it. Somewhere round about must lie the civil settlement in which a temple of Jupiter Dolichenus was uncovered, but this, too, must have been destroyed or at least abandoned in short order at the time of the Alamannic raid which brought the occupation of the fort to an end.

At the junction of the Regen and Danube rivers, 50 kilometres to the east of Vetoniana, lay the legionary fortress of Castra Regina, which, many centuries later, has transmuted into the attractive riverside city of Regensburg. Its alternative name, Ratisbon, probably derives from a Celtic root, which alludes to an earlier Celtic settlement on the site. At the time of Vespasian, an auxiliary fort was built to protect an important crossing of the Danube, which was then reconstructed in stone under Hadrian. The garrison from the time of Trajan appears to have been the *Cohors III Bracaraugustanorum*,[13] a mixed cavalry and infantry unit from Portugal. The original fort, which lay south of the modern city centre at Kumpfmühl, was destroyed during the Marcomannic Wars in the 170s, and this time a legionary camp was built on a site nearer the Danube, which housed the III Italica legion. Although the commander of this legion was governor of Raetia, his official residence remained further south at Augusta Vindelicorum (Augsburg), safely away from the *limes* line.

In an exposed position on the central Danube, Regensburg suffered terribly during Alamannic invasions in 233 and 259–60, and major repairs were needed to the camp after the second assault. The III Italica seems to have remained in place until at least the beginning of the 5th century, although after Diocletian's reign *vexillationes* (detachments) were stationed elsewhere (including at Cambodonum/Kempten), so the effective strength of the Castra Regina garrison was reduced.

Although the Roman city has mostly disappeared beneath the medieval and above all the modern settlements, Castra Regina still peeps out from between the beer-cellars and baroque charm of this Bavarian town. It has retained vestiges of the Roman street grid and the *decumanus* along the line of the modern Fröhliche Türkengasse. At Maximilianstraße, down some steps in a shallow depression, stretches a 15-metre-long section of the south-east Roman fortress wall, with part of a rounded corner tower. The blocks of the tower stand to a couple of metres in places, and give a real sense of how massive the fortifications must have been when fully intact. A few broken column drums lie, partly obscured by an untidy carpet of grass. This little nook retained some defensive importance, for in 1383 another tower was erected on the spot, and its outline partly obliterates that of its Roman predecessor. Overshadowed by a little square lined with an optician's shop and a car park, they both seem largely forgotten.

Next to the chapel of Saint Georg and Afra, on a very busy road junction, lies another section of the Roman wall, but the pride of Roman Regensburg – lying half-concealed on Unter den Schwibbögen, a narrow street of souvenir shops behind the 13th-century cathedral – is the Porta

Praetoria. It consists of a gateway and part of a gate tower, whose semi-circular outline is embedded into a modern hotel. It is the rounded single section of what must have been a double-tower, one entrance having almost totally disappeared save for a few fragments. The left-hand side, however, rises to a second partly arcaded storey, belonging to a structure that was probably built in the 4th century, not dissimilar in style and intent to the great Porta Nigra in Trier.

The capital of Raetia, Augusta Vindelicum (Augsburg), lay on a protected spit of land between the Wertach and Lech rivers some 115 kilometres to the south-west of Regensburg and far behind the safety of the *limes*. It took its name from the Vindelici, the Celtic tribe who had dominated the area before the Roman conquest. During the conquest, it was the first Roman forward base in the area, and the site of a short-lived legionary camp for a quarter of a century from around 10 BC. Although it became the provincial capital, Augusta Vindelicum did not receive a formal constitution until the time of Hadrian, when it became a *municipium*. It remained the administrative centre of the province right up until the 5th century, after which the fate of the town is difficult to trace.

The 'Augsburg Victory Altar', which lies in the city's Roman museum, sheds light on a dark phase in the town's history.[14] It is dated April 260, and shows the taking of Augsburg from the Semnoni and Iuthungi after those barbarians had held it for a while in the face of a Roman siege. Interestingly, it honours not the official emperor at the time, Gallienus, but Postumus, who had declared himself Emperor in the Gallic provinces just a few months before, and whose authority seems, for a time at least, to have extended this far eastwards. But he cannot have held Augusta Vindelicum for long, as this would have resulted in an unacceptable encirclement of the Italian peninsula.

Also in the museum a case of 'hack-silver' dates from this time. This consists of parts of finely decorated plates that have been cut into pieces and divided, probably by barbarian raiders who were not so much concerned with the level of workmanship as with the raw value of the metal of which they were made. There is also a suitably celebratory dedication stone of 281, which commemorates Probus as the *Restitutor provinciarum et operum publicorum* ('Restorer of the provinces and of public works'). After half a century of near-anarchy in which barbarian raiders had not had to dread the full might of the legions, the citizens of Augusta Vindelicum must have breathed a hearty sigh of relief.

The only fragments of Roman Augsburg that can be seen above ground sit outside the Dom, the cathedral, a masterpiece of the German

Gothic style, which was begun around 1275 on the site of a yet earlier Romanesque church, and which lies more or less on the site of the old forum. Set against a wall (the 'Römische Mauer') a miscellany of pieces includes the grave of Marcus Aurelius Carus, who was an Augustal priest, (and so ministered to the imperial cult) in the 2nd century, and an altar of the Romano-Celtic hybrid god Apollo Grannus. Another dedicated to the sun god commemorates Julius Avitus Alexianus, who was the husband of Julia Maesa, and thus the grandfather of the Emperor Elagabalus.[15]

Just opposite the wall lies a jumble of ruins, all that remains of the Johannis chapel, which was demolished in 1808, but which had itself been built on the site of a very early Christian baptistery. It was here, in a small square well-shaft which the Christian community adapted as a font, that Saint Afra was baptised in the early 4th century. According to her *Acta*, Afra had originally come from Cyprus and worked as a prostitute in the Temple of Venus in Augusta Vindelicum.[16] She was converted to Christianity and weaned away from her unseemly profession by the offices of the Spanish bishop Narcissus of Gerona. When the Great Persecution broke out in 303, she and her mother concealed the bishop in their house, but Afra was detected and as a punishment tied to a tree on an island in the Lech river and then burnt to death.

The veneration accorded to Afra in the city is mentioned by Venantius Fortunatus, a 6th-century Bishop of Poitiers, who travelled from Italy to Gaul in 565, and who reported that the cult of Afra was still remembered at Augsburg. He also hints that the Bavarians, then in possession of Augusta Vindelicum, impeded the passage of travellers. However, while his journey may well have been fraught with perils, it does at least provide concrete evidence that a settled community of some kind remained in the city around 150 years after the collapse of Roman rule.

Running alongside the cathedral square is a curious reminder of the history of the study of the *limes*, for the road is named Peutingerstraße, in honour of Martin Peutinger, who was a citizen of Augsburg. His acquisition[17] of the medieval copy of a late-Roman map, which detailed itineraries throughout the Empire, revolutionised scholars' understanding of the detailed topography of the provinces and has proved a fertile quarry ever since for those locating 'lost' Roman sites or seeking to attribute names to those that have long since been found.

Back on the line of the Danube, the stretch to the border of modern Austria was defended by forts at Sorviodurum (modern Straubing), 25 kilometres to the east of Castra Regina, and at Quintana (Künzing), where a timber castle built under Domitian seems to have been destroyed so suddenly by an Alamannic attack around 242–4 that the soldiers were unable to retrieve their weapons from the armoury before disaster struck.[18]

Although there is nothing to see of the fort of Sorviodurum itself, which was built under Vespasian and garrisoned in the 2nd century by a detachment of Syrian archers, excavations at a villa to the west of the town revealed the most extraordinary treasure. Hidden in a bronze basin was a collection of lavish pieces of armour, including seven parade helmets. These were a Roman cavalryman's 'best' display armour, in the form of a bronze mask that concealed the features, reserved for special occasions and very definitely not battlefield wear. At Sorviodurum, four of the masks have wavy Grecian-style hair, lips slightly curled, with an otherwise impassive expression, while the other three sport more tightly curled hair styled in a conical form, which seems almost Persian in effect. The rest of the collection includes barding for the horses, and a series of cuirasses and greaves, one of which shows a fine figure of Mars standing on a giant, a symbol perhaps of the capacity of the wearer to triumph even in the face of enormous odds.

This area of the frontier, Sorviodurum not excluded, suffered grievously from raids by the Alamanns, beginning in the 230s. Despite Caracalla's success against them on the Rhine in 213, by 235/6 they were raiding extensively in Raetia, and in Noricum further to the east. By the late 250s, the Danube frontier and large stretches of the Rhine were in serious danger of being overrun by both the Alamanns and other groups such as the Iuthungi. The Raetian frontier was probably never held in anything like the same strength after 260, and some frontier positions were abandoned to the Alamanns. The tribes were always politically fragmented however, being ruled by a number of *reguli* or sub-kings and so the threat that they posed to the Roman Danube and Upper Rhine provinces remained intermittent.

The final point in the defensive system of Raetia, and indeed the border of the province, was at Castra Batavorum (known in later Roman sources as Batavis), which is buried under modern Passau. It derived its name from its early garrison, the *Cohors IX Batavorum milliaria equitata*, a mixed infantry-cavalry regiment from the lower Rhineland. It lies where the River Inn flows into the Danube, creating a protected spit of land just where the two waterways meet. At the very tip, the Ortsspitze, an early Roman fort was placed under Domitian; it is now a quiet waterside park populated by late-afternoon joggers and those wishing merely to contemplate the counter-flows and eddies caused by the joining together of the two rivers with yet a third, the Ilz, which flows down to here from the Bavarian forests to the north.

For the main, Passau is a picturesque university town, dominated by the bishop's fortress-cum-palace on the north bank of the Danube and the 17th century baroque bulk of St Stephen's Cathedral, which holds the second-largest church organ in the world. A later fort at Castra Batavorum was sited further west, near the Römerplatz, now a rather nondescript piazza with a little park overlooking the main bridge over the Danube. While the rest of the *limes* was collapsing, the Batavian cohort continued to hold the line here, and they seem to have remained in their station until the early 5th century, by which time the fort must have been little more than a refuge for the desperate populations nearby, and an ambivalent symbol of a far away emperor who could, in reality, do little to protect them.

Noricum

The border line between the provinces of Raetia and Noricum lay at modern Passau (Castra Batavorum), on the modern German-Austrian border. The Bavarian Passau lies within the provincial boundary of Raetia, while Passau Instatt (Boiodurum), the Austrian section of the city, sits at the western edge of what was Noricum. The eastern border of that province ran between the modern towns of Zeiselmauer (ancient Astura) and Vienna (Vindobona) much further east along the Danube. It was not one of Rome's most glamorous provinces and its annexation came about not through a series of hard-fought campaigns, but by an almost peaceful process of absorption.

The *Regnum Noricum* that was annexed by Tiberius, probably in 15 BC,[19] had its beginnings in the mid-4th century BC, when Celtic peoples began to filter down from Raetia into the territory of Salzburg and Upper and Lower Austria, and was securely established before 186 BC, when the Noricans sent an embassy to Rome.[20] It was only under the early Empire that Roman attention turned towards securing the alpine passages into Italy and achieving a frontier on the Danube which might block raids that threatened the peninsula, such as the Celtic incursions that had been so troublesome in the early 2nd century BC.

According to Cassius Dio, the pretext for the annexation of Noricum was an attack on Istria in 16 BC, which brought Roman retribution the next year and an end to the Noricans' independence.[21] Not all of the former kingdom was absorbed within the new province: the area north of the Danube was not occupied, while territory in the east was attached to Pannonia. Carnuntum (Petronell), which the Romans established as a legionary base, remained in Noricum until the XV Apollinaris was posted there in AD 14, when it, too, was transferred to Pannonia.

At first Noricum seems to have been garrisoned by small detachments from Pannonia, with the provincial administration based at the Magdalensburg fort in the south of the province. Later, under Claudius, Virunum became the provincial capital, and the normal apparatus of provincial administration was established, with Noricum being governed by a procurator.[22] It was at this time, too, that Noricum, which had previously possessed few towns, began to urbanise, with the establishment of *municipia* at Virunum, Celeia (Celje), Teurnia (Tiburnia), Aguntum and Iuvavum (Salzburg), all of them safely away from the frontier. The interior of the province was now largely demilitarised, with the construction of new forts along the line of the Danube, particularly at Lentia (Linz) and Lauriacum (Enns-Lorch); the forts at Boiodurum, Faviana (Mautern) and Commagena (Tulln) probably came later, possibly during Flavian times.

The province seems, thereafter, to have developed smoothly, but in an unspectacular fashion. As elsewhere in the Empire, (or at least those areas along the frontier that had not previously possessed a flourishing civic culture), Romanisation spread from the urban centres, radiating outwards into the rest of the province. Latin names came to predominate quite rapidly, although many of them are in fact only Latinised versions of Celtic forms, such as Acceptus, Avitus and Ingenuus.[23]

It was only under Hadrian that urban settlement crept further north towards the Danube, with the foundation of Ovilava (modern Wels) in the valley of the Traun, at the point where traditional routes leading down from the Danube and then towards Virunum and Iuvavum crossed. Hadrian did not operate on a blank slate, for there seems already to have been a merchant settlement at Ovilava, but a new street-plan was laid out, which can be dimly discerned in the grid system of the modern town.[24]

The peace of Noricum was only really disturbed during Marcus Aurelius's Marcomannic Wars (166–80), and while it was not a main theatre of that war, some destruction identified in the northern sectors of the province from around 166 to 170 might be ascribable to it, particularly at Lentia, Ovilava and Lauriacum in the west, and at Faviana and Augustiana (Traismauer) in the east. It was in an effort to keep the Marcomanni out of Italy, and to prevent a recurrence of their damaging descent through Pannonia towards the alpine passes, that Noricum received its own legion for the first time, at Ločica, where the II Italica legion – first raised in 166 – was stationed from 171.[25]

Situated west of Celeia, Ločica dominated the road that led south-west towards Emona (modern Ljubljana in Slovenia) and ultimately into Italy. The legion did not stay there long, being moved within three years to Albing, 7 kilometres from Lauriacum and near the mouth of the River Enns. Its new station was short-lived, too, for some time before 191 the unit was transferred to its final posting at Lauriacum. As a result, Noricum's administrative status was promoted, for whereas as a province with only auxiliary troops it could be governed by a man of equestrian rank, now that it had a legion its top official was a legionary legate, and hence of senatorial rank. This situation continued until some time after 255 (when the last attested imperial legate, Macrinius Decianus, served),[26] after which governors of equestrian rank supervised the province.

Alamannic raids began to hit Noricum from the second quarter of the 3rd century, and coin-hoards buried at Iuvavum around 235 may be a sign of this. It seems that Maximinus Thrax had siphoned off elements of the Norican garrisons for campaigns further east along the Danube, and – stripped of the means to fight off the barbarian raids – Noricum paid a heavy price. At the time of the general reforms of provincial administration by Diocletian at the end of the 3rd century, Noricum was split into two, with the northern part becoming Noricum Ripense and the southern (with its capital at Virunum) being reorganised as Noricum Mediterraneum; both of the new provinces came under the Diocese of Illyricum. Most of the army units remained stationed in the Noricum Ripense, with the addition of a new legion (I Noricorum) at Ad Iuvense (Ybbs) to see to the security of the eastern sector of the *limes*.[27]

The frontier was again strengthened under Valentinian I in the 370s, with the construction of new watchtowers, but from the time of Gratian the garrison seems to have been run down and Noricum was debatable territory by the early 5th century. In 407, Alaric and his Gothic followers occupied a large part of the province, formally requesting that the Emperor Honorius officially hand over the territory to them, baldly stating that Noricum was of no worth to the Romans as it was not paying any taxes.[28]

Alaric was a typical product of the late-Roman world, occupying a position of great ambiguity, in which his aims were extremely unclear. It may have been his intent to damage the Empire, extract as much profit from it for himself and his followers as he could, or to obtain a hand-somely rewarded official position within it.

Alaric led a people, the Goths, whose origins are much disputed. Around 150, Ptolemy records a people known as the Gutones settled somewhere between the Danube and the Vistula, but there is no trace of them for the next century. Writing in the 6th century, Jordanes puts their origins somewhere in southern Scandinavia; but attempts to trace the migration of any groups of people from there to the Danube have been problematic.[29]

Probably from the 230s the Goths began to migrate from their then homeland around the western Ukraine and the Black Sea,[30] though whether pushed from behind by tribes in search of land or pulled towards the Roman frontier by the lure of the undoubted riches to be obtained in the Empire is unclear. Only from the mid- to late 3rd century, when they began to raid the Empire, can their progress be traced with anything approaching precision. At the time they were not divided into the groups that would later establish kingdoms in Italy and Spain (the Ostrogoths and Visigoths respectively), but were constituted in a series of tribal confederacies, the principal amongst which were the Tervingi and Greuthingi.

In 238, they had first definitively emerged into the historical record with a raid on Olbia and Tyras. By 255, the Goths had acquired the use of a fleet, and for the next three years raided at will around the Black Sea, capturing Trebizond on the southern coast in 256 when its garrison, alarmed at the appearance of shipborne barbarians, simply turned tail and fled

After a turbulent eruption back into Roman territory in the 370s, which led to their defeat of the Romans at the Battle of Adrianople in 378[31] and the peace treaty four years later, the Goths subside for a time into the background.[32] Alaric first comes to the notice of the sources in around 395, though he may have been active in an attack by Gothic marauders on Theodosius I as he travelled to Constantinople from the west in 391. Four years later, he seems to have been serving in the Roman army that fought at the Frigidus river against the usurper Eugenius, a battle in which the Goths had taken terrible casualties.

Alaric was probably angered that he received neither recognition nor promotion for his role in the conflict, and he rose up in revolt.[33] He proceeded to march on Constantinople, but turned aside – either intimidated by the strength of its defences or, according to the poet Claudian, bribed by the praetorian prefect Rufinus – and set to plundering Macedonia and Thessaly. For the next two years Alaric pillaged at will, his raiding parties reaching as far south as the Peloponnese. Then, in 397, when the western military strongman Stilicho was poised to act against him, Alaric received some kind of recognition in a military position (which may have been that of *magister militum per Illyricum*) from Eutropius, the eunuch who then dominated the eastern government and was not at all keen on Stilicho extending his influence into the Balkans.[34] Until 401, therefore, Alaric's illegal raiding in the Balkans was replaced by the obligation on the citizens of the provinces to provide him, as a lawful representative of the government, with military supplies, which may in the end have amounted to pretty much the same thing. In November 401, for reasons that are not entirely clear,[35] Alaric crossed the Alps into Italy. Stilicho beat him twice, at Pollentia and Verona, but on both occasions the Goth gave the Roman general the slip, finally fleeing into Pannonia, where he rebuilt his forces over a couple of years, smouldering with resentment.

Probably in 404 or 405, Stilicho appointed him to a military office, thereby seeking to co-opt the Goths in the game of tug-of-war between Eastern and Western Empires over the Balkans. In 407, however, Alaric – sensing that Stilicho, weakened by the usurpation of Constantine III in Britain and Gaul, might be amenable to pressure – invaded Italy once more. A complicated series of negotiations with the Senate and Stilicho were interrupted by the latter's murder in August 408 at the hands of Honorius. Stilicho's barbarian followers were massacred in large numbers throughout Italy and the remnants fled to Alaric, who found himself bereft of his principal negotiation partner in the wake of Stilicho's death, and at the same time bolstered by the acquisition of a large number of fresh warriors. He laid siege to Rome in late 408, a blockade during which Serena, the widow of Stilicho, was strangled to death on the orders of the Senate, who could not quite get it into their heads that negotiation and compromise were the only means to avoid disaster.

Finally, at Rimini in 409, the praetorian prefect Jovius[36] agreed to talks, at which Alaric insisted on being appointed to the supreme command of the Roman army (as *magister utriusque militiae*) and receiving a hefty sum in cash. Honorius, needless to say, refused, resulting in a year of increasingly desperate manoeuvres by both sides, in which Alaric raised up a usurper – a senator named Priscus Attalus – found that his new protégé was not nearly as compliant as hoped, deposed him and then discovered that Honorius (given fresh heart by a new draft of reinforcements from the East) was now refusing to negotiate at all.[37] Angry and frustrated, Alaric marched on Rome, and gave his followers free rein for three days to loot and pillage the Eternal City.

The Romans had suffered nothing like it since the capture of the city by the Gauls in 390 BC, and the shock was profound. Yet despite its seeming portentous significance and a collective gnashing of teeth by contemporary writers,[38] the sack of Rome resolved nothing. As Hannibal had six centuries before, Alaric headed to the south of Italy, largely for want of anything better to do, but possibly intending to cross into Africa. There, near Consentia (Cosenza), he contracted a fever and died soon afterwards. Alaric, who had campaigned for two decades across the Balkans and Italy, had in the end achieved little, save landing a few body-blows on his would-be paymaster, the Empire, and taking its prestige down a good few notches by his capture of the capital.

The journey east along the Norican *limes* begins where the River Inn (or Aenus to the Romans) meets the Danube. Here the *castellum* of Boiodurum dominated the Norican side, mirroring its twin of Castrum Batavorum on the Raetian bank. Just as it had been a provincial boundary in Roman times, so this stretch of water continued to mark the separation between realms, marking out the border between German Bavaria and Austria. The footbridge that runs over the German side of the Inn to Austria leads first to the church of Saint Severin, a saint who has a much higher profile in the latter country than elsewhere (and who should not be confused with the Bishop of Cologne, or the 4th-century Bishop of Bordeaux who is remembered in the church of Saint Séverin in Paris). The life of the saint, who operated in Noricum Ripense from around 460[39] is told in the *Vita Sancti Severini*, written by Eugippius around 511, a text that gives a unique portrayal of the twilight of Roman rule in the area.

Severin was said to have come to the province 'at God's command', but from exactly where is not recorded. He would stay in Noricum until his death in 482, travelling widely within the province and acting as a rallying point for the Romanised population in the face of the near-total collapse of the official administration. During the early years of Severin's stay in Noricum, there are scattered references to Roman troops, to the garrison at Boiodorum across the border in Raetia, and to a *tribunus* called Mamertinus who was based at Faviana (Mauern) with a small force at his disposal, but who soon afterwards gave up the military life and became a bishop.[40]

Elsewhere in the province, unlike Mamertinus with his small military force, the people had to rely on their own resources to defend them-selves in the late 5th century, and it was not enough. The Rugii occupied Commagena (Tulln); Astura (Zeiselmauer) was destroyed around 460; and by 480 the whole of the western sector of the *limes* had been overrun. The very end of the Roman army in the area is poignantly described by Eugippius in a scene that must have been repeated a number of times throughout the Empire.[41] The pay for the garrison at Batavis had failed to arrive, and some of the soldiers set off towards Italy to see what the problem might be. On their way, they were set upon by barbarians and murdered and some time later their bodies were washed up by the river near Passau. Their former comrades, realising that there would now be no reinforcements or money from the central government in Rome, simply disbanded. In places such as this, the soldiers may have continued to cluster together in the fort, but in the absence of any organised support, their numbers would soon have dwindled away. Some lived off the local populations and their depredations become indistinguishable from those of the barbarians whom they were once supposed to have kept at bay.

With the disappearance of the Batavis garrison, Boiodurum was captured by the Thuringians, and in response Severin organised the evacuation of the whole frontier region and resettled the surviving population in and around Lauriacum, where, however, they were still at the mercy of the local Rugian king. By 476, the Western Empire itself had ceased to exist, and so what remained of 'Roman' Noricum now fell to Odovacar. A leader of the Germanic Scirians, he had led a group of *foederati* in the 470s, and by the middle of the decade was in effect the commander of the Roman army in Italy. When the patrician Orestes tried to pre-empt his authority by setting his own son Romulus on the imperial throne in 475, Odovacer in exasperation deposed the hapless young emperor within a year, and, choosing not to rule the rump of Roman territory in Italy through an imperial puppet, exercised power himself directly as a king. A few years later, Noricum became entangled in the Eastern Empire's first serious attempt to do something about the situation. The Eastern Emperor Zeno (474–5, 477–91) called upon Feletheus, the King of the Rugians, who were in effective control of Noricum, to invade Italy and drive Odovacar out. Odovacar, however, defeated the Rugians in 487, and the following year launched an invasion of Noricum to finish the task. However, his brother Onoulfus, who was in charge of the expedition, decided that the province could not be effectively defended and so ordered all the 'Romani' to leave Noricum and evacuate to Italy. The body of Saint Severin accompanied the refugees, carried by the monks of his monastery of Favianae as far as Naples, where it ultimately came to rest in the Abbey of San Severino.[42]

Amidst the well-kept graveyard, and the memorials of white and sombre black marble enlivened by faded photographs of the deceased, the Passau church is a plain and simple structure, its wall washed with a pretty shade of pink, but to the right of the main door is evidence of the Roman town that lies everywhere underneath. The memorial to Faustinianus, who was a customs officer, conjures up the image of a man who supervised the border between Illyria, which began here (from the fiscal point of view), and the German customs area to the west. He would have reported ultimately to the headquarters of the Norican customs office, which lay in the provincial capital at Virunum.[43] The river crossing and the now-vanished customs house would have marked the point at which tolls due for carrying goods across the provincial border would have to be paid.

The riverside is populated with narrow streets and plain-fronted houses. A stretch of ancient stone wall and the adjacent round bulk of the 'Saint-Severin Tower' are in fact late-medieval constructions, from around 1412. A short way off lies the remains of Boiotro, a late-Roman fort built around 300 to replace an earlier one destroyed by the Alamanns in about 240. This is the place where Saint Severin is reported to have built his monastery in the 5th century. He is not forgotten here, either. Inside the ruined shell of the walls a pleasant garden has been laid out with what looks like Roman foundations adapted as tower-like planters for a variety of shrubs and flowers. In one corner of this rather municipal-seeming place, presiding over it all, is a 20th-century statue of the saint, arm outstretched as though to say, 'Look how well I preserved the land that I sought to protect.'

Much of the interior of the fort has disappeared and the outlines of the buildings are marked out with chalked lines. Small sections of the south-east and south-west towers remain intact, together with a substantial portion of the south tower, the ruins quietly enclosed and hidden by the surrounding houses. It was from a vantage point such as this that the last garrison troops of Noricum would have watched as the administrative infrastructure of the Empire diminished and dwindled to nothing.

Around a kilometre's walk along the line of the Danube lay the earlier Roman fort of Boiodurum. It began its life under Domitian, initially as a wood and earth construction, and probably housed the V Breucorum cohort after the reign of Marcus Aurelius. Later rebuilt in stone, it was destroyed by an Alamannic incursion in the 240s and was not directly rebuilt, as the new site of Boiotro was instead chosen to replace it. The church of Saint Aegid, on whose ground the fort lay, is now a private house, situated besides a car park dotted with some bedraggled-looking recycling bins. A bold 'Privatgrund' sign prevents any latter-day Alamanns from investigation of the former castle ground, while only the oddly basilical shape of the house betrays any hint of its subsequent history as a church.

East of the Passau area, the Danube flows through a thick gorge, which makes crossing perilous, and thus for around 60 kilometres the Romans did not find it necessary to site significant forces, with just small units at Stanacum (Oberanna) and Ad Mauros (Eferding) to defend this whole sector. At Lentia, however, which has mutated into modern Linz, the normal density of fortifications resumed. Here the initial construction was a cavalry fort in open country suitable for a mounted detachment, and was first established under Claudius.[44]

Now Austria's third-largest city, with around 200,000 people, Linz's Roman heritage has suffered the fate of most antique cities that have subsequently thrived and been completely built over. Its principal monuments are pretty baroque churches, topped with green onion domes, and a 20-metre-high column erected in thanks for the delivery of Linz from an outbreak of plague in 1713. The Roman remains that have been found were largely brought to light through the destruction of more modern buildings during the Second World War. A temple complex and a *mithraeum*, together with the *capitolium*, were all identified, but nothing of them can really be seen today. Instead there are only fragments and guesses, but it seems the civil settlement lay beneath today's Hauptplatz. Lentia suffered widespread destruction during the Marcomannic Wars in the 160s, but probably revived before too long. It does not feature in the life of Saint Severin, so its age of prosperity had most likely ended long before the start of the 5th century.

Around 30 kilometres to the south-west of Lentia, in the interior of the province, Ovilava (modern Wels) had become an important road junction, because the route from Aquileia in Italy that led through Virunum crossed here with one that ran parallel to the *limes* from Boiodurum and Lentia to Lauriacum further east. Under Hadrian, Ovilava attained the rank of *municipium*, suitably honouring him by its new name of Municipium Aelium Ovilava, taken from 'Aelius', one of the Emperor's own names. It achieved further promotion as a result of the Marcomannic Wars, when many of the civilian offices of the provincial governor moved here.[45]

Under Caracalla, the town became a *colonia* (as Aurelia Antoniana) and it may have been at this time that it received its city wall. Ovilava reached the summit that a provincial city could hope to achieve when, during the reign of Diocletian, it became the capital of Noricum Ripense. That it continued to flourish, as far as the uncertain times of the 3rd to 5th centuries would permit, is demonstrated by a visit from Gratian in 378 and the town's appearance in the *Vita Sancti Severini* as one of the remaining places where something like normal urban life still staggered on. By the 7th century, however, all vestiges of Rome had gone, and the town was settled by Germanic-speaking Bavarians, the ancestors of today's residents.

Now a modest-sized town of about 50,000 people, Wels's main square is an elongated oval surrounded by lovely plaster façades done up in pastel colours. At the far end lies the Lederturm, the last surviving town gateway, dating from the 14th century, its white rectangular tower soaring above the other buildings. Just a small portion of Roman Ovilava can

be viewed in the basement of the Minoritenkirche museum on the main
square. Excavations in 1988–90 around the church unearthed part of the
Roman layer, though extensively overlaid by the remains of the
Romanesque church. Part of a mosaic floor, some water pipes and tile
stamps are all that remain. In the main museum, pieces of a large equestrian statue dragged out of the Traun river nearby may have come from
the town's forum, possible evidence of the damage caused by barbarian
raiders in the 3rd century.

The legionary fortress at Lauriacum (Lorch), around 30 kilometres
south-east from Lentia, was situated near the confluence of the Enns
and the Danube. It is a position of great strategic importance, lying on
the road that ran parallel to the *limes* between Carnuntum and Castra
Batavorum in the east of the province, and along the head of the route
that led from Aquileia in Istria all the way north across the Danube. The
original auxiliary fort here was destroyed during the Marcomannic Wars,
and was rebuilt as a legionary fortress. Irregularly shaped, at around 600
x 400 metres, it varied somewhat from the classic 'playing-card' shape
and housed the II Italica until the end of the Roman period. The civil
settlement that grew up around it may have been granted the status of
municipium under Caracalla around 212, and the forum of this settlement
is believed to have been in the area of the modern Saint Laurenz church.

The church itself is the successor to a basilica that was constructed
in the early 4th century on the site of a Gallo-Roman temple that was
certainly still standing around 197.[46] It lies down a quiet suburban street,
at the end of which lies a section of 2nd- to 3rd-century Roman housing,
a few walls and two column fragments representing scant survivals
of the Roman civil settlement. Perched on one section of wall is the
ubiquitous statue of Saint Severin, still carrying about him a vaguely
protective air in case any late and stray barbarians should happen by.

Inside the basilica itself, in a corner of which a charnel house is adorned
with a splendid carving of Pontius Pilate dressed in Ottoman gear, the
main altar has been moved forward to expose the remains of the church's
ancient predecessors. Part of the hypocaust of a Roman heating system
and some 2nd-century walls are clearly visible, the latter once believed
to belong to a Romano-Celtic temple from 175 to 192 (dated by an altar
stone), but now thought more likely to be a private house. Cutting
through it is the clear apse shape of an early Christian basilica and,
forming a kind of outer ring, another larger apse. The first church is
believed to date from around 370, and was destroyed during the Hunnish
invasions of the 440s, but rebuilt soon thereafter. A new church was then
erected on the site during the 8th century, to be replaced ultimately by

the present model. It all provides a neat summary of the career of Lauriacum itself, from Roman legionary fortress to the modern-day Austrian town.

The Christianisation of Noricum is further represented by the life of Saint Florian, who, according to the *Acta* composed about his life, was martyred at Lauriacum. A high-ranking official during the era of the Great Persecution, though whether he was a soldier or civilian is unclear, Florian had converted to Christianity. On hearing of the tribulations suffered by his co-religionists at Lauriacum, where some forty of them had been arrested, he resolved to hand himself over to the authorities in order to share their fate. He was then hauled before the governor, Aquilinus, and provocatively declared that although Aquilinus might have possession of his body, his soul was still in the hands of God. For this he was beaten, his shoulder blades broken, a bonfire lit underneath him and, when none of this dampened his ardour for confessing himself a Christian, Aquilinus ordered a heavy rock to be tied around Florian's neck, and that he then be hurled into the River Enns, where he drowned. The river is said to have thrown up his body the next day. It was found by a devout local Christian widow, Valeria, and transported to a place a short way away from Lentia, where later the Abbey of Saint Florian was built. For his trial by fire, and his immersion in water – and hence, by transference, a presumed ability to douse or protect from flames – Florian later became the patron saint of both firefighters and chimney sweeps.[47]

Lauriacum suffered badly during the uncertainty of the 3rd century, and seems to have been burnt down three times. During the widespread raids by the Alamanni and Iuthungi, which penetrated Raetia to the west in the 270s, Lauriacum was razed once more. However, it recovered and was rebuilt, and in the 4th century both Constantius II (in 341) and Gratian (in 378) stayed here.

To the east of Lauriacum, the land was more open, a broad plain that provided easy access for hostile incursions, especially, in the 2nd century, by the Marcomanni. It was thus more heavily fortified, by posts at Faviana (Mautern) in the west and by Commagena (Tulln) and Astura (Zeiselmauer) in the east. Tulln, around 120 kilometres along the river from Lauriacum (Enns), is an attractive small town on Austria's central stretch of Danube. Down by the riverside walk, a pretty housing estate groups around the Marc-Aurelstraße, while nearby a Mark-Aurel Parc stretches, both named in honour of the 2nd-century emperor. A modern equestrian statue has Marcus pointing his sword out into the Danube in a vaguely menacing gesture, an air that is punctured by the toy train that wends its way by each Saturday half-hour, transporting tourists around Tulln's main sites. A short walk down the Danube shore – the river not exerting itself unduly as it flows lazily by – is the Salzturm (or 'salt tower'), heavily rebuilt in medieval times, but preserving the horseshoe shape of one of the interval towers of the Roman fort's west wall.

The *Ala I Commagenorum*, after whom Commagena took its name, was certainly present here by 96, around fifteen years after the fort itself was built. It came as part of a new draft of troops to Noricum[48] which included the transfer of the *Cohors I Asturum* (originally from Spain) to Astura and of the *Cohors I Aelia Brittonum* to Faviana some time during the reign of Hadrian. Around the back of the town museum under a glass roof are sheltered a few fragments of the camp's *porta principalis dextra*, a gate that was bricked up in about 370, in a sign of increasing insecurity in the area.

Commagena did survive in some fashion, however, as it is mentioned as one of the places that Saint Severin visited. Although only in a later literary fancy, it did play a significant role in the age of migrations, for in one version of the *Nibelungenlied*, the south-German epic saga, it was at Commagena that Attila the Hun proposed to Gudrun, his future wife, who was loosely modelled around Ildico, the real Hun ruler's last spouse; it was not a happy match, for on their wedding night Attila choked to death in bed.

Noricum, meanwhile was left to the successive depredations of the Goths, Huns, Lombards, Avars and Slavs. Only in the former Noricum Mediterraneum to the south did urban life persist in anything like its previous form. However, by 600, even those few places had collapsed and been abandoned; only at Celeia in the far south-east of the province is there any sign of continuous occupation. Noricum now returned to much the state it had been in before the Romans had taken it in 15 BC: a small population, economically unsophisticated and centred around hill fortifications, which were used in (the lamentably frequent) times of trouble.

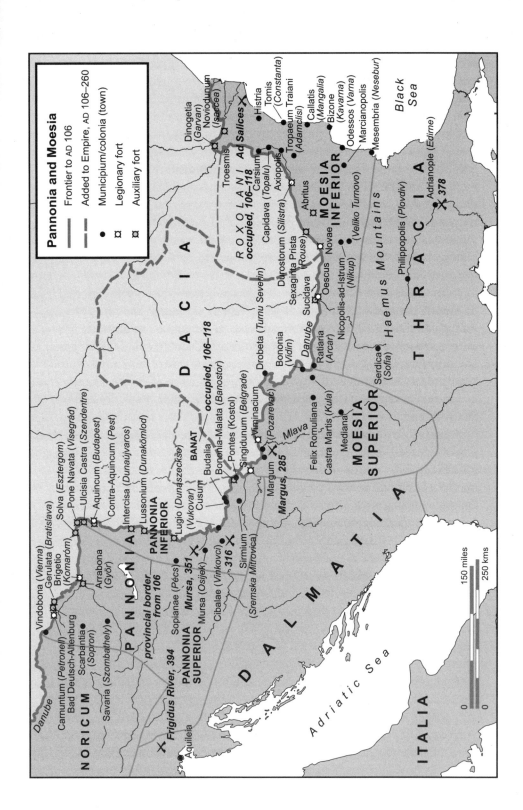

Pannonia and Moesia

Frontier to AD 106
Added to Empire, AD 106–260
Municipium/colonia (town)
Legionary fort
Auxiliary fort

Black Sea

Dinogetia (*Garvan*)
Noviodunum (*Isaccea*)
Ad Salices ✕
Histria
Tomis (*Constanta*)
Tropaeum Traiani (*Adamclisi*)
Callatis (*Mangalia*)
Bizone (*Kavarna*)
Odessos (*Varna*)
Marcianopolis
Mesembria (*Nesebur*)

Troesmis

R O X O L A N I occupied, 106–118
Carsium
Capidava (*Topalu*)
Axiopolis
Durostorum (*Silistra*)
Sexaginta Prista
Abritus
Sucidava
Oescus
Novae
Nicopolis-ad-Istrum (*Nikup*)

MOESIA INFERIOR
(*Veliko Tumovo*)

Adrianople (*Edirne*)
✕ 378

Philippopolis (*Plovdiv*)

H a e m u s M o u n t a i n s

T H R A C I A

D A C I A

occupied, 106–118

Drobeta (*Turnu Severin*)
Bononia (*Vidin*)
Ratiaria (*Arcar*)
Danube

BANAT
Budalia
Bononia-Malata (*Banostor*)
Pontes (*Kostol*)
Singidunum (*Belgrade*)
Viminacium
Margum (*Pozarevac*)
Mlava
Margus, 285 ✕
Margus, 285
Felix Romuliana
Castra Martis (*Kula*)
Mediana

MOESIA SUPERIOR

Serdica (*Sofia*)

Ulcisia Castra (*Szendentre*)
Pone Navata (*Visegrád*)
Solva (*Esztergom*)
Aquincum (*Budapest*)
Contra-Aquincum (*Pest*)
Intercisa (*Dunaújvaros*)
Lussonium (*Dunakömlod*)

PANNONIA INFERIOR

Lugio (*Dunaszeckso*)
Cusum
(*Vukovar*)

Sirmium
(*Sremska Mitrovica*)

provincial border from 106

Vindobona (*Vienna*)
Carnuntum (*Petronell*)
Bad Deutsch-Altenburg
Gerulata (*Bratislava*)
Brigetio (*Komárom*)
Arrabona (*Győr*)
Scarbantia (*Sopron*)
Savaria (*Szombathely*)

N O R I C U M

Danube

Sopianae (*Pécs*)
Mursa, 351 ✕
Mursa (Osijek)
Cibalae (*Vinkovci*)
✕ 316

PANNONIA SUPERIOR

Frigidus River, 394
✕

Aquileia

I T A L I A

Adriatic Sea

D A L M A T I A

150 miles
250 kms

0
0

CHAPTER 4

Pannonia and Moesia

His eyes, his voice, his colour, his gestures, expressed the violence of his ungoverned fury; and, while his whole frame was agitated with convulsive passion, a large blood-vessel suddenly burst in his body, and Valentinian fell speechless into the arms of his attendants. Their pious care immediately concealed his situation from the crowd; but, in a few minutes, the emperor of the west expired in an agony of pain . . .
Edward Gibbon, *Decline and Fall of the Roman Empire*[1]

The Roman provinces of Pannonia and Moesia occupied portions of the modern countries of Austria, Hungary, Slovakia, Croatia, Serbia, Bulgaria and Romania, with Pannonia taking up the western portion from Vindobona (Vienna) to Singidunum (Belgrade in Serbia), and Moesia the eastern section as far as the Danube delta. The river formed the traditional boundary of these provinces in the face of *barbaricum*[2] – a position that was only really modified by the annexation of Dacia by Trajan in AD 106 and the occupation of that new province for a century and a half.

Pannonia and Upper Moesia along the Middle Danube first came to Roman attention following the defeat of Perseus, the last King of Macedonia, at Pydna in 168 BC. Friction now arose with Celtic tribes such as the Scordisci and Boii, whose lands lay further north towards the Danube plain.[3] The Romans were drawn deeper into the Balkans, and during a war against the Dardanians in 76–73 BC a Roman army reached the Danube for the first time, possibly somewhere near the valley of the Oescus.[4] There they encountered a tribe called the Moesi, whose name the Roman province would in time take.

Much of Pannonia and Moesia came under the influence of the Dacian king, Burebista, in the 60s BC, and the expansion of his domains threatened to block off Roman access to the northern Balkans, but after his death in 44 BC (at about the same time as Julius Caesar's assassination) the confederation he had built fell apart. This opened the region to a serious extension of Roman power, and in 35 BC Octavian (as Augustus was still known) marched eastwards from Aquileia in northern Italy and captured the Pannonian stronghold of Siscia (modern Sisak in Croatia). The Romans then pushed further northwards and westwards from their bases in Macedonia; in 29 BC, Marcus Licinius Crassus defeated King Cotiso of the Dacians and subdued a whole swathe of tribal peoples, including the Dardanians and Moesians.

Following a campaign by the young Tiberius in 15 BC, Pannonia was officially annexed in 11 BC – although this had not stopped Octavian, in his morale-raising speech to the troops at Actium in 31 BC claiming that Roman might had reached the Danube two years beforehand. The first governor of Moesia, Poppaeus Sabinus, was not, however, appointed for around half a century after Crassus's 29 BC campaign. The process by which that province was subsumed into the Empire is therefore somewhat obscure,[5] although it was probably characterised by a gradual northwards advance towards the line of the Danube.

In AD 6, Roman armies marched north across the Danube, aiming to stem the rise of the Marcomannic kingdom of Maroboduus which had established a powerful confederacy in the area of modern Bohemia. The Danube force under Tiberius coordinated its attack with a pincer movement from Raetia in the west under Sentennius Saturninus. The campaign – which, if successful, might have established a strong Roman presence across the Danube – failed because of an uprising in the rear by the still-restive Pannonians, which was not finally suppressed until AD 12.[6] The near-catastrophe of the revolt, coupled with the disastrous defeat of Varus in the Teutoberger Wald, in effect put paid to any Roman designs to occupy the area of Germany between the Rhine and the Elbe. These two events probably did more than anything to halt the Roman army in its tracks, and the advances of the previous half-century would prove difficult indeed to replicate.

It was after this campaign that the Romans came to understand the importance of controlling the routes that carried into Dacia and the ancient Amber Trade Road across the Danube, a realisation that led them to the stronger occupation of the river line and the establishment of a military presence at Carnuntum. The acquisition of eastern Pannonia, however, took much longer and may not have been firmly achieved until the reign of Claudius (41–54).[7]

The Roman military presence in Pannonia and Moesia was then substantially strengthened under Domitian, with the establishment of a string of auxiliary forts along the Danube,[8] although the Romans experienced a serious setback when a resurgent Dacian kingdom under Decebalus began to raid south of the river in 85. Having seen this threat off three years later,[9] Domitian faced further trouble from the Sarmatians in the late 80s and in 92–3, although he emerged victorious and celebrated an ovation, a lesser version of a triumph.[10]

Trajan's Dacian Wars in 101–2 and 105–6 also resulted in a significant reorganisation of the Pannonian frontier. In 106, the Emperor divided the province into two, with Pannonia Superior to the west (stretching from Vindobona (Vienna) to Cirpi (modern Dunabogdány) having three legions (initially the XIII Gemina Martia at Vindobona, XV Apollinaris at Carnuntum and XXX Ulpia Victrix at Brigetio)[11] to defend against what was perceived as the greater danger from the Germans; meanwhile the governor of Pannonia Inferior in the east had to make do with a single legion at Aquincum (Budapest). This province reached as far as a point just west of Singidunum (modern Belgrade in Serbia).

A further emergency took place in 118 when the Sarmatians threatened the border but were beaten back.[12] After that, this critical portion of the frontier was largely quiet until the reign of Marcus Aurelius, who fought a prolonged fourteen-year campaign against the Marcomanni and Quadi, peoples who would still be causing trouble on this stretch of the *limes* two centuries later. On the death of Marcus in 180, his son and successor, Commodus, brought the war to an abrupt end, but it was some years before the damage caused by the conflict could be restored. An indication of the disruption is that, as part of the peace settlement, the Iazyges are said to have returned 100,000 prisoners to the Romans.[13]

The frontier remained relatively tranquil for four decades, with only an invasion by Carpi and Vandals in 212 or 213 recorded in the sources. In 214, a slight reorganisation occurred, by which Brigetio[14] was shifted into Pannonia Inferior, resulting in both Pannonian provinces now having two legions. It was part of a process by which the Severans[15] did away with three-legion provinces, which had provided too tempting a platform for overambitious generals to mount bids for the imperial throne, a route to power that Septimius Severus, the founder of the dynasty, had himself followed when he was governor of Pannonia Superior in 192.

In the end, the soldiers and the military governors were to have the last laugh, for in the half-century of disorder following the assassination of Alexander Severus in 235, the majority of emperors came from Pannonia and Moesia, particularly from the area around Sirmium (Sremska Mitrovica). The tradition would be a long-standing one: the last of these military strongmen was Valentinian in the latter part of the 4th century. Although the Pannonian and Moesian provinces achieved a much higher profile politically during this century, it was also a period of great troubles. Wars against the Carpi in 247–8 were followed by a disastrous conflict against the Goths in 250–1 in which the Emperor Decius perished,[16] and in 258–60 attacks by Suebi and Sarmatians caused enormous damage. The latter represented a particularly grave threat, for the eastern provinces were slipping away from Rome after a signal Persian victory in 260, and the Gaulish provinces had broken away in 259, so the loss of control over the Balkans would have left Gallienus, the Emperor unlucky enough to have to deal with these concurrent crises, as a ruler without a realm.

Even after this emergency was overcome, and the imperial administration was placed on a firmer footing under the Tetrarchy, Pannonia was not spared. Diocletian had to spend a great deal of time in the period 289–94 conducting yet another war against the Sarmatians.[17] It was probably shortly after this that the Pannonian provinces were further subdivided, creating four new provinces (Pannonia Prima, Pannonia Secunda, Savaria and Valeria). Moesia Superior had already had a slice of its eastern portion cut off in the 270s to make way for Dacia Ripensis, the Roman state's way of obscuring the fact that it had evacuated (and therefore lost) the real Dacia to the north of the Danube.[18] Under Diocletian, the remaining western part of Moesia Superior was renamed Moesia Prima, and the former Moesia Inferior became Moesia Secunda (with its easternmost portion, the modern Dobrudja, lopped off to become Scythia), while Dacia Ripensis continued to occupy the middle ground. If it was all very confusing, it at least provided additional jobs for the bureaucrats, for each of the provinces needed its own governor and administrators.

The mid-4th century brought further woes, and Constantius II was forced into major operations across the Danube in 358–9 to deal with the Sarmatians and Quadi. By the 370s, the tribes were at it again, and Valentinian I ordered the building of forts in Sarmatian territory to bring them finally to book. One such may have been located as far as 60 kilometres north of the Danube,[19] but generally the refortification was on the Roman side of the river. After the Emperor's death and the influx of Goths across the river in 376, the Romans were never really able to bring Pannonia and Upper Moesia firmly back under their control. Although the Danube remained in formal terms the border of the Empire, the settlement of barbarian federates in the border areas meant that the matter of whether the Romans really controlled the area or could exert any significant level of day-to-day influence there became confused.

In around 400, the poet Claudian praises the half-Vandal patrician Stilicho as restorer of peace to Pannonia,[20] but whether this is mere poetic hyperbole or a reflection of a real consolidation of the frontier is unclear. The migrations of Vandals through Pannonia in 401 and the movement of the Goths under Alaric into Italy the next year must have severely taxed any remnants of the Roman administration that still remained in the province. The invasion of Italy under the Goth Radagaisus in 405 also passed this way, although by then Alaric had been given control of portions of Pannonia by Stilicho, and it had in effect become the prize for competing barbarian groups rather than a part, in any real sense, of the Empire. A *dux* of Pannonia Prima is, however, still listed in the *Notitia Dignitatum* (though his command is a joint one with Noricum Ripensis to the west),[21] and so there may still have been some Roman garrisons operating even in the early 5th century.

In 427, it seems that the eastern Roman army temporarily regained control of Pannonia,[22] although it was lost to the Huns once more in 433. In 437, the enfeebled western government ceded its rights to Sirmium to the Eastern Emperor at Constantinople, but by the 450s such concessions were rendered meaningless, as the Hunnish advance had swept away everything south of the Danube as far as Naissus (Niš). In 455, Avitus did try to recover the province for the Western Empire, but it was a last fitful act of exertion on the part of a hopelessly weakened administration, and it did not succeed.

The situation in Moesia Inferior to the east was somewhat different. The barbarian raids there were never as bad as those that afflicted Pannonia and Moesia Superior, and the Gothic and Hunnish hordes in particular never devoted much attention to the province. Since it fell securely into the domain of the Eastern Emperors, the resources available for its defence were also greater. Nonetheless, by the end of the 6th century, raids by Avars, Slavs and Bulgars had made the Roman hold very insecure and most of the towns were abandoned. The restoration of Byzantine control here in the 9th century was over a much-changed political and social landscape, and it makes little sense to speak of a *limes* in the sense of the one that had existed along the Danube until the 5th century.

Pannonia

Just 20 kilometres or so down the Danube from the border with Noricum, lies Pannonia's first significant fortification, and one of its historical success stories. Vindobona – or Vienna, as it has become – survived the fall of the Roman Empire, maintained itself in the early Middle Ages and then flourished to become the capital of another empire, that of the Habsburgs, which self-consciously borrowed some of the symbolism of its Roman predecessor.[23] In one sense, therefore, Vindobona only ceased to be an imperial city in 1918, when the Austro-Hungarian monarchy collapsed in the chaotic conditions following the end of the First World War.

Reminders of this second imperial period are hard to avoid in modern Vienna, from the grandiose bulk of the Hofburg, half-bastion and half-palace, which acted as the seat of the Habsburg sovereigns from 1279, to the rococo masterpiece of Schönbrunn Palace, where Franz Josef I – whose sixty-eight-year reign spanned both the zenith and the nadir of the empire – spent most of his life until his demise in 1916. The Schönbrunn even has its own 'Roman Ruin', a Romantic folly that was installed in the palace grounds in 1778 during a period when enlightened European tastes craved reminders of the classical heritage, which they were just then coming to rediscover and to value – feelings that would, at their most developed, feed into the ideology of Napoleon in his recreation of a Gallic Empire in France in 1804. Referred to commonly at the time as the 'Ruins of Carthage', their construction was supposed to represent Rome's triumph over that city, a reminder that the Habsburgs claimed, as Holy Roman Emperors (an office the dynasty had held, without a break, since 1452), some sense of continuity with the Roman imperial past.

The Schönbrunn ruins, although largely a creation of the craftsmen and artists of the late 18th century, did contain a real nucleus of the Roman past. Elements of a Roman palace that had existed in the centre of Vienna had been reused by Maximilian I in the 16th century for his Neugebaude Palace, and a few Corinthian columns and other architectural features were then transferred to the Schönbrunn's fanciful recreation of the original. The glimpses of more authentic Roman antiquities in Vienna are equally tantalising, peeping out between the Gothic or baroque exteriors, or half-drowned out by the insistent demands of modernity.

Vienna's antecedents, however, are ancient indeed. There were Celtic hill-fort *oppida* on the Leopoldsberg hill next to Vienna, which were occupied by the Boii, although these seem to have been abandoned around 20 BC, some time before the Romans arrived at this point on the Danube. Exactly when they first occupied the area around Vindobona is unclear, but it may well have been in association with Tiberius's abortive expedition against Maroboduus of the Marcomanni in AD 6. A fort for a cavalry unit (the *Ala I Britannica milliaria*) was probably built under Domitian, and soon thereafter Vindobona became a legionary base with the construction of a fortress by the XIII Gemina legion around 89.[24] After

the accession of Hadrian, however, the X Gemina became the permanent garrison, and the legion was stationed here from around 115 until
the end of Roman rule in Pannonia in the 5th century.

Vindobona remained relatively peaceful, apart from its use as a base by
Marcus Aurelius during his Marcomannic Wars. Although the reign of
Marcus was later idealised as something of a Golden Age, at least in
contrast with what was to come, the cracks were already beginning to
show for those who knew where to look, and his years in power were a
relentless struggle – in the east, in Germany and on the Rhineland – to
hold the line rather than to effect any significant advance in Roman power.

That Marcus has a reputation as a philosopher-statesman as well as a
dogged but effective military commander is because, uniquely, he left a
kind of private philosophical manifesto, the *Meditations*, which has
survived to transmit the Emperor's most private thoughts. They seem
to have been composed during the final years of his reign, and were not
known to Cassius Dio, who composed the only really contemporary
historical account in the first quarter of the 3rd century. Tellingly, Marcus
wrote this private work in Greek, for that was widely regarded as the
language of philosophy. It is not a diary or journal, and no coherent
narrative of his reign can be constructed from it. Yet it does argue powerfully for the virtues of self-control and self-scrutiny, both attributes highly
valued by the Stoics.[25]

In the *Meditations* themselves there is much general musing on the
futility of struggling against the cares of the world, and on the useless-
ness of a life that is not spent at least in part in self-examination. There
are a few distant echoes, too, of the lessons and consolations that the
Emperor must have drawn during the seemingly incessant campaigns
on the northern frontier. Individual fame is seen as futile in the face of
time itself, which will utterly erase all such vaunted achievements.[26] In
the chapters on the deaths of great men, Marcus remarks on how many
renowned soldiers and philosophers have died, a telling remark from a
man who himself constantly ran the risk of such a fate.[27]

The first Marcomannic War broke out in 166 and lasted, with some
intervals, for the best part of a decade and a half, bringing destruction
to many areas along the Danube line and exposing the weakness of a
frontier that was better placed for forward supervision and the repelling
of occasional raids than for such long-term warfare. In the end it seemed
that victory was within the Emperor's grasp, for in the campaigning
season of 178–9 he achieved the kind of decisive victory over the
Bohemians that had long eluded him. It looked as if his plans for the
organisation of the new provinces of Quadia and Marcomannia, which

would project Roman power far beyond the Danube and perhaps even permit the long-abandoned lands of the German interior to be re-annexed, would come to fruition.[28]

Yet in 180 Marcus fell ill and died at Vindobona. Rumour had it that he was assisted in his passing by Commodus, who choked his ailing father to death with a pillow.[29] Marcus's unstoic attachment to his own flesh and blood in promoting his son to imperial honours (making him co-Emperor in 177) turned out to have been particularly unfortunate. As well as degenerating – in the eyes of contemporary historians – into tyranny, Commodus abandoned his father's plans for a final solution on the Danube. Perhaps he was just making a point that his father would well have understood: that excessive regard for one's own achievements will ultimately end only in disappointment.

In general, however, Vindobona was overshadowed by Carnuntum (Petronell), its neighbour some 40 kilometres to the east, and it may only have reached the status of *municipium* some time in the early 3rd century.[30] The plan of the Vindobona fortress is barely recognisable from the modern street plan of the city. It was sited on the high plateau of the Hohe Markt and at its northern end, which fronted onto the Danube, was protected by a dyke, near which the military harbour was located. The south-eastern edge of the camp lay just near the Stephansdom, the imposing cathedral of Vienna, outside which a series of Roman-inspired stone busts of the Evangelists and the double-headed eagle of the Habsburgs are reminders of the imperial iconography that the Austrian Empire inherited. The *principia* of the camp lay a little to the south of modern Wipplingerstraße, while the *via decumana* probably ran north from the modern Kohlmarkt. The Wipplingerstraße passes on a high road bridge over the Tiefer Graben and marks the point where the legionary camp was defended by additional ditchworks to the west. As traffic whizzes by in a somewhat polluted and untouristed section of the city centre, it is extremely hard to summon up any image of the past.

At the Michaelerplatz, just short of the entrance to the Hofburg Palace, a few foundations have been unearthed from houses of the legionary *cannabae*,[31] that grew up to the south-east of the camp itself. Above the exiguous ruins, the hemispherical sweep of the Hofburg entrance looms, with huge statues of what looks like Heracles and his labours, one with the hero wielding a large club. Alongside the small square, Viennese horse carriages trot by, decked out in mock 19th-century style for the benefit of the tourists. For a brief moment all these times in Vindobona's history seem to telescope and collapse into one.

To the west of the Hohe Markt, close to what would become the forum, lies one of the more unusual settings for Roman remains on the *limes*. The elaborate clock on the market square parades round ornately painted and gilded figures from Vienna's past at set times of the morning and afternoon. For those with Roman interests, ten o'clock is the hour, as Marcus Aurelius makes his round then, while those of a more medieval bent might come at two o'clock when it is Charlemagne's turn. Those nostalgically hankering after the Habsburg apogee should turn up at eleven o'clock to see Empress Maria Theresa, while anyone with more eclectic interests can see the whole parade of historical figures at midday.

Just next door, at No. 3 Hohemarkt, downstairs from an Asian noodle bar, lie the remains of several Roman officers' houses, one of them with a hypocaust visible and the faint remains of plaster still clinging to the walls. The grandest of them was probably the house of a *tribunus laticlavius*,[32] the senior commander of the legion. Down below the level of the street, the ruins, despite their highly unlikely setting, exude a sense of calm. A few pieces of Mithraic altar, and also one to Neptune, indicate the religious preferences of the senior soldiery, while a gravestone of a camp prefect of the X Gemina from Rimini (later reused as a millstone) is evidence of the decline of the site, when the sanctity of such memorials was ignored in favour of their recycling for much more mundane purposes.

The camp was last repaired during the time of Valentinian in the 370s. Some time in the early 5th century it became the base of the section of the Danube fleet that had been stationed previously at Carnuntum, but this was Vindobona's last moment of glory. Presumably, though, the legionary fortress managed to shelter the remains of the city's population against the depredations of successive waves of Germanic barbarians, and so it was that Vindobona was able to re-establish itself in the early Middle Ages and grow into the Vienna of today.

It is barely an hour by car or train east from Vienna to the modern village of Petronell, within which the ruins of the legionary fort and *vicus* of Carnuntum lie. It is fairly flat and unassuming countryside, in which the predominance of viticulture is evident and where the touristic labels of 'Weinstraße' and 'Limesstraße' seem to compete for pre-eminence. The village itself historically depended on agriculture, and every other driveway seems to have a tractor parked in it. Unlike Vienna, it never developed to any great size after the collapse of the Empire, and it was this failure to thrive that has enabled it to preserve so much of its ancient structure.

Situated more or less at the point where the Amber Road crossed the

Danube on its way to the Baltic, and at the crossroads with routes that led to the Adriatic, Carnuntum was of primary strategic importance, and its use as a base by Tiberius for his attacks on Maroboduus in AD 6 confirmed its usefulness to the Romans. As early as AD 14, the XV Apollinaris legion moved here from Emona (Ljubljana) to build the first fortress on the site, at about the same time that Carnuntum, which had fallen to Rome in the conquest of the Norican kingdom, was transferred to the province of Pannonia.[33] After being moved in the early 60s AD and replaced by a succession of short-lived garrisons, XV Apollinaris was back in station in AD 71, and the legion stayed at Carnuntum until it was replaced by the XIV Gemina legion,[34] which then remained here until the end of Roman rule in the 5th century.

Carnuntum's profile was massively raised in 106, when the province was divided by Trajan, as the town became the seat of the governor of Pannonia Superior. The civilian settlement that had arisen west of the camp was raised to the rank of *municipium* by Hadrian in 124 (as Municipium Aelium Carnuntum), and it was while based here that Marcus Aurelius wrote one of the books of his *Meditations*. It was also at Carnuntum in 193 that Septimius Severus, who was then governor of Pannonia Superior, was proclaimed Emperor by his troops,[35] less than two weeks after the murder of his predecessor, Pertinax.

Once he finally reached Rome, the new Emperor summoned the praetorian guard to a meeting on the parade ground of their camp in the centre. They expected a welcoming speech and, no doubt, a handy donative (a 'present' due on the accession of a new emperor or the anniversary of his rule) to add to a massive pay-off they had received from Didius Julianus just eight weeks before. Instead they were disarmed by Septimius's men, who had surrounded the camp, and the former guardsmen were then exiled to beyond the hundredth milestone from Rome on pain of death. Septimius had learnt the lesson of the past twelve months and would brook no mutinous troops subverting his position at the very heart of the Empire. However, it took a further two years for him to be totally secure, as he needed to see off the parallel attempts to seize power by Clodius Albinus and Pescennius Niger, the governors of Britain and Syria.[36]

In memory of the place where his rise to the imperial throne began, Septimius awarded Carnuntum the rank of *colonia*, with the suitably florid title of Colonia Septimia Aurelia Antoniniana Carnuntum. Carnuntum next saw an imperial proclamation in 258 or 260 (the date is uncertain) when the rather less successful usurpation of Regalianus[37] broke out on the Danube. He seems to have struggled to attract support, for coins minted in his name cluster around Carnuntum and Vindobona and are hardly found elsewhere. In the end his demise was swift, possibly in battle against the Roxolani, or even deposed by his own supporters.

The central excavated site at Carnuntum represents part of the civil town; the legionary fort itself lies 2 kilometres further to the east. The gaps between the town *insulae* and the gentle downward slope beside the unearthed buildings are laid out with manicured lawns and pretty flower beds, while the roofs of the reconstructed buildings with their ochre-orange tiles make it seem like a quaintly old-fashioned Mediterranean village transplanted to the Danube, which is in a sense exactly what Carnuntum was.

'House I', near the entrance to the site, demonstrates the longevity of the settlement, for it was in use right up until the 5th century, and sometimes in the early 4th century a mosaic room was installed after the house had been badly damaged by fire. Its outline can still be seen in a geometric pattern, with broken *terra sigillata* used to delineate the outer border of the design. A little garden beside House I is planted with the same flowers whose seeds were found in the Roman-era level of the soil, including *Lilium candidum* (the Madonna lily) and what looks like a pink geranium, creating some sense of the domesticity – rather than just the imposing architectural presence – of the Roman town. 'House II', next door, has been totally reconstructed, and it looks just as if the inhabitants had departed in unseemly haste. Herbs, onions and garlic hang in the kitchen, and the door to the shrine of the *lares*, the household gods, stands open. To the east, Houses III and IV are un-reconstructed and lie, mere outlines of walls and foundations, much as the archaeologists found them.

The baths in the central section of the site are being re-excavacted, and it is hard, therefore, to gain much sense of the shape of this vital civic amenity. Next to it runs a road of large cobbles, roughened with age, left almost as it was the day the settlement was abandoned, the ruts of the cart wheels that plied the Amber Road[38] still visible on the stone. Along the north road, which led to the Danube, a reconstructed portico has been erected, on the site of which were recently found 150 pieces of raw, unworked amber, a sign of the importance of Carnuntum to the trade. Beside the portico lay a temple (in which a head of Diana was found, perhaps indicating the deity to whom it was dedicated), and shops, all part of a busy, noisy commercial quarter.

Much of the rest of the city is lost in fields and woods. On a peaceful country path to the west of the main site sits the brooding baroque bulk of Schloss Petronell. Its peeling plaster and shuttered windows enclose

the shell of an 11th-century castle, which was constructed on the probable site of Carnuntum's old Roman forum and later massively
reconstructed in the 17th century. Although the forum has largely
vanished, some of the buildings associated with it remain, known as the
'Palace Ruins', overgrown with spring flowers in a quiet glade a few
hundred metres away. The ruins are difficult to disentangle, being badly
eroded, but one of them may be a *macellum*, or public market, and others
are certainly associated with the city's largest public baths. The remains
of an octagon and a round building could be a temple or meeting hall.

It was in these unlikely surroundings that the Conference of
Carnuntum, one of the most extraordinary meetings of the Later Roman
Empire, took place in 308, bringing together the retired emperors
Diocletian and Maximian, and Galerius, who had been appointed
Augustus and ruler of the eastern provinces when the two former rulers
had stepped down. It was this abdication of power by Diocletian and
Maximian, carried out in coordinated ceremonies in Milan and Nicomedia
in May 305, that was at the root of the problem, for it had very definitely been Diocletian's idea that he and his co-Augustus should do what
no other Roman emperors had willingly done and stand aside from the
throne. This ignoring of dynastic claims in the new arrangement had
doubtless added to the unease of Maximian's son, Maxentius, who felt
that he was being passed over.

The events following the death of Constantius I, who had been selected
as the new Augustus in the West, which was followed by the troops'
proclamation of his son, Constantine I, as Emperor in July 306, must
have aggravated both Maximian's and Maxentius's sense of grievance.
On 28 October 306, Maxentius engineered his own declaration as Emperor
by a section of the Rome garrison, and at the same time ordered that
his father, who had been skulking in less-than-happy retirement in Lucania
in southern Italy, be conveyed to Rome.[39] In February, Maximian resumed
the purple as co-Augustus with his son, a move as utterly illegitimate as
it was bound to bring down upon him the wrath of both Constantine
and Galerius. After an attempt to dislodge Maxentius from Rome failed,
with fatal consequences for Severus, the Western Augustus, Galerius
tried in person late in 307; but, unable to contemplate storming the walls
of Rome or an extensive siege, his army retreated with its tail between
its legs.

Meanwhile, Constantine took advantage of the constitutional confusion to forge an unlikely alliance with Maximian. The old Emperor came
north across the Alps to Trier to arrange the marriage of his daughter,
Fausta, to Constantine. He also gave his blessing to his new son-in-law's

elevation from Caesar to Augustus, meaning that there were now no fewer than three claimants to this rank in the West: Constantine, Maximian himself and Maxentius. On his return to Rome, however, Maximian quarrelled with his son and attempted to strip him of his imperial robes, fleeing in the ensuing chaos back to Constantine's court. It was all an appalling mess, and Galerius looked on askance as Diocletian's orderly scheme for the imperial succession fell apart in an unseemly outbreak of family quarrels, constitutional coups and over-lapping jurisdictions.

Finally, Galerius turned to the architect of the Tetrarchy to restore his blueprint to working order. Diocletian was coaxed out of retirement at Salonae and travelled to a conference at Carnuntum on 11 November 308. The old Augustus resolutely refused to return to power as Maximian had done, and indeed ordered that his old colleague abdicate once more.[40] Constantine was demoted from Augustus to Caesar, and Licinius, a former colleague of Galerius, became the new Augustus in the West. Maximin Daia, who had been loyally serving Galerius as Caesar in the East, thus failed to gain promotion, a slight that rankled greatly with him. Constantine, too, believing he should have kept the senior rank of Augustus, felt aggrieved, while Maxentius (who had received nothing out of the settlement) and his father Maximian (who resented being pushed back into retirement) resolved immediately to do whatever they could to undermine the Conference's decision.

Within two years, the incorrigible Maximian had declared himself Emperor for a third time, been chased down by Constantine in southern Gaul and forced to commit suicide, while Constantine himself – refusing to accept his demotion from Augustus – was joined in that rank by Maximin Daia, who had his troops acclaim his promotion to the rank of senior emperors. By 310, therefore, there were just as many Augusti as there had been at the time of the Carnuntum Conference, and the confusion and bitterness between the notional imperial partners was, if anything, even more marked. Meanwhile, Diocletian disappeared into obscurity. Despite the recognition he has rightly received for his re-engineering of the Roman state and army, and his establishment of the institution of joint emperorship on a firm basis, even the date of his death is uncertain. It was probably in 316 that he passed away, no doubt disillusioned that the only power he possessed was that to survey the frustration of his designs.[41]

The absolute impotence of the former Emperor is amply demon-strated by the fate of his daughter Valeria (widowed in 311 on the death of Galerius),[42] who roamed the Balkans as a fugitive after the death of her husband before being put to death on the orders of Licinius in 315. Her father – or his memory, if he was already dead – could do nothing to protect her. Diocletian's great palace at Salonae also passes into obscurity. It had one last moment in the limelight, when it formed the headquarters of Julius Nepos, the last lawfully appointed Emperor in the West, who based himself in Illyricum after his expulsion from Italy in 475, claiming, in vain, until his death in 480 – and especially after the deposition of Romulus Augustulus in 476 – that it was he who was still the Emperor.

Carnuntum's civil amphitheatre is a short walk to the south-west of the Palace Ruins. Cutting along narrow country lanes and through fields, the way seems totally divorced from the urban settlement behind, and the building itself is only marked out by the grassy banks where the seats (calculated to hold 13,000 spectators) once lay. Only part of the main supporting walls and some auxiliary buildings to the south remain, though a hexagonal pool was discovered in excavations, composed of reused parts of the original building, and may have been a baptismal font.[43]

Much more resonant of Carnuntum's Roman past is the Heidentor ('Heathen's gate'). Splendidly isolated in fields beyond a railway track, this quadriform arch is all the more striking for being orphaned of its original context. It strikes a dramatic silhouette against the sky, a touch shorter than its original 15-metre height, but still imposing from afar and even more impressive close up. The top of the arch, from which soar the stumps of a second storey, was probably decorated with relief figures in marble. It has been dated to the reign of Constantius II (351–61)[44] and might have had some military function for official parades or the assembly of troops. The arch has long piqued the interest of those with an eye for classical antiquity and was mentioned as long ago as 1551 by the humanist Wolfgang Lazius, while its appealing and mysterious image appears in a prominent position on all of the modern publicity for the Carnuntum site.

The legionary camp itself lies beneath fields halfway between Petronell and the next-door settlement of Bad-Deutsch Altenburg. Situated on a raised plateau, its walls described an irregular quadrilateral, much longer on one of the sides. Although the normal camp buildings have been identified from aerial photography and from a series of excavations in the 1960s and 1970s, there is little to be seen on the ground. The only building that has been restored is the military amphitheatre, just a hundred metres or so from the fortress perimeter and laid out in a slight depression. The original structure was wooden and rebuilt in stone in the 2nd century, with funds donated by a town councillor named Caius Domitius Zmaragdus, who originated from Syria. The grassed-over arena is an oval around 70 x 45 metres, and part of the podium where the legionary legate's box would have stood survives to the west side. All around the stone supports of the seating tiers and the facing of the arena walls are still intact, and an inscription atop the main entrance memorialises the *quattorviri*, or municipal magistrates, of the Municipium Aelium Carnuntum, a name for the city that dates the inscription to before the reign of Septimius Severus.

The amphitheatre's small museum contains an admirable display on the training and life of Roman gladiators, a caste who were alternately lionised and despised by Roman authors. The Christian Tertullian, regarding the whole thing as scandalous, acidly commented that 'Men offer them their hearts and women their bodies.'[45] Gladiatorial contests had their origin in ancient Etruscan funeral rites of the 6th century BC, in which prisoners of war fought to the death to propitiate the shades of departed warriors.[46] The custom was taken over by the Romans, whose very early history included a phase of Etruscan dominance at Rome. They fastidiously made a distinction between *ludi* (processions and chariot-races), which were regarded as genuinely Roman, and *munera* (the gladiatorial version), for whose development the Etruscans were credited (or blamed).[47] By 55 BC, the *ludi* were so well established and elaborate that a set put on by Pompey for his consulship involved the slaughter of a thousand lions and leopards and the first public display of an Indian rhinoceros in Europe.[48]

The gladiatorial *munera* developed more slowly; the funeral of Marcus Aemilius Lepidus in 216 BC featured twenty-two pairs of gladiators, and that for the father of Titus Flaminius in 174 BC had thirty-seven pairs fighting over three days,[49] but these were essentially private affairs. It was only really under the Empire that the gladiatorial games received official sponsorship.[50] By that time amphitheatres, the normal venue for such contests, with their oval shape surrounded on all sides by seats (in contrast to the hemispherical shape of theatres for less bloody spectacles) dotted the Empire, most especially in the western provinces and North Africa.[51] They provided a hugely popular form of entertainment and a vent for the frustrations of the lower orders, who could scream out from the crowd slogans satirising the administration of the day, an act that would in any other context have led to summary punishment.

The gladiators themselves were a mixture of prisoners of war, condemned criminals and slaves, who had often been captured beyond the boundaries of the Empire. Occasionally – producing a particular frisson amongst the Roman chattering classes – free men put themselves into the arena, in effect enslaving themselves to the gladiatorial school to which they had signed up. Even Mark Antony's brother Lucius fought in the arena, in Asia Minor, much to the patrician sneering of Cicero.[52] The most extraordinary manifestation of the desire amongst the well-to-do to experience the thrills and danger of the arena, and the admiration of the baying crowd, was the Emperor Commodus, who spent long days fighting as a 'gladiator' – in little or no danger of being injured, however, so handpicked, drugged or terrified were his opponents.

Most Roman public officials were forced to put on games as part of their magistracy, and so there was a healthy market in gladiators and a respectable profit to be made. Under Augustus, there were sixty-six days a year given over to some form of public spectacle, and by the reign of Marcus Aurelius this had risen to 135.[53] The greatest games were given by Trajan to celebrate his conquest of Dacia; they lasted more than four months and included the sending of 10,000 gladiators into the arena, together with the slaughter of more than 10,000 wild animals.[54] By no means all contests ended in the death of one of the fighters, but nonetheless the carnage (and the cost) must have been prodigious.

The gladiatorial industry became a highly technical affair, with specialist schools and the fights themselves becoming increasingly ritualised, the appointed equipment of the gladiators sometimes aping that of various of Rome's defeated opponents. The 'Samnite', for example, wore a large oblong shield, a helmet with a visor and prominent crest, and a metal greave on the left; the 'Thracian' sported a curved sickle-shaped sword, a smaller round shield and greaves on both legs; the *retiarius* fought with a trident-shaped harpoon and a net to ensnare his opponent. The shows were overseen by an *editor* who supervised the general organisation, while the pairings of gladiators were generally done by lot. After the day's bloodshed was done, careful lists were made, some of which survive, noting against the names of the gladiators P (for *periit*, 'perished'), V (for *vicit*, 'won') or M (for *missus*, 'spared') – the last-named being those who lost but whom the senior magistrate present had decided should be spared, often at the behest of the crowd.

After Constantine I's acceptance of Christianity, gladiatorial games gradually withered away. An edict of his in 326 purported to abolish them, but its lack of effectiveness is indicated by another law of Constantius II in 357, which forbade soldiers to fight in the arena.[55] The gladiatorial schools were closed by Honorius in 399, but such spectacles sputtered on for a few years, and the last recorded games at Rome took place in 404.[56] The arenas were even then not shut down completely and were used for *venationes* (wild-beast spectacles), in which men hunted ferocious animals, sometimes at the cost of their own lives. By 440, the Christian writer Salvian, in a bitter attack on public shows, mentions *venationes* and chariot-racing, but not gladiatorial shows, implying that by then they had ceased.[57] At Rome, the last such recorded beast-show came as late as 523.[58]

At the Carnuntum amphitheatre, a small troupe of Austrian school-children is decked out in gladiatorial array (with a detachment of mini-legionaries, presumably on guard duty). Someone, however, has forgotten the swords, and there is a great deal of chaotic running backwards and forwards to recover the weapons for the programmed mock-combats. To while away the time the legionaries lock their wooden shields together over their heads to make an impromptu *testudo*, the Roman army's 'tortoise' defensive formation, which protected against projectiles and objects hurled from the battlements of cities under siege. This manoeuvre, it must be presumed, formed part of last week's lesson.

Only a kilometre east of the main legionary camp lay a fort for a cavalry *ala*, originally based here in the 1st century AD, which then occupied the camp until at least the mid-3rd century. Although little save the outline of the camp's ditches can be made out, the positions of the main buildings during its four phases of rebuilding have been established[59] and the situation of another significant military force shows how vitally important the Carnuntum area was.

The next fort along the Pannonian *limes* was around 60 kilometres from Carnuntum at Gerulata, to the south of Bratislava, situated in modern Slovakia's exiguous strip of land south of the Danube. It lies in the quiet village of Rusovce, now in effect a suburb of the Slovak capital, and Gerulata itself never achieved the glorious afterlife of the more substantial army camps at Vindobona (Vienna) and Aquincum (Budapest). It sits down a quiet tree-lined side-street, near a twin-towered baroque church whose peeling frontage has seen better times, and close to the old course of the Danube, which has since shifted a little southwards. It was probably first erected during the reign of Domitian and by the early 2nd century housed a garrison of the *Ala I Milliaria Cananefatium*,[60] who hailed from the far west of the continental *limes* at distant Forum Hadriani (Voorburg) on the coast of the Netherlands.

Relatively little remains of the fort, with its ruins a mixture of the 2nd-century stone phase of the site and a late-antique smaller fortlet, which was subsequently built in the north corner of the earlier walls, cannibalising stones from its predecessor as well as a medley of tombstones, altars and whatever other building material lay easily to hand. A small section of the north-eastern angle of this later fort survives to just a few restored courses, with a peristyle courtyard in the interior of the building. Set asymmetrically in the centre of this lies a deep well, providing the security of water supplies for the soldiers and eliminating the need, in the less secure circumstances of the 3rd and 4th centuries, to leave their camp.

Around 75 kilometres to the south-west of Gerulata lay the important town of Scarbantia, now modern Sopron in Hungary, which was one of Upper Pannonia's chief settlements. It began life as a road station on the route that led from the Adriatic and Istria up to the Danube, and was initially assigned under Tiberius to the province of Noricum, being transferred by the reign of Vespasian to Pannonia, at around the time it reached the rank of *municipium*.[61]

The old town of Sopron is an attractive place with a predominantly baroque feeling, its most impressive monument, the late-medieval Fire Tower, squatting faintly phallus-like over the town centre. Watchers stationed at the neoclassical balustrade towards its summit could spot and warn of any conflagrations before they burnt out of control. Its base is also built in part over the remains of the Roman city wall beside the northern gate. A little further into the old town, butted right against the medieval wall and hemmed in by later, early modern buildings, are the remains of Scarbantia's forum. A couple of *insulae* are clearly demarcated on either side of the remains of a road; in one of them evidence of a bronze workshop was found. From the Roman wall itself one fan-shaped and one horseshoe tower survived, which were built over in the 14th century when the old fortifications were renewed.

Off to the right lay another defensive structure, which again had the remains of a medieval breastwork built over it. An outer ring is early medieval, but then, later in the 15th century, the Roman circuit (which was ignored by the earlier builders) was reused. One round projecting bastion, patrolled by a few cats prowling in the low grassy moat, was incorporated in all the phases. This complex of Roman walls represents the Constantinian defences of the city, at a time when the town defended the northernmost reaches of Pannonia Prima, after Pannonia had been subdivided by Diocletian in 296.

Somewhere nearby, the remains of an amphitheatre, a *horreum* and a Temple of Isis were uncovered by archaeologists, all part of the normal panoply of civic life, and a testament to the high level of Romanisation in the area. Concealed in the basement of a bank building, down a staircase reached by squeezing behind a set of desks and metal filing cabinets, hides another remnant of the forum. Here fragments from a sanctuary to Silvanus, god of the woodlands, sit beside the main roadway into the forum, marked out with a line of reconstructed portico columns. To one side is the base of what must have been a monumental equestrian statue. Its sheer size could only have been appropriate for a person of the highest eminence, and probably it carried an official portrait of one of the emperors. The roadway and another weed-choked portion of it visible through an iron grille above ground on the other side of the square were once – strange though it might seem in their current straitened circumstances – part of an ancient and vital trade route, the Amber Road.

Trade in the attractive fire-coloured gem, with its strange electric qualities, was no easy matter, for the principal source of the stone in ancient times lay along the shores of the Baltic Sea, many days' journey into *barbaricum*. The origin of amber was believed, as far back as the time of Herodotus in the 6th century BC, to be a 'river Eridanus'.[62] Pliny recounts the expressive tale of how, when Phaethon, the son of Helios the sun god, stole his father's chariot and allowed it to veer out of control – incidentally creating the Sahara Desert where it scorched North Africa, and turning the Ethiopians' skins black – Zeus was forced to strike him with a thunderbolt to bring his fiery joyride to an end. So besides themselves with grief were his sisters that they turned into poplars, which each year shed viscous tears on the banks of the Eridanus river, tears that were called *electrum*, in other words, amber.

The best account of the trade in amber and the search for its origins comes from the time of Nero, when a Roman member of the equestrian class was despatched by Julianus, a businessman, to try and transport back a huge quantity of amber.[63] This probably represented an attempt to make direct contact with the tribes at the head of the route and so cut out some of the middlemen along the way. It is unclear whether it was successful, and with the constantly shifting patterns of migrations of peoples to which the central European plain between the Danube and the Baltic was prone, any attempt to reach agreements with the tribes there to allow direct Roman access to the amber sources would have been like trying to tame the wind.

The route in ancient times carried the amber down via the estuary of the Vistula either to the Black Sea or through the Moravian Gate (the flat area between the mountains of the Sudetenland and the Carpathians) on towards the Danube near Carnuntum and Gerulata, and thence south (via Scarbantia) to the Italian peninsula. However, once the *limes* became porous in the late 4th century and collapsed completely in the late 5th century, the settlements that had depended on the trade, such as Scarbantia and Savaria (Szombathely), the provincial capital of Pannonia Prima 40 kilometres to the south, diminished in importance, and the trade in amber dwindled away to nothing.[64]

Scarbantia was vulnerable as early as the 2nd century and, to cap its earlier sacking during the Marcomannic Wars (166–80), it was overrun by the Goths in the early 5th century and was thereafter effectively lost to the Empire. Ninety kilometres to its east, and 60 kilometres to the south-east of Gerulata, Arrabona (modern Győr) lay on a tributary of the Danube. Its pleasant old lanes, baroque-style churches, squares and riverside walks totally conceal its heritage as a Roman *castrum* and a key link in the line between the legionary fortresses of Carnuntum and Brigetio. The earliest fort seems to have been built under Tiberius,[65] and the site, which was later rebuilt in stone, was occupied until late-Roman times by a variety of garrisons, principally cavalry regiments (such as the *Ala I Augusta Ituraeorum sagittariorum* from Syria), which were well placed to take advantage of the flat conditions on the Hungarian plain.

It is a short trip along the river to Brigetio, which began life as an auxiliary camp in the mid-1st century AD, before becoming a legionary fortress in 101 with the posting of the XI Claudia legion there, to be replaced five years later by XXX Ulpia Victrix and then, finally (before 119), by the I Adiutrix. Its very name has a Celtic root (*Brig-*) meaning 'fort'. Despite the subsequent rich history of the camp, and the town that grew up alongside it, there is relatively little left to see.

The fort sits alongside a factory compound in a park of neatly manicured hedges overlooked by an enormous housing estate in the modern settlement of Komárom (a suburb of Szöny), which nestles alongside the Danube, the southern section being in Hungary and the northern part (Komarno) in Slovakia. A few sarcophagi without inscriptions lie scattered around, together with a modern carved stone that marks the visit in 375 by Valentinian during his campaign against the Quadi, which ended in his death after an apoplectic fit. Of the fortress buildings, nothing remains, all backfilled after excavations, while the housing estate, built in the 1940s, has swallowed the southern portion.

More evocative are the wall paintings in the small local museum. One from a peristyle house, dated by a coin of Antoninus Pius to the period after the mid-2nd century, shows a man bearing a tray with a blue background, holding something in his hand, poised as though to bite into it, his curly hair and confident face clearly delineated. Another less clearly outlined figure and a lion-skin stretch out across part of the floor. In another scene, Pegasus and Andromeda are depicted in a central medallion, while at the corners of the painting beautifully refined women's faces represent the Four Seasons, creating a star-shaped composition of great elegance.

Of the line of forts that guarded the Danube *limes* between Brigetio and the next legionary fortress of Aquincum, little has remained, particularly where the situation was of sufficient strategic importance (as at Esztergom, or ancient Solva, 55 kilometres to the east of Brigetio) to encourage continued occupation in medieval times. Solva itself, originally founded in the 2nd century, remained in use until the 430s, but suffered particularly badly as it lay on the site of the palace of the Hungarian kings in the Middle Ages, with further destruction being wrought when a 19th-century basilical church was built on top of the fort mound.

Twenty kilometres east along the Danube towards the modern town of Visegrád, the country becomes hillier and more wooded, differentiating itself from the unbroken plain behind. Here, too, a medieval palace was built, occupying a prime position in the centre of town. Yet elements of the late-Roman castle of Pone Navata have survived, high up on a 170-metre plateau overlooking the river. It is not quite the biggest hill in the vicinity; that honour goes to a slightly higher promontory next door, to which a medieval fortress clings, almost inaccessible, even to its defenders. Pone Navata was one of the more important fortifications in this section during the Later Empire, probably built under Constantine I in the 320s or 330s,[66] and it remained in use at least until the 380s (the *Notitia Dignitatum* lists its garrison as the *auxilia Ursarensia*). Around this time most of the fort was abandoned and only a watchtower built around the main gateway continued in use. From there, the remaining soldiers watched as their hold on the territory of the middle Danube grew ever weaker. By the 5th century, barbarian hut dwellings clustered on the southern side of the fort, as Roman control in this region collapsed for ever.

Of Pone Navata, one main line of walls survives to about 30 centimetres high, running for about 10 metres before disappearing into the ground, together with three horseshoe-shaped projecting towers. One of the fort's gates survives, and beyond it is a curious small, round structure with wall-spurs projecting from it. This section of the Danube, where it changes direction and bends round to flow north–south, rather than east–west, was densely defended, with the auxiliary castle of Ulcisia Castra (modern Szentendre) lying between Pone Navata and the main base on this part of the river, some 35 kilometres to the south at Aquincum.

Both the twin capitals of the Austro-Hungarian monarchy, Budapest and Vienna, owe their existence to their origins as Roman legionary camps, sites whose location was so strategically placed that their associated civil settlements survived the catastrophe of the Empire's fall in the West, continued to grow and eventually became capital cities. It is a singular history, which only Belgrade in Serbia unambiguously shares (although Gerulata near Bratislava at least lies near its successor, even if occupation was not continuous, and Bonna on the Rhine frontier did give birth to what was the capital of West Germany until German reunification). The earliest fort, which would ultimately give rise to Buda, was founded under Tiberius for a cavalry detachment, which was replaced by the fortress of the II Adiutrix legion under Domitian.[67] The second of Budapest's constituent cities, Pest, derives in turn from Contra-Aquincum, which was established as a bridgehead fort across the Danube in the late 2nd century.

The main civil settlement of Aquincum lies to the north-west of the centre of Buda, the rattling ride on the city's HEV light-railway system an incongruous entry into the Roman *municipium*. From its status as mere legionary camp, Aquincum rose to become the capital of Pannonia Inferior at the time of Trajan's division of the province into two parts in 106. The first governor of the province, and therefore a resident of Aquincum for several years, was none other than Trajan's young protégé, the future Emperor Hadrian. It did not, however, reach the rank of *municipium* until 124 (when it took the name Municipium Aelium Aquincum), and had to wait until 194 during the reign of Septimius Severus to reach the level of *colonia*.

Only the eastern section of the ancient town has been extensively excavated, and the consolidated walls of this section, bordering a very busy main road, have a slightly sombre, pensive feel about them. So close to the centre of a capital city, the ruins are well visited and a procession of day-trippers and schoolchildren lounge against urban villa walls or run excitedly along the *decumanus*, barely pausing to examine an altar or explanatory plaque. In the museum the most striking exhibit is a Roman water-organ, a recreation of one found on the site. The original was given by a certain Iulius Victorinus to the firemen's guild in 228. Even though the inscription discovered with it referred to it as a water-organ, its workings (using fifty-two pipes) are in fact pneumatic. An old newsreel plays out a concert given by a reconstructed version of the organ, the music creating a rather haunting and distant atmosphere. Elsewhere in the museum, a statue of a man clad in a toga has a handy stone slot at the neck for screwing on a replacement head, no doubt a very useful fixture in the 3rd century when emperors changed almost every other year and the city could thus economise on commissioning an entirely new statue by simply replacing the old head with the latest imperial bust.

Close to the museum lies the lapidarium (stone repository) of Aquincum, an awesome collection which takes up a stretch several hundred metres long, arrayed with tombs, altars, milestones, sarcophagi, lintels, architraves, statues and all the other stonework and masonry that a provincial capital might produce over several hundred years. It is a veritable graveyard of the city, and in a way more evocative than the ruins themselves, as the hopes, fears and life stories of the citizens are pressed together in a jumble of memories.

Just opposite the museum is the *mithraeum* of Symphorus and Marcus, its central hall with the side-rooms clearly visible, but the middle section now lacking the altars that must once have stood there. It was one of four shrines to the god in the town, a sign of military influence in Aquincum, for the cult was always particularly popular amongst the military, as evidenced by the other *mithraea* along the frontier. Beyond it, a substantial section of the *decumanus* survives, principally in a quarter composed of craftsmen's and traders' shops and dwellings, including a *macellum* for the butchers. The colonnade of the *decumanus* runs alongside a grassy bank all the way back to the site entrance, and beside it sit the 'Great Baths', the largest of half a dozen such complexes found in the city. Part of the building close to the hypocaust seems charred, perhaps evidence of the destruction of Aquincum in the 3rd- and 4th-century disorders.[68]

A small forum at the end of the *decumanus*, the main east–west axis of the city where it crossed the *cardo*, the principal north–south street, possesses a shrine of uncertain dedication, with a very weathered altar still *in situ*, together with the town's *curia* and the fragmentary remains of the basilica and law courts. On the north-west outskirts of town lay the civil amphitheatre, now missing its seats, but with the stone piers that supported them, the entrance gate and enclosing wall still intact. Around 30 metres in length on its longest side, it seems now to serve principally as a pleasant walking and running track.

The legionary camp that gave birth to Aquincum was sited a little way from the Danube. Built in stone under Hadrian to replace the early Domitianic fort, it remained in use until the time of Constantine, when a new stronghold was constructed on the banks of the river. This, in turn, was abandoned and replaced with a simple watchtower under Valentinian I. Although excavated intermittently during the 20th century as the demolition of older buildings permitted, only small parts are now visible. The largest surviving section, wedged under a spaghetti-like complex of flyovers and overpasses, is that housing the camp baths, which were enlarged in 268 and then partly adapted in the 4th century to be the palace of the *Dux Ripae Pannoniae*. To wander through a two-millennia-old bathhouse 10 metres beneath a road over which thunders the heavy traffic of modernity is a surreal experience. Dramatic stripes of shaded and sunlit stones caused by the criss-crossing of the roads above create a confused impression of walls and columns, obscuring any wide-ranging viewpoint of the site.

In an underpass beside the nearby metro stop, the life of the camp fleshes itself out somewhat with the tombstone of an auxiliary soldier tacked to the wall next to a snack bar, with a very unmilitary purple teddy bear perched on a seat propped up against it. Outside the precinct of the metro, on a totally neglected patch of ground, lie the remains of the south gate of the camp and the re-erected pillar of the house of one of the senior officers. As commuters rush to and from their daily office grind, no one at all seems to notice the stones, the earliest evidence of their home city.

Of Contra Aquincum, the great-grandfather of Pest, the remains are even sparser, although it was always a smaller fortress, a mere bridge-head on the barbarian side of the Danube. It now sits in a depression in the centre of Budapest-Eskü Square, the outline of a round projecting tower with wall spurs about 3–4 metres long still visible. Hemmed in by the buildings of the square and overlooked by incurious office-workers consuming their lunchtime snacks, these remains are of a later Roman fort. It was originally about 85 metres square, and probably constructed on the site of a larger 2nd-century fort, as the *limes* was strengthened in the late 3rd or 4th century, but at a point when there were no longer sufficient resources to build or garrison the larger military installations of former times.

After the reforms of the late 2nd-century, the provincial administration moved away from the town, with Sopianae (Pecs) or Gorsium (Tác) becoming the capital of Valeria.[69] The town diminished, and the proconsul's palace was abandoned. The palace of the *dux* of the Pannonian *limes* was moved away to the military camp, and the civil settlement was left bereft of patronage. In the 370s, when Valentinian I passed through on his campaign of refortification of the Danube *limes*, he found Aquincum so impoverished that he could not have his winter quarters in the city.[70] By the time the *Notitia Dignitatum* was composed at the end of the 4th century, Aquincum's legion had been transferred to Gaul, and the town had probably been overrun by Germanic tribes and then by the Huns in the early 5th century. The Romanised civilian population evidently did not evacuate entirely, for it must have formed the core of the settlement that would, many centuries later, evolve into modern Budapest.

From Budapest the Danube strikes in a more or less straight line southwards. The land here is again very flat and was vulnerable to nomadic incursions, particularly horseborne ones. The principal civilian town in this sector, set around 75 kilometres to the south-west of Aquincum, and 30 kilometres west of the Danube, was Gorsium, where around AD 50 a military camp was built on the banks of the Sárvíz river.[71] Over time it was transformed into a civilian settlement as the main garrison moved up to the line of the river, although a new camp, for the *Cohors Alpinorum equitata*, was built just to the south of it. When Pannonia was partitioned by Trajan in 106, Gorsium became the centre for the imperial cult in Pannonia Inferior and a new and more intense phase of construction began. Severely damaged by a Sarmatian raid in 178, the settlement was then completely destroyed by the Roxolani in 260, and had to be entirely rebuilt on the ashes and wreckage of the old town. It was then renamed Herculia, a name very much in keeping with the spirit of the times, for it was with Hercules that the Emperor Maximian was identified in the official ideology of the Tetrarchy.

Far away from any modern settlement, Gorsium has a much more tranquil air to it than Aquincum, set amongst fields and bordered by small clumps of trees, and it is far easier here to gain a sense of the whole life of the ancient city. It is mainly the late-Roman settlement that can now be seen, its predecessor having been so comprehensively erased both by the barbarians and by the rebuilding of the site. At the entrance a rounded projecting angle tower survives, its stones seeming to gleam impossibly white in the mid-afternoon sun. The port that serviced Gorsium was situated nearby, but it seems lost in a tangle of undergrowth and mud; the modern river has moved 200 metres or more away, but its ancient course lay much closer to the city. As Gorsium/Herculia was rebuilt, large urban villas were sited within it, a sign perhaps of the growing social division between the *potentes* who possessed power and social distinction and the *humiliores*, who, even if they belonged to groups that had been enfranchised and (certainly after 212) had citizenship, gradually slipped into a position of inferiority. This division was even recognised by the law, which, for example, permitted the humbler (but free) classes to be tortured, whereas no such sanction was applicable to their social betters.

The largest of the villas, in the north-west of the town, was some

60 metres long, a maze-like complex of state apartments, baths and work-shops, so grand as to be termed a 'palace'. Several of the rooms have apses, and one in particular has the feeling of an audience chamber. It is possible, once Pannonia Inferior was divided in two by Diocletian, that this was the headquarters of the governor of the new province of Valeria.[72] To the east of it, preserved under a shelter, are the remains of a series of wall frescoes, one preserving the shape of a winged figure, the other a simple geometrical pattern. Around this survives the curve of an early Christian basilica, probably built not long after official govern-ment recognition of the religion under Constantine in 311.

Along the *decumanus*, past a *nymphaeum*, with what looks curiously like a stone trilobite shell placed on top of it as part of the modern restoration, lie the remains of the forum, the only area whose use was conserved intact from the pre-3rd-century phase of the city, bordered by four columns of a pagan-style temple dedicated to Rome and Augustus. As this area seems to have constituted the official provincial religious centre, the remains of a podium to the south of the *decumanus* have been taken to have some purpose associated with the imperial cult.[73]

This cult, exploited in the frontier provinces as a handy agent of Romanisation and a means to promote provincial loyalty to the ruling classes, centred on posthumous worship of the emperors as gods. Deification had an ancient pedigree in Roman tradition, for Romulus – Rome's first founder and first king – was regarded as a god after his death and worshipped under the name Quirinus. Republican leaders underwent no such elevation, although overenthusiastic subjects had occasionally come close to worshipping them,[74] especially in the East, where such cults had a heritage stretching back to Alexander the Great and before. It took until the accession of Augustus as first Emperor for the tradition to be revived at Rome. His adoptive father, Julius Caesar, was posthumously recognised as divine in 42 BC,[75] strengthening Augustus's position as not only the son of a great military leader, but of a god as well. The honorific *divus* ('deified') was accorded to Augustus after his death and the deifica-tion of subsequent emperors became almost routine, although not without an occasional hint of controversy. Antoninus Pius had to threaten to abdi-cate in order to cajole the Senate into deifying Hadrian, with whom that august body had latterly been on bad terms. Similarly, emperors univer-sally regarded with execration, such as Domitian and Caracalla, were denied their immortality as gods. Emperors whose accession could be regarded as of dubious legitimacy, such as Septimius Severus – who, for all his virtues, had taken the throne by force – could try to associate themselves with a previous regime by proclaiming a predecessor to be a god.

Hence, in 193 Septimius tried to acquire a veneer of lawfulness by having the title *divus* accorded to Pertinax, who had received wide support amongst the senate prior to his murder, and pointedly denying it to Didius Julianus, his immediate predecessor whom he had overthrown. Whether the divine status of former emperors was taken particularly seriously is unclear, but it did form a central part of the imperial cult, which focused, as time went on, on the worship of the deified emperors as a group. Only the most notable, such as Augustus himself, received their own individual temples. The role of priest of the imperial cult was an attractive means of social advancement for ambitious provincials, and even more so for the fact that it was one of the few prestigious positions that were not denied to freedmen.[76]

The direct worship of living emperors continued to be frowned upon, but a means around this was found through the veneration of certain aspects of the Emperor's personality, such as his *genius* (or spirit) and his *numen* (or divine presence). Even in relatively conservative Italy, altars were dedicated to the *numen* of Augustus, in which sacrifices to his 'divine presence' would only have been distinguishable from actual worship to the most pedantic.[77]

An arch comment on the whole business came from one of its beneficiaries, Vespasian, who, as he lay dying in AD 79 is reported to have said, 'I can feel myself becoming a god.'[78] More satirically, Seneca penned a piece entitled 'On the Pumpkinification of Claudius', in which the dead Emperor pleads unsuccessfully before a court of the gods to be allowed to join their number.[79] The Christianisation of the Empire in the 4th century rendered deification redundant and Emperor-worship highly suspect. Even so the notion was so embedded in the popular psyche that Constantine himself was referred to in inscriptions as *divus*, although by this time it had more the connotation of 'the late' than any sense that he was in any way the equal of the one God, whose worship he had so greatly promoted on Earth.

In the east of Gorsium, the town walls are less well preserved. Around 378, after the security of the western Balkans had been gravely compromised by the Gothic victory at Adrianople, a large part of the civilian population that had been living in suburbs outside the city walls moved inside the shelter of the fortifications. A great number of poor-quality houses were built, often against the inside of the ramparts, and the southern suburbs of the town were entirely deserted. Sometime between 380 and 430, this area was converted into a cemetery; mingled amongst the ruins of the abandoned buildings are dozens of humble graves, *tegulae*, made of tiles propped together into a triangular shape, with a light infill of earth. They look like a hundred little huts for the dead and, together with the broken-down houses of this former residential quarter, lend to this area of Gorsium a very eerie feeling indeed.

Intercisa, one of the larger auxiliary forts on the Pannonian *limes*, lies around 50 kilometres to the south-east of Gorsium, transformed now into the rather depressing town of Dunaújvaros, its centre almost entirely composed of high-rise blocks, and where the museum has a whole wing still devoted to the glorification of the locality under the communist regime (for a while it even renamed itself for the Soviet dictator as Sztalinvaros). The remains of the camp lie at the edge of one of the huge apartment complexes. Not much of it survives, except the grassy outline of the ramparts and one north-eastern tower overlooking the Danube (and a fetching panorama of an industrial complex packed with cranes).

A few stone outlines of the interior buildings are still intact, one situated near where the camp *principia* should be. Otherwise there are just slight indentations in the ground to indicate the principal buildings of the fort. The baths lay elsewhere, five minutes' walk away, in an older, more agricultural quarter of Dunaújvaros. The surviving section, a rather dusty-looking affair, must be the old *caldarium*, judging from the number of tiles scattered around, which would have been used to raise the floor level, beneath which the hot air used to heat the building circulated. Looking away from the crane-lined riverbank, it all seems very peaceful and tranquil, a couple of sarcophagi quietly sitting in the small lapidary garden next to the guardian's house.

Intercisa did not have a particularly peaceful history, however; it was probably destroyed during an action by the Iazyges in 117–18, and was then burnt again by the Marcomanni during their war against Marcus Aurelius around 178, only to be put to the torch once more by the Roxolani in 260. It was partly reconstructed under the Tetrarchy, but more comprehensively so under Constantine I between 325 and 330. Further repairs were then necessary under Valentinian I, that great refortifier of the Danube *limes*. It is not clear exactly when Intercisa was abandoned, but it was probably some time in the early 5th century. The town had probably been garrisoned in the last years of its existence by Germanic federate troops, and, with the Western Emperors' decreasing ability to guarantee military pay, the army units may simply have dissolved rather than suffered any catastrophic local defeat.

From Intercisa, southward along the river through 40 kilometres of flat fields, woods and a few low hills, the auxiliary fort of Lussonium, near the modern village of Dunakömlőd, sits on a bluff overlooking what was in ancient times the gorge of the Danube, though the river has now moved several hundred metres further to the east. At the north gateway of the fort, a crew of workmen are busily plastering and mortaring, creating a reconstruction of the north entrance, and have just reached part of one projecting tower, so that before too much time has elapsed, Lussonium, or its gate at least, will be restored to its former glory. Although the camp was first occupied by a wooden building in the 1st century, the visible stones date from the late-Roman period.

The western part of the fort collapsed due to erosion caused by the river's course at the foot of the hill and was further damaged by defensive works built on the hill under the Habsburgs in the 18th century. The fort therefore has an elongated strip feeling about it, and the shape of the ruins is further confused by the superimposition of a massive tower at the end of the 4th century when the rest of the fort was demolished. Some 10 metres square, the tower had 2-metre-thick walls and at least two storeys, and was characteristic of the type of fortification built along the Danube in the last years of reasonably secure Roman control here. Its situation atop the hill and the additional height provided by the tower must have given the garrison an excellent view of what was going on across the Danube, though with their presumably limited numbers it is doubtful what, if anything, these border troops could have done to intercept any incursions.

A good example of the fate of many of the forts along the *limes* is to be found at Lugio, around 70 kilometres south on a bend in the river in Dunaszeckslő county. The fort stands (or stood) on top of the Várhegy ('castle') hill, but the crest of this is entirely covered in a vineyard, and the sides of the slope are thickly wooded. Somewhere in here, apparently, are the remains of walls, and a frescoed house and hypocaust were found, but they remain resolutely concealed amongst the trees. On the opposite side of the river a cluster of ruins makes up the remains of the bridge-head fort in *barbaricum*, Contra Florentiam (a name which indicates that Lugio itself was renamed as Florentia during the late-Roman period).

Lugio makes up for the paucity of its remains by its most spectacular find, a bronze statue bust of Marcus Aurelius (now in the museum at Pécs), a masterpiece that depicts the Emperor at about thirty or forty years of age. He sports curly hair and an ample philosopher's beard, his brow furrowed and his eyes cast slightly upwards. He seems just a little weary, but still strong and enduring, his expression at the same time knowing and compassionate. It is an exquisite embodiment of the spirit of the Emperor, which comes across so strongly in his *Meditations*, mired in a seemingly incessant war with the Marcomanni, when he would much rather have been tending to his own inner contemplative life.

Around 40 kilometres almost due west of Lugio lies Sopianae, which was the principal town of the area and evolved in due course into the city of Pécs, Hungary's fifth-largest, with about 150,000 inhabitants. The town's name may perhaps derive from a Celtic root that means 'swamp', but it does not seem to have been a major settlement until Roman times, when it grew on the junction of roads that led north towards Aquincum, and east–west towards Sirmium and the Italian peninsula. The modern town completely overlays ancient Sopianae, and so excavation has only given a partial impression of the antique city.[80]

The majority of the remains that have been located date from the late-Roman period, when the town probably rose in status, and most of these are associated with its Christian cemeteries. These mainly lie clustered around the modern basilical church, indicating that this was early on the nucleus of Christianity's development in Sopianae. The main area is known as the Cella Septichora, from a seven-apsed structure built in the late 4th or early 5th century, which forms the centrepiece of an extensive cemetery complex. With its sterile modern lights, and arrayed with modern metal benches, it still manages to retain an aura of mystery, its walls in some places surviving to greater than head height. In passageways that lead off in each direction are a variety of early Christian tombs, some plain burials, others in carefully crafted mausolea.

The highlight of all is the Saint Peter and Paul burial chamber, its barrel vault visible one level up in the multi-storey catacomb, its interior ceiling decorated with frescoes of the two saints – clad in Roman robes, with wide-bordered tunics – and the Virgin Mary, faded to an almost chalk-like consistency. Across the square from the city's basilica lies another early Christian mausoleum excavated in the 1950s. It is a single vaulted tomb, with one large sarcophagus and a collection of exquisite frescoes from the 4th century. To the left the temptation of Adam and Eve is shown, together with Daniel, in imminent danger of being consumed by the lions.[81]

The Christian burial chapels at Sopianae survived in use into the Age of Migration, (when large numbers of Germanic and other barbarian peoples moved south and westwards into Roman territory), and there are some 8th- or 9th-century frescoes on a few of the tombs. The medieval name of the town, Quinque Basilicae ('Five Churches') probably indicates a continuity of use in the vast Christian complex. In the 9th century, however, a second wave of invaders from the East swept through the

Pannonian plain. By the time the Magyars crossed the Carpathian basin in 895, the Roman province was but a far-off memory.

The journey through the flat Pannonian plain to the south and east of Sopianae crosses agriculturally rich territory dotted with the small, nondescript villages of the eastern Slavonian province of Croatia. It has long been debatable territory between the Balkans (or the steppes) and the lands further west. It lay along the most obvious routes towards the Italian peninsula, and usurpers or legitimate emperors intending to secure Rome from a base in Constantinople (or vice versa) were forced to traverse it. Just a little further east, one of Europe's most persistent fault lines appears. To its west, in Croatia, lies the area that formed, in general, part of the western Roman provinces, largely Latin-speaking, whilst to its east, in Serbia, lay the Eastern Emperor's lands, which were or became predominantly Greek-speaking. The division persisted in the line between the Habsburg Austria-Hungary and the Ottoman Turkish lands in the Balkans, and between the Roman Catholic majority in Croatia and the Eastern Orthodox of Serbia. The passage of time has not erased the area's strategic importance; it was bitterly fought over during the civil wars that accompanied the break-up of Yugoslavia in the 1990s. Empty lots and charred and burnt-out shells of buildings mark the passing of the fighting, while an even more sinister reminder of the conflict lurks to either side of certain stretches of roadway, in the red or black skull-and-crossbones symbols that warn of uncleared mine-fields amongst the gently swaying trees.

Osijek, the regional capital, is a gracious 19th-century city lying near the confluence of the Danube and Drava rivers, its main square scattered with statues honouring the forefathers of Croatian nationalism, the tower of the Saint Peter and Paul Cathedral at one end still pock-marked by bullet and shrapnel holes from the bombardment during the civil war. The remains of Mursa, part-excavated, lie in the eastern section of town around 300 metres south of the hospital on an open lot, though with little to rival the more spectacular finds of sites such as Carnuntum or Viminacium (Kostolac). Granted the status of a *colonia* by Hadrian in 133, Mursa remained a prosperous outpost near the *limes* into the 4th century. Its political life was uneventful, though the area outside the city twice saw major battles that were the undoing of a usurper, with the defeat in 258 or 259 of Ingenuus,[82] and the bloody suppression of the revolt of Magnentius in 351.[83]

To the south-east of Osijek along the highway that leads a short distance later into Serbia, Cibalae (Vinkovci) was badly damaged during the Yugoslav civil war, but not destroyed like its near-neighbour Vukovar.

The scant remains of baths and hypocausted houses that have been excavated hardly do justice to its real importance as the birthplace of Valens and Valentinian, brothers who both became Emperor in 363.

The Balkan provinces of Pannonia, Moesia and Illyricum did, indeed, become something of a cradle for emperors from the 3rd century. After the demise of Alexander Severus in 235, emperors were largely made (and as often murdered) by the soldiers. And what better replacement for an unsatisfactory emperor than their own general, whom they most often trusted, sometimes even admired, but from whom they could be absolutely sure of a suitable financial reward for their elevation of him to the highest office? In this fashion Trajan Decius, from the small village of Budalia (Martinci) between Cibalae (Vinkovci) and Sirmium (Sremska Mitrovica), became Emperor in 249, while Aurelian (270–5) may have been from Sirmium, Probus (276–82) was born near the same city, and Diocletian's colleague Maximian (286–305) hailed from the surrounding area. Constantine I (306–37), in turn, was born at Mediana outside Naissus (Nis) in Moesia.

It was, therefore, hardly shocking when Valentinian, born at Cibalae, became Emperor, and eminently predictable that when, urged by the troops to appoint a colleague to support him, his choice fell on his own brother, Valens. He was advised by Dagalaifus, a senior military officer, to choose Valens if his first concern was for his own family, but someone else if his primary loyalty was to the Empire. Blood, as so often, won out over reason.[84] The general was wise not to press the point against his new Emperor, for Valentinian had a notoriously bad temper. Once firmly ensconced in the palace in Constantinople, he is said to have procured two bears, which he had stationed outside his audience chamber, and, should someone cause him too much annoyance, he would allow the beasts literally to tear them apart.[85]

Valentinian had a great deal to keep him occupied. He allocated the government of the eastern provinces to his brother, who had little military experience, and set off to deal with a renewed threat from the Alamanns in the west. Their king, Vithicabius, had been assassinated and Valentinian took advantage of the confusion in their ranks to lead a preemptive expedition into their territories. By 374 the Emperor had brokered a tenuous peace with Macrianus, the new Alamannic ruler, and the Rhine frontier thereafter remained quiescent. Valentinian then turned eastwards to face a new danger threatening his own homeland.

The Quadi and the Sarmatians, the latter an Iranian-speaking people whose mounted warriors fought in chainmail armour, were vexed that Valentinian had ordered the erection of forts in what they regarded as their territory on the northern bank of the Danube. In 374, the barbarians tried to negotiate, but their humour was hardly helped by the murder of their king, Gabinius, at a banquet given by the local Roman commanders.[86] Unsurprisingly, the Quadi streamed across the river and plundered the neighbouring towns. One of their marauding bands very nearly intercepted the carriage transporting Constantia, the granddaughter of Constantine I, to her planned wedding with Gratian, Valentinian's eldest son.

The outrage to imperial dignity was unsupportable, and Valentinian moved his headquarters from Trier into Illyricum to be closer to the frontier and as a means to intimidate the troublesome barbarians. Faced with the full might of the legions, the Sarmatians wisely sent envoys begging for forgiveness. The Emperor merely promised to investigate their claims and sent them away, neither forgiven nor chastised. Valentinian then crossed over into the territory of the Quadi at Aquincum (Budapest) and set enthusiastically to laying waste their lands. The Quadi, seeing that they were beaten, or at least that they would starve if matters were left unchecked, sent a deputation to the Emperor, who was by now in Pannonia at Sirmium. Curious portents attended their arrival; lightning struck the imperial palace, and Valentinian dreamt that he had seen his wife – who was in Gaul – attired in mourning clothes.

At their meeting, it was agreed that in return for supplying recruits to the Roman army, the Quadi would be left to enjoy what was left of their lands in peace. Before departing, the envoys were granted a personal audience with the Emperor. Unwisely, but understandably, they insisted that the cause of the conflict had been the Romans' building of forts on their tribal land. To be addressed in this way was an appalling breach of protocol and Valentinian was enraged – as far the Romans were concerned, all these tribes were subjects of Rome, albeit sometimes rather badly behaved ones. He had a fit of apoplexy, followed by a stroke, and died that very night, 17 November 375. The hapless envoys were rushed away before they could witness Valentinian's death agony.

Colonia Aurelia Cibalae, as Osijek city had become on its elevation to colonial status in the 2nd century,[87] was a modestly prosperous town, some 56 hectares in extent, around which Valentinian's father Gratian had held extensive estates before they were confiscated on the grounds of his suspected involvement in the rebellion of Magnentius. However, it was comprehensively outshone by Sirmium, its neighbour some 70 kilometres to the south-east, which became a favoured imperial residence under Diocletian and the Tetrarchy, as well as at the time of Constantine and his successors.

Sirmium lay just on the edge of two worlds, within striking distance of both East and West, and so it became a location of massive strategic importance for the 3rd- and 4th-century emperors, right up to the time when there was so little left to preserve of the Western Empire that maintaining such a stronghold at its border ceased to have much purpose. Today the medium-sized town of Sremska Mitrovica in Serbia's Vojvodina province, it was first settled by the Romans in the early 1st century AD on the site of a former Pannonian settlement. With its strategic position on the Sava river, it became a *colonia* in Flavian times, and found frequent use as the headquarters for expeditions against the tribes across the Danube.

A short walk from the Sava, where a Roman port was located, lie the excavated remains of a 'trading quarter' set in a small shop-lined square. The buildings are from the 2nd or 3rd century and represent just a couple of *insulae* of the quarter, the stones remaining to about five or six courses high, set in a grassy dip surveyed by a gaggle of inquisitive pensioners seated on the surrounding benches. With its section of roadway, an exposed water channel with brick-built arches, and parts of several small but well-built houses, it is a mundane representation of what was for many years a working imperial capital.

Sirmium's administrative importance long pre-dates the Tetrarchy. In 103, when the province of Pannonia was split into two, the city became the capital of Lower Pannonia, and with Diocletian's further subdivision of Pannonia into four provinces in the 290s, it was made the capital of Pannonia Secunda, and also of the Vicariate of Illyricum. During the 2nd-century it saw frequent imperial visits from Marcus Aurelius, who used it as his headquarters during his decade-long Rhine and Danubian campaigns. During the Tetrarchy itself, Sirmium acted as the capital of Galerius, who, on the retirement of Diocletian and Maximian, became, in effect, the senior emperor. Sirmium, rather than Rome, was thus now the political centre for the whole Empire.

The remains of Galerius's palace lie just a few hundred metres from the trading quarter, split into two sections by the modern street. Set in a deep pit surrounded by a high concrete and wooden fence against the prying of curious eyes, it is really only a section of what must have been a much grander building. These are the baths of the imperial palace, their original function given away by the preservation of the bricks of a hypocaust in one corner and the telltale curved apses of the various pools. Low walls enclose grass-filled interiors, and here and there a few decorated pieces from friezes or pediments lie scattered on the ground, together with fragments of pinky-orange marble and a few bits of deep-purple imperial porphyry. In one section, small hexagonal floor tiles have broken up, leaving their six-sided cylinders as just a thousand pieces in some nightmarish jigsaw puzzle.

The only clue to the former inhabitants is a paw-mark on the border of some floor tiles, imprinted by a dog that ran over them as they dried around 1,800 years ago. It is hard in such an abandoned place, staring down at the ruins and up at the orange-tiled roofs of the surrounding modern houses surmounted by the white, round stains of their satellite dishes, to conjure up the atmosphere of an imperial palace in all its complexity, bustle and backdoors intrigue. However, the place does still excite interest, and a Serbian television crew listen intently as the layout is explained to them, taking panoramic shots to create a broad sweep of the past and as much visual drama as their cameras can muster.

Yet more ruinous is the small section of the palace on the other side of the road, where under a lattice-like wooden framework, its protective sheath of translucent plastic lying shredded in strips all over the ground, are a few more rooms, clothed in grandiose metre thick monumental walls. Somewhere, too, under the houses of Sremska Mitrovica lies one of the largest hippodromes in the ancient world; a section of its central barrier – the *spina* – has been found, and it is calculated that the arena must have been more than 300 metres long.

Sirmium was served by a port at Bononia-Malata (Banoštor), 40 kilometres to the north along the Danube, which also housed a fortress and, according to the *Notitia Dignitatum*, had units of the V Iovia legion as its garrison. Further east along the river, at modern Novi Sad, the massive complex of the Petrovaradin Fortress rears up. Composed of multiple defensive rings around the high point of the citadel hill, it was begun in the late 17th century and, by its completion around 1776, represented the very height of military architectural sophistication. Unfortunately, by this time the threat from the Ottoman Turks, to defend against whom it had been built, had receded so far that they never attacked it in its completed form. Somewhere deep beneath the impressive, pointless stonework may lie the remains of the small Roman fort of Cusum,[88] which, at 16 Roman miles from Bononia, hosted a small cavalry unit of *equites Dalmatae* that saw to the security of this sector in the 4th century.

Moesia Superior

Singidunum (modern Belgrade), some 75 kilometres south-west of Novi Sad, was one of the frontier's most important military stations, and

marks the westernmost point of Moesia Superior. The Roman settlement was situated on the high ground that overlooks the confluence of
the Sava and Danube rivers. The Romans originally established a
legionary fortress here in AD 86 for the IV Flavia Felix legion,[89] and small
parts of it can still be discerned in the bulk of the Kalemegdan fortress
that broods over the city, but the town's very survival as a viable settlement in the Middle Ages, and its growth to become the capital of
Yugoslavia and then of Serbia, have obliterated almost all trace of its
ancient forebear. The Roman Danube fleet, the *Classis Moesica*, had its
base here after its transfer from Viminacium to the north-east, and the
city became a *municipium* in 169, by which time Trajan's conquest of
Dacia meant that it was no longer a frontier position. Singidunum was
finally elevated to become a *colonia* in 239, but was always overshadowed
by Sirmium, its grander neighbour to the west, and by the legionary
fortress of Viminacium to the east. In contrast to Sirmium, it can claim
to be the birthplace of just one emperor, Jovian, the short-lived successor
to Julian in the 360s.

From the 4th century, Singidunum experienced a dizzy series of swings
in fortune and political control. It fell to the Huns in 441,[90] during Attila's
victorious campaign that swept away Roman control along a wide band
of territory south of the Danube. In the chaotic times following the Hun
khan's death, the eastern Roman army recaptured the fortress in 454,
only to be pushed out almost immediately by the Sarmatians. They in
turn were expelled by the Ostrogoths under Theoderic the Amal, who,
when they invaded Italy in 488 at the invitation of Emperor Zeno, ceded
Singidunum to the Gepids. The Byzantine Empire regained the city in
510, and around 535 Justinian rebuilt the fortress, only for it to be sacked
once more by the Avars in 584.[91] Finally, in the 7th century, after a brief
period of Byzantine reoccupation, it was settled by the Slavs, under
whom it became Beograd, the 'White City'. A large and noisy capital,
there is little white about it now; its suburbs are swathed in a band of
undifferentiated grey apartment blocks, the gift of socialist town planning to most cities of the region.

Outside of Belgrade's urban sprawl, the landscape is more rural,
though dotted with the shells of redundant industrial installations and
factories built according to the inscrutable requirements of the socialist
command economy. The sector east of Singidunum was guarded by
the fort at Margum (Dubravica), which, according to Ptolemy,[92] served
as the winter quarters of the VII Claudia legion in the mid-2nd century.
Although destroyed by the Huns in 441, the fort (and the *municipium* of
Aurelium Augustum Margum that had grown up around it) managed

to recover and by 505 was serving as the headquarters of the *magister militum* of Illyricum. It formed a key part of the *limes* of Djerdap, the defensive system in this part of the Danube, for which a significant upgrading of the road network was undertaken during the reigns of Tiberius, Claudius and Domitian. Once the trans-Danubian province of Dacia had been conquered, the fort lost its significance, but nearby another crucial and impressive structure appeared. A massive bridge was constructed between Pontes (Kostol) and Drobeta (Turnu Severin in Romania), where remains of some of the supporting structures can still be seen.[93]

Finally, just near the Danube, and about 12 kilometres from Pozarevac – most notable for being the birthplace of Slobodan Milosevic, Serbia's nationalist leader and the bringer of war to the Balkans – lies Viminacium. Just outside the small modern town of Kostolac, the old legionary fortress is situated on a plain beside the Mlava river, overshadowed by a power-plant whose chimneys pump a constant stream of white vapour-clouds out into the atmosphere, with the view further scarred by a coal mine in the distant hills. Amidst the often underfunded, neglected and badly presented Roman sites in the Balkans, Viminacium stands out as an exception, and it is, paradoxically, precisely the eyesore of a power-station that has been its salvation. The money provided for rescue excavation as a *quid pro quo* for permitting the building of the station on a site of such known archaeological sensitivity meant that there were funds for a modern visitor centre and the effective presentation of finds from the large-scale Roman necropolis that was discovered, in part on the site now obliterated by the power-plant itself.

Viminacium is first mentioned in the sources in Ptolemy's *Geography*. By early in the 1st century the Romans had built a military camp there, which became the base first for the IV Flavia legion and then the VII Claudia legion, one of the two with which Julius Caesar had invaded Britain in 55 BC, and which had subsequently acquired the nickname *pia fidelis*, for its loyalty to Claudius in the face of a revolt in AD 42. Viminacium served as the headquarters for Trajan in 98–9 before his First Dacian War, and, safely behind the shelter of the new province of Dacia, it developed rapidly as a civilian centre during the 2nd century, being granted the status of a *municipium* by Hadrian, in whose honour it became known as Municipium Aelium Viminacium.

Rapid, largely untroubled development followed for Viminacium in the early 3rd century, and under Gordian III it reached the status of *colonia*, at the same time being granted the prestigious right to mint its own copper coins (a right that would be revoked by Gallienus for the town's involvement in the revolt of Ingenuus).[94] During the reign of Philip, Viminacium briefly became the centre of the usurpation of Pacatianus, an officer in the Danube army (whom Zosimus says was of low rank), who persuaded the soldiers to raise him to the imperial eminence, possibly because Philip was seen to be ineffective in countering the threat posed by the Goths across the Danube.[95] They then did away with Pacatianus and threw in their lot instead with Trajan Decius, the very general whom Philip had despatched to suppress the revolt.

Having seen off Philip, who was killed in battle near Verona in 249, Decius enjoyed the position for only about two years before he, in turn, died fighting the Goths near Abritus in Moesia in 251.[96] With him perished his older son, Herennius Etruscus, leaving just his fifteen-year-old younger son Hostilianus, who was declared Emperor in Rome. The Danube armies, by now exercising their practically biennial right to pick a new sovereign, opted instead for the senior general Trebonianus Gallus. He acted cautiously, recognising Hostilianus's right to rule, while also appointing his own son Volusianus as co-Emperor. Shortly afterwards the whole terrible muddle of emperors was greatly simplified by the death at Viminacium of Hostilianus (and his mother, the splendidly named Herennia Cupresennia Etruscilla) in an outbreak of plague.

There is an intriguing possibility that Hostilianus might have been buried at Viminacium, and that one of the 13,000 graves that were located in the eastern necropolis belonged to him. The presentation of the site is spectacular. A modern shell of steel and plastic encloses the whole; inside, a stone wall of large, well-cut and dressed stones surrounds more than a dozen tombs, all grouped around a central mausoleum with an opening formed by a truncated triangle, now closed off with a metal grate. The central tomb is certainly of some prestigious personage, and seems to date from the mid-3rd century, so the theory that it is Hostilianus's grave is a plausible one. Against this, the stock of the former imperial family might not have been so high after his death (and the seizure of power by Trebonianus Gallus and his son) as to attract others to bury their dead near Hostilianus's mausoleum.

In the silence and the slightly grey-brown dust of the floor, it seems a secret, hidden place, despite the open nature of its display. One of the other tombs has a barrel vault that makes it look like a basket, while others have rounded roofs that give them the strange appearance of a dog-kennel. A few more conventional sarcophagi lie around, some of them with lids missing. Other poorer, 'free' burials were discovered, with just the skeleton and no sarcophagus, which it has not been possible, on the whole, to conserve. The earliest grave found here was from about

250, and the cemetery enclosure remained in use for about another century or so after that. Arrayed outside it was another selection of graves, some with the skeletons *in situ*, crouched as though trying to defend themselves from their inevitable fate.

Downstairs in the darkness a member of the site staff plays Charon, hooded cloak and scythe leading the visitor on into the Underworld. Here three tombs were found, complete with their original frescoes (two sets of which had to be moved to the museum at Pozarevac, while one remains in its original position). Two of them incorporate Christian symbolism into the wall decorations: in one a pair of peacocks, in the other a Christogram. The third contains a portrait of the 'Lady of Viminacium', the undoubted masterpiece of the site. She is richly dressed in a draped cloak, her hair in an elaborate coiffure, with pearl earrings, her eyes turned slightly to the right. Analysis of the bones found in the tomb have indicated that the woman – if this was her portrait – was at least partly paralysed in the later years of her life. On the opposite wall is the figure of a young man bearing offerings on a tray. An imaginative interpretation of the frescoes – which one of the archaeologists, in a break from the tangible world of cold, back-breaking digging, made into a film – is that he is the painter of the tomb, and had fallen madly in love with his subject opposite, a love that, because of social differences, could never be requited.

The area around Viminacium (or possibly closer to Margum) saw the denouement of another 3rd-century power struggle, when the armies of Carinus were defeated by those of the 'usurper' Diocletian near the River Margus in April 285. Carinus's father, Carus, had died the previous year fighting the Persians, and his brother Numerian had perished in suspicious circumstances while leading the army back to Constantinople; some pointed the finger of responsibility at Diocles (as Diocletian was then known), head of the palace guard, who had the next day engineered his proclamation as Emperor by the troops. Then, in a theatrical gesture he executed Aper, the praetorian prefect – who might have known the truth behind Numerian's death – by lopping off his head on the podium before the assembled army.

Constantine I is recorded to have visited Viminacium twice, in 321 and 334, while his son Constantius II graced the city with his presence in 338 and 358. From the later 4th century, however, emperors simply travelled less. The death of Valens in battle against the Goths in 378 led to a reaction against the idea that the Emperor should lead his troops in person; the consequences of an imperial death on the battlefield were too grave to risk it occurring again. Henceforth, emperors were largely confined to their capitals, or the areas around them, and the last to visit Viminacium was Gratian (the nephew of Valens) in 382. From this 4th-century period of guarded security dates a section of the legionary camp's *porta praetoria*. It lies across virtually open fields from the necropolis building, the landscape of the ancient city and fortress visible only in gentle undulations and bumps in the grass that suggest the presence of ancient stones beneath. In the light early-autumn drizzle, and the first faint hints of a biting winter wind, it instantly instils a desire to huddle against some warming camp fire.

Under another cover, fragments of the paving of one tower are visible, as well as part of a water channel that led down to the Danube. It was once believed that the area between the fortress and the river was marshy, but subsequent finds have indicated that it was dry and that the banks of the river were reasonably accessible. A little way on from the camp gate lies a shallow bowl-shaped indentation in the grass, which indicates the location of the amphitheatre. The baths nearby, and under another cover, are in good condition, but represent several different stages of building and so are hard to read at first. There are in fact no fewer than five different floor levels, and two different layers of hypocaust are visible in what might be the *caldarium*. The whole complex, 30 metres long and 15–20 metres wide, represented a substantial amenity for the citizens.

Viminacium was destroyed by Attila and the Huns in 441, in a campaign that devastated most of the urban settlements in this part of Moesia. Although it was reoccupied and refortified as part of Justinian's programme to strengthen the Danube *limes* in the early decades of the 6th century, within 100 years it had once again been overrun, this time by Slavic invaders, and it was not reoccupied.

Opposite Drobeta (Turnu-Severin in Romania) the river changes direction, turning southwards, before kinking east again to form the border between modern Bulgaria and Romania. Around 100 kilometres south of the river, and so well back from the *limes* itself, lay ancient Naissus (now modern Niš), the third-largest city in Serbia. The town was founded in the late 1st century BC after the subjugation of the indigenous Dardanians, at a relatively early stage in Rome's gradual absorption of the Balkans. After the establishment of the province of Moesia Inferior in AD 15, Naissus became one of its most important centres and experienced several centuries of quiet prosperity before the crises of the 3rd century.

Naissus's most famous son, the future Constantine I, was born around 273 – his birthday would be later celebrated as 27 February, but the precise date is uncertain[97] – and spent at least part of his childhood in a villa at

Mediana, just outside Naissus. His mother, Helena, was the daughter of an innkeeper, and the taint of such ignoble ancestry was an early handicap that Constantine struggled to overcome. When his father became Caesar in 293, he was forced to marry his senior colleague Maximian's stepdaughter Theodora and thus divorce Constantine's mother. Helena and her son were then packed off to Byzantium, out of the way, but where a close eye could be kept on their activities.

The remains of the villa are sited around 5 kilometres out of town along a minor highway. Lying on the south bank of the Sava river, this was the main route through the Balkans to Serdica in Thracia, and Mediana became the favoured location for the out-of-town properties of those wishing to escape the bustle and unhealthy atmosphere of the larger Roman settlement. The site lies in a wooded park, separated from the road by low walls. Approaching from a track, the low remains of a peristyle courtyard come into view. The site guardian is clearly not expecting much in the way of visitors and only reluctantly opens the museum, before warming to his task with a torrent of information delivered in Balkan-inflected French. The museum building houses Mediana's star piece, and the object around which the building itself was constructed. A Constantinian-era mosaic occupies a large central roundel several metres across, with three circular apse-shaped extensions creating private corners. Bands of lotus flowers and a series of crosses, swirls, knot-patterns and meanders fill the space of the black-and-white mosaic, whose high quality speaks of the prosperity of the villa's owners. This may indeed have been Constantine's private *triclinium*, a personal retreat when he returned to this place of his childhood.

The main villa complex was clearly very large, with a number of rooms set around the peristyle, but only the outlines and a couple of courses of brickwork have been reconstructed. Further to the east, a long rectangular building with double rows of internal columns and huge jars set into the ground must have been some kind of storage chamber. Nearby, a larger complex represents the imperial baths, with a rectangular room still possessing a hypocaust and a small semicircular apse for a pool. The rest of the site is largely unexcavated, a great expanse of field pitted with excavators' trenches and a few wooden shelters where structures of particular importance have been unearthed. Under one of them lies a recently discovered palaeo-Christian church, the floor of the apse just visible beneath plastic sheeting.

It is scarcely surprising to find an early Christian church in the birthplace of Constantine, who has found everlasting fame as the first Christian emperor. It is hard now to untangle the route by which Constantine reached Christianity and his motives in espousing the new religion, or indeed the real level of his commitment to it. The 2nd and 3rd centuries had seen an increase in the popularity of 'mystery cults' and in the occurrence of inscriptions that invoked gods such as Zeus Hypistos (Zeus the Greatest)[98] – a tendency towards recognising one of the deities in the pantheon as the supreme one, which is referred to as henotheism (as opposed to monotheism, which only accepts the existence of a single god and denies the reality of the rest). Three decades before Constantine, Aurelian seems to have favoured the worship of the Sun (Sol Invictus) as a single unifying cult for the Empire,[99] while under the Tetrarchy the promotion of the cults of Jove and Hercules, the protectors respectively of Diocletian and Maximian, seems to indicate official imperial support for a simplified pantheon, which might help bolster the position of a new imperial system.

Narratives that were written during Constantine's reign, such as the *Vita Constantini* of Eusebius, Bishop of Caesarea, have something of the hagiographical about them, and the bishop even implies that Constantine's father, Constantius Chlorus, was practically a Christian himself. Constantine, though, had shown little evidence of Christian sympathies during the early stages of his rise. The panegyrist who delivered a speech in praise of him in 310 was happily able to claim that the Emperor had received a vision of Apollo, who had offered him a laurel wreath in token of a reign that would last many years,[100] while the coinage of the time depicts him as being associated with Hercules and Mars. Then, from 310 Constantine promoted the image of the sun god, of whom Aurelian had been so fond.

By summer 311, the appalling political mess that had followed Diocletian and Maximian's abdication in 305 had begun to resolve itself somewhat, with the untimely death of Galerius. He had been suffering from some kind of malignant ulcer in his genitals, which may have been associated with bowel cancer and caused him the most indescribable torment – a fact that Christian authors related with unholy relish, ascribing it to God's revenge for the persecutions he had earlier unleashed on their co-religionists.[101] On 30 April 311, as he lay dying, Galerius issued an edict in which he ordered an end to the persecutions and allowed the Christians to return to the worship of their God. It did him no good, for a few days later he died in the utmost agony. Constantine now made a bargain with Licinius, one of the surviving emperors in the East, that in exchange for his support against Maximin Daia there, Constantine would be given a free rein to deal with Maxentius in the West. To seal the alliance, Licinius was to marry Constantine's sister Constantia.

It was at some point during his march against Maxentius that Constantine appears to have received – or believed he had – some kind of vision from the Christian God. Advancing rapidly with a relatively small force, and brushing aside Maxentius's army near Segusio (Susa), he reached Rome in late October 312. It might well have been here that the Constantinian enterprise ended, for he had nothing like the strength to invest Rome completely, so all Maxentius had to do was wait for his opponent's supplies to dry up or for the support of his legions to ebb away. Constantine would then have faced ignominious retreat, or worse. Maxentius had seen off previous challenges by Severus (whom he actually succeeded in capturing) early in 307 and by Galerius later that year, precisely by waiting behind Rome's powerful fortifications and watching the loyalty of his opponents' troops waver.

Yet this time he made the fatal error of marching out of Rome to give battle. Things were not so favourable for him as in 307; he was deprived of the residual loyalty to his father, the former Augustus Maximian, who had committed suicide in 310, and Maxentius had unleashed his praetorian guard on the population of Rome after a fire at the Temple of Fortuna in 309, leading to the death of perhaps 6,000 civilians and irreparably damaging a crucial reservoir of support for his regime. On 28 October, at Saxa Rubra, 14 kilometres from Rome, his army was routed and in its retreat back to the city was caught in the bottleneck over the Milvian Bridge crossing, and huge numbers were slaughtered or drowned, including Maxentius himself, whose body washed up the next day and whose head was then paraded on a pike.

The dedicator of the Arch of Constantine in the Forum at Rome ascribed his victory to 'the inspiration of a divinity' (*instinctu divinitatis*), a suitably vague formulation, which might as well apply to a pagan deity as to a Christian one. Lactantius,[102] however, writes that Constantine received a dream shortly before the Battle of the Milvian Bridge in which he was told to have all his soldiers mark the 'heavenly sign of God' upon their shields in the form of a Cross with a hook that formed a P-shape. This 'Chi-Rho' monogram was subsequently to become a characteristic symbol of those claiming Christian allegiance. According to the version in Eusebius, Constantine – overcome by the weight of the task facing him in dislodging Maxentius from his Roman stronghold – had prayed to the Christian God, asking for a sign.[103] After he did so, he saw a fiery cross in the sky, and alongside it the message *In hoc signo victor eris* ('By this sign you will conquer').

Although accounts of these portents were written down some years later and with the benefit of hindsight, it is clear that Constantine ascribed some role to the Christian God in his victory over Maxentius, for on taking control of Rome he promptly exempted the clergy from civic duties and ordered a lavish programme of construction of new Christian buildings. He ordered the barracks that had housed Maxentius's cavalry guard to be demolished and on the site was erected a grand new basilica – the traditional form of a civic meeting house – as a place of worship for the Christians. This new cathedral, initially known as the Basilica Constantiniana, would later (from its proximity to the imperial Lateran Palace) take on the name of San Giovanni in Laterano. Within a decade, work had also begun on the Church of Saint Peter over the site of the martyr shrine of the apostle, which would, in time, become the headquarters of the Western Christian Church.

Constantine now cemented his accord with Licinius by celebrating the previously agreed marriage of Licinius and his sister Constantia at Milan. After the festivities the two emperors agreed on the issuing of a decree of religious toleration, which has become known as 'The Edict of Milan'.[104] It was specifically aimed at permitting Christian activity, for it refers to freedom of worship for 'Christians and to all people', and repeals point by point the disabilities under which Christians had laboured since Diocletian had launched the Great Persecution in 303.

Once Constantine had finally disposed of Licinius in 324,[105] he issued further edicts to enforce the restitution of any property in the eastern provinces that had been confiscated from Christian individuals or churches on the grounds of their religion. Christianity was now free of persecution and the unchallenged religion of the victorious ruling clique. Anyone who wanted to curry favour with the Emperor would find it convenient to be a Christian. There would be pagan reactions in the future, most notably under Julian in the mid-360s, but within two generations the Christian Church had established itself so securely that dislodging it from its central religious (and, increasingly, social and political) role would prove impossible. Within a century the pagan temples had closed, public sacrifice had been forbidden on pain of death and, while there were still pagans in positions of public authority,[106] they had no power – or mostly any intention – to turn back the tide of religious policy in favour of the traditional cults. Rites such as the *Parilia*, the celebration of the birthday of Rome, would persist into the early Middle Ages, but more as traditional folk festivals than as any real survival of pagan practice and belief.

Aside from Mediana, precious little survives of ancient Naissus. A curious reminder of the great Emperor stands, however, some kilometres from it. Niš airport is officially named 'Constantine the Great' (or Konstantin Veliki in Serbian). It is the only such facility anywhere to have been named after a Roman emperor, and so, uniquely, travellers from the terminal flying off to Switzerland or Montenegro can pause a moment for contemplation of perhaps the most famous Serbian of them all.

The Turkish fortress dominates the older part of town near the river. Its ramparts are forbiddingly high, but only a single ditch protects it. Inside, in the late-afternoon chill, a couple of open-air cafés and souvenir stalls struggle on, and beyond them in a section a few metres square are some Roman remains, parts of brick piers and walls. Another similar area lies scooped out from the basement of a disused mosque. Beyond, up a slight slope leading away from the main path through the fort, is a longer structure with large rectangular rooms or vaults, each one with an arch. Above these a double-arched entrance leads into yet another rubble and rubbish-choked chamber. It is clear that the fortress mound must be honeycombed with Roman remains, but they lie undisturbed beneath the coffee-houses and the tread of locals taking a quick evening stroll before darkness falls. In the centre of the fort-park, a Roman necropolis was unearthed and a selection of the finds has been arrayed in a somewhat neglected lapidary garden. One tombstone memorialises two sisters, both called Attidia, while another sports a delicately carved dolphin-like sea monster.

Naissus was to be the birthplace of two more Roman emperors: Constantius III, one of the West's last really able military commanders,[107] and Justin, one of the first of the renaissance of the Empire in the East, who was born in the nearby settlement of Bederiania. Around 470, he set out from Naissus with two companions, Zimarchus and Dityvistus, to try and seek their fortunes at Constantinople. Of Justin's two friends, nothing further was heard, but he managed to secure himself a position in the *Excubitores*, the new palace guard that Emperor Leo (457–74) was then establishing. Over time Justin rose to be the commander of the unit, and he brought over his young nephew Petrus Sabbatius[108] to take advantage of his good fortune. In due course, and certainly before 520, he adopted the young man, who then changed his name to Justinianus (known, in turn, to historians as Justinian). The accession of his uncle to the throne in 518 opened the way for the young Justinian to become one of the Eastern Empire's most successful rulers.[109]

It was to be Naissus's last moment of glory. The new Emperor refortified the town, though not particularly out of any sense of nostalgia, for he strengthened the Danube defences in general. However, it fell to the Slavs in 578 and then to the Avars in the late 6th century, after which organised occupation of the site ceased. Instead Justinian lavished his

imperial building instincts on Constantinople and on the town of
Justiniana Prima, which lay near his birthplace. The latter's location is
not certain, but is probably the extensive site that lies near Caričin Grad,
close to Lescovac in southern Serbia.[110]

From Niš, the road climbs gradually, crossing over the edge of the
Stara Planina, the mountain range that strikes across central Bulgaria
and which divided Moesia from the plain of Thrace to the south-east.
Around 10 kilometres west of modern Zaječar, and about 70 from the
line of the Danube, lies the 4th-century palace complex of Felix
Romuliana, built by Galerius near the village where he had been born,
and which he intended to be his place of retirement. Diocletian had set
the precedent in 305 when he stepped down voluntarily from the imperial office, maintaining that he had achieved all that he wished and that
he was tired – an unprecedented relinquishing of supreme power. He
had the vast fortified palace at Spalato (Split) prepared for this eventuality, and there he spent his last years, tending (as he claimed on his one
brief foray back into imperial politics) his cabbages.[111]

From the parking lot, the bulk of two large, round projecting towers
greet visitors to the site of Felix Romuliana, a token that this was not
just any old imperial residence. The retirement of former emperors had
proved a troublesome affair, as Maximian's misbehaviour before and after
the Carnuntum Conference in 308 had proven, and the towers are a
reminder of the military detachment that would have manned the palace
complex; though ostensibly their job would have been to maintain an
appropriate sense of dignity and the basic security of such an eminent
person, it might equally have been to keep an eye on any intrigues in
which he might become involved.

The wall on this side of the palace is almost complete, punctuated
by interval towers, presenting a formal obstacle for casual marauders,
though not perhaps much of an impediment for more organised forces.
The double-gateway has a further interior tower, for additional protection, and, inside a whole array of remains, in a huge area some 6 hectares
in extent,[112] presents itself: basilicas, temples and baths. Everything, in
short, that an ex-emperor could possibly desire, save the power that he
had voluntarily laid down. Now inaccessible on a hillside a kilometre
away, the track to it cut off by mud caused by heavy rain and snow, lies
the Margura, the mausoleum that Galerius constructed for his mother,
Romula, so that, during his declining years, he would be able to gaze
upon and visit her last resting place. The name of the palace, too, derives
from Galerius's sense of filial piety: Felix Romuliana ('the fortunate place
of Romula'), but it was never so lucky for him.

Galerius's rise to fortune had been rapid, one of the almost common-place success stories of the hard school of the Danubian armies in the 3rd century. Having begun his career as a herdsman, an occupation that he inherited from his father, Galerius sought better prospects in the army and fought with some distinction under Aurelius and Probus. When Diocletian established the Tetrarchy, Galerius was well known to him and was an obvious choice to be the Caesar, or junior Emperor, to Maximian in the East. His base was to be Illyricum and the Balkans.

In 305, when Maximian and Diocletian retired and Galerius became Augustus (together with Constantius I in the West), he chose his nephew Maximin Daia, another local lad, to be his Caesar. It was probably Galerius who had been responsible for persuading Diocletian to unleash the Great Persecution against the Christians in 303 and, now that he was answer-able to no one, his thirst for targeting them increased. He is, indeed, one of the principal targets of the Christian writer Lactantius in his *De Mortibus Persecutorum* ('On the Death of the Persecutors'). Yet Galerius's ambitions to rule the Empire as the pre-eminent among the four emperors, just as Diocletian had done, were ultimately thwarted by the upstart Constantine. Even Galerius's move to cut off Constantine's route to the top by appointing Licinius (another Moesian) as the second Augustus in 308 was unable to stop his young rival's rise. Galerius never lived to enjoy his peaceful retirement at Felix Romuliana, dying in 312. Once Constantine had eliminated all his rival emperors by 324, the Tetrarchy – and with it the tradition of emperors' retiring once they had reached an appropriate age – was never again revived or proposed.

The little site museum preserves a few architectural fragments; on one the name of the palace is inscribed in a wreath supported by two peacocks sporting crowns and, most notably, a beautiful bust of Galerius in imperial porphyry, its deep-purple colour lightly speckled in white. The Emperor seems stern, and the sketchy, stylised lines of his facial features give him a faintly surprised and suffering air, as though resigned to the trials that overcame him almost the moment he achieved supreme power.

The first section of the palace has a peristyle courtyard, off which leads the unmistakable shape of a basilica. The presence of churches on the site, despite Galerius's persecuting policy, is not a surprise, for the palace remained in use as a garrison and then a small town into the 7th century, and the former palace buildings were adapted, including through the construction of Christian places of worship.

Steps to the west lead up to a largish platform, which is indeed a pagan one, possibly a temple of Cybele.[113] To the side of this lies another hall with an apse, partly cut off, later reduced in size by the building of walls of a different stone from the left and right wings. The far wall of the town, opposite the main entrance, is less impressively preserved, just an earthwork rampart still standing, with only the gateway surviving in stone. Off from this the remains of a colonnade lead to a bulky rectangular structure on a podium with no apparent means of entrance.

With the premature death of Galerius, and the small town that grew up on the palace site suffering so severely from barbarian attacks from the 4th century onwards, Felix Romuliana never acquired the degree of permanency of settlements such as Singidunum, Vindobona or, for that matter, Diocletian's own palace at Salonae (Split). Galerius did at least come home to Felix Romuliana in death, for he was interred in a second mausoleum at Margura, next to his mother. As we leave, a mist descends and a haunting otherworldly lament wafts in from somewhere amongst the hills, sweet, yet chilling. It is probably the song of a shepherdess, but it seems instead to be a lament on the pain endured by an emperor, and the power that brought him no joy.

The road from Serbia passes east along the Danube into Bulgaria not far from the small town of Kula, about 30 kilometres east of Felix Romuliana. The run-down main street is made more attractive by a carpet of snow and swirling wind-blown flakes that promise an even deeper covering. Alongside its main square sits the remains of the fort of Castra Martis, a military station on the ancient road from Naissus to Bononia (Vidin). It never housed a large garrison, nor was it in itself of huge importance, but the loneliness and grandeur of its ruins in such an unlikely setting are one of the secret gems of the Danubian *limes*. Its sides 30 metres long, the square fort in its current form dates from around the late 3rd or early 4th century. Inside the bulky curtain walls, two rows of barracks with a central pier run down the middle. One's eye, though, is immediately drawn to the angle tower to the south-east, which soars to more than 16 metres high in one part, probably lacking only a metre or so of its original height. For three-quarters of its diameter more of the tower's top portions are missing, and the great ruined silhouette pushes out dramatically against the snow-laden sky. It is one of the most striking pieces of military architecture on the frontier.

Castra Martis's efforts to remain a discrete and untroubled garrison fortress were rudely brought to an end in 408, with the first serious irruption of the Huns across the Danube into the Empire. Pushing forward from a homeland somewhere in central Asia, the Huns were involved in a complex movement of peoples that was part domino effect, as one group pushed forward in search of new lands and propelled those in front of them further from the steppes and towards the Mediterranean littoral, and part the magnetic pull of the Roman Empire, which attracted 'barbarian' groups with its promise of easy wealth and an end to the constant struggle for land and food to which they had grown accustomed.

Attempts to link the Huns to the 'Xiongnu' on China's northern frontier in the 1st century BC are somewhat tenuous, but do reveal that the challenges facing the Roman Empire were not dissimilar to those experienced by its late Han Chinese counterpart. Wherever they came from, the Huns became the bogeymen of late antiquity. Ammianus Marcellinus describes them as squat, with thick necks and so ugly that they seemed like figures crudely carved out of wood.[114] They cut the cheeks of their boys to create patterns of scars, and their legs were bowed from constant life on horseback, so that they found it uncomfortable to dismount and walk. Of course, Ammianus most likely had little direct experience of the Huns himself, and his descriptions are purely conventional ones. Yet, real or not, these attributes were melded with a reputation for ferocity that, once they had united under the leadership of Attila, made them the barbarians whom the Romans most feared.

In 395, they had given notice of their future intentions when they rode around the Black Sea and descended on Georgia, Armenia and even into Syria. Saint Jerome in his Bethlehem monastery referred to them as 'wolves of the North', who ranged so widely and rapidly that no one knew where to expect their arrival next.[115] By 400 the Huns were led by Uldin, who is first recorded for his killing in that year of Gainas, the refugee Gothic former *magister militum* and effective head of the government at Constantinople, who had fallen foul of an anti-barbarian coup in the city. In 404–5, Uldin crossed the Danube and ravaged part of Moesia, and then, three years later, he crossed in greater force, capturing Castra Martis, before his raiding band was broken up by a Roman army that was rushed to the scene and he was forced back across the Danube.

Little more was heard of the Huns for some decades, as they seem to have expended their energies on consolidating control over other tribes in central and eastern Europe, rather than on confronting the Romans directly. It was around this time that the teenage Aëtius spent some years as a hostage amongst them, and his subsequent use of them as mercenaries in the 420s may actually have revived their interest in the gain to be had from plundering or blackmailing the Roman state.[116] By the 430s they were led by Ruga, who had expanded Hunnish control over a large area based on a heartland in central Hungary before he was, according to a dramatic account given by the Church historian Socrates, struck dead by lightning.[117] If it was divine retribution for his crimes, then God may later have had cause to reconsider, for Ruga was succeeded by his nephews Bleda and Attila, the latter of whom would become infamous as the *Flagellum Dei* ('scourge of God').

The pretext for the brothers' assault, and the start of a fifteen-year campaign that would almost bring the Empire to its knees, seems to have been a little freelance looting on the part of the Bishop of Margum, who was alleged to have connived in the ransacking of certain royal tombs across the Danube. They were probably not Hunnish graves, but it represented an intrusion into their domain that Attila and Bleda chose not to tolerate. In response, they led a great force south of the Danube, capturing and sacking Viminacium (Kostolac), Singidunum (Belgrade) and a great number of other towns, including Margum itself, whose gates the treacherous bishop left open in return for being allowed to escape. The Huns finally turned back, mollified by the promise of a satisfying stream of tribute.

The respite was strictly temporary, and before long a vast swathe of territory to the south of the Danube was laid waste and the area fell so much under the dominion of the Huns that Attila later claimed that the boundary between the Hunnish and Roman territory lay not, as it traditionally had, on the Danube, but at Naissus, some three days' journey to the south. And so it remained until 449. In that year, an embassy from Attila to Theodosius II arrived in Constantinople.[118] The return embassy included the historian and diplomat Priscus, who left a detailed account of his journey (in a more general history of the Empire of which, unfortunately, only fragments survive).[119] His description of Attila's headquarters, which have been variously located in Hungary[120] or even close to Kula,[121] contains the surprising revelation that it included a bath complex, built in stone by a Roman architect captured at Sirmium.[122]

The impression that Attila's was no mere crude encampment, but had achieved a level of sophistication that belies the Huns' reputation for gross barbarity, is reinforced by Priscus's encounter with a merchant from Viminacium. Captured by the Huns in the recent wars, he had set up business again on the Hunnish side of the *limes* and, even though he had amassed enough wealth to buy his freedom, was doing sufficiently well that he chose not to return to Roman territory and face the oppressive taxation and capricious bureaucracy that he insisted he would find there.[123]

It is just 35 kilometres north-east from Kula to Vidin, which was the settlement of Bononia in Roman times, its Latin name sharing a root with its much more famous cousins of Bologna in Italy and Boulogne in France. The Ottoman-era Baba Vida fortress, its rounded towers and deep moat dominating the riverside section of the old town, incorporates what remains of Bononia – indeed, at the base of the north-west wall traces of much older masonry may hint at the original Roman fort that stood on the site to protect this stretch of the Danube *limes*.

Half an hour to the east along a loop in the river lay Ratiaria, once a legionary fortress, now surviving in much-reduced circumstances near the small village of Arcar, some 25 kilometres to the south-east of Vidin. It started life as a garrison camp in the late 1st century AD, and after Trajan's conquest of Dacia was demilitarised and raised to the rank of a *colonia* as Colonia Ulpia Traiana Ratiaria. After the evacuation of Dacia in the 270s, Ratiaria became the capital of the newly created province of Dacia Ripensis on the south bank of the Danube, and once again received a garrison, this time the XIII Gemina legion. In 441 it was captured and destroyed by the Huns, but restored in the late 5th century under Anastasius, in whose honour it took the name Anastasiana Ratiaria. It was finally overrun by the Avars in 586, following which it was abandoned.

The only evidence today from the road of the formerly prosperous town is a café named 'Ratiaria'. Here enquiries about the ancient fortress are met with blank, self-conscious looks; finally one old lady has no idea about a Roman site, but wonders if we want the place 'where the gold-seekers are digging'. To the north of the road, in dense undergrowth, we still find no trace of the Roman remains, but encounter a boy of about fourteen, dragging behind him a dilapidated-looking metal detector; the contraption itself, rust-caked and mud-spattered, seems to merit the label of antiquity. He rather cagily dismisses the notion of a Roman site and directs us in another direction. Here an aged shepherd, his face lined by years in the outdoors performing an honest occupation, at last knows what we are looking for. He himself had worked as a driver on the excavation of Ratiaria in the 1980s, and had transported a whole sarcophagus down to the national museum in Sofia.

Back on the other side of the road, up a low, sloping side-road, an open area stretches out besides a terrace of single-storey houses. It seems composed of a series of small grassy hummocks stretching out as far as the eye can see. Walking a short way into this field, it is clear that we are not the first visitors. The whole place is pitted with holes and trenches, some shallow, others metres deep. The hummocks we saw at first are simply the areas where the 'gold-seekers' of whom the old lady spoke have not yet dug. The ground is soft underfoot as we step over the spoil of these illicit excavations, the brown mud disturbed by their works caking our boots.

Ratiaria was researched properly in the 1980s, particularly in the south-western corner, where several *insulae* were dug up, including a bath complex, and sections of the 4th-century wall and fortifications were revealed.[124] But in 1992, in the wake of the collapse of the communist regime in Bulgaria, the money for such research dried up. Once the official archaeologists had packed their bags and left the site, unofficial digs began on a grand scale. The result was the total destruction of an antique city, with trenches and holes sunk throughout the area of the original excavations and across an area many times its size – which did reveal, incidentally, that estimates of the area covered by Ratiaria gained from aerial photography were more or less correct.

Everywhere now there are bits of pot and tile, the remains of everyday life in Ratiaria considered by the looters not attractive enough for the international market in stolen antiquities. Here and there a fragment of green marble and a larger piece of white-flecked marble about 15 centi-metres long pokes out from the side of a robber trench. Occasionally pieces of stonework protrude, largely undisturbed, for the skeleton of the city did not interest the treasure-seekers, but only the flesh they could easily strip from its bones. One part seems to be the remains of a rectangular building with four or five courses of stone, but it seems like a stranded survivor amongst the scene of utter devastation.

The pockmarks of the illicit dig stretch for more than a kilometre and some of the trenches seem relatively recent. The destruction of the Roman city stands as one of Europe's cultural disgraces and it is hard not to form the impression that, after destruction by the Huns and the Avars, Ratiaria has suffered its third and most comprehensive sacking only in the last fifteen years.

The Huns were by no means the last nomadic group to arise on the central Asian steppes, sweep westwards and create havoc on the Roman frontier. The Avars first appeared in the area of modern Ukraine around the 550s, viewed by the Byzantines as potentially useful allies in the volatile mix of nomads swirling around the northern Balkans. They were soon apprised of their mistake as the Avars smashed first the Kutrigurs and Utrigurs, and then in 567 proceeded to destroy the Gepids.[125] The Avars' own Lombard allies, afraid that they were to be next, migrated en masse southwards into Italy, knocking over at a stroke the Byzantine control of the peninsula that had been so painfully won in the Gothic Wars just fifteen years previously.

The Avars did not rest on their laurels, pushing south over the Danube

Hadrian's Wall, near Vercovicium (Housesteads) fort, Britannia

Hadrian's Wall, looking towards
Housesteads Crags

The *mithraeum* at
Carrawburgh, Britannia

The chalet-style
barracks at
Cilurnum (Chesters)
fort, Britannia

Interior ditches and wall, Rutupiae (Richborough) fort, Britannia

South wall, Rutupiae (Richborough)

Ditch and embankment of the Antonine Wall at Watling Lodge, Britannia

The Porta Nigra, Augusta Treverorum (Trier), Gallia Belgica

Pfäffikon fort, Germania Superior

Reconstructed watchtower and palisade at Grab, Germania Superior

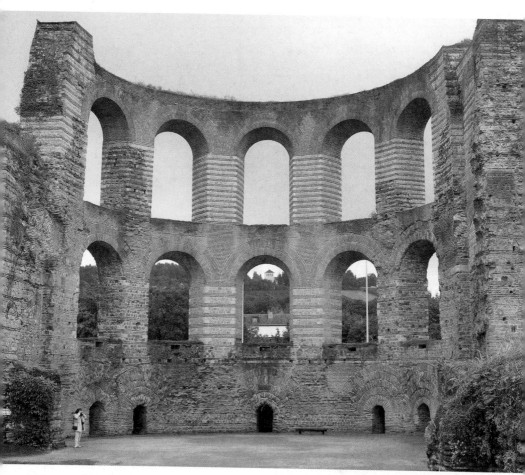

Caldarium of the Kaiserthermen,
Augusta Treverorum (Trier),
Gallia Belgica

Roman wall tower, Bodobriga
(Boppard), Germania Superior

Reconstructed city gate, Colonia Ulpia Traiana (Xanten), Germania Inferior

Reconstructed west wall and tower, Pfünz, Raetia

The *porta praetoria* at Castra Regina (Regensburg), Raetia

Statue of Saint Severinus, Boiotro (Passau) fort, Noricum

Section of the Raetian wall in Mahdholz woods, Raetia

Castra Martis (Kula) fort, Moesia Superior

The Heidentor, Carnuntum (Petronell), Pannonia Superior

Decumanus maximus of Nicopolis-ad-Istrum, Thracia / Moesia Inferior

Porphyry bust of Galerius from Felix Romuliana, Moesia Superior

Metope from the Tropaeum Traiani (Adamclisi), Moesia Inferior

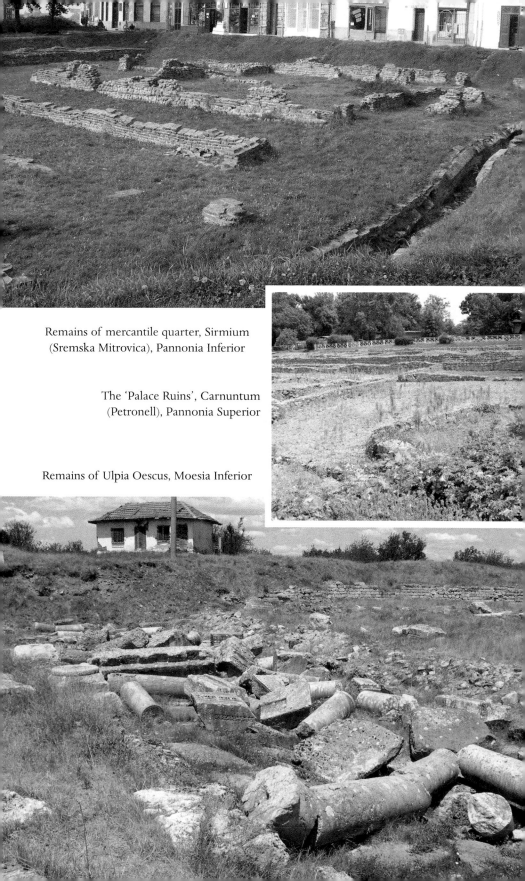

Remains of mercantile quarter, Sirmium
(Sremska Mitrovica), Pannonia Inferior

The 'Palace Ruins', Carnuntum
(Petronell), Pannonia Superior

Remains of Ulpia Oescus, Moesia Inferior

Modern monumental
sculpture of
Decebalus, Dacia

Remains of Roman
bridge, Drobeta
(Turnu-Severin), Dacia

Dacian temple, Sarmizegetusa Regia, Dacia

Amphitheatre, Porolissum, Dacia

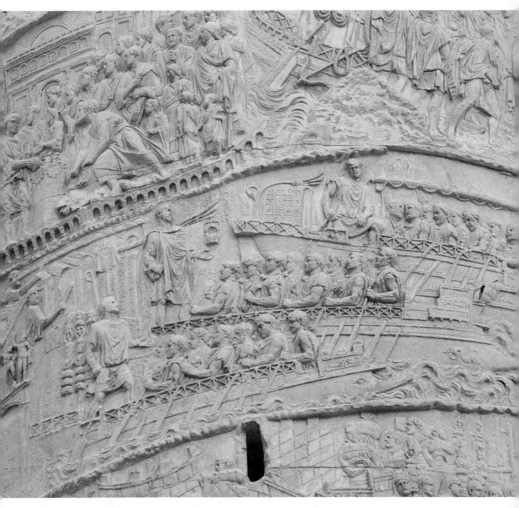

The Romans cross the Danube. Trajan's Column, Rome

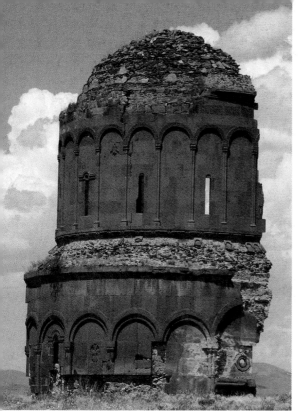

Church of Our Saviour, Ani, Armenia

Ruins at Satala (Sadagh), Cappadocia

The *Hierothesion* at Nemrud Dagh, Cappadocia

Palace of the
Comneni,
(Trebizond)
Trabzon,
Cappadocia

Frescoes at Soumela
monastery, Cappadocia

Roman bridge at
Cendere, Cappadocia

The 'catapult', Edessa (Sanliurfa), Osroene

Church of Meryemanna in the Tur Abdin, Mesopotamia

and capturing Sirmium in 581–2, thus providing them with a bridgehead from which they could raid at will into the Balkan plains. Their expansion also displaced the Slavs, who had occupied the plain between the lower Danube and the Carpathians in the 6th century, but who now moved southwards in earnest, switching from small-scale raids from their forest hideouts to full-scale ravaging of the southern Balkans. Only in 591 did a peace treaty with the Sassanid Persians enable Emperor Maurice to switch his military resources westwards and begin to repair the much-breached frontier.[126]

The renewed Sassanid invasion in 602 undermined this policy and the Avars resumed their expansion southwards towards the Peloponnese. In 623, Heraclius, desperate for peace on his western flank in order to reverse the devastating Persian advances that had overrun almost the whole of the East, arranged a parley with the Avar leader, the kagan, in Thrace. The Avar ruler, scenting weakness, instead tried to capture the Byzantine Emperor and Heraclius was forced to beat a humiliating retreat to Constantinople, and then watch the Avars as they ravaged the suburbs of the capital. Only a timely payment of 200,000 numismata per year was able to buy off the barbarians. It was not enough, and three years later the kagan moved on the imperial city once more, this time orchestrated with a Persian assault from the east. With Heraclius campaigning far away in Armenia, it looked as if the Empire was finished. But the Avars' attempts at a seaborne assault on the city wall using light canoes were broken up by the Byzantine fleet, and their confused bid to ferry the Persians over ended in a similar disaster. Disenchanted at being robbed of a prize that seemed so easily within their grasp, the Slavs in the Avar force revolted, and the whole army withdrew from Constantinople in disarray.

The Slavs themselves were to prove rather more durable than the Avars, who were finally smashed by Charlemagne's Franks in the early 9th century. They formed part of a second wave of barbarian invasions that threatened to overwhelm the Eastern Roman Empire in the 500s, just as it appeared to have weathered the storm that overcame the western provinces in the previous century. It is possible that there were Slavs in the multi-ethnic confederacy that made up the Hunnish Empire, and some allusions in Priscus (who visited Attila's court in 448) have been taken to refer to them, such as the use of *monoxyles*, or boats scooped out from hollow logs.[127]

By the 6th century, Justinian was having to deal with a group called the Sclavini (most likely the Slavs) who streamed into the Balkan peninsula from their lands north of the Danube;[128] by 528 they were menacing

Thrace, and a particularly severe raid in 550–1 even threatened Constantinople. Tiberius (578–82) was so desperate that he enlisted the kagan Baian of the Avars to push the Sclavini out of the Balkan provinces. Despite cutting a destructive swathe through the Balkans and looting and sacking Slav outposts, the Avars were unsuccessful in their main mission, and within a decade were making common cause with the Sclavini in causing mayhem south of the Danube. Throughout eastern Pannonia, Moesia and Thrace the Sclavini came to stay, forming the nucleus of the modern Slavic-speaking countries in those areas.

In the east they merged with the Bulgars, who had first appeared in the guise of the Kutrigurs and Utrigurs during the reign of Zeno and who were to form the principal challenge to the re-establishment of Byzantine dominance in Thrace during the early medieval period. Although the Byzantines managed to recover the southern Balkans from the Slav tribes by the 8th century, in the areas of modern Serbia and Bulgaria they ever afterwards had to contend with Slav tribal confeder- acies that ultimately coalesced, in the early Middle Ages, into kingdoms. If there was a victory, it was a cultural one, for in the end the Slav king- doms – such as Serbia, and most particularly Bulgaria – came to form part of a 'Byzantine commonwealth', influenced in religion, language and expectations by the norms of Constantinople. Ultimately this Byzantine inflection was transmitted even to Russia, which was unashamedly able to declare itself the 'Third Rome' after the fall of Constantinople in 1453.

Moesia Inferior

Around 150 kilometres south-east down the Danube from Vidin, and about 40 kilometres north of modern Pleven, lies the legionary fort of Oescus. It served as one of the two legionary bases for Moesia Inferior, whose western border lay just to the east of Ratiaria (Arcar). To travel along this stretch of the river is truly to take a step back in time. The main roads become an obstacle course of ruts and potholes, the prin- cipal traffic on them ceases to be motorised, as horse-drawn carts predominate, and on chimneys and other architectural high-points, fami- lies of storks lazily watch the world go slowly by. Oescus itself sits on a low plateau set back a few kilometres from the Danube, and was ori- ginally a Thracian settlement, referred to by the geographer Ptolemy as Oescus Triballorum.[129]

The first Roman fortification in stone may have been built here under Domitian about 85–6, at the time of his invasion of Dacia, or else at the start of the 2nd century, shortly before Oescus's garrison (the V Macedonica) departed following Trajan's more successful Dacian campaign. The city, now a civilian settlement, was made a *colonia* by Trajan, and took on his family name of Ulpius to become Ulpia Oescus. It underwent rapid expansion, though it suffered badly during the Gothic invasion of 250–1, and its wall needed to be repaired afterwards. Within twenty years or so, however, Dacia had been evacuated and Oescus got back its legion – much, it must be presumed, to the relief of its inhabitants.

There is little to be seen of the walls now. Backing onto their original location, towards the main gate, lies the 'extra-mural' complex, constructed, as its name suggests, beyond the original city perimeter. It is a massive collection of largely rectangular rooms, with two apsed chambers to one end. The outside walls are solid and bulky, but the inside ones have internal corridors penetrated by pipes. It is unclear what purpose these served, although one plausible theory is to allow for extra ventilation.

The first significant buildings visible in the eastern sector of the city are the baths, built in the 2nd century, of which the only restored section is a rectangular room, bordered by two smaller ones, in which a square stone basin sits. On the day of our visit, the area around is being cleared by teams of local ladies, for a television team is visiting the next day to do a feature on Oescus, and this high-level visit has prompted some fitful hoeing in the almost forty-degree heat.

In the city centre, to the south of what is probably the forum, lie the remains of the Temple of Fortuna, one of Oescus's principal public buildings. Once a splendid affair, some 30 metres long with a Corinthian portico, it was erected under Commodus, but is now utterly ruined. Whether it was destroyed by raiding Goths or as part of one of the outbreaks of temple-sacking by Christians in the late 4th century is unclear, but whichever party was responsible, the job was thorough. Fractured columns lie in heaps, shattered architraves keeping company with bits of pediment and smaller piles of inscrutable fragments. The sole area that retains any sense of order was in fact cleared in the 12th century to create space on which to construct a church. Out of the devastation peep floral designs, garlands, Medusa heads and eagles, all melancholy reminders of the temple at the height of its splendour.

Another structure nearby, more than 70 metres long, occupied a whole city block. There remain just the traces of hypocausts with brick piers and an apsed room more than 20 metres long. Here was found a mosaic

showing a scene from the *Achaeans* by the playwright Menander. The
chance nature of the survival of ancient manuscripts is highlighted by
the fact that, until the mosaic depiction was discovered, the play itself
was totally unknown (and its text has been completely lost). To the
north lies the forum itself, where huge sections of columns and capitals mark the portico, and beside it the council chamber. This would
have been a place humming with life, but apart from the women clearing
the weeds beside the baths, Oescus's only inhabitants today are a couple
of startled rabbits, which at our approach make a break for the city's
gate.

At the edge of the excavated area of the city, a low mound gives a
good view over the plain that leads down to the Danube a few kilometres away. It was here that Constantine came in July 328 to inaugurate
a new bridge across the Danube, linking Oescus with the bridgehead
fort at Sucidava in modern Romania.[130] It was a massive undertaking, at
2,400 metres long the longest bridge in classical antiquity, and indicates
that communication with (and possible conquest of) the northern bank
was still very much on the Roman agenda. It coincided with a general
strengthening of the Danube *limes*, which was experiencing a period of
relative stability between the storms of the mid-3rd century invasions
and the disastrous Gothic incursions a century later.

Fifty kilometres further east along the river – but, with the lament-
able state of the roads in the region, a much longer journey than one
might suppose – lies the legionary camp at Novae.[131] For roughly the
first two decades of its career, from AD 46 to 69, it housed the VIII
Augusta legion, but after that unit's support for Otho during the 'Year
of the Four Emperors' the legion was transferred away to the Rhineland,
where it then spent the best part of three centuries based at Argentorate
(Strasbourg). Its replacement was the I Italica legion, which in turn resided
for almost 300 years at its Novae base.

Originally a Thracian settlement – of which nothing survives – Novae
was situated at a strategic road junction and in a position to dominate
one of the easier crossings over the Danube. Together with Oescus, it
marks one of the densest concentrations of legionary force anywhere
in the Empire – at least once the double legionary fortresses had been
abolished – and is a strong testament to the strategically vital nature of
the Danube *limes*.

A recent influx of archaeological investment in Bulgaria, much of it
the fruit of European Union funding, has seen Novae build a smart new
glass-domed visitor centre, the fort's most significant development in
one and a half millennia. The main entrance to the site, through the

camp's west gate, was originally a simple affair. In the 4th century, however, gate-towers were added, making it a much grander portal – the largest surviving one in Moesia – its outline still clear amid the carpet of grass and encroaching shrubs that threaten to engulf it. Along part of the curtain wall that joins onto the gate, large holes and indentations betray a vaulted passage, which might be used by the defenders as a sally port to catch attackers unawares and assail them from behind. The path through the site then diverts slightly into a small wood, before cutting north back into the fortress, which lies on a slight incline running down to the Danube. A chaotic jumble of walls, probably of several stages of construction, represents the officers' housing, which was replaced in the early 4th century by some kind of public building and later by a church.

The most splendid surviving vestige of ancient Novae is the *valetudinarium*, the hospital complex, a series of rectangular rooms, their walls restored and consolidated to above a metre high, arrayed around a central (presumably colonnaded) courtyard.[132] With the Danube just a hundred or so metres away and the opposite, Romanian bank, lined with a thin screen of trees, it seems an idyllic setting in which to spend some time recovering from wounds or fever. Beside it, a quick scramble down the 3-metre slope formed by the archaeologists' trenching to uncover the site, are the baths, solidly constructed but with little to indicate their original purpose, save a rectangular stone basin. In the corner of the hospital complex, just by the Danube, is the toilet, which must have had alarming consequences for the legionary water supply if its outflow went straight into the river.

A *municipium* from the time of Marcus Aurelius, Novae first experienced the uncertain times that lay ahead in the middle of the 3rd century, when it saw some fighting associated with the Gothic invasion under Cniva in 250–1. However, it remained throughout a legionary fortress, so the inhabitants of the town that grew up around it must have drawn some comfort from the presence of the troops, while less militarised parts of Pannonia and Moesia were easy prey for barbarian raiding.

Throughout this time, the I Italica stayed at Novae, although units of it had previously taken part in a series of external campaigns, from Trajan's conquest of Dacia in 101–6 to his later Parthian War, and possibly in Hadrian's suppression of the Bar Kochba revolt in Palestine in 132–5. By the end of its career at Novae, the legion had been split, with a portion of it based further east, at the Danube fleet base of Sexaginta Prista (modern Ruse). The pushing of the frontier of the Dacian province 50 kilometres eastward beyond the River Olt under Caracalla then almost created a situation where Novae, south of the Danube, would no longer have been on the frontier. But the Roman holdings in Dacia did not advance beyond its new *Limes Transalutanus*,[133] and Novae remained a military settlement.

Across the modern main road is the southern part of the camp, where the remains are, if anything, more extensive, sitting in a large, almost rectangular clearing about 150 x 200 metres. The portion nearest the road was originally the site of more baths,[134] but these were later supplanted by a huge Christian basilica, one of the largest in the Balkans at over 45 metres in length and about 25 metres or so in width,[135] a bulk that is impressive, even in its current overgrown state. A rank of brick stumps marks the base of the columns that delineated the aisles, but little else of the internal structure of the building is discernible. Novae was indeed the seat of a bishopric in the 5th and 6th centuries,[136] and to warrant a basilica as grand as this, the civilian population of the town must have been reasonably substantial.

Beyond these remains lie an almshouse and a pilgrims' hostel, only the outline remaining in a couple of stone courses, but their existence implies that the grand ecclesiastical complex attracted Christian visitors from far afield. Just visible in one corner, the remains of a furnace survive from the baths submerged beneath the Christian development. Next to the main basilica is a much more modest church, the 'Small basilica', only 12 metres or so in length; in the grass beside it pokes up a column on which the inscription 'SS MARI[A]' is just visible, possibly evidence of a church dedicated to Mary. Off to the east lie the remains of the *principia* of the original legionary camp; now an undifferentiated collection of stones, but a reminder that, whatever its subsequent growth, Novae always remained at heart a military centre.[137]

By the late 5th century the Roman hold on Moesia was growing weak. Already in 441 the Huns had passed through, devastating the area. Although the Hunnish Empire had collapsed into fratricidal squabbling following Attila's death in 453, the Romans were still not able to reassert full control over the area. Consequently, from 476 until 483, Novae served as the capital of the Ostrogothic king, Theoderic the Amal.[138] Once ensconced here, the Goths threatened the north–south routes over the Haemus mountains (the Stara Planina), allowing easy intervention in Thrace and permitting Theoderic a little judicious meddling in imperial politics to advance his cause even further. His large, well-organised barbarian kingdom based to the south of the Danube posed a potentially fatal challenge to the eastern Roman government, and Zeno came up with a cunning and mutually satisfactory ruse to persuade the Ostrogoths to move elsewhere.

It had been more than a decade since Odovacar, the Scirian general, had taken control of Italy. After his coup in 476, he had chosen not to elevate a new emperor; the dizzying succession of ineffectual imperial candidates had by the 470s become something of a nuisance for their barbarian sponsors. Instead, wishing to rule directly himself, but still conscious of diplomatic niceties, he despatched the imperial regalia back to Constantinople, in effect acknowledging Zeno as the sole Emperor, and implying that Odovacar ruled Italy on his behalf.

Zeno, however, muddied the issue by replying that there was still a legitimate Western Emperor, Julius Nepos, who had been pushed out of Italy in 475 and still skulked in the Illyrian province that had been the domain of his father, Count Marcellinus. But Nepos died in 480, and so there was then no obstacle to Zeno's despatch of Theoderic and his Ostrogoths into Italy. The campaign was prolonged, initially held up by the Gepids, who obstructed the Gothic advance near the modern city of Vukovar. But by 493 Theoderic was victorious and had Odovacar murdered at a banquet, displaying his grasp of table manners by cutting his guest in half with a single blow of his sword. More importantly, from Zeno's point of view, it opened the way for the reoccupation of the northern Balkans.

By Justinian's day, a quarter of a century later, Novae was back in eastern Roman hands, and, according to Procopius, new fortifications were built, though there is little evidence of these later defensive structures on the ground. Although most of the Christian buildings date from the late 5th or 6th centuries, and so the city was clearly occupied at the time, it seems that by the 7th century the effort required to hold it against waves of Slav, Bulgar and Avar invaders was just too great, and it was abandoned.

Around 50 kilometres south of the Danube at Novae, and lying just inside the province of Thrace at the foot of the Haemus mountains, the town of Nicopolis-ad-Istrum was founded by Trajan as the 'city of victory' in 102, in celebration of the battle that brought an end to the first Dacian War. It was part of a programme intended to strengthen the urban framework and economy of the Thracian plain. From here roads lead northwards to Novae and to Sexaginta Prista and southwards across the Stara Planina to Philippopolis (Plovdiv) in Thrace. It also stood on a road that led east–west to Odessos (Varna) on the Black Sea. To this day it stands on much more accessible routes than the poorly maintained arteries that sluggishly link the majority of towns along the Danube, and here, unlike the tourist deserts of Oescus or Novae, the occasional accent from Manchester or Manhattan is to be heard.

Close to the modern town of Nikup, in whose main square a few rather dusty and neglected column bases sit in a tiny sculpture garden, the remains of Nicopolis lie near a bend in the Rositsa river, down a country lane that is more pothole than thoroughfare. The main approach is through the remnants of the ancient city's western gate, up the former *decumanus*, its wide slabs smoothed with age. The area to the left is a combination of slightly overgrown grass and trees, with a few mounds and hummocks marking what must have been the southern edge of the city.

A collection of fallen columns, altars and the lids of monumental sarcophagi litter the ground, inscribed in Greek. Away from the influence of the Danube-based army, for whom Latin long persisted as the language of command, this part of Thrace was firmly in the Greek-speaking portion of the Empire, a tendency exacerbated by the pull of the old Greek settlements of the Black Sea coast, which were only a couple of days' journey away. Almost every educated Roman was expected to show some knowledge of Greek, and many were in practice bilingual. From the reign of Hadrian, this tendency became even more pronounced.

The process was not a two-way one, and many in the Greek-speaking East spent their careers, if they were not in the central government, without displaying any evident knowledge of Latin. At many of the church councils in the 4th and 5th centuries the business was clearly done in Greek, and the minority of bishops who turned up from the West required interpreters if they could not, as was becoming more common by then, speak (or at least understand) Greek.[139] In the early 6th century, Justinian recognised the inevitable and decided that the language of governance should henceforth be Greek. It probably did not help his cause in trying to resecure the lost provinces of Italy, North Africa and Spain that they had been (and still were) Latin-speaking territories, and therefore their acquisition by a new set of Byzantine officials might seem all the more alien, and not like the restoration of the old Roman Empire at all. With the loss of Carthage to the Arabs in 698, the Empire held almost no land that had been Latin-speaking in the 5th century, while the Arab conquest of the Syriac-speaking lands on its eastern border (and the Copts of Egypt) meant that it had become a wholly Greek affair.

Accentuating this imperial trend to Greekness, Nicopolis-ad-Istrum was established by Trajan not as a *colonia* or a *municipium*, but as a Hellenistic foundation, mirroring the constitutions of the ancient Greek city-states of the coast (and of Greece proper), rather than being organised on strictly speaking Roman lines.[140] Founded on a low plateau, it was laid out on a traditional grid pattern, with its north-eastern corner truncated as it sloped down to the River Rositsa, forming a rather irregular pentagonal shape. Only the central section around the forum (or *agora*) has been investigated, and an odd-shaped enclosure to the west of the main walls, revealed by aerial photography, might or might not be a fort.[141]

At the point where the *decumanus* crosses the *cardo*, the main excavated area is a large rectangle, scattered with stones, part overgrown with grass and weeds and bordered by straggly copses of low trees. Huge sections of architrave inscribed with floral decorations (and in just a few cases with fragments of inscription) lie everywhere, mostly sculpted from the limestone available in the nearby quarries at Honitsa. The architraves must have formed part of the portico of the forum, and much of this is missing. It seems hard to believe that such huge sections of stone could have been robbed, so sections of it must still lie buried.

Around the northern edge of the forum, a strip of the portico is more intact, with a few pieces of column still lying in place. Ahead, at the east, four great Corinthian columns rear up, forming a *propylaeum*, the monumental entrance to the forum. An inscription revealed that it was set up by Nicopolis in 145 in honour of Antoninus Pius and Marcus Aurelius. Behind lay the council house of the city, the *bouleuterion*, the remains of whose decrees, set in stone, sit now beneath a little shelter, as though stacked and filed in neat rows for easier consultation. The councillors' chambers and their seating, in contrast, lie mostly ruined.

To the south of the *bouleuterion* are the remains of a little theatre or *odeon*, whose orchestra was only a little over 9 metres in diameter. The seating is long gone, and only the semicircle of the raised platform on which it stood survives, rising about a metre from the ground, which makes it most unlikely that the place was ever used for gladiatorial spectacles, as it would have left the audience dangerously exposed. Behind are the ruins of shops and taverns, a few doorways still standing, one of them, in marble, totally unattached to any supporting wall, and looking like a ghostly portal into another world. A little way beyond the *odeon*, the excavated portion of the site peters out. Low mounds from which protrude telltale pieces of stone and the detritus of shattered columns, all tangled in increasingly thick undergrowth, betray the presence of as-yet-uncovered sections of the city.

The evidence of inscriptions from Nicopolis seems to indicate a heavy oriental influence, with immigrants coming predominantly from the eastern portion of the Empire. Votive dedications commemorate cults identified with the East, such as Serapis, Mithras, Magna Mater and Priapus. Interestingly, no Christian churches have so far been discovered here, although this may simply represent mere chance, with so much of the site yet to be excavated.

Already raised to the status of a *municipium* by Hadrian, Nicopolis received further imperial favours under Septimius Severus, who transferred it from the provincial authority of Thrace to that of Moesia,[142] and visited the city in 202, receiving in honour of his stay there a huge gift of 700,000 sesterces from the 'grateful' citizenry. By the mid-3rd century, however, prosperity gave way to uncertainty and then to fear, as the Goths laid siege to Nicopolis in 250 and 270, though they failed to take it on both occasions. There is some evidence that buildings begun at this time were simply not finished, a clear indication of economic retraction.[143] In the troubled times after the Gothic invasion of 376 and the Roman defeat at Adrianople in 378, the countryside in this area of Moesia must have been devastated and the towns, even if they held out, were cut off from their rural hinterlands. Justinian may have ordered the refortification of the city, though, and a bishop is certainly attested in 458.[144] But it seems that the population gradually drifted 20 kilometres southwards to a more defensible position at Veliko Turnovo, where a Byzantine fortress survived into the reign of Heraclius (610–41), and which was later to become one of the most important centres of the Bulgarian kingdom in the Middle Ages.

Around 70 kilometres to the north-east of Nicopolis, the town of Abritus (Razgrad) – some 60 kilometres south of the Danube *limes* – saw the Empire's worst disaster for three centuries, with the first-ever death of a reigning emperor in combat. Decius was almost sixty when he seized power in 249, making him one of the oldest men to assume the purple, but his death just two years later left him far down in the league of ages achieved by emperors.[145] A senator and one who had achieved a modicum of military success on the Danube, Decius might, with better luck and the continued support of the army, have built a coalition of factions that would have put an end to the revolving-door nature of 3rd-century imperial politics. As a token of his intent (ill-omened as it turned out), he took the additional name of Trajan, as if to show his hopes of bringing glory to the Empire to equal those won by the great warrior-emperor more than a century before.

Cniva, the first leader of the Goths whose name is known, headed a host that crossed the Danube in 249. At first trying their hand at plundering Novae, the Goths were repelled by the governor of Moesia Inferior, one Trebonianus Gallus, and they then moved southwards to

Philippopolis (Plovdiv). After Decius's army was badly beaten north-east
of the city, its commander, Lucius Priscus, the governor of Thrace, gave
the city up. Cniva was left in possession of his prize all winter before
seeking the next spring to push back north across the Danube. Decius
had ordered the crossing points to be secured to prevent Cniva escaping
into *barbaricum*.

At Abritus (modern Razgrad) he cornered his quarry. The Goths hid
a portion of their force in a swamp, and the Romans, having defeated a
section of the remaining barbarians, advanced incautiously through the
marshy ground, believing it to be undefended. Weighed down by their
armour and utterly surprised, Decius and most of his army were cut to
pieces. The Emperor's body was never found, nor that of his son
Herennius Etruscus. The loss of an emperor for the first time in battle
created a dangerous moment of crisis. The Moesian legions, casting
about for a new ruler, proclaimed Trebonianus Gallus, the same man
who had earlier had some success against the Goths at Novae. There
were, understandably, some nasty rumours that he might have played a
part in Decius's downfall, but to allay these he acknowledged his predecessor's younger son, Hostilianus, as Caesar along with, for the sake
of family harmony, his own son Volusianus.

The Abritus fort, set some way back from the frontier itself, was in
fact built in the late 3rd or early 4th century,[146] and so was not there at
all when Decius met his untimely end. The communist-era authorities
in Razgrad thoughtfully permitted the building of an enormous pharmaceutical factory right across the site, slicing it in two, making
excavations next to impossible over much of it and gifting it with the
eyesore of a 60-metre-high steam-billowing tower.

However, much of the wall survives, solid and thick, typical later
imperial work, originally 3 metres thick and 12 metres high, with the
regulation four gates at each of the compass points. Only two gates are
in place now, and of the interior buildings the most important is a large
town house, grand enough to be that of a leading citizen, its reconstructed walls stretching for 400 square metres or more, and with an
apsidal room that may have been an audience chamber of some kind.
A few hundred metres from the site's central area, overlooked by a set
of ramshackle chalets, an indistinct scatter of ruins marks a site that
was in use first as a palaeo-Christian basilica and then as an early medieval
Bulgarian church.[147]

Back along the Danube and an hour or so east of Novae, Ruse is
another of the region's riverside settlements that has clearly seen better
days. It was once Bulgaria's third city – after Sofia and Plovdiv – and the

peeling, fading remains of the once-splendid opera house on the main square speak eloquently of a town that is rather down on its luck. Local knowledge of its Roman past is rather faded, too, for though a few passers-by seem to remember something about an antique fort, no one actually knows where it is. Finally, in a down-at-heel part of town, just along a slope that leads to the railroad track which hugs the Danube on its slow way eastwards, a tree-covered and unpromising-looking promontory houses what is left of Sexaginta Prista.

A military camp was established here under Vespasian, which was later garrisoned by the *Cohors II Flavia Brittanorum equitata*, a part-mounted detachment, and then by the *Cohors II Mattiacorum* composed of troops from faraway Germania Superior. By the 5th century, at the time of the *Notitia Dignitatum*, a unit of the I Italica legion was stationed here.[148] It was also a base for the Moesian fleet, the *Classis Flavia Moesiana*, and the name of the site derives from a type of fast reconnaissance vessel (*Prista*)[149] and the Latin for sixty (*sexaginta*), presumably referring to the size of the flotilla based here.

Sited as it is on a steep bluff, whose cliffs overlook the Danube far below, the fort would have been fairly impregnable to a river-based assault, though vulnerable from the rear. And so, over time it proved. Now just a narrow strip of the site remains, most of it swallowed up by the growth of Ruse in the 19th and 20th centuries, buried under the foundations of buildings or, in part, by a large copse of trees. The remains of barracks and one of the gates are still visible in a patch some 5 metres or so across. The site guardian, sporting a magnificent walrus moustache and sideburns, is most keen to show us the site's 'surprise'. This turns out to be a reconstruction of a *mithraeum* situated in a bunker of Second World War vintage, whose building must itself have taken another bite out of the Roman fort. A few altar fragments and a rather fetching brown and dark-blue colour scheme attempt to resurrect the air of mystery surrounding the cult. Some votive stelae for Mithras were found during excavations at Ruse, and so the supposition of a *mithraeum* at the fort is not entirely fanciful.

Just where the Danube begins to turn north, protected by wide marshes, Durostorum, some 125 kilometres east of Sexaginta Prista, protected the entrance to the area now known as the Dobrudja, which acted as a Roman-held salient pushing northwards towards the Crimea. Though this wide finger of land was terribly exposed to barbarian attacks, it did not lie on the most direct or accessible routes, either towards Thrace and the Western Empire or to Constantinople itself. The attacks therefore tended to be on a lesser scale and, coupled with the possibility of river- or seaborne reinforcements to the forts and cities here, this helped the lower Danube, which marked out the Dobrudja territory, to remain virtually the last part of the river over which the Byzantine authorities were able to exert control. Generally, the cities around Durostorum resisted conquest by the barbarians until the late 6th or even the 7th century, around a hundred years later than the frontier outposts further to the west.

The modern city of Silistra has long obliterated almost all that remained of Durostorum, but here and there tantalising elements survive. The legionary camp, which became home to the XI Claudia legion following its posting around 102 after Trajan's First Dacian War, was reconstructed during the reign of Aurelian, and its wall strengthened from about 1.5 metres to 2.5 metres in thickness. Already the Dobrudja had felt the chill wind of insecurity coming in from the steppes, for in 170 it had suffered the ravages of the Costobocci, one of the tribes whose incursions Marcus Aurelius struggled for decades to contain.[150] When the V Macedonica legion was transferred from Troesmis, Durostorum was left as the only legionary base along the Danube to the east of Novae, and so was of critical importance to Rome's hold on the section of river nearest the delta. It was probably during the reign of Marcus – or possibly that of Caracalla in the early 3rd century – that the town was elevated to the rank of *municipium*. Further raids by a combined group of Carpi, Goths and Sarmatians occurred during the reign of Gordian III, following the death of Decius in 251 and during the rule of Aurelian.

Close to the town centre of Silistra lie the remains of a *villa urbana*, set on a grassy patch below a couple of apartment blocks. The complex, including parts of a set of baths, dates from the 5th or 6th century, evidence that urban life was still flourishing here at that late stage. Durostorum's most spectacular archaeological discovery came about as a result of a chance find in 1942. It lies to the south-east of the city centre in a nondescript housing estate of low barrack-like concrete blocks, an unbroken forest of grey slabs. The small rectangular structure that sits on top of the late-Roman tomb makes it look more like a miniature church than a mausoleum, but inside and downstairs its purpose is clear.

Visible from a square hole punched into the original tomb chamber when it was opened, a Roman master and his wife stare out, flanked by a male and female slave, with further household slaves arrayed on the right and left walls. The tomb, which is generally dated to the second half of the 4th century, was never actually used, and since the very point on the wall where an inscription might have been located was destroyed when the tomb was first opened, the identity of the mausoleum's owner is something of a mystery. The man's gaze is stern, his clothing that of an aristocrat, a long tunic under a mantle that is fastened at the shoulder with a fibula (a type of brooch). In his hands he bears a codicil, probably commemorating his appointment to some senior official position. Such signs of appointment to high office were so valued and revered that they were often put on public display, set on cushions and bracketed by candles, as a visible token of the eminence of their owner.[151] It has been speculated that the tomb dates to shortly before the disastrous Roman defeat at Adrianople and that the man intended to be buried here was lost in that battle and his body never recovered. The truth will probably never be known.

After 1,600 years, the colours are amazingly vivid; an unused tomb would not have been attractive to grave-robbers, and thus its opening in the 20th century was the first time that the frescoes had been exposed to the air since the chamber was sealed. The mistress of the house seems to have been painted in later, for reasons that are unclear, and her face is obscured by a veil so that her features cannot clearly be seen; the female slaves to her right hold items for her bath, including a mirror and a towel, while the male slaves who flank her husband carry items of his clothing, such as his cloak and a *cingulum*, a badge of military office and a further indication of the man's importance.[152] Four boys and young men are depicted in roundels on the wall, possibly portraits of the master at various stages in his life; in one of them he is shown holding a spear, apparently hunting a bear.

Above the couple's portrait, set in a lunette, two peacocks are shown drinking from a vase. The image is such a commonplace of Christian iconography that it is taken – together with the east–west orientation of the tomb – as an indication that the owners may well have been Christians. Durostorum did have something of a reputation as a citadel of the new religion, producing its own rich crop of martyrs. A curious tale relates the story of Dasius, a legionary who refused to take part in a celebration associated with the feast of Saturnalia. Although well known as a time of inversion when the normal social order was turned upside down, in this extraordinary form of the rite, lots were drawn and the winner became 'king' for a month, during which period he was allowed to indulge in whatever pleasures he chose. At the end of the thirty-day period, the 'king' would be beheaded. Dasius, a staunch Christian (whose actual historical existence is doubtful),[153] is said to have refused to take part after the lot fell upon him, and was thrown into prison and executed.

Durostorum's brand of Christianity was not always orthodox. In 380, it received a new bishop, Auxentius, who was a leading supporter of the

Arian creed. Amongst the tortuous theological controversies that afflicted Christendom in the century after its adoption as an official religion, one of the most bitter was the question of whether God the Father took primacy amongst the members of the Trinity and created the other two, or whether instead Jesus Christ and the Holy Spirit were coeval with him and uncreated.

Arius, a Christian priest from Alexandria who lived in the mid-3rd century, taught the former and acquired a strong body of adherents before he was roundly condemned as a heretic at the Council of Nicaea in 325.[154] His teaching, however, lived on, particularly beyond the borders of the Empire, where his disciples had experienced notable success in evangelising the barbarians. Most prominent was Ulfilas, who preached amongst the Goths from the 340s and translated the Bible into Gothic. His story is muddied by the competing claims of orthodox historians (such as Sozomen and Zosimus) who maintain that Ulfilas actually converted the Goths to orthodox Christianity[155] and only turned to Arianism in the 370s at the behest of the Emperor Valens, who strongly supported that creed. Yet the Goths were certainly Arian by the end of the 4th century, and both the Visigoths in Spain and the Ostrogoths in Italy (together with the Vandals in North Africa) established kingdoms that derived some of their strength from their self-conscious identification with Arianism in opposition to the 'Roman' Nicene Church.

Auxentius – who was, as it happens, Ulfilas's foster son – was certainly a strong partisan of Arianism, and a letter that he wrote around 400 is one of the chief sources from the Arian side for the nature of their theology.[156] Later appointed as the Arian Bishop of Milan, Auxentius had the misfortune to be the contemporary of Saint Ambrose, an exceptionally able and pugnacious defender of the Nicene cause, who comprehensively outplayed his milder opponent in 386 over which of the two creeds had the right to celebrate mass in Milan's principal basilica.

Durostorum's other famous son was Flavius Aëtius, one of the Western Empire's last really capable military leaders. Born a little after 390 from a partly noble background,[157] as a young man Aëtius was held for a time as a hostage at various barbarian courts, first that of the Goths and then, more significantly, in the entourage of Rugila, King of the Huns. There he made important contacts and learnt something of Hunnish organisation and tactics, lessons that would stand him in great stead later in his career. He owed his initial rise to prominence to his reputation as a man who could deal with the Huns, taking advantage of the confused period that followed the death of Honorius in 423.

Castinus, who had been Honorius's *magister militum*, decided, on the death of his master, that his interests would not be best served by the raising of the infant Valentinian III to the imperial throne. Instead he elevated Ioannes, a relatively minor civil servant,[158] to become Emperor. When it was clear that the Eastern Emperor Theodosius I would vigorously oppose this move, Aëtius was despatched to recruit a force of Huns to deal with the inevitable conflict. By the time he returned, having duly mustered a large host, the eastern general Aspar had already captured the western capital, Ravenna, and had Ioannes executed. Aëtius's presence was now menacing rather than fortuitous and he was bought off with a large donative for his Hunnish mercenaries and his own appointment as *magister militum per Gallias*.[159] Valentinian III was installed on the throne, although at the tender age of six he was the plaything of competing factions, one of them led by Aëtius.

It took time for Aëtius to cement his influence at court, but by 430 he had managed to dispose of his first rival Felix, whom he had murdered that year.[160] He then engaged in a violent struggle with Boniface, who had held Africa for the legitimate government of Valentinian III during the usurpation of Ioannes, and who thus held an ace card in his relations with the Emperor's mother, Galla Placidia. It appears that Aëtius attempted to trick Boniface into rebelling, by fabricating letters showing that Galla Placidia was about to execute her former favourite.[161] But in the end the plot came to nothing, and instead, in 432, Boniface was given the title of 'patrician', the most prestigious position short of Emperor. A chastened Aëtius fled to Pannonia and thence to the Hunnish court. There he obtained from Ruga a fresh military force, with which he then marched on Italy, suffering a tactical defeat near Rimini in which Boniface was (luckily for Aëtius) mortally wounded.

Now without effective rivals, Aëtius came to dominate the government of the Empire for the next twenty years, during which time the Emperor, Valentinian III, remained firmly in the background. Aëtius received the almost unparalleled honour – for a non-member of the imperial family – of a third consulate in 446, and struggled with all his might for two decades to hold back the Hunnish genie, which he himself had first unleashed in 423. The principal arena of his activities was in Gaul, against which the Huns, led from 435 by Attila and his brother Bleda (and from 445 by Attila alone), pressed incessantly. Aëtius made able use of other barbarian groups in an effort to create buffers against their growing power. In 440, he settled a number of Alans on lands around Valence that had become deserted, and in 443 he placed the remnants of the Burgundians (whose power had been smashed by the Huns in 437) in Sapaudia (modern Savoy).[162]

The climactic struggle of Attila's career came about as the result of an extraordinary piece of court intrigue. Valentinian III's sister, Honoria, is said to have become pregnant by her household steward Eugenius. In order to avoid a scandal, he was executed and the Emperor's sister betrothed to a senator of consular rank with absolutely no hint of ambition about him. Outraged, Honoria had a ring despatched to Attila, saying that in exchange for a huge quantity of gold, he should come and rescue her; the clear implication was that she would also marry him. At this point the Eastern Emperor, Theodosius, who had advised Valentinian to pack his sister off to Attila and have done with the troublesome princess, died after a bad fall from his horse.[163] He had no male heir, and after the predictable period of jockeying for power, his sister Pulcheria effectively gifted the throne to a senator from Thrace named Marcian by marrying him. The new Emperor adopted a much harsher policy towards the Huns, to whom the Eastern Empire had been paying large subsidies each year, and cut off the supply of gold.

Faced with the drying-up of a handy source of payment for his growing horde, Attila did not (as might have been expected) turn on Marcian and make him pay for his insolence. Instead, he brought up the matter of Honoria, deciding that now was the time to assert his marriage rights over her. At the very least, he might have supposed, a massive payment would be in order to buy him off. In the end, he demanded the whole of Gaul in exchange for turning back his huge army, which was even then marching in the direction of the province. Aëtius, whose power base Gaul had always been, could never countenance such a move. He hastily cobbled together a coalition of all those who stood to lose by Attila's ultimate victory: the Visigoths under Theoderic, the Franks, Saxons and Burgundians, the men of Brittany and a motley collection of other minor barbarian clans. There was even a contingent of genuinely Roman soldiers.

The two armies met in June 451 on the Catalaunian Fields, some 50 kilometres from Châlons (or Catalaunum). The Huns were already somewhat on the defensive, having been forced to withdraw from the gates of Orléans, and they were tired. The Visigoths managed to occupy a slight rise on the plain, giving Aëtius's forces a significant advantage in the bitter hand-to-hand fighting that followed. Gradually Attila was forced back to his army's wagons, stationed in the rear. Just when it looked as if the Visigoths might press home their advantage – despite the death of Theoderic – Aëtius called them off and allowed the bloodied Huns to escape.

He had, perhaps, no intention of allowing any one barbarian group to become dominant and thought that some advantage might still be gained from manipulating the Huns – with whom, after all, he had a long history of involvement – at some later convenient moment. In 452, however, Attila was back, laying siege to Aquileia and blazing a trail through Italy as far as the River Po, where an embassy from Rome, including Pope Leo I, persuaded him to turn back. Attila's departure probably had more to do with the plague and famine then afflicting the Italian peninsula than with any sudden attack of piety on his part, when faced with the papal pleas to leave the Eternal City in peace.[164]

The next year, though, the great Hun was dead and the Hunnish confederacy shattered, its subjects no longer held in check by their almost superstitious fear of Attila's wrath. His sons struggled to keep even a much-diminished realm together, and in the 460s the two survivors, Dengizich and Hernac, asked leave to bring their remaining followers to settle south of the Danube. At first this was summarily refused, and in the end it was only Hernac who was permitted to bring a much-reduced band to settle in the Dobrudja as federates.[165] Thus, within two decades of the death of Attila, the Huns had disappeared almost entirely as a political force.

The ignominious removal of his great rival might have been considered a moment for Aëtius to relish. Yet just as he had first involved the Huns in Roman politics, so their removal from the equation meant that, for a brief moment, he was vulnerable, as his longtime clients-cum-enemies could no longer be invoked either as a threat or as the unlikely saviours of the Roman state. In September 454, Valentinian summoned his overmighty general to a meeting to discuss some accounts, and there stabbed Aëtius to death with his own hand. Procopius acidly remarks that the Emperor had thereby cut off his own right hand with his left.[166] While clearly out to advance his own best interests, Aëtius had also juggled the competing challenges facing the Empire with at least reasonable success. His defeat of Attila may have saved the Gallic provinces from premature loss to the Empire, and though he could not preserve Africa, in Gaul he did at least retain one of the two best revenue-raising areas that the Empire still possessed. From provincial obscurity, Aëtius had risen to the highest rank and truly earnt the epithet often attached to his name, 'the last Roman'.

Apart from its southern extremity, the Dobrudja now lies largely within the territory of modern Romania. The Romans first entered the area in 72–71 BC during their war against Mithridates, ruler of Pontus on the southern Black Sea coast, whose power had grown to encompass a series of Hellenistic cities on the western shores of the sea, such as Tomis (Constanţa), Callatis (Mangalia) and Histria (Istros). The great Pontic ruler, as well as being vexingly hard to unthrone, held two kingly records. The first, his ability to speak all twenty-two of the languages of his subjects and address each soldier in his army by name and in his own tongue, would have left him a wide range of options for a place of exile in which he could converse with ease.[167] The second, much more ambivalent gift was his immunity to all then-known poisons. This tolerance he had, ironically, built up on account of his fear of assassination and consequent self-administration of small doses of venom throughout his adult life, which created an immunity to the otherwise lethal substances. When finally facing capture by the Romans, his attempts to poison himself failed miserably and in the end he had to call on his friend Bituitus to kill him.[168] Although the historians do not record it, one can well imagine him cursing heartily and creatively in all those twenty-two languages.

Marcus Terentius Varro Lucullus, the Roman general who had been victorious against Mithridates, forced a treaty of alliance on a number of cities. This certainly included Callatis (for the text of the inscription survives) and quite possibly Tomis and Histria, too, promising mutual assistance in case of attack, and providing a useful guarantee for Roman expansionist moves in Macedonia and Thrace. A revolt in Macedonia led to the defeat of Gaius Antonius Hybrida in 61 BC near Histria and this, together with the expansion of the native Dacian state that grew up under Burebista in the 60s and 50s BC, led to a temporary diminution of Roman influence in the area. It took a campaign by Marcus Licinius Crassus[169] in 29–28 BC to restore the situation, and the trio of Greek-speaking cities on the coast – Callatis, Histria and Tomis – were now effectively annexed by Rome, although nominally retaining their freedom.

Under Tiberius, the Dobrudja was incorporated into Moesia during the province's formal organisation in AD 15. Apart from an invasion by the Roxolani in 67–8,[170] the area remained relatively tranquil under the early Empire, although, in a token of things to come, Plautius Silvanus Aelianus (governor of Moesia from 57 to 67) is said to have transported 100,000 tribespeople from beyond the Danube to replenish provincial manpower resources,[171] establishing a precedent for the *receptio* of barbarians into the Empire that would become a regular feature during the more troubled times of the 4th and 5th centuries.[172] The Roman authorities always sought to present the settling of barbarians within the Empire in a positive light, rather than as an act into which they had been forced. The settling of the Ubii on the left bank of the Rhine by Augustus in 38 BC had been a model for this, but the process became so frequent from the 2nd century that imperial propagandists struggled to present *receptio* as a positive thing. Marcus Aurelius allowed a large number of Naristae into the Empire around 180, Probus permitting 100,000 Bastarnae to enter the Empire, and Constantine capping it all with the settlement of 300,000 Sarmatians.[173] After the Roman defeat at Adrianople in 378, and the large-scale migration of unintegrated Goths that resulted, the panegyricist Themistius made the best of it by opining that it was far better that Thrace should be filled with barbarian farmers than by hostile warriors.

Even though the province was further enlarged after Claudius annexed the kingdom of Thrace in AD 46, appending to Moesia those parts of it that lay north of the central Balkan range, there is not much evidence for Roman troops being stationed in Dobrudja until the time of Vespasian. Once Dacia was occupied by Trajan by 106, and the central sector of the Danube between Durostorum and Novae (which had hitherto been heavily militarised) no longer lay on an external frontier, troops were released, both for the occupation of Dacia itself and to provide a legionary garrison for the first time for Dobrudja. A string of forts was built at Axiopolis (Cernavoda), Carsium (Hirsova) and Troesmis (Igliţa), which continued to defend the Dobrudja into the reign of Justinian, long after the forts on the central Danube to the west had been overrun by successive waves of barbarian invasions. As well as the V Macedonica legion, which was despatched to Troesmis (only to be withdrawn and sent to Dacia around 167), a number of auxiliary cohorts were sent to reinforce the defence of the area, including the *Cohors I Germanorum* at Capidava.[174]

During the Diocletianic reforms Moesia Inferior was renamed Scythia Minor, and from here on, reinforced by new legionary forces (the I Iovia and II Herculea), it acted as a Romanised bastion. There was some destruction by the Huns, but it was nothing like as severe as the swathe of land south of the Danube towards Naissus had to endure. The area suffered the depredations of the Goths' naval campaign in 257, and a large contingent of Sarmatians was settled in Scythia Minor between 340 and 360 to bolster the security of the province. However, even after the disastrous defeat by the Goths at Adrianople in 378, the Dobrudja remained resolutely Roman. It was only in the late 6th century with the advent of the Avars, and even more so in the 7th and early 8th centuries, that Constantinople's grip on the area finally weakened. Even so, cities in southern Dobrudja and northern Thrace such as Odessos (Varna) and Mesembria (Nesebur) remained Byzantine, with interruptions, almost to the very end of the Empire in 1453.

Some way into the interior of the province, around 100 kilometres east of the Danube at Silistra, along a Roman road that bypasses both the Danube and the Black Sea coast, resolutely refusing both sea and river, lies one of the most extraordinary monuments to Roman imperialism anywhere in the Empire. In a part of Romania where low chalet-style houses and horse-drawn carts seem the height of modernity, somewhat blurring the line between antiquity and the present, the small village of Adamclisi houses a monument of wholly unexpected grandeur. In 109, at a place that became known as Tropaeum Traiani, Trajan erected a stone trophy to celebrate his recent victory over the Dacians. Unlike the refined depictions on the column he set up in his forum in Rome, with its cartoon-strip narrative of the Dacian Wars, this account is rawer and bloodier, the art more provincial, but carrying more power and authenticity for lacking the filter of a refined disdain for the realities of war.

A reconstructed version of the monument stands a little way outside the village. A 40-metre-diameter marble drum some 10–12 metres high is set on a platform, which adds a further 8 metres to the monument. Topping it, a statue of Mars Ultor, the avenging god of war, is festooned with the trophies of battle, arms and armour captured from dead Dacians. It is a reflection of an ancient Roman tradition, by which the arms of slain opponents would be hung from a tree on the battlefield, so sending a grizzly message to anyone who might oppose the young city-state's rise to power, while at the same time glorifying the achievement of the victorious general.[175] All around, on fifty-four panels, were depicted scenes from the execution of the war. Even if the carvings themselves could not have been seen at any great distance, the Tropaeum would have been visible over a huge area, an ever-present – and presumably galling – reminder to the Dacians that they were no longer a free people.

The originals of the panels are held in the Adamclisi museum where, though divorced from their original context, they are more easily comprehensible than the replacements that encircle the reconstructed monument. They are weathered by long exposure to the atmosphere, but their patina of age lends them a disturbing immediacy. Here a bearded Dacian wields a *falx*, the characteristic sickle-shaped sword of his people; there a Roman legionary in chain armour thrusts his *gladius* into the chest of a bearded and kilted warrior, whose stone image writhes and twists in its death agony. On one panel a Dacian seems to hang in the air, almost flying, while on another the *cornicularii*, the legionary trumpeters. sound the advance. Trajan, meanwhile, watches and waits to receive the victorious cohorts at the end of the campaign.

The final panels show Dacian prisoners bound and shackled, with Roman soldiers leading them into captivity, while two Dacian women, one bearing a baby, are depicted standing apart, perhaps watching their husbands being led into slavery. It is all a brutal depiction of the subjugation of a nation and the ugliness of war, made all the more unsavoury for its triumphalist tone. Yet, from the Roman point of view, they had done nothing more than punish the Dacians for breaking a treaty and had brought 'peace' to the new province. Just a few hundred metres away to the east, the Romans erected a more personal monument to the losses they had endured in the taking of Dacia; the names of almost 4,000 soldiers who died in the campaign were set up on a square altar, together with a rectangular mound, presumably the burial tumulus of a senior commander who had fallen in the fighting.[176]

Tropaeum Traiani was not simply the trophy. The place lay at an important crossroads between Tomis and Durostorum, and Trajan settled veterans from his Dacian campaign there, establishing a fortress as well as a civil town, certainly before 115–16 when the inhabitants, the 'Traianenses Tropaeenses' dedicated a statue to their patron emperor. Under Antoninus Pius it became home to a detachment of the XI Claudia legion, and its increasing importance is shown by its promotion to the rank of *municipium* around 180 during the reign of Marcus Aurelius.

Tropaeum Traiani's exposed position, however, meant that it did not prosper during the 3rd century and had to be rebuilt almost from scratch during the time of Constantine the Great and Licinius.[177] A dedication survives to the two emperors, in which Constantine tellingly takes precedence (just a few years later, in 317, he would defeat Licinius in the first of two fratricidal wars between them). The place staggered on until it was destroyed by the Avars at the end of the 6th century. At what point the trophy was thrown down, and what the reactions of the local population might have been to the overturning of this symbol of their subjugation, it is hard to say. They may have been more ambivalent than expected, for Rome's fall did not mean Dacia's rise, and the conditions that prevailed after the collapse of the *limes* on the Danube were hardly conducive to basic survival, let alone fine proto-nationalist sentiment.

The town lies just a couple of kilometres away, on a low rise from which a fantastic view can be had of the trophy itself and on to the high plateau up to the east. It is protected on three sides by a natural slope, which was reinforced in the 4th century by a defensive wall studded with horseshoe-shaped towers. In the mid-afternoon summer sun, it seems an exposed place, the carpet of grass and tangle of weeds threatening to blur and obscure the indistinct outlines of its surviving buildings, while here and there the ground is scarred with the trenches from various archaeological campaigns.

On the town's main street, around 200 metres from the principal gate (which survives only in its rubble core and a few facing blocks), lies the *basilica forensis*, the civilian basilica, marked out by two rows of column bases that formed the portico of the building. The forum, alongside which the basilica must have lain, is obscured by a jumble of ruins. Nearby, four Christian basilicas from the 4th to 6th centuries are evidence of the Christian life of the city. One, the 'Cistern Basilica', was adapted in late-Roman times from a pre-existing water cistern, which provided a convenient and well-built rectangular structure without the need for extensive new building. Across the main street again are the ruins of the 'Marble Basilica', clear only from the shape of its apse, the rest being just an undifferentiated mass of stones.

The east gate of the city and the adjacent wall have been reconstructed and one tower stands incongruously whole. Leaving the site from the south side, a single jagged arch of a gateway survives, divorced from any surviving stones of the walls, from where a slight scramble leads down to the modern roadway. Unvisited and half-shapeless with age, Tropaeum Traiani is a stark reminder that the proud boasts of emperors could do nothing to prevent the collapse of the frontier and the overwhelming of such towns by the tide of time.

The modern road along the Danube is subject to exactly the same vagaries that periodically damaged many of the forts and at the same time contributed to their security. The fort at Capidava (modern Topalu), which lies on the Danube 55 kilometres north of Tropaeum Traiani, was first constructed under Trajan at the start of the 2nd century, but is now rendered somewhat more difficult to find by a flood that has washed away the riverside road, necessitating a slanting detour inland before the mound of the fort appears, unexpectedly, at the side of the new highway around 20 kilometres beyond Cernavodă. The ruins, as at so many places that the Romans occupied for several centuries, are something of a multi-layered prospect, with the Trajanic phase almost entirely built over by a reconstruction under Diocletian or Constantine, which in turn has been obscured by a heavy overlay of buildings from the 8th to the 11th centuries. It is certainly a testament to the obduracy of the Roman and Byzantine hold on the place.

Entering from the western side, parts of one horseshoe-shaped projecting tower have been reconstructed a little further to the east, while the others lie in ruins. Inside the main circuit, many of the buildings are dwellings from the 8th to 10th centuries, when the fort was adapted for civilian use. In the south-west of the wall, an earthwork mound represents the late-Roman fort, which, like many fortifications of the time, occupied a restricted area; partly because the size of garrisons was reduced, and partly because those troops might actually be expected to defend their bases against attack. It all offers a fine view over the Danube, flowing tranquilly by.

The first garrison here (until 243) was the *Cohors I Ubiorum* from near Cologne, which was replaced by the *Cohors Germanorum civium romanorum*, again from Germany. The fort was destroyed by the Goths during an incursion in the mid-3rd-century. It was razed again by the Huns in the mid-4th, and the place was only revived when Justinian built the smaller fort in the 5th century. Capidava was by then the centre of a bishopric, and a basilica with three apses has been unearthed. After being on the receiving end of another sacking, from the Avars in the late 6th century, Capidava was then temporarily abandoned, to be further devastated by an earthquake in the 7th century. It was only reoccupied when Byzantine control returned to this section of the Danube in the 9th century and, from the evidence of the hut-like dwellings half-sunken into the ground that made up the predominant type of housing of this phase in Capidava's history, it was not a very prosperous era. By the 11th century even these petered out, and presumably the site was abandoned.

The lynchpin of the *Limes Scythiae*, which formed the defensive system of Dobrudja, was Troesmis (Igliţa), some 75 kilometres north along the *limes* from Capidava. The V Macedonica legion was based here after its transfer from Oescus around 102 until it was sent to Dacia in the 160s.[178] It gave rise to two civilian settlements, one based around the legionary *cannabae*, the other, a more purely civilian town, a *municipium* under Marcus Aurelius.[179] Its citadel, at a strategic position on the lower Danube around 50 kilometres from the point where it finally bends eastwards for the last stage of its journey to the delta, was first excavated in the 1860s by a Frenchman, Desiré More, who claimed that the local Turks were so hostile to him that one of them even shot off his right thumb.[180]

Situated near this final bend, a few kilometres from modern Garvăn, is the fortress of Dinogetia, which lies on a broad plateau above what was once an ancient tributary of the Danube, and which retained an isolated garrison amidst all the vicissitudes of the ages of invasions, right up until the end of the 6th century. It was built over the remains of a pre-existing Geto-Dacian[181] settlement, and was certainly constructed before the mid-2nd century, when it is mentioned in Ptolemy's *Geographia*.[182] Extensive reconstruction was carried out under Diocletian, and large numbers of tile stamps of the I Iovia legion have been found. It was again rebuilt during the reigns of Anastasius and Justinian, as the part of the general strengthening of the Danube *limes*, but was burnt to the ground during an invasion by the Kutrigurs in 559. Although it was reoccupied, Dinogetia limped on in a fairly poor state. A medieval basilica of the 11th or 12th century occupies part of the central area of the site, evidence of the last stage of its existence.

The fort lies a few hundred metres from the main road, occupying a prime site on a low promontory, its 12-metre-high walls and semicircular towers making it seem as if a siege would still present a formidable challenge. The guardian, who farms in the locality, as did his father for twenty years before him, says that the area was far marshier in ancient times, so the approach to the citadel would have been even more treacherous. Despite the relatively complete state presented by it exterior, Dinogetia is splendidly ruinous inside, grassed over and quietly decaying. Roughly in the centre a square building probably represents the *praetorium*, next to which another structure could have been the house of some local notable built within the fort precincts in the 4th century, and which, in common with the rest, was sacked by the Huns around 375.[183] The gate facing the roadway was blocked up in Byzantine times, evidence of the increasing insecurity experienced by all such outposts as this.

A few hundred metres from the fort, past fields of waving corn, lies the bath-complex. Partly protected by a metal-roofed shelter, the remains are overgrown, although the hypocaust, the best-preserved in Romania, can just be made out. The ruins here are made more confusing by the fact that in the 6th century they were partly cannibalised to make a Christian chapel on the site. Presumably by then, the ritual of bathing was less central to a civic life that was becoming divorced from its classical antecedents. It is a process that continues even today, as the guardian acidly points out that whilst his forebears of Roman times had enough water to run such an establishment, he has lived here for forty years without ever once having access to mains running water.

A further 25 kilometres east along the river, close to modern Isaccea, lies Noviodunum, which was the main base of the *Classis Flavia Moesica*, the Moesian fleet that patrolled the lower section of the Danube.[184] The fort was built to control the last easy crossing point of the river before it begins to divide into the confusing web of waterways that make up the river's delta. The high promontory on which it was erected was later used for an Ottoman-era fortress, and the visible Roman remains are scant, a large part of the northern sector of the walls having simply slid into the Danube. One of the interval towers of the late-Roman stage of the fort, which may originally have been built at the time of Nero, but certainly by the time of the Flavians, can still be made out. On the riverside humps and mounds in the grass probably represent the remains of the fort's interior buildings, but there is little actually visible above the ground. At this point, the Danube forms the border between Romania and the Ukraine, and across the wide expanse of river the wooded bank opposite seems peaceful, although since 2007 it once more represents a kind of boundary with *barbaricum*, as the Romanian side forms part of the economically advantaged club of the European Union, while a few kilometres away the Ukrainians are the wrong side of a tariff barrier, just as they were in Roman times.[185]

Noviodunum's moment of greatest fame came in 369, when the Emperor Valens met the Gothic chieftain Athanaric on a boat moored in the river outside the fortress to agree a treaty between their two peoples. Valens had been engaged in a campaign against the Goths for almost three years, and had earlier the same year crossed over into *barbaricum* on a bridge of boats that he had ordered constructed at Noviodunum.[186] The Goths were tired of fighting, and their supplies were exhausted. Athanaric finally came to sue for peace in person. Yet many years before he had sworn an oath to his father that he would never set foot on Roman territory, and in deference to the aged chieftain's pious wish not to violate his vow, Valens agreed to meet him midstream.

Temporarily, it seemed that the Gothic menace had been turned aside, and that peace might return to the Balkans. Less than ten years later, however, the Eastern Empire was overwhelmed by total catastrophe. Its origin lies precisely in dissatisfaction with the terms of the treaty brokered with Valens. A group of Goths under Fritigern revolted against the rule of Athanaric, who, by suing for peace at the hands of the Romans, had proved himself unworthy as a war leader. As a result the Tervingi, the leading faction of the Goths, which Athanaric had dominated, began to break up into their component sub-tribes. It was particularly unfortunate that this process coincided with aggressive advances by the Huns and their Alan allies, who were pressing in on the Gothic rear from their lands east of the Don.

The Tervingi, having largely abandoned Athanaric, and now under the leadership of Alavivus and Fritigern, flooded towards the Danube.[187] They demanded refuge in the Empire, and the panicked local authorities ordered them to stay put whilst the Emperor, far away in Antioch (Antakya in modern Turkey), was consulted. Eventually, permission was given for the Tervingi to cross, probably in the area of Durostorum, a complicated procedure during which many of them drowned in the swollen river. Once there, they faced terrible privations. Far from giving them adequate supplies, as the Emperor had commanded, the local military leaders

Lupicinus (the *comes per Thracias*) and Maximus (probably the *dux* of Moesia) pocketed the funds intended to pay for the Goths' upkeep and let their new charges simply starve, thus beginning a long and dishonourable tradition of the mistreatment of political refugees. Parents are said to have exchanged their children for dog-meat, and huge numbers of Goths were sold into slavery.[188] In the meantime, the Tervingi were joined on the north bank of the Danube by another Gothic group, the Greuthingi under Alatheus and Saphrax. However, these newcomers were denied entry into imperial territory.

Further embittered by the paltry shelter offered to them in the face of a bitter winter, Gothic hearts turned from gratitude for their sanctuary to burning hatred at the arrogance and cruelty of their hosts. Fritigern restrained his followers from any intemperate violence and directed his Goths south-eastwards towards Marcianopolis, inland from the great port of Odessos (Varna) on the Black Sea coast. Lupicinus, who was still supervising the movements of the Tervingi, invited Fritigern to a banquet inside the town, but forbade the Gothic chieftain's followers to accompany him. Fritigern narrowly avoided assassination, for the feast had been a trap, and in the ensuing battle outside the town walls Lupicinus and his army were roundly defeated. The Goths, who could take no more Roman perfidy, set to plundering Thrace and Moesia with an enthusiasm redoubled by their treacherous treatment.

It took until 378 for Valens to assemble a sufficient force to face down the Goths, who in the meantime had dealt a stinging blow to the local Roman forces at Ad Salices in the summer of 377. The problem was now, if anything, even worse, for the Greuthingi had also crossed the Danube (probably near Noviodunum) and joined up with Fritigern's horde. Held up by trouble in Isauria in Asia Minor, and by a revolt in Palestine, Valens only set out from Constantinople in the second week of June[189] while reinforcements from Gratian in the west were delayed by the need to deal with an Alamannic invasion.[190] Faced with a move by Fritigern to bypass him and block his return route to Constantinople, Valens decided, against the advice of some of his senior generals, to seek battle as soon as possible. On 9 August, he found the Goths camped around 12 kilometres from Adrianople (Edirne in Turkey). Fritigern seems to have played for time, asking for a parley whilst he called back scattered bands of warriors to rejoin his central force; he is even said to have set fires to create a choking blanket of smoke to wear down the Romans' morale.

When fighting did break out, it was confused. Valens was unaware of the true numbers of Goths and ordered an ill-judged attack on their camp, which was thrown back once the large cavalry force led by Alatheus and Saphrax returned to the fray after a foraging expedition. The Roman cavalry broke and the infantry, despite prolonged and dogged resistance, were eventually cut to pieces. Ammianus recounts that the crush was so great that troops slipped on the blood of those who had fallen and were impaled on the weapons of their own comrades.[191] Valens's own bodyguard appears to have fled as resistance crumbled, and a last-ditch stand by the cavalry commander Victor to rescue the Emperor failed. Those Romans who could made a disorderly escape from the battlefield.

The carnage was appalling: two-thirds of the Roman army is thought to have fallen. One estimate gives up to 26,000 Roman dead out of the 40,000 or so who started the battle, including the two *magistri militum* Traianus and Sebastianus and Valens himself, whose body was never found.[192] At a stroke the eastern field army was cut to pieces and, to make matters worse, the Emperor was dead, many of the senior military officers who might be expected to rally the remainder of the army and select a new leader had also perished, while a large force of Goths, fired on by the elation of such a rare and total victory, was on the loose near the imperial capital.

Yet the desperate times called forth the measures necessary to ensure the Empire's survival. Julius, one of the few surviving very senior military officers, summoned the large numbers of Goths who were enrolled in the Roman army and stationed near Constantinople to a special parade. Once assembled, they were tricked into disarming and then massacred to a man, so ensuring that there would be no Gothic fifth column to join up with Fritigern's victorious horde. Gratian, meanwhile, who could easily have kept the job within his family – since he had a seven-year-old cousin, Valentinian II, with whom, nominally, he shared power in the West – chose expediency over the ties of blood. He summoned the capable Spanish army officer Theodosius, who had been in exile on his family's estates since the disgrace and execution of his father in 374,[193] to become *magister equitum*. Then, at Sirmium in January 379, he had Theodosius crowned Augustus, with control of the Eastern Empire. After a series of difficult campaigns, by 382 the Goths sued for peace and were given land on which to settle in Thrace.

Old Athanaric, who had by now been marginalised and deserted by most of his former followers, overcame his qualms and finally entered the territory of the Empire late in 380. Theodosius gave the venerable Goth asylum and welcomed him to Constantinople, where he passed away just two weeks later on 14 January 381 and was given a state funeral. The 'Gothic problem', however, had not been solved, merely shelved, and within fifteen years would erupt again under Alaric with, if anything, even more destructive consequences.[194]

The littoral of the Black Sea coast seems a world away from the winding and twisting river passages of the Danube delta and the forts that fronted the Roman defence against *barbaricum*, yet the ancient Greek cities which lay along it formed the original core of Roman power here and remained the most important settlements in Lower Moesia (and then Scythia Minor). The approach to Istros (or Histria), one of the most important of these, is fringed with reed beds, giving it a much more maritime air than the mound-hugging marsh-beset fortresses to the north. It lies about 100 kilometres to the south-west of Noviodunum (Isaccea), to which it was connected by a direct road that avoided the need to circumnavigate the fringes of the delta.

Istros's beginnings are antique indeed; it was founded by Greek colonists from Miletus in the 7th century BC, and the settlement survived into the 7th century AD, not long after its destruction by the Avars in 586. In between, it experienced alternating periods of prosperity and disaster, suffering a sack by the Getae in the 1st century BC and by the Goths in the mid-3rd century AD. It became Roman in the late 1st century BC, together with its neighbouring Hellenistic cities of Tomis and Callatis.[195]

The outermost set of city walls dates from the period after the Gothic sack in the 3rd century (it was the fourth such circuit, the others being built at the colony's Hellenistic foundation, and under the early Roman occupation). The defences are impressively strong, composed of large blocks, which reused material from earlier phases of the city, including a couple of dedication stones that were incorporated into the gates as lintels. Inside, the city contains remains from throughout its 1,500-year history, creating a confusing jumble of interleaved phases. From its earliest period come a wealth of Greek inscriptions, some one-third of the total found in the Dobrudja,[196] and a sacred area, including the very broken-down remains of a temple of Zeus.

Around the 3rd century BC the harbour at Istros began to silt up, and in 262 BC the city lost a long-running battle with Byzantium over who controlled the harbour at Tomis to the south. A long depression set in, which was compounded after a sacking by Getic allies of the Dacian King Burebista in the 50s BC, and only began to lift once the Romans had securely occupied the city later in that century.

Just inside the town's main gate lies a late-Roman official quarter of the city, with the outlines of several large civic basilicas, a bath building and a small colonnaded square surviving. One of the basilicas sits in a dusty 4-metre-deep depression with just a couple of columns in place. Along an uncertain path, the *palaestra* of the bath-complex with its open space and portico is clear, and the remains of brick arches mark the remaining buildings. Beyond this there is a somewhat poorer quarter, with undifferentiated rectangular dwellings composed of smallish blocks. A larger ecclesiastical district dates from the 4th to 6th centuries and includes the Great Basilica, the largest in the Dobrudja, of which only the outline survives, marking out the nave and the apse, with the rest just architectural shards and fragments, columns and pieces of marble architrave lying hither and thither.

Deeper into the city lies a 6th-century residential area, from the very last years of Istros's existence. Rectangular rubble walls and a small colonnaded square speak of a life that was still at least modestly prosperous, despite the city's reduced circumstances. While in the western Balkans, and the riverine settlements of Upper Moesia, building activity had virtually ceased, here it still went on unabated, and the walls were reinforced several times.[197] Evidence from coins suggest that Istros managed to survive into the reign of Heraclius, though when control over the Danube frontier was achieved once more during the 9th century, the venerable ruins of the city were not reoccupied.

It is only around an hour's journey down the Black Sea coast from Istros to its long-time rival Tomis, but the fate of the two cities since the ending of Roman rule could hardly be more different. While Istros was totally abandoned, settlement at Tomis (or Constanţa as it became) continued. It is now a city of more than 300,000 inhabitants, with the largest harbour on the Black Sea (and one of the biggest in Europe), caught between the competing pulls of a rapid modernisation, the decaying remnants of the heavy industry that communism bequeathed to it and a much more ancient heritage as a Greek foundation of the 6th century BC.

After the Roman annexation in the 1st century BC, Tomis rapidly became the chief town of the Dobrudja, eclipsing its neighbours Istros and Callatis as the centre for the whole region. It is from this period that a unique testament to early-Roman Tomis comes. Publius Ovidius Naso, known to English-speaking posterity as Ovid, was one of the greatest poets of Rome's literary golden age. The author of masterworks such as the *Metamorphoses*, a collection of myths linked together by the theme of transformation, he was sent into exile in AD 8 to the far-flung shores of the Black Sea at Tomis, about as far from the cosmopolitan luxuries of Rome as it was possible to imagine. He spent the rest of his life there, continuing to pen poetry, including the poignant *Tristia*, a set of reflections on exile and pleas for forgiveness.

The slight to the Emperor for which Ovid was banished to his Scythian purgatory has never been securely established. Ovid himself indicated that it was because of a poem (the *Ars Amatoria*) and some kind of political error he had made. It is possible that certain passages in the poem, which seem to promote adultery, may have fallen foul of a new puritanical morality that Augustus was trying to promote, as evidenced by a law he promulgated which decreed severe penalties for adultery; in 2 BC the Emperor even banished his own daughter Julia to a remote island for the crime.[198] Perhaps the most plausible theory for Ovid's exile is that he knew somehow of Julia's adulterous affair with Junius Silanus, that it may even have had more seditious undertones as the basis for conspiracy against the Emperor himself, and that the poet, whilst not directly implicated, chose not to reveal what he knew.[199]

The picture Ovid paints of Tomis is of a city swarming with barbarous types, Getae and Sarmatians, dressed in furs against the winter cold.[200] The inclement weather and the barbarians were a constant preoccupation for the poet during his years of exile, unwelcome contrasts with the world he had left behind for ever at Rome. It took until May of AD 9 for Ovid to arrive in his place of exile, and within a year he was even called upon to don arms as a member of the city militia, to fight off one of the sporadic raids from the neighbouring Getae.

In the end, though, Ovid made the best of it. He carried on a constant stream of correspondence with friends in Rome, as a literary substitute for seeing them on a daily basis, and produced nine volumes of the *Tristia* ('Sadnesses') and of *Epistulae ex Ponto* ('Letters from the Pontus'). He even learnt some Getic, and was capable of conversing in the language – a necessary compromise in a place where, at least according to Ovid, Latin was rarely heard. His exile never ended, for after eight years, and the disappointment of the accession of Tiberius in 14, which did not bring a reversal of Augustus's obdurate refusal to pardon him, Ovid died in 17. His poetry, however, lived on, and neither his unknown crime nor his Pontic exile served to dent his reputation. As the poet himself wrote, '*Tempus edax rerum*' (Time is the devourer of all things).[201]

Ovid still gazes over Tomis, but now in the form of a statue erected on a lofty plinth in front of the city's main museum on Piaţa Ovidiu, the square named in his honour. It is a sad last resting place for a poet in the place of his bitter-sweet exile, as taxis whizz by and groups of adolescents lounge idly, waiting for their tourist coaches to collect them, the odd one curious enough to take a snap of the old bronze statue behind. The museum, from which the poet averts his gaze, houses a collection of priceless relics, mostly from the Greek phase of the city, including a statue of the snake god Glykon, the guardian of temples, his sinuous stone coils taut and ready to spring, whilst around his face fall disturbing, almost dreadlock-like, marble curls of hair. The Roman exhibits peter away around 702, when the city finally fell and was temporarily abandoned, while a run of medieval and modern rooms curiously stutters to a halt in 1939. History resumes in 1989 after the fall of the communist autarch Nicolae Ceauşescu, for, at least in museum circles, a reappraisal of the Second World War years and the communist era is clearly still under way.

The vestiges of ancient Tomis are thin on the ground, unsurprisingly so for a city that has been occupied almost constantly for 2,500 years. Just by the museum, a little sculpture park shares space in a square with a couple of travel agencies, displaying a few of the grave monuments found in the area. Much more spectacular is the 'Roman Edifice' a few metres away, which houses one of the largest extant mosaics in the Roman world, a geometric affair some 100 metres long and 20 metres wide. The building itself has walls some half a metre thick, which still stand to about 3–4 metres on one side. The storey beneath this consisted of around eleven vaulted rooms in which a variety of amphorae were found, indicating some kind of storeroom, but the splendour of the mosaic speaks of a much grander function. The geometric pattern, in black, white and yellow, includes ivy leaves, spirals, vases, shields and double-headed axes in its decoration, although what must once have been a mesmerising expanse of tesserae is now somewhat broken up by the buckling of the floor, caused by the shifting of the earth beneath, perhaps through an earthquake.

The mosaic was laid in the 4th or 5th century AD, by which time the city had been renamed Constantiana, possibly under the Emperor Constantius II (337–61). Down below, fronting the port, sections of the city's sea wall survive, surmounted by modern housing, while nearby fragments of a bath-complex moulder quietly in a green expanse of park beside the harbour road.

A larger section of the late-Roman wall, restored under Diocletian or Constantine, survives inland in a small park, its western gate clear, with a 2-metre-wide opening and the threshold still in place. The south gate also remains, though the section of extant wall here is much lower. Around 50 metres away the 'Butcher's Tower' was originally built during a later, Justinianic refortification, showing that efforts to keep the defences of Tomis in good shape were still under way into the 6th century.

A string of other Hellenistic foundations guarded the Black Sea coast down from Tomis, including Callatis (Mangalia), Bizone (Kavarna in Bulgaria) and the most important city of coastal Thrace, Odessos (modern

Varna). Like Constanța, Varna boomed in the 19th and 20th centuries, and is now the third-largest city in Bulgaria, counting some 350,000 inhabitants, a mass that has almost wholly effaced its classical heritage. Founded in around 585 BC, again by colonists from Miletus, the town fell under the domination of the Macedonians during the time of Alexander the Great's father, Philip II.

Along with many of the other Greek cities of the Black Sea coast, it came under the suzerainty of Rome in around 27 BC, and then, with the definitive suppression of the Thracian kingdom by Claudius in AD 46, it was attached to the new Roman province of Thrace. After the division of Moesia by Domitian around 85, Odessos was then transferred to the new province of Moesia Inferior. Although Trajan re-established the neighbouring town of Parthenopolis, 30 kilometres away, renaming it Marcianopolis in honour of his sister, Odessos's maritime trade enabled it to continue to flourish, complementing rather than competing directly with its upstart neighbour.

In one of Varna's main pedestrianised streets, half-obscured by the chairs of the neighbouring pavement cafés, sits a small piece of the Roman level roadway, more now the target of those seeking a quick depository for their litter than of any antiquarian curiosity. Somewhere under here, and in the streets leading down to the harbour, lay the original Greek quarter of the city. A section of Roman wall and several buildings sit in a pit by the side of an apartment block, where a tenant has forged an ersatz flowerpot from a very eroded column base. The remains themselves are utterly overgrown with grass and weeds. In the back courtyard of another apartment block, totally cut off from the eye of passers-by, a Roman tower lurks, standing to around half a metre in height, and crowded around by the parked cars of the modern inhabitants of the place.

Nearby are the main Roman baths, some of the finest surviving anywhere in the Balkans. It is a huge complex, some 3–4 metres below present street level, and stretching over some 7,000 square metres, although a section at both ends has been cut off by a later church. Down several flights of steps, part of the subterranean supporting structure survives, its brick vaults dank and water-stained. Up again, the square *apodyterium* or changing room leads into a vestibule with walls surviving up to a height of two storeys, and sections of an arch on both sides creating a hugely impressive silhouette. At the back the normal procession of *frigidarium*, *tepidarium* and *caldarium* is mirrored on both sides of the symmetrical complex. In the rear section of the baths, piles of broken sections of architrave and other architectural fragments lie in heaps. Most impressive of all are the remains of the furnace for the *caldarium* and, down beneath it, a forest of hypocaust tiles and ceramic pipes for moving the hot steam around the building. So intact does the system appear that it seems almost possible that a brief plumbing job might restore the steam room to working order.

The baths were built around the middle of the 2nd century, possibly at the same time as a new aqueduct was constructed for the city in 157.[202] Coins have been found here from the reign of Gordian III (238–44), so the amenities were clearly then still in use, but some time before the end of the 4th century they probably ceased operation. Small, poor dwellings were then constructed around them, making use of the superior-quality masonry, and these in turn collapsed, possibly after an earthquake in 544.[203]

Odessos remained important into the 6th century. In 536, Justinian made it the headquarters of a curious union of the province of Moesia Secunda, Cyprus, the Cyclades and Caria, united by little common interest save their maritime heritages.[204] As late as 595, it was still in use as a military base during a campaign by Peter, the brother of the Emperor Maurice, against the Slavs and Avars. Thereafter it changed hands several times between the Byzantines and the nascent Bulgarian Empire, before falling definitively to the Bulgarians in the 11th century.

Odessos did in fact briefly become a Byzantine city once more in the early 15th century, when it was ceded to Manuel II Palaiologos in 1413, nearly 1,500 years after it had first known Roman administration. The Empire had precious little time left to run, and its territory had shrunk almost to vanishing point, but a few towns further to the south of Odessos represented a continuing hold on the Black Sea coast and a tenuous justification for the continued use of the label 'Empire'.

Mesembria (modern Nesebur in Bulgaria), some 70 kilometres south of Odessos, was almost the last of them, a final outpost on the frontier, when the *limes* had all but collapsed to the front steps of the imperial palace on the Golden Horn. It fell to Mehmet II's Ottoman army in February 1453, just two months before the final siege and fall of Constantinople, a day still referred to by Greeks as the 'Great Disaster'.

In Nesebur a largely reconstructed set of Byzantine city walls encircles part of the old town, in which large numbers of souvenir stalls compete for the attention of day-trippers with a dozen or more medieval churches. The oldest of these churches, the 'Old Metropolitan' constructed between the 5th and 8th centuries, is genuinely Byzantine, rather than a Greek-Bulgarian hybrid. It is a triple-apsed basilica with the nave and aisles separated by massive and still-standing two-storey piers. No decoration survives, though to the right of the principal apse, faint remains of what might be polychrome plaster still cling to the walls. The first church on the site, possibly from the 5th century, was razed and rebuilt in grander fashion in the 7th century, showing a city still able to contemplate major construction projects. A set of Roman baths nearby were, indeed, built only in the 6th century and were still in use as late as the 8th century, when such installations further north in Moesia had long been abandoned.

One of the last inhabitants of Byzantine Mesembria is buried in Saint Spas, a lovely little 15th-century church, whose walls are covered in frescoes of a vast array of saints and holy men. Mataissa Cantacuzina Palaiologina, who combines in her name that of two of Byzantium's last ruling dynasties,[205] died in 1441, and was originally buried in the Old Metropolitan Church, before her tomb was transferred to avoid its being cannibalised by the Turkish authorities for building materials. It seems to have been moved first to a church of the Analepsis, which in turn disappeared by the 1930s, before coming to its final resting place at Saint Spas.[206] Exactly who the princess was is unclear; she was misidentified in the 19th century with a daughter of Tsar John Alexander of Bulgaria, who became the wife of Andronikos IV Palaiologos (1376–9).[207] But she was obviously a woman of great status, laying claim to kinship with two of the families who ruled over the very last years of the Empire, and the survival of her tomb and her name seems almost symbolic, a distorted echo that is virtually inaudible against the tourist hordes of Nesebur.

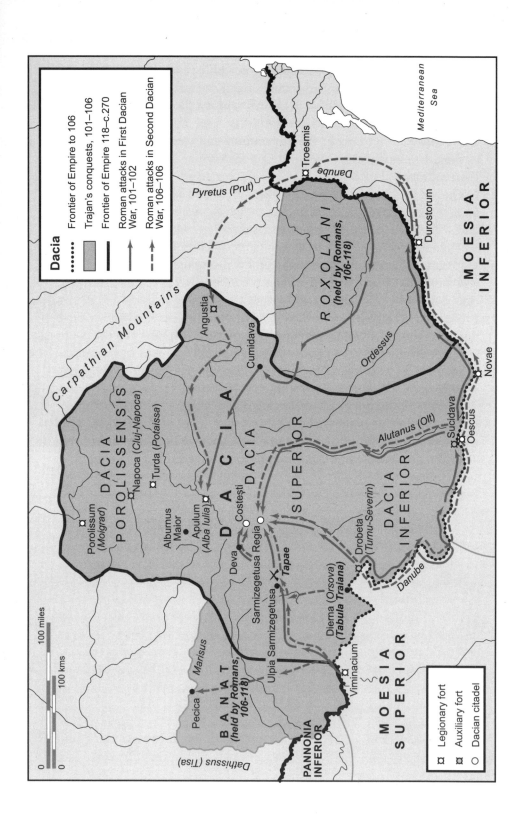

Dacia

- ⋯⋯⋯ Frontier of Empire to 106
- Trajan's conquests, 101–106
- ——— Frontier of Empire 118–c.270
- ⟶ Roman attacks in First Dacian War, 101–102
- ⇢ Roman attacks in Second Dacian War, 106–106

Mediterranean Sea

MOESIA INFERIOR

Troesmis

Danube

Pyretus (Prut)

Durostorum

ROXOLANI (held by Romans, 106–118)

Ordessus

Novae

Carpathian Mountains

Angustia

Cumidava

DACIA POROLISSENSIS

Napoca (Cluj-Napoca)

Turda (Potaissa)

DACIA SUPERIOR

Alutanus (Olt)

Sucidava

Oescus

Alburnus Maior

Apulum (Alba Iulia)

Costeşti

Deva

Sarmizegetusa Regia

Tapae

DACIA INFERIOR

Drobeta (Turnu-Severin)

Danube

Ulpia Sarmizegetusa

Dierna (Orsova) (Tabula Traiana)

Viminacium

MOESIA SUPERIOR

Marisus

Pecica

BANAT (held by Romans, 106–118)

Dathissus (Tisa)

PANNONIA INFERIOR

100 miles

100 kms

- ⌖ Legionary fort
- ⌖ Auxiliary fort
- ○ Dacian citadel

CHAPTER 5

Dacia

*Trajan constructed over the Ister a stone bridge for which I cannot suffi-
ciently admire him. Brilliant indeed are his other achievements, yet this
surpasses them ... This too, then is one of the achievements that show
the magnitude of Trajan's designs, though the bridge is of no use to us;
for merely the piers are standing, affording no means of crossing, as if
they had been erected for the sole purpose of demonstrating that there is
nothing which human ingenuity cannot accomplish.*

Cassius Dio, *Roman History*[1]

The medium-sized town of Turnu-Severin, far from Romania's political
centre at Bucharest, and long marooned in an awkwardly strategic location
near the point where Bulgaria, Romania and Serbia meet, lies at the root
of the problem that is Dacia and the struggle over the self-identification of
an entire people. It was here, in 101, that one of the columns of Trajan's
expeditionary force crossed into the territory of the Dacians. The army
was intent on teaching a lesson to their overly successful and aggressive
king, Decebalus, who was seen as posing a threat to the neighbouring
Roman provinces of Pannonia and Moesia that was too great to be ignored.
It was a campaign that would ultimately end in the conquest and annexation of Dacia, and the establishment of a Roman presence that would
endure for almost 170 years.

The Dacians and the Romans already had a long history of tension.
Sheltered in the Transylvanian plain behind the high protective cradle
of the Carpathian mountains, the Dacians had prospered, exploiting the
richness of their land in gold and silver resources, and harnessing new
techniques of craftsmanship and engineering that filtered through to
them from the Greek colonies on the Black Sea coast. Out of this they
developed their own indigenous civilisation, which, when united under
a strong political leadership, threatened to pose an awkward block on
any Roman expansive designs north of the Danube and to provide an
alternative power centre for any malcontents south of the river line.

Under King Burebista, the first really unified Dacian state had already expanded into Transylvania and even attacked Olbia in the Crimea.[2] Julius Caesar may have been squaring up to deal with this growing menace of the Dacians before his assassination in 44 BC, particularly as Burebista had offered assistance to his arch-enemy Pompey in 48 BC during the Civil War, but the death of the Dacian king the same year as Caesar reduced the urgency of taking immediate action. Dacia gradually fragmented into a number of warring factions, and what territory Burebista had captured south of the Danube was seized by Marcus Licinius Crassus in 27 BC.[3]

Intermittent raids by the Dacians across the river did continue, but they presented only localised problems, until the kingdom once more united under Decebalus in about AD 86. The previous year, a Dacian raid had resulted in the death of the governor of Moesia, Oppius Sabinus, and the Romans felt that it was high time to revenge him. Domitian therefore despatched his praetorian prefect Cornelius Fuscus to deal with Decebalus. However, at Tapae, about 100 kilometres to the north of Turnu-Severin, the Romans were badly mauled, resulting in the death of Fuscus and the loss of almost an entire legion. So the next year Tettus Iulianus was sent to finish the job, and he defeated Decebalus in more or less the same area.[4] The launching of another campaign against the Suebi and Iazyges to the west of Dacia meant that Domitian had insufficient resources to impose his will fully on Decebalus. The resulting treaty was something of a compromise, and one that the Dacians could even present as a victory, for the Romans handed over a large sum of money to Decebalus to keep him quiet and, possibly more importantly, sent craftsmen and artisans to the royal capital at Sarmizegetusa, some of whom may have been skilled in siegecraft and counter-measures.[5]

Dacia was, therefore, very much unfinished business when Trajan decided to launch his invasion in 101. Exactly what the Emperor's motives were has been the subject of much speculation. Allegedly Decebalus had been harbouring Roman deserters and had employed the engineers provided by the peace in 89 to construct impregnable strongholds; a more likely explanation is simply that he resented the affront to Roman dignity and the expense caused by the continued payment of subsidies to Decebalus,[6] and that he planned a limited campaign to put the Dacian king in his place. It was not in any case a sudden decision, as the logistics necessary to mount such an expeditionary force must have taken several years to arrange, and Trajan appointed safe pairs of hands to govern the neighbouring provinces (and to the command of their legions), including Marcus Laberius Maximus in Moesia Inferior. Estimates of the force involved vary from 50,000 to 100,000.[7] Whatever the true number, it was one of the greatest Roman armies ever gathered together for a single campaign.

The first assault was probably mounted in April. The sources for the campaign are surprisingly slight; the historians Dio Chrysostom and Appian both wrote accounts of the campaign, but they are wholly lost, while of Trajan's own narrative of the Dacian War, but a single sentence survives. Instead, apart from incidental mentions in more general histories, we are forced to rely on one of the most unique military narratives in Roman history. After his final victory in the Second Dacian War in 106, Trajan ordered the erection of a column to commemorate the victory. It was to be the centrepiece of his new forum, which had been started in Rome and sits opposite the older forums of Augustus and Julius Caesar, and adjacent to that of his adoptive father Nerva (the Forum Transitoria). At more than 30 metres high, and made up of seventeen marble drums, Trajan's Column was intended to be the last resting place of the funerary urns for Trajan and his wife Plotina. Whether it was in fact used for this purpose is unclear, but the reliefs, which run in a spiral from the base to the top of the column in around 400 frames, present an official visual history of the Dacian Wars.[8] The column was dedicated in 113 and was originally surmounted by a gilt statue of the emperor; which was replaced by the current portrait of Saint Peter in 1588.

The panels on the column have proved a fertile mine for students of Roman military tactics and equipment, in some cases providing the only really good depiction of such legionary activities as making a camp, entrenching or foraging. But their value in determining a chronological narrative of the Dacian Wars is hard to assess without corroborating evidence, which is, for the most part, lacking. The extent to which it simply depicts commonplace themes that were expected in such a publicly visible glorification of the Emperor is unknowable, but it is likely that, in general terms, the events shown have some relation to the real war, even if attempts to tie down exactly where a skirmish or battle took place are exceedingly difficult. These scenes are, however, a unique resource, and though other emperors (such as Galerius with his arch at Thessaloniki) depicted their campaigns in sequences of panels on stone, none of them approaches the breadth, ambition or completeness of Trajan's Column.

There is other evidence for the engineering work that was necessary for the military operation. Around 40 kilometres west along the river from Turnu-Severin, and 10 kilometres south-west of Orşova on the Serbian side (at ancient Dierna), an inscription records how the Emperor had a roadway excavated out of the bare rock of the cliffs, an extraordinary engineering achievement. A reproduction of the inscription, the *Tabula Traiana* is just visible from the Romanian side, decorated with an architrave as though a temple front; but the original was moved when the Djerdap dam was built and threatened to inundate the monument, and now sits more inaccessibly in a display some way off at Lepenski Vir.[9]

It seems that detachments of at least twelve legions may have been involved in the war,[10] a prodigious number, and – coupled with the large number of auxiliary cohorts and *alae*, plus the allied troops Trajan had assembled – this left Decebalus with very little choice but to fight a fundamentally defensive campaign and avoid full battlefield confrontations. The war as depicted in stone on Trajan's Column seems, therefore, to have an almost leisurely feel about it at first, showing the massing and mustering of the troops and their crossing on pontoon bridges, surveyed benignly by a personification of the Danube. Trajan is depicted on Panel VIII as holding a council of war, seated on a podium surrounded by his personal guard; then, in the next panel, he presides over the sacrifice of an ox and a sheep, a *suovetaurilia*, the proper offering for the successful undertaking of a military campaign. Yet before long, battle scenes appear; in one Jupiter is shown hurling a thunderbolt down against the Dacians, who are duly routed; soon afterwards a Dacian fortress is fired and an embassy composed of long-haired Dacian nobles is seen being received and sent away empty-handed.

Trajan seems to have won a major victory at Tapae, the same location as the two battles in the Domitianic war against the Dacians, but his losses were great enough to mean that he could not press home this advantage and a second year's campaigning was necessary. Further Roman successes led to the taking of at least two fortresses, in the storming of the second of which (on Panel LXVIII) the Romans are seen forming up in the *testudo* (or 'tortoise'), with shields locked together above and to the sides for protection as they near the ramparts.

It appears that Sarmizegetusa, the capital, was now dangerously exposed and Decebalus sued for peace. According to Cassius Dio, he was ordered to surrender the engineers he had previously been allowed by Domitian, to dismantle his forts and to hand over Roman deserters.[11] The Romans did not evacuate the whole of Dacia, retaining an area to the south, the modern Banat, and establishing military camps, possibly including the precursor of the legionary fortress at Sarmizegetusa Ulpia, in a salient threatening Decebalus's capital.[12]

Although Trajan had himself awarded the title Dacicus in honour of his victory and celebrated a triumph in December 102, Decebalus was not content to let things lie. In 103, he invaded the territory of the Iazyges (who had supported the Romans), and began to acquire arms again. In 105, he seems to have launched a direct attack on the Roman garrisons in southern Dacia.[13] There was also an alleged assassination attempt on Trajan and, more tangibly, a senior Roman officer was kidnapped by the Dacians after being tricked into attending peace negotiations in person. It is more than likely that this was the former consul Cnaeus Pompeius Longinus, who had been governor of Pannonia until 98 and so represented a prize hostage indeed.[14] Decebalus offered to parley Longinus's safe return in exchange for a Roman withdrawal south of the Danube. In the true spirit of Roman heroes of earlier times, Longinus took poison, preferring death to a dishonourable part in any exchange of territory for his own survival.

Trajan had had enough. An even larger army was assembled and despatched to Dacia. In the early spring of 106, the army crossed, after the requisite *suovetaurilia* was performed. The target would be the Dacian capital and Decebalus himself. The crossing of the Danube was immeasurably assisted by the construction of a fixed bridge across the river. The architect of the column, Apollodorus of Damascus, a Syrian and a favourite of Trajan, was also responsible for the great bridge (as well as for most of the other elements in Trajan's forum). Unfortunately, he was not so popular with his master's successor, Hadrian, who not only ordered the bridge thrown down, for fear that the Dacians might use it to strike more easily south of the river should they ever rebel, but also did not take kindly to some perceived criticism by Apollodorus concerning his own architectural tastes. The architect was summarily exiled and shortly thereafter Hadrian had him killed.[15]

The bridge was an astonishing feat of engineering. At around 1,100 metres long, it had to be supported by twenty massive piles driven into the river. In order to construct it, the course of the river was diverted by vast dams, which allowed the placing of the piles and arches. Unsurprisingly, its dedication takes pride of place in one of the scenes on Trajan's Column. At the same time the bridge was built, the first Roman stone camp in Dacia was established around the northern bridgehead at Drobeta. First garrisoned by the *Cohors I Antiochensium*, it, together with the bridge, spelled doom for Decebalus.

The second war began with an attempt by Decebalus to cut the Drobeta bridge,[16] and thus sever the vital artery of the entire Roman operation, but it failed. The Roman army then struck north, probably marching through the valley of the Olt to invest Sarmizegetusa from the south and east. Decebalus again avoided direct confrontation where he could, seeking to wear down the Roman through guerrilla-style attacks, hoping that he could survive until winter, and then once again patch up some kind of peace or enlist the support of further allies amongst the neighbouring barbarian tribes. Through hilly defiles and almost inaccessible approaches, the legions and cohorts finally reached Sarmizegetusa. Whether Decebalus defended his capital against a determined Roman assault, or simply fled when his leading warriors looked as if they were losing heart, depends on the interpretation of Trajan's Column.[17] Yet what is clear is that Decebalus escaped the fall of his royal capital in about July 106 alive and fled northwards to carry on the resistance.

Although he continued to defend (and lose) a string of other hill forts, many of his nobles must have defected, including one Biklis, whom Cassius Dio relates betrayed the whereabouts of the royal treasure, a bitter blow for any hopes that Decebalus may have held of buying assistance from outside Dacia.[18] The hoard had been concealed by diverting the Sargetias river, burying it and then rechannelling the river into its old bed.[19] When recovered, it was found (according to one source) to consist of five million pounds of gold and ten million of silver.[20] Even if exaggerated, the true sum must still have been vast, as it went a great deal of the way to defraying the costs of the whole campaign.

Decebalus was by now down to his last few diehard supporters. On 6 September 106, a mounted Roman detachment caught up with him in wooded territory, a scene dramatically depicted on the Column. The Roman cavalrymen desperately try to reach their quarry, but Decebalus, seeing that things are hopeless, slits his throat with his own *falx*, the characteristic curved sword of the Dacians. Astonishingly, corroboration of this account came to light when the tombstone of the very man who had commanded the cavalry in their failed attempt to capture the King was found in 1965 at Philippi in Macedonia.[21] Tiberius Claudius Maximus had been decorated for bravery in Domitian's Dacian War and fought in both of Trajan's campaigns in the *Ala II Pannoniorum*. He was probably about forty-five years old at the time of the exploit that has immortalised his name, and for which he received a further decoration. He would be honoured once more for bravery in Trajan's Parthian War of 115–17, making him one of the most decorated Roman soldiers known. Decebalus's severed head, meanwhile, was sent to Trajan's encampment at an unidentified place named Ranisstorum, together with his two children. The head was later hurled down the Gemonian steps at Rome, a fate reserved for the most heinous amongst Rome's enemies.[22]

Once the Roman conquest was complete, the camp at Drobeta hosted a variety of garrisons, including the *Cohors III Campestris* in the 2nd century, and the *Cohors I sagittariorum milliaria*, a double-strength cohort of archers, in the 3rd.[23] The auxiliary fort grew into a city, which was granted municipal status by Hadrian in 118–19,[24] before becoming a *colonia* under Septimius Severus some time around 200. The remains of the civilian settlement at Drobeta, however, have been wholly swallowed up by the modern town. The square perimeter of the camp is in place, but the several phases of rebuilding have confused somewhat the original neat plan. When the rest of Dacia was evacuated in 270, Drobeta – in common with a couple of other bridgehead forts (including Sucidava (Celei) to the east, opposite Oescus in Moesia) – was retained to provide control over a possible crossing point over the Danube where barbarians might strike southwards, but equally from which Roman armies might more easily launch punitive raids northwards against any troublesome barbarians.

The fort was rebuilt under Constantine I in the early 4th century, but was devastated during the Hunnish invasions of the 440s. It was then restored one last time under Justinian, when a simple defensive tower was constructed here, but so decayed was Drobeta itself by this time that it was given the new name Theodora. Exactly when it was abandoned is unclear, although the other bridgehead fort at Sucidava has yielded finds of coins up until 596–7 in the time of Emperor Maurice, which implies that it was pressure from the Slavs and Avars in the early 7th century that caused the final evacuation of the Byzantine positions to the north of the Danube.

Amongst the ruins, a series of barrack blocks by the river are visible, while the central *praetorium* seems fairly intact, and it is even possible to make out the curved apsidal podium of the temple of the standards. A large, round tower facing the river is of 13th-century vintage, but a less prominent one in the south-west belongs to the reconstruction under Justinian; it even incorporates gravestones from the earlier fort. Of the main fort, part of the gate towers of the *porta principalis dextra* survives, but more impressive by far are the piers of the original bridge that lie beached beside the modern river's course. They sit a little uneasily beyond a railway line, partly encased in modern concrete for protection against erosion. The larger one is as big as a house, part of it torn off, giving it the sinister effect of an insincere smile. Looking across to the Serbian bank, there are further remains towards the southern beachhead at ancient Pontes, but a grey-brown sky, limned with searing flashes of lightning, allows only intermittent glimpses of the point from which Trajan embarked on his invasion of Dacia.

From Turnu-Severin the road northwards is flat at first, but soon starts to climb into the foothills of the Carpathians. The countryside is afflicted by a curious schizophrenia, dotted with abandoned factories, rusting dinosaurs, already half-forgotten testaments to Nicolae Ceauşescu's policy of bringing heavy industry into the countryside. Yet alongside these, horse-drawn carts ply the roads between the villages, an easy and time-tested means of transportation when the money for flash cars or even for fuel is short. And superimposed upon this is a level of new prosperity, as gaudy villas line the roadside and the ever-present hoardings for mobile-phone companies insist on the arrival of a new economic era. Amidst all this, it would be little surprise to encounter a Roman legionary en route to Sarmizegetusa.

Although the Romans tried to lay claim to the Dacian heritage by naming the new town they founded on the lower ground as Sarmizegetusa Ulpia Regia (about 100 kilometres north of Drobeta), they were never really able to claim the uplands, and certainly not its soul. At Oraştie, the nearest main town to the site of Decebalus's capital, known for convenience as Sarmizegetusa Regia, those who do not have fond feelings towards the 170-year-long Roman occupation of Dacia have erected a statue to Burebista, the first of the Dacian kings to cause trouble for Rome.

Whether the Dacians benefited from the Roman occupation, how much native influence survived it, and in turn to what extent Dacia continued to be shaped by the Romans after the Empire evacuated the province have become the subject of a lively and sometimes bitter debate, which verges on the polemic. The traditional standpoint, at least in Romania, has been that the Romanian language (which is quite clearly a Romance tongue, like French or Spanish) is sufficient evidence that a Romanised population persisted in the area after the 3rd century and that today's Dacians are therefore lineal descendants of the settlers who flooded into the province after its annexation. Some neighbouring countries – and this is an attitude particularly prevalent in Hungary – have sniped that this is all nonsense and that Latin could not have survived in the face of widespread barbarian settlement, and without the support of a government infrastructure that Dacia signally lacked after 270. Finally, to add a third corner to a very vexed triangle, there are those in Romania who argue that really the two other camps are asking the wrong questions and that Romanian culture as it emerged into the Middle Ages had a strong component of the original Dacian about it, that the Roman invasion should not be celebrated as a 'liberation', that the Roman abandonment of the province was a good thing, and that in general Romanians should be celebrating Decebalus and his heroic struggle in preference to Trajan and his legionary blitzkrieg.

For the visit to Sarmizegetusa, I am, for the sake of excluding bias (or of including both biases), accompanied by representatives of both pro-Roman and pro-Dacian camps. Really it is a matter of emphasis, and no one doubts that the Dacians were amongst the most advanced of the 'barbarians' that the Romans encountered, and that the imperial occupation of Dacia did leave traces that echo down to the present day. The citadel lies at around 1,200 metres altitude, the first 1,000 metres just about accessible along a very rough road with a four-wheel-drive and a determined driver. Work on a tarmac road, which for the moment makes the ascent even more challenging, will eventually make one of Dacia's most hidden secrets within easy reach of all, with inevitably deleterious effects on the air of mystery that currently shrouds its wood-clad slopes.

The car park, such as it is, is in a narrow glade on a terrace, over-looked by a thin canopy of trees. A few scattered blocks mark the remains of the camp of a *vexillation* of the IV Flavia Felix legion, which occupied a position here for around half a century after the defeat of Decebalus.[25] However, once it was clear that the hill country had been genuinely subjugated and there was to be no Dacian resurgence, such lofty outposts were largely abandoned.[26]

Alongside stands a section of the original Dacian fortress wall, built using a system known as *murus dacicus*, which involved the construction of a double-wall joined together by timber struts with a packed-earth and rubble core between them for extra strength. The grooves and slots along the interior of the stones can still be seen where the timbers were originally laid between the two layers of wall. It was the erection of fortresses using such advanced techniques as this that had so exercised the Romans before the First Dacian War, and that had led to their demands that they be dismantled as part of the peace that resulted in the temporary cessation of hostilities in 102. Reused column drums integrated into the wall also indicate that it was built employing earlier, dismantled structures from the fortress.

A short distance away, the paved stones of a Sacred Way lead further up into the citadel. Sarmizegetusa was primarily a cult site, and the main area that has been investigated by archaeologists relates to its role at the heart of Dacian religious life. The Sacred Way led, originally, to this main sanctuary enclosure a few hundred metres away, which was first used during the time of Burebista. It continued to be maintained and embellished until the end under Decebalus, by which time the political and religious centres of Dacia had been consolidated into this one site, of such vital importance that its capture became the primary focus of Trajan's second war.

The temple enclosure is built on a double-terrace, which holds a series of shrines dating from different stages in Sarmizegetusa's development. The uppermost is the latest, almost certainly dating from the reign of Decebalus. It is composed (as are most of the Dacian temples) of several aisles of columns, which commonly had an upper and lower storey. Here, just the stumps of the columns remain, testament to the comprehensive sacking to which the Romans must have subjected the Dacians' sacred place (and their probable subsequent harnessing of the temple ruins for their own construction needs) – indeed, on the whole site only one more or less complete column is visible. On the lower terrace a number of older aisled temples sit in a wide, open space surrounded by a thick screen of trees.

Among them, one anomalous building stands out. A 7-metre-wide, flat disc, cracked with age, has a tail composed of rectangular blocks leading off from it, making it seem like a great stone lollipop. It is in fact a solar indicator. If a stick is placed in the middle of the disc at noon, its shadow will always fall along the stone 'tail', though the shadow's length will vary depending on the time of year, being shortest at the summer solstice and longest at the winter solstice.

As well as another aisled temple, which represents a pre-Decebelan phase, a curious circular sanctuary sits in the middle of the terrace. It has rows of concentric circles, one of larger stone blocks, then immediately inside this one of smaller stones – almost stone pegs – each seventh one being bigger than the rest. It is believed that these represent the Dacian solar year.[27] Intermediate circles are made up of wooden posts of varying heights, which create a kind of ripple effect. Any speculation that this might have had a particular religious significance is dampened by the revelation that they were in fact placed at Sarmizegetusa by the director of a film made about Burebista in the early 1980s.

At the centre of the temple lies a horseshoe-shaped inner sanctuary with its closed end pointing west, the normal orientation for Dacian temples. Exactly which gods were worshipped here is not clear. The 'Dacian' camp maintains that gods such as Zamolxis and Bendis were honoured at these shrines. Zamolxis is mentioned by Herodotus[28] as the supreme god of the Thracians, who was originally mortal and a disciple of Pythagoras, but who, after his death, was miraculously resurrected and became the subject of a long-lasting cult. Bendis was a goddess of the moon much revered by the Thracians, but to place her and Zamolxis's worship here involves translating the religious practices observed by Herodotus amongst the Thracians of the 5th century BC to those of the Dacians of the 1st century AD, a leap fraught with supposition. It is probable that the reality is much more complex, with groups of mixed Geto-Thracian heritage moving northwards over time and mingling with Celtic influences to create the high 'Dacian' culture of Burebista and Decebalus.

Down below the temple terrace, further sections of *murus dacicus* are visible amongst the trees and undergrowth. Only around 5 per cent of the site has been excavated, and much remains unknown of its governmental buildings and functions, and indeed of the civil population who must have made up the majority of its inhabitants.

Only about 10 kilometres as the crow flies from Sarmizegetusa, but a far longer journey from the summit of one hill fort to the crown of the other to its north-west, lies Costeşti, which was very probably the original capital of the Dacian kingdom under Burebista before its transfer to Sarmizegetusa. The climb here is more modest, a 750-metre hike up a gently sloping track from the guardian's house. The fort was again built using a series of concentric terraces, the topmost of which was surmounted by a palisade of oak logs above an earthwork stronghold and contained the royal palace.

On the second terrace, the grassed-over remnants of a *murus dacicus* defensive wall sit, together with stone blocks forming the outline of one of the gate towers. From a flat section of terrace nearby there is a sublime view of the forested hills opposite. It is an indication of the unfriendliness of the terrain that the Romans had to overcome; the large army groups that Trajan despatched into Dacia must have struggled to make headway in such terrain of wood and hill, yet any smaller units would have risked falling prey to Dacian guerrilla strikes and would have lacked the muscle to invest or storm the hill-fort complexes that dot the Oraştie mountains of the Dacian heartland.

The royal terrace further up retains two towers, one of which originally had an upper storey of brick, but this was badly damaged by fire and has collapsed. A second, larger tower lies 200 metres further off, in which sections of the upper storey survive, together with a porch of four broken columns. It has been interpreted as the royal palace of Burebista, from which he directed the Dacian armies that first threw down the gauntlet against Rome.[29] On a lower terrace nearby, in a quiet, damp glade, sits the largest Dacian temple still in its original location. Many of the smooth, round stones that mark the sites of the columns are covered in little blooms of moss and it seems a very peaceful place, from which the tide of war has long ago receded.

Once Decebalus had been defeated, the Roman armies occupied most of his kingdom, including an area in the east that had been annexed by the Dacians from the Sarmatians in the previous decade; Trajan ignored the latter's protest that their lands should be restored to them, in favour of holding a better defensive line for the Empire. The outline of the new province was dictated very much by the geography of the region. As Jordanes would later say in his *Getica*, 'This country lies across the Danube within sight of Moesia, and is surrounded by a crown of mountains.'[30] The Roman territory formed a rough horseshoe from the Dathissus (Tisa) river on the west, up past the gold-mining centre of Alburnus Maior to Porolissum in the north at the edge of the Apuseni mountains. It then ran along the foothills of the Carpathians to an eastern point at Angustia, at which it was closest to the north-western point of Moesia Inferior in the Dobrudja, though separated by several hundred kilometres of unfriendly territory. A string of fortifications on the Alutus river then took the *limes* to the Danube at a point roughly equidistant between the Moesian forts of Oescus and Novae. An area to the east of the Alutus, which had initially been occupied under Trajan (and attached to Moesia Inferior), was then abandoned by Hadrian in the 130s, before Septimius Severus pushed the frontier 10 or so kilometres east of the river to create a *Limes Transalutanus*. It seems likely that this latter was the first part of the province to be abandoned and was lost by the Romans around the reign of Gordian III (238–44).[31]

A portion of the old Dacian kingdom to the north-west, which was open to the central European plain, was left unoccupied and became known as the land of the 'Free' Dacians. To the north and east of this lay the territory of the Carpi and the route to the Ukraine and the central Asian steppes. It was unfortunate for the Romans that this became a sort of barbarian 'super-highway' along which successive waves of invaders moved. Dacia was thus terribly exposed and required a great outlay of resources to defend it. The province did at least have the merit (apart from its mineral riches in gold and iron) of acting as a lightning conductor, for barbarians would have to travel through it across hundreds of kilometres of Roman territory and past the defending legion and auxiliary units before they ever reached the Danube and the rich pickings of the cities that lay beyond it.

Sarmizegetusa Ulpia Traiana, the most important early centre of Romanisation was about 30 kilometres from modern Hunedoara, and 40 kilometres west of the old Dacian capital of Sarmizegetusa Regia, from which it borrowed its name. It was in fact originally founded (between 108 and 110) as Colonia Dacia, and only acquired its new name under Hadrian. It was the residence of the governor of Dacia, and thus the chief city of the province, before it was divided into three under

Marcus Aurelius. The new subdivisions of Dacia Apulensis (with its capital at Apulum)[32] in the west, of Dacia Porolissensis (with its governor resident at Porolissum) and of Dacia Malvensis in the south (with its centre possibly at Romula) excluded Sarmizegetusa from the direct line of political authority, but it was compensated with a position as metropolis for all Dacia and the focal point for the council of all Dacia (*Tres Daciae*), for which it was the designated meeting point.[33]

The city received a wall as early as the reign of Trajan, a sure sign that it was already recognised that defending the province might prove a challenge. On a rich agricultural plain overlooked by low, forested hills, it encloses an area of some 32 hectares, only part of which has been excavated. Indeed, the site seems like a curious mixture of museum and country park, the buildings infilled with grass, and parts of the ancient city still occupied by orchards and fields dotted with haystacks sculpted in the shape of an upside-down golf tee. The walls have been consolidated with mortar to stop erosion, but this gives them the disturbing appearance that they have been tamed and are now rather sulky. To the left of the main entrance lie a glass workshop and a small temple to the woodland god Silvanus, now with just the fragments of a courtyard and *cella* remaining. Nearby a larger shrine, the 'Great Temple', retains two Corinthian columns of its original colonnade, but the dedication of the god worshipped here is unknown.

Of more interest is the forum, extensively excavated and now a mixture of partly reconstructed and wholly ruinous buildings. The most important of these was the Aedes Augustalium, the palace of the priests of the imperial cult, one of the few such to have been identified throughout the Empire (another example was unearthed at Herculaneum, near Pompeii). The cult, which was ministered to by imperial freedmen (ex-slaves), was a prestigious sign of Romanisation and it is no surprise to find it here, in an area that was subjected to such a heavy military presence.

Among the heaps of fragments and column pieces lying around the forum, one is clearly a dedication by the *duumvirs*, the joint magistrates who presided over the city in provincial imitation of Rome's pair of annual consuls. Just outside the city walls lie the remnants of the Temple of Nemesis, adjacent to the amphitheatre – a juxtaposition of the deity of retribution and the arena that recurs time and again throughout the Roman Empire. The amphitheatre itself, a large curving expanse of brick and stone, seems oddly devoid of soul. There is no seating remaining and it is impossible to make out anything of its internal structure. It was built during the first half of the second century and had a capacity of around 5,000 spectators. It was repaired in 158 and remained in use quite

late; the discovery of a 4th-century coin hoard and the conversion of
the amphitheatre to some kind of fortress at about that time are rare
signs of the residual urban life of Dacia following the Roman withdrawal
some decades before.[34]

Most of the defensive installations in Dacia were in fact auxiliary forts
(in the north primarily garrisoned by mounted units) or watchtowers,
many built during the phase following the initial occupation (except in
the *Limes Transalutanus*), but dating them any more precisely than the
period 120–200 is difficult, and some at least may have been built later
as part of a reorganisation or to fill in gaps in the line. There were,
however, probably three legions in Dacia in the immediate aftermath of
the Trajanic conquest: XIII Gemina, IV Flavia and I Adiutrix.[35] By 118–20,
two of those had transferred to the eastern frontier, where they were
needed for the Emperor's new war against the Parthians, and the XIII
Gemina remained the sole legionary garrison until 168, when V
Macedonica was transferred from Moesia Inferior to Dacia Porolissensis.[36]

Not far from Deva, the regional centre nearest Sarmizegetusa Regia,
a large monument in honour of the Dacian king Decebalus, sickle-sword
in hand, stands on the way into northern Transylvania. From here it is
only around 60 kilometres to Alba Iulia, a handsome town, whose historical centre is in large part based around a Vauban-style fortress that was
built by the Austrian Habsburg rulers of Romania in the 18th century.
Its bastions and counterscarps lie precisely on top of the presumed
fortress of the XIII Gemina legion and the town of Apulum that later
developed from it. Under Marcus Aurelius, the town was elevated to
become Municipium Aurelium Apulense.[37] It became a *colonia* under
Commodus, and inscriptions have been found dating from as late as 253,
just two decades before the Roman administration must have evacuated
it. Uniquely, Apulum gave rise to two *coloniae*, the second of which, to
the north-east of the legionary camp, reached that exalted status under
Trajan Decius in the late 240s and was – with singular pragmatism, if
not imagination – named Nova Apulensis. It remained long after the
Roman era a focus for pan-Dacian (or Romanian) feeling, and it was
here that in 1599 the unification of Romania was proclaimed by King
Michael the Brave, and the first King and Queen of modern Romania
were crowned in 1922. In the Catholic cathedral there, a Gothic structure with soaring barrel vaults, a discreet marble tomb contains the body
of Janos Hunyadi (or Ioan de Hunedoara to Romanians) who, as King
of Hungary, almost single-handedly held back the Ottoman Turks in the
north-western Balkans for the best part of a decade in the 1440s.

The principal visible Roman relic of Apulum is one of the gates of the legionary fortress, the *porta principalis dextra*, which lay in the centre of the right-hand wall of the camp. In the throes of a major restoration, it lies in a grassy area alongside some of the 18th-century ramparts. Part of the Roman wall stands to about 5 metres high, and the two side-towers of the gate (covered in modern protective canopies) and its central arch are visible. Beneath them ditches have been excavated whose purpose looks defensive, but they are more closely associated with archaeological soundings than the original Roman structure. The walkways around the gate are patrolled by a small posse of 'soldiers' dressed in 18th-century Austrian garb, who act as guides to the Vaubanesque fortifications. On the day of our visit there were, unfortunately, no Roman legionaries in evidence.

It is only around 65 kilometres' drive north-east, along what was the Roman military road from Alba Iulia, to Turda, which was in Roman times the town of Potaissa and from 167 to 268 home to the V Macedonica legion.[38] Until then it had been a comparatively small settlement, but soon thereafter was promoted to become a *municipium* under Septimius Severus. Modern Turda is neat and well kept, but its tourism industry depends much more heavily on Dracula tours than it does on Romans, for the lore of the legendary vampire has spawned a large Dracula-themed restaurant and hotel in the centre, while Trajan, Hadrian and Marcus Aurelius merit scarcely a mention.

The site of the Roman camp lies on a plateau up a steep hill just to the south-west of the town centre. On a large rectangular area of grass, on which a couple of cows contentedly munch, and bordered by a row of single-storey houses, a gas holder or storage tower perches besides the Roman remains. The south-west corner tower lies visible in the grass besides the storage tower, then further back towards the east is the consolidated *principia*, really just the outline, though with the apse of what might have been a podium or the temple of the standards clearly discernible. Arrayed alongside it are small rectangular rooms, probably representing offices. Across a track from here are recent excavations, including what seems to be a bathhouse, with a scattering of ceramic pipes. There is clearly still much more to see, for from an obviously artificial mound on which a shrubby bush is growing, large numbers of pieces of tiles peek out, and throughout the fields in which the legionary camp now lies there are small pieces of pottery strewn everywhere.

Potaissa reached the rank of a *colonia* under Caracalla.[39] Coins from the time of Philip I (244–9) indicate that the camp was occupied at least until then, and pottery found on the site, together with indications from burials in a necropolis to the north-east of the town, show signs that Potaissa was not totally abandoned in the wake of the Roman withdrawal.

Some 30 kilometres further north-west lay Napoca, now Cluj-Napoca, the capital of Transylvania. Despite its importance in Roman times, the growth of a thriving medieval town, including the splendid 14th-century church of Saint Michael that dominates the main square, has all but obliterated its ancient parent settlement. It was, however, made a *municipium* by Hadrian in 124, and in common with other towns that their predecessor had raised to that rank, was elevated to *colonia* by Marcus Aurelius or Commodus.

The terminus of the military road that led all the way through the province, coming ultimately from Aquincum (Budapest) in Pannonia, was Porolissum, the administrative centre of the region and the capital of the later province of Dacia Porolissensis. It lies north-west of Zalău, some 80 kilometres to the north-west of Napoca, in countryside popu-lated with low-rise villages with orange-ochre tiled roofs, each one of them with a pretty white- or cream-faced church mounted with metal crosses and almost onion-style domes. Porolissum itself was defended by auxiliary units, including the *Cohors I Brittanorum milliaria Ulpia Torquata pia fidelis civium Romanorum*, a unit from far-off Britain, which must have the honour of one of the longest Roman military names on record.[40] The civilian settlement, amongst whose inhabitants was a strong presence of military veterans, grew up to the south and west of the fort. The possibilities for making a profit from the trade across the border into *barbaricum* must also have drawn merchants and would-be entre-preneurs from much further afield.

The little museum in Zalău maps the seven military forts and sixty-six watchtowers or signal-towers in just this sector alone. The *limes* consisted largely of an earthwork, with a north-facing ditch, studded with strongpoints and observation towers, in distant echo of Britannia's Antonine Wall. The first signs of the camp complex, some 10 kilo-metres away near Moigrad, are a few vestiges of a rectangular building with a gated entry (now surrounded by barbed wire). This building, outside the camp itself, and just a few kilometres from the military fron-tier, was the customs house, at which dues could be levied on anyone entering or leaving the Empire, a tax known as *portoria*. The level of this could reach as much as 25 per cent, and it was distinct from any impo-sitions exacted by individual cities (most notably Palmyra in Syria) for goods passing through their territory. *Portoria* dues were also occasion-ally levied on inter-provincial trade.

It was one of the most effective means of raising revenue that the

Empire possessed, for the government did not, in general, raise taxes based on income (which was difficult to prove), but preferred to attack more tangible assets, such as land and, as in this case, physical goods that were being transported. An additional set of taxes, called *vicesima* and payable at 5 per cent of the value, were levied on the manumission of slaves and as an inheritance duty. One of these, the *vicesima hereditatium*, was only payable by Roman citizens, and it is quite possible that Caracalla's decision in 212 to grant citizenship to all free males in the Empire was motivated by a desire to expand the base of this taxation, an argument made all the more plausible by the fact that he simultaneously increased the rate to 10 per cent.[41]

To the left of the track that leads on towards the fort itself lies another area of remains, with just the foundations and a section of wall surviving. This was originally a sacred enclosure that housed temples to Liber Pater and Baal, the latter evidence of a strong Syrian presence in the town. This structure belonged to the civilian settlement of Porolissum, which, although it became a *municipium* under Septimius Severus, never quite made the final leap to *colonia* status.

The fort sits on Pomet hill, a slight eminence to the north and east of the *municipium*. To the north again a series of wooded ridges formed the actual *limes*, while to the north-west lies a gap in the hills, another 'Iron Gate' into Dacia, analogous to that along the Danube that led Trajan's troops into the province during the war of conquest. It is the need to guard this second opening that explains the heavy Roman military presence in the area. Across the valley, on Citera hill, another smaller Roman fortlet (probably built under Trajan)[42] stood, but, although excavated, the trees and bushes have long since grown back to reclaim the mound as their own.

The *porta principalis* of the main fort has been heavily reconstructed, its two projecting rounded towers somewhat reminiscent of a miniature version of the Porta Nigra at Trier. The surrounding circuit wall, however, is largely gone, leaving just a steep earth bank as a reminder of the once-formidable ramparts. In the centre of the camp the foundations of the *principia* have survived, as well as the podium from which in 214 Caracalla ordered the murder of Gabaromathus, King of the Quadi, who had been invited to Porolissum for peace negotiations.[43] It was a clear indication that Rome's word was best trusted at a very safe distance.

The partly restored *porta decumanus* leads out of the fort to the amphitheatre, which was reconstructed in the late 1990s. It was originally built in stone over an earlier earthen structure in about 157. The level of the original can be made out by a wavy white line in the stones, above which is all modern stonework, albeit quarried locally from the same sources as were used in the Roman building.

Outside the fort to the west, past a partly preserved angle-tower, lies an area that was a tavern and, down some stairs beside it, a shrine to Jupiter Dolichenus. This, and the probable presence of a Temple of Mithras near the *principia*, are evidence of the influence of the military on the religious life of the town. A more mainstream public temple, that of the Imperial Cult, also lay south of the *principia*, which was in turn adapted to become an early Christian basilica once emperor-worship was no longer de rigueur. Porolissum was one of the most exposed outposts on the *limes*, but it still survived right until the end of the Roman period, with coins as late as Gallienus occurring there. It was probably inhabited beyond the withdrawal of the imperial administration, for coins have been found from the reign of Valens (364–78), while in 2007 a large deposit of materials dating to the late 4th and early 5th centuries was discovered.

In the mid-2nd century, persistent pressure by barbarian groups in the Carpathians and along the Danube led to a terrible dilemma for the Roman state. Raids by the Carpi in the 240s and the Goths in the late 240s and 250s had become ever more pressing and there were not the resources to fight on every front at once, particularly when the tax base was subsequently reduced by the breaking away of the Gallic provinces and then of almost the whole of the east during Zenobia of Palmyra's rebellion from 268. Dacia was simply too exposed, vulnerable to attack on three sides, and sometime between the 250s and 270 a pull-out from some of the forts may have begun. The chronology is unclear, but the forts on the Alutus river may have gone first.[44] Porolissum was certainly restored under Trajan Decius (between 248 and 251) and so may have been held comparatively late. Sometime during the reign of Aurelian (270–5), however, the Romans finally evacuated Dacia.[45] It was not a move that the Emperor was particularly disposed to publicise widely; even the slightest success might be celebrated on coins, or trumpeted in triumphs or ovations, but failure was normally quietly forgotten. Indeed, the province of Dacia was 'revived' south of the Danube by Aurelian's establishment of two new provinces of 'Dacia', both carved out of Moesia. Whether any of the population of the abandoned province was transferred to Dacia Ripensis and Dacia Mediterranea is unclear, but it was at least a useful propaganda exercise for the Emperor; it could now be claimed that Dacia had not been lost; it had merely moved a little.

Black Sea

Byzantium

Sinope (Sinop)

Amisus (Samsun)

BITHYNIA ET PONTUS

Ancyra (Ankara)

GALATIA

Amaseia (Amasya)

Megalopolis (Sivas)

CAPPADOCIA

Satala (Sadagh)

Soumela Monastery

Trapezus/ Trebizond (Trabzon)

ARMENIA

Artaxata

Euphrates

Melitene (Malatya)

Nemrut Dagh

Karakus

Samosata (Samsat)

Edessa (Urfa)

annexed 244

Carrhae (Harran)

ASIA

LYCIA ET PAMPHYLIA

Taurus Mountains

Antitaurus Mountains

CILICIA

Laodicea

Antioch

Cyprus

Mediterranean Sea

SYRIA

Palmyra

OSROENE

Suayb

Sogmatar

MESOPOTAMIA

Edessa (Urfa)

Amida (Diyarbakir)

ARZENENE

TUR ABDIN

Mor Gabriel

Dara

Nisibis (Nusaybin)

CORDUENE

Midyat

ZABDICENE

Castra Maurorum

Singara

Tigris

PERSIA

Euphrates

Circesium

Dura Europos

Seleucia on the Tigris

Ctesiphon

Cappadocia, Mesopotamia and Osroene

- – – – Frontier of Empire, c.165
- ——— Frontier of Empire, c.195
- ▨ Added to Empire, 298
- ••••••• Frontier of Empire, 408

200 miles
300 kms

CHAPTER 6

Cappadocia

They put arsenic in his meat
And stared aghast to watch him eat;
They poured strychnine in his cup
And shook to see him drink it up:
They shook, they stared as white's their shirt:
Them it was their poison hurt.
– I tell the tale that I heard told.
Mithridates, he died old.
　　　　A. E. Housman, *A Shropshire Lad*, LXII

Rome's long involvement with Asia Minor began in 133 BC with the legacy bequeathed by Attalus III of Pergamum of his kingdom in western Asia Minor to the Roman Republic.[1] Such posthumous gifts – real or concocted – were not uncommon and served as a way of guaranteeing present security against meddling neighbours (or family), all at the expense, of course, of future independence. By the time of Attalus, the hegemony of Alexander the Great's Seleucid successors in the 3rd century BC had long since broken up into a kaleidoscope of fractious Hellenic kinglets, and once Rome was involved, the temptation to them of involving an external power-broker in their quarrels proved both alluring and, ultimately, disastrous.[2] Not particularly keen on annexation, the citizens of Pergamum rose under Aristonicus, and saw off one consul (Publius Licinius Crassus Mucianus), only to be defeated in 130 BC by his successor, Marcus Perperna.[3]

Rome's second acquisition in the area came in a similar fashion when Nicomedes IV of Bithynia (in north-west Asia Minor) willed his kingdom to Rome in 74 BC. From the windfall acquisition of this western coastal region, Rome's tentacles spread gradually inland. But during the next decade the Republic was nearly pushed from Asia by the rising power of Mithridates of Pontus, and it took a hard series of campaigns – and the military prowess of the most famous general of the age, Pompey the Great – to bring him down and in 64 BC establish the structures by which the Romans would dominate the area for a century.

The core of Mithridates's kingdom lay along the Black Sea coast and, extending as far down as the mountainous interior of central Anatolia, became the province of Pontus, while a stretch – including Trebizond (Trabzon) – was handed over to the client king Deiotarus of Galatia; and further south Rome's interests were safeguarded by King Ariobarzanes I of Cappadocia. Under Augustus, the province of Asia became one of the few really prestigious posts left open to senators, and to achieve the proconsulate here – or in Africa – was the summit of many senatorial careers. For the most part Augustus left the minor principalities of Asia untouched, despite the adherence of many of the petty monarchs to the cause of Mark Antony.

Under Tiberius, the huge central kingdom of Cappadocia was annexed to Asia in AD 15,[4] while the kingdom of Commagene – similarly absorbed after the death of its philo-Roman king Antiochos III in 17 – was given to the province of Syria.[5] Cappadocia was initially governed by a procurator (as had been the recent acquisitions of Raetia and Noricum in Europe), so rendering its treasury directly accessible to the Emperor. After a brief experiment under Caligula at reviving the client kingdoms as a means of governing the region,[6] the provincial organisation was finally stabilised by Vespasian, who established Cappadocia as the province covering the greater part of the Anatolian plateau, with Armenia Minor joining it in 72 to guard the north-eastern flank against the Persians.[7]

As the area where Roman power came up against that of Persia, the only state with the resources to truly rival Rome in the long term, expansion beyond the Euphrates, which became marked as an unofficial borderline between the two, was fitful and fraught with difficulties. Despite the strength of the Persians, the Romans did succeed in pushing the frontier forward. Trajan, with brief success in 115–17, and Septimius Severus, with more lasting effect in 197–9,[8] advanced the border to the Tigris, thereby creating the provinces of Mesopotamia and Osroene and an exposed salient into Persian territory to the east and south-east, whose defence would cause far more insecurity than it relieved.

The Cappadocian and Armenian frontier is one of the longest stretches in the Empire, and one of the most rugged. Largely defined by the Euphrates, as the river meanders through modern Turkey and on into Syria, it is comparatively little explored. From the prosperous coastal fringes of the Black Sea, the *limes* snaked, generally southwards, through coastal hills and then through the much more forbidding ranges of the Antitaurus and Taurus mountains, before descending finally into the fringes of the desert in northern Syria. Compared to many of the other sections of the frontier, there are relatively few visible remains in Cappadocia, though the cities that have grown up over the ruins of their Roman (and frequently much older) ancestors have very rich heritages indeed and often played a key role in the history of the Roman East.

Around 150 kilometres south of the Black Sea lay Amaseia (modern Amasya), the capital of the Pontic kingdom for a century after its foundation around 300 BC. It nestles at the foot of a dramatic gorge formed by two sets of cliffs towering above the River Yeşilırmak (the ancient Iris). Its ancient acropolis suffered a vengeful sacking by Lucullus's troops in 70 BC, no doubt frustrated at their inability to run the Pontic King Mithridates to ground. One of Rome's most implacable enemies, Mithridates, having provoked war through a massacre of Roman citizens in western Anatolia in 88 BC[9] – never a wise career move for an oriental despot – saw off Sulla and Lucullus in successive Mithridatic Wars before finally being brought to book by Pompey the Great in 65 BC.

After a brief period of direct occupation, Amaseia fell to a local client king, before being annexed directly to the province of Galatia in 2 BC. The town's most famous son, the geographer Strabo, was born here sometime around 64 BC,[10] just after the initial Roman conquest. An exceptional polymath, Strabo travelled widely, particularly in the Eastern Empire, and lived in Rome for at least nine years, from 44 BC. In 25 BC he travelled down the Nile with Aelius Gallus, the prefect of the province,[11] collecting information for his great seventeen-volume *Geographica*, which combines an account of the geography of the regions he visited with an eclectic mixture of history, mathematics, philosophy and political theorising. It is probable that it was through his relationship with Gallus that Strabo acquired his Roman citizenship (not a given, in an essentially Hellenistic *polis* such as Amaseia).[12] His acute observations included the all-too-true aside that the sun almost never seems to shine in Britain, while about his home town he proudly wrote, 'My city . . . both by human foresight and by nature it is an admirable devised city.'[13] Alongside the riverside walk where Amasyans take an evening stroll to help forget the oppressive midday summer heat, statues have been erected of the town's historic worthies. That for Strabo is robed in distinctly un-Roman garb, making him look like a botched hybrid, half-Oxbridge don, half-Mongol overlord.

The cliff face below the acropolis summit is pockmarked with tombs carved deep into the rock. Known as the 'Tombs of the Pontic Kings', there are five, accessible by staircases leading up the precipitous slope, in one of which an inscription was found dedicated by Metrodoros, the commander of the fort, to Pharnaces I.[14] All that now survive are plain rooms with niches cut into the back, either for the corpses themselves or, more likely, for cult statues. Two of the tombs share a cave, excavated out at the top, with the remains of a carved zigzag pattern in the facing wall to indicate the former presence of steps that would permit access to the roof of the chambers. After the removal of the royal capital to Sinope on the Black Sea coast in the later 2nd century BC, no other kings were buried here. Of Mithridates VI himself, we only know that Pompey ordered a decent funeral and that he was buried 'in the tombs of his forefathers',[15] but as to whether this was at Sinope, or indeed whether the royal necropolis at Amaseia was used for the illustrious last monarch of his line, the Roman historian Appian is studiously vague.

The final Roman frontier lay some 400 kilometres to the east of Amaseia, beginning its long course on the Black Sea coast near the city of Trapezus (later known as Trebizond, and now the modern city of Trabzon).[16] In the first century AD, Trebizond had served the Romans as a vital border conduit for the road over the mountains via the Zigana pass into Armenia, and, although notionally independent under Polemo I of Pontus, it provided a convenient base for Corbulo's campaign against the latter kingdom in AD 58.[17] It was, however, only six years later that the city was formally annexed as part of the province of Galatia.[18] As the frontier pushed eastwards under Vespasian and Hadrian, further roads were built into Persia and Mesopotamia and the city was extensively remodelled under Hadrian. Trebizond then experienced several centuries of quiet prosperity until the Goths, in a surprising eastward extension of their plunderers' progress, sacked it in 256. Finding the garrison drunk and the defences largely unmanned, they were able to break the barbarians' generally bad run at storming walled cities.

By the 13th century Trebizond had fallen to the Comneni, a noble family who since 1204 had presided over a wayward fragment of the greater Byzantine *imperium*, which had escaped the clutches of the Fourth Crusaders and had somehow never quite returned to the fold. Appending the suffix 'Megas' (great) to their family name, the Trapezuntine Comneni survived principally on a diet of absurdly inflated self-belief, cleverly calculated intrigue and an almost inexhaustible supply of princesses whom they used to cement alliances with their predatory neighbours. For all the Comneni's manoeuvring and grandiose statements that it was they, rather than the Palaiologi – the family that had actually recaptured the imperial city of Constantinople from the Crusaders in 1261 – who were the true heirs of Constantine, no one took their Lilliputian empire seriously and their position became ever more parlous.

The total population of the city itself had probably slipped by the 15th century to just 4,000, mainly as a result of the mortality caused by the Black Death. In the early 1450s, a Turkish emir from Erdebil besieged it, and Emperor John IV found only fifty of his subjects remaining, as the rest of the defenders, prizing survival over a valorous end, had simply slipped away.[19]

After the fall of Constantinople to Mehmet II in 1453, the Trapezuntines tried to keep a low profile. David, who came to the throne in 1458, effected an unfortunate change of policy and began to seek salvation through aggressive alliances with the western powers.[20] Being neither particularly interested in the charms of the Comneni daughters, nor in any position to offer concrete assistance, David's new friends – who included Philip the Good, the Duke of Burgundy – were entirely unable to fend off the inevitable denouement, and the offended Ottoman sultan marched on Trebizond in the summer of 1461. In vain David offered one of his daughters in marriage to the sultan, but this traditional gambit had long had its day, and Mehmet, unimpressed, declined.

After a month-long siege, David took the option of dishonourable exile and ordered the gates opened. Mehmet's janissaries streamed in to take possession of the town, and David, his family and most of the surviving nobility were packed off in ships to Constantinople. It was, in a sense, the day the Roman Empire died.

Two years later, angered at a letter that seemed to indicate a plot to restore the Comneni to power, Mehmet had David and seven of his sons beheaded in a single night.[21] The man who betrayed the letter, and who had also undermined David's will to resist the Ottoman siege, was his former treasurer and cousin, George Amoiroutzes. By a bizarre twist of fate, it was Amoiroutzes's son, George, known as Skanderbeg, who would lead decades of resistance to Ottoman advances in the Balkans, in some way making up by his bravery for the perfidy of his father.[22]

Shielded by the Pontic Alps, the Black Sea coast retained a strong and individualistic culture that held back Turkish advances for centuries, and even after the loss of its political independence it retained a vibrant separate identity until its Greek-speaking population was deported wholesale as a result of the Treaty of Lausanne, which formally ended the First World War in the region in 1923. Considered one of the most attractive cities in Asia Minor, Trebizond was described by a panegyricist as 'the apple of the eye of all Asia'.[23] Very little of this splendour now survives. A gate pierces the wall of the lower citadel – there were two – close to a congested square near the former Russian consulate, the immediate interior of old Trebizond being choked with traffic and lined with an unromantic assortment of travel agencies, spare-parts yards and tailors' shops. The square gate bastions project incongruously into another era, much restored and then blackened by the fumes.

Of the 'Golden Palace' of the Comneni there appears to be no trace. Even the most authoritative greybeards shake their heads sadly and offer this mosque or that madrasa as a worthy substitute. Further and further up the citadel slope, where surely the palace must have been sited, its marble great hall decorated with sumptuous portraits of the Grand Comneni,[24] there is still no sign. Finally, a local schoolteacher points us in the direction of the Kraal Köskü ('the King's Pavilion'), which sounds at least as if a dim memory of the palace has survived. So, uphill and past a small mosque, the clear remains of an enclosure wall of some antiquity face the road. In the 1920s, this area was comparatively clear and the palace ruins faced onto an open square called Epiphania, but now a whole suburb has grown around to conceal the ancient secret, making it much trickier to enter.

We plunge down a side-alley, into a kitchen garden with chickens scratching around a collection of ramshackle hutches, and a stand of vegetables struggling away in a gloomy corner. Pulling aside a makeshift barrier of wooden planks, we discover a way into the palace itself. Only shells of rooms now remain, the interior of the structure a shapeless maze of half-collapsed masonry, enclosed by the more substantial exterior walls, which stand in places to around 4 metres high. After a brief ramble around the broken palace interior, egress from the palace precinct is gained by another domestic yard, the modern residences supported in part by the old Byzantine wall. Looking back after another 50 metres, there is nothing to be seen, and the Golden Palace has disappeared behind a screen of modest apartment blocks. It is almost as if the Ottomans had taken until 1461 to storm the Comnenid citadel, for the simple reason that they could never quite find it.

Although at first intent on regaining the great prize of Constantinople, the Comneni soon recognised the practical needs of more localised aspirations by building themselves suitably grand churches in Trebizond. They could not resist, however, giving one the same dedication as the great cathedral of Hagia Sophia in the lost metropolis. Now set in a square well back from the traffic and bustle, the 13th-century monastery church is an island of calm. It is of a cross-in-square design, with a narthex at the west end, along which a gallery of beautiful medieval frescoes are arrayed, while inside, another set includes a very damaged depiction of Pontius Pilate washing his hand, and Saint Thomas feeling Christ's wounds. Although cleaned and restored in recent decades, their survival over seven centuries has something of the miraculous about it.

Hagia Sophia is not, however, Trebizond's oldest surviving church, for that accolade goes to Saint Anne's in the east of the old town. A worn relief slab on its south door depicts a soldier with outstretched sword standing alongside an angel, with an inscription stating that the church was restored in 883/4. The basilica remained a functioning church until 1923,[25] but its once-painted interior has been gutted, and it now remains firmly barred, its courtyard providing handy extra space for the neighbouring parade of coffee-houses.

The city's most important church, the largest of all and the venue for imperial coronations, was the Theotokos Chrysokephalos ('the Golden-headed Mother of Christ'). Its foundation is traditionally attributed to Hannibalianus, nephew of Constantine the Great, and the city's legionary fortress may have occupied an area subsequently used for the building of the church,[26] but its history can really only be traced to the 10th century. Converted soon after the Turkish conquest into a mosque, the Fatih Ortahisar Camii, its plain interior has a pleasing sense of tranquillity about it. Yet in truth the centuries have not been kind to it, and its hidden past jostles for attention in the background. The soaring dome is a reminder of the painting of Christ Pantocrator that must surely once have presided over it. Only a few decades ago, moreover, the walls were plastered over, obliterating a series of wall paintings and mosaics in the apse. Just a section of floor covered in *opus sectile* – cut sections of marble in black and white – gives direct evidence of the original church's decoration. For those intent on further scrutiny, the lower courses of the western wall of the mosque are composed of the original Roman stonework.

South of Trabzon, the road passes high into the Pontic Alps, the way winding through almost alpine forests, increasingly remote from the commercial and urban life of the Greek coastal colonies. Finally, after about 40 kilometres and at about 1,200 metres altitude, there lies the monastery complex of Panayia Soumela, the most spectacular of the many that dotted the Trapezuntine landscape, and among which it is the best representative of the age-old tradition of Christian piety that populated Asia Minor with monastic foundations, both lofty (as here) and (in modern Cappadocia) troglodyte.

From a distance the buildings seem to cling to the rock, as likely to promote vertigo as any sense of religious awe. Said to have been founded in 386, during the reign of Theodosius I, by Barnabas and Sophronius, two Athenian monks,[27] the monastery was long the recipient of high-ranking patronage. Its restoration and enlargement in the 6th century were attributed to Justinian's favourite general, Belisarius. After the establishment of the Empire of Trebizond, the monastery church became if anything an even greater focus for imperial favours, being accessible to Comnenid largesse in a way that the basilicas of Constantinople no longer were. Alexios III Comnenos refortified Soumela in 1360, claiming on his inscription, which survived until 1650 on the monastery's outside gate, the rather overoptimistic title of 'Emperor of all the East and Iberia'.[28]

Soumela survived the Turkish conquest and almost five centuries of Ottoman rule before the transfer of populations in 1923 deprived it of its loyal Greek-speaking flock, and it was abandoned. Today the site is largely based on a remodelling in the 13th century, although many of the buildings were destroyed in a fire in 1929 and have been substantially restored in recent decades. This has not stopped dozens of the fresco panels being defaced by visitors more careful for their own transient fame than the preservation of a priceless cultural heritage. Saints look down amid a score of scrawled names and messages, their frozen stares and stylised poses mercifully betraying no sense of the indignity to which their images have been subjected. Some graffiti pre-date the end of the active life in the monastery in the 1920s, but an upsurge of vandalism in the 1960s was accompanied by predominantly local names, save the proud, neat and disgraceful contribution by a visiting US Air Force man in 1965. Those frescoes sited higher up have largely escaped damage, and the Rock Chapel, which formed the original core of the monastery, retains its biblical scenes mostly intact amid the gloomy half-darkness and distant sensation of a place once drenched in piety, now almost devoid of any hint of the sacred.

The legionary fortress of Satala lay, then, as now, on the route south-wards from Trebizond, which ultimately took travellers skirting the frontier down as far as Antioch, a distance of more than 600 kilometres. The verdant hills of the Black Sea coast gradually become less fertile, browner and more arid in appearance until at length they take on the look of a lunar landscape, scored and furrowed with erosion channels. Finally, the hills descend into the plain of Kelkit, about 90 kilometres south of Soumela, and close by lies the unassuming village of Sadagh, its older houses in part built from stones acquired from the Roman fortress. Until the 1960s, indeed, the former Roman baths were still being used as the village's bakery.[29] Procopius, in his account of Justinian's 6th-century reconstruction of Satala, describes a topography that is instantly recognisable: 'it also lies in a low-lying plain and is dominated by many hills which tower around it'.[30]

Satala seems an unlikely place for a famous Roman victory. Indeed, the fact that it once housed a legionary fortress, a significant civilian settlement, and was the lynchpin of the Roman frontier defences in central Cappadocia seems to risk a severe attack of incredulity. When Alfred Biliotti, the British vice-consul at Trebizond, came here in 1874, there was far more to see.[31] He reported substantial sections of wall remaining, some 6 metres high and more than 4 metres wide. Of all this abundance of remains, most has now vanished.

Upon the annexation of the central Anatolian kingdom of Commagene to the Empire by Vespasian in AD 72, the whole of the upper Euphrates became a frontier area, although in part shielded by the client state of Armenia from direct confrontation with the Parthians. Of the other legionary fortresses that guarded Cappadocia, Zeugma and Samosata, the bases of III Scythica and VI Ferrata respectively, have been inundated by the waters of the Atatürk Dam, while Malatya has been encroached on by the modern city, and so Satala's survival is of unique importance. It became the base of XV Apollinaris, probably under Trajan,[32] who passed through during his Parthian campaign of 115–17, and the legion remained there even after the town's destruction around 256 by the Persian shah Shapur I during his rampage around the Roman East. According to the Notitia Dignitatum, they were still on garrison duty there at the end of the 4th century.[33]

The area remained contested by Sassanid Persians and Romans throughout the 3rd century. In 298, Galerius rescued his reputation with his senior colleague Diocletian when he defeated the Persian ruler Narses in the vicinity of Satala, capturing the royal harem and treasury for good measure. He thus made up for a stinging defeat that he had suffered at the Persians' hands two years before, not far from Carrhae (Harran in south-eastern Turkey). So annoyed had Diocletian allegedly been at the damage to Roman prestige on that occasion that he had made Galerius, clad in full imperial regalia, walk on foot in front of his chariot as the two Tetrarchs entered Antioch.[34]

After the Persians suffered a further defeat in 530 in front of Satala, Justinian decided to give it new fortifications, and it is the remains of these that can be seen today. The civilian settlement seems to have been largely swallowed up by the modern village, but perched on a gentle slope that ultimately leads across the fields down to the Kelkit river lies the fort, the surviving banks and stones of its ramparts forming a plat-form on which a sea of golden wheat ears wave tranquilly in the breeze. The interior of the fort, in part cut away at its western end by the village houses, is impenetrable until harvest time, though Biliotti reported a 'substantial house' there, which a century of agriculture must have eroded away entirely. The rubble-core of the north-east corner towers is substan-tially intact, standing upright up like a lonely chess piece, its game long over. Just a few courses of stone remain of the rest of the circuit, uncertainly ringing the mound, a scattering of the rest lying at the edge of another field to the east of the fort.

A few hundred metres to the south-east, deep in the middle of another field, sit four arches, only one of them still carrying a channel or lintel on top. A little further on, small piles of stones mark the former site of a fifth arch and, doubtless, further in the agricultural undergrowth lie the remains of many more. After resisting for many centuries, in 1784 the bulk of the structure seems to have been plundered for stones to help repair damage caused by a large earthquake in the regional capital of Erzincan.

There has been a great deal of debate as to whether this is an aqueduct or the remains of a basilical church. Biliotti certainly thought it was a church, but subsequent scholars seem to have favoured the aqueduct, before a recent swing back to regarding it as a religious building.[35] The pair of shepherds who shyly regard our unlikely progress are with Biliotti, and maintain adamantly that it is a former Christian church and that it must be, for their grandfathers told them so. The hillsides, they say, are dotted with tombs and there are inscribed stones to be seen by those who know where to look. People from the government came some years back and took away stones in army helicopters, though whether this was an officially sanctioned excavation or a strictly freelance enterprise they do not know or, diplomatically, will not say.

Biliotti faced similar ambiguities more than a century ago. A bronze head that he had discovered was confiscated by the governor of Erzerum and sent on to Istanbul, where it was sold to a private collector, for which Biliotti received the grand sum of eight Turkish pounds. Immediately after the British consul's departure, the headman of Sadagh set to his own excavations, which apparently yielded him no harvest whatsoever.

The site is still littered with minor treasures. Near the aqueduct or basilica, someone has excavated a deep pit, exposing the remains of an ancient wall. In the debris piled up around the hole lie carved mouldings from friezes with zigzag patterns and a couple of fragmentary tile stamps carved with 'X', which might possibly be part of XV for the Apollinaris legion, Satala's garrison. The fort's final fate is obscure; it was probably abandoned after being sacked by Khusraw II in 607, but what became of its civilian community, which was large enough to send a bishop to the Council of Nicaea in 325, is utterly obscure.

Lying to the south and east of Satala, in a mountainous region of eastern Anatolia bordering the upper Euphrates, the kingdom of Commagene was able for several centuries to exploit its lofty and

inaccessible position to avoid the clutches of its more powerful neighbours. In the second century BC, the Seleucid Empire, one of the successor
states that carved up Alexander the Great's conquests after his death in
323 BC, began to fragment. Ptolemaios, the Seleucid governor, took the
opportunity to declare independence around 162 BC. He founded
Commagene and gradually extended its domain southwards to include
Samosata (300 kilometres south-west of the Kelkit plain),[36] and the
kingdom reached its cultural apogee under Antiochos I, who ruled it
from about 69 BC.[37]

In AD 17, however, Commagene was annexed by Tiberius and appended
to Syria. It was gifted a further three decades of independence by Caligula
in 41, who confirmed Antiochos IV as its ruler. But in 72, Antiochos was
accused by Caesennius Paetus, the governor of Syria, of conspiring with
the Parthians, and Vespasian permitted his legate to annex Commagene
once more. Direct Roman control now extended down the middle
Euphrates, probably as far as its confluence with the Balkh, and Samosata
was renamed Flavia Samosata to indicate its new allegiance. The
Commagene royal family was packed off to Greece, where it regained
a momentary fame when Antiochos's grandson – who rejoiced in the
delightfully Hellenistic-Roman mish-mash name of Gaius Julius
Antiochos Epiphanes Philopappos – was appointed suffect consul in 109.[38]

A much more spectacular legacy lies hidden in the hills to the north
of Samsat, where the Commagene royal house erected a series of memorials and cult installations. The most famous of these is at Nemrud Dagh,
about 100 kilometres to the north-east, where two terraces of decapitated divine heads lie neatly arranged on a platform beneath a massive
tumulus of loose stones. Constructed under Antiochos I, this cult site,
known as a *hierothesion*, involved an enormous effort to carve the terraces
from the living rock and heap up the huge amount of debris to form
the tumulus itself (although whether it actually contains a tomb has not
been determined).[39] The heads propped on the ground and the larger-
than-life-size bodies that once supported them, represent Heracles,
Apollo, Zeus, Tyche (goddess of fortune) and Antiochos, whose divine
nature is thus hinted at by the company he keeps. Most of the gods, in
the syncretistic way of the times, can be identified also with deities from
the Iranian pantheon, such as Mithras for Apollo and Ahuramazda for
Zeus. Elsewhere a set of reliefs shows the illustrious royal ancestry of
Antiochos, from the Achaemenids Darius I and Artaxerxes II, down to
various Seleucids, and also including Alexander the Great, from whom
Antiochos claimed descent on his mother's side.[40] On others the king is
shown greeting various gods in what are charmingly described locally

as 'hand-shaking' scenes,[41] while a relief of a striding lion contains zodiac symbols and a pattern of stars that indicate a precise date, most probably 7 July 62 BC, though both the date and its precise significance have been much disputed.[42]

However, more than any individual piece, it is the ensemble that is striking, and the enormous diversion of resources that must have been necessary to achieve its construction. Antiochos, though, can never have dreamt that his grand project, to which only a limited number of his Commagene subjects can ever have come via a series of difficult processional ways, would become an enormous tourist magnet. At sunrise in particular the slopes are congested with backpackers seeking to witness the first rays touch the sacred sculptures and infuse them with a tint of rosy-yellow. Far more than his Roman conquerors, then, Antiochos has truly achieved immortality.

Around 50 kilometres to the south-west, and on a clear day offering a view of the terraces at Nemrud Dagh itself, is yet another tumulus, this time constructed by Mithridates II, the son of Antiochos I, quite possibly for his sister Laodice. The main feature is two pairs of columns – there were once three – one of which contains the extremely weathered figure of an eagle. It is from a rather creative misinterpretation of the identity of the bird that actually surmounts the column, that the place gets its Turkish name, Karakuş – the tumulus of the blackbird.

As Commagene was absorbed into the Roman provincial structure, it became necessary to provide it with a road network, particularly to reinforce the military spine running down from the Black Sea to Antioch. A few kilometres west of the Commagene royal summer capital of Arsameia (itself about 20 kilometres west of Nemrud Dagh) – where more 'hand-shaking' scenes are visible amidst the tumbled stones – lies the Roman bridge at Cendere, which carried the military road that followed the Cappadocian border via one of the few convenient crossing points over the Kahta river. From the side, as it spans a largely dry riverbed, the awkwardly humped construction with its facing of brick seems to resemble any other bridge of uncertain antiquity, but it still carries traffic, and is thus one of the oldest major river bridges anywhere in the world still in use for vehicles. Coming closer, three columns resolve themselves from the surrounding haze, one at the eastern end and two on the western bank. The bridge was constructed by the legate of the XV Apollinaris legion in the early 3rd century, and the columns (there were originally four) were dedicated for the Emperor Septimius Severus, his wife Julia Domna and sons Caracalla and Geta.

When Caracalla had Geta murdered after their father's death, he decreed that his brother's name be erased from all monuments throughout the Empire, and thus, here at Cendere, one of the columns would have been defaced. Its actual removal, though, is probably more to do with the vicissitudes of time than evidence of a particularly thorough job in removing all trace of Geta's memorial. It is a practice known as *damnatio memoriae*, the Romans' way of literally erasing from history those who had, for one reason or another, fallen into disfavour. It has its antecedents in Greek practice, where as early as the 5th century BC inscriptions were modified to shade out disgraced politicians or remove other unwanted references.[43]

With the extreme political instability and the frequent changes of regime that characterised the later Roman Republic, the use of devices to target opponents posthumously (such as depriving their heirs of the right to inherit or throwing down their statues) became ever more common. Upon the defeat of Mark Antony, the Senate declared that inscriptions mentioning his name should be destroyed (or his name simply erased), the first major example of this type of sanction.[44] They also declared for good measure that the name Marcus should henceforth be banned from use by the Antonii, the disgraced triumvir's family. Thereafter, both those who fell foul of the Emperor, such as Cnaeus Calpurnius Piso[45] (who was convicted of treason under Tiberius), and the emperors themselves if unpopular could find inscriptions in their honour being erased (but the latter only after their deaths). The normal form would be for the Senate, generally at the prompting of the Emperor (but in exceptional circumstance on its own initiative), to vote the target of the *damnatio* as an enemy of the Roman people, and to impose the erasure of inscriptions as an additional sanction.

Emperors who suffered *damnatio* included Nero, Commodus and Caracalla, while during the 3rd-century military anarchy, the ordering of the defacements of a predecessor's monuments became almost a rite of passage. Whilst normally only individuals suffered this penalty, the unique case of an entire legion – the III Augusta – stands out. Its monuments were defaced in the mid-3rd century on the orders of Gordian III, who blamed them for the death of his relatives Gordian I and Gordian II in an uprising that the legion had put down.[46]

To the north and east of Commagene lay the kingdom of Armenia. For the Romans, it was a client state too far. It first came into the sights of Rome through the tacit support of its king Tigranes for Mithridates of Pontus in his own wars against Rome during the 70s BC.[47] Faced with the threat of total occupation of Armenia, Tigranes submitted to Pompey,

laying his diadem at the Roman general's feet. He was permitted to
retain the core of his kingdom, but his recent acquisitions in Mesopotamia
and the borders of Parthia – which were probably what had the Romans
worried all along – were handed over.

So began Rome's on–off relationship with Armenia. For more than
600 years the Romans sought to pull Armenia out of the Persian sphere
of influence, sometimes shadow-boxing, at other times outright slug-
ging it out. In 20 BC, Augustus intervened to oust a pro-Parthian monarch,
Artaxias II, and replace him by his more pliant brother, Tigranes II. And
so it continued.

Nero's general Corbulo campaigned here in AD 60, again securing
Roman predominance and extracting an agreement that, whilst the
Armenian king might be a Parthian and selected by the Parthian shah,
he should nonetheless seek Roman confirmation of his rule and receive
his crown at Roman hands. The high tide of Roman success in Armenia
came in AD 163, when Statius Priscus stormed Artaxata, the northern
Armenian capital (now Artashat in modern Armenia), during Lucius
Verus's general campaigns against the Parthians.[48] A new capital, Kaine
Polis – which means, imaginatively enough, 'New Capital' – was established and a Roman senator, albeit related to the Parthian royal family,[49]
placed on the throne.

Armenian-Roman relations were given a further twist in the early 3rd
century when the ruling Arsacid Parthian dynasty in Persia was overthrown by the Sassanids. In Armenia, a branch of the Arsacid family
clung on to power, so that now, although the territory remained within
the Persian cultural sphere, there was an irretrievable cleavage between
its own political interests and those of (as the Arsacids saw it) the Sassanid
usurpers in Ctesiphon, the capital they established on the east bank of
the Tigris (some 30 kilometres south of modern Baghdad). The coming
of Christianity to Armenia further accentuated the differences with
Persia; the baptism of Tiridates III of Armenia in 314 raised the unpalatable prospect of a permanently pro-Roman state on the Sassanids'
northern flank. Under Constantine I, there was even a plan to annex
Armenia by declaring his nephew Hannabalianus as king. The Emperor's
unexpected death in 337, however, put an end to this, and Hannabalianus
was murdered along with most of Constantine's more distant male relatives by his three ambitious sons.

The disastrous death of Julian in 363 on campaign against the Persians,[50]
and the subsequent humiliating peace, left the Romans promising not
to intervene further in Armenia. Yet under Valens conflict broke out
once more, as the Romans placed their nominee, Pap, on the throne in

370. It was an extremely short-lived policy success, as Pap was murdered five years later, leading to the installation of yet another Persian-backed king.[51] The game of royal musical chairs was temporarily halted by a treaty in 387 by which Armenia was in effect partitioned between two kingdoms, one with a pro-Roman king, the other with a Persian-backed ruler. The western portion was soon absorbed into the Empire as the province of Armenia Minor in 428, while the remaining four-fifths became the Persian satrapy of Persarmenia.

Finally, in 590 the forces of Emperor Maurice defeated the Sassanid shah Vahram VI and, with the support of the Armenian nobles, annexed the whole of Armenia. Although they finally had the prize that had long eluded them, the Byzantines had little time to enjoy it. A brief dispos-session by the Persians in the 620s was followed by a more definitive expulsion of the Byzantine authorities by the Arabs in the 640s. Brief flickers of independence from 657 to 661 and in the 680s were soon snuffed out.

Arab rule led over time to the destruction of many of the traditional noble class, the *naksharars*, and the consolidation of authority in the hands of a single family, the Bagratunids, culminating in the appoint-ment of one of their number, Ashot I, as 'prince of princes' in 885.[52] For 200 years the Bagratunids performed a delicate juggling act, balancing the competing interests of their nominal Arab suzerains, their religious brothers in the Byzantine Empire, and the fractious squabbling of the resurgent *naksharars*. Ashot, memorialised by the nickname 'the Great', and his son Smbat were reasonably successful, although the latter finally found himself on the losing end of a civil war and was disposed of in 913 by Yusuf, the Arab governor of neighbouring Azerbaijan.[53] Although restored with Byzantine assistance, the Bagratunids were rarely able to reassert their authority over an area as wide as that dominated by Ashot the Great. What Armenia lacked in political unity in the 10th century, however, it made up for in a dazzling cultural and artistic renaissance. In 964, Ashot III 'the Merciful' transferred the Armenian capital to a new site at Ani in the southern portion of the kingdom.

Until the collapse of the Soviet Union in 1991, the site of Ashot's new capital (some 350 kilometres east of Trabzon, and 50 kilometres east of the provincial capital of Kars) was very hard to visit, with the taking of photo-graphs (and even the visible writing of notes) forbidden on pain of confiscation by Turkish border guards; and, for those who strayed too near the Cold War border, the prospect of being shot by their Soviet counter-parts. Ani still sits on the frontier, between Turkey and its new neighbour, the Republic of Armenia, divided by the snaking line of the Arpa Cayi river. Relations between the two countries, poisoned by the deaths of huge numbers of Armenians during the chaotic era that followed Ottoman Turkey's defeat in the First World War, are suspicious in the extreme. There have even been accusations from the Armenian side that damage caused to the Ani monuments was connived at by local Turkish authorities, whose attitude to a cultural monument to a people that many accuse the Ottomans of trying to wipe out is decidedly ambivalent.

Passing through the Lion Gate, an Ayyubid gateway – together with the rather too pristine restored walls, the Portakabin ticket office and the gang of juvenile trinket-sellers – gives little promise of what lies ahead. For whether damaged, neglected or unloved, Ani reveals itself as a breathtaking spiritual landscape. Its secular buildings have long ago decayed or are inaccessible, but the remains (in some cases skeletal) of the churches are poignant witnesses to a piety and devotion that sustained this kingdom in its long, and ultimately unsuccessful, defence of its position at the very edge of the Christian world.

At a distance the buildings have the curious appearance of a low, thickset dwelling surmounted by a conical cap, the trademark dome of the characteristic centralised Armenian church architecture. Close to the city's entrance, the church of the Holy Apostles seems curiously chunky and rectangular, but the effect is attributable to a later Seljuk caravanserai bolted onto the ancient church, a building also responsible for the stone portal carved with stalactite-like stone projections at its entrance. Inside, the main church boasts a superb riot of ceiling ribbing, counterpointed with a two-coloured pattern of mosaics and a scattering of Armenian inscriptions. Visible from here, the imposing hill of the town's citadel dominated the skyline, but both this and a monastery beyond lie in a forbidden military zone.

The Menüçehir Camii, towards the southern end of the site, is said to be the earliest Seljuk mosque in Anatolia, dating from the mid-11th century, with a rather funnel-like brick minaret. But inside there is no *mihrab*, save one sculpted out of the bricks of the original gallery, while the same bichromatic black and red work as in the Holy Apostles church, and an inlaid mosaic ceiling, give rise to the suspicion that this was originally an Armenian building, possibly a meeting hall. Climbing of the minaret is strictly forbidden, on account, it is said, of a tourist who some years ago leapt to his death from its summit.

Close to the ravine that delimits the city's plateau on the opposite side from the river gorge lies the church of Saint Gregory of Abughamir, a building restored to its final form in 1040 by a member of the Pahlavuni family, which thrived in the last decades of Ani's independent existence.

Its conical dome is punctuated by mouldings that surround windows in the drum to create blind arcades, a technique which the Armenians made almost their signature flourish. Inside, an arrangement of six apses was intended to focus attention on the central nave, which may have housed the Pahlavuni family tombs.

Ani's main cathedral, near the city's southern edge, lies squat and bulky, very different from the conical structures that otherwise dot the landscape – a little deceptive, for the church did originally have a dome, but it was brought down by an earthquake in 1319, one of a series that have contributed to the generally ruinous state of Ani. Ribs rising up from the arches to support the dome bring to mind the Gothic cathedrals of western Europe, though the process by which it might have influenced Western styles is obscure; perhaps the Crusaders saw Armenian churches in Cilicia, further to the south, and brought back memories of the structures on their return home from the Holy Land.

Nearby lies one of Ani's most famous structures, the church of Our Saviour, known more for the particular nature of its destruction than for the unusually large dimensions of its dome. Built around 1035/6, the church survived (although much decayed through age and general neglect) until the 1950s, when it was struck by lightning during a storm and the façade was literally rent asunder. The surviving half of the church looks, from the correct angle, as if it forms part of a complete whole, yet shift your perspective by a few degrees and it is clear that the other half of the building is simply missing. The stones of the destroyed portion still lie around in a crumpled heap, giving the whole the air of some bizarre Hollywood film set.

Down by the river lies another of Ani's surviving gems, the church of Saint Gregory the Illuminator, named in honour of the saint who brought Christianity to Armenia, himself of a noble Parthian family. It is also known as the Tigran Honents church, for the merchant who dedicated the church in 1215 and paid for its lavish frescoes. Constructed at a late stage in Ani's history, it shows some influence from Georgia, Armenia's Christian neighbour in the Caucasus, which had experienced rather more success in holding back Turkish attempts to absorb it. A pair of saints arched over the baptistery stare out at another trio over the church's main door, their faces gouged out by some unknown iconoclast.

Inside, the frescoes depict scenes from the life of Christ and that of Saint Gregory. Tradition relates that the saint refused to sacrifice to the pagan goddess Anahid – from whom Ani takes its name – and so enraged King Tiridates by his refusal that he was subjected to a brutal sequence of tortures, including suspension upside down over a mound of burning dung, and shredding the flesh on his thighs by gashing them with iron spikes. Finding that Gregory would still not abjure his faith, the King had him consigned to a darkened pit for fourteen years, an ordeal that he survived only because a pious widow threw a loaf of bread down to him each day. Finally, Tiridates went insane, perhaps sent mad by the strain of devising ever more inventive torments for Gregory, and it was only the intervention of the saint, who prayed for his royal tormentor, that cured the King. Suitably impressed, Tiridates released him, became a Christian and began a tradition of royal patronage that would last almost 800 years.

Further down towards the river another little monastery clings, together with the scattered remains of churches that collapsed long ago and sent their stones tumbling down to the edge of the gorge. On the Arpa river itself a pair of end abutments of a bridge that once connected the two sections of Ani sit alone, the void between them a symbol of the fractured relations between Turkey and Armenia, a gulf almost impossible to pass. Over on the other bank, amidst the rumble of machinery and the roar of excavators, in a potent political gesture, the modern Armenians are building a replica Ani, complete with imitations of the principal churches on the Turkish side.

In 1045, Armenian independence was snuffed out by the Byzantine Emperor Constantine IX, keen to reassert Constantinople's influence in the region after a hiatus of some four centuries. But, just as it had so many times in Roman history, the removal of a client state, or at least a sympathetic one, brought direct confrontation with a much more dangerous enemy. With the defensive bulwark of Armenia removed, the Byzantines had to face head-on the depredations of the Seljuk Turks in the region. In 1064, a Seljuk army took Ani after a three-week siege. Sacks by the Mongols in 1237 and by Tamerlane in the 1380s, combined with the effect of a series of earthquakes, consigned the city to a twilight existence in which the inhabitants were scarcely greater in number than the tally of its churches.

Three hundred kilometres to the west of Ani, the main line of the *limes* initially followed the Euphrates southwards. Under Septimius Severus at the end of the 2nd century, however, the border was pushed eastwards, with the annexation of territory between the Euphrates and Tigris. It was a region that the Romans had fought over before, under Trajan, and formed one of the principal approach avenues for expeditions aimed at the Persian heartland and its capital, Ctesiphon.

A hundred kilometres east of the Euphrates and sitting on the Tigris,

at the very edge of the territory acqured by Septimius Severus, the great
fortress of Amida, modern Diyarbakir, perched on a bluff at the end of
the navigable portion of the Tigris. Occupying such a strategic location,
it was a frequent target for Persian attacks, particularly after its walls were
reinforced by Constantius I while he was still only a Caesar in the 320s.
A much-reconstructed version of these still girds the town, the great
bastions of black stone exuding a mixture of pride and menace to outsiders.

During Shapur II's campaign of 359, the capture of the town, which
together with its southern neighbour Nisibis dominated the region, was
a major priority. Its garrison, the V Parthica legion, was boosted by the
reinforcement of no fewer than six further legions.[54] The Persians made
preparations to besiege the city. However, it soon looked to Shapur as
though his cause might be better served by thrusting deeper into the
Empire, but fate intervened. A fortunate – although, as it turned out in
the end, unlucky – shot from a ballista mounted on the walls of Amida
struck the son of one of Shapur's key allies. In order to give the bereaved
father satisfaction and save face himself, Shapur could no longer raise
the siege and pressed on with it for a further two months.[55]

The defence is vividly chronicled by Ammianus Marcellinus, one of
the Later Roman Empire's greatest historians, and one of the few from
whom a continuous narrative has survived. Although of Greek descent,
born in Antioch, Ammianus wrote in Latin, which was still the language
of command in the army. His early career was evidently a success, for
by the time his history begins, he was serving on the staff of the general
Ursicinus in Asia Minor, and he stayed with him when the senior officer
was sent to Gaul and on his despatch back to the East in 357.

Ammianus arrived at Amida to find the siege of the city just beginning. He describes in compelling detail the gradual tightening of the
Persian noose, as outlying positions were stormed and defensive artillery
had to be employed to repel attacks on the walls themselves.[56] In the
end a mound, built by the defenders to reinforce the wall and provide
a vantage point from which to fire on the enemy ramps that were
approaching the defences, collapsed and enabled the Persians to gain
entry. Ammianus and a few companions hid in a deserted corner of the
city whilst the Persians engaged in an orgy of unrestrained slaughter.
As Ammianus puts it, soldiers and civilians 'without any distinction of
age or sex were slaughtered like sheep.'[57] Ammianus and his companions somehow managed to escape, cross the Persian lines and trek,
constantly afflicted by thirst, to the comparative safety of Roman-held
Melitene (Malatya), nearly 200 kilometres to the west.

For the historiography of the Roman Empire, Ammianus's survival was a fortunate chance, for contemporary reliable accounts of the events of the 4th century are thin on the ground, with alternative sources coming from epitomes, summaries often compiled centuries after the event, or lurking on the pages of saints' lives, rich in anecdote, but failing to provide anything remotely like a coherent political narrative. When Ammianus's account comes to an end after the Battle of Adrianople in 378, Edward Gibbon, the majestic 18th-century chronicler of the Roman Empire, laments, 'It is not without the most sincere regret, that I must now take leave of an accurate and faithful guide, who has composed the history of his own times, without indulging the prejudices and passions, which usually affect the mind of a contemporary.'[58]

Nusaybin, a small Turkish town butted up just against the Syrian border some 120 kilometres south of Diyarbakir, is no stranger to life as a frontier outpost. Like Nisibis, its ancient predecessor, it long sat just at the very edge of the Roman and Persian spheres of control, dominated by one and then the other, before finally ending up under Sassanid Persian control in 363. Although Lucullus had first captured it in the 60s BC, it was not until Trajan marched through here in AD 115 that the Romans made a serious effort to make their presence permanent. As Rome's control over the East had grown tighter, with the annexation of client states such as Commagene, the room for ambiguity in terms of who controlled – or claimed – exactly what grew slighter, and friction between Rome and the ruling Parthian dynasty of Persia grew greater. The Romans had never really forgiven the Parthians for their humiliation of Crassus in 53 BC, and this – combined with the tendency of successive Roman emperors to dream that they would, somehow, recreate the Eastern domains of Alexander the Great – meant that Persia was an obvious target for an emperor in search of a war.

Trajan combined ambition with a good dose of military ability, and the service of effective generals such as the Moorish cavalry commander Lusus Quietus. After softening-up campaigns in 114 and 115, he struck out in 116 for the Tigris, bridging it with a pontoon made of wood stockpiled the previous winter near Nisibis, then pushed south via Dura Europos and captured the twin cities of Seleucia and the Parthian capital of Ctesiphon against relatively light resistance.[59] Then, going further than any Roman emperor before or since, Trajan sailed down the Tigris to the Erythrean Sea (the Persian Gulf), reaching the river mouth at Spasinou Charax (modern Basra in Iraq), where he is said to have caught sight of a ship setting sail east across the sea and lamented – no doubt for public consumption – that had he only been younger, he would have been able to follow in Alexander's footsteps all the way to India.[60]

Pausing on his return journey to pay homage at the house in Babylon where Alexander had died, Trajan found that rebellion had already broken out in the newly captured territories of Mesopotamia and Assyria. Although the initial uprising, under Sanatruces, a nephew of the deposed Parthian king Osroes, was put down and a client king installed on the throne in Ctesiphon, Trajan was too ill to campaign in 117 and died in August while returning on the long voyage to Rome. Although marked on many maps as Roman 'provinces', Mesopotamia and Assyria had no more received a normal Roman provincial government than had Germany between the Rhine and the Elbe early in Augustus's reign, and Roman control of these Parthian territories was most ephemeral.

Having slipped back under the control of Persia, Nisibis was next taken by the Romans in 194 during Septimius Severus's projection of Roman control – this time more permanently – across the Euphrates into Mesopotamia. It was promoted to the rank of *colonia* at some point during Severus's reign[61] and may have been for a short time the base of the newly raised III Parthica legion. The first Sassanid ruler of Persia, Ardashir (224–40), adopted a much more aggressive posture than his Parthian predecessors and captured a number of cities of Roman Mesopotamia, including Nisibis (although the Romans were soon able to recover it). As a token of his intentions, he also seized Spasinou Charax, which had served as a principal entrepôt for trade coming from Roman-controlled Palmyra, thus choking off a major source of wealth entering the Roman Empire.

The Persians took Nisibis again during the reign of Ardashir's successor, Shapur I (241–72). As part of the treaty that followed Galerius's defeat of the Persian shah, Narses, in 298, Nisibis was restored to the Roman Empire and became the designated point for all trade between Persian- and Roman-controlled territory.[62] It was transferred again, however, to the Sassanids in the treaty forced upon Jovian in 363 in order to extricate the battered remnants of the dead Emperor Julian's army from Persian territory. The Romans were permitted to evacuate the inhabitants, so they did not fall into Persian hands, but they were forced to abandon all their property. The Roman interpretation of the treaty was that the city should revert to its former allegiance after 120 years, but in 483 the Persians refused to hand it over, leading to several Roman attempts to wrest back control, most notably in 572 under Justin II (565–78).[63] Nisibis, however, remained stubbornly Persian (and then Arab) until its capture by the Emperor Nicephorus Phocas in 969, after which the Byzantines held a tenuous control over northern Syria for a century.

Ancient Nisibis has all but vanished. Amid the mixture of chaos and enterprise typical of this region of Turkey, almost all memory that it ever was a Roman town has been erased, and enquiries about its antiquities – save for a couple of Jacobite Christian churches – are met with puzzled stares. Yet precisely in no-man's-land between Turkey and Syria, overlooked by a Turkish watchtower and barred off by swathes of barbed wire and a squad of soldiers from the respective sides, sit the remains of a four-way arch, possibly a tetrapylon, or even a triumphal arch. Five columns and three Corinthian capitals remain, all tantalisingly off-limits, as the cross-border traffic shuffles by, eyes focused on the challenges of passport control, and not one casting a sidelong glance at the town's most important monument.

Around 15 kilometres of straight desert highway west of Nisibis, the way turns off into a series of rural backwater roads, more populated by herds of sheep and waddling troupes of ducks than any modern traffic. It was here, 28 stades (5,174 metres) from the Persian border – more or less the same distance that its ruins occupy from the present Syrian frontiers – that Emperor Anastasius decided to solve a tricky strategic problem. Ever since the loss of Nisibis in 363, the Persians had possessed a major fortified base right against Byzantine territory, a most convenient launching pad for raids and outright invasions. Kavadh's success in the war of 503–6, which resulted in the sack of several major cities, including Amida (Diyarbakir), and the extraction of an annual payment of 500 pounds of gold annually for seven years persuaded the Emperor that something had to be done.[64] Work therefore began on converting the little village of Dara into a fortified outpost, which would match and neutralise Nisibis. By 509 the fortress was largely complete, and Kavadh, who had been distracted by a Hunnish attack on his own eastern frontier, was forced to accept a fait accompli. To persuade him to allow the building of such a defensive bulwark, however, took an additional large payment from the Byzantine side as compensation for their violation of the 442 treaty, which had forbidden just such construction of new fortresses in the border regions.[65]

The city, named initially for its founder as Anastasiopolis, was embellished with the normal civic amenities such as baths, churches and – a necessity in this arid clime – water cisterns. It was provided with a strong garrison and became the base for the *dux* of Mesopotamia. But the walls proved inadequate, and, although the Byzantines under the great general Belisarius won a signal victory against the Persians near the city in 530, Justinian decided that Anastasiopolis could do with some serious reconstruction. Never shy at claiming the credit for his building projects – and occasionally those of others – the Emperor permitted the city to be renamed Iustiniana Nova. Although the extent of the work may have been exaggerated by Procopius in his *Buildings* (which was essentially a panegyric for Justinian),[66] the walls of Dara withstood major Persian sieges in 540 and 544, at a time when even Antioch fell to the Sassanids. But in 573, the Persians managed to break their way into the city. For a week the defenders fought inside the walls, behaving quite uncharacteristically for ancient armies, for whom an attempt at surrender or flight would have been more normal at this point.

When he heard of this disaster, Emperor Justin II, at whose behest the war had been initiated in the first place, is said to have lost his mind.[67] His wife Sophia sent the Emperor's doctor to Persia with a message that it would demean Shah Khusraw I's honour to carry on fighting against a defenceless woman. With the addition of a hefty payment, the Persians agreed to a one-year truce, but did not give up possession of Dara. The city remained theirs until 591 when the Byzantines got it back in exchange for giving Khusraw II support to topple Vahram, a usurper who had unseated him. When the Arabs swept through the area in the late 630s, Dara lost its purpose completely. It had risen from being a small village, but, deprived of imperial subsistence and the purchasing power of its garrison, it relapsed once more into that state.

The modern village at Dara seems to have grown organically from the old, and become completely intertwined with it. Every house is in part composed of ancient stones, column drums and friezes, some almost entirely, and it is hard to discern whether a field wall fell down last week or a thousand years ago. Beyond the edge of the village, a huge quarry has been scored into the rock face, the successive campaigns of extraction creating a curious stepped-contour effect, and it is from here that doubtless much of the construction material for the fort and the new city was carried.

The ruins are best preserved in the north-east sector of the walls' irregular perimeter,[68] close to the point at which a barrel-shaped arch carries the defences over the dried-up bed of the Dara Çay stream, itself now strewn with rubble from fallen buildings just inside the city. The bulk of the walls stands intact at this point, punctuated after about 100 metres by a U-shaped tower, still complete with a circular chamber inside topped by a plain pattern of white mosaic tiles.

From the walls the remains of a well-built road strikes straight for 50 metres or so, before coming to a full stop against a later dividing wall. Although now a confusing jumble of ruins, the place has a sense of forlorn grandeur, of an opportunity vanished, that contrasts with the sheer impoverished helplessness of the modern settlement. Further south-west within the old city walls lies a series of ancient cisterns, without whose water storage the place would have become uninhabitable in the heat of summer. The first is exposed to the air, three large vats each at least 20 metres high and 50 long, dwarfing the modern dwellings that surround it.

Further into the village, one of the houses conceals an astonishing secret. The owner – his attention attracted by the crowd of local boys who are making the most of practising their dozen English words over and over again with their eccentrically attired visitors – comes down and offers to show us the 'dungeon'. It is, he attests, a prison used by people in the 'old times' to hold malefactors. At the foot of his house, just visible above the ground, are the tops of arches of some ancient structure, so it seems worth a look. Descending by torchlight down well-cut steps (both staircase and walls slippery from an inflow of water), we reach the 'dungeon'. It is a breathtaking space, the size of a small cathedral, with towering arches creating a triple-aisle and supporting a roof some 40 metres or more above. Far from being a prison, it seems to be another water cistern, but this time staggeringly well preserved. On the floor is a small scattering of column bases, fragments of drums and other worked (but extremely faded) stone. The owner is insistent that his wholly unexpected cellar was used for confining criminals and points out a much smaller side-chamber – which has, however, no door – where he is convinced they were kept.

At the edge of the village lies the necropolis, a complex of rock tombs replete with stone-carved crosses and biblical imagery, for by the 6th century the inhabitants would almost all have been at least nominally Christian. The best of these sits on a carved portal, the arch incised with egg-and-dart patterns, and above it a relief of an angel holding a child and standing above a pile of skulls, to its right a man holding down another child on the point of cutting its throat with a knife. It seems a clear reference to Abraham's sacrifice of Isaac, which the angel has presumably just intervened to prevent. It is speculated that some, at least, of the necropolis complex may have been built in the later 6th century, by citizens of Dara who were deported in 573 after the Persian conquest of the city and then, later, dedicated a series of carvings as an offering of thanks on their safe return.[69]

By this time, the whole plateau to the north of Dara had become a Christian stronghold, and fertile ground for the spread of that late-antique brand of monasticism which seemed to thrive in soil that nurtured little else. Now known as the Tur Abdin, many of its monastic foundations from the 5th and 6th centuries have survived to this day. A small population of the faithful weathered all the vicissitudes of the Islamic conquest, Arab domination, Ottoman rule and then the increasingly unfriendly environment of the later 20th century for the shrinking Christian communities in the Middle East. Latterly, they have been joined by small numbers of the faithful who have begun to drift back, either permanently or to visit their spiritual homeland and, for those who have prospered, to assist in the restoration and upkeep of the churches and monasteries; for those less fortunate, the Tur Abdin still exerts a powerful pull as a place of pilgrimage.[70]

Most of the surviving active monasteries cluster around the regional town of Midyat, 35 kilometres to the north-west of Dara. The monastery of Mar Yakoub, around 25 kilometres north-east of Midyat, is one of the most venerable, founded in the late 4th or early 5th century; it was clearly functioning by 421 when its eponymous founder, Yakoub, died. The current church, however, probably dates from no earlier than the 6th century. On the day of our visit, a couple of aged, black-swathed nuns sit listlessly in a portico, sheltering from the blistering sun, whose heat seems magnified by the white-cream walls of the church and monastery buildings. A couple of stone crosses and a finely carved fili-gree stone tower shimmer in the heat, as a local Syrian Christian man, who lives in one of the nearby villages, explains something of its history. All, he says, was well until the 15th century when the Christians started to lose their land, only to have it restored in the 1850s. Then, during the First World War, many were massacred, part of the chaos during the break-up of the Ottoman Empire, which brought disaster for the Syrian Christians, although not on the same scale with which it visited the Armenians further to the north.

In the original church, a deliciously cool transverse chamber with three sanctuaries, two crosses flanking a sun are said to represent a solar symbol taken over from the traditional pagan beliefs of the countryside. One part of this ancient church seems still in use, with a Bible set on a stone podium with a red cloth carefully placed beneath it; the rest, with stone crosses carved on the wall, exudes an aura of sacred neglect.

The church of the Virgin, or Meryemanna as it is known locally, sits in the village of Hah, around 3 kilometres north of Mar Yakoub, which for a time until the early 7th century was the seat of the patriarch of the Tur Abdin. It is an isolated place, some 30 kilometres off the main road, and at the entrance to the small settlement a Turkish *jandarma* or police post scrutinises newcomers – intended, presumably, to protect the village's half-dozen or so Christian sites from those inclined to persecute or vandalise evidence of the country's pre-Muslim past. The existing church dates from the 7th century,[71] though the monastery associated with it may date from the 4th century. From the outside its two-storey construction makes it look like an awkwardly placed wedding cake, the niches indenting its exterior, some of them bearing eagles and other symbols of the Evangelists, all adding to the air of nuptial finery. Inside, it is an architectural gem: its walls delicately carved, and a pattern of tiles set in the ceiling to form the outline of a flower or star. The burning of candles lit by the devout and the enveloping gloom of the interior enhance the sense of a place encrusted with centuries-deep layers of devotion.

Around 25 kilometres to the south-east of Midyat, Mor Gabriel, built around 397, is amongst the oldest, and most eminent of the surviving monasteries, being the seat of the Metropolitan bishop of the Tur Abdin.[72] The monastery precinct is ringed around by a high wall, which gives the place even more of a sense of isolation than its position 3 kilometres off the main road on a side-way that seems to lead nowhere and loses itself amid low hills covered in olive groves. Inside, the outer courtyard presents a blank face, little indication of the treasure within, populated mainly by the cars of pilgrims and other visitors; among them is a battered mini-van from Syria, bearing a prominent portrait of President Bashar al-Assad. It takes several rounds of ringing and pleas to be admitted, for there is a service taking place and it is before regular visiting hours, so no one is readily available to show us round. Finally, a volunteer prepared to forego the morning devotions comes forward and we are allowed in.

The monastery was originally founded by Samuel, a monk who may have been from Persia, and a companion, Simeon, who came from the neighbouring village. An angel appeared to Simeon and inspired him to build the monastery on the site of a former pagan temple.[73] The new foundation subsequently received rich endowments from Arcadius (395–408) and particularly from Theodosius II (408–50), who gave the money for a complex of buildings that still survive to the north-west of the monastery. The main church was endowed in 512 by Anastasius and still forms the principal place of worship. The monastery, however, took its name from a 7th-century abbot, Gabriel, who was said to have performed a number of miracles, and whose body was interred in the crypt of the church.

To the north of the main courtyard, the Dome of Theodora, or the 'Octagon', is an unusual eight-sided affair, which probably began life as a baptistery. That it has taken on Theodora's name is a tribute to Justinian's wife, who, despite the strong-willed nature of her husband, adhered stubbornly throughout her life to the non-orthodox, Monophysite creed, which had established a tenacious hold in the south-eastern portions of the Empire, and for which she acted as high-placed sponsor (even sending envoys to proselytise Ethiopia, who got there before Justinian's 'official' party and set the course of the Christian Church there for centuries to come).

The argument about the nature of Christ (whether he was fully human, fully divine or a mixture of the two), although seemingly an abstruse matter to modern eyes, was the question of utmost concern in the early Christian Church and the subject of bitter and prolonged wrangling, which threatened to – and finally did – split the community into rival factions. The 4th-century bishop Gregory of Nyssa (whose see lay in modern Cappadocia) satirised this by remarking that a visitor to Constantinople might ask a local the price of bread and be greeted instead with a discourse on the Trinity.[74] Debates over the nature of the Christian Trinity, God the Father, God the Son (Jesus Christ) and God the Holy Spirit, almost tore the early Church apart. It is hard now to recreate the sense of fervour that could lead to riots over the implication that Mary was not the literal mother of Jesus – and so the cherished epithet *Theotokos* ('Bearer of God') should not be used – or the savage arguments in church councils over the single iota (in the Greek) of difference over whether Jesus was *homoousios* (of the same substance) with God the Father or merely *homoiousios* (of similar substance).[75]

Once Christianity had become in effect the official religion of the Empire and gained access to the benefits of patronage, the problem of defining who exactly made up the orthodox community – and so could benefit from imperial and civic largesse – became more pressing. Particularly bitterly contested was the theology of Arius, a clergyman from Alexandria, who maintained that God the Father preceded all else, that Christ was created, that there was a time when he did not exist. At the Council of Nicaea, called by Constantine in 325 to thrash out a creed to which all orthodox Christians should subscribe, Arius was branded a heretic and excommunicated.[76] For decades, though, the controversy rumbled on, the principal defender of the Nicene cause being Athanasius, the patriarch of Alexandria from 328.

From the early 5th century, the battleground shifted from the relationship between the members of the Trinity to the nature of Christ's humanity – in other words, how it was possible that he could have a divine and a human nature at the same time. In 428, Nestorius, originally from Antioch, was elected Bishop of Constantinople. In his preaching he began to stress the differences between Christ's two natures, maintaining that they needed to be considered as separate.[77] Cyril, the Bishop of Alexandria, responded furiously that Nestorius was reducing

Jesus to a shell behind which separate natures lurk, and not truly a union of divine and human natures. The Council of Ephesus, called in 431 to resolve the issue, broke into Cyrillian and Nestorian counter-councils and only aggravated the division.

It was not until the Council of Chalcedon in 451 that a formula was agreed, that Christ is 'one person in two natures', but critically this point of view was rejected by the bulk of the Egyptian Church, which supported the stance that Christ had only one single nature, a position described (by its opponents) as Monophysite.[78] In Egypt, the Church splintered between Monophysites and Chalcedonians, who accepted the position of the council, but were in a distinct minority. Both groups heartily rejected the extremist Nestorian position, though the Monophysites took great delight in implying that their Chalcedonian opponents were secret followers of the creed of Nestorius.

Successive attempts to bridge the gap between the two factions always foundered, beginning with Emperor Zeno's *Henotikon* in 482, which fudged the matter by stating that while Christ was of the same 'nature' as God the Father, he combined a human nature within him.[79] Efforts at reconciliation gathered pace under Justinian, who, though he may not have had a personal commitment to the Chalcedonian creed – and his wife, Theodora, was an active Monophysite – was most keen to bring the competing Christian factions together for the sake of imperial harmony. They finished with the Council of Constantinople in 553,[80] which ended disastrously as it failed to reconcile the Monophysites and also alienated the Western Church, which considered that its eastern counterpart had backtracked on the doctrinal purity of Chalcedon.[81]

The Monophysite faction gave rise to the Coptic Orthodox Church in Egypt, which derived great strength from the monasteries and the rural areas, and acquired something of the nature of a national Church, a char- acteristic that enabled it to weather the storm of the Arab Muslim invasion in the 7th century. It also gave birth to many of the local churches of the Near East, including the Syrian Orthodox, whose monasteries dot the hills and valleys of the Tur Abdin. At first a beleaguered if staunch group of believers, the Monophysite cause was permanently bolstered by Theodora's connivance in the consecration of two bishops for the Ghassanid sheikh al-Harith (who was a Monophysite, like many Arabs). One of these, Jacob Baradaeus, who became Bishop of Edessa, traversed the entire Near East from Egypt to Armenia, consecrating priests and ordaining Monophysite bishops, in effect establishing an alternative hierarchy that was to form the backbone of the Monophysite churches of the future (and in honour of whose activities the Syrian Orthodox Church is often termed 'Jacobite').[82]

Down a flight of stairs near the monastery's octagon lies Mor Gabriel's crypt. At its entrance rests the tomb of the last bishop, who died in 1984 and was buried in a crouching position, a burial posture unique to the Syrian Orthodox metropolitans. The plain and simple niches for the remains of further bishops lie nearby, and also somewhere down here are the bones of '10,000 martyrs' resting near the grave of Mor Gabriel himself.

Back in the main church, a service is still going on, the priest officiating from the sanctuary, an apse-like room set away from the main congregation. Those present are a mixture of young and old, predominantly women wearing black-lace mantillas, many of them visiting here from abroad, particularly the United States, where a strong Syrian Orthodox community thrives. The liturgy is given in Syriac, a close relation to the Aramaic that was probably Jesus's mother tongue; the intoning of the prayers in a rhythmic, almost chant-like fashion certainly exerts a tug at the soul similar to that inspired by the few surviving islands of the Latin rite in western Europe.

The canopy over the altar was originally gilded, but this has been almost totally stripped off, leaving just small portions of gold leaf to represent the rest. It happened, says our guide, at the same time that a tree with branches entirely made of gold and silver vanished. It sounds like a recent act of desecration, but when pressed he admits that this happened during the time of Tamerlane, the last Mongol ravager of Asia Minor in the early 15th century. In a place as ancient as this, 500 years ago is regarded almost as recent history.

At the end of the service the forty-strong congregation troops up to kiss the Bible and then an icon concealed behind a curtain, which turns out to depict a military saint saddled on a white charger. As they depart, the church is left deserted, its nave rather bare, with the decorations principally in the three sanctuaries that run off it. In the corner a large stone trough has been placed, but it is not a baptismal font, merely a stone on which dough was made that was brought up from the monastery kitchen some decades ago and left here in the church. That it dates from the 8th century is almost an afterthought, the kind of antique detritus that litters the corridors and courtyards of these ancient places of worship.

It is sites such as the monastery of Tur Abdin that preserved elements of the late-Roman religious culture of the province, long after the central authorities had relinquished it to the conquering waves of Arabs in the 640s. For more than thirteen centuries their rites remained almost unchanged and they clung tenaciously to their lands and churches. Here, above all, it is possible to gain an insight into how life felt, at least on a

religious level, and to connect with one aspect of the Roman past in a
way that the ruins – however appealing or romantic – cannot inspire.

Around 250 kilometres west of Midyat lies Sanliurfa (also known as Urfa),
one of the most important of the Roman possessions east of the
Euphrates. The imprint of piety weighs heavily upon the city, Roman
Edessa, and successive religions – paganism, Christianity and Islam –
have all sought to claim its allegiance as a cornerstone of their presence
in the region. At the heart of its mystical life lie two sacred carp pools,
great oblong cisterns today surrounded by later mosque buildings, but
the fish themselves, grown numerous and fat on the titbits offered by
visiting pilgrims, are the descendants of a very ancient cult indeed. High
up above the throng of visitors, curious or devout, and the parade of
kebab restaurants that minister to them, the steep cliffs of Edessa's citadel
soar, and on them perches the city's most curious sight.

Two columns strike up against the skyline, entirely bereft of companions, as though the rest of the colonnade to which they once belonged
had simply tumbled down the cliff face.[83] Local legend relates that
Abraham came to settle in Urfa, whose similarity in sound – even closer
in its Semitic form, Orhai – to his much better-attested residence at Ur
may have caused confusion and the assimilation of his legends to Edessa.
Nimrod, the local ruler, became angry at Abraham for his piety and
refusal to worship idols, a prissiness that rather showed up the dissolute-
ness of his own lifestyle, and resolved to do away with him. Using the
two columns on the citadel hill to create a giant catapult, the citizens
of Urfa propelled Abraham towards a fiery death in a furnace which
they had lit down below. However, God transformed the fire into water,
and the burning pieces of wood into fish, and thus Abraham – far from
being incinerated – merely went for a dip in the sacred carp pool.[84]

The city's position, dominating one main route towards Persia, has
long been a strategic one, a fact recognised by Seleucus I Nicator around
303 BC when he sited his new foundation of Edessa close to an existing
native settlement there.[85] Although it had acquired the name 'Antioch by
the Callirhoe' by the mid-2nd century BC, the multiplicity of Antiochs in
the region meant that it soon reverted to plain Edessa. About this time,
also, it became the capital of an Arab kingdom governed by a succession
of rulers who mostly bore the name Abgar. The fifth king of that name
features in an early Christian legend, which relates that he engaged in an
exchange of letters with Jesus Christ and was so enthused by what he
learnt that he passed on the message to the Emperor Tiberius, to the
King of 'Assyria' and the ruler of Persia.[86] After the crucifixion, Abgar V

is alleged to have converted to Christianity under the influence of Saint Thaddeus, making Edessa by some margin the first Christian country. Sadly, there is no concrete evidence for all this and the correspondence between Jesus and Abgar, apparently still intact in the state archive in the 4th century, has long since vanished. More credible, but still unproven, are claims that Abgar VIII the Great (177–212) became Christian a century before Constantine's conversion heralded the Christianisation of the Roman Empire itself.

Edessa's religious heritage was complex. Long renowned as a centre for the worship of the gods Nebo and Bel, it also hosted large-scale cults of the Sun and Moon, the latter of which had its main centres further east at Harran and Sogmatar. The cult of Atargatis seems even more exotic. Its male devotees were given, at times of ecstatic reverie, to self-emasculation – clearly a once-only act of sacrifice to the goddess, and a practice which caused such controversy that it was outlawed under Abgar the Great. Another of the rites of Atargatis involved the ascent by holy men of two wooden columns at the temple entrance, where they would remain for several days, a practice which foreshadows that of Saint Simeon Stylites and his followers many centuries later.[87] The 'catapult' up on the citadel may, indeed, be the remains of an Atargatis temple, just as the sacred carp pools may originally have been associated with the cult (although other scholars have supposed they were simply a part of Abgar the Great's winter palace).[88] The pools, however, survived both Abgarid and pagan rule, and the 5th-century Christian pilgrim Egeria,[89] who visited on her way to the Holy Land, noted that she had never seen fish 'of so great size, so bright and of so great flavour'.[90] To this day, it is regarded as extremely unlucky to eat one.

The Abgarids were briefly supplanted by a pro-Roman Parthian prince named Parthamaspat in 117–23, in part as a punishment for Edessa's role in the revolt of Trajan's newly acquired Mesopotamian province the moment the Emperor's back was turned. Then in 193, suspected of complicity with Pescennius Niger in his attempt to oppose Septimius Severus's seizure of the imperial throne (or at least of taking advantage of the disorder to make territorial gains), Abgar VIII had his wings firmly clipped and most of his possessions, save a rump around Edessa, were incorporated as the province of Osroene.[91] The King affected the unimpeachably Roman name of Lucius Aelius Aurelius Septimus and feigned at least enough gratitude for his punishment to be allowed, for the time being, to retain his throne.

Edessa's long period of quasi-independence as one of the last Roman client kingdoms came to an end in 213, when Caracalla, in preparation for his expedition against the Parthians, called King Abgar IX to Rome, where he summarily deposed him, annexing Edessa to Osroene, which had for decades completely surrounded it. In compensation, Edessa was given the title of *colonia*, although as this was the very same year of the Antonine Constitution, the grant of citizenship to the free male population of Edessa in practice meant very little. A brief restoration of 'independence' under Gordian III between 239 and 242 brought a new Abgar (X) to the throne, but Gordian had probably only permitted this as a means of recruiting additional support in the East for his attack on Persia in 242–3, and even before this offensive had got under way, Roman municipal administration was restored and the Abgarids were summarily pushed aside once more.[92]

Somewhere outside Edessa, the Romans suffered their worst military setback since Crassus's death at Carrhae. On a rock relief at Bishapur in modern Iran, Shapur I celebrated his victories over three Roman emperors. His horse is shown trampling one, Gordian III, who had, according to the Persian side of the story, been killed in battle against the Sassanid army at Misiche in 244.[93] A second emperor kneels in supplication before Shapur I. This is Philip, who was forced to conclude a highly unfavourable peace to extricate the Roman army from the debacle of Gordian's death. The third of the trio, Valerian, whose wrist Shapur is seen clutching, suffered the worst fate. It seems that, while leading an army to head off Shapur's invasion of Syria in 260, Valerian was defeated in the vicinity of Edessa, and in the aftermath opened negotiations with the Persian side.[94] He made the fateful mistake of turning up in person at the talks and, seeing this, Shapur had him arrested and carried off into a humiliating and unprecedented imprisonment at the Sassanid court.

Tradition relates that Shapur used the captive former emperor as a mounting stool whenever he wished to get on his horse, and, when the hapless Valerian finally died, had his skin flayed, dyed purple and mounted as a trophy. Valerian's son, Gallienus, made absolutely no attempt to rescue his father. A Roman emperor who had endured the loss of dignity that Valerian had suffered was not a man who could remotely expect to inspire the army's loyalty ever again.

A breathless climb up a claustrophobic enclosed staircase inside the citadel cliff leads visitors to the site of the catapult columns. A series of undifferentiated ruins lies scattered about, shaping indistinct outlines of buildings that may once have formed part of Abgar's palace. The columns are the only undamaged structures, topped with weathered Corinthian capitals, the surface of their drums broken by pimple-like protrusions, which make them this close up seem as if they are scarred by the pox. On one of these there survives an inscription in Syriac, the language of Edessa, in which the dedication by Apthtuha the *nuhadra* (a royal official) states that the column bore a statue of Queen Shelmath, daughter of Ma'nu, the *pasgriba* (or heir to the throne). It is all a long way from Abraham and his catapult.[95]

Edessa's religious ferment continued into the age of Christianity. Among the key figures in its early development is Bardaisan.[96] Born into a well-to-do Edessene family around 155, he became a Christian in the 180s and bequeathed to the Syrian Church a rich legacy of more than 150 metrical hymns, set to music by his charmingly named son, Harmonius. His complex theology, later denounced as heretical, denied the bodily resurrection of the dead, and maintained that God had made all the elements of the universe, but that light and darkness had become inextricably muddled up in his new creation. After 6,000 years order would be restored and creation would revert to its pristine state, one in which light would be separated out and the matter of corporeal bodies would have no place. Such original speculations were commonplace in the independent Syriac Christian Church of the time, drawing freely on dualistic notions of great antiquity. But once Edessa was drawn into the Roman mainstream in the 3rd century and the Christian Church began to take on the mantle of an established religion, this free-thinking came to be regarded as unwise or downright dangerous.

Edessa was besieged a number of times by the Persians in the 6th century, as the grip of the authorities in Constantinople on their eastern possessions grew gradually more tenuous. It withstood sieges in 503, 544 and 580,[97] before a brief Persian occupation in 609 during the civil war following the murder of the Emperor Maurice by his successor Phocas. Heraclius recovered the city in 628, just eleven years before his garrison was swept out by the unstoppable tide of the Muslim Arab armies, who in their turn held it until 1032 when the Byzantines managed to retake the citadel and surrounding territory and maintain it for fifty years. Edessa was then incorporated into a Crusader principality during the First Crusade in 1098.

A dusty 40-kilometre drive to the south-east of Edessa, Harran – or, as the Romans knew it, Carrhae – has an ancient heritage indeed. First mentioned in the Bible as the place where Abraham and Sarah dwelt for a while after leaving Ur, the city is still dotted with curious beehive-shaped buildings of mud-brick whose traditional form may date back to the time of the patriarch, although they are now more often used for storage or for impressing tourists. It was later to Harran that Jacob fled from his brother Esau,[98] and his well (or its alleged location) is still there. A jumble of undifferentiated ruins surrounded by an unsympathetic wall enfold a rubbish-choked hole, a few steps leading to a pool of dubious-looking water, on which bob a collection of very unbiblical plastic water bottles.

More resonant of Harran's past is the citadel, sections of wall and a precarious arched gateway surviving, much restored and rebuilt by the town's various ancient, classical and medieval occupiers. Here in a corner that the Crusaders later turned into a redoubt – for the shortest-lived of their Levantine principalities was based here in the 12th century – is the site of the Temple of the Moon or 'Sin'. Ancient already in the 6th century BC, when it was restored by the Babylonian ruler Nabonidus, it was known as E-hul-hul ('the Temple of Rejoicing') and was magnificently roofed in cedar of Lebanon. Nothing remains of this, hidden somewhere deep inside the dusty mound on which the ruined Crusader fortress has imprinted a broken maze of stone. Visitors are so few and far between in the height of summer that our arrival provokes some curiosity and a slightly crazed local enquires over the reason for our presence.

The temple mound long remained a sacred site. Harran was the centre for the group who later became known as the Sabaeans, recidivist pagans who continued the old worship long after others had taken to different faiths. So resistant were the old ways here that when a delegation was sent to negotiate surrender to the Arabs in 639, it was found that all of its members were pagan.[99] The Koran mentions them in the 7th century as a 'people of the book', who were thus entitled to toleration of their beliefs (along with Jews, Christians and Zoroastrians), and around 830 the caliph Marwan is said to have encountered a group who claimed that they were Sabaeans – on the advice of a local jurist – to avoid being slaughtered or converted for their distinctly heterodox beliefs and practices.

The Sabaean religious life, as far as it can be reconstructed, was complex, but much of the information is derived from later Arab sources, such as the 9th-century writer ibn al-Tayyib. They believed in a single, supreme power beyond direct worship, who had delegated the actual running of the universe to the planets. Although this does not sound like classical paganism, in fact there was an increasing tendency in later antiquity to identify one god who was supreme, but not the only god. If Greeks revered Zeus Hypistos ('the highest') and Romans Jupiter Optimus Maximus ('the best and greatest'), than the Sabaeans clearly had their own variant.

Their planetary temples were each said to have been of a special shape and colour; that of Saturn was a black hexagon, while that of

Venus was a rectangle containing a square of green. The shrine of the Moon was in turn a silver octagon. Sabaean festivals seem to have involved much symbolic use of fire; each 26 September the believers would make vows and then tie a flaming torch to a chicken. The hapless fowl would then, naturally, run around, and if it was burnt to death before the torch went out, the vows were deemed accepted by the 'Lord of Luck'. The Sabaeans would never eat the chicken, for this (together with pigeons, fish, garlic and broad beans) was a forbidden food, making them difficult dinner guests.[100]

Further evidence of the Sabaean inhabitants has been found underneath Harran's Great Mosque, where another of their temples once stood. It also seems that the Emperor Caracalla came to the Moon Temple in the Citadel to sacrifice in 217. In common with a number of Roman emperors, he was an admirer of, indeed even modelled himself on, Alexander the Great, and also had his eyes on securing victories to rival those of his illustrious predecessor Trajan. Taking advantage of a split in the Parthian royal house, between Artabanus V and his brother Vologeses V (who controlled the capital, Ctesiphon), Caracalla sowed further dissension by proposing a marriage alliance with Artabanus's daughter.[101]

When his offer was rebuffed, Caracalla used this as a pretext for launching an expedition against Parthia late in 216. At first this came under the command of one of his favourites, a former dancer named Theocritus, and then, when – predictably – little was achieved, under his own personal direction. Even so, no direct gains were made against Parthia, although the buffer state of Osroene was annexed. Retiring for the winter to Edessa, Caracalla ignored the mounting grumbles in the army at his lack of martial prowess and his increasingly erratic behaviour. On 6 April, the Emperor went to pay his devotions at Carrhae. Two days later, during the journey to yet another moon temple a few kilometres from the city, Caracalla left the convoy to relieve himself amongst some bushes beside the road. There he was killed by a soldier named Martialis, who had a grudge against the Emperor, and who had been assigned to Caracalla's personal guard by the praetorian prefect Opellius Macrinus, himself motivated by fear that the Emperor was about to have him murdered.[102] It was an undignified end for the son of the great Septimius Severus, but after four days of feigned reluctance, Macrinus allowed the troops to declare him Emperor, thereby becoming the first member of the equestrian class to reach that position.

Perhaps Caracalla should have known better, as Carrhae was not exactly a well-omened place for the Romans. It was on the plains somewhere outside the city that Rome suffered its most disastrous defeat since the Punic Wars. Marcus Licinius Crassus, one of the triumvirs who shared power with Julius Caesar and Pompey the Great, rather smarting at his rivals' high profile as military leaders, and in particular at Caesar's successes in Gaul, decided to belie his reputation as a financier and little else, and teach the Parthians a lesson. After some initial successes in Upper Mesopotamia in 54 BC, he was lured outside Carrhae the following spring, where the open country made ideal territory for light cavalry, which the Parthian army had in great abundance, and of which Crassus's legions possessed a much more modest complement.

Hails of arrows from horse-mounted archers and repeated probing cavalry attacks broke the Romans' spirit and they fled: 20,000 were killed (including Crassus), 10,000 captured and only a quarter of the original force escaped towards Antioch. Even more humiliatingly, a number of the legionary eagle standards, the emblems of Roman martial glory imbued with an almost sacral symbolism, were also taken by the Parthians. Although their advance into Syria was largely halted by Crassus's surviving legate, Cassius, the Parthians held on to the standards for more than thirty years, and it took some strenuous diplomacy by Augustus to have them finally returned in 20 BC.[103]

Carrhae saw another Roman ruler on his way to hoped-for victories against the Persians, when the Emperor Julian visited in 363. Just like Caracalla, Julian was drawn by the desire to sacrifice at the Temple of the Moon. The Emperor had spent much of the previous year attempting to restore the old gods in their place at the centre of Roman public life, and to undo the Christianisation of the Empire by Constantine and his successors.[104]

Although he could not openly espouse paganism whilst his uncle the Emperor Constantius II lived, once he himself had become Emperor in November 360, Julian set about rolling back the privileges that the Christian Church had been given. In March 362 he ordered that Christian clergy no longer be immune from their civic duty as *curiales*,[105] and he further commanded that the cities have restored to them the public estates that had generated the revenues for the upkeep of the temples. A few months later, in June, he legislated for the appointment of qualified teachers in the cities, no doubt to promote traditional – polytheistic – learning. Christian teachers were forbidden to give lessons on the traditional curriculum, on the grounds that they did not believe in it and, as the Emperor put it, 'they should either show piety towards the gods or withdraw to the churches of the Galileans to expound Matthew and Luke'.[106]

Many saw Julian's measures as unduly divisive, and even the pagan historian Ammianus Marcellinus commented that it was a 'harsh act which should be buried in lasting oblivion'.[107] A certain amount of anti-Christian violence was sparked off by the new regime's policies; in Alexandria, Bishop Athanasius was expelled, and Bishop George of Cappadocia, the Emperor's old tutor, was lynched by a mob. Julian responded with a mere rebuke, and an instruction to the Prefect of Egypt to acquire George's extensive book collection and have it sent to Constantinople.[108] As scattered opposition grew, the Emperor became more resolute. He penned a treatise entitled *Against the Galileans* setting out his position, and he moved against cities that showed too strong an attachment to Christianity. At Bostra in Arabia, the bishop was hounded out. He demoted Caesarea in Cappadocia from its civic status because of its inhabitants' violence against pagan temples, and promoted Gaza to the rank of a *colonia* as a reward for its steadfast polytheist majority.[109] As a further spite to Christian sentiment, in 363 Julian permitted a start to be made on the rebuilding of the Jewish Temple in Jerusalem. An earthquake, the lack of enthusiasm of the rabbinate for a project that would have undermined their authority, and the death of the Emperor meant the project never in fact got very far.

As a counter to the well-organised Christian hierarchies, Julian tried to re-establish the pagan priesthood on a similar, structured and disciplined basis. In some ways, his Christian education was showing through in his attempt to fight spirit with spirit, and the heritage of his early years influenced him in other ways, too. Rumour had it that when the apostate Emperor was scared, he actually made the sign of the cross.[110] Yet Julian's template did not fit very well onto the massive diversity of pagan belief and practice, and in any case it all came much too late. For in March 363, Julian set out from Antioch for a new war against the Persians.

Motivated by the same desire as Caracalla to emulate Alexander the Great, and in particular by a wish for revenge against Shapur for his seizure of the great fortress city of Dara in 359, Julian may not have had clear objectives for his campaign. As emperors before him had done, such as Carus in 283, Julian struck out at Ctesiphon with little apparent idea what he might do once he had captured it. Although a number of towns were taken, the Persians hindered the Roman army's progress by flooding irrigation ditches, and Shapur's army was still undefeated when Julian reached the Persian capital.

A prolonged siege was out of the question, and the Romans marched north to meet another column under the command of Procopius, which was moving via Armenia to reinforce them. Shapur had, however, ordered the area north of Ctesiphon laid waste to deny his enemy supplies, and constant harrying attacks by the Persians added to the

Romans' discomfort. On 26 June, somewhere near modern Samarra in Iraq, the Persians attacked again. Julian, alerted to the danger, rushed out of his tent to rally resistance, but in his haste neglected to don his breastplate. In the ensuing skirmish the Emperor was mortally wounded by a spear-thrust.[111] As he lay dying, Julian is said to have discoursed lucidly with his former philosophy teacher Maximus on the nobility of the soul, but his inevitable end came within hours. Later, jubilant Christian writers would claim that the end of the 'Apostate' came at the hands of a Christian soldier, and indeed that it was the work of a saint, variously identified as Saint Sergius, Theodore or, more commonly, Mercurius.[112]

Whoever was responsible for Julian's death, any real chance of a re-establishment of paganism was ended. The Roman army, meanwhile, found itself leaderless and beleaguered, still far from friendly territory. A rapid council of war offered the crown to the praetorian prefect Secundus Salutius, who declined on the grounds of his advanced age; in some confusion the senior officials than lighted on a compromise candidate, Jovian, the *primicerius domesticorum*[113] of the imperial guard. Desperate to escape back across the borders of the Empire – not least because he needed rapidly to build a coalition of support amongst the power-brokers in Constantinople and the provinces, who might not regard his hasty elevation particularly favourably – Jovian opened negotiations with Shapur.

To secure his safe passage, the new Emperor gave up five Roman provinces across the Tigris (Arzanene, Moxoene, Zabdicene, Rehimene and Corduene), the cities of Nisibis (Nusaybin), Singara and Castra Maurorum (Seh Qubba), and further agreed that he would give no military assistance to Arsaces, King of Armenia.[114] The new Emperor's surrender of these territories was seen as hugely shameful; when a messenger reached Carrhae with the news, the citizenry was so enraged that they killed him.[115] Ammianus Marcellinus bitterly – and wrongly – commented that it was the first time Rome had ever voluntarily given up land it had won in war.[116] Jovian, meanwhile, did not even survive long enough to reach his imperial capital. On the morning of 2 January 364, halfway between Ancyra (Ankara) and Nicaea (Iznik), and still more than 200 kilometres from Constantinople, he was found dead in his bedchamber. Poisoned mushrooms or the fumes from a brazier close to his bed were blamed, but a suspicion lingered that those who did not approve of the army's battlefield choice had Jovian murdered.

It seems a long, hot road from Harran to Sogmatar (if in reality it is only 30 kilometres to the north-east), passing barren dusty hills and parched land from which scratching a living seems scarcely worth the effort. Past Suayb, a village burrowed into the rock for protection from the searing sun, occupied from Roman times – with a jumble of subter-ranean dwellings, crude steps and niches, which might as well have been abandoned twenty years ago as 2,000 – the way leads on to Sogmatar Harabesi itself. The modern village, a clutch of single-storey mud-brick dwellings at its heart, more modern but no more assuming at its edges, gives little clue to its ancient secret.

The village is ringed by a series of low hills, on at least several of which lie the ruins of ancient structures. Up the nearest of these the remains of a circuit wall of large blocks and possibly a corner tower give a sense of a defended place, but on the crest a jumble of blocks, pillars and a section of frieze lying among the sun-bleached grass are all that is left of the temple. A single ragged-trousered boy stares at the visitors, too amazed that anyone should visit these abandoned stones even to beg for a pen or some small change.

Similar structures visible on the other mounds once ringed a sacred precinct in the heart of the village, with seven hilltop sanctuaries, one for each of the planets. On a shrine here have been found inscriptions in Syriac and a reference to a dedication by 'Tiridates, son of Adona, ruler of the Arabs', who 'built this altar and set a pillar to Marilaha for the life of my lord the king', dated to AD 165,[117] the very year in which the Romans occupied Edessa and began to bring an end to the vitality of this ancient cult.

It is an eerie feeling, that this may have been the last place where prayers were offered to the traditional pagan deities, suppressed else-where by the monotheist certainties and intolerance of, first, Christianity, and then Islam. Far away from the mainstream of history, it is in such hidden-away places that the most poignant glimpses of the past can truly be had, and the most immediate insights into the religious feelings which inspired the mass of the population of the Empire, before Christianity swept aside the old beliefs and relegated them to mere folk tales and superstitions.

Melitene

CAPPADOCIA

CILICIA

0   50 miles
0   80 kms

Euphrates

Zeugma

Cyrrhus

S Y R I A

MESOPOTAMIA

Antioch
(*Antakya*)
Daphne
Seleucia Pieria   Qalb Loze   Qirkbize

Telanissos (*Deir Semaan*)
Beroea (*Aleppo*)

C O E L E

Euphrates

Sura

Serjilla

Sergiopolis
(*Resafe*)

Zenobia
(*Halabiye*)

Orontes

Laodicea
(*Latakia*)

Apamea

Qasr Ibn Wardan

Dura Europos

Emesa (*Homs*)

Palmyra

Mediterranean

Sea

S Y R I A

P H O E N I C E

Diocletiana

Strata

Berytus
(*Beirut*)

Dumeir

Damascus

Arabian Desert

Tyre

Sea of
Galilee

Jordan

Bostra

A R A B I A

SYRIA
PALAESTINA

Syria

Frontier of Empire, c.165

new provinces under
Septimius Severus

CHAPTER 7

Syria

Cenobia, of Palmyerie queene,
Of Kynges blood of Perce is she descended
I seye nat that she hadde moost fairnesse
But of hir shap she myghte nat been amended . . .
Hir riche array ne myghte nat be told,
As wel in vessel as in hire clothyng,
She was al clad in perree and in gold . . .
Geoffrey Chaucer, *The Canterbury Tales*, 'The Monk's Tale'[1]

Roman Syria swept down in an arc from the edge of Asia Minor and
the Euphrates down to the Gulf of Aqaba, always shaped and defined
by the desert to the east and in its northern portions by the Mediterranean
Sea to the west.[2] It was defined by three principal regions: the fertile
coastal strip, which was bordered by a mountainous region, and then to
the east and south by the desert. The main towns, such as Antioch
(Antakya), Damascus, Emesa (Homs) and Apamea (Afamya), clustered
close to the coast or the valley of the Orontes, with a secondary area
of dense settlement running from Beroea (Aleppo) down the Euphrates
to the south-east.

Although never at the heart of any of the ancient civilisations on the
fringes of whose domains it sat, such as the Hittites, Assyrians, Babylonians
or Persians, Syria supported cities of time-defying antiquity such as
Damascus, and, whenever the central authority of its various suzerains
weakened, it gave rise to indigenous kinglets whose aspirations were
almost always greater than the reach of their power. Once Alexander the
Great had claimed the former domains of the Persian Achaemenids in
the 330s BC, Syria fell to him, and then, after his untimely death in 323 BC,
it landed in the portion of Seleucus, one of his principal lieutenants.

The large numbers of Greek colonists who, over time, made Syria (and
indeed much of the rest of the Near East) their home brought profound
changes to the urban landscapes of the area. Many new Greek-style *poleis*

(or 'city-states') were founded and others adapted themselves to Greek-style constitutions with citizen-assemblies and annually elected magistrates. Quite how far this process of Hellenisation penetrated into the countryside is hard to say, but when the Romans did eventually arrive in Syria, they ingested the existing arrangements almost wholesale. Their ancient conceit that the Empire was in fact made up of a patchwork of 'independent' cities, which just happened to conform to the wishes of the principal amongst them (in other words, Rome), suited them very well in Syria.

Although the Romans' acquisition of territories in western Asia Minor and then Cappadocia[3] brought them into contact with the Seleucid heartland further to the east and south in Syria, they came at first as diplomats rather than conquerors. The interference in 168 BC by Gaius Popillius Laenas in the Seleucid Antiochus IV's attempt to annex Ptolemaic Egypt established a status quo in which the local potentates had only limited freedom of action, always inviting Roman intervention should they overstep the bounds of their traditional territories.[4] It was really only the expansion of Tigranes of Armenia from 95 BC, who added huge swathes of Cappadocia and Syria (traditionally Seleucid lands) to his kingdom, that upset the balance of power, and, once they had disentangled themselves from the Mithridatic Wars, caused the Romans to enter definitively into Syria.

With the annexation of Antioch in 64 BC, a new province of Syria was established by Ptolemy,[5] although at first a complex patchwork of client states and independent cities obscured the realities of Roman power.[6] Further progress in organising and expanding the Syrian base was hampered by the civil wars between Caesar and Pompey, and then between the leaders of the second triumvirate and Caesar's assassins. The disastrous defeat of Crassus at Carrhae in 53 BC[7] led to the partial occupation of Syria by the Parthians, who even succeeded in seizing Antioch itself.[8] By 50 BC, though, the Parthians had been chased out, and ultimately Syria fell into the domains of Antony, meaning that it once more became entangled in a Roman civil war, this time between him and Augustus, and was only restored to central control after the Battle of Actium in 31 BC.

Once Augustus had established himself in power, he ceded control of some provinces back to the Senate, but only those without a significant military presence, and from which, therefore, no bid to unseat him could be effectively mounted. Syria, as a province with a significant garrison, fell to the Emperor and was governed by a number of distinguished imperial legates, including Varus (the Roman commander at the disastrous defeat at the Teutoberger Wald in Germany) and Calpurnius Piso (who was executed for treason in AD 65). At first client states such as that of the Samsigeramids at Emesa or, more important, that of Herod in Judaea were not absorbed, leading to blocs of Roman provincial territory being surrounded by the domains of those kings, and an administrative system of almost nightmarish complexity.[9] The province initially stretched far to the south, including cities such as Gerasa and Philadelphia that would, once the Nabataean kingdom was annexed by Trajan in 106,[10] form part of the province of Arabia.

After the great Jewish revolt of AD 66–70 had been put down, the new Emperor Vespasian, who had been the commander of the Roman forces in the initial stages of the campaign, set about simplifying the situation. A new province was established in Palestine, while at about this time Emesa was annexed and its royal dynasty deposed.[11] Under Trajan, the province seemed to have reached its final boundaries, with the slicing-off of a section to form the northern reaches of Arabia, but during the reign of Septimius Severus, the province was split into two portions, with the northern part becoming Coele Syria (or 'Hollow' Syria) and the southern part Syria Phoenice, in an effort to avoid the concentra-tion of power in the hands of a single governor that had so threatened Septimius's own bid for imperial power.[12] After the disorders of the 3rd century, which saw Zenobia, Queen of Palmyra, seize almost the whole of the East, the Syrian provinces were further subdivided under Diocletian, who also sponsored a large-scale fortification of the route down from Sura on the Euphrates to Damascus, which formed part of the system that has become known as the Strata Diocletiana.[13]

Although vulnerable to periodic Persian incursions, particularly after the advent of the Sassanids as the ruling dynasty in the mid-3rd century, Syria seemed a bulwark of the Eastern Roman Empire right until the early 7th century, when the invading armies of Arab Muslims swept away in just a few short years what it had taken the Romans almost three-quarters of a millennium to construct.

Antioch-on-the-Orontes, the principal city of Syria, was one of the great cities of the Empire, not on a par with Rome or Constantinople, but equal in size and eminence to Carthage or Alexandria and with a population that, at its height, may have reached several hundred thou-sand.[14] Its lineal descendant, Antakya, is now a substantial Turkish city, situated in the Hatay, a strip of land that was detached from Syria by the French mandate authorities in the late 1930s.[15] Founded, as so many other towns in the region,[16] by Seleucus I Nicator in the 300s BC,[17] it occupied a sheltered position between the heights of Mount Silpius and the River Orontes in the northern coastal regions of the province. The twin foundation of Seleucia Pieria (Samandaği), some 30 kilometres to the west on the coast, provided a port, for the river was not navigable as far as Antioch itself.

In the 60s BC, Antioch served as the capital of the last two Seleucid kings, Antiochus XIII and Philip II, who squabbled viciously over a rapidly diminishing circle of Syrian land, unaware or uncaring that the world was rapidly moving on and that the Romans were quickly closing in. In 64 BC, following his defeat of Tigranes of Armenia, Pompey the Great arrived in Antioch, and he granted the city *libertas* ('freedom'), a liberty that was to result in seven centuries of Roman rule, regularised by the appointment of Lucius Marcius Philippus as the new province's first governor in 58 BC. He also abolished the previous 'Seleucid' era of the city, which had calculated dates from 312 BC,[18] and replaced it with a modestly named Pompeian era, which, with a deft piece of mathematics, was deemed to begin in 66 BC (when Pompey had defeated Tigranes of Armenia, leaving Syria without alternative patrons and effectively at his mercy). From the time of the early Empire, Antioch came to be the headquarters of the imperial province, with its legate directly in command of several legions and often *de facto* commander of the whole Roman East.

Freed of its rather uncomfortable position as the capital of the collapsing Seleucid state, Antioch then prospered, receiving embellishments such as the building by Julius Caesar of the earliest-known basilica in the region (the Kaisarion),[19] and the establishment of a local Olympic Games under Augustus, which would in due course become one of the most celebrated festivals in the eastern half of the Empire. The city, however, was devastated by a particularly damaging series of earthquakes, starting with one under Gaius Caligula in April 37; it had to be rebuilt by Trajan in 115, by Leo I in 458 and again by Justinian in 526 and 528.

The December 115 earthquake struck whilst Trajan was actually staying in the city before his expedition against the Parthians. The Emperor was only slightly hurt, although one of the consuls, Marcus Pedo Vergilianus, was killed. Trajan was said to have been led safely from his bedroom by a supernatural spirit of extraordinary size,[20] quite possibly, it was believed, Zeus himself. In the aftermath of this earthquake, a spasm of persecution broke out against the Christians, blamed for provoking divine wrath by their impiety, which led the following year to the martyrdom of Ignatius, who had been Bishop of Antioch since around 67. This seismic instability, damage caused by the Persians who seized Antioch in 540 and its loss to the Arabs in 636 eventually deprived Antioch of political significance and it fell into complete decline. When the Byzantines retook the city in 969 under Nicephorus Phocas there was little left worth preserving and they started again on a nearby uninhabited site.

The ancient monuments are thus largely known, not through excavation, but from the testament of ancient texts, principally those by Antioch's most famous son, the orator Libanius.[21] Perhaps the most noted was the colonnaded street, some 3 kilometres long, that ran right through the heart of the city and was rivalled in its magnificence only by the mighty colonnade of Apamea in central Syria. Begun under Augustus, though possibly under the auspices of Herod Antipas, the client king of Judaea, it was completed in the reign of Tiberius and rebuilt in the 2nd century under Trajan and Antoninus Pius.

Control of Antioch acted as a key to the whole Roman East, and it was thus the target for successive attempts by the Persians to capture it.[22] Following Shapur's taking of the city in 260, he deported part of the population to Persia, where he set them to rebuilding the decayed town of Gondeshapur, which he then out of pride – and with a particular eye to annoying the Romans – renamed Beh-az-Andew-i-Sapur[23] or 'Shapur's better-than-Antioch town.'[24] Antioch was also seized by the Palmyrenes under Zenobia in 270, and used by a string of usurpers as a springboard in their attempts to secure imperial power. Avidius Cassius, for instance, found support here and, following his defeat in 175,[25] the city was consequently punished, briefly deprived of the right to stage its games. More seriously, Pescennius Niger, the eastern rival to Septimius Severus in the civil war of 192–3, used Antioch as his base. After his defeat at Issus – site of Alexander the Great's more famous victory against the Persians in 333 BC – Pescennius fled back to Antioch, where he was apprehended and rapidly put to death.[26] As a punishment for its adherence to his opponent's cause, Septimius demoted the city from the rank of metropolis to a mere village under the jurisdiction of Laodicea, its neighbour and bitter rival, whose loyalty to the Severan cause had been notable.

With the increasing tendency of emperors from the Tetrarchy onwards to base themselves closer to the frontiers, Antioch's importance rose dramatically. Diocletian spent several winters here around 298–301 and supervised the construction of a great palace – now lost – on an island in the Orontes. In a sign of the increasing strength and demands of the imperial bureaucracy, an arms factory and granaries were also built, as well as no fewer than five baths.[27]

Amongst Antioch's surviving hidden secrets is evidence of the very earliest emergence of Christianity. It was in Antioch, according to the

Byzantine chronicler John Malalas, that the followers of Jesus were first called Christians, a name given to the faithful by Evodios, who succeeded Peter as bishop around AD 41.[28] As a cosmopolitan city, which had a well-established Jewish community and a heavy veneer of Hellenistic culture, it was receptive to precisely the kind of social and intellectual ferment that gave birth to the new Church in the middle decades of the 1st century.

Set high on a mountainside, with stunning views over the chaos of the modern metropolis, lies the church of Saint Peter. The first Christians are said to have met here secretly, taking advantage of a natural cave, and adapting and extending it for their services. Peter himself spent a year in Antioch, according to the Acts of the Apostles, and he is traditionally credited as the city's first bishop.[29] An unpromising modern courtyard, and a flat Crusader-era façade punctuated with stylised crosses and stars, gives way to the cave itself. It is a simple place, imbued with a deeply spiritual atmosphere, furnished with a bare altar, a statue of Peter – both modern – and the merest hint of wall painting on the back wall, eroded away by the centuries and faint trickles of water, which give the whole a damp as well as holy atmosphere. The tunnel through which the Christians are said to have escaped from would-be persecutors is nowhere in evidence, doubtless long ago blocked up.

As a Christian stronghold, Antioch was perhaps an inauspicious selection for Julian's headquarters in summer 362[30] immediately prior to his assault on Persia. His desire to re-establish pagan shrines and sweep away Christian accretions and usurpations of sacred spots led him to a catastrophic error of judgement. He ordered that the bones of Babylas, the 3rd-century martyr and much-revered Bishop of Antioch, be removed from their resting place at Daphne just outside the city. The Christians responded by putting on a massive show of defiance, as the relics were processed to a newly prepared tomb free of pagan taint or imperial spite. Not long afterwards, the Temple of Apollo at Daphne, from the environs of which Babylas's bones had been so publicly expelled, caught fire and burnt down, an event for which the Emperor understandably – although, as it turned out, mistakenly – blamed the Christians.[31]

Traditionalists were upset by Julian's refusal to attend public spectacles such as the theatre, while the whole populace was affected by the Emperor's attempt to fix the price of grain to dampen the inflation caused by the presence of his army, an intervention that led to landowners refusing to sell their produce, resulting in escalating food shortages. In response to the clear antipathy that his Antiochene subjects felt for him, Julian penned a remarkable, almost self-satirical treatise in his defence, the *Misopogon* ('Beard-Hater'), which he had posted in public outside the imperial palace, and which provoked a grovelling apology from the town council of Antioch.[32]

Antioch's troubled relationship with authority continued in 387, when, after a letter was read out announcing the imposition of additional heavy taxes on the city, a mob pulled down the statues of the Emperor Theodosius and the imperial family that stood outside the governor's palace. Such an act of *lèse-majesté* was intolerable and the perpetrators were immediately arrested, tried and soon afterwards executed by burning or being thrown to the beasts in the amphitheatre.[33] The ruling class of Antioch quailed, fearing that the Emperor's anger at such an unprece-dented slight would fall heavily upon them. A deputation was sent off to Constantinople to plead the city's cause, and Libanius tried to deflect responsibility by attributing the 'Riot of the Statues' to the intervention of demons or, almost as heinously one presumes, to foreigners.[34] Theodosius confined his punishment of Antioch to demoting it once more to a village under the jurisdiction of Laodicea. The city's baths and circus also shut down, but the measures were only temporary, for within months the injunctions against it were lifted. Antioch escaped lightly for, just three years later, the same emperor, angered at the murder of the garrison commander in the Greek city of Thessalonica, gave his troops free rein to exact vengeance. Within three hours, around 7,000 people had been slaughtered, while Theodosius himself suffered an eight-month-long excommunication from the Church until he was deemed to have repented sufficiently.[35]

Of Daphne, from which Julian had expelled the remains of Babylas, little survives. It was a favourite, shaded spot for the city's elite, where they built villas and enjoyed the waters of the sacred spring of Castalia. After brief moments of excitement when Zenobia's rearguard fought a delaying action here to permit their queen's escape back to Palmyra, and the crisis caused by Julian's attempt to reopen the holy spring in 363, Daphne relapsed into quiet decay. Indeed, when Julian arrived at such an important pagan shrine, he expected to be greeted by a large crowd and a sumptuous sacrifice, but instead all that came was a single, elderly priest, bearing a rather scrawny duck.[36] It was, the old man explained to the Emperor, all that he could afford. Daphne is still a leafy, compara-tively calm retreat from the hustle of Antakya, its pleasant and cool riverside walkways providing a sense, if no direct evidence, of the role it played in Roman times.

Still visible today is the Emperor Titus's impact on the city. Besides giving Antioch a share of the booty taken during the capture of Jerusalem after the Jewish revolt of AD 66–9 (including, it is said, bronze figures of Cherubim looted from the temple itself),[37] he also supervised the building of a canal that connected the area of the port at Seleucia with the Orontes. The construction, known locally as 'the Channel of Titus', is still there, treacherous in rainy weather, scarcely less so in summer. At up to 10 metres in height, the walls of the gorge, now rubble-choked, give way to a tunnel, on occasion eerily lit by the fire of those who fear to tolerate its darkness. The course of the waterwork loses itself in overgrown fields and orchards beyond. A building inscription at the point where the tunnel finally emerges into the light commemorates 'Divus Titus', and so was clearly inscribed after that emperor's death and deification. The whole, therefore, must still have been under construction during the reign of his brother, Domitian.

Just within the borders of the province of Syria at its north-easternmost reach, the site of Roman Zeugma (Belkis) is a melancholy place. It lies along the Euphrates, 175 kilometres to the north-east of Antioch, and some 30 kilometres north of the border with modern Syria. Founded around 300 BC by Seleucus I Nicator, a prolific establisher of cities in Syria and its surrounds, its official name was Seleucia-on-the-Euphrates, but it came to be known as Zeugma ('the bridge') for the important river-crossing that it guarded.

The site was almost totally flooded by the rising waters of Turkey's Atatürk Dam Project in the late 1990s and a clear blue expanse of water conceals the temples, forum and markets of the city below – a case where it is man's recent actions rather than the slow chiselling of time that have obliterated the past. A few fragments of buildings, which must have been on the highest parts of Zeugma, cling precariously to slopes at the water's edge: at one point an arch, perhaps part of the supporting structure of a house, at another a fragment of geometric mosaic carefully preserved on a little jetty that projects beyond the waterline. At the edge of the site, behind a barbed-wire fence, further architectural flotsam, pillars and bases of capitals, have been gathered together, untended, unmarked and disappearing beneath a rapidly growing carpet of grass.

It is hard to credit that this was once a thriving legionary base and city. The Romans controlled it from at least 31 BC, marking the point at which the Euphrates became the commonly accepted boundary of their territory in this region.[38] It first received a legionary garrison in the late 60s, probably initially the X Fretensis,[39] and, after that unit was sent to suppress the Jewish revolt in 66–7, the IV Scythica guarded the crossing until some time in the 3rd century. Only the necropolis at the edge of the city, itself partly cut through by the modern road, survives remotely intact. To gain some sense of the city's ancient life the modern visitor has to go to nearby Gaziantep, where the mosaics rescued from the rapidly sinking site were taken, including the city's finest, from which the piercing-eyed gaze of Zeugma's most-reproduced image seems to follow visitors around the museum. Dubbed the 'gypsy girl', she is, in all likelihood, an embodiment of Gaia, the spirit of the earth.

Around 80 kilometres to the south-west of Zeugma, the Roman road that led south towards Antioch crossed the River Subun just east of the legionary fortress of Cyrrhus (Nabi Khouri). A six-arched Roman bridge still stands, with an exaggerated hump, among low hills planted with a scattering of olive trees on a scarcely frequented route, an ancient artery that carries precious little modern blood. The city was yet another foundation of Seleucus Nicator around 300 BC, named for a town in his Macedonian homeland, and it too fell to Pompey in 64 BC. It became the winter quarters of the Legio X Fretensis in AD 18, retaining its garrison until the aftermath of the Jewish revolt of the late 60s, when the legion was transferred to Judaea.[40]

The final approach to this ancient city, even on a spring day, is a muddy one, the remaining pillars of the south gate mired in deep rainwater pools. From here the *cardo*, once colonnaded, with scattered column fragments a reminder of its former status, leads on into the heart of the city. To the west the brooding massif of the acropolis rears, ringed with late-Roman fortifications, a final sanctuary for the north Syrian populace. The citadel has yielded an inscription of Justinianic date commemorating the construction of the acropolis around 530, but it is probable that by then much of the city had been abandoned and that it had become little more than a hilltop refuge.[41]

In the lee of the hill a cluster of nomad tents clings, threatening at any moment to succumb to the tearing wind. While sheep munch contentedly, and their owners eye any visitors warily from a safe distance, their handiwork (or that of their confederates) is clear. The whole site is pockmarked by holes and small trenches, exposing here an acanthus-leaf-clad column, there a curved section of a well, all marred and spattered by upcast from the illicit excavations. Further to the north a ruin-field lies, stones scattered without apparent form or rhythm. A lonely arch surveys the olive fields, and nearby a still-upstanding structure, itself arched, marks one of Cyrrhus's two located churches, sited just by the remains of a large sanctuary to an unknown god. To the south of this, closer to the city centre lie the most impressive remains by far, those of the theatre. At just over 110 metres in diameter, it has a dozen rows of seating still largely intact, but the stage and *scaenae frons* have been utterly cast down by earthquakes, huge blocks strewn hither and thither as though hurled carelessly by an especially petulant giant.

For much of antiquity the record is silent on Cyrrhus. Its one brief flaring of notoriety came late in the reign of Marcus Aurelius, with the revolt of Avidius Casssius, the governor of Syria, who was a native of the city. Apparently egged on by Faustina, the Emperor's wife – who was concerned that, should her husband die, other factions at Rome might seize the throne and deny her young son, Caracalla – Cassius was considering the merits of assuming the imperial mantle himself. Precipitated into an untimely decision by rumours of Marcus's death that reached the East in April 175, he soon learnt the unfortunate truth that the Emperor still lived. By then it was too late to go back. Declared an enemy of the state by the Senate, Cassius sought and received support from Egypt – where he was recognised as Emperor by 3 May (and an edict has been unearthed rejoicing at his accession)[42] – from Arabia and of course from Syria, giving him the potential support of seven legions. But, critically, he failed to recruit Martius Verus, the governor of Cappadocia, a comrade of his from Marcus's Parthian War.

Cassius's efforts to build a wider coalition were also rebuffed: his letter to the distinguished Athenian senator Herodes Atticus met with the laconic reply 'You are mad!'[43] Marcus gave an emotional speech to his troops, in which he lamented the disloyalty of 'a dear friend' and mused that he would happily have given up the Empire to Cassius if the Senate willed it and it were for 'the common good'.[44] The Emperor was clearly winning the propaganda war, and the usurper's legions succumbed to such grave doubts that a centurion murdered him – probably in early July – and despatched his head on a plate to Marcus. The Emperor, saddened, but no doubt relieved, tastefully refused to receive the trophy and ordered it buried.[45] Martius Verus, meanwhile, marched on Syria, took Cassius's headquarters unopposed and made haste to burn the rebel's correspondence, coincidentally thereby removing any incriminating references to himself or his supporters.[46]

The circuit of walls that girdle the whole site, now largely disappeared, did not keep out the Persians in 256, but this was a fate shared by many Syrian cities at the time and does not speak of any particular vulnerability in Cyrrhus's defences. For a century, little is known, other than that the city acquired a bishopric and sent its prelate to the Council of Nicaea in 325. But in around 423, Cyrrhus received a new bishop, the renowned theologian Theodoret. Born in Antioch around 393, his major work, the *Historia Religiosa*, is an invaluable account of the lives of Syrian ascetics. Theodoret became embroiled in the bitter controversies concerning the nature of Christ that tore apart the Church in the mid-5th century.[47] As a result, the Second Council of Ephesus (449), known to its detractors as the 'Robber Council',[48] deprived him of his see and he went into exile in a monastery at Apamea. Rehabilitated at the Council of Chalcedon in 451, he died six years later, content that his orthodoxy had been established, but little knowing that the Christological controversy would rage for a century yet and claim him as a posthumous victim, for in 553 the Council of Constantinople condemned his writings against Cyril, as part of the last-ditch effort to patch up differences between the contending Monophysite and orthodox Nicene factions.[49]

South from Cyrrhus, the land continues to be fertile, its rural richness an echo of late antiquity, when northern Syria underwent a boom, partly fuelled by the production of olive oil, and prosperous villages and small towns proliferated, only to find themselves in a troubled border-zone after the Arab invasions of the 7th century. They dwindled, were abandoned, but, in the absence of local populations to rob them for building materials, they did not decay.[50] They remain, a shadow-land of 'Dead Cities' strung across the Syrian landscape in two belts, one running north of Beroea (Aleppo) – itself some 80 kilometres south of Cyrrhus – and one to its south-west, forming a collection of stone ghosts, each one with church and solidly constructed houses looking as if a few light repairs might restore them to the state when their residents left just the day before yesterday.

As well as agricultural settlements, the area was highly productive in piety, producing rich harvests of monks and holy men. Theodoret of Cyrrhus enumerated them in the *Historia Religiosa*, but the one who most captured the imagination both then and since is Saint Simeon Stylites. Born somewhere near Antioch around 390, Simeon joined a community of monks at Telanissos around 412, where he made a nuisance of himself by such acts of ascetic athleticism as standing upright on one leg for as long as he could bear his weight, taking no food and drink at all during Lent, and binding a rope of palm fronds so tightly around his waist that the fibres entered the wound and began to fester, an act of self-mortification that resulted in his temporary expulsion from the monastery.

Readmitted to the community, but feeling his spiritual efforts hampered by the increasing throng who came to see him, Simeon adopted the simple but effective expedient of building a pillar and ascending it, thus rendering himself simultaneously closer to God and further from his earthly admirers. At first 3 metres seemed enough, but the clamour below grew ever greater, and he built ever higher, finally reaching a height of

20 metres.[51] The saint lived over thirty years atop this perch, twice daily delivering lengthy and powerful sermons to the stream of visitors for whom, if he himself was out of physical reach, his spiritual message was certainly accessible.

It seems that things could get pretty heated. Theodoret recounts that Bedouin would come to see Simeon in great groups 200–300 strong, smash their idols in front of the pillar and, for good measure, renounce the eating of camel-meat.[52] On one occasion, Theodoret himself was nearly trampled to death by an onrush of enthusiastic nomads, tugging at his beard and cloak in their eagerness to get as close as possible to the holy man on the pillar.[53] Upon Simeon's death, the citizens of Antioch managed to lay claim to his remains and carried them off in a solemn procession to a new resting place in the city. His example spawned a whole series of copycat stylites, among whom the most famous was Simeon the Younger (521–92), who, fittingly, practised his aerial vocation at a monastery between Antioch and the sea, a short journey from the elder Simeon's tomb.[54]

There is little left of the pillar at Deir Semaan now, if indeed the egg-shaped stone about half a metre high perched awkwardly on a column base actually is the remains of Simeon's earthly home. Guides were showing the pillar fragment as early as 1905, when Gertrude Bell spent a contemplative moment seated upon it whilst her Bedouin servants pitched camp.[55] There is no way of telling if it is the genuine article, yet its strange shape does seem almost as if a million believing hands had brushed away a tiny fragment of its sanctity, and it is undeniable that after the saint's death in 459, an enormous complex grew up, for the worship of God, the veneration of the Simeon's remains and the accommodation of the countless pilgrims drawn to the place.

A unique ensemble of four basilicas was constructed, creating a cruciform effect around the central shrine of the pillar. From the south basilica, richly adorned with blown acanthus decorations on the capitals, a typically Syrian flourish, the pilgrim – or modern visitor – gains the first view of the pillar. A whole series of piers and framing arches give extravagant architectural form to the basilicas, but still leave centre stage to the column itself. That four churches were needed is itself evidence of the vast numbers who came to worship here, for evidently they could not be accommodated in just one. The building of the western basilica even involved the effort of levelling off the hillside to enable it to be the same length as the others, its now-ruined state permitting striking views over the plain below that were impossible in the 5th century. The architects were innovators in other ways, too: on the eastern basilica, the apse's curve projects beyond the building to create a *chevet*, possibly the earliest example of such a feature in Syria.

To the south and east of the basilical complex lies a monastery, for those favoured enough to live or lodge so close to the shrine itself. Standing up to three storeys, using blocks and lintels, only the façade remains, giving the impression of a giant monastic noughts-and-crosses board. Beyond, and on the way to Deir Semaan – the lower town, where most had to stay – is the baptistery, containing a font built into the floor with steps to either side, possibly for the more rapid processing of the catechumens in a 'walk-through' baptism.

Deir Semaan, the monastery of Semaan (or Simeon), grew up on the site of the original Telanissos. A shattered monumental arch marks the start of the sacred way that led pilgrims up to the shrine itself. Beyond this lie the churches, monasteries and hostels, which made the place a veritable pilgrim city. In various states of ruination now, their arches alarmingly cracked, keystones wobbling and naves filled with the rubble of earthquake-induced collapse, carpeted in thorn-bushes and spring flowers, they still have the power to awe. The Great Pandocheion, the largest monastery – which also acted as a hostel for travellers – is surrounded by a two-storey portico, and the multiple arcades in the structure give the strange sensation of a building yet to be completed, and not of one in the process of falling down.

Earthquakes had, indeed, damaged the buildings as early as 526 or 528, possibly leading to the collapse of the roof over the pillar shrine itself, and the complex went into a decline after the Arab invasions.[56] A brief Byzantine reoccupation in the 10th century is evidenced by a crude defensive wall around the upper churches, but it was recaptured and sacked by a Muslim Hamdanid army in 985, and thereafter abandoned, leaving the saint's spirit to a final few centuries of silent contemplation.[57]

To enter into the life of a Byzantine holy man is to cross the threshold of a world both similar and yet profoundly different from our own. The ascetic piety, the mortification of the flesh, the longing to be rid of the trammels of a mortal body and to achieve by conspicuous piety the radiant garment of a saint or, better still, of a martyr – all these seem utterly at odds with our materialistic society. Yet the direct appeal over the heads of traditional authorities to the masses, the concern for those dispossessed or left out by the march of 'progress' in the fancy cities, the role of mediator between villages and the elites, the utter unconcern for traditional proprieties and etiquette, these are the hallmarks of the charismatic leader. But for the small matter of a thirty-year stint on top of a stone pillar, Simon Stylites could well, in a modern incarnation, have been a Kennedy or a Castro.

Deir Semaan is not an isolated phenomenon. It sits close to the northernmost extension of the Dead Cities, a crown atop a landscape that, though populated only by the deceased, seems curiously alive and vibrant. It is the most vivid witness anywhere to the diversity of rural life in the Later Roman Empire. Much debate has centred over exactly when the villages and small towns that made up this dense network of agricultural settlements began to decline, whether they retained their vitality into the 8th century – and thus beyond the Islamic invasion – or were already decaying in the early 7th.[58] That they grew, and flourished, is undeniable. Some 800 villages have been counted, and there may be more, most of them fairly small, with around fifty or so houses, and with no centralised plan, a far cry from the rigid grids – or at least the attempts to impose them on unwilling topography – that are the norm for larger cities in the region. The well-built houses, often with olive presses attached, speak of a comfortable existence, even of prosperity, while the absence of walls, and in general of fortifications save a few watchtowers, indicates a reasonably secure existence untroubled by imperial crises or external raiders.

Burj Haidar, which lies around 10 kilometres east of Deir Semaan, off a minor road winding south-eastwards towards Aleppo, is not untypical. A settlement first recorded in 298 as Kaprokera,[59] it boasts an unusually large number of churches for a comparatively small place, the most extraordinary of which is a chapel that clings limpet-like to the side of a slope overlooking the modern road. A huddle of bad-tempered dogs guard a tent that has been pitched inside the church, denying entrance. Two walls of a single tower remain, standing to a precarious height and listing at an alarming angle, surveying the rich arable land below, which once supplied the village's wealth.

Dar Qita, 50 kilometres west of Aleppo, seems from the road a small settlement, the walls of its houses merging into a vista of scattered rocks that stretches to the horizon. But on approaching it resolves itself into groups of neat, well-built dwellings, mostly two-storeyed, with the slots for wooden beams to support the upper floors still visible. A spring rain drizzles down, making the stone pathways slippery and treacherous and rendering the exploration of each house a hazardous adventure. Grey stone slabs form the lintels, set on uprights to create doorways that seem like miniature dolmens. In many cases only the roofs have collapsed, the rest of the structure remaining almost totally intact, creating the sensation that the inhabitants stepped out just a minute or two ago and made their way down to the fields with the firm intention of returning quite soon. The village church, complete only on its western side, has a heavily ornamented window decorated with almost spaghetti-like loops of stone. The doorways are all beautifully carved with intricate mouldings of acanthus and other plants. Inside are the remains of a *bema*, a semicircular raised platform of stone, somewhat overgrown, from which the clergy would read the lessons or deliver the sermons to their congregation of prosperous, pious farmers.

Around 20 kilometres further to the south-west lies the church of Qalb Loze. Its Arabic name means 'heart of the almond', though an alternative theory holds that it derives from Qal Baal Uze or 'the light of Baal Uze'. It is in a very poor settlement, at the edge of a village whose general state of repair seems almost worse than that of the 1,500-year-old church. A pile of discarded vaccine packs from the World Health Organisation is a sign that, once agriculturally independent and capable of sponsoring innovative ecclesiastical architecture, this place now very much depends on others for any flicker of prosperity. The church building stands isolated, the rest of the ancient settlement having disappeared, and it probably pre-dates the main church at Saint Simeon by a couple of decades. Around the outside of the rectangular basilica flow three corded bands of decoration, and the outline of the church is broken by a chevet. Inside, three dramatically swept arches divide the space into three aisles, the two at the sides still retaining some of the original flat roofing slabs. As one of the Dead Cities' most ambitious structures, it seems curiously muted and alone.

Just a couple of kilometres north is Qirkbize, in many ways indistinguishable from its many fellow Dead Cities. Yet the solidity of its buildings is still compelling, and on the top of the hill lies a fair-sized 3rd-century private house, converted at some point (probably early in the 4th century) into a church, with the remains of a *bema* still intact in the nave.[60] Incised on a fallen and almost inaccessible slab lies a little cross, a poignant reminder of the village's religious heritage. As we leave, a local imam, splendidly bearded, steps from a nearby van, curious as to what a foreigner is doing quite so far off the beaten track. The response clearly finds favour and he anoints our hands with perfume, kisses our foreheads and duly pronounces upon us sincerely intoned blessings. It is a just reward for a dozen Dead City churches visited.

In the southernmost group of Dead Cities, one more than any other merits the designation of city. Serjilla, around 50 kilometres south of Aleppo, lies in a basin between low hills, whose rocky appearance has been accentuated by their almost total loss of topsoil, long ago blown away and deposited in the valleys, leaving once-fertile slopes barren and lifeless. The settlement seems to flow down the hill, with well-preserved (or, rather, reconstructed) buildings standing tall amidst the debris of their fallen neighbours. In the centre of the site a miniature baths, with the largest room only 15 metres long, butts up against a two-storey building with a double-portico. With its beautifully carved Corinthian columns, this building, the *andron*, or men's meeting house, clearly had a lot of attention and expense lavished on it by the local dignitary who had it built some time in the late 5th century.[61] Even out here, far from the cosmopolitan life of the big cities, life's little luxuries were not neglected.

Around a dozen other houses still stand, some veritable villas; one, just up from the church with a double-frontage and a Corinthian colonnade façade looking out onto a courtyard, must have belonged to a prosperous family indeed; the remains of an olive press behind their residence perhaps give a clue to the source of their wealth. Yet all this passed away. Outside the church lie a couple of stone sarcophagi, hardly decorated save for ornate crosses, with the stone closing slab of one of them pushed slightly ajar, as though its occupant had, at the last moment, tried to flee.

By the 7th century, it seems, there was little chance of escape from the outside forces that were threatening the economic livelihood of these towns and villages. The big cities had been struggling since the 4th century, with little building of new municipal facilities, and by the 6th the decline was palpable. This great rural hinterland needed the possibilities offered by trade and some form of market economy, and, as the arteries of the Empire furred up and were then snapped, first by the Persians and then by Arab invasions, the opportunities for amassing surplus production and converting it into wealth locally disappeared. The monasteries, offering refuge both for the body and the spirit, and a convenient depository to gift what wealth there was, probably survived in more reasonable shape until the 10th century. The villages, too, were inhabited on a lesser scale than before, and it may have been that the final *coups de grâce* were delivered by the disruption caused first by the Crusades in the 11th and 12th centuries, and then by the Mongol invasions of the 13th.

The traveller who moves east from Beroea, rather than south-west towards Serjilla, passes down a road punctuated by villages and small towns, all dependent on the irrigation projects undertaken by the Syrian government over the past decades, tinting the desert fringes with smudges of green. Fifty kilometres to the east the road touches the Euphrates and, 125 kilometres further on, a side-branch leads to the ancient town of Sergiopolis (Resafe), 30 kilometres to the south. It all seems a long way from the modern government in Damascus, and it must have appeared just as distant in Roman times from the authorities in Rome, Constantinople or, at best, Antioch. Sergiopolis formed part of a chain of desert outposts established under Diocletian as part of the Strata Diocletiana, which led from Sura on the Euphrates south to Palmyra and thence as far as Damascus. It created a sort of outer *limes*, a trip-wire, while still retaining the security of a system of fortifications further inside provincial territory.[62] By the 5th century, however, most of the auxiliary and legionary troops had been moved up to this outer line, creating a bristling, threatening border, more like the fixed riverine frontiers of the Rhine and Danube than the traditional fluid desert lines of old. But then the outer posts were abandoned, in some cases entrusted to the guardianship of the Romans' Arab allies such as the Ghassanids, in others forsaken completely. It was thus a very thin force indeed that faced renewed Persian thrusts in the late 6th century, and one that depended on the field army or local initiatives to throw back invaders. When either or both of these failed, as they did against Khusraw from 610, the results were catastrophic.

The walls of Sergiopolis enclose a far greater area than was needed for the modest garrison of the 5th century, the brown bulk of the city's buttresses standing out starkly against the desert sands. The reason for this metropolis in the desert was the martyrdom of Saint Sergius, a Roman soldier who refused to make a sacrifice to the gods in 305, during the Great Persecution under Diocletian.[63] Sergius's martyr-shrine soon became a major centre of pilgrimage, drawing crowds from all over Syria and beyond, and churches, hostels and other facilities had to be constructed to service them. Under Anastasius (491–518), the settlement was renamed after the soldier-saint and the mud-brick walls were replaced with stone, using a gypsum that seems to catch the rays of the summer sun and reflect them back at onlookers with intermittent dazzling bursts of white. The walls were further reinforced under Justinian, but inside the arcaded galleries give them a curious light feeling despite their width and bulk. The north gate of the city is one of the finest extant examples of Byzantine military architecture; projecting from the wall, it protects an inner gateway decorated with a complex of arches and vine-branch patterns, more sculptor's tour de force than practical portal.

The principal buildings of Sergiopolis were of course ecclesiastical and the interior of the city is scattered with the skeletal remains of the

great pilgrimage basilicas. The most important of these, the church of
the Holy Cross, lies in the south-east of the city; some 30 metres long,
its sweeping lateral arches are reinforced by smaller arches resting on
columns, for the proneness of the region to earthquakes, and the uncertainty of the architects in handling this relatively new technique for
dividing nave from side-aisles, meant that remedial reinforcement was
necessary. In Basilica B to the west, coloured fragments of fresco have
survived against all the odds, depicting indistinct saints' heads, though
sadly scarred and obscured by quite recent graffiti. In the northern sector
of the city are three huge water cisterns, the largest of which is nearly
60 metres in length, with an estimated capacity of 15,000 cubic metres,
proof that Sergiopolis was well equipped to withstand an extended siege
or period of drought.[64]

Just outside the north gate of the city lies the building known as the
praetorium of the Ghassanids, or the palace of al-Mundhir. It is a low
rectangular structure, probably an audience chamber, its east wall interrupted by an apse. As early as the end of the 3rd century, with the
removal of the buffer that Palmyra had provided,[65] the Roman East
became ever more vulnerable to desert raiders or to the depredations
of more organised confederacies that began to grow up. The Romans
were forced to pay subsidies to Arab allies, a legally sanctioned form of
extortion, to make the desert safe, or at least passable, for their troops
and merchants. They had had relations with Arab peoples for many
centuries, but these were generally settled groups such as the Nabataeans
of Petra, the Edessans and the Palmyrenes, which sheltered the Roman
provinces from direct dealings with the more fractious nomadic or semi-
nomadic groups of the Arabian peninsula itself. Once the Romans
annexed the caravan cities of Petra, Edessa and Palmyra – in 106, 244
and 272 respectively – it became necessary to adopt new strategies to
cope with the direct responsibility for security of the desert regions over
which they had now assumed control.

The success of Diocletian's colleague Galerius in forcing the cession
in 298 by the Persians of five satrapies across the Tigris only aggravated
the situation. Both Rome and Persia were now in effect forced to
recruit the desert Arab tribes directly to their cause. By the early 6th
century, the Persians were allied with the Lakhmid confederacy, a group
who had its main base at Hira, south-west of the Euphrates in the Iraqi
desert, and the Byzantine government placed its faith in the Ghassanids,
originally a south Arabian group, which had migrated gradually northwards to the vicinity of Damascus.[66] The chief Ghassanid sheikh was
granted the title *phylarch* and substantial payments in exchange for safe-

guarding imperial interest from the Persians and Lakhmids, and for keeping his own followers from raiding Byzantine towns or convoys. The Ghassanids had converted to Christianity, although to its Monophysite form, a confessional choice that distanced them from the central orthodoxy of Constantinople, although it may have made them more acceptable to the heavily Monophysite populace of rural Syria. Part of their duties must have involved the protection of the pilgrims who came to worship at the shrine of Saint Sergius.

The al-Mundhir named in an inscription at the Sergiopolis palace (his name transliterated into Greek as Alumanduros) ruled over the Ghassanids from 569 to 582 and was arrested and exiled to Sicily by the Emperor Tiberius on suspicion of disloyalty, to be followed in short order by the overthrow of Nu'man, his son and successor.[67] Already in the mid-6th century the Byzantines had grown exasperated at the fickleness of their supposed allies; a treaty of 561 points the finger at the Ghassanids, accusing them of all manner of misdemeanours and threatening them with severe punishment if they transgressed again.[68] Two decades later the relationship had broken down altogether and the Byzantines were content to sit back as the Ghassanid confederation broke up into a score of squabbling factions. By doing so, however, they connived in the removal of the one effective barrier against those Arabs whose domains lay deeper still in the desert. This was not a problem whilst those tribes were disunited and disinclined to anything more damaging than the odd pillaging raid, but when in the early 7th century the advent of Islam gave those groups a new, united purpose, there was little to hold them back.

Sergiopolis had performed its role well as a breakwater against possible Persian incursions, save for its capture by Khusraw II in 616. Against the Arab invasions, however, it was powerless. The city continued to prosper modestly, performing for a time a role as a favoured retreat for the Umayyad caliphs, particularly under Hisham (724–43). But when the Abbasids came to power in 750, their army looted Sergiopolis and ransacked the palace that Hisham had built there – its remains lie beyond the palace of al-Mundhir – sending the city into a steep decline, which became terminal when the Mongols finished the destruction in the 13th century.

Two hundred kilometres further to the south-east down the Euphrates, Dura Europos lies at the very extreme of the Roman Empire, almost its greatest physical projection,[69] a fortress thrust deep into the heart of formerly Parthian territory, and a position that the Romans only held, precariously, for eighty years or so. In many ways, therefore, it is scarcely a Roman city, mingling Hellenistic, Parthian and Semitic influences in a cosmopolitan and unique mixture. The fortress-city lies on the west bank of the Euphrates, just 60 kilometres north-west of the border crossing with Iraq, its huge bulk dominating the view over a wide expanse of river and desert, seeming from a distance as though a mud-flow had spilt over, solidified, baked and then started to crumble back into the dust. It is this great western wall that provides the first, and abiding, impression of the site; on the other three sides Dura was protected by lower walls, steep gorges or the river itself.[70]

The probably founder of Dura was Nicanor, one of the generals of Seleucus I, who named it for Europos, his patron's birthplace in the Macedonian homeland.[71] The other half of its double-barrelled name probably derives from *dur*, a Semitic word meaning 'fort'. From its strategic position on a rocky plateau some 30–40 metres above the river plain below, it was an effective means to control the caravan routes, and consequently attracted the attention of the Parthians, who certainly held it at the time of a treaty with the Romans in 20 BC (which assigned Circesium, 50 kilometres upriver, as the forward Roman position).[72] Trajan's army passed through during his campaign of annexation against Parthia, leading to a brief Roman occupation in 115–17, but all that remains of this stay is a crumbling triumphal arch.

More definitive Roman control began in 164, when Lucius Verus (Marcus Aurelius's less philosophically inclined co-Emperor) captured it, as the Romans pushed ever further down the Euphrates. When the Sassanid dynasty came to power in Persia in 226, it initiated a more aggressive policy against its Roman neighbours, who had largely had their own way in Roman-Persian encounters since the Parthian victory at Carrhae in 53 BC. It seems the city may have been taken in 253, but revolted and, when Shapur recaptured it in 256, he did not permit the inhabitants any second chance to throw off Persian rule; the city was razed and its citizens deported elsewhere in his empire. So total was the destruction that when Julian passed through in 363 on his way to attack Ctesiphon, the Persian capital, there was no trace at all to be found of the town.[73]

It was the desperate efforts to reinforce Dura against this second Sassanid siege that preserved the most important archaeological finds there, for a great earth ramp was thrown up against the walls in a vain attempt to provide greater strength, thereby burying all the buildings at the edge of the city and preserving them from destruction. The intensity of the defenders' struggle was dramatically highlighted by the discovery of a tunnel beneath Tower 19, in which a group of skeletons lay, their armour still in place, three of them with purses full of coins about their bodies, their remains charred by the force of the fire that caused the tunnel supports to collapse.[74] Although it is unclear whether these were Roman defenders digging a countermine to block Persian tunnelling or Sassanid troops trying to undermine the tower, the bitter and fatal fight certainly ended in the city's fall.[75] The nearby bastion is riven by a great crack; though tempting to assign it to destruction during the siege, the damage was as likely caused by subsequent earthquakes.

The main or 'Palmyra' gate leads to the most important finds, a jumble of foundations and wall fragments that housed some of the city's many spectacular religious buildings. The first significant discovery here was made by Captain Murphy, a British soldier in the region as part of the post-First World War carve-up of the Middle East by the western European powers. He wrote to his superior officer that 'The paintings are in the west corner of the fort and consist of life-size figures of three men, one woman and three other figures partly obliterated.'[76] The British hurriedly despatched an archaeological team – for they were about to hand the area over to French control – which found further frescoes, including a depiction of Tyche, but by the time the French were able to commence excavation in earnest in 1922, the local Bedouin had defaced the exposed wall paintings. In a campaign of digs that stretched across fifteen years, Dura yielded an astonishing harvest. There were temples to the Palmyrene gods, a *mithraeum* (probably a legacy of the Roman military occupation) as well as temples to Zeus Kyrios ('the Lord'), Artemis, Zeus Megistos ('the Greatest') and more exotic deities, such as Gaddé, Azzanathkona, Atargatis and Artemis-Nanaia – all now represented by grassed-over walls, indistinct mounds and half-filled excavation pits.

The Durans' eclectic religious life was rounded off by a synagogue and a Christian chapel, both prize examples of their genre. The chapel seems to have been incorporated into a private building (it would have been unwise to advertise a Christian building in public at such an early stage) and is either from the late 2nd century or the first part of the 3rd; a graffito gives the date as 230/1.[77] It is amongst the earliest Christian buildings in the world, and was decorated with biblical scenes including the good shepherd and his flock, the story of Adam and Eve and representations of Jesus and the disciples.

On the other side of the gate lay a Jewish synagogue. The presence of a Jewish community is not in itself unusual, particularly in a cosmopolitan trading post such as Dura, but what is extraordinary is the series of beautifully crafted figurative paintings discovered there, dating from around 244,[78] just a decade before the city's destruction. Judaism would later have an aversion – just as did Islam – to depicting the human form, and so this fresco cycle is highly unusual,[79] perhaps evidence of an accommodation with Hellenistic ideas, perhaps just a sign of the Durans' self-confident individualism. The frescoes have long been removed from the site and can only be viewed in a side-room of the Damascus museum, supervised by a conspiratorial museum guard in a blue-peaked cap. The reds and yellows have survived most strongly, giving the depictions of biblical scenes a warmth and sadness. The whole gamut of stories is present here, from the finding of Moses in the Nile, to King David garbed in a suitably imperial purple robe and the judgement of Solomon.

When the Romans occupied Dura, they very unusually constructed their camp within the walls, sectioning off the whole of the north-west quarter of the city and building a *praetorium* and military baths there. Alongside the Seleucid-era 'new' citadel, the Romans built a fort for the military official who directed the garrison from around 211,[80] the *Dux Ripae* ('Duke of the Shore'). An early example of the *duces* who came to have particular commands along the frontier, the *Dux Ripae* kept watch for any Persian incursions – safe, as he thought, behind the thick, now partly fallen walls.

The archive of the auxiliary unit stationed here, the *Cohors XX Palmyrenorum*, has, thanks to the dry conditions and lack of subsequent occupation, provided a high proportion of the everyday military documents found anywhere in the Empire. These include guard rosters and quartermasters' records, but the most evocative of all is the *Feriale Duranum*, the military calendar of Dura.[81] A corollary of the founding of a permanent standing army under Augustus had been the establishment of an official calendar of religious observances for the soldiers. Aside from major Roman festivals, such as the Vestalia in June,[82] the birthday of Rome was commemorated on 21 April, while on 3 January the soldiers took vows for the health of the Emperor and the security of the Empire, a show of loyalty that, perhaps not coincidentally, took place four days before the army received its first pay-instalment of the year.[83] The date of accession (the *dies imperii*) of former emperors, most of them deified, was also celebrated, including Trajan, Antoninus Pius, Marcus Aurelius and Septimius Severus, but not Commodus, whose memory was universally reviled, or, more surprisingly, Hadrian. Thus from Dura in Mesopotamia to Durostorum in Moesia and Dubris in Britannia, the corporate identity of the army was reinforced by a common round of rituals and sacrifices.

At Dura Europos, the line could not hold, however, and after 256 the Romans never again secured a position quite so far forward on the Euphrates. By the 6th century the Roman border with the Persians ran close to a series of fortified cities further up the river, most notably Zenobia (modern Halabiye, 200 kilometres north-west of Dura Europos), named for the Queen of Palmyra whose territorial ambitions would seriously threaten Rome's control over Syria in the 270s. Here the river runs between two sets of hills, making it a suitable choke-point for blocking waterborne traffic or, indeed, for impeding land forces hugging the course of the Euphrates to take advantage of the ease of resupply that it offered. The set of walls facing the river has long ago been washed way. But the south wall, the longest of Zenobia's irregular triangular perimeter, retains almost all of its bastions, which march like stone pegs high up to the hill on which stands the city's bulky citadel, the last refuge for its defenders. The place is not much visited now; the ticket collector wearily complains that the year's total visitor tally has only just reached a hundred. Immediately below the citadel lies the *praetorium* in this late-Roman incarnation of a military camp, not centrally placed, but squatting at the edge of the city, and, reached by a flight of 120 precipitous steps, not easy of access for those in full armour. Inside, lovely barrel vaulting and clear views of the river compensate for the darkness and the thoughtless defacement of the walls with swastikas.

According to Procopius, the man responsible for the refortification and embellishment of Zenobia was Isidore the younger, the nephew of Isidore of Miletus, the architect of the dome of the great church of Hagia Sophia in Constantinople, and who had himself restored the great church after an earthquake caused its collapse in 558.[84] With such an illustrious architect, Zenobia was clearly a prestige project. Now lost in silence, it is hard to picture the place at the height of its prosperity. The fragments of a bathhouse are evidence of the municipal facilities that all such cities, no matter how remote, demanded, whilst as an outpost dating from the Christian era of the Empire it has its fair share of churches. One basilica, the large blocks of its nave and precarious tower seeming to teeter on the edge of imminent collapse, looks to be principally supported by a warped and buckled old plank.

Zenobia largely fulfilled its purpose, falling to the Persians only in 610 at a time when they seized almost the whole of the Near East. When the Arabs came, the frontier was lightly held, if at all; and, for all the strength of its walls and loftiness of its citadel, Zenobia could not hold them back.

Palmyra is a desert town, lying 300 kilometres across the desert south-west of Zenobia, its wealth derived from the basic need of travellers to rest and stop for water. Its name seems almost impossibly romantic, a distillation of all our preconceptions of the East. Take its alternative name, Tadmor (meaning 'the city of dates'), mix in the story of Queen Zenobia and the cocktail becomes irresistible. Palmyra's glory was built on trade, its sheltered oasis a convenient stopping point on the desert trade routes. Spices, precious metals, slaves – all travelled through here, destined for the insatiable appetite of Rome.

The approach to the town passes through a monotonous, desolate landscape of sand, distant dust-clouds and the debris of past travellers. The journey through the Syrian desert to the refuge of the Palmyrene oasis now takes just four hours from Zenobia, but in ancient times traders would spend days navigating their camel-borne cargoes through the wastelands. It is no wonder that the city was able to grow rich on the tariffs it levied on passing traders – after just an hour in the baking heat of the desert, almost any price for a sip of water sounds a reasonable one. The luscious dates, which gave the town its Palmyrene name and which enthusiastic vendors still hawk today, would have seemed an almost sensuous luxury.

Palmyra's past stretches back into almost unimaginable antiquity. It is first mentioned in records from Mari in the 18th century BC, and the name of Tadmor crops up in Assyrian archives a millennium later.[85] After a stint as a satrapy of the Achaemenid Empire, the city fell into the hands of Alexander the Great's conquering Macedonians around 330 BC. When Alexander died and his subordinates fell (as generals will) to quarrelling over the spoils, Tadmor, in common with much of Syria, found itself in the apportionment of Seleucus. In 64 BC, Pompey the Great, his career still on the upswing before his losing contest with Julius Caesar, lost patience and abolished the Seleucid Empire, at a stroke annexing its territories. It was not until 41 BC, however, that Palymra's enormous wealth tempted the Romans to replace theoretical sovereignty with practical occupation and plunder. Mark Antony tried to seize the oasis in that year, but found all the inhabitants fled and its treasure gone.[86] Disappointed, he left the Palmyrenes in peace and turned his mind to the sensuous delights of Egypt.

The city long formed a kind of buffer zone between Rome and the Parthian Empire to the east, where goods and information could be safely exchanged – needless to say, the Palmyrenes took a cut on each transaction. The bent for commerce and relieving travellers of a portion of their hard-earnt pounds or denarii survives today. Whilst the only real trade now is the tourist business, the ancestors of the modern hoteliers, guides and touts would doubtless be proud of their descendants' ability to mint new money from the distant echo of their forebears' ancient prosperity.

While retaining a neutrality between Parthia to the east and Rome to the west, Palmyra gradually found itself drawn closer to the Roman sphere of influence. The city had a studiously vague status that makes it frustratingly difficult to determine exactly when it became part of the Empire. Augustus's nephew Germanicus visited in AD 17, and this is probably the earliest date possible, while a milestone on the road north to Sura on the Euphrates of AD 75 is taken to indicate that Palmyra was clearly within Roman territory at this date.[87] Yet whatever the year of its actual absorption, Palmyra was allowed to keep its own army and ruling aristocracy and to carry on its business of growing rich on passing trade for at least another two centuries Ambitious merchants poured their wealth into the public buildings that make Palmyra, even in its ruined state, one of the most profoundly impressive sites on the Roman frontier.

The ruins themselves represent both three centuries of Roman interest in the town and the strength of local traditions and political power. Enclosed by the remains of a Roman wall, the site is almost semicircular, bounded to the north by the desert and to the west by rocky hills, on one of which a ruined Arab castle presides. The modern town of Tadmor barely intrudes, save in the guise of guides, vendors and hawkers. Unlike at the pyramids of Giza – where a fixed stare in one particular direction is needed to ignore the urban sprawl of Cairo – at Palmyra it needs no conscious effort to turn your eyes towards the past.

The wealth that ambitious local merchants accrued was poured into grandiose buildings as a public testament to their wealth and a bid for monumental immortality. Even half-buried under the sands, as they were for a thousand years, these magnificent ruins impressed later travellers. The first-recorded English visitors, a party from the Levant Company led by one Dr Huntington in 1678, scarcely had time to enjoy the ruins because, just after their arrival, they were stripped naked and chased through the desert by some unsporting local Bedouin.[88] A more leisurely inspection was achieved by Dr Halifax in 1691, but the most celebrated visit came in 1751 when the Englishmen James Dawkins and Robert Wood reached the city – then under Ottoman dominion – and were struck by 'the quantity of ruins . . . all of white, and beyond them towards the Euphrates a flat waste, as far as the eye could reach, without any object which showed either life or motion'.[89] It was as if Palmyra was the last remnant of some antique disaster that had reduced everything to dust, leaving only the shattered Corinthian pillars and fragmentary walls as testament.

The pillars and columns – now much restored from Wood's and

Dawkins's time – still seem from afar like the vertebrae of a great beached whale. On drawing closer, the field of ruins distinguishes itself into half-ruined temples, walls, houses and the grid pattern of a Roman town, with the vivid colonnaded gash of the Roman *decumanus maximus* forming the antique cetacean's backbone. The colonnaded street is an unmistakable sign that we are in the East, for it is a form of urban layout that is not found in the Western, Latin part of the Empire and, with its porticoes lined by shops, is probably the ancestor of the bazaar to be found today throughout the Greek and Semitic areas of the former Roman dominions.

Perhaps the most striking and symbolic ruin is the Temple of Bel, its great columns standing on a site that had been occupied for at least a millennium before the Romans came. Until the late 1920s, the temple shared its hallowed grounds with the mud-built houses of the local residents. Its conversion by the Mamelukes into a fortress in the 12th century was the principal reason for its survival in such an intact condition. Now standing alone on the southern edge of the main colonnaded street, it perches on a slight hill formed by the remains of previous sanctuaries – for the site has been regarded as sacred for at least 4,000 years. It was probably begun around AD 17 and was completed by AD 32, as its dedication makes clear.[90]

A massive paved courtyard surrounded by colonnaded porticoes leads to the temple itself, which the Arabs turned into a mosque and a fortress. In the southern chamber of the temple the ceiling decoration still survives in the form of octagons, roses, swastikas and at the centre a huge acanthus leaf. A plate of this was included in Dawkins's and Wood's book of their Eastern travels and was so admired that its reproduction in plaster appeared in a host of grand 19th-century English country houses.[91] Our Roman heritage comes back to us by the strangest of routes.

Guides to the site delight in pointing out a carving of three Syrian women heavily veiled from head to toe – a forerunner, they will say, of the Islamic custom, although these particular women may simply be in mourning.[92] Beside them walks a camel bearing on its back a type of high pavilion, which probably housed the sacred cult idol of the temple. The god worshipped here, Bel (more familiar from the Bible as Baal) shared the crowded Palmyrene pantheon with a host of others – Allat from Arabia, Balshaamin from Phoenicia – but Bel was supreme, and the magnificence of his temple shows it. Ancient gods were certainly not above vanity. Nearby are a series of friezes depicting Bel with a variety of other deities, including Yarhibol (the Sun) and Aglibol (the Moon), for the association of gods into triads was a habit deeply ingrained in the religious observance of the Near East, making the acceptance, if not the precise comprehension, of the Christian Trinity that much easier.

Just a short walk to the north-west lies the Temple of Nebu, a wisdom god from Mesopotamia. Only the podium of the temple really now survives, the rest of the sanctuary – on a much more modest scale than that of Bel – providing a strategic view of the great monumental arch which stands at this point on the colonnaded street. An enormous structure, the arch is in fact slightly wedge-shaped to mask a change of direction in the street, which was needed to preserve the axis based on the Bel Temple. Erected under Septimius Severus at the end of the 2nd century, its richly decorated façade is studded with niches for the exposition of imperial statuary. Even here, it did to pay lip service, at least, to the Emperor.

To the west of the colonnaded street lie two structures without which no city of the Greek-speaking East would have felt itself truly complete, the theatre and the *agora*. The former was probably restored and embellished in the 2nd century. Now complete to nine rows of seating and with an elaborate *scaenae frons*, its extravagant portico and stage entrance with ornate architrave make it look more miniature temple than theatre backdrop.

The *agora*, which was sprinkled, to judge from the column bases found there, with the statues of more than 200 local dignitaries, is adjoined by a much more intriguing space, the Tariff Court. It was here that a decree of AD 137 listing the taxes to be paid by passing trading caravans was displayed. The impression given, however, is hardly one of sumptuousness, for the goods listed are often humdrum. Wheat, wine, olive oil and salt are not the stuff of a despot's dream, but they did ensure the survival of this city, far away from the richer agricultural soils of the Mediterranean littoral. The import of unguent is a more hopeful sign of luxury goods, taxed at 25 denarii the camel-load (or, curiously, at just 13 denarii if carried in goatskins). Slaves, if intended for re-export, were taxed at 12 denarii a head, while, as Palmyra's commerce did not discriminate on moral grounds, prostitutes who charged one denarius or more for their services were themselves to be taxed at one denarius.[93] On how the assessors determined the prostitutes' normal charge, the tariff law is silent.[94]

The Temple of Balshaamin, which lies further to the north of the city, five minutes walk up the *decumanus*, is dedicated to the divine Phoenician import. Its restoration and the tree that has grown up to provide shade for a chirping multitude of local birds give it an almost Gothic quality. Smaller and more ruined than the Temple of Bel, it probably once bore

busts of the seven planetary deities and has an inscription recording a
three-week visit by the 'divine Hadrian' in AD 129. In gratitude for the
hospitality he received there, the Emperor declared Palmyra a 'free city',
and, to ensure that his visit was not forgotten, he renamed it Palmyra
Hadriana.[95] The Palmyrenes probably breathed a sigh of relief when he
left, and they most certainly ignored their city's new imperial nomenclature. Roman control was, for the first few centuries, a relatively light yoke.
It was only after the Parthian Wars of 162–7 that a permanent Roman
garrison was stationed there, whilst a decline in the caravan trade led to
the city gaining more the air of a military encampment and less that of
an entrepôt.

As Rome's hold on her eastern provinces weakened in the mid-3rd
century against the encroaching power of a new Persian dynasty, the
Sassanids, the lifeblood of Palmyra – its control of the trade routes –
was slowly strangled. After a Sassanid army defeated and killed the
Emperor Valerian in 260, the situation became ever more precarious.
The timing could hardly have been worse for Valerian's son, Gallienus,
who now took over as sole Emperor. Only the previous year, Postumus
had wrested the Gallic provinces away from central control, and there
were certainly not sufficient resources to fight on two fronts at once.
Meanwhile, the remnants of the defeated Roman army in the East
took the understandable view that local self-help was the only viable
option and elected as co-Emperors the two sons of Macrianus, one of
Valerian's generals, who himself refused the diadem on account of his
advanced age.[96]

Although he defeated one of the usurpers' armies in the Balkans (a
battle in which the two Macriani were killed), Gallienus still had to rely
on Septimius Odaenathus, who had emerged as the exarch of Palmyra
around 257–8, to mop up the rebellion in the East. Odaenathus saw the
advantage of supporting a Roman emperor desperate enough to show
suitable gratitude for his services, yet far enough away not to jib at a
little local expansion of Palmyra's power base. He turned his attention
to Shapur's Sassanid army, still in possession of large swathes of Roman
provincial territory. Despite the modest size of Palmyra's army, he
deployed it and co-opted remnants of the Roman eastern legions to great
effect, driving the Persians from Armenia and Mesopotamia and almost
advancing as far as Ctesiphon, the Persian capital.

Having driven the Persians out of Syria, he was showered by the
grateful Romans with high-sounding titles such as 'Corrector of the East'.[97]
Odaenathus, for whom modesty was clearly not an issue, styled himself
mlk mlk – 'King of Kings'. The Romans were probably not unduly

concerned by this assumption of a high-sounding indigenous title. More worrying would have been the aping of Roman imperial nomenclature, and this Odaenathus did not do. In fact, it is Shapur who is more likely to have been offended, as the Palmyrene's new style mimicked that of the Persian royal court.[98]

In 267 Odaenathus and his eldest son Herodian were murdered under mysterious circumstances. The chief benefactor, coincidentally, was his widow, Zenobia, who took it upon herself to make her husband's self-given title a reality. For two years, Zenobia's armies carried all before them. It seemed for a time that she might seize the whole of the East and abolish the power of Rome for good. Her armies pushed as far west as Ancyra in Cappadocia and as far south as Egypt, where she defeated the loyalist governor Tenagio Probus in 269. Perhaps in order to arouse local sympathies, she claimed, according to one source, descent from the Ptolemies.

A number of cities turned coat, and it would have seemed preferable for the rest to express, at best, a studied neutrality until the situation became clear. The Empire had seen many usurpations, both failed and successful, over the past half-century, and ending up on the winning side in the various civil wars required a good mixture of foresight, diplomacy, ruthlessness and luck. At first Zenobia, despite the onward march of her armies, did not make the break with Rome official. Exploiting to the full all the opportunities offered by numismatic diplomacy, she initially had coins minted for her son Vaballathus at Antioch, which showed him dressed as a Roman general, and bearing an inscription that can probably be deciphered as 'Rex, Imperator, Dux Imperatorum'.[99] Crucially, Aurelian, who had become Emperor in 270, is depicted on the reverse of the coin with the title Augustus.[100] It seems that Zenobia, believing the new Emperor to have been as unable as Gallienus (and his immediate successor Claudius Gothicus) to reassert his authority in the East, was hoping for some recognition of her position. Only in 271/2 did the title 'Augustus' appear on Vaballathus's coins, showing that Zenobia was now prepared to assert what she could not gain through diplomatic means.[101] She even had her son claim Odaenathus's old title of *Corrector Totius Orientis*, to which he emphatically had no legitimate claim.

Aurelian was a skilled and tough campaigner. Leaving behind him the unfinished business of the breakaway Gallic empire, he marched east. An initial engagement near Antioch went badly for the Palmyrenes. Zenobia's general, Zabdas, only got away by parading an Aurelian look-alike through the streets of the city, claiming that he had captured the Emperor, and thus duping the Antiochenes long enough to make his escape. At Immae, north-west of Antioch, the Palmyrene cavalry was put to flight, and then at Emesa their main force was badly mauled. As quickly as it had appeared, the aura of inevitability about Zenobia's hold on power dissipated and her former allies fell over themselves in the rush to prove that actually they had been loyal to Aurelian all along. The Roman army pursued its royal prey all the way back to Palmyra.

The *Historia Augusta* preserves an exchange of letters between Aurelian and his foe, which, if fictional in its details, may preserve the Emperor's desire to co-opt rather than crush Zenobia, or at least force a bloodless surrender. His demand is peremptory: 'You should have done of your own free will what I now command in my letter. For I bid you surrender, promising that your lives shall be spared, and with the condition that you, Zenobia, together with your children shall dwell wherever I, acting in accordance with the wish of the most noble senate, shall appoint a place.'[102] Zenobia replied with haughty pride: 'From Zenobia, Queen of the East, to Aurelian Augustus. None save yourself has ever demanded by letter what you demand. Whatever must be accomplished in matters of war must be done by valour alone. You demand my surrender as though you were not aware that Cleopatra preferred to die a Queen rather than remain alive, however high her rank. We shall not lack reinforcements from Persia, which we are even now expecting.'[103] Historians' frequent comparisons of Zenobia's career with that of Cleopatra clearly has the most respectable sanction, that of the Palmyrene queen herself.

No aid came from the Sassanids, however, and so, with her Armenian allies having deserted her, the Palmyrene queen went in search of the Persians. She failed to find a boatman to ferry her small party over the Euphrates, and the Romans, to whom her flight had been betrayed, captured her. Taken to Rome, she was displayed to the public in Aurelian's triumph in 274, accompanied in the procession by ten captive Gothic women dressed as Amazon warriors, and by Tetricus, the former Gallic Emperor, whose territory had been recaptured by Aurelian the year before. Rather than suffer strangulation after the triumph, the more traditional fate of defeated chieftains, Zenobia was permitted to live the rest of her life in obscure retirement in a villa near Rome. According to the historian Eutropius – and the less reliable testimony of the *Historia Augusta* – she may have remarried, her descendants still living in Rome at the time of Valens, a century later.[104]

Over the centuries her legend was relayed and embellished by a succession of writers, including Chaucer, becoming more attractive with every retelling. Gibbon wrote of her, with a nice combination of chauvinism and swooning admiration: '. . . Zenobia is perhaps the only female, whose superior genius broke through the servile indolence imposed on her sex by the climate and manners of Asia . . . She was of a dark complexion . . . Her teeth were of a pearly whiteness, and her large black eyes sparkled with uncommon fire, tempered by the most attractive sweetness.'[105]

In 1813, Lady Hester Stanhope, the niece of Prime Minister William Pitt the Younger, paid a visit to Palmyra during an eccentric progress through the Orient, accompanied by a train of twenty-five camels. In a splendid ceremony, in which Bedouin warriors stood guard on the column brackets, Lady Hester came to believe that she was, in some sense, a reincarnation of Zenobia. 'I have been crowned Queen of the Desert under the triumphal arch at Palmyra,' she wrote. 'I am the sun, the star, the pearl, the Lion, the light from heaven, and the Queen.'[106] In exchange for their paying such extravagant court to her compulsively self-regarding fancies, she awarded the local Arab tribe the 'right' to levy a toll on any subsequent travellers who might pass through Palmyra – a tax that, need-less to say, successive sheikhs were more than happy to exact, brandishing in their support a tattered paper of authorisation from the English 'Desert Queen'. When the British naval officers Charles Irby and James Mangles visited the site in 1818, they found that her largesse had set something of a floor on the price to be paid for a safe-conduct through the desert and they were forced to part with 600 piastres, a hundred more than Lady Hester herself.[107]

On the central colonnaded street of the town, close to the Temple of Bel, where old shop doorways can still be made out, is evidence of Palmyra's most famous resident. Just before the tetrapylon – a virtuoso construction of four pedestals, each supporting four huge columns – is a smaller column that originally bore a statue, and an inscription for Zenobia (which the Romans had removed after her defeat). Next to it, the inscription for Odaenathus, her husband and predecessor in power, was left intact by them, an acknowledgement, no doubt, that whilst his wife had done Rome a great disservice, the 'Corrector of the Orient' himself had probably saved the eastern provinces from long-term Persian occupation. Nearby, another dedication commemorates Julius Aurelius Zenobia, who may have been the great queen's father.

After Zenobia's fall, the Romans' military grip became tighter as the Palmyrenes' income from trade fell. The garrison Aurelian had left in the town was massacred in an uprising in spring 273, and, once Palmyra was recaptured, the Emperor showed no second clemency, permitting a large-scale massacre of the inhabitants and the plunder of the Temple of Bel. A wall was built around the city, parts of which still survive, and a legion was permanently based here. Diocletian has given his name to a part of the ruins, known as 'Diocletian's Camp', which houses the remains of the camp for the new garrison, the I Illyricorum legion, its accommodation and temples. A monumental staircase looking as though it has melted in some tremendous furnace into a buckled and folded mass leads up to a massive Temple of the Standards.[108] No inconspicuous shrine such as those found in the legionary camps of the west, this one is huge in scale, the stairs leading up to a platform on which survives a chamber ending in an apse. Here, the sacred eagle and other standards of the legion would be set, in an unmistakable display that the Roman military presence had come to stay, overshadowing the much more modest temple of the south Arabian goddess Allat down below.

Just to the east is the ancient residential quarter of the city. It is an especially broken and desolate place, little more than a field of broken stones, collapsed columns and distant dreams. However, not much has been excavated and it is an almost fitting symbol of the end of Palymra's prosperity, a long, slow decline into night.

For Palmyra the twilight was to be a long one. As the frontier regions that had hosted trade and exchange with the powers further east became military garrisons and closed defensive zones, they became a drain on imperial funds and the city's cultural resources diminished. A few churches were constructed to the north of the city, and the Temple of Baalshamin was converted to Christian use, while under Justinian the walls were strengthened, but already most of the city had collapsed into ruins. In 634, the Roman period came to an end for Palmyra as the armies of the first caliph, Abu Bakr, seized it on their victorious sweep through the province of Syria.[109] Urban life clearly continued for a time, as the Jewish traveller Benjamin of Tudela reports that he found 2,000 Jews living there when he visited in 1192.[110] After that, Palmyra was left to be washed over by a sea of sand and was forgotten, so that when William Halifax visited from Aleppo in 1691, he found just forty families living in hovels crowded together in the Temple of Bel.

To the west of Palmyra's main monuments lies the Valley of the Tombs, a landscape oddly reminiscent of *Star Wars*, peppered with strange funerary towers poking up from amongst the desert dunes. There are underground tombs, too. The whole valley is peopled with the dead and they are still being discovered. A few years ago a lorry skidded off the road and caused the roof of a hidden tomb to collapse, and both vehicle and driver tumbled into the newly revealed necropolis. The driver's thoughts at escaping death only to be confronted by the stylised and faintly smiling statues of his ancestors can only be imagined.

Even in death the Palmyrenes knew how to cut a deal. Inside the tower tombs a central corridor leads onto narrow passages in which the remains of the deceased were stacked, one compartment on top of another, in a kind of bizarre filing cabinet. Some families even funded their own grandiose tombs by selling spaces in these 'loculi' to others less well-off, but still keen for their stake in immortality. The largest remaining is the Tomb of Elahbel, completed in 103,[111] a solid, soaring tower, which had a capacity for some 300 inmates in an underground *hypogeum*, with four overground storeys stacked on top of it. One of the best preserved of the purely underground structures is the Hypogeum of the Three Brothers, at the foot of whose stairway an inscription unabashedly reports that the necropolis was constructed by the three siblings[112] as a commercial venture. Further into the tomb a fresco shows the fraternal entrepreneurs, depicted in frames supported by winged victories.[113] In death, victory – or at the very least, profit. One of the brothers, Malé, found his rest here in 142, and the tomb remained open for business for more than a century, up to 259.

It is in the tombs that we come face-to-face with the ancient Palmyrenes. They wear carefully arranged tunics and draped cloaks, with their names and ancestry inscribed above their shoulders, almost universally in Palmyrene, for the use of Greek in such private contexts was extremely rare. The men, from the 2nd century generally bearded, often turn their glance to the side, as though not to look visitors in the eye. The women are depicted veiled, wearing an elaborate headdress with a turban, and ornate brooches and earrings. In earlier examples, the women often hold spindles and distaffs, signs of domesticity, or carry a little child. One hand normally holds the two sides of the veils together with the fingers resting against the cheek, a gesture of touching intimacy.

The best time of day to view the tombs and the ruins in general is at sunset and dusk, when the rosy light and deep-hued shadows lend the site an air of melancholy, and the sounds of the desert night give the impression that the gossiping and hawking of the ancient inhabitants are only just out of reach. The finest vantage point is from the hill that towers over the site to the south, from the ramparts of the Arab castle originally built in the 13th century to ward off a Crusader invasion that never quite came. Local Syrian families come to take tea, exchange gossip and watch the sun go down over the final homes of their illustrious ancestors.

The Bedouin still camp in the ruins of Palmyra. Ragged children herd black-fleeced sheep in Diocletian's camp, their refusal to be overwhelmed by the past lending a wistfulness to the imposing marble blocks. Their animals wander through a forum that was once as busy as Rome's or

Antioch's, and by night the barking of their dogs imbues the otherwise tranquil ruins with a sense of threat. Yet any tourist who approaches too closely will be met by demands for money for a photo of shepherd and flock, or even offered a set of grubby postcards of Palmyra for a few pounds a packet. Entrepreneurs come in all shapes and sizes. There is also still an oasis at Palmyra, and its warren-like maze of watered gardens behind low walls exude a timelessness. If *their* walls have fallen and *their* grandeur faded, they seem to say, our Palmyra never changes.

During the last period of Byzantine occupation of Syria, a number of administrative and military complexes were built to secure control over a region that was no longer as heavily militarised as during its 3rd-century heyday. Almost contemporary with the 6th-century stage of Halibiye-Zenobia, the fortified centre at Qasr ibn Wardan lay around 200 kilometres north-west of Palmyra. Completed in 564 – an inscription records the precise day of its dedication – the structures, church, totally ruined barracks and palace have a surprising grace and fragility, surrounded by arid fields that, in antique times, must have produced enough to support at least a small garrison.

It seems that workmen from Constantinople may have been brought in to build Qasr ibn Wardan; the size of its bricks match exactly moulds used in the capital. The main portal of the palace (or *praetorium*) boasts the date inscription which proclaims that all this was made 'for the glory of God', and a surrounding wreath of Alphas and Omegas leaves no doubt as to the Christian allegiances of the workmen. The building is laid out around a central courtyard with a variety of vaulted rooms, which probably ranged from stables to reception halls. The sleeping accommodation was upstairs, now roofless, but providing impressive vistas across the dry scrub of the surrounds.

A short way from the palace lies the church and this is indeed an impressive desert find, entered through a door on which is inscribed (in Greek), 'This is the door which God made through which all the faithful will enter.'[114] Originally two or three storeys tall with a series of internal galleries and arcades lending an illusion of further height, the basic ground plan is square despite the circular dome. Of the latter only one arch survives, pointing heavenwards as though the whole building had been seized and somehow stretched in that direction. A compact gem, its alternating brown and grey levels of brickwork lending it a little the air of a layer cake, the Qasr ibn Wardan church seems to cry out for a larger congregation than the desert, and its Bedouin guardian, can provide.

Emesa (now Homs), Syria's third-largest city, which lies 100 kilometres to the south-west of Qasr Ibn Wardan, back in the more heavily settled western portion of the province, was one Syria's most important cities, and had a venerable pre-Roman past. It was founded far back in the Bronze Age, but achieved prominence under the native Samsigeramid dynasty, who seized control in the mid-2nd century BC as the power of the Seleucids waned. The Romans incorporated it into the province of Syria in AD 78[115] and deposed the last Samsigeramus, his family retreating into the sacred realm, retaining authority as the hereditary high priests of the god Elagabal, symbolised as a black stone that resided in a sumptuous temple, an image renowned throughout the Empire. Of it not the slightest trace has been found, save representations on coins from the time of Antoninus Pius that depict an eagle perched on the black stone.[116]

It was in Emesa that Septimius Severus found his second wife, the formidable Julia Domna, herself a daughter of the high priest. Septimius allegedly married her in 187 because an oracle had declared that she 'would marry a king'[117] and, with an eye for supernatural assistance, he believed this might aid him in one day achieving royal – or imperial – status. A striking woman, Julia Domna and her female relatives were to be an important force in imperial politics for half a century. Of her undoubted charms, Gibbon gushed that she had 'the attractions of beauty, and united to a lively imagination a firmness of mind and strength of judgement, seldom bestowed on her sex'.[118]

It was her great-nephew who would, in effect, be the undoing of her dynastic hopes. Julia Domna died in 217, allegedly starving herself to death in protest at the usurpation of Macrinus following the death of her son Caracalla. Her sister Julia Maesa, and her niece, yet another Julia (Soaemias), contrived to present the troops encamped near Emesa with Julia Soaemias's son, Varius Avitus, who, as the latest high priest of Elagabal, was more commonly referred to by the name of the god he served. Once Macrinus had been disposed of, the thirteen-year-old boy duly took the imperial title of Marcus Aurelius Severus Alexander Augustus, claiming – at the instigation of his mother – to be the illegitimate son of Caracalla,[119] but it is as Elagabalus that he is universally known.

Multiple divorces and remarriages, allegations of open homosexuality and a general collapse of morality in the court eventually undermined any respect for Elagabalus,[120] and in June 221 his grandmother Julia Maesa forced him to adopt his younger cousin Bassianus Alexianus as Caesar.[121] The following year the praetorian guard rioted, murdered Elagabalus and, for good measure, his mother too, and then installed Alexianus as sole Emperor under the name Alexander Severus. The Roman army and aristocracy most probably breathed a collective – if short-lived – sigh of relief and the sacred black stone was despatched back to Emesa, where it remained in place at least long enough for Aurelian to visit it in 272 and (according to the *Historia Augusta*) gain divine assistance from it in his struggle against Zenobia.[122]

One hundred and fifty kilometres to the south of Homs, and almost in the extreme south-west of ancient Syria, Damascus lays claim to being one of the oldest continuously inhabited cities in the world; it is first mentioned as 'Dimashqa' in the archives of Mari around 2500 BC,[123] and remained an important regional centre until its conquest by the Achaemenid Cyrus of Persia in 539 BC. For a time from about 85 BC it marked the northernmost extension of the Nabataeans, the northern Arabian kingdom that had grown rich on the spice trade,[124] and in common with most of the rest of Syria, it became Roman in 64 BC by Pompey's conquest. But it was never the chief city of the Roman province, that honour being accorded to the former Seleucid capital of Antioch on the Orontes.

Although the noise, the urban sprawl and the exuberant chaos of the modern capital city seem utterly to drown out the past, some traces of ancient Damascus still survive, centred around the old walled city. The plan of the ancient town can be detected in the Hellenistic and Roman outline, including the walls – where traces of Roman blocks can be seen at the very bases – and in an underpass just outside Bab Sharqi, the eastern gate, where part of an original Roman angle-tower has been excavated, some 20 metres from the line of the medieval perimeter. The alignment of the gates is closer than the walls to that of the Roman originals, seven of the nine gateways being originally named for the planets: Bab Sharqi itself was the Gate of the Sun, which was numbered among the planets in Roman cosmology.

More resonant of Roman Damascus is its most important holy place, now the site of the Ummayad mosque. Deep inside the old city, it is enclosed within a busy bazaar, selling all those necessities of daily life, from hunks of camel meat to spices, beaten copper trays, wedding dresses and, for the tourists, an almost endless array of carpets. Little has changed over the years, for the mosque's predecessor, the Temple of Jupiter Haddad, also lay within the city's chief market district, while the porticoes of the sanctuary would have been used as classrooms by professional rhetors, just as the columns of the current mosque act as the focus for impromptu Koranic instruction classes. The remains of a *propylaeum* or triumphal arch sit outside the west entrance of the mosque, which may originally have reached to a height of 12 metres. The outer wall of the mosque compound retains, for the most part, that of the *temenos*, the inner temple enclosure of the Jupiter sanctuary.[125] Incorporated within it are several Roman-era inscriptions, including one in Greek declaring that 'Thy Kingdom O Christ is an everlasting kingdom'.[126] Probably during the reign of Theodosius I (379–95) the temple was converted into a Christian church, dedicated to Saint John the Baptist. Almost all trace of this was swept away when, after an uneasy seventy-year cohabitation following the Muslim conquest of Damascus in 636, Caliph al-Walid ordered the building of the present mosque. The reverence for the Baptist, however, survived, and inside the prayer hall is a shrine marking the spot where his head is believed to have been buried after its grizzly presentation by Salome to Herod on a plate.

The Umayyad mosque holds a special place in the development of the mosque's form. Its domed roof vies with the al-Aqsa in Jerusalem as the very earliest example of the type, almost certainly an imitation of the domes of the great Byzantine centralised churches, such as that of Saint Simeon at Deir Semaan. The angle-towers that lined the *temenos* (enclosed sacred space) of the temple, themselves an echo of the ancient Semitic tradition of worship on high places, are said to have influenced the development of the minaret, which was not a feature of the earliest mosques. On the exterior surface of the prayer hall, however, is an embellishment that was not to be replicated so widely, but is nonetheless a sign of the mixed culture within which early Islam flourished in Syria.

The mosaics are the glory of the Umayyad mosque. Against a shimmering golden backdrop, a rich landscape is woven, of fields, orchards, streams, palaces, towers and cities, all bound together with winding trails of acanthus leaves. Much of the surface of the mosaics was lost through fires – most notably in 1893 – and reconstruction, but the original workmen were probably the heirs to a tradition that stretched back to Hellenistic times. They placed the tiny coloured tesserae on the great canvas of the mosque frontage, just as their great-grandfathers had probably done for the adornment of late-Byzantine palaces and churches.

The old town retains other vestiges of its Christian heritage, which was all played out under Roman rule. The 'Street called Straight', which is mentioned by name in the Acts of the Apostles,[127] served as the *decumanus maximus* of the city, cutting westwards through its heart from the Bab Sharqi. It is, as irony demands, not entirely straight, its course changing axis twice along its length, masked in typical Roman fashion by memorial arches, one of which survives as a slightly undignified car-parking space. Mark Twain acerbically commented that the street was 'straighter than a corkscrew, but not as straight as a rainbow'.[128] The pot of gold at its end for anyone braving the traffic that pushes erratically through the congested single-carriage lane is the chapel of Ananias, a subterranean crypt where Saint Paul is said to have taken refuge after his blinding on the road to Damascus. On recovering his sight, Paul took to preaching the new religion in the synagogues of the city, which, as a practice clearly designed to win converts away from their number, angered the Jewish notables of Damascus. The place where tradition holds that he was lowered from the city walls in a basket, to escape their plot to kill him, is marked in a chapel just a few hundred metres away from that of Ananias. For those who have not quite got their bearings, the church has provided a very large (and modern) wicker basket in commemoration of the legend.

In 613, Damascus fell to the Persians. It was one of the first major losses to a resurgent Persia, under the leadership of Khusraw II, which looked set finally to emerge victorious from its seven-century-long struggle with Rome for dominance in the region. Yet in March 630 the Emperor Heraclius made a triumphant ceremonial entrance into Jerusalem. At the head of the procession went the True Cross, the very wood on which Christ had been crucified, seized by Khusraw II when the Persians took the city in 614, and now being restored to its place of honour in the church of the Holy Sepulchre. Negotiations the year before in connection with the restoration of the sacred relic had seemed to presage the conversion of Persia to Christianity,[129] which would have confirmed the Byzantines' absolute victory in religious as well as political terms. Less than a decade later, in 638, the caliph Umar took possession of Jerusalem for Islam, while the final Sassanid opposition to the Muslim armies was swept aside at Nehavand in 641. The age-old rivalry between Persia and Rome was rendered irrelevant and Byzantine control over the Near East and North Africa was swept aside with terrifying rapidity. How had it come to this?

Both principal empires in the Near East were exhausted by thirty years of campaigning, which had seen the Byzantine Empire on the point of collapse before a remarkable swing of fortune left it more able to impose its terms on the prostrate Persians than at any time since Trajan's victories in the early 2nd century.[130] Yet the Byzantines had had just a few years in which to rebuild the administrative structures and re-establish the networks of loyalty that had been swept aside by the Persian occupation. In the meantime, the Arabs of the peninsula had been uniting behind the banner of the religion of Islam, under the inspirational leadership of the prophet Muhammad. The removal in the late 6th century of the buffer presented by the Byzantine and Sassanids' Arab allies, the Ghassanids and Lakhmids, and the previous evacuation of the frontier forts in Syria and Arabia by the Byzantine central army left little to shield those provinces from the new force.

The new religion, by offering tolerance to those Jews and Christians who chose not to convert, and economic benefits – in exemption from the *jizya* or poll-tax – for those who did, undermined what little residual loyalty there was to the central regime in Constantinople. The prevalence of Monophysitism in those provinces bordering on the Arabian peninsula also meant that those Christians who continued to cling to their faith may have felt they were just as well served outside the direct political control of an empire that officially espoused a creed antithetical to their own.

The disastrous defeat of the Byzantine field army at Yarmuk (in the north of modern Jordan) in 636 meant there was no force left to hold the Arab armies back.[131] When a defensive line was finally established in the mid-7th century it was across central Anatolia, where the Empire was able to reorganise the territory into military provinces, or 'themes', and rely on the martial tradition of the mountain tribes to supply them with fresh troops. Syria, Arabia and most of North Africa (save an outlying fragment around Carthage that resisted for a further half-century) were utterly lost.

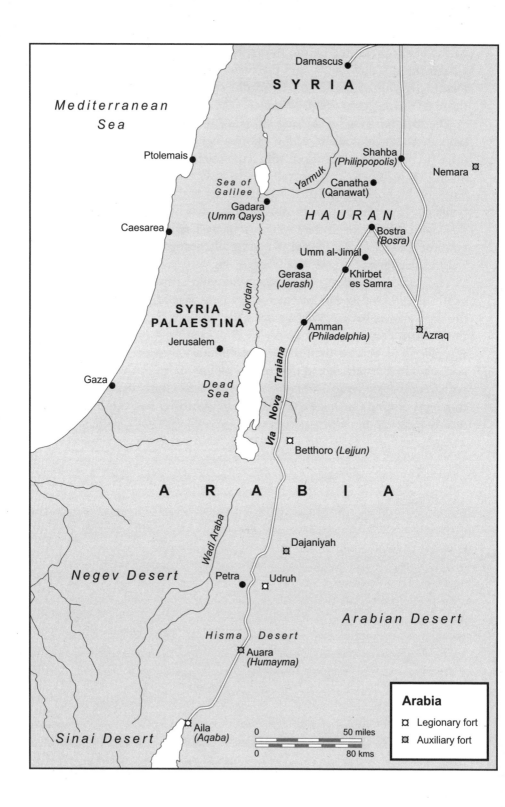

Mediterranean
Sea

SYRIA

Damascus

Ptolemais

Sea of
Galilee

Yarmuk

Shahba
(Philippopolis)

Nemara

Canatha
(Qanawat)

Gadara
(Umm Qays)

HAURAN

Caesarea

Bostra
(Bosra)

Umm al-Jimal

Gerasa
(Jerash)

Khirbet
es Samra

SYRIA
PALAESTINA

Jordan

Amman
(Philadelphia)

Azraq

Jerusalem

Gaza

Dead
Sea

Via Nova Traiana

Betthoro (Lejjun)

ARABIA

Wadi Araba

Dajaniyah

Negev Desert

Petra

Udruh

Arabian Desert

Hisma   Desert

Auara
(Humayma)

Aila
(Aqaba)

Sinai Desert

0   50 miles

0   80 kms

Arabia

¤ Legionary fort

¤ Auxiliary fort

CHAPTER 8

Arabia

They seem no work of Man's creative hand,
Where Labour wrought as wayward Fancy planned;
But from the rock as if by magic grown,
Eternal – silent – beautiful – alone!
Not virgin white – like that old Doric shrine,
Where once Athena held her rites divine:
Not saintly grey – like many a minster fane,
That crowns the hill, or sanctifies the plain:
But rosy-red – as if the blush of dawn
Which first beheld them were not yet withdrawn:
The hues of youth upon a brow of woe,
Which men call'd old two thousand years ago!
Match me such marvel save in Eastern clime,
A rose-red city half as old as time.

John William Burgon 'Petra'[1]

Arabia was amongst the least troublesome of Roman acquisitions. Most of this vast tract of land from the basalt plateau of the Hauran mountains down across the wadi-scored terrain of the Jordan valley and the fringes of the Sinai, Negev and Arabian deserts had been occupied by the Nabataean kingdom, with its capital first at Petra and then latterly at Bostra, and it seems to have fallen without much – if any – of a fight. In AD 106, it was simply annexed by Trajan, its royal family disenfranchised and its territory organised as a new Roman province.

The Nabataeans had occupied at least part of the area since the 4th century BC. Petra was settled originally by the Edomites in the late 8th century BC, but it is not clear what relationship (if any) the Nabataeans had with them. In 312 BC, Antigonus Monopthalmos ('the One-Eyed'), one of Alexander the Great's former generals, sent a raiding force into their territory, since he had heard that they gathered annually at 'a certain rock' (which might have meant Petra).[2] His troops carried off a substantial haul of spices and silver, but the Nabataeans caught up with them somewhere in the desert, mauled the Greeks badly and retrieved their goods. The account of the geographer Strabo, probably relating to a period a century or two later, paints a picture of a more settled folk, whose king lived in a certain style.[3]

The apogee of the Nabataean kingdom ran from the mid-1st century BC to the end of the 1st century AD, or at least the great monuments for which Petra is so justly famous can be dated to that period. It was their command of the spice trade, more than the masterful mausoleums that they constructed at Petra, their capital, that marked out the Nabataeans as the richest of the petty kingdoms of the desert fringe. Exploiting a marginal position between two of the bickering successor kingdoms to Alexander the Great, the Ptolemies and the Seleucids, and lying almost at the head of the spice route that ran from distant Arabia Felix (Yemen), the Nabataeans extracted a suitable cut for permitting the precious cargo to transit northwards to Palmyra and thence to the Roman Empire. Rich, shrewd and adept at balancing the interests of more militarily powerful neighbours, the Nabataeans succeeded for many decades in escaping the avaricious grasp of the legions.

This great wealth enabled the Nabataean monarchs to do more than hold their own against the neighbouring Jewish Hasmonaean state. They faced their first real crisis when it seemed in 63 BC as if Pompey might be looking to add Petra to his list of conquests. He had confidently announced his intention of paying the Nabataeans a visit that year, presumably to extract at least plunder, and possibly even to terminate their independent existence. Fortunately, he was distracted by the opportunities presented by a civil war in the next-door Hasmonaean kingdom and by the far greater prospects for financial gain offered by seizing Jerusalem and taking the Jewish Temple.[4] Two years later, Pompey despatched his lieutenant Aemilius Scaurus against Petra, but – having burnt the harvests and thereby deprived himself, as well as the Nabataeans, of ready sources of food – he settled for extorting a payment of 300 talents to be on his way.[5] At his triumph in Rome, however, the triumvir included Arabia in the list of those areas he had overcome, so that, at least from his point of view, he really had subdued the Nabataeans.

Yet already by the mid-1st century AD, more and more trade was going by sea, either up the Red Sea and along the coast of Africa to Roman Egypt, or heading eastwards to land at the head of the Persian Gulf and thence either east into the Parthian Empire or west via Palmyra, up to the Euphrates and into the Roman Empire. The discovery, around the 1st century, of the monsoon winds, and thus of an all-maritime route to India, accelerated this trend,[6] much to the detriment of the Nabataeans.

After the Roman annexation of Egypt in 30 BC, the Nabataeans faced Roman provinces to the north (in Syria and Judaea) and to the west (in Egypt). It may well be that Augustus planned to annex the kingdom outright, but the Romans were distracted by an expedition in 24 BC against the kingdom of Sabaea in modern Yemen, a land then also known for its legendary wealth as Arabia Felix ('Lucky Arabia'). It could be that the Emperor reasoned that taking control of the source of the precious spices in south Arabia would be even more lucrative than seizing the lands of the Nabataean middlemen, whose role would then be rendered at a stroke superfluous. If so, it may have been a tad unwise for Aelius Gallus, the Prefect of Egypt tasked with the expedition, to choose Syllaeus, the chief minister of Obodas, the Nabataean king, as his advisor and guide to the unfamiliar Sabaean lands.[7]

The whole thing was a fiasco from start to finish. Gallus dallied all winter at the African Red Sea port of Leuke Kome, ordering the construction of warships that were irrelevant to the kind of fighting he would be likely to face. It then took six months to reach the border of the Sabaean kingdom, a journey the historian Strabo alleges was significantly extended by the tortuous route over which Syllaeus led the Romans.[8] By the time Gallus laid siege to the town of Mariaba, his forces were severely weakened by losses to disease and desperately short of water. After just six days, Gallus threw in the towel and retreated, reaching Alexandria in a comparatively speedy seventy-one days, which must have given him at least some pause for thought concerning the prolonged nature of the outward journey. He had also stopped just two days' march short of the spice-producing regions of the Sabaean heartland, the securing of which was presumably the whole purpose of the expedition. As a demonstration of Roman power – which, coincidentally, reached its furthest ever projection south at Mariaba – it was hardly likely to make Rome's neighbours quail.[9]

A gap in the Nabataean coins series in the years 3–1 BC, which coincided with an expedition to Arabia by Gaius Caesar, Augustus's grandson, has been used to suggest a temporary annexation by the Romans, but nothing is proven.[10] At any rate the coinage (and, if the annexation theory really is correct, the monarchy) was restored, and many of the important Nabataean monuments date to the long reign of Aretas IV (8 BC–AD 40). Under Rabbel II, from AD 71,[11] the kingdom seemed to go into a decline; it may be that the spice routes were already shifting eastwards and the Nabataeans' prosperity was fraying at the edges.

The annexation in 106 was a quiet affair, and Trajan failed to order any coins minted to celebrate it until 111.[12] More importantly, work began on the construction of the *Via Nova Traiana*, a defensive road that ran all the way from Bostra – 150 kilometres south of Damascus – to the port of Aila on the Gulf of Aqaba (a southward journey of some 350 kilometres), facilitating any necessary rapid transfer of troops. The Romans annexed territory further south, possibly as far as Ruwaffa, north of the Nabataeans' secondary capital at Medain Saleh in modern Saudi Arabia (and some 250 kilometres to the south of Aqaba). A temple to the emperors Marcus Aurelius and Lucius Verus has been found there, dedicated by a confederation of Arab tribes (the 'Thamud') during the governorship of Claudius Modestus.[13] Here, however, as in the Jordanian desert, the actual border was undefined by any physical features. If the tribes acknowledged Roman power, then they were, in a sense, part of the Empire. Arabia of course received a Roman garrison to shield Judaea and Egypt from attacks from the east. This seems to have been made up of around twelve auxiliary units, including at least one of camel troops (*ala dromedariorium*) and infantry cohorts drafted in from Egypt and Syria.[14] The legionary garrison consisted, at least in the early stages, of III Cyrenaica, which had its main base at Bostra in the very north of the province.

With the disorder caused by successive Persian invasions in the 3rd century, and the temporary loss of control over the whole East during the revolt of Zenobia, the Romans came more and more to depend on dominating or cajoling a succession of Arab allied tribes to take responsibility for the defence of the desert approaches. Although Diocletian defeated the most threatening of the 'Saracen' groups around 290, he was still forced to reorganise Arabia, partitioning the province around 295 to make its separate parts easier to administer, and to construct the Strata Diocletiana, a militarised road system further to the east.[15] During the 6th century, however, a full hundred years before the Arabs swept Byzantine political control away, the military presence on the frontier was drastically reduced, possibly as a result of the financial demands caused by Justinian's campaigns in Italy and North Africa.[16] When the end came, in the 630s, it was terrifyingly swift.

Ninety kilometres south-east of Damascus, and just into the province of Arabia, nestled at the north end of the Hauran mountains, lies the small town of Shahba, a place destined for utter obscurity, had it not been for one of its sons who achieved an improbable elevation to the imperial throne. Marcus Julius Philippus, known to historians as Philip, was a typical product of the military and political turmoil that gripped the Empire in the mid-3rd century. He accompanied the expedition of Gordian III against the Sassanids in 243–4, which aimed to push Shapur I back from the key cities in Syria, such as Carrhae and Edessa, that the Persians had captured in the preceding years. Philip took over as praetorian prefect when Timesitheus fell ill and died late in 243, sharing the post with his brother Julius Priscus.[17]

When the army was defeated somewhere near Ctesiphon and Gordian III was killed, Philip was the most obvious candidate close at hand to succeed him. Paying the whopping ransom of 500,000 denarii for his and the army's safe-passage, he made in haste for the capital before alternative factions could dispute his right to power, leaving Priscus as commander in the east with the *ad hoc* title of *rector orientis*, a kind of deputy Emperor.[18] Philip is commonly nicknamed 'the Arab', and, though probably he was born into a local family with no visible Latin antecedents, there is no sign during his reign of any self-conscious promotion of an Arab identity. Of course he heaped favours on his home regions – few emperors could avoid the temptation – but his ethnic origin is more important as a sign that the hold on power of the traditional senatorial elites, in Italy and the provinces, was fatally weakening.

The most notable feature of his four-year reign were the celebrations for Rome's one-thousandth birthday in 248, an anniversary that also gave rise to unfortunate millenarian currents that may have fed into the revolt of Pacatianus in Moesia, following which Philip was overthrown by his own general, Decius. Philip achieved posthumous fame amongst Christian writers, most notably Eusebius, as the first emperor to convert to the new religion. The evidence for his pre-emption of Constantine is slight, however, and he certainly proclaimed nothing in public.[19] It may well all have been no more than a literary device to contrast him with Decius, who indisputably was an enthusiastic persecutor of Christianity.

Philip's home village thus enjoyed only a few years of glory before construction was stopped, and the place (renamed Philippopolis) was restored to its position as a backwater. Many of the buildings were probably never completed, some not even begun, but what survives makes striking use of the local black basaltic stone, which lends a certain sternness and sombreness to the architecture. Philippopolis is a classic Roman city built in negative, all dark colours that suck in the light instead of reflecting it. Three stumps of a grand triple-gateway draw visitors in along the *cardo*, now a humdrum modern street of low concrete blocks.[20]

A little way up, the street begins to climb and alongside it, perched on the lower storey of a modern building, four bold basalt columns probably mark the site of a temple façade. The street then opens up into a broad square, once the civic heart of Philippopolis, now host to nothing more bustling than an impromptu football match between a crowd of local boys, none of them, assuredly, with their sights set on emulating their imperial forebear. To the west of the square lies a curious structure, a triple façade of basalt almost forming a semicircle inset with deep niches. It is a *kalybe*, a form typical of the province of Arabia and probably having Nabataean antecedents.[21] Most probably the niches were for the exposition of statues of the imperial family, with some form of cult ritual taking place in the open space just in front of the *kalybe*.

Just behind lie the shattered remains of what may have been an imperial palace, but more impressive is the temple at the south end of the square, the Philippeion, erected in honour of the Emperor's father. As the dedication inscription reveals, Philip was not content with his possible elevation to godhead after his death, but saw fit to revere his own father, Julius Marinus, as a god. Not, it must be remarked, the kind of action consistent with his alleged conversion to Christianity. A simple rectangle with a colonnade in front – a prostyle – the temple inside has a quiet, dark dignity. Groups of niches flanked by arches were again probably for the display of family statues, particularly the divine Julius Marinus, while internal steps give the place more the feeling of an intimate theatre than a place of worship.

Philippopolis's real theatre is just a few metres away to the south. It is comparatively small, only about 42 metres in diameter, with seating for just 1,000 spectators, and was one of the last Roman theatres built in the East. In common with the nearby bathhouse, it has a certain starkness. Basalt is a very hard stone and does not lend itself easily to ornate carving, and the stage backdrop here is almost entirely blank. Whether the citizens of Philippopolis were actually able to enjoy extensive theatrical performances, once their imperial patronage was withdrawn so soon after it had been bestowed, is unclear.

The one real insight into the life and wealth of the city comes from the mosaics located in a villa in the town and now housed in the local museum. The vibrant colours of Tethys, the sea goddess, her winding locks surrounded by a swirling crowd of sea creatures, and of Aphrodite and Ares caught in an illicit tryst, as cupids divest the war god of his armour, are of the finest quality. Covered in sand to protect them once the villa was abandoned, some at least seem to date from the early 4th century, so the town did retain some wealthy residents after its brush with imperial fame.

Climbing high up into the Hauran range, the territory becomes more rugged, and some 12 kilometres south of Shahba lies the town of

Qanawat, ancient Canatha. It was a leading member of the Decapolis ('the ten cities'), a grouping of Hellenistic cities, most of them lying further south in modern Jordan. Unfortunately for historians and archaeologists of a precise bent of mind, the exact membership of this grouping is unclear; some counts reach fourteen cities, and some of those mentioned in the lists – such as Dion – have not been identified on the ground. Nor, indeed, is there much evidence for any official federation or formal organisation. It was probably just a convenient term to group together Greek cities in the region, and one that the writer of the Gospel of Matthew took up.[22] Canatha, however, was always regarded as belonging to it, as were Damascus and, further to the south, Gadara (Umm Qays), Gerasa (Jerash) and Pella.

Perched high on a ravine, the city has been extensively built over, and even some of the buildings reported by travellers in the 19th century have since disappeared. In the modern town centre lies a small square fringed by a few coffee shops where impossibly old men and their aged sons while away undifferentiated days smoking, arguing and dreaming. At its centre, railings and a barred gate form a perimeter around the Serail, the 'palace', the principal remaining structure of ancient Canatha. For those fortunate enough to locate the guardian amongst his coffee-sipping peers, entrance reveals a Roman civil basilica, dated by an inscription to AD 124,[23] later converted into a Christian complex. A pre-existing building was adapted in the 5th century by the addition of an apse to change its orientation to east–west. Puddles of melted wax and a few faintly burning candles indicate that someone, at least, still regards the place with reverence. To one side of the Serail lies an atrium, and across it cuts a wall beyond which lies another church, its main entrance beautified with a swirl of floral and vine patterns, the lintel decorated with swastikas, at the time a symbol of good luck and eternity and untainted by the 20th-century associations with anti-Semitic violence. Around the church lie a jumble of chambers that could have been housing for the clergy, almshouses or storerooms. At the far end of the compound is a tower so eroded and ruined that what remains has the air of a rather forlorn arch that would collapse this very minute if only it could muster the energy.

On the south-eastern outskirts of Qanawat, at the edge of the deep ravine of the Wadi al-Ghar,[24] lies the restored outline of a *nymphaeum*, or ornamental fountain, and close by an *odeon*, with about eight or ten rows of seats, both dated to the 3rd century AD.[25] Not far off, next to a busy road just at the edge of town, sits the platform and half a dozen standing columns of the Temple of Helios. Its rubbish-strewn approach and the encroaching concrete skeletons of half-completed apartment blocks mask any sense of mystery or the divine.

Just 30 kilometres south-west of Qanawat and almost into modern Jordan lay the capital of the Arabian province. Although there has been a settlement here since at least the Bronze Age, Bostra – now Bosra in Syrian – only reached real prominence during the later Nabataean period in the 1st century AD, when for a time it supplanted Petra as the capital of the kingdom. It retained its position of primacy in the new Roman province of Arabia, although Trajan granted Petra the title of metropolis as compensation for its downgrading. The Nabataean town originally sprawled slightly to the east of the existing ruins, and to its west the Romans laid out a more orderly grid-like street pattern for the new city, which they named Nova Traiana Bostra. It was favoured with a visit by Hadrian in 129, and was elevated to the rank of a *colonia* under Alexander Severus.

The approach to the site today is unpromising; ringed by the modern town, Bostra appears as an isolated island among the motorcycles, noise and market stalls. The main gate, at its western entrance, is a solidly reconstructed single arch with empty statue niches to either side, constructed in black basalt. From this entry point, the Bab el Hawa ('gate of the winds'), the *decumanus* stretches east, originally colonnaded, with the remains of pillars strewn, stacked and occasionally arranged to either side of it. Proceeding further onwards, it is clear that the ancient town and the new are inextricably intertwined, with columns incorporated into walls and Ionic capitals employed as garden ornaments. Shops selling crisps and chequer-pattern footballs strung up in threes occupy the place of former porticoes and temple precincts, while bicycles are propped up against modern houses whose foundations clearly comprise wholly ancient stonework. It all seems as though the antique city has suffered some great disaster, and in the aftermath the new town has sprung up, scavenging off the old for spare parts. When the government and archaeologists have their way, of course, the residents will be cleared out and the whole restored to a more pristine state, gaining in grandeur what it loses in charm.

An area of ancient shops is marked off by a *cryptoporticus*, an underground colonnade, barred off by grilles, with something of the air of a disused subterranean cloister. The more substantial ruins are further to the east, beginning with the Bab Qandil ('Lantern Arch'), an imposing triple-arch, probably built in the 3rd century and dedicated by the III Cyrenaica legion.[26] It has lost its facing on one side, exposing a cruder brickwork sub-structure, which in contrast to the smooth and polished surface on the other gives it a strange 'before-and-after' look. Around this are grouped most of the city's other major monuments. Four huge columns some 12 metres high and, unusually for basalt work, carved with the more ornate Corinthian capitals, mark the remains of a *nymphaeum*, an ornamental public fountain, while opposite, at the junction with the north–south *cardo*, lies a solid rectangular ruin, whose external walls are punctuated by external niches. This, called locally 'the Palace of the Daughter of the King', is most likely a *kalybe*, similar in purpose to that at Philippopolis further north and intended for the exposition of imperial cult statues. However, the distribution of such *kalybes* in former Nabataean territory gives rise to the suspicion that this was a pre-Roman practice adapted by the new masters as a convenient vehicle for imperial propagandising. Back across the *decumanus* are the city's South Baths, its domed *apodyterium* (changing room) surviving largely intact, but the main bathing areas being far more ruined, both still impressive testaments to the urge to showiness in municipal construction.

Northwards up the *cardo*, flanked by the remains of another colonnade, the way leads to a set of important, early Islamic monuments. The much-reconstructed Mosque of Umar was once attributed to the second caliph, who ruled from 634 to 644, which would make it a relic from the very dawn of Islam. It is now believed to date more probably from the reign of Caliph Yazid II, around 720, still making it a rare survival from the Muslim religion's first century. Indeed, the interior has many reused columns; the position of the mosque may mean that these originally formed part of the portico of the *cardo*. The caretaker proudly points out some of green-streaked *cipollino* (finely veined Italian marble), and a couple with faded, barely legible Greek inscriptions.

A hundred metres or so further east lies another witness to the earliest Islamic period. The basilica probably dates to the 3rd century, and was originally a Roman civic building used by the city magistrates, before being converted in the 4th or 5th century for use as a Christian church. It is an austere and simple place, almost unadorned, its ground-plan broken only by an apse and an old well or cistern long since bricked up. What lends it significance is a meeting alleged to have taken place here around 580 between the Nestorian monk Bahira and the young prophet Muhammad, who was travelling with his uncle as part of a merchant caravan. Bahira noticed stigmata on the youthful trader and predicted that these miraculous marks meant that God had singled him out to become a great prophet. Subsequently a polemic broke out between Christian and Muslim authors as to the significance of this event. As Bahira belonged to a sect that had been condemned as heretical after the Council of Chalcedon in 451,[27] orthodox writers had no hesitation in blackening his name – or, as an alternative approach, doing everything they could to imply that he had taught Muhammad about the Christian faith and that this had been filtered in a distorted form into Islam. Muslim scholars countered with a much more straightforward affirmation of the original story.[28] Whatever the truth about the encounter, this unassuming place may have hosted one of the most portentous meetings in religious history. Bostra went on to become one of the first towns captured by the Muslim armies as they advanced out of the Arabian peninsula, falling to them in 632.

A little to the south sits the cathedral of Bostra, again constructed in dark, subdued shades of basalt. Dedicated to the saints Sergius, Bacchus and Leontius, it was built in 512, and is a transitional type between the earliest rectangular basilicas and the square, centralised form that was to become more fashionable in the eastern Greek-influenced Christian world. The church has lost its roof and most of its interior columns, but part of the walls survives, and in the apse, astonishingly, a few faded frescoes cling on, their colours reduced by sun and rain to red lines and ochre smudges, but with the halo of a saint just visible, and figures seated at a table, possibly portraying the Last Supper.

South again from here, and back on the east–west *decumanus*, lies the Nabataean arch, a rather simpler affair than the other two, with just a single opening, but a complex of niches and columns built into the structure at the sides. It probably formed the eastern end of a processional way, which in Nabataean times ran along what the Romans later converted into the Roman city's *cardo*. Beyond is a much more ruined quarter, which was probably the heart of Nabataean Bostra. The encroachment of modern settlement seems greater here, the dusty streets more rubbish-strewn, the football-playing youths and the grazing sheep look more like the hosts than the guests they appear as further to the west. Another ruined proto-centralised church lies totally neglected nearby, but much more significant is the building referred to locally as the 'governor's palace'. Built around a grand central courtyard, the palace stood at least two storeys high, with official rooms leading off the main court, including the remains of a grand formal dining hall or *triclinium*. It seems possible that this was originally the palace of Rabbel II, the Nabataean king who transferred the capital here from Petra around AD 70, though doubtless as one of the more prestigious buildings in the city it could well have been modified for the use of Roman governors after the annexation of the province.[29]

Almost nothing remains of the legionary camp of III Cyrenaica just to the north of the city, save field walls built from basalt, some of the stones artfully shaped as though they have just been plundered from a more grandiose structure. Of all the fort buildings, its hospital, granaries, barracks, roads and ramparts, nothing can be seen.[30] Bostra's greatest glory is similarly concealed, again just outside the central area of the antique city, this time to the south. The remains of the theatre are preserved within a medieval fortress that encloses it like a jacket, using the bulk of the ancient structure for strength, and at the same time protecting it from stone-robbing and other depredations. It sits now alongside a cleared plaza, frequented largely by postcard-sellers and a huddle of horse-drawn carriages, plying for a trade that never seems to come.

Once through the gloomy passageways of the Ayyubid fort, the theatre's interior is a glorious surprise, all of its forty tiers of seats totally intact (and originally providing places for some 6,000 spectators). The stage backdrop is almost complete, the towering basalt walls dramatically offset by colonnades of white limestone to each side of three stage entrances. From the top row of seating the view is stunning and, albeit in parts restored, this is a perfect gem of an ancient theatre – the ideal place from which to survey one of the more complete remaining Roman provincial capitals.

In the wake of the destruction of Palmyra in 273,[31] the Romans were deprived of a vital ally in their constant struggle to render the desert trade routes secure, and soon other Arab groups had appeared to contest Palmyra's monopoly on extracting wealth from passing traders – which it had done through the legally respectable imposition of tolls, rather than the more traditional mode of simple plunder.

Towards the end of the 3rd century, the Tanukh confederacy emerged as one of the most powerful groups on the desert fringes, gradually migrating north-east towards their final home in the region of Hira in modern Iraq. The Tanukh had a particularly bitter history with the Palmyrans. At the time of Zenobia, their ruler was, according to Arab sources, Jadhima.[32] During the brief period of Palmyrene supremacy, Zenobia's army defeated and captured the Tanukh sheikh and, finely balancing cruelty and refinement, she had his veins cut and the blood gathered into a golden cup. That there was now ill-feeling between the Palmyra and the Tanukh is probably something of an understatement.[33] Arab tradition holds that Jadhima's nephew 'Amr ibn 'Adi avenged his uncle by allying himself with Aurelian against Zenobia,[34] although the claim that he actually killed the Palmyrene queen is contradicted by

the Roman historians' narrative that she died in comfortable retirement in Italy.

Whatever the truth, 'Amr ibn 'Adi's son, Imru' al-Qays, seems to
have inherited the mantle of leading regional power-broker, this time
in alliance with the Sassanids. Yet at the end of a long life he moved
southwards, to the edge of the Arabian desert, apparently becoming a
Roman ally and participating in the campaigns of Diocletian and Galerius
against his former masters.[35] He may even have converted to Christianity,
and it is plausible that this caused friction with his former suzerain
Shapur II.[36] In any case, it is at Nemara that he settled, at a spot where
under Diocletian a fort had been erected for a detachment of the III
Cyrenaica legion.

It is in death, however, that Imru' al-Qays achieved his most lasting
fame. His tomb inscription, dated 328, discovered at Nemara, some 100
kilometres east of Shahba, is carved in cursive lettering that has been
considered a precursor of classical Arabic script. The language itself is
undoubtedly Arabic, which here makes its first appearance in the
epigraphic record.[37] Imru's epitaph makes the normal kinds of modest
claims for his earthly achievements, declaring him to have been 'King of
all the Arabs' and reeling off a list of the places under his authority,
which might – the inscription is very hard to decipher – include territory as far-flung as the southern Hejaz.[38]

Although only a couple of hours' drive east of Shahba, Nemara seems
a totally different world. East of the Hauran hills, the landscape becomes
flatter, but the terrain is desolate, the fields increasingly filled with basalt
rocks, at first a scattering, then columns, stacks and finally whole mounds
of the stuff, which at a distance make the ground look as though it is
covered by some black, alien crop. The road snakes through kilometre
after kilometre of this harsh, relentless land, which lends true meaning
to the term 'lava field' that geologists and archaeologists give it. An
enticing well-tarmacked route off to the left leads nowhere, a gift by a
local man turned provincial governor to his home village, a few modest
houses with no visible livelihood. Finally in the baking heat, just as the
road gives out completely, a jumble of basalt-built walls offer the faint
impression of an ordered design. Great chunks of dark rock lie strewn
around its edges, and, standing either too far away or too close, the structure merges into the sharp tangle of the solidified lava flow. There is no
one around to confirm that this is Nemara, and doubtless few ever pass
this way, but at just the right distance, one can almost feel the proud
exile and clamorous boasts of Imru' al-Qays.

Back to the south of Bostra, but across a tricky international frontier

between Jordan and Syria, the hills of the Hauran begin to impose themselves more fully on the landscape. Buckled and folded outcrops of grim,
tar-black basalt with their hidden reaches, and the isolation of the water-
poor terrain, long provided a refuge for bandits and discontents in a
territory the Romans knew as the Auranitis.

Lying in the heart of this region, Umm al-Jimal – whose expressive
Arabic name 'Mother of the Camels' is a clue to its origins as a Nabataean
post on the trading routes at the northernmost extremity of their
kingdom – is gifted with a multiplicity of modern nicknames, including
'the black gem' and 'the black oasis'. All struggle to capture the real
feeling of these shattered remains of a city built of black basalt, great
blocks scattered about as though in some disorderly giant's dice game,
the jagged silhouettes of its surviving buildings contrasting dramatically
with a blue-on-azure sky. It is as if Tolkien's Mordor had redesigned the
city of Bath.

It is a far cry from the large, cosmopolitan cities of Syria and Arabia.
Very little of note occurred here and, indeed, such is the historical
anonymity of Umm al-Jimal that even its ancient name is unknown.[39]
The nearest it comes to troubling the written records is a Nabataean
inscription hidden on the wall of an anonymous-looking house that
commemorates Fihr, the tutor of Gadhimat, chief of the Tanukh.[40] This
probably refers to Jadhima, the Tanukh sheikh allegedly murdered by
Zenobia for daring to cross her.[41]

The hardness of the basalt made it suitable for constructing multi-
storeyed buildings, with the lower levels often used for storage and stabling
of the animals, and only the upper parts for living accommodation. Access
to these was gained by external staircases, the remains of which hang
outside many buildings here, often leading the way up to ghost floors,
long vanished and collapsed into piles of rubble. To support the weight
of the floors, stone corbels were built out from the walls, or supporting
arches constructed, on top of which wooden beams were laid.

The site was first fortified in about 180, but the original defences may
have been destroyed during the invasion of the area by the Palmyrenes
in 270. The village was rebuilt, using the ruins of the old one as a stone-
quarry, and provided with a remarkable network of churches, some
fourteen of which have been identified for a population estimated at just
8,000 or so. The most remarkable of these is the West Church, a dramatic
arch of piers thrusting outwards towards the modern village, and the
Cathedral, built in 556, of which but a shell remains, preserving a small
patch of polychrome mosaic in its aisle. Everywhere the regular houses
are marked with crosses incised above and alongside their doors.

Around 300 a new fort was built,[42] a great dark rectangular block, with one angle-tower still standing, giving the town a focus that its chaotic layout otherwise lacks. An inscription reused on the door lintel of the Cathedral refers to the building of a watchtower by a detachment of *equites Dalmatorum* (Dalmatian cavalry) and so it is possible that these, for a time, formed the garrison of the town. Scrambling through the ankle-twisting ruins involves a great number of detours, as there is no comforting street-grid to guide travellers, and our wayward progress through the site attracts the attention of the local guardians, who are convinced that we must be in search of some treasure, for why else would anyone come to such a place?

The Romans pushed further east into the desert from the 2nd and 3rd centuries, particularly under Diocletian, building a string of forts to screen the more settled areas of the province's interior from nomadic incursions or, should the eventuality arise, from Persian aggression. One of the most important of these was the fort in the oasis of Azraq, 100 kilometres to the south-east of Umm al-Jimal. Deriving its name from an Arabic word meaning 'blue', Azraq was long famed for the purity of its oasis lake, a boon for thirsty travellers through the Jordanian desert and a useful resource to dominate by means of a military presence. Those days are long past, and water is now scarce, the lake shrunk to a mere collection of muddy puddles. The reinforcement of the Roman frontier here happened under Diocletian, and Azraq is associated with his construction of the Strata Diocletiana.[43]

Today the fort is essentially an Ayyubid construction from the 13th or 14th century, a stolid square of large dark bricks, punctuated by arrow-slits, looking every inch as though the French Foreign Legion were about to emerge to chase down some Arab renegades. Aerial photography has definitely revealed an earlier Roman construction beneath this, however, and a collection of inscribed stones just inside the fort provides some evidence of it. One includes the terms 'Iovii' and 'Herculii', a reference to the symbolic association between Diocletian and his colleague Maximian and those two gods, and also the name of two elite legionary units. Another commemorates the rebuilding of the fort sometime around 326/7 under Constantine I, when it had fallen into considerable disrepair.

The interior of the fort bakes beneath the summer sun, the grey-black dust that carpets it seeming to radiate the heat back into the face of visitors, while the mosque constructed in the centre of the courtyard provides no escape. The most welcoming and shaded spot at Azraq is immediately over the main gate, where a staircase leads to a little room that provides both an unsurpassed view over the oasis and a refreshingly cool refuge. So it was during the First World War, when T. E. Lawrence ('Lawrence of Arabia') used the old fort as a military base during his raising of the Arab Revolt against the Ottoman Turks. The spot is inevitably called by local guides 'Lawrence's Room', but in this case there is for once some justification to their stories, since in *Seven Pillars of Wisdom* (his account of the revolt) Lawrence writes how he established himself in the southern tower, which his Arab helpers obligingly reroofed. So much did Lawrence love the place that he was afflicted by a particularly purple passage in this description of it: 'Azrak's unfathomable silence was steeped in knowledge of wandering poets, champions, lost kingdoms, all the crime and chivalry and dead magnificence of Hira and Ghassan. Each stone or blade of it was radiant with half-memory of the luminous silky Eden, which had passed so long ago.'[44] Of its atmosphere he further opines, 'Numen inest' – that there is a sense of the divine spirit here. Nowadays that sense is much attenuated, and if anyone's spirit can be felt to dwell in the place, it is Lawrence's.

Jerash, ancient Gerasa, around forty kilometres west of Umm al-Jimal is one of the best-preserved Roman cities in the Middle East. Indeed, if appearances were anything to go by, it would seem a much more important place even than Antioch, and of greater significance than Bostra, the capital of Arabia. Yet appearances are deceptive. Massively wealthy Gerasa may have been, but it was of strictly limited political and administrative importance. Yet it is a harsh heart that would deny Gerasa its colonnaded streets, its large temple of Zeus, even grander sanctuary of Artemis, and a host of other partly reconstructed monuments that give – as nowhere else but Palmyra in the region can – a real sense of how a Roman city functioned and was organised.

Gerasa's origins lay far off in the Bronze Age, when a settlement grew up on a nearby hill, but tradition has it that it was refounded by Perdiccas, one of Alexander the Great's generals, who gave it the name Antioch by the Chrysorrhoas ('the golden river'). There seems to have been a major building programme under the Seleucid Antiochos IV Epiphanes (175–164 BC), so it was a town of some grandeur when it fell to Pompey in 64 BC. At first part of Roman Syria, after the annexation of the Nabataean kingdom it was allocated, together with most of the other towns of the Decapolis, to the new province of Arabia.[45]

The main entrance to the city today lies through the Arch of Hadrian, built by the citizens of Gerasa to commemorate a visit by that Emperor in 129/30, the first time the city had been graced by an imperial presence. It is a splendid affair, the central entrance arch matched by two subsidiary passages, both topped by niches (for imperial statues) framed between engaged pillars, above which are a frieze and architrave, a visual reference in miniature to the whole of the arch itself. An inscription in Greek honouring Hadrian is matched by the find of one in Latin – the language of the army – by the *equites singulares*, his personal bodyguard. Coins commemorated his sojourn in the province with the legend *Adventus Aug Arabiae* ('the visit of the Emperor to Arabia').

It may well have been at this time that Hadrian conceived one of his least successful policies, aimed at finally suppressing Jewish resistance to Roman rule in the next-door province of Judaea. The plan was to refound Jerusalem as a *colonia*, a purely Roman establishment, to close down the Jewish Temple and replace it with a temple to Capitoline Jupiter and, for good measure, to ban the practice of circumcision and forbid any Jews from living in their former sacred city. Needless to say, the reaction was furious, and a rebellion broke out in 132. It took three and a half years to suppress the revolt, which was brilliantly directed by the guerrilla leader Simon Bar Kochba ('Son of a Star'),[46] and the involvement of at least four legions, including the local force, the III Cyrenaica from Bostra.

The Gerasenes, too, appear to have been somewhat overoptimistic with their arch. It is possible that they hoped the city would grow to encompass the grand new monument, or at least reach it, but the arch remained outside the municipal bounds, and Gerasa, or Antioch-by-the-Chrysorrhoas (as the inscription, with a resolute antiquarian insistence, continues to name it), remained more or less within the same circuit from the 1st century onwards. Nearby lies the Hippodrome, until quite recently just a grassy collection of earth banks, but now reconstructed for the hourly presentation of shows by a troupe of Jordanian re-enactors. Clutching shiny helmets and sporting polished *lorica segmentata* armour and blunted (one hopes) *gladii*, they mingle among the tourist crowds hoping to drum up business. Late in the day an incongruous crocodile of tired-looking Roman soldiers drifts back towards Hadrian's Arch, weary of the past until tomorrow. The Hippodrome itself has yielded some indication of the late period of Gerasa's history, after the Persians took it in 614 during their victorious sweep through the Byzantine Near East. Evidence has been unearthed that, unimpressed by their conquered enemies' predilection for horse-racing, they converted the Hippodrome into a polo field.[47]

Just inside the city, the Oval Piazza is one of the Roman world's most spectacular urban spaces. Its slightly irregular shape creates a series of curves, which draw the eye onward and seem to enlarge the area far beyond reality. The stones of the piazza's surface bend round too, as does its encircling portico of plain Ionic columns, all accentuating the effect. The unusual shape was used to mask the change of direction of the road between the south entrance gate and the *cardo*, which would otherwise form an awkward dog-leg, an angle caused by the need to preserve an axis oriented on the Temple of Zeus that pre-dated the laying-out of the urban grid on Roman lines. The Oval Piazza, indeed, is not truly a Roman innovation. Such semicircular or oval plazas are characteristic of the East, not appearing in the Western Empire – with the possible exception of Leptis Magna – and they were perhaps associated with processional ways leading to important temples. Once more, the oriental pops out from beneath a seemingly smooth Roman façade.

To the west of the piazza lies the sanctuary of the Temple of Zeus, beneath which evidence of the earliest Macedonian settlers has been found, and beside it Gerasa's Southern Theatre, a highly restored specimen, with a foundation dedication to Domitian. Inside is honoured the gift of 3,000 drachmas by Titus Flavius Dionysius, a magistrate who can hardly have imagined that his beloved theatre would ever be taken over by a Bedouin military band playing a most un-Roman medley of Scottish bagpipe favourites.

Far more ambitious than the Zeus Temple was that of Artemis, further north into the city and, had it ever been completed, one of the largest and most splendid urban sanctuaries anywhere in the Roman world. An elaborate *propylaeum*, a ceremonial gateway now largely vanished, leads up through a broad staircase of seven-times-seven steps to the temple platform itself. It all formed part of a processional Sacred Way, which was cut off in the 6th century by the building of a church right across the area in front of the *propylaeum*. Looking eastwards away from the temple is a melancholy sight now; the *decumanus*, a slightly overgrown forest of pillars, stretches out towards the modern city of Jerash, whose sprawl of apartment blocks seems in imminent danger of engulfing its ancient counterpart.

Around the central *cella* of the Artemis Sanctuary a peristyle six columns wide, each some 13 metres high, makes an unmistakable statement of the wealth of the temple and of Gerasa itself. The columns themselves, with capitals delicately carved despite their immense size, were designed to withstand earthquakes, a fact alarmingly demonstrated by placing a key or spoon in the gaps between the drums, for it will then move up and down as the structure is moved almost imperceptibly by the wind. Lest any visitors be seized by a surfeit of divine ecstasy, a sign beside the main podium warns, 'For the safety of all visitors. Don't pick any of the herbs of the site.'

Once the pagan temples had been closed down or sidelined, the eminence on which the Artemis Sanctuary lies was commandeered by a series of Christian churches, including the Cathedral, amongst whose ruins lies the basin of a fountain where Christians celebrated the miracle of the wedding feast at Cana. During the ceremony, the fountain would, it was alleged, flow with wine instead of water. It is surely no coincidence that the church was built over a former shrine to Dionysus, the pagan god most associated with the vine, and a previous pagan feast was no doubt adapted and continued under the aegis of the Church, a borrowing made much easier by the parallel importance of wine in both belief systems.

Further up the *decumanus* a *tetrakoinion*, a splendid four-way arch used in the East to mark major street intersections, draws the visitor towards the North Theatre, originally a small *odeon* for around 800 spectators, which was enlarged in the 2nd century with the addition of an imposing forecourt bordered by a portico of Corinthian columns. Everything is on a majestic scale for such a modestly important place, a sobering thought when one considers how Antioch, Alexandria or Rome might have looked if their monumental structure had been recoverable to anything like the same extent.

Of Gerasa's final era of prosperity, the Christian churches are ample witness. Towards the northern edge of town lies a cluster of these, including the church of Cosmas and Damian, dedicated in 533 by a Bishop Paul.[48] From the floor stare out portraits of Theodore the *paramonarios* (church-warden) and his wife Giorgia, forever frozen in a pious gesture. The last church seems to have been built around 611, and less than three decades later the Byzantines were swept from this part of Syria. Some occupation did continue under the new masters; pottery kilns and houses of Umayyad date have been found near the North Theatre, the tetrapylon and grouped around the Oval Piazza. Deprived of the comfortable cushion of Roman provincial life, however, there was no real reason for Gerasa to survive, and, damaged beyond the power of its remaining inhabitants to repair, it was finally abandoned by the 10th century.

Further to the east, the Via Nova Traiana snaked down, defended by a series of strongpoints such as Khirbet es Samra and Philadelphia (modern Amman). Sited halfway between today's King's Highway and the Desert Highway, the principal arteries of modern Jordanian travel (the former of which follows roughly the line of the Roman Via Nova Traiana), and roughly 100 kilometres south of Amman, lies the legionary fortress of Lejjun, its name probably a corruption of the Latin *legio* or legion. The Romans knew it as Betthoro and chose the site in around 300 for the construction of a base for the IV Martia legion as part of the general reinforcement of the *limes* in this central section of Arabia. Lying just alongside the Wadi al-Lejjun, with its perennial spring and fertile valley, Lejjun was well situated in a region where the lack of water presented a major difficulty in the long-term supply of large bodies of troops.

On this stretch my guide has given to waving airily at any broken-down buildings of any vintage older than the 1950s and pronouncing, 'Here, ruins!' and at Lejjun he identifies a set of half-collapsed cottages on the hillside beside the road as clear evidence of Roman occupation. They are at least a sign that others recognised the strategic importance of the place, for they are the remains of an Ottoman police post built around 1910,[49] and my guide is only half-wrong, for they were doubtless constructed using stones from the handiest source around, namely the Betthoro fort.

Little remains of the fort save the shattered outlines of the wall, only partly now delimiting the site, although with a lot of patience four corner towers and some of the original twenty interval towers can be made out. The interior is a seeming chaos of disordered stones. Amidst all this archaeologists identified at least the *principia*, the legionary headquarters, though no evidence was found of the great basilical cross-hall characteristic of such buildings,[50] perhaps a sign that during the later Empire less rigorous attention was paid to the old ways of doing things. The barracks buildings, too, are a sign of changing times; divided into six main blocks, they seem to have provided accommodation for around 1,500 men, around one-third of the classic legion's complement of 5,000.[51] IV Martia was probably raised under Diocletian, and although there are clear signs that he increased the overall numbers in the army, the additional legions he raised were probably of this smaller size.[52]

The site suffered badly from natural disasters. The discovery in one building of a level of ash caused by a fire is datable to 502, the same time as an earthquake devastated the fort. Much of the fort collapsed after another earthquake in 551,[53] although the military seem already to have abandoned it twenty years earlier.[54] What subsequent occupation there was seems, to judge from pottery and other artefacts unearthed, to have been non-military, another sign that, after a century of heavy military presence in late-Roman times, the Byzantine authorities retrenched, relying on little more than prestige and the uncertain word of their Arab *phylarch* allies.

Dajaniyah, 80 or so kilometres further south along the desert highway, is a much smaller fort, though dating from the same period and performing in miniature much the same function as Lejjun. Yet it is far more spectacular. From Lejjun the route to Dajaniyah is relentlessly flat and arid, a desert landscape that must have offered the Roman soldiers little in the way of relief. Low, single-storey blocks straggle in untidy clusters alongside the road, many of them Bedouin settlements established as part of the government's programme to encourage the semi-nomadic peoples finally to settle down in one place. Hidden behind one such, the road veers off straight into the desert towards the very distant silhouette of Dajaniyah, one wall visible across the wasteland, a great hole gouged from its central section as though smashed by some massive hammer-blow. My driver will not proceed, his vehicle defeated by the ruts and potholes that bar the way to the fort. I have to rely on the kind service of a local, a former naval officer fortuitously settled in this remote place, to break through the desert barrier. Bones shaken and van's axle buckled, it takes twenty minutes to cover the couple of kilometres to the fort perimeter.

Attached to one corner of the fort is a Bedouin encampment with a couple of tents, presumably inhabited by a few families who wish to retain at least a foothold in their traditional world. The fort is of basalt, the black rock seeming to suck in the burning sun and glow even more darkly for it. The wall circuit is largely intact, but the gateways have gone and entrance now is through the great gash gouged in the south wall, huge chunks of black stone strewn all around. It is still possible to venture onto the parapet walk for an auxiliary's-eye-view of the desert. Looking around, the setting seems the bleakest imaginable, with nothing save the fort itself and the roadside village to break the monotony, while the heat is so severe that it sets up a cruelly inviting haze, suggesting low clouds or even water-courses that are simply not there.

Back in the fort the main artery, the *via principalis*, is reasonably free of debris, and a structure in the middle must be the *principia*, where the *aedes*, the temple of the legionary standards, has been identified – a sign of the military observance that linked desert soldiers at Dajaniyah to their brothers on the Danube and in the chilly northern climes of Britannia. By the 6th century it, too, seems to have been abandoned and left to fall, too far even from major settlements to provide an attractive target for the robbing of stones.

From here the King's Highway continues to mimic the route of the Via Nova Traiana, leading 30 kilometres or so south to Petra, with the landscape, if not exactly inviting, gradually relaxing its relentlessly harsh grip.

William Burgon's poem with its reference to 'a rose-red city half as old as time' has become one of the most-quoted, and misattributed, poetic references to a Roman city. Yet, if not quite half as old as time, Petra is inescapably rose-red. As the rays of the desert sun die in the sandy gloom, the colonnaded and pillared tombs of Petra's city of the dead do absorb the light, become suffused with a golden rosy hue and hold a promise of daylight's return.

The Nabataeans, who inhabited ancient Petra, have become, perhaps unfairly, irredeemably associated with funerary monuments. It is hardly surprising considering the splendour of the final resting places they constructed for their elite, and the paucity of more mundane evidence of their everyday life. It is a narrow passage from the world of mushrooming hotels and the cosmopolitan blandness of tourist menus to the melancholy splendour of the ancient Nabataean capital. Its very name, Petra, may be linked to the Greek for 'rocks', so it is fitting that the entranceway should be a narrow defile through the mountain, the siq, a kilometre-long canyon that constricts in places to a mere 2 metres in width, lined all the way with niches that once bore images of the chief Nabataean god, Dusares, whose catch-all portfolio of divine responsibilities included the sky, the rain and the fertility of the soil. His name may mean 'he of the Shara', one of the mountain peaks that tower over Petra. In his earliest incarnation he was worshipped in the form of a betyl ('house of the god'), a solid stone block. Even before modern visitors reach the siq a couple of monumental 'god-blocks' are a reminder of the Nabataeans' predilection for aniconic representation of their deities.[55]

In spring 1858, Edward Lear visited Petra in the company of his faithful Greek servant Giorgio. On first sighting the beautifully variegated and striated hues of the rock-tombs, Giorgio was overcome with emotion and exclaimed, 'We have come into a world where everything is made of chocolate, ham, curry powder and salmon',[56] a sentiment worthy of his poetic master. A reaction every bit as extravagant, if perhaps less expressive, is apt to trip off the lips on first sighting Petra's signature monument, which lies exactly at the point where the siq opens out into the great valley in which Petra's principal buildings sit. The Khazneh (or 'Treasury') is so named because the local Bedouin believed that it must have contained the treasury of Pharaoh, the semi-mythical personage whose name was liberally sprinkled about the Petra landscape, lending mystery to a culture that subsequent inhabitants of the place simply could not comprehend.

The Khazneh is a tour de force, a classicising extravaganza that is unafraid to borrow local motifs and mix them into what should by rights be a total mish-mash, but in fact holds together to create a façade of arresting power. A colonnade of six columns seems to support a second level (a false impression, for the whole is cut into the rock and is not free-standing at all). Upon this sit three kiosks: to the left and right two rectangular and surmounted by half-pediments, and in the centre a semi-circular drum containing a shattered statue, possibly of Isis, on top of which perches a stone trophy. It was within this that the Bedouin believed the Pharaoh had concealed his fortune and, once the march of progress had blessed them with firearms, they took to taking pot-shots at the monument in the hope of cracking it and causing a shower of gold and jewels to issue forth. A further subterranean level of the Khazneh has recently been discovered by archaeologists, but so far the fabled treasure has remained elusive.

Framed by the rock-face through which the *siq* cleaves and by other promontories that surround and shelter Petra, the Khazneh's location is impossibly romantic, and it is almost hard to criticise those visitors whose pressing schedule for the return to their cruise ships docked at Aqaba means they barely progress any further. The first European since Roman times to see the site was Johann Ludwig Burckhardt, a Swiss orientalist who, intent on travelling in Africa, had decided that passing himself off as a Muslim traveller would be a most useful disguise, and to that end spent several years travelling in the Near East, immersing himself in the culture as thoroughly as he could. When he heard of the Wadi Mousa, the valley outside Petra, and of the nearby antiquities, he feigned a desire to sacrifice a goat at the Shrine of Aaron on the Jebel Haroun, which would involve walking right the way through the monuments.[57] With admirable restraint, Burckhardt describes the Khazneh as 'one of the most elegant remains of antiquity existing in Syria'[58] although his enthusiasm may have been dampened by his Bedouin guides, who were deeply mistrustful of their travelling companion's habit of gawking at ruined buildings. They suspected him of prospecting for treasure and, even more dangerously, of a magical ability to detect hidden gold.

Nonetheless, Burckhardt was able to enter the Khazneh, make drawings on a notebook hidden in his robes and visit several of the other Petra ruins, before being struck with a tactical case of weariness when faced with the hard, steep climb to the top of the Jebel Haroun. The goat was sacrificed at the base of the mountain, instead of its top, at 'Aaron's terrace', a place deemed to be of sufficient sanctity and far less onerous to reach than the shrine itself. Unlike Burckhardt, we were able to reach the shrine, though it is a hard slog on horseback in the late-morning heat and on several stretches the horse must walk without a mount, for the footing is treacherous. Past side-valleys scored with the façades of funerary monuments we struggle, many of the structures along the route having Bedouin tents pegged outside them, because, unlike on the main tourist drag, here the authorities have not cleared the local people away from their traditional use of the tombs as additional storage space and a cool refuge from the sun. Most notable amongst these is the 'Snake Monument' near the base of the Jebel Haroun, a squat bulbous stone idol, its ossified coils still looking threatening, as though about to squeeze the life out of any who approach it.

On finally reaching the summit, a small green-domed mosque lies firmly locked, and it is a long way down to find the guardian who might hold the key. The view back over towards Petra, its temple façades just visible as matchstick-like constructions almost lost in the folding mountain valleys, gives a spectacular panorama of the sheer ruggedness of the terrain and helps explain why, in their rocky fastness, the Nabataeans were able to elude the grasp of their more powerful neighbours for quite so long.

From the Khazneh, which has been dated to the time of Aretas IV (9/8 BC–AD 40–1),[59] the 'Outer Siq' opens out, flanked by a number of façades decorated with a characteristic crow's-step pattern of crenellations, a style believed to have originated in Assyria. Around the corner lies the 'Street of Façades', with dozens and dozens more tombs, the strong impression of a City of the Dead broken only by the equally numerous stalls set up to hawk jewellery, trinkets and, on a strictly under-the-counter basis, genuine coins and antiquities that the local people have scavenged from the site. A gaggle of juvenile camel herdsmen offering rides, and a string of donkeys braying with legs buckling under the substantial weight of well-fed tourists, all combine to give some sense of a bazaar, and perhaps, for all its raucous quality, a genuine idea of the past mercantile life of the place.

The theatre rises up to the left, built around the same time as the Khazneh, the *cavea* containing the seats simply slicing through the entrances of several pre-existing tombs. The back rows of seats are very worn now, while the stage backdrop is utterly ruined, having collapsed at the time of an earthquake in 363. To the right the Jebel al-Khubtha, whose heights contain the best vantage points for viewing the Khazneh from above, shelters a series of Petra's finest tombs: the Silk Tomb, the multicoloured striations in whose rock lend it the name; the Corinthian, so called for its use of Corinthian columns in its façade; and the Palace Tomb, an attempt at grandiose classicism whose curiously squat upper level renders the whole effect less than harmonious. The Urn Tomb is a much simpler affair, and inside contains an inscription revealing that the room was converted to use as a church by Bishop Jason in 447.[60]

Though Petra lost its royal family, and the *raison d'être* for its grandest tombs, the life of the city carried on, more modestly than before, but still retaining a certain level of prosperity. Despite no longer being the provincial capital, Petra was still visited by senior officials, and one of them, Titus Aninius Sextius Florentinus, who was governor of Arabia in 127, is buried in a tomb further east, alongside the Jebel al-Khubtha. It exhibits no particularly Roman elements, and could well not have been purpose-built for him at all. Yet, on his death in 129, he (or his family) chose a Nabataean-style burial, lending his name an immortality that neither he nor his successor governors at Bostra could have imagined.

The remains of a colonnaded street, a 300-metre-long artery originally paved with slabs of limestone and marble, much trafficked now by donkeys and camels, leads to Petra's single substantial free-standing monument, the Qasr al-Bint ('Castle of the Daughter of Pharaoh'). This solid rectangular block, with little of the appeal of the tomb façades, was in origin a temple, and the remains of the arch through which the colonnaded street passes probably marks out the road as a processional way to the sanctuary. Exactly which god of the Nabataean pantheon was worshipped here is not clear. It may have been Dusares, the chief deity, or equally the goddess al-'Uzza,[61] equated by the Romans with Aphrodite, and for whom it is known that there was a temple somewhere in Petra. Strabo relates that at the chief temple in Petra – presumably this one – thirteen adepts of the god would preside over banquets and the King himself would serve the guests at the sacred meal.[62] The temple continued in use in Roman times, for an inscription has been found to Zeus Hypistos, as well as a dedication to an unspecified emperor. The earthquake that struck Petra in May 363 severely damaged the sanctuary, and another in the 6th century completed its destruction.

More characteristic of Nabataean worship, and that of the region more generally, was the veneration accorded to 'High Places', and Petra, with its multiplicity of peaks, has a surfeit of these. Ed-Deir ('the Monastery'), sits high up on a promontory at the north-west edge of Petra, requiring an hour's weary climb to reach its summit. It takes its name from the inscribed crosses scratched into the wall in places, but it is without doubt a Nabataean funerary monument. One theory associates it with the last king, Rabbel II, who, though he ruled from Bostra, could have been returned on his death to his ancestral necropolis.[63] The façade, complete with urn and side-kiosks, seems like an attempt to recreate the Khazneh at a higher level, but the columns at ground level are carved into the rock and not free-standing, while the whole, despite its massive scale, contrives to give an impression of brooding squatness totally at variance with the elegant grace of the Treasury. Outside, the great plaza is not natural, but was levelled to accommodate rituals, presumably associated with the cult of the dead king.

Positioned overlooking the Outer Siq is the 'High Place of Sacrifice', Petra's best-known aerial temple, which offers wonderful views over the bleak wilderness valleys of the Wadi Araba. It is a comparatively simple affair, with a stone platform on which sits an altar raised on a podium of four steps, with a basin set beside it. Despite lurid guides' tales of human sacrifice, there is no evidence that the Nabataeans did more than offer animals to their gods here. The Romans, who tended to get huffy about the alleged sacral murder performed by other less-civilised races such as the Celtic Druid priests or the Carthaginians in North Africa, were apt to forget that they themselves were on record as having performed such bloody rites. When Hannibal threatened to march on Rome after his crushing victory at Cannae in 216 BC, the Roman magistrates ordered that two Greeks and two Gauls be sacrificed to ward off the disaster. The poor unfortunates were buried alive in a pit, so that Romans of a more squeamish or moralistic tendency could maintain that they had not actually been killed, but merely left to die.

An alternative way down from the High Place leads through the Wadi Farasa, past a number of other Nabataean tomb façades, most notably the Garden Tomb – an ancient water cistern lying broken and empty in front of it an indication of the nearby residence of the supervisor of the city's water supply. Beside it lies the Roman Soldier's tomb, named for a headless male torso clad in a Roman-style military cuirass, which projects from above its door. Although the dating of the tomb is most likely from the independent Nabataean period and thus the 'Roman' soldier probably served in the local army, it is pleasant to speculate that he may have served as an auxiliary in a Roman cohort and retired to his home town to die, leaving instructions that his military service be remembered in his funerary monument. Whoever he was, he was clearly a man of some substance, as both the tomb itself and the *triclinium* opposite, with carefully carved fluted columns in a riot of mauves and pinks, show a high level of workmanship.

The Petrans dedicated a new temple of Artemis in 150, and Epiphanius, in the 4th century, writes that the inhabitants were still wedded to the cult of Dusares, but these traditional ways did not last for ever and by the 6th century Christianity had established a firm hold here. Up on the north slope from the colonnaded street lie a cluster of churches, evidence of this late phase in Petra's development. The Petra Church, a Byzantine construction of the 5th century, is a fairly typical three-aisled basilica, though enclosed, for its better conservation, in an alarming spider-like sheath of plastic and glass. The floor retains part of its original mosaic covering, on the right a series of beautifully studied personifications of the seasons, on the other side various animals, intended to show the bounty of nature, including a cameleopard, a strange mutant hybrid between a camel and a leopard. A fire at the end of the 6th century caused part of the building to collapse and buried a precious archive of papyrus scrolls, partly carbonised, but containing details of land sales, tax payments and all the other mundane transactions, which shed some light on the minutiae of a community clearly still functioning, if not exactly flourishing.[64]

The Blue Church, named for the blue Egyptian marble columns used in its construction, and the Ridge Church at the highest point of the slope are mostly ruinous, but offer a viewpoint over the very edge of Petra and its perimeter of city walls. Massively built in sandstone blocks, these Nabataean works defended the settlement from attacks to the north. Snaking across the ridges, these unglamorous remains are reminders of a side of Nabataean life about which the grand façades of the Royal Tombs are mute. In the end, it seems they were built in vain, for only one source (Cassius Dio) hints at any kind of fighting during the Roman occupations,[65] and coins issued to commemorate the annexation bear the legend *Arabia Capta* ('Arabia captured') rather than *Arabia Victa* ('Arabia defeated').[66] As the Roman imperial propaganda machine was rarely backward in proclaiming even modest military successes as occasions for celebration, it is safe to presume that its defence was a very brief one.

A dim light on the transition to Roman rule and the early years of the province is shed by an archive of scrolls found in a cave in the Negev desert in the early 1960s. Babatha, to whom the documents belonged, was a rich landowner from a Nabataean-controlled village at Mazoa, south of the Dead Sea. The documents span a period from before the Roman annexation, with the scrolls written in Nabataean, to 132 (when Babatha is presumed to have died), by which time Greek – the language of administration in the eastern portion of the Empire – had taken over. They make reference to a *boule* (town council) at Petra, indicating that a Romanised form of urban administration was then functioning. Interesting, too, are the constant references to Roman soldiers in the region. Babatha goes to the prefect of a cavalry *ala* to register her holding of date-groves during the census carried out in Arabia in 127, while a

Roman centurion is recorded as lending money at an interest rate of 12 per cent to Babatha's second husband, an indication of the army's involvement in the local economy at an informal level.[67]

Babatha's presumed end was not a peaceful one. When the Romans put down the revolt of Simon Bar Kochba in 135, which for three years had torn through Palestine and threatened briefly to herald the restoration of Jewish independence, the surviving fighters scattered into inaccessible hideouts in the desert. Probably caught up somehow in the crisis, and sharing her last days with the rebels, was Babatha, whose remains could be amongst the twenty skeletons unearthed at the cave where her archive was found. Between her death and the establishment of the Petra Church archive, little is known. Then, just forty years after the fire that tore through the Christian complex, the Arabs seized the area. Earthquakes and the shattering of the water-management systems that had allowed the Nabataeans to husband what little moisture the near-desert provided left Petra's astonishing city of the dead as the haunt of just a few Bedouin families.

It is with a certain sadness that one leaves Petra, weary legs carrying the tomb-surfeited visitors away through the *siq* on to the more insistently pressing claims of the modern town. For the most exhausted, a tidy sum in Jordanian dinars claims a place in a carriage, whose clattering wheels break the silence of the route with cries and redoubled echoes. The best way of all to leave the ancient city, however, is on horseback, a mode of transport that requires permission in triplicate and involves incredulous checking of the paperwork by the guards, and jealous stares from those who have been firmly told by their guides that such a practice is strictly forbidden. Yet, a metre above the crowds and the carriages, gently rocked by the sway of the horse's back, it is still possible to feel like a real explorer, and experience just a hint of the wonder with which Burckhardt must first have cast eyes upon the Nabataeans' hidden capital.

Beyond Petra the landscape once more turns arid, transforming into the forbidding Hisma desert of southern Jordan. It was areas such as this that the Romans needed to dominate if they were successfully to hold on to their new Arabian province. Originally a Nabataean settlement, Humayma, 60 kilometres south of Petra, was founded by Aretas III around 80 BC and named Auara, 'the white place', for the vision of a man riding on a white camel that he is said to have seen there.[68] Under the Roman occupation, Auara found itself in a strategic position along the Via Nova Traiana, and one of the earliest Roman forts in Jordan was built here, the first garrison transferring from Egypt, its

presence evidenced by a collection of ankhs and other characteristically Egyptian votive symbols. In the *Notitia Dignitatum* the garrison
of Auara (or Haurae) is listed as the *equites sagittarii indigenae*, a unit
of native horse archers.[69]

The way to Humayma leads through barren limestone outcrops into
a land that somehow provides sustenance to the Bedouin's herds of sheep
and goats, and which, for those like the Nabataeans who were masters
of water husbandry, can actually provide a modest living. Annual rainfall in the area is just 90 millimetres. Yet, set down amid the most
parched-looking landscape fringed by wrinkled and gullied hills, already
baking in the late-winter heat, it seems impossible to conceive of anyone
voluntarily settling here. A short way into the site lies the indistinct
outline of the earlier Roman camp, a square shape possibly indicating
the *principia*, with less-distinct rubble piles to indicate the barracks. A
small building just outside, and equally ruinous, is one of the Byzantine
churches that indicate continuity of settlement in this bleak outpost at
least into the 6th century. Indeed, a tax edict of the mid-5th century indicated that the place was considered prosperous – the levy it was required
to pay, some forty-three gold pieces, being the second-highest in the
Transjordan, an amount exceeded only by Udruh, Arabia's other main
legionary camp, 20 kilometres east of Petra.[70]

A Bedouin shepherdess scrutinises us uncertainly as we approach the
Nabataean reservoir, the cistern still full of water and with intact piping
still leading off from it. Beyond lies another larger, but unroofed, structure marking the Abbasid *qasr*. Arab tradition has it that during the early
Islamic period, the former Byzantine settlement at Auara became the residence of the Abbasid family, who claimed descent from one of the uncles
of the Prophet Muhammad. During the 730s, they used it as a safe base
for their conspiracy against the ruling Umayyad caliphate, and when in
749 they succeeded in seizing power and becoming caliphs themselves,
they abandoned Humayma for the rather more urban delights of Baghdad.

Sited at the northern end of the Red Sea, on the Gulf that bears its
name and just 50 kilometres to the south-west of Humayma, Aqaba has
been an important trading and naval station throughout its history. Even
today it has become a free port, as the Jordanian authorities attempt to
pump life into an economy undermined by successive Middle East crises.
Mentioned in the Bible as a trading post on the way to 'Ophir', the
earliest settlement at Aqaba lies at Tell el-Khuleifa to the west of the
modern centre, and was superseded by a Ptolemaic port at Berenice,
and then, after the annexation of Arabia, by the town of Ailana, which
lies buried beneath the heart of the modern city.

Off the café-fringed cornice, the beach thickly populated with bathers despite the scorching heat, lies Aqaba's partly ruined fort. Originally of late-Abbasid construction (from the mid-12th century), it is most famous for the raid carried out on it by Lawrence of Arabia in July 1917, which drove the Ottoman Turks from the town. Aqaba has been Muslim-held since 630, when its bishop, Yuhanna ibn Ru'ba, brokered a treaty with the Prophet Muhammad, by which the town allowed safe-passage to the Muslim armies and access to its wells, and agreed to pay a tribute of one solidus for each of its non-Muslim inhabitants – which meant, one presumes, virtually the entire population.[71] Such localised agreements and the spirit of self-help and implied disloyalty to the central government's cause must have been typical of the way in which Byzantine control over Arabia and Palestine simply dissolved away. If the government could not protect the towns, the locals would pay tribute to those who could; as for the tribes of the desert fringes, they would fight under the banner of the side that was, in their view, most likely to win.

At such a strategic location, Roman Ailana soon found itself garrisoned by the III Cyrenaica legion, detached from duty in Egypt. The town sat at the southernmost extension of the Via Nova Traiana, and milestones from the construction of that road dated 112 have been found at Aqaba. When Diocletian reorganised the administration of the region, Ailana found itself a part of the new province of Palaestina, with its garrison the X Fretensis legion, which, from the evidence of the *Notitia Dignitatum*, was then stationed there at least until the end of the 4th century. Aqaba remained an important trading centre and a stop on the route for pilgrims making the arduous journey to the monastery of Saint Catherine in the Sinai desert.

But security in the region grew ever shakier. During the reign of Leo (457–74), a tribal sheikh named Amorkesus[72] seized the island of Iotabe in the Gulf of Aqaba and proceeded to levy tolls on all shipping that desired to pass. In order to get rid of this nuisance, the Byzantine government was forced to acquiesce to Amorkesus's demand to be appointed *phylarch* of Palaestina Tertia, the lands around Petra, in effect rewarding his piratical act with an officially recognised position.[73] It took further action on the part of Romanus, *dux* of Palestine, to reassert full control over Iotabe, but by 530 Justinian had in effect demobilised this eastern frontier, handing over primary responsibility for its policing to his Ghassanid Arab allies.

Ailana, therefore, was by 630 hardly defended at all. The remains of the Byzantine walls can be seen around 500 metres from the modern shore, complete with fragments of a projecting tower. It was probably here that the X Fretensis legion was based. The ruins sit utterly unregarded on a dusty traffic island at the side of a busy road. Over the way, jumbled fragments of Byzantine Ailana's more domestic life lie in a mouldering heap of mud-brick constructions and the more substantial shattered stones of several churches. The Arab *misr* or fortified encampment – which became known as Ayla – that was set up in the 630s just by the shore has survived in better condition, although hemmed in by modern hotels and a yacht club, which has swallowed up part of its perimeter. The Egypt gate, with two horseshoe-shaped towers intact, and the ruins of the congregational mosque manage to give at least some sense of the settlement that finally put an end to the career of Roman Ailana. Secure in a base such as this, and having acquired the rest of Palestine with the capture of Jerusalem in 634, the Arabs were free to turn their attention to the conquest of still-Byzantine Egypt.

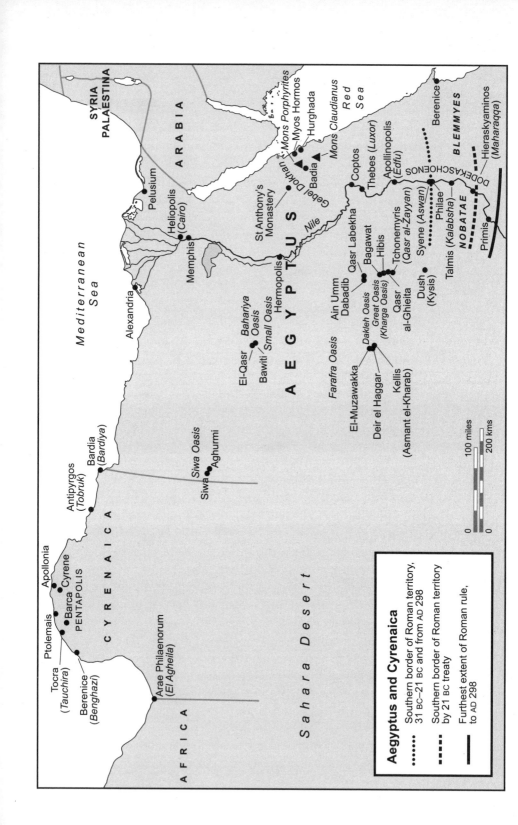

Aegyptus and Cyrenaica

- .... Southern border of Roman territory, 31 BC–21 BC and from AD 298
- - - - - Southern border of Roman territory by 21 BC treaty
- ▬▬▬▬ Furthest extent of Roman rule, to AD 298

SYRIA
PALAESTINA

ARABIA

Mediterranean Sea

Pelusium

Heliopolis (Cairo)

Memphis

Alexandria

St Anthony's Monastery

Gebel Dokhan

Mons Porphyrites

Myos Hormos

Hurghada

Mons Claudianus

Red Sea

Badia

Berenice

BLEMMYES

Hieraskyaminos (Maharraqa)

Coptos

Thebes (Luxor)

Apollinopolis (Edfu)

DODEKASCHOENOS

AEGYPTUS

Nile

Hermopolis

Baharija Oasis

El-Qasr

Bawiti Small Oasis

Ain Umm Dabadib

Qasr Labekha

Bagawat

Hibis

Tchonemyris (Qasr al-Zayyan)

Syene (Aswan)

Philae

Talmis (Kalabsha)

NOBATAE

Primis

Farafra Oasis

El-Muzawakka

Deir el Haggar

Dakleh Oasis

Great Oasis (Kharga Oasis)

Qasr al-Ghieita

Kellis (Asmant el-Kharab)

Dush (Kysis)

Siwa Oasis

Siwa Aghurmi

Bardia (Bardiya)

Antipyrgos (Tobruk)

CYRENAICA

Apollonia

Cyrene

Barca

PENTAPOLIS

Ptolemais

Tocra (Tauchira)

Berenice (Benghazi)

Arae Philaenorum (El Agheila)

AFRICA

Sahara Desert

0   100 miles
0   200 kms

CHAPTER 9

Aegyptus and Cyrenaica

The barge she sat in, like a burnished throne
Burned on the water. The poop was beaten gold;
Purple the sails, and so perfumed that
The winds were lovesick with them. The oars were silver,
Which to the tunes of flutes kept stroke, and made
The water which they beat to follow faster,
As amorous of their strokes. For her own person
It beggared all description: she did lie
In her pavilion – cloth of gold, of tissue –
O'erpicturing that Venus where we see
The fancy outwork nature . . .

William Shakespeare, *Antony and Cleopatra*[1]

Egypt always seemed to the Romans a mysterious, atypical place, radically opposed to the 'Roman' way of doing things, a country that entangled, entrapped and mesmerised. During the civil wars of the 1st century BC, it certainly did ensnare such successive aspirants of supreme power as Julius Caesar and Mark Antony. Before this, though, in 210 BC, the Romans had tried to secure grain supplies from Ptolemy IV, and so vital did Egypt subsequently become as a source of food for the teeming populace of Rome that in 168 BC they intervened directly to demand that the Seleucid king of Syria, Antiochus IV, who was trying to annex his neighbour, withdraw his forces and his governor from the country.

Thenceforth, Egypt was always independent more or less at the whim of Rome, and the next century and a half consisted of a 'will they, won't they' diplomatic dance between the Romans and Egyptians, the latter alternately fending off and then inviting Roman occupation. In 55 BC, Pompey was drawn into Egyptian affairs when he had his lieutenant Gabinius restore Ptolemy XIII, who had fled the country following one of the bitter (and quite commonly fatal) feuds that periodically afflicted the Ptolemaic ruling house. If Pompey thought Ptolemy would be grateful, he was rudely disabused when he sought refuge with his old 'ally' following his defeat against Julius Caesar at the Battle of Pharsalus in 48 BC. In an attempt to curry favour with the Caesarian side, Ptolemy – far from sheltering Pompey – had him murdered and sent his head on a dish to Caesar, when he in turn arrived in Egypt. Ptolemy, though, received the just reward for his perfidy, as Caesar had him executed and promoted his half-sister Cleopatra VII to the throne.[2]

Cleopatra, just seventeen at the time of her accession, flirted with and charmed the middle-aged triumvir, seeking thereby to entwine her own ambitions so inextricably with his that her beloved country's independence would be safeguarded. But Caesar finally returned to Rome, leaving as the product of his little adventure a son, dubbed Ptolemy Caesarion. Undeterred, Cleopatra turned her attention, following Caesar's assassination in 44 BC, to the leading star in the rising new generation of Roman strongmen, Mark Antony. A man seemingly of much more volatile temperament than Caesar, Antony appears for a while to have contemplated dismantling the edifice of Roman provincial authority and returning to the system of management through clients which had previously served the Romans so well in the East.

This may have been the motive in 34 BC for the 'Donations of Alexandria', when Antony, seated on a dais in Alexandria and dressed like an oriental potentate, dished out the eastern provinces to Cleopatra and the children he had fathered on her, the twins Cleopatra Selene ('the moon') and Alexander Helios ('the sun') and the youngest, Ptolemy Philadelphos. Even little Caesarion received his share. Needless to say, this did not go down at all well in Rome, where Antony was widely (and hardly inaccurately) regarded as having 'gone native'. It all handed a propaganda coup to Antony's rival Octavian, and Antony's belated pamphlet attempting to defend himself against accusations of betraying Roman morals and interests was tellingly entitled De sua ebrietate ('On his Drunkenness').[3] In 31 BC Antony and his Egyptian queen were defeated at the naval Battle of Actium, and in its aftermath both committed suicide, but not before Cleopatra had tried a half-hearted tilt at enticing Octavian into a relationship, an attempt that was firmly rebuffed.

So, in August 30 BC, on the first day of the Egyptian New Year, the country became a Roman province. Octavian – or Augustus, as he would soon become – at once decided that Egypt was too vital to Rome's interests to be treated as just another province. It was not therefore handed over to a governor of senatorial rank, but, uniquely for the time, was to be administered by an equestrian prefect, who would also have command of Egypt's legionary complement – at first three, then reduced to two in AD 23. So tightly held was the rein on Egypt that no senator was even allowed to set foot there without prior authorisation from the Emperor. That the relationship with Egypt was always going to be an ambivalent and occasionally troubled one was presaged when Augustus decided to do a bit of tourism, visiting the tomb of Alexander the Great in Alexandria. He touched the illustrious corpse's face and, most unfortunately, broke off the great man's nose.[4]

Many aspects of Ptolemaic governance were retained, at least for a time, and Roman government officials in Egypt acquired anomalous titles, such as the *strategoi* who supervised the *nomes*, the traditional administrative divisions of the country. The peculiarities of Egypt, combined with the dry desert conditions that have favoured the survival here (as almost nowhere else) of a mass of local archives on papyrus, mean that evidence is almost superabundant, but it cannot always be translated to understand practices elsewhere in the Empire.[5]

After a long period of relative tranquillity, the later 2nd and 3rd centuries brought more troubled times to Egypt. The revolt of Avidius Cassius in 175, although based in Syria, touched Egypt, as he sought to cut off the grain supply from there to Rome, thereby reminding the central government of the vital strategic necessity of keeping a firm grip on the province. Consequently, Septimius Severus visited in 199, implementing an important series of administrative changes, which included the grant of a city council (or *boule*) to Alexandria, a privilege that it had long been denied (and long lobbied vigorously to be awarded).[6] The Emperor must have rather put a dampener on the citizens' celebrations, however, as he also conceded town councils to the chief settlement in each *nome*, some of which the cosmopolitan Alexandrians probably regarded as barely better than native villages.

Egypt, along with much of the rest of the Near East, fell into the hands of Zenobia's Palmyrenes in 269, and a further revolt, under Firmus, demanded the personal attention of Aurelian in 273–4. The province had, therefore, barely been back within the fold of the Empire for two decades when trouble broke out anew. It was probably sparked off by an edict of Diocletian of 297, which reformed the basis of the taxation system, from a purely headcount-based one to a hybrid in which both the productivity of the land and the number of people living there were taken into account (known as *capitatio-iugatio*).[7] Although this was a rational attempt to reform the budgetary system by allowing the central authorities to adjust the amount of revenue raised, depending on the needs of the time (something that, astonishingly, the Empire had not up until that time been able to do), it was seen in many circles as a naked attempt to extort more money out of the long-suffering provincials.

The immediate result was a revolt by one Lucius Domitius Domitianus, probably in the summer of 297, but this was put down early the following year by Diocletian himself.[8] Galvanised by his victory, the Emperor followed his initial reforms with a more radical overhaul of Egyptian bureaucracy and administration generally, which continued with the implementation of a problematic new system of tax assessment. It saw the introduction of a fifteen-year taxation cycle, known as indictions, whose use was to survive in one shape or another into the Middle Ages.[9] Besides these reforms, Diocletian significantly reinforced the military presence in Egypt with units now stationed in the Delta around Pelusium (Tell el-Farama), in the western oases, and at Philae, where the island became a legionary base. In Thebes (Luxor) the main temple complex was converted in part to house a legionary detachment.[10] Egypt was also now for the first time subdivided, first into two (Egypt and the Thebaid), and then later into three or even four provinces.[11]

Egypt escaped the barbarian incursions and occupation that were the fate of Roman North Africa west of Cyrenaica, and the Vandals never sought to penetrate this far east.[12] Although there is evidence of increased activity on the part of nomadic groups such as the Nobatae and Blemmyes in the far south and the eastern desert, and the abandonment of some forward positions, Roman Egypt on the whole remained prosperous (and loyal) throughout the 5th and 6th centuries. The disasters of the 7th century, therefore, must have been a complete shock to the Byzantine emperors who had come to rely so completely on Egyptian taxes, and particularly on the annual shipments of grain from Alexandria to Constantinople.

Roman Egypt fell with barely the shadow of resistance. Heraclius had in fact had little chance to re-establish central authority after the Persian occupation of the province from 617 to 627, before, a bare thirteen years later, a 4,000-strong Arab Muslim army under Amr invaded the province.[13] The imperial army was defeated at Heliopolis in July, and within two months the fortress of Babylon, the Empire's stronghold in Cairo, was under siege. The man chosen by Heraclius to lead the defence was the patriarch, Cyrus, a cleric more adept at theological hair-splitting than military stratagems. He had played a leading role in the propagation of the doctrine of Monothelitism at the Emperor's behest, a belated and ultimately futile attempt to reconcile the Monophysites and the official 'two-nature' Chalcedonians.[14] Christ, Cyrus averred,[15] although he had within him two natures, human and divine, was possessed of but a single united will (or *thelos*).[16]

Those who understood Cyrus's position protested at the unwarranted blurring of their own creeds, while, for the mass of believers, it seemed but a piece of imperially sponsored trickery. Still, his position at the helm of the Roman defence did absolutely nothing to shore up support for Byzantine rule in Egypt, while his vigorous persecution of the Coptic hierarchy undermined what little credibility he possessed. Perhaps recognising this, Cyrus negotiated the surrender of all of Egypt except Alexandria. As the Byzantine troops evacuated Babylon on Easter Day 641, they ensured that any remaining stock of goodwill amongst the Egyptians evaporated by massacring the Coptic prisoners they had been holding in the fortress prison. It took just a year for the final collapse of Alexandria to occur. Cyrus brokered a treaty with Amr in November 641, agreeing an eleven-month armistice after which all Byzantine troops would leave the city and the province would be abandoned to Arab control. In September 642, the imperial fleet weighed anchor and sailed for Constantinople, bringing to an end almost seven centuries of Roman rule.[17] Both Cyrus and Heraclius were by now dead, so neither lived to see Amr take possession of Alexandria, which, he reported to his master Omar, possessed '4,000 palaces, 4,000 baths, 400 theatres, 12,000 sellers of green vegetables, and 40,000 tributary Jews'.[18]

The city lay at the heart of Roman Egypt, as at the core of its Ptolemaic predecessor. It was one of the Empire's great urban centres; indeed, before the rise to prominence of Constantinople it was the only other metropolis that could truly be said to have rivalled Rome in wealth and splendour. However, the centuries have not been kind to the place and, since the Middle Ages, it has been Cairo that has occupied the heart of Egypt's political and cultural life. Alexandria therefore wears its past almost self-consciously, an era of greatness that has slipped frustratingly out of reach, but of which only a fugitive shadow can ever be really grasped.

The history of Alexandria began with a small fishing village named Rakotis, constructed around 1300 BC. When Alexander the Great captured Egypt from the Persians – who had held it for the best part of two centuries – in 332 BC, he at once identified the sheltered harbour as the ideal capital for his new province, one that would look outward to the eastern Mediterranean world, rather than inward to the Nile valley. It became, ultimately, the acropolis of Alexandria. The Roman city, which may have had between 200,000 and 300,000 inhabitants,[19] must have been a truly wondrous as well as a troubled place, becoming as renowned for its boisterousness and riots as for the marvels of its monuments. It was laid out on a grid pattern, with the wide main east–west street known as the Via Canopica. Beside the massive double-harbour – made up of the Great Harbour to the east, and the Eunostos to the west – lay the Caesareum, a temple honouring the memory of the deified Julius Caesar, with three huge obelisks in front, one of which now graces New York's Central Park; the other two sit on London's Embankment and in Paris on the place de la Concorde.[20]

In a bay just north of the Great Harbour lay the Pharos of Alexandria, one of the Seven Wonders of the Ancient World. Its light was visible far out to sea, employing mirrors by day[21] and a fire by night to guide mariners safely to land. It was still intact as late as the 7th century when Arculf, a Frankish pilgrim, described it.[22] Shortly thereafter, the lantern of the lighthouse came crashing down and the Alexandrians used it as a stone quarry, so that by the 12th century only the square base remained. An earthquake in 1365 finished the destruction,[23] and the rubble was removed to provide material for the Mamluk Fort Qait Bey, which now towers up block-like on the promontory. Stonework from the lighthouse still lies in the bay, and locals stroll up and down the promenade here enjoying a cooling ice-cream, surveying the scant remains of one of the ancient world's most celebrated buildings.

Another of the city's prominent landmarks was the Great Library, founded by Ptolemy I Soter as part of his Mouseion, where court-sponsored scholars could pursue philosophical research to the greater glory of the ruling house.[24] It was badly damaged during Caesar's operations against Pompey in 48 BC, although Mark Antony obligingly made matters up to Cleopatra by sequestering the almost-as-renowned collection of the Ionian city of Pergamum. But during the troubles at the end of the 4th century the whole thing was burnt to the ground, destroying a priceless trove of ancient works, the survival of even a fraction of which would have filled many of the huge gaps in our knowledge of antiquity, and the loss of which is enough to make grown classicists weep. Nothing of the old building survives, but down by the sea front, looking more like a beached whale than the 'flowing glass' promised by its publicity, the Biblioteca Alexandrina has been built in an attempt to recreate the spirit of the old. Its current selection of half a million volumes just about matches the level of its ancient model more than 2,000 years ago.

Now sitting in a poor district of the city, the surrounding streets potholed and narrow, encroached upon by a lively array of shops hung with plastic awnings, the main archaeological reserve of Alexandria, dusty and sun-baked, feels more like a building site than a window into Roman Egypt's past. The apartment blocks that crowd about on one side, and the city's public cemetery, which threatens to burst in from the other, complete the hemmed-in, claustrophobic feeling.

Two structures of great importance are located here, one Alexandria's most misnamed relic, the other perhaps its most overlooked. The first, 'Pompey's Pillar', a single towering monolith some 28 metres high, constructed of red Aswan granite and topped with a showy Corinthian capital, dominates the whole hill. Although universally known as such, it has absolutely nothing to do with Pompey.[25] When the Crusaders, in a late attempt to regain a foothold in the Levant, occupied Alexandria in 1365, they found the acropolis almost totally ruined save for the pillar. Since it was clearly of Roman origin, they simply attached to it the identity of a great Roman whose name was familiar to them, and their attractive but erroneous attribution has stuck over the centuries. Local tradition amplified this with the legend that it was put up by Caesar as an honour to his dead foe, slain on the coast not far from here.

The column was in fact erected for Diocletian, possibly around 298, as an inscription on its west side reveals.[26] It probably celebrates his suppression of the revolt of Domitius Domitianus. When the rebel leader died, his deputy, Achilleus, carried on the resistance, specifically around Alexandria, for a further three months. Diocletian was so furious at the delay in taking Alexandria that when the city finally fell, he swore to punish the citizens so severely that the massacre would not cease until the blood reached to his knees – a threat that was thwarted by his horse, which stumbled as it passed the walls, causing the Emperor's legs to touch the ground.[27]

Nearby the foundations of the Serapeum, the temple to Serapis, have been exposed,[28] but now just a jumble of drums and foundations survive, together with a subterranean annex consisting of a passage lined with niches, at one end of which a golden image of the god in the form of the bull Apis was unearthed. These unpromising remains conceal one of the last great pagan shrines in Egypt and, to boot, the final location of the Great Library of Alexandria. The temple was probably built in the time of Ptolemy III Euergetes (246–221 BC), and the worship of Serapis became almost a dynastic cult for the Ptolemaic pharaohs.[29] It seems to have been an attempt to fuse elements of the traditional Greek religious practice with traditional Egyptian beliefs, much as the Ptolemies themselves were Hellenic grafts onto an ancient Egyptian monarchy.

Just as Serapis was associated with the King, so the Ptolemaic queens became identified with Isis, and temples to the two divinities are often, as here, found together. Worship of the 'new' god Serapis spread far and wide throughout the Empire, with a temple to him and Isis being constructed some time in the first century AD on the Campus Martius in Rome. The priests were clearly identified by their shaven heads, and followed what were, to non-believing Romans, rather strange dietary restrictions, being forbidden pork, fish and wine. More startling still was the priestly habit of jumping in the River Tiber.[30] Long after the worship of many of the other traditional gods had ossified, Serapis found favour and, indeed his cult seems to have experienced something of a renaissance in the 3rd century. Amongst diehard pagans, the Serapeum at Alexandria became a symbol of resistance to the seemingly unstoppable advance of Christianity.

After years of obfuscation, some of it disingenuous, about whether private pagan worship was to be tolerated, in 391 Theodosius decided to clamp down once and for all. In a series of constitutions he decreed that sacrifices were to be banned – although this simply repeated earlier laws – at any time, day or night and in any place, including private houses. Even the lighting of fires to the traditional Roman household gods, the *lares* and *penates*, was forbidden, as were a variety of other practices regarded as pagan superstition, such as the tying of ribbons around trees and the building of impromptu altars of turf in rural areas. Theodosius did not specifically decree the destruction of pagan temples – indeed, a law of 399 enjoins their protection as public 'ornaments',[31] – but one of the Emperor's constitutions had been specifically directed to Alexandria, and there Bishop Theophilus interpreted matters quite differently.[32]

Already from 384 to 388 Maternus Cynegius, the praetorian prefect of the East, had connived in or actively encouraged attacks on pagan temples, so in Egypt the groundwork for Theophilus's notionally illegal Christian act of demolition had been well laid. The bishop led round a mob to the Serapeum, into which the pagans had barricaded themselves for protection, though Theophilus accused them of using it as a fortress from which to attack his flock. Finally, the Christians broke into the temple, but, for a brief instant, dared not attack the great cult statue of Serapis itself.[33] The pagans mocked them, saying that if they did assault it, the god would strike them down. Tentative at first, the Christians broke off the statue's jaw and, when no thunderbolt smote them, and the earth failed to open up and swallow them, they levered down the whole great image.[34] Serapis's spell was broken and many of the god's followers instantly accepted baptism. Those that did not tried to turn the whole event round to their own advantage by claiming that Serapis, saddened at the blasphemy of the Christians in violating his sanctuary, had now 'withdrawn' from Alexandria. In the shadowy and persecuted world of late-pagan piety, it may have consoled them, but it did nothing to improve their position or reverse their defeat.

Alexandria saw one of the more shocking (to modern eyes) acts of religiously inspired violence in the ancient world. Cyril, the Alexandrian patriarch from 412, had built up a body of monks, the *parabalani*, who acted as his own private army of enforcers, terrorising all who opposed him, Christian and pagan alike.[35] The city retained an elite, well-educated pagan community into the 5th century, despite all the temple-toppling and the forbidding of traditional rites. Prominent amongst them was the philosopher Hypatia, who was so well 'integrated' that her friends included even Synesius, the Bishop of Cyrene. In 415 a Christian mob that included a sprinkling of pious *parabalani* thugs attacked her carriage and dragged her to the Caesareum, where she was stripped naked, stoned to death and then her body mutilated by the mob.[36] Although the imperial government condemned the atrocity, in practice reprisals were limited to capping the membership of the *parabalani* at 500 and insisting that in future the Prefect of Egypt vet recruits.[37] Hypatia's murder, however, seemed to mark a watershed, at least in Egypt, beyond which to operate as a publicly prominent pagan became next to impossible.

Another victim of the demolition of the Serapeum was the Great Library. After the destruction of the original building in 48 BC, much of the collection that was acquired to replace the destroyed scrolls was housed here (and guides will, improbably, maintain that the whole thing was stored in the niches of the surviving underground section of the temple). When Theophilus's men demolished the rest of the temple in 391, the library's collection, which would have contained many pagan texts, but presumably little or nothing in the way of Christian writings, mostly perished with it. A later, Christian-inspired legend[38] attempted to put the blame on the Arabs in the 7th century, but the subsequent Muslim role in copying and transmitting many precious ancient texts indicates that, had they found the library intact, they would almost certainly have saved it.

The colonnade of the Serapeum was, unlike the temple itself, preserved, and a martyr memorial and small church may have been built outside the area of the original shrine. By the 12th century, however, the whole area was neglected, and in 1167 Saladin removed the pillars from the colonnade to act as an ersatz sea wall against the encroaching waves of the Mediterranean. Only 'Pompey's' (or, rather, Diocletian's) column was left in place.

A few hundred metres south-west of the pillar lies the catacomb of Kom es-Shoqafa ('the hill of potsherds'), a Roman-era necropolis of the 1st or 2nd century AD,[39] and the largest such to be located in Alexandria. The place gets its name from the enormous quantity of broken antique pottery fragments discovered here, believed to be the containers used to transport the elements of funerary (or memorial) feasts and then smashed as being too unlucky to take home because of the association they had acquired with the dead.

The entrance hardly promises much; the hill has been largely cut away to aid the excavations, leaving a flat area dotted with sarcophagi unrelated to the site, which have been gathered together from other locations in Alexandria. Above the way into the catacomb itself sits a kind of glass structure with radial struts, looking more like something out of a 1960s municipal baths than a tomb entrance. The necropolis has three levels (the lowermost flooded), and is accessed by a well down which coffins were lowered by a rope, but where modern steps now obligingly lead in a tight spiral to the first level. Almost immediately a vestibule opens out, with two alcoves to either side topped with conch-shell patterns, and down beyond this another well to allow coffins to be let down onto the second floor. This level is studded with *loculi*, niches for coffins, some hundreds in the complex as a whole. These were for richer folk; the poor were relegated to pit-burials in the floor, while the truly wealthy received memorials such as the elaborate room just to the right of the vestibule.

Two bearded serpents, *Agathodaimones*, guard the way to the left and right of this chamber, above each of them a little Medusa head to transform any intruders into stone. Inside, there are three sarcophagi, although – curiously for such a grand monument – none of them seems ever to have been occupied. The interior walls are decorated with mummification scenes, supervised by two of the gods of the dead: Sobek, the crocodile, dressed in military garb with a cloak and spear, and Anubis, the jackal god, who is robed in a more identifiably Roman military uniform, with cuirass, *gladius* and *pilum* (the Roman legionary's throwing javelin). On the tomb chamber's right-hand niche a man, possibly a prince, is shown wearing the twin crown that represents Upper and Lower Egypt, making an offering to an Apis bull. The intended occupant of the tomb must therefore have been a man with high connections, and it has been speculated that this could have been Tiberius Julius Alexander, the prefect under Nero in 66–9, who was instrumental in the suppression of a Jewish revolt centred on the city, which is said to have cost 50,000 lives.[40]

Adjacent to the main complex, and originally accessed via a separate entrance, is the area known locally as the 'Knights' tomb'.[41] A large quantity of human and equine bones were found interred together here, and it is speculated, without too firm a basis, that these were the victims of an atrocity perpetrated by the Emperor Caracalla when he visited the city in 215. Initially all had gone well, and the Emperor had visited the tomb of Alexander, decreeing that it should be blocked up, so that he himself would be the last person to gaze on the corpse of the great Macedonian. Unfortunately, the Alexandrians' joking references to Caracalla as a fratricide for his (very real) involvement in the murder of his brother Geta were rather too pungent for the Emperor's taste.[42] He ordered a massacre of the citizenry, which even resulted, in the ensuing chaos, in the deaths of a number of his own companions, whom the soldiers indiscriminately slaughtered.

In the 'tomb' itself a series of plain *loculi* and, in one corner, a relief with the remains of four murals are scant reminders of whatever did occur in this place. On the upper register of one there is a mummification scene, the deceased protected by Isis and Nephthys with wings outstretched. Below is a Greco-Roman scene, with three goddesses identified as Hera, Athene and Aphrodite, which could be a reference to the Judgement of Paris. It is not even clearly a funerary scene – though ultraviolet photography has shown the otherwise obscured figure of Persephone, a more appropriate harbinger of the Underworld – and offers no reference or hints to a holocaust of 3rd-century Alexandrians.

None of Alexandria's great public buildings have been excavated, as the sprawl of the modern conurbation makes opportunities for the investigation of its ancient predecessor all but impossible. However, in the Kom el Dikka quarter, about a kilometre through crowded streets north-east of the Serapeum, a collection of the city's more mundane buildings has given an invaluable insight into its everyday life during the 5th and 6th centuries. Its name, 'the Hill of Benches', may be taken from the rows of seats of the partly restored *odeon* (a smaller version of a theatre intended for more intimate, possibly musical, performances), which is its centrepiece. Greek characters on these, intended to show positions reserved for particular divisions of citizens or for notables, are all jumbled up and sometimes upside down, evidence of some long-ago restoration. To one side is a series of rooms, each of which has sets of benches around the wall; it is speculated that these may have served as lecture halls. In a city as famed for scholarship as Alexandria, this is not an idle supposition.[43]

Beyond this again rises the ruined shell of a medium-sized bath-complex, only the brick dome of the *caldarium* really surviving anything like intact. Much of it was badly damaged during the Persian capture of the city in 619.[44] Arrayed on the rim of the valley that has been formed by the excavations are a collection of artefacts unearthed from Alexandria harbour, including some very worn royal heads and sphinxes. The Mediterranean has only just begun to give up the remnants of the northern part of Ptolemaic and Roman Alexandria[45] romanticised as 'the City of

Cleopatra', which were inundated through successive earthquakes, and a hugely ambitious plan to build an underwater museum may one day enable visitors to view the shattered remains of the Pharos as stone fish in an archaeological aquarium.

A world away from the cooling breezes of the Mediterranean coast, the Eastern Desert is an unforgiving place in the summer, when the temperature rises above forty degrees Centigrade and there is little shade to be found. The harsh conditions attracted monks, such as Saint Anthony, the first of the Desert Fathers, who, in the early 4th century, retired deep into the desert, among the hills behind the Red Sea, where the community that grew up still survives as the oldest active monastic community in the world.[46] Save for a harvest of sand and souls, however, there seems precious little reason to linger in such a place. The Roman army must heartily have wished to spend as little time as possible here. Yet come they did, building forts and importing large workforces.

Besides the need to patrol and secure the roads leading from the Nile valley to ports such as Berenice on the Red Sea (far in the south of modern Egypt), the lure that drew the Romans here was the mineral wealth of the Eastern Desert, in particular granite and, most precious of all, porphyry. An igneous rock, formed by the cooling of volcanic magma, its purple form, 'imperial' porphyry, could only be found in a single quarry, Mons Porphyrites, in the shadow of the Gebel Dokhan ('the Hills of Smoke'), some 45 kilometres west of the Read Sea, close to modern Hurghada. An inscription unearthed in the area states that the quarries were found by a certain Caius Cominius Leugas in AD 18, during the reign of Tiberius.[47] So precious was the stone, and the imperial connotations of its colour, that it was used only for prestige projects, such as the statue of the Tetrarchs that stands at the corner of Saint Mark's Cathedral in Venice, the coffin of Constantine's mother Helena, and for imperial statuary, such as the bust of Galerius at Felix Romuliana in Moesia.[48] The imperial birthing chamber at the Palace in Constantinople was also lined in porphyry, giving rise to the term Porphyrogenitus to an imperial prince born there – by definition, after his father had become resident in the palace and thus Emperor – and thus to the English term 'born in the purple'.

From Hurghada (325 kilometres south-east of Suez along the Red Sea coast), with its ultra-modern sprawl of diving resorts and 'family' hotels insulated entirely from Egypt, both ancient and modern, the journey to Mons Porphyrites requires a strong stomach. Twisting, turning and bumping along desert tracks that seem to disappear as soon as they are

found, the way leads past one of the Roman roads that originally facili-
tated the transportation of porphyry, both to the coast and to the Nile
valley. Small piles of stones to either side show its width, and the criss-
cross tracks of four-wheel-drive vehicles mark where modern travellers
have made some use of this partially sand-buried ancient route. More
muttered curses, oaths and frantic discussions lead us finally to the Wadi
Umm Sidri, the gateway to the Gebel Dokhan. Here, in a bleak and
scorched stony desert valley overlooked by the barren jagged peaks of
the Gebel, lies a loading ramp, some 2 metres high and 20 metres long,
looking incongruously like the horse-mounting ramp at Petra. But the
desert is not good horse country, and it would have been camels or mules
that brought the porphyry from the mines, to be transferred here to
larger carts for the far longer stage westwards to the Nile.[49]

Half an hour to the west lies the fort of Badia, which stood guard
on the desert road just south of the main settlements at Mons
Porphyrites. On one side of the fort 'the Hills of Smoke' rise up in the
distance, while to the south the mountains of the Wadi Qattar tower,
giving a sense of grimness and, if this is possible in the wide-open
desert, of claustrophobia. The fort, built of dark local stone, standing
out starkly against the yellow ochre of the desert, is about 40 metres
square, with the remains of eight or nine towers still visible, the stones
used to construct it looking as though they are struggling to keep their
heads above the encroaching sands. The interior buildings are all ruinous,
but pottery and coins indicate that the fort may have been retained as
late as the 6th century.[50]

About 50 metres to the west of the main fort is a curious circular
enclosure, surrounded by a wall around 4 metres high constructed of
small stones. In the centre stands a rocky outcrop, on the top of which
a large hole has been gouged. My guide insists that this was made by
the local Bedouin digging for treasure, but they must have had strong
shovels indeed to dent the rock, and the alternative theory that it was
blasted away with dynamite carries more credibility. Still, quite why the
Romans chose to build a wall around a rock in the first place is unclear.

Finally, a series of upright columns on a rise in the wadi mark the
castle that guarded the settlement at Mons Porphyrites itself. Comforting
plans drawn in the 1950s[51] show a typical square shape with projecting
circular angle-towers, and well-defined rooms. An awkward scramble up
the *castellum*'s mound, which is itself slowly collapsing into the wadi
below, reveals that the five columns are part of the structure of a water
cistern some 2 metres deep. The rest is a chaos of collapsed walls and
maze-like passages.

Descending from the fort, slipping and sliding, we see that the treacherous stones are mixed with a stratum of ancient pottery and even, in
places, with small chunks of the precious porphyry, its white-flecked
purple core standing out clearly against the more subdued colours of
the fort's building material. Just beside the fort lie the shattered remains
of a small Isis temple,[52] while a more substantial testament to the spiritual needs of the original inhabitants, a temple to Serapis, sits on a small
promontory 100 metres down the wadi. Several fallen columns and a
couple of column bases lie scattered around, but the stone itself is bright
and smooth, looking astonishingly as though it was cut only a few weeks
ago. A fallen lintel bears a dedication to 'Zeus Helios Great Serapis' and
carries the name of Rammius Martialis, which dates it to 117–19, when
he was governor of Egypt.[53]

Down on the wadi floor, five pillars ring an ancient well, now dried
up and stuffed full of rubbish and debris. On several of the pillars are
scratched stylised pictures of sailing ships, although from what era they
come is not immediately clear. The place was certainly used as a watering
hole, probably for many centuries after the Romans abandoned the mines
in the 4th century.

Who exactly provided the workforce for Mons Porphyrites and for its
sister quarries at Mons Claudianus 50 kilometres or so to the south has
been the matter of some debate. The theory that the workers were
convicts seems logical to anyone who has spent more than five minutes
in the direct sunlight of the wadi basin, but *ostraka* – discarded pot-sherds
used like notepaper – found at Mons Claudianus indicate that the workers
there, at least, were free.[54] One has to presume that the rates of pay to
attract the miners to this desolate spot must have been significantly over
the norm. They were certainly well provided for in other ways; the
remains of food found at Mons Claudianus indicate a surprisingly rich
diet, including such luxury items as artichokes, walnuts, watermelons
and oysters.

On the way to Mons Claudianus we come across a modern counterpart to the ancient quarry-workers, for the Egyptian government has
opened up mines at several points in the area to exploit the still-rich
mineral seams. He is walking to the nearest café and says it will take
him two hours to get there. Sadly we are going in the opposite direction and can offer him only water and a cigarette. By truck, the 50
kilometres still take more than two hours, for we are cutting south across
the desert roads made by the Romans and so are again caught up in a
confusing succession of switchbacks, false trails and detours to reach
our destination. Every so often we pass by a flimsy lean-to of wood or,

on occasion, of plastic sheeting propped against pillars. A few Bedouin families still live in this wilderness, but diminished rainfall over the last thirty years has made life all but impossible, and only the hardiest or most desperate still eke out a living here.

Although the name of Mons Claudianus implies that it was founded during the reign of Claudius, there is in fact no evidence of settlement before the time of Domitian.[55] The Romans came for the high quality of the white granite to be found here, exporting some of the columns as far afield as Rome itself, where they were used in the construction of Trajan's forum. The fort that guarded the village and quarries sits in the Wadi Umm Hussein, around 70 metres square, and is well preserved, its walls retaining some of the original interval towers. Inside, less is clear; a labyrinthine assortment of rooms wind through the interior, some still with the original stone slabs used as lintels for the door. The roofs, however, are long gone; they may originally have been made from rush matting, providing much-needed shade against the relentless sun.

The outline of wall foundations to the west of the fort, looking like a sun-scorched chequers board, is in fact what remains of the accommodation for those animals unlucky enough to spend their hot and thirsty lives here. To the north, up the slope that leads to the granite quarries themselves, lies a ruined Temple of Serapis. A few fallen column bases and part of the gable end of the building are all that survive, together with a part-buried altar containing an inscription by Annius Rufus, prefect of the XV Apollinaris legion, who was superintendent of the works of Mons Claudianus during the time of Trajan. It was here, in the abandoned stone, that the earliest known mention of the quarry's name was found.[56]

Up the hillside, the remains of the ramp along which the huge granite columns were brought from the quarry are visible, with metre-high cairns of stones to either side, presumably as part of a system to stop the columns rolling away uncontrollably down the ramp and onto the unfortunate camp below. Scattered around this area are more than 100 quarries, and here and there lie the remains of the workings, blocks that were left behind because they cracked during the extraction process or had other defects. Quarrying the stone involved digging trenches into the rock with hammers and picks, and then using chisels to cut wedge-holes into the granite. In one small quarry north-east of the fortress lie the remains of a monumental column, which would have been nearly 20 metres long had it not cracked during its excavation. So determined were the quarrymen to save this leviathan, however, that they used giant iron rods to staple together the cracked section, but it must have split again and they were forced to abandon it for good. Had it not shattered, it must have been destined for a truly massive structure, rivalling that of the Temple of Jupiter in Baalbek, which contains the highest surviving columns in the Roman world.[57]

From the quarry ramps there is a spectacular view over the fort and the wadi below. As the workers here seem to have been free men, they were paid between 28 and 47 drachmae a month, to encourage them to operate in such an unforgiving climate – somewhat more (but not spectacularly so) than the average civilian labourer in the country as a whole.[58] One is again struck by the sheer arid desolation of the place. Indeed, it may have been a shortage of water that caused the Romans to abandon Mons Claudianus some time in the mid-3rd century. It was certainly not the exhaustion of the granite mines, for quarrying still goes on today. Although Mons Porphyrites was probably active for at least a century longer, the cessation of this important economic activity in the Eastern Desert probably also had a connection with a decreasing level of security in the province generally, as nomadic tribes such as the Blemmyes and Nobatae to the south became increasingly emboldened in their raiding.

From Hurghada, it is a hot 240-kilometre drive south-west across the desert to Luxor that brings the convoys of foreigners to the Nile valley, its palm trees and the lush vegetation lining the river coming as a shock to incomers from both east and west. The relief must have been great in antiquity to travellers whose budgeting of food and water to sustain them marked time in days rather than the hours of today's air-conditioned tourists. It is impossible in Luxor not to be conscious of ancient Egypt and its native culture. The huge hypostyle hall of the Karnak temple, with its enormous columns and their mushroom-like capitals and the rows of sphinxes that led in a ceremonial way to the temple entrance; the huge pylon (gateway) to the Luxor temple; not to mention the funerary temples of the Valley of the Kings on the west bank of the Nile – all these (though not of course, the spectacular tomb painting that we now know was contained in pharaonic tombs such as that of Tutankhamun) would have been visible to the Roman rulers of Egypt. It is almost overwhelming, and it is little surprise that in Egypt, of all places, Roman culture and monuments – except in the very latest period – seem to hang back in the shadows, peeping out discreetly, and often deliberately blending themselves in with pre-existing temples and other buildings.

At the back of the Luxor temple lies a temple court that was converted during the late 3rd century to serve as a hall for the imperial cult, with an apse sliced into the back of the pharaonic stone. Barely visible are the remains of frescoes showing four men dressed in rich, late-Roman court costume. Beneath the coloured plaster, the earlier hieroglyphic inscriptions poke through; much was stripped away in the 19th century by souvenir-seekers, who were more interested in the earlier Egyptian layers than the Roman accretions. The modifications were probably made around 298, after the revolt of Domitianus, when Diocletian was keen to stamp his authority (and his image) on the province.

The four figures are in fact the Tetrarchs: Maximian, Galerius, Constantius I and, carrying a golden sceptre, Diocletian himself. Drawings made before the frescoes were destroyed also show an array of richly attired courtiers, with the hems of their robes beautifully decorated and wearing the *cingula*,[59] the elaborate belts that signified senior office (both civilian and military). When Diocletian travelled down the Nile (as Hadrian had before him) in 298, he passed as far as Aswan, although whether he stopped at Luxor is unclear. For the most part, the province rarely saw Roman emperors, although – as the dedication for Constantine I by a *dux* of Thebes (the Roman name of Luxor) reveals – it was as politic here as anywhere to display loyalty to the centre in as public and enduring a fashion as possible.

The principal Roman settlement in the far south of Egypt was (as it had been in pharaonic times) more than 200 kilometres upstream from Thebes, at Syene, which now largely lies under the rapidly growing city of Aswan. This far to the south, the blue strip of the Nile barely cools those sailing upon it, let alone the tired legs of those trudging the corniche beside its banks. Even the hustlers importuning passers-by to attend the Nubian market nearby (which is 'only on today, tomorrow gone') seem to do so with a weary air, calculating that too unmeasured a motion will be punished harshly by the sun's pitiless gaze. Colonisation in this region was a slow business, and the territory between here and Primis (Qasr Ibrim) some 150 kilometres further south, saw an ebb and flow of Roman control over the centuries that caused far less drama than similar adjustments elsewhere in the Empire. The strategic nature of Syene itself stemmed from its location at the first cataract of the Nile, a set of rapids that made river transportation further south impossible without a time-consuming portage to the clear water beyond the obstacle. It served as a most convenient trading centre, and a springboard for expeditions further south; and, though the Romans did maintain garrisons further into Nubia – a general region that included the lands both to the north and south of the provincial border – Syene was as far as their writ could be said to have run securely.

Almost nothing now remains of Roman Syene, although as late as 1839 the artist David Roberts reported that a Roman-era wall could be seen on a promontory on the island of Elephantine, which sits in the Nile just opposite Aswan.[60] To reach it, with its Egyptian settlement predating even that of Syene, requires a short voyage in a felucca, the traditional shallow-bottomed sailboat that plies the Nile around Aswan, whose captains' roguish airs and all-too-expected demands for extra baksheesh are one of the area's less endearing charms. The scattered remains, baking in forty-degree heat, seem to sweat a light dust that cakes both them and any visitors importunate enough to brave the midday blaze. The ancient town of Yebu, which dates from early dynastic times, covers the whole of the south of the island, and its most impressive remains are the Temple of Khnum, dating from the Middle Kingdom (around 1500 BC). Under the Roman occupation the temple was embellished by Antoninus Pius, although Roman troops who were garrisoned on the island also converted part of the area around the temple to act as barracks,[61] and in 391, under Theodosius, a portion of the precinct was converted into a church, in line with that emperor's avowed policy of closing down those pagan places of worship that still functioned.[62]

On the side of the island facing Syene lies a Nilometer down a set of restored steps. This was a device for predicting the rise of the river during its annual inundation, thereby determining the likely abundance (or dearth) of the succeeding harvest and so allowing the government to assess the amount of taxes it was likely to receive. As Pliny the Elder noted, a rise of 5.5 metres meant famine, one of 6.75 metres was pleasing, while one of 7 metres brought great delight; the highest on record was one of 8 metres during the reign of Claudius.[63]

Syene acted as the gateway to Roman Nubia. It was in this region that the only really serious threat to Roman control of southern Egypt lay under the early Empire. The kingdom of Meroë, whose base was several hundred kilometres down the Nile towards the fourth cataract, and whose culture had been strongly influenced by that of later pharaonic Egypt, was at the peak of its power in the 1st century BC and 1st century AD. Relations with its new neighbour to the north were at first quite hostile. In 29 BC, a peace treaty between the two sides established a buffer state between the first and second cataracts,[64] so that the border of Roman Egypt lay officially just south of Syene. The arrangement did not last, and in 25 BC the Meroites invaded Egypt. The Romans were finally victorious, penetrating as far as the Meroite capital of Napata, some 500 kilometres south of Aswan. In the ensuing treaty of 21 BC, which this time did largely hold, the buffer state was abolished and the border transferred further south to lie at Hieraskyaminos (Maharaqqa), at an intermediate point between the first and second cataracts.[65]

The land in this region is much poorer than in the Nile valley to the north. The cliffs of the desert plateau hem in the river, providing little space for agriculture, in contrast to the fertile flood plain that permitted such rich harvests in the lower reaches of Egypt. Between Syene and Hieraskyaminos the Romans built around a dozen settlements and forts in a region they named the Dodekaschoeonos. Much of this area, however, has been inundated by the rise in water level associated with the construction of the Aswan High Dam. This led to the creation of Lake Nasser, beneath whose waters those monuments that were not rescued and transferred elsewhere now lie.

As time wore on, the main threat to Roman control of the region came not from the Meroites, whose centre of political gravity shifted further south, but from the Blemmyes of the Eastern Desert, who exploited the power vacuum that arose. The tribe has received a generally bad press in ancient sources. Pliny the Elder, in his *Historia Naturalis*, reports that they had no heads, and that their eyes, noses and mouths were instead situated on their chests.[66] Subsequent accounts do not confirm Pliny's fantastical physiognomy, but the group remained forever just outside the imperial ken, never as menacing as the tribes of the Rhine or Danube, but posing just enough of a threat to security to make life in the south of Egypt somewhat uneasy.

The Romans' hold on the isolated positions of Hieraskyaminos and Primis was growing tenuous by the mid-3rd century and the Blemmyes launched an invasion at the time of Decius and again during Aurelian's reign, when the Empire's position in the whole of Egypt was critically endangered. At the time of Probus, a Blemmye expeditionary force captured several cities in Upper Egypt and it took a major military effort to dislodge them.[67] It was thus that Diocletian – after his victory over Domitius Domitianus in 298, and a journey to the south that included a series of punitive raids on the Blemmyes and other desert tribes – decided that Roman forces would be withdrawn from Nubia.[68]

Diocletian then tried to use the Nubians as a buffer against the Blemmyes, though the rights of the latter to travel to their traditional cult centre at the Temple of Isis at Philae were guaranteed, presumably as a means of maintaining at least some level of contact with them. Even the most persecuting of Christian emperors, such as Constantius II and Theodosius I, took no action against the Philae temple, when the idols were being overthrown all over the rest of the Empire. It was only in 532 that Justinian finally dared order the doors of the shrine to be shut, snuffing out the last spark of organised paganism in the Empire.

During the latter part of his reign, Theodosius II had been forced to take the radical step of uniting the civilian and military administrations of the province of Thebais, which included all of southern Egypt from Thebes (Luxor) to Syene (Aswan), reversing the tendency since Diocletian to keep them separate. It seems that there must have been something approaching an emergency. Indeed, it was in 450 that the cleric Nestorius wrote of the Blemmye raid that temporarily took him prisoner.[69] The same year the Blemmyes and their neighbours, the Nobatae, were defeated by the *dux* Marcianus and agreed to a peace treaty, but when one of the Roman envoys, Maximianus, died, they took this as an excuse to begin their raids anew.

Other accounts of the Blemmyes are rather sparse, but the poet and diplomat Olympiodorus of Thebes spent a few days among them in 421. The Blemmye chieftains had been so impressed by his reputation that, when they heard he was staying at Syene, they issued an invitation for him to visit in person. The poet asked the tribe's priests, who probably served at the Temple of Isis and Mandulis at Talmis, for permission to see the emerald mines about which he had heard. The Blemmye king, unfortunately, refused to allow it, and after five days Olympiodorus went on his way. His work, which survives only in fragments, also includes an account of an embassy that he accompanied to Donatus, King of the Huns, in 412–13, where he noted the excellent archery ability of the Hunnish warriors. Whether Olympiodorus was accompanied on either occasion by his pet parrot, which he writes about with fondness and which he had taught to sing sea-shanties, dance and say its owner's name, is not recorded.[70]

The temple complex at Philae, the first major archaeological site to the south of Syene and one of Egypt's most splendid relics, lay just beyond the first cataract of the Nile, and was connected to Syene by a road on the east bank, since the rapids made communication by river impossible. Close by was the legionary camp of the I Maximiana, one of the new units established under the Tetrarchs to complement the three auxiliary cohorts that had previously patrolled the area. The camp was enclosed within a protective wall that ran right the way up to Syene, defending the road from marauders. It was not a Roman system in origin, for the walled road may date from the Middle Kingdom, but it was certainly maintained at least until the 4th century AD.[71]

The complex rises up on an island in the Nile, its buildings sharply defined against the river and the searing blue of the sky. This is not in fact the original island, for that was nearly drowned by the Aswan High Dam works, and the archaeologists moved the monuments wholesale to a neighbouring one, which they then landscaped to be as close as possible to the original. It is a little smaller, however, and so the main axis of the temple was not entirely preserved.

Despite the light scatter of early-morning tourists zipping to and fro in motor launches, which rather shatter the fragile tranquillity of the place, it is still a hugely impressive complex. The fancy that the Victorian traveller Amelia Edwards said that a 'procession of white-robed priests bearing aloft the veiled ark of God' might well come round the corner is, though, just a little too whimsical.[72] The Temple of Isis, that last bastion of Blemmye paganism, is of course the most important building, entered by a vestibule constructed under Nectanebo (360–343 BC) during the 30th Dynasty, which features a striking row of columns crowned with capitals in the form of the cow-headed goddess Hathor. To the right of the main pylon, an inscription incised by Napoleon's troops on their victorious entry into Egypt in 1799 defaces the wall, but it is beyond this, in the main part of the sanctuary, that the principal Roman interest lies.

In 9 BC, Augustus permitted a small temple to be built at the north end of the island, thereby beginning the involvement of several emperors in cult worship at Philae. On its walls, Augustus himself is shown in a relief with Buto, goddess of the north. Later, Claudius ordered the erection of a temple to the minor god Harendotes, and successive additions were made under Trajan, Hadrian and as late as Diocletian's reign.

The hypostyle hall – its dark atmosphere, barely penetrated by the sun, offering a cool retreat to visitors and twittering birds alike – was partly converted into a church in Coptic times, with the remains of frescoes of Jesus and Mary just showing, together with more boldly incised crosses on the columns. In the eastern corner of the hall, an altar and a niche have been carved out, evidence that the temple was not completely abandoned in the period after the final suppression of pagan worship in the 530s, and that the adherents of the new religion commandeered it to expunge it of its (to them) demonic connections.

Just outside the main temple to the west is a small gateway overlooking the river, constructed under Hadrian (from whom it takes its popular name of 'Hadrian's gate') near the Claudian Temple of Harendotes. On it is an unusual depiction of the cataract of the Nile, opposite which Isis and Nephthys are seen presenting the two crowns of Upper and Lower Egypt to the falcon-headed sky god Horus, all quite canonical scenes and apparently uninfluenced by the new Roman benefactors, who are themselves immortalised in relief around the corner. On the eastern part of the island lies Philae's most imposing Roman structure, the Kiosk of Trajan – which remained unfinished by the time of the Emperor's death. It is an almost perfect classical-style peripteral temple, but with rather (for a Roman) anomalous acanthus-leaf capitals, its solid and angular bulk gracing a hundred posters of Philae. Inside, the walls are scored by dozens of graffiti from less-than-punctilious travellers, including one, in impeccable Latin, for Tsar Alexander I of Russia.

Off by the waterside, the ruins of a triumphal arch – just the side-entrances now staring out towards the river – represent the 'Gate of Diocletian', the last major Roman construction on the island, commemorating the emperor whose decision to pull out of Nubia and bring the frontier back to Syene left Philae in the hands of the Blemmyes. It was really only the penetration of Christianity further south into Nubia (sponsored by Theodora, Justinian's wife) that neutralised opposition from the desert tribes and permitted the final closure of the Philae temples in the mid-6th century.

It was an inscription at Philae that commemorated the Romans' furthest southward thrust from Egypt, when Caius Petronius was prefect of the province, probably in late 25 BC. Although in the end Petronius's attack on Meroë came to nothing, a curious expedition was despatched in AD 61, during the reign of Nero, consisting of a small number of the praetorian guard, including two centurions.[73] They penetrated even further than Petronius had done, first reaching the city of Meroë itself, only 150 kilometres north of modern Khartoum. On their route they saw parakeets, monkeys and rhinoceroses, and, once at Meroë, were given guides who led them south down the White Nile to an area of 'great marshes', which has been interpreted to mean an area near Malakal, more than 500 kilometres south of Khartoum. The purpose of the expedition is unclear, but there are indications in 68 that Nero had sent additional troops to Egypt to prepare for a campaign in the south, only to be forced to recall them when the revolt of Vindex broke out in Gaul.[74] To have contemplated annexing such a huge swathe of territory would probably have exceeded even the grand designs of the mercurial Nero. Whatever the reason, the little group of praetorians penetrated further into Africa than any Romans before or after them, and probably further than any other European power would reach until the Portuguese in the 16th century.

The Temple of Kalabsha (or Talmis, its ancient name) originally lay about 50 kilometres down the Nile from Philae, but since the construction of the Aswan High Dam it has sat on an island just to the south of the dam itself. The boatman who takes us there on his rather decrepit-looking motor-launch (optimistically named *Cleopatra*, for it is definitely not a thing of beauty) confides that we are the first visitors he has ferried for more than a week, as busy schedules will not permit most tourists more than a cursory look at Philae before they move on elsewhere.

The temple was cut into 13,000 blocks for its transportation north, but does not seem much the worse for it. Approached by a rather precipitous bridge with a steeply angled hump, the main pylon at the front of the temple has a noticeable tilt, leading into an open courtyard, closely set with pillars and decorated with reliefs of Horus and Thoth, the ibis-headed scribe of the gods. Although begun under Tuthmosis III in the 15th century BC, a great deal of it was constructed under Augustus (who is shown standing before Horus), with Caligula and Trajan in turn adding reliefs to the temple decorations. The open court also served as a suitably public place for inscriptions intended for a wider audience. These include one set in the wall facing the main pylon by Silko, King of the Nobatae, in about 543, boasting of his defeat of the Blemmyes.[75] Poor Silko, his inscription is almost always referred to as being in 'bad Greek', with his grammatical infelicities immortalised for all to see. Even worse for his reputation, a papyrus found at Primis (Qasr Ibrim) in the very far south of the province indicates that it was Phonene, King of the Blemmyes, who won the victory and not Silko at all.[76] On the next-door wall is a text by Aurelius Besarion, who was governor around 248,[77] in which he commands the exclusion of all pigs from the temple grounds, an injunction that conjures up a rather strange image of the situation before he had the swine chased out of the shrine. The small hypostyle hall features an image of Trajan offering sacrifice to Mandulis (the Kushite god to whom the temple is dedicated) and a beautiful series of reliefs in a small chapel at the back.

Two hundred and eighty kilometres north-west of Aswan, Kharga was known by the Romans simply as 'The Oasis'. It was the closest to the Nile valley of the settlements in the Western Desert and therefore the easiest of access. Nonetheless, it was still extremely remote and this, and the burning summer heat, made it a favourite place of exile for those who had fallen into imperial disfavour. The satirist Juvenal, who unwisely angered the rather touchy Emperor Domitian, was exiled to Egypt and seems to have spent part of his banishment in Kharga. In the mid-5th century Nestorius, the deposed patriarch of Alexandria, spent some of his years of banishment here, rather than the originally designated and substantially more comfortable place of exile at Petra.[78]

The capital of the oasis in antiquity was Hibis, where one of the most ancient buildings in the oasis, the Temple of Amon-Ra, stands, probably begun by the pharaoh Apries around 588 BC. Discovered here was the official report of a commission sent out in AD 246/9 to investigate the agricultural resources of Egypt. Addressed to Marcellus and Salutaris (the heads of the commission, based in Alexandria), it found that the majority of water sources and reservoirs in the oasis were on land that was uncultivated or had been abandoned. It was a sign, perhaps, of a contracting economy, and a hint of trouble in the oases.[79] By the mid-4th century there were indications of disturbances, with a layer of burning in the Christian buildings that had sprung up outside the Hibis temple. More incontrovertible evidence of insecurity comes in 450 when the Blemmyes invaded and carried off a large number of prisoners, including Nestorius.

Just a kilometre from the temple of Hibis, in the central part of the oasis, lies the early-Christian necropolis at Bagawat, containing hundreds of tombs grouped around a central church. It is a veritable city of the dead, set on a low sandy slope, the landscape studded with low, square blocks of mud-brick. The fancier tombs have arcaded façades and their architectural embellishments make them seem more like a monastic cloister than a graveyard. Between the mausolea run narrow lanes, accentuating the eerie feeling that somewhere, just around the corner, a brown-clad monk will walk by intoning the Coptic liturgy.

The cemetery was in use from pharaonic times, and there are tombs as old as the 6th Dynasty.[80] When the Christians took it over, they did not abandon their ancestral practice of mummification, despite the fact that the religious motivation for embalming the dead had vanished. Perhaps the early-Christian focus on the actual physical resurrection of the body touched a chord with more traditionally minded Egyptians, who considered that they had best ensure that the corpse was kept in good condition for its judgement date with the almighty. The actual graves, which were pits dug into the earth floor of the surrounding mausoleum, were, sadly, mostly robbed and ransacked long ago, but the internal decoration of several survives.

The Chapel of Peace's frescoes, faded now despite the roof and the cool, dry conditions in the tomb, depict Adam and Eve after their expulsion from the Garden, the sacrifice of Isaac and a dozen other biblical scenes. The nearby Chapel of Exodus, one of the oldest of the Christian chapels,[81] contains another wealth of beautifully crafted wall paintings crammed into the dome of a space no greater than 3 metres square. Moses is seen leading the Israelites out of Egypt, pursued by a rather dapper-looking pharaoh sporting a very fine headdress. Jonah, meanwhile, is depicted being swallowed up by the whale, which looks rather more like an irritated dragon than a sea creature. Here, in the deep desert, where temperatures regularly soar over forty degrees, the monkish artists can be forgiven for having their imaginations turned far more to fire than water.

Christianity has a very ancient pedigree in Egypt, and experienced a development all of its own. Egyptian tradition claims Saint Mark as the founder of their church, drawn by a vision to sail from Cyrene, his native town (in modern Libya), to Alexandria, where he preached for two years before the local pagans dragged him through the streets until he died.[82] It is more than likely that Christianity first took hold among the Greek-speaking Jews of Alexandria, but after this community was decimated during the Jewish revolt of 115–117 the new faith was forced to look more widely, and into the countryside, for adherents. Egypt produced more than its fair share of theologians, including one of the very earliest, Origen – whose name actually means 'Born of Horus' – who flourished in the early 3rd century and whose doctrine of the pre-existence of souls before the creation of the physical universe influenced later mysticism, but led to the eventual condemnation of his writings under Justinian in 543.[83]

Egypt suffered, too, at the time of the persecutions ordered by Decius in 250, and by Diocletian in 303. So harsh were conditions during Diocletian's Great Persecution, and so many Christians killed by the authorities, that the Egyptian Coptic Church for ever after dated its calendar, the Era of the Martyrs, from its beginning. The aftermath of the persecution led to a bitter split in the Egyptian Church, not dissimilar to the Donatist schism that simultaneously afflicted the Latin-speaking provinces further west.[84] Its root was the flight of Peter, the Bishop of Alexandria in 304, who was seeking to escape a possible death sentence for refusing to make sacrifice to the Emperor, as decreed by the persecuting imperial edicts. The more rigorist Bishop of Lycopolis,[85] Melitius, viewed this as a betrayal of the faith. Even though Peter was in fact eventually martyred in 311, Melitius established what was in effect an alternative Church, which by 327 had as many bishops as the official one. In 334, the Melitians even attempted to depose the orthodox patriarch of Alexandria, Athanasius, by accusing him of murdering a bishop named Arsenius. The patriarch, however, was able to prove incontrovertibly that the charges against him were trumped up, by having his agents seize the still-living Arsenius from his bolthole in Berytus (Beirut). Athanasius was, however, deposed by the Synod of Tyre the next year on charges – quite possibly entirely justified[86] – of having his followers beat up Melitian bishops. On and off over the next forty years he would spend fifteen years in exile, suffering no fewer than five sentences of banishment.[87]

The Melitians, meanwhile – unlike the parallel Donatist movements in the provinces of Numidia and Africa – faded away. There were quite enough Christian viewpoints competing for primacy in the Egyptian Church, with Arians and Monophysites and others all striving to present themselves as national champions in opposition to the central church authorities in Constantinople; and Melitianism, differentiated only in matters of hierarchy rather than doctrine, found insufficient room to take root in the long term.

Around 50 kilometres to the north-west of Bagawat lies Qasr Labekha, one of the chain of forts by which the Romans supervised the desert routes, this one placed strategically athwart the junction between two roads, one leading south towards the capital at Hibis, and the other to the west towards the Dakhleh oasis. Approaching on dirt roads that seem to wend aimlessly across the flat stony ground, the fort comes into sight on the prominent mound on the floor of a wadi. Beyond it, low hills and escarpments stretch red-brown fingers through the desert as far as the eye can see. From a distance the fort's high walls and massive round towers seem complete, save for the part obscured by a huge bank of sand piled up against it by the biting wind. Yet, rounding the corner, this turns out to be an illusion, and on two sides the walls are missing and the interior of the fort consists of mounds of rubble. It is, nonetheless, an impressive site, where conditions for the soldiers would have been difficult on account of the heat, but not as utterly remote as it seems, for it was just 20 kilometres to the west to the neighbouring fort of Ain Umm Dabadib (whose rectangular rather than round towers are unique in the Western Desert).[88]

In the southern portion of the Great Oasis security was provided by the large fort of Qasr al-Ghieita ('Fort of the Little Garden'), which, as was common practice in the Western Desert, was constructed around a much earlier temple, of the gods Amun, Mutt and Khans, that was built during the Persian occupation of Egypt under Darius I (552–486 BC), but was maintained into late-Ptolemaic times. More direct evidence of Roman involvement in the upkeep of the traditional Egyptian cults is provided by Tchonemyris (Qasr al-Zaiyan), a short distance to the south of al-Ghieita. Partly enclosed by a mud-brick wall, the sanctuary has something of the appearance of a small fort from the outside, but a processional way leads through to a much more obviously religious structure, a low kiosk temple, built in Ptolemaic times and dedicated to

'Amun of Hibis'. An inscription commemorates its restoration at the time of Antoninus Pius, during the governorate of Avidius Heliodorus.[89]

Right at the southern edge of the Great Oasis, beyond which to the south there is only desert, lie the temple and fort of Dush (ancient Kysis). Atop a hill the broken remains of the fort may originally date from Ptolemaic times, but it was at the very least adapted and may have been enlarged for Roman use to supervise the route that led eastwards towards the Nile at Edfu, a week's march away, and another that went southwards towards Darfur, a road that in the Middle Ages became known as the Darb al-Arbain, 'the forty days' road', after the length of time it took to traverse it, and which became a principal conduit for the slave trade.

The ground between the fort and the temple contains a scattering of building foundations, but is covered with a mass of pottery remains, from small fragments to almost complete pots, which it takes great concentration on the part of the visitor not to crunch underfoot. The view across the desert here is alluring and disturbing in equal measure, for there is nothing to break the monotony of the endless desolation, save a few minor variations in the intensity of the sand's browny-orange. The temple comes almost as a surprise, for while all else here seems to be subsiding slowly into the earth, or being ground away by the desert winds, the courtyard and hypostyle hall are oddly fresh and complete. Built under Domitian, additions were made by Trajan and Hadrian and the temple, originally for Osiris, also honoured the cult of Serapis.[90]

From the Temple at Hibis, the modern road west roughly follows the line of the traditional route from Kharga to the Dakhleh Oasis. Largely flat, the unremitting desert does not invite travellers to linger, though here and there Roman-era caravan halts existed, a reminder that ancient travellers did not have the luxury of moving from one oasis to the other within a few hours; for them it meant long, hot and thirsty days in the desert – prey, once out of the protective orbit of the nearest forts, to any passing bandit that took a fancy to their goods. Known in ancient times as the 'Small Oasis', Dakhleh – whose eastern reaches lie around 120 kilometres west of Kharga – possessed a reasonably large population supporting four major settlements, and seems to have undergone something of a boom in the early Roman period.

Once a prosperous market town, Kellis, or Asmant el-Kharab ('the ruined'), lies a kilometre down a dirt track off the main road on the eastern edge of the oasis. It looks in ever-present danger of final inundation by the fine sand that blows in from deeper in the desert, its buildings engaged in a constant game of hide-and-seek between concealment by nature and excavation by archaeologists. By the guardian's hut, partly uncovered, a series of barrel vaults seem like the roof of a bath-house. Two low rectangular structures are temples, one with small fragments of wall plaster surviving in yellows and sky-blues, but little trace of the original internal structure. In the main temple complex an inscription was discovered, dedicating it both to Tithoes, the 'Master of the Demons', and to the 'son of the divine Hadrian' – that is to say, Antoninus Pius. One wonders what the sedate and gentle Antoninus would have thought of the juxtaposition.

Nearby, over fields of pottery, abandoned for the many centuries of Kellis's settlement, lies a palaeo-Christian church, newly excavated. Already the desert has begun to reclaim it, and only part of the columns of two aisles and a small apse poke out of the sand. More visible are the remains of the oldest church in the oasis, and one of the most ancient in Egypt, built inside a Ptolemaic-era temple, and occupying around one-third of the original structure's 50-metre length. The later, lower-quality bricks stand out against the fineness of the sandstone used to build its predecessor. The church dates from the middle of the 4th century, and so, although from after the period of the Great Persecution, it is a vener-able place of worship indeed.

It was in a comparatively humble residential area that Kellis gave up its greatest and most unexpected treasure to date.[91] A large quantity of Manichaean documents from the mid-4th century have been found among the houses, including at least eighteen psalms and a number of catechisms in both Greek and Coptic. Their letters, full of phrases such as 'the members of the Holy Church', indicate that they saw themselves as a chosen elect and the true followers of Jesus Christ, in a sense the only real Christians. Other Christians most certainly did not regard the Manichaeans as in any way belonging to their number and particularly reviled them, failing to accord them the same toleration that they them-selves received after the Edict of Milan in 313. It seems that a fair proportion of the towns' populations may have subscribed to the dualist creed, but by the 4th century Manichaeism, which had arrived in Egypt via Alexandria around 260,[92] was very much a community under siege, and Kellis may have been one of its last strongholds in the province. Life there was not all about religion, however, and equally valuable papyri were found detailing a mass of financial and legal transactions, including what is possibly the last-recorded sale of a slave in Egypt, by Aurelius Psais of an unnamed girl to Aurelius Tithoes, a carpenter, in AD 362.[93]

Dakhleh in general lacks the Roman-era forts that dot the rest of the oases, but a section of the town's wall still stands, some 15–20 metres long, with 8 metres or so poking out of the sand, which must have provided some level of security for Kellis. Further exploration of the walls' internal chambers is discouraged by the nest of vipers that do service for the long-departed guards.

The largest Roman necropolis in Dakhleh lies in the west at El-Muzawakka ('the decorated hill'), which takes its name from the painted tombs of Petosiris and Petubastis, the most notable in the cemetery, and in which Petosiris is depicted dressed Roman-style, but otherwise surrounded by Egyptian funerary imagery. The key to the burial chambers has, however, been confiscated by a French archaeologist, afraid of the effect of the breath of too many casual visitors on the fragile wall paintings, and instead the guardian shows us a selection of grizzled mummies and several graves dotted around the hillside that are open to the air, and from which an embalmed hand or a mummified head sticks out, staring balefully through a sand-bleared haze at the modern intruders.

At Magoub, on the western edge of the Dakhleh Oasis, is another of its Roman treasures, once more displaying the accommodation between Roman and traditional beliefs. The temple at Deir el-Haggar (the 'monastery of stone') lies solitary at the edge of the desert, its processional way marked out with the stumps of sandstone columns and a partly reconstructed pylon. It seems every inch the late-pharaonic or late-Ptolemaic temple, but was in fact built under Nero, between AD 54 and 68. As part of the adaptation of their imperial iconography to local Egyptian traditions, the emperors' names frequently appear in temple dedication inscriptions, not in their traditional Latin style, but in the form of a cartouche containing the 'birth' name and 'throne' (or Ra) name of the ruler in Egyptian hieroglyphics. Right from the start, Augustus consented to his depiction as a traditional Egyptian pharaoh, and as the Empire consolidated its hold in North Africa, the establishment of the imperial cult acted as a substitute for the direct worship of the pharaohs that had been the norm in Ptolemaic Egypt.[94] Deir el-Haggar received imperial attention through a number of reigns, and the temple walls also carry cartouches for Vespasian and Titus.[95]

The main gateway, redecorated under Domitian, leads into a small courtyard, and thence to the main temple. The final set of columns on the approach bear a particularly distinguished graffito, that of the German explorer Gerhardt Rolfs, who visited in 1873 (and who, legend has it, made off with a great treasure after placating the temple's spirits by the human sacrifice of one of his servants).[96] The now-unroofed temple is closely decorated with hieroglyphs and faint traces of the colour of the original wall paintings. Better preserved in a small room at one end is an astrological ceiling, set against a deep-blue background; the snake-like god Geb, who represents the Earth, curls around all the other divine beings represented, including a centaur and the constellation of the giant Orion. The ceiling was painted during the reign of Hadrian, whose visit to Egypt in 130 sparked the Emperor's interest in the religious mysteries of the country, which would later be reflected in the decoration of his rural retreat at Tivoli outside Rome.

From Dakhleh, the road passes 200 kilometres north-westwards to Farafra, the most compact of the main oases, and regarded by the Romans as forming part of the 'Small Oasis' (*Oasis Parva*) together with Bahariya. From here on, extreme desert conditions begin to form weird terrains, capricious and colourful flights of fancy for those who have braved the journey this far into the wilds. The 'White Desert', possibly the remains of an ancient lake, is crusted with salt crystals that leach to the surface and make it seem as if the desert has received an impossible coating of snow. In places, the salt has accumulated into strange formations, blasted by the wind and snow, many looking like fantastic mushrooms, or boats beached far out in the sands. Further north-west there is the 'Black Desert', an area of dark, volcanic sand, which stretches for more than 100 kilometres, as if someone has very carefully and evenly sprinkled out volcanic lava from an immense shaker; to the sides of the road small conical mounds sit, for all the world like an array of cadet volcanoes.

Bahariya, 175 kilometres north-east of Farafra, comes as a welcome relief from the visual rigours of the desert, in which a glance in any direction is to be rewarded by a stern and unrelenting beauty. The oasis, first showing itself as a small fence here, a donkey cart there, and then groves of date palms and a dusty main street, was a comparatively poor relation in terms of Roman remains. All that changed in 1996 when an antiquities guard accidentally lighted upon a tomb chamber near the temple he was protecting. It turned out to be part of a huge 1st- and 2nd-century AD Greco-Roman necropolis, which might contain thousands of graves when fully excavated.

Even more extraordinary than this were the richest burials from the cemetery, of mummies encased in cartonnage – layers of plaster and fibre – and with gold leaf and semi-precious stones applied to the topmost layer. A dozen or so of them are now kept in the storehouse of the Antiquities Department in Bawiti, the capital of Bahariya. A strange and nauseating smell pervades the place, literally the stench of death, as decay and preservative chemicals mix in equally unwholesome measure. Some mummies are badly damaged from their sojourn in the tomb or excavation, the faces painted on the coffin lids collapsed into a rather perturbed or worried half-expression, while others are nearly complete, with funereally staring eyes of a more cheerful disposition.

At El-Qasr village in the centre of the oasis lies one of Roman Egypt's unlikeliest gems, a triumphal arch that may have formed part of a larger fortress, long since disappeared. When described by the British antiquarian G. Hoskins in the 1830s, it was much more complete, with a cornice, attic and other architectural features.[97] Now, even finding it is something of an achievement. Down through the narrow back streets of the village that has utterly concealed it and then into an area of palm gardens, the way is blocked by crowds of children, gently trudging donkeys, and finally by an iron gate. In order to gain access, our guide slides nimbly over an irrigation ditch and scrambles up a slippery slope that leads into one of the palm gardens. And there it sits, utterly engulfed within the village, two piers of stone, their joining arch long since fallen, one side propped up by the trunk of a date palm, as though the locals fear that it too is on the point of tumbling over. Few of the facing stones now remain, so the rubble core of the arch is exposed, slowly crumbling into the garden below. Of the winding staircase, niches and columns that Hoskins also described, there is nothing left.

A couple of kilometres to the north of El-Qasr lies a building which, though not Roman, commemorates perhaps Egypt's most famous ever ruler.[98] The temple at the small village of Qasr al-Migyhbah, probably built in the early Ptolemaic period, seems a very plain structure, a platform accessed by a short flight of steps, with walls rising to 5–6 metres. Around this lie the remains of rooms from a much larger complex. The whole is dedicated to Alexander the Great, and once had a cartouche honouring him, the only one to be found in the Western Desert (not even Siwa, much more closely associated with the Macedonian conqueror, had one). The cartouche itself, it is claimed, has been 'eroded' by the elements, but a large hole in the wall where it is said to have been looks as though it has been literally gouged away.

A monotonous and searing stretch of desert makes up the 400-kilometre, eight-hour drive west from Bahariya to Siwa, dotted with military checkpoints that aim, in the manner of a fly swatting an elephant, to choke off the smuggling trade through the Western Desert, and which provide for the security of those few travellers allowed down the military road. Siwa was perhaps the least Romanised of the oases; indeed, it had long resisted integration into the pharaonic kingdom and even now retains a way of life that is distinct from that of the Nile-valley dwellers, if now more closely linked to the centre by transportation and telecommunications than it has been at any time in its history. The people here have stronger ethnic ties with the Berber groups to the west in Libya, Algeria and Morocco. Their isolation is accentuated by the Great Sand Sea to the south, a stretch of nearly impassable dune fields, into which the army of Cambyses of Persia was swallowed in 524 BC when he tried to cross it to conquer the Siwans.[99] Herodotus claims that 50,000 men perished, doubtless something of an exaggeration, but much effort has been expended, fruitlessly, in trying to find any trace at all of the lost Persian host.

Siwa has always had something of an air of mystery about it, principally as the site of one of the ancient world's most renowned oracles, whose existence was recorded as far back as the 18th Dynasty (1550–1292 BC).[100] The most famous visitor of all was Alexander the Great, who came in 331 BC,[101] aided by miraculous desert rains, which ensured that his troops did not perish of thirst like so many before them. The accounts of his visit to the oracle vary frustratingly, but it seems that he asked if the 'empire of the world' was destined to be his, to which the priest's reply was positive. The priest is also said to have referred to Alexander as 'O pais Diou' ('the son of Jupiter'), which pleased the Macedonian despot greatly, even though it may have been an innocent mispronunciation of 'O paidion' ('My child').[102]

The Temple of the Oracle lies today a little way from the central settlement of Siwa, at the end of a palm-fringed road. Over time, the medieval settlement of Aghurmi grew around and over the remains of the temple, much of its mud-brick encrustation not being removed until the second half of the 20th century, and a good deal of it surviving today to obscure the contours of the ancient temple. The inner sanctuary, a large court, adjoined by two smaller courtyards (from which the priests are said to have whispered the responses of the god), is only about 6 x 3 metres and perches on the edge of a cliff-face down which it threatens at any moment to tumble. It is a curiously soulless place now, and it is hard to gain much sense of the awe inspired by the ancient oracle, and the power it wielded through its influence on the judgements of the ancient world's mightiest rulers.[103]

When Strabo visited in 23 BC he reported that the oracle was in a serious state of decline.[104] It was, however, clearly functioning in some form in AD 160, when Pausanias wrote that the priests and oracle were still present. Certainly, by the time of Justinian's order to close the last pagan temples, the oracle must have ceased to operate, and it may well have fallen victim to earlier waves of anti-pagan feeling, such as the bouts of temple-smashing during the reign of Theodosius I. Much earlier, in 48 BC, the Stoic politician Cato the Younger arrived in Siwa, while on the run from Julius Caesar after the death of Pompey at Pharsalus. He tried to provoke the oracle, and no doubt public opinion at home, by asking about the 'freedom of Rome'. The oracle wisely remained silent, in turn not wishing to incur the wrath of Caesar, the almost certain victor in the civil war. On the other hand, perhaps the priest foresaw the collapse of the Republic, the inauguration of the Empire and the fate of Rome under emperors such as Caligula, Commodus and Caracalla, and so his silence expressed most eloquently the amount of freedom that Romans could expect to enjoy in the future.

Once the Siwans had abandoned Aghurmi and left the Temple of the Oracle mute and unregarded, they constructed a new town called Shali, itself now a heap of crumbling mud in the centre of modern Siwa. Built of *kharsif*, a type of mud-brick made using salt, which is extremely susceptible to collapse if not maintained, it is a good example of the type of construction that native villages throughout the region would have employed. After severe rains damaged it in 1942, the Siwans left their old home to decay, a confusing maze of alleyways that, given a few decades, will subside back into the mud from which it was created.

Siwa has given rise to one of the more unsavoury spats in the history of modern archaeology. In 1995, a Greek archaeologist who had been excavating in the al-Marqi district of Siwa, some 25 kilometres from the centre, made the astonishing claim that an unprepossessing and out-of-the-way temple was in fact the location of Alexander the Great's tomb, and that inscriptions at the site for Ptolemy I, who had been one of Alexander's chief lieutenants (and went on to be ruler of Egypt), confirmed the connection with Alexander and stated that the Macedonian king had died of poisoning in Babylon. Alexander, it was claimed, had wanted to be buried near his mystical 'father'. After the finding received initial, guarded support from the Egyptian Antiquities Department, a delegation from the Greek Culture Ministry came to investigate. They concluded that the tablets found were not of Ptolemy I, that there was no mention of Alexander or poisoning, and that the temple was not even Macedonian at all.

The available ancient literary evidence all points, in fact, to Alexander being buried in the city named for him, Alexandria. The tomb, which was known as the Soma (from the Greek for 'body'), and which was mentioned by a number of ancient writers, was clearly situated near the centre of the city, and was visited by Augustus, Caligula, Septimius Severus and Caracalla.[105] Thereafter, accounts of the tomb, and knowledge of its whereabouts, gradually fade from the record. By the Middle Ages, the Arabs of Alexandria were venerating a Prophet Eskander (or

Alexander), and in the early 16th century the traveller Leo Africanus was shown a small building where Eskander was venerated.[106] From then on, visits or searches for the 'tomb' of Alexander became something of a cottage industry, with leading candidates being the Attarine mosque (the former church of Athanasius) and the mosque of Nabi Daniel, where in 1850 a Greek dragoman-interpreter named Scilitzis claimed to have seen a skeleton interred in a secret passage in the crypt, crowned with a golden diadem.[107] The search goes on, and even Venice has been touted as a possible last resting place of Alexander's mortal remains. However, the Siwan theory has generally been discounted, and the Greek archaeologist responsible for announcing the 'discovery' of the tomb there had her licence to excavate revoked.

A short drive west, as the fertility of the soil dwindles to nothing and the green splashes of the oasis seem a distant memory, lies evidence of the late-Roman phase in Siwa's history. Among cliffs dotted with tombs, and rock formations that themselves seem like giant Roman walls, a substantial settlement once stood. All that remains now is a single wall some 7–8 metres high, scarred with a triangular-shaped hole that may once have been an entrance. On the other side, two supporting internal walls may have formed part of a Doric temple some 25 metres long, which was described as being relatively intact by 18th- and 19th-century travellers. An alternative theory is that this is in fact the remains of a church.[108] Christianity came late to Siwa; its location as the centre of a great pagan oracle may have retarded the advance of the new faith, and there is little evidence of Christianisation even by the end of the 3rd century. Having long failed to accept Christianity, the Siwans gained a similar reputation for resisting the advance of Islam, and there are indications that they repulsed an Arab army as late as 708.[109] Balad al-Rum, which means 'Town of the Romans', may, therefore, have been one of the last Christian bastions in the region.

Cyrenaica

From Siwa, it is a further hot 300-kilometre drive to the mercifully cooling waters of the Mediterranean at Mersa Matruh, ancient Paraetonium. It is roughly here that the Roman province of Cyrenaica began, nowadays more normally accessed by a lonely coastal road that runs through the Second World War battlefields at El Alamein and Sidi Barrani. Cut off from Egypt by the Western Desert, and from Africa by the Syrtic Desert to its west, Cyrenaica's narrow coastal fringe failed to share in the massive prosperity of its two agriculturally rich neighbours. Even the relatively large number of secure harbours in the central part of the region provided only a limited boost, for lateral communications between them were difficult in the broken terrain.

Colonised by the Greeks as early as the 7th century, Cyrenaica had five main settlements (Cyrene, Apollonia, Teucheira, Berenice and Barca), from which it acquired its customary designation as the Pentapolis. Just as in Asia Minor, Roman involvement in Cyrenaica came about as the result of a bequest: its last ruler, Ptolemy Apion, bequeathed his kingdom to the Romans, and so they acquired it upon his death in 96 BC.[110] After some decades of muddle over the exact nature of the administration of the new territory, Cyrenaica was formally constituted as a province in 74 BC and a quaestor was despatched to govern it. After the Roman acquisition of Crete in 67 BC, the two areas were normally bundled together as a single province, an odd transmarine pairing, which must have made the life of the governor rather difficult. It was a senatorial province with no permanent legionary garrison under the early Empire.

An abortive Jewish uprising in 73 was a foretaste of much more serious things to come, as the region thrust itself unexpectedly and brutally to the forefront of imperial preoccupations in 115, with the outbreak of a much bigger Jewish revolt. This soon spread into Egypt, where the considerably larger Jewish population of Alexandria, and the closer proximity of Palestine, posed a serious challenge to the Emperor Trajan. Aggravated by long-standing ill-feeling between the Greek and Jewish populations of the Near East, a series of massacres ensued, and 220,000 Greeks are said to have perished.[111] The suppression of the revolt was bloody in the extreme, and thereafter little was heard of the Jewish population of Cyrenaica, which had previously been extremely prosperous (and numerous).

Cyrenaica was then quiet for two centuries apart from an incursion by the nomadic Marmaridae around 268, which required the intervention of the governor of Egypt to put down.[112] In the 280s or 290s, Diocletian reformed the administration of Cyrenaica, as he did in so many other areas of the Empire, dividing the region into two provinces: Libya Superior (or Cyrenaica) based at Ptolemais in the west and Libya Inferior (or Libya Sicca, 'dry Libya') to the east, with its capital at Paraetonium (Mersa Matruh). A screen of forts was constructed south of Berenice (Benghazi).[113] This outer ring of defences for the Pentapolis and signs of increased fortification in the cities[114] mark a struggle to hold back an upsurge of activity by the nomadic tribes of the desert fringe. From the 390s, Cyrenaica suffered particularly badly from the depredations of the Austuriani, a group probably originating from near the Gulf of Sirte, who had expanded their field of operations from initial raiding around Leptis Magna in 363–5. A *dux* 'of the Two Libyas'[115] had already been appointed in the 380s to organise the defence of the region, and by the 470s Cyrenaica had a *dux* of its own.

The principal city of the Greek Pentapolis was Cyrene, nearly 600 kilometres west along the coast from Paraetonium, through terrain both monotonous and forbidding. Cyrene itself has always had a reputation as a green respite from the harsh rigours of the desert; the Arabic name of the prominence on which it sits, Gebel Akhdar, means 'Green Mountain'. Founded by Dorian Greeks in the 630s BC, it was ruled for the first two centuries by kings who, confusingly, alternated between the names Battus and Arcesilaus. Conquered by Alexander the Great in 331 BC, Cyrene fell, save for a few decades of independence, to the Ptolemaic kings of Egypt, and was ruled by a cadet branch of that family from 163 BC to 96 BC.[116] After the Roman acquisition of Cyrenaica in 96 BC, control was light at first, only strengthened after the arrival of the quaestor Cornelius Marcellinus in Cyrene in 74 BC. Thereafter the city enjoyed almost two centuries of uninterrupted growth until the Jewish revolt of 115, when it suffered massive damage. Hadrian gave it the title of metropolis in 134, in recognition of its continued importance, but when the province of Cyrenaica was established, it was Ptolemais and not Cyrene that was made the capital. A severe earthquake in 262 destroyed many buildings, and another in 365 threw down the great sanctuary of Apollo.[117] For the next three centuries there was little building, even after Justinian's reconquest of North Africa had restored a modicum of security, and the city then began a rapid decline into an abandoned backwater.

The first glimpse of the site for modern visitors in the extensive necropolis, a mass of broken stonework and tumbledown tombs that populate the whole of the hillside approach to Cyrene. A few of them retain their pedestals, whilst of others only a sarcophagus survives, creating the eerie and melancholy feeling that something has been sorting through them in search of an unknowable treasure. Close to the site entrance lie the imposing ruins of the Temple of Zeus, with two rows of enormous Doric columns set about its more than 70-metre-long sanctuary. Inside, part of a Latin inscription survives commemorating its partial restoration under Augustus, though, like much of the city, it was destroyed in the Jewish revolt of 115.

The *agora* of Cyrene is a large open square surrounded on two sides by a colonnade, which was then adapted to be a forum in Roman times. The ruinous remains of an altar at one end probably come from a temple built to honour the imperial family during the reign of Tiberius. On the eastern side of the square was erected a victory monument to celebrate Octavian's triumph at the Battle of Actium in 31 BC, which led to his mastery of North Africa (and the rest of the Roman world). Here, so close to Egypt, the battle and its aftermath must have had a particular resonance. The founder of the city, Battus I, was by tradition buried in this area also, and what was believed to be his tomb still survives, down a short flight of steps, with a triangular-shaped roof that has an archaic, almost Mycenaean feel, and which marked a place already ancient by the time the rest of the monuments in the forum were built.

To its east lies the most impressive of the private residences excavated in the city, known as the House of Jason Magnus. Dated to the reign of Commodus, it was owned by an influential priest of Apollo, who also held a number of other public positions, including that of gymnasiarch (the magistrate in charge of public works, who would have been expected to lavish a fair amount of his own personal wealth upon them). Its main surviving feature is a mosaic of the Four Seasons, which gathers dust under a rather unattractive metal protective roof, but the rest of the house, with lovely marble pavements, sections in *cipollino* and yellow marble alternating across an area some metres square, speaks of vast wealth and an unabashed desire to display it.

The road that runs alongside Jason Magnus's house was one of the most prestigious in the city, known as the Skyrota, bordered by a colonnade bearing statues of Hercules and Hermes, alternating at each new column: the former a stout, almost portly hero bearing a club that he seems rather too unfit to carry; the latter a more elegant youth who appears almost ashamed of his proximity to his chubby companion. Alongside the street lie several of the city's five theatres; to one side a very ruinous one, a little beyond it a small gem of an *odeon* for more intimate performances.

Cyrene also contains the normal complement of baths, basilicas and other public buildings appropriate for a city of its wealth and position. Undoubtedly the most impressive of these is the sanctuary of Apollo, approached by a steep flight of steps, which lead down into a spring and fountain dedicated to the god. At the entrance to the cave from which the spring issues, a series of Greek inscriptions can still be made out in his honour. Just beyond, the temple itself has several columns standing and marble slabs laid around, which may have been used for sacrifices. Another fountain for Apollo sits adjacent, made up of two lions, one of which is being strangled and out of whose mouth the water issues.

Cyrene, like many North African towns, succumbed relatively early to the spread of Christianity, after which its new monuments were churches rather than temples or theatres. During the 6th century, two Christian basilicas were constructed in the city centre, whilst a large cathedral was built at the eastern end of the town, although this was not included in the new circuit of walls built in Byzantine times.

Cyrene's most famous and unlikely cleric was Synesius, who was born in the city in 370 and retained close ties with it throughout his career. Close to the house of Jason Magnus lie the ruins of the home of Synesius's friend Hesychius, who was president of the provincial council at the start of the 5th century.[118] As a member of the provincial aristocracy, Synesius would have been expected, along with his peers, to serve on the city council. He received his higher education in Alexandria, and became a pupil of the eminent female philosopher Hypatia, who would later be torn apart by a Christian mob in the city.[119] He must have performed well in his studies, for around 397 he was selected to participate in an embassy from the cities of the Pentapolis, which was to present at court the Cyrenaican cities' *aurum coronarium*, a 'gift' due from the provinces every five years of each imperial reign to honour the Emperor's reaching such an auspicious milestone.[120] By the late 4th century the gift had become an onerous due, and the embassy in which Synesius participated was also intended to plea for a remission from Emperor Arcadius of the general taxation that Cyrene owed. He stayed in the city for four years, only returning home in 401, having composed a treatise *On Kingship*, which was intended for presentation to Arcadius himself.[121]

Synesius returned home, got married and settled into the comfortable life of a provincial aristocrat, taking time off to compose a selection of philosophical treatises heavily influenced by Neoplatonism.[122] As the security situation in Cyrenaica deteriorated, with the increasing frequency of raids by the nomadic Austuriani from the desert fringes, so Synesius became increasingly involved with the defence of Cyrene. In 410, however, he was proclaimed Bishop of Ptolemais, a settlement near his native city, at the behest of Theophilus, the patriarch of Alexandria.[123] It was by no means uncommon for a provincial notable with no previous experience of church leadership to be elevated to the episcopacy. Often, local citizens would take the initiative themselves, seeking to co-opt the network of influences possessed by an influential and successful secular noble and to retain or divert them to the protection of their home town. The phenomenon became particularly prevalent in the later 4th century, when traditional civic leaders seemed to wane in authority, so that, backed by the growing power and geographical reach of the Church, bishops might be more effective and activist guardians of local interests. Such was the fate of Saint Ambrose at Milan and Saint Augustine at Hippo, both of whom were at first most unwilling prelates.

As a condition of accepting the position, Synesius extracted a concession from Theophilus that he would be permitted to retain his personal beliefs about whether or not the soul had been created, and whether the next life meant the literal resurrection of the bodies of the deceased[124] – areas where his Neoplatonist tendencies would normally have led to his being labelled a heretic – as long as his sermons contained a leavening of more orthodox interpretations. Synesius continued to be a tireless advocate for Cyrenaica, organising stout resistance against the depredations of the Austuriani. His letters, many of which survive, recount his standing guard on one occasion on the walls of nearby Ptolemais, awaiting the anticipated arrival of one such raid.[125] However, evidence of any committed conviction to Christianity on an emotional level is sparse indeed in his writings, and so his career acts as a fascinating insight into the transition during late antiquity from a Christianity that was beleaguered, yet fierce in the depth of its belief, to one that became increasingly bureaucratised and subsumed into a parallel hierarchy of power.

Ptolemais lies about 75 kilometres west along the coast road from Cyrene. The settlement, although founded in the 7th century BC, only became really prosperous under Ptolemy III (246–221 BC), who refounded it. It was not until the reign of Diocletian that it became an administrative centre, when it was selected to be the capital of the new province of Libya Superior (or Cyrenaica), thereby promoting it over Cyrene, which had traditionally been the pre-eminent city. Though hugely evocative, Ptolemais is only partly excavated and the approaches are hedged about by the broken-down stone houses of a settlement that grew up here during the Italian colonial occupation of Libya, many of them incorporating the odd arch or column from the ruins of the city and now inhabited by more recent migrants from sub-Saharan Africa.

The museum, among its collection of relics discovered on the site, contains a copy of the Price Edict of Diocletian, a failed attempt by the Emperor to control the raging inflation that was endangering the Empire's prosperity. Published in 301, it sets the maximum prices permitted for a thousand different commodities, as well as fixing wages for labourers and skilled artisans. Its preface expresses exasperation with the 'uncontrolled madmen' whose avarice fleeces the honest citizens of the Empire.[126] Tellingly, the Emperor complains that soldiers are separated from their pay and donative within a single day, so high are the price levels set by the profiteers. Diocletian's edict portrays an idealised world in which a labourer would earn 20 denarii a day, enough to buy himself a couple of pounds of meat or sufficient grain for his family.[127] Of course, since the level that the Emperor sought to impose on prices was probably considerably lower than that prevailing in the marketplace, the new policy served only to throttle the supply of goods that producers were no longer willing to sell, and so it was quietly dropped.[128]

Ptolemais contains several Roman triumphal arches along its *decumanus maximus*, including one dedicated for Constantine, which would originally have been a triple-arch, with two side-ways for pedestrians, and which was made up of twelve columns of black marble that lie strewn about nearby. The *decumanus*, known as the 'Via Monumentale' by the Italian excavators, is littered all the way with a scatter of broken columns and the fragments of Greek inscriptions. The level of the pavement during Byzantine times is clearly visible atop the original paving stones. The prosperity of the town, even at this late stage, is indicated by a set of 6th-century baths, with a large *frigidarium* whose ruins survive nearby, with some of the cracked marble paving still remaining *in situ*, including fine, deep-green-veined *cipollino*.

Around 200 metres down a subsidiary *cardo* lie the solid ruins of a 5th-century structure known as the 'Fortress of Athanasius', named for the eminent Bishop of Alexandria. Next door in an unexcavated building, mosaics are clearly visible under the soil, in black and white, including the indistinct outline of a flower just waiting to be dug up. All around the site, indeed, lie large chunks of tesserae that have broken away from unconsolidated mosaics, as Ptolemais gradually decays away into nothingness.

The cisterns of Ptolemais are among its most impressive monuments. No fewer than seventeen have been unearthed, many of them built during Roman times or adapted from Hellenistic predecessors. The dividing level between the two eras, with the upper portions (the Roman) built in brick and cement, is clearly visible, and the cavernous vaults would have enabled the city to hold out for some time in case of siege or drought. By the 640s and the advent of the Arabs, cities such as Ptolemais were scarcely contested, as the circuit of their walls was too large to be held by the overstretched garrison of the province. At the very end, the governor retired to Tocra (Teucheira), about 40 kilometres further west, a comparatively modest settlement, but one in which he thought (incorrectly) he might be able to resist.[129]

One hundred and twenty-five kilometres to the west of Ptolemais, along the deceptively green coastline, Berenice is the rather more romantic name of modern Benghazi in Libya. Its original and even more evocative designation was Euhesperides, the name given it by the founding Greek fathers some time around 540 BC to evoke the mythical

Alleged column of Saint Simeon, Saint Simeon's monastery, Syria

Temple of the Standards, Palmyra, Syria

Walls of Resafe, Syria

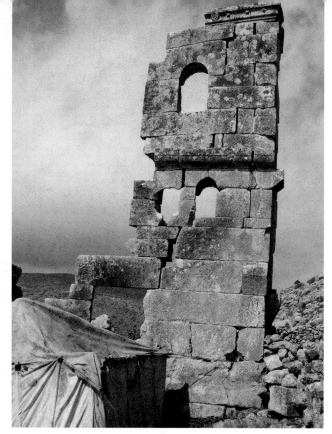

Ruined church, Kaprokera (Burj Haidar), Syria

The theatre, Cyrrhus (Nabi Khouri), Syria

The Valley of the Tombs, Palmyra, Syria

Colonnade of the *decumanus maximus*, Palmyra, Syria

Theatre stage and backdrop, Bostra, Arabia

Colonnade of the *cardo maximus*, Gerasa (Jerash), Arabia

The Oval Piazza, Gerasa (Jerash), Arabia

Dajaniyah auxiliary fort, Arabia

Tomb façades at Petra, Arabia

Ed-Deir ('the Monastery'), Petra, Arabia

'Pompey's Pillar', Alexandria, Aegyptus

Qasr Labekha fort,
Kharga Oasis, Aegyptus

Fresco of the Tetrarchs,
the Luxor temple, Aegyptus

Palaeo-Christian church,
Kellis (Asmant el-Kharab),
Dakhleh Oasis, Aegyptus

Fort at Mons Claudianus, Aegyptus

Abandoned granite columns in quarry,
Mons Claudianus, Aegyptus

Remains of triumphal arch,
El-Qasr, Bahariya Oasis,
Aegyptus

Kiosk of Trajan, Philae,
Aegyptus

Temple of Zeus, Cyrene, Cyrenaica

The Sanctuary of Apollo and lower town, Cyrene, Cyrenaica

The amphitheatre,
Thysdrus (El Djem),
Africa Proconsularis

The Severan arch,
Leptis Magna,
Tripolitania

Modern bronze sculpture
of Philaeni brother, Madina
Sultan, Cyrenaica

Punic tophet, Carthage,
Africa Proconsularis

Ras al-Ghoul fort, Tripolitani

Cuicul (Djemila),
Numidia

Garum vats, Cotta,
Mauretania Tingitana

'Arch of the Basilica',
forum of Banasa,
Mauretania Tingitana

Castellum Tidditanorum
(Tiddis), Numidia

Thamugadi (Timgad), Numidia

western paradise. It is a place full of fabulous connections, for a few kilometres to the north of Benghazi, near the current Libyan Military Academy, lies the site traditionally identified as the beginning of the River Lethe,[130] one of the rivers of the Underworld whose amnesiac draught caused the shades of the dead to forget the cares and triumphs of their former life. Its alleged location was on the edge of the Sebka es-Selmani lagoon, which dried up gradually in antiquity, leading in 246 BC to the moving of the settlement closer to the sea. Benghazi, now Libya's second-largest city and a bustling port, combines fading Italian colonial architecture with a powerfully fetid miasma in the vicinity of the waterfront, but there is precious little in the way of vestiges of its antique past.

Ptolemy III renamed the city for his wife Berenice II in the 3rd century BC. In true Ptolemaic style, she had fabulously unhappy relations with her family. Her mother, Apama (the wife of Magas, King of Cyrene), had set her heart on marrying the young Berenice off to Demetrios the Fair, grandson of Ptolemy I. As ill-luck would have it, Demetrios was not nicknamed the 'Fair' for nothing, and Apama herself fell madly in love with the young prince. On discovering the affair, the sixteen-year-old Berenice had Demetrios put to death, while sparing her mother, who, it must be presumed, resolved firmly never again to mess with her daughter's boyfriends. The city was badly damaged by the Vandals in the 5th century, and, although refortified under Justinian, the brittle hold of the Byzantine authorities had not solidified into sustainable control and prolonged prosperity before it succumbed to Arab invaders in 641–2.

The traditional boundary between the territories of Cyrene and Carthage – the great rival of the Greeks for control of the North African coast – lay at a place named Arae Philaenorum ('the altars of the Philaeni'), somewhere along the south-eastern coastline of the Gulf of Sirte. Legend related that, in order to settle the quarrel between the two cities about where their border lay, it was agreed that two pairs of athletes would set out from their respective home cities and run towards the other; the frontier would be set wherever they met. The Philaeni brothers, the representatives of Carthage, reached much further than the halfway point between the cities, and the Cyrenaicans complained that they had cheated. In response, the Philaeni offered to be buried alive if their run, and the point it had reached, was acknowledged to be legitimate.[131] Their sacrifice on behalf of their mother city was commemorated by an altar, and the spot was, indeed, ever after accepted as the border between Cyrenaica and the Carthaginian lands, becoming the frontier of the Roman province of Africa (and subsequently of Tripolitania).

The precise position of the Arae Philaenorum is unknown,[132] but it certainly lay in the central or eastern sector of the Gulf of Sirte. Undaunted by the problem of its precise location, the Italian dictator Mussolini built a commemorative arch some 40 kilometres west of El Agheila. It was his dream to reconstitute the Roman Empire, or as much of it as his German ally Hitler would permit him, and the mimicking of Roman architectural styles formed a part of his grandiose vision. The new construction, which resembled a high imperial triumphal arch, spanned the coastal road from 1936 until its demolition by the Libyan regime of Colonel Qaddafi in 1973, and was wittily dubbed 'Marble Arch' by the British troops who successively advanced, retreated and advanced again beneath it during the Second World War.

The new Arae, or its remains, is situated in a modest museum near Madinat Sultan, a small jerry-built coastal settlement. Two bronze figures lie in the courtyard, Italian Fascism's representation of the Philaeni brothers, naked, muscular and with expressions both tortured and triumphant at the knowledge that their glorious sacrifice also signifies a terrible death. Lying abandoned in a field, partly overgrown by tiny thorn bushes, are parts of the arch, with the figure of Mussolini taking a salute clearly visible, and representations of the principal buildings of Rome. A frieze of Mussolini shows the *fasces*, the Roman symbol representing the power of magistrates to impose the death sentence, while an inscription proclaims that this is a 'stage in our journey to march in peace towards tomorrow'.[133] At least in its ruination, Mussolini's arch has reached some equality with the broken Roman monuments elsewhere in Africa, but his new Roman Empire lasted but a decade before the Allies swept him out of Libya in 1943.

Africa

Approximate limit of Carthaginian control

Roman boundary under Augustus, c. 20 BC

Roman boundary, 1st and 2nd centuries AD

Approximate extent of greatest Roman control, c. AD 225

¤ Legionary fortress

200 miles

400 kms

Mediterranean

Sea

Sicily

Malta

CYRENAICA

Bardia
(*Bardiya*)

Antipyrgos
(*Tobruk*)

Cyrenaica

Arae Philaenorum

Fossa Regia

Hippo
Regius

Utica

×*Tricamarum*

×*Ad Decimum*

Carthage

Tunis

Thugga (*Dougga*)

Hadrumetum

Mactaris
(*Mactar*)

Leptis Minor

Thysdrus (*El Djem*)

Cirta
(*Algeria*)

Madauros

Ammaedara ¤

Theveste ¤

Kairouan

Sufetula
(*Sbeitla*)

AFRICA

PROCONSULARIS

Tacapae (*Gabes*)

Ad Maiores

GAETULIANS

Cidamus
(*Ghadames*)

Ras al-Ghoul

Sabratha

Oea (*Tripoli*)

Leptis
Magna

TRIPOLITANIA

Gheria
el-Garbia

Gholaia
(*Bu Ngem*)

GARAMANTES

G e b e l

CHAPTER 10

Africa

It was at Megara, a suburb of Carthage, in the gardens of Hamilcar. The soldiers whom he had commanded in Sicily were having a great feast to celebrate the anniversary of the battle of Eryx, and as the master was away, and they were numerous, they ate and drank with perfect freedom.
                                        Gustave Flaubert, *Salammbô*[1]

It is a considerable irony that the strongest common thread running through Roman Africa is its previous occupation by the Carthaginians, Rome's most dangerous opponents in its earliest expansion in the western Mediterranean. From the Arae Philaenorum in the east, Carthage's writ ran along the coastal strip of Tripolitania, encompassing the rich trading cities of Leptis Magna, Sabratha and Oea (now modern Tripoli in Libya), through to the richer agricultural lands of present-day Tunisia, coming to a halt at the edge of the Algerian plateau, where opposition from native Numidian tribes prevented their further expansion.[2]

The occupation of this territory was Rome's first truly imperial venture. Although the defeat of the great Carthaginian general Hannibal in the Second Punic War (218–201 BC) brought Rome lands in Spain and the Balearics, Africa remained stubbornly under the rule of Carthage. It took until the Roman victory in the Third Punic War (149–146 BC) for them to establish a permanent military presence on the southern shores of the Mediterranean for the first time.

The land the Romans had now acquired was a very varied one, characterised by a fertile strip along the coast, backed by a series of mountain ranges, known in Libya and the east as the Jebel, and behind these the plateau of the Sahara, which in places on its edges permits limited agriculture but, further south, descends into the great sand plains of the deep desert, where only occasional oases allow anything like a settled form of life. In the 'pre-desert' areas between the coastal strip and the desert plateau, semi-nomadic groups continued throughout the Roman period to engage in their age-old practice of transhumance, by which their families and flocks would be moved northwards in late spring to more clement pastures and then southwards in the winter as the bitter heat of the summer abated. The central core of the province, which included Carthage, was much richer, with a broader agricultural hinterland that covered much of modern Tunisia, and possessed a much denser network of urban settlements.

The Roman *limes* in Africa, therefore, is not characterised by long fixed barriers as in Britain, river frontiers as in much of Europe, or even dense networks of forts as in Syria or northern Arabia; the topography of the land could simply not support this. Instead, the Romans concentrated on providing security for the principal settlements on the coast and, inland, on controlling and funnelling the movements of nomadic groups. The viable routes that possessed sufficient water resources were few, and so, throughout most of the Roman period, the whole area west of Egypt was controlled by but a single legion (the III Augusta), together with supporting auxiliary units.[3]

This new province became known as 'Africa', and acted as the nucleus from which Roman territory expanded, surprisingly slowly, over the course of 300 years, until it reached its final extension into the fringes of the Sahara Desert during the reign of Septimius Severus. The frontiers of this first province were defined by a ditch (which became known as the *fossa regia*) dug on the orders of Scipio Aemilianus, the victor in the Third Punic War.[4]

The Roman civil wars of the late Republic brought a further expansion of its territory, as another slice of land was obtained from Numidia to the west, when the Numidian king Juba I chose to ally himself with Pompey instead of Caesar. Two years after his patron had been defeated at Pharsalus in 48 BC, the rump Pompeian forces, including Juba's Numidians, were smashed by Caesar at Thapsus[5] (10 kilometres east of Moknine in modern Tunisia). In the aftermath of this disaster, the eastern part of Numidia was annexed, the new territory being dubbed Africa Nova, to distinguish it from Africa Vetus ('Old Africa'), the existing Roman province.

After Augustus became Emperor in 27 BC, Africa fell amongst those provinces allocated to the Senate, indicating that it was not really viewed as an active frontier region that required a substantial garrison (and therefore direct rule by the Emperor). The two provinces of Africa Vetus and Africa Nova were joined together and assigned to the rule of a proconsul, an official appointed by the Senate. This became known thereafter (until its reorganisation under Diocletian) as Africa Proconsularis. The coastal cities of Tripolitania, which had previously existed in a kind of semi-autonomous state, were now more firmly incorporated into the province. Africa Proconsularis then remained securely in Roman hands, save for the revolt of Tacfarinas in AD 17. Like so many rebellions under the early Empire, this was led by a man who had served as a Roman auxiliary. It took eight years, and a succession of disasters, before the Romans adapted themselves to his guerrilla tactics and Tacfarinas was captured and killed by Publius Dolabella in AD 24.

The security of Africa Proconsularis was greatly enhanced by the annexation in AD 40 of the neighbouring kingdom of Mauretania to the west (which was divided into the provinces of Numidia and Mauretania).[6] The frontier then gradually moved southwards, particularly under Septimius Severus, who ordered the occupation of a string of forward positions deep into the desert, such as Gholaia (Bu Ngem), Gheria el-Garbia[7] and Cidamus (Ghadames) in Libya. Although these advanced positions were largely evacuated at the time of the general imperial crisis of the mid-3rd century, and the coastal cities (deprived of this buffer) began to suffer more from nomadic raids, Africa was one of the most secure regions of the Empire throughout the 4th and early 5th centuries, providing vital revenues and supplies of grain to the beleaguered central administration in Italy. Around 303, Diocletian gave the final administrative form to the Roman possessions in Africa, when he subdivided Africa Proconsularis into Zeugitana (northern Tunisia), Byzacena (southern Tunisia) and Tripolitania (western Libya, including Leptis Magna).

Yet North Africa slipped out of Rome's grasp in the 420s, falling victim to a massive migration by the Vandals. Having broken through the Roman *limes* on the Rhine in 405–6,[8] they pushed through Gaul and on into Spain. Alarmed at the loss of control of such large swathes of territory to the Vandals and their Alan allies, the Roman government had invited the Visigoths to help re-establish central control. In 417/18, the Alans suffered a massive defeat,[9] after which they ceased to be an effective independent political force, and the Vandals – whose Siling sub-group had received similar treatment at the hands of the Visigoths – faced being squeezed into oblivion. It was a particular stroke of luck, therefore, when the power struggle between Aëtius and Count Boniface[10] led, in 429, to the latter's inviting Gaiseric, the Vandal king, to cross over to Africa. Gaiseric did not confine himself to despatching a few hand-picked troops, but instead ferried over – according to Victor of Vita[11] – the whole Vandal nation, some 80,000 men, women and children.

The barbarians swept eastwards through North Africa, and Boniface, by now reconciled with Galla Placidia, sought in vain to persuade them to leave. By summer 430 they had reached the gates of Hippo Regius, blockading the citizenry, including the city's bishop, Saint Augustine, inside its gates. The eminent theologian's principal work, *On the City of God*, is intimately connected to the travails of the later Roman Empire, for it concerns the relationship between Christianity and a secular society, meditations inspired by the fall of Rome to the Goths in 410. As the preface puts it, 'For to this earthly city belong the enemies against whom I have to defend the city of God'.[12] Augustine's City of God remained intact, but the wordly city of Hippo was devastated after the Vandals finally took it in 431 following an eighteen-month siege. Augustine, perhaps mercifully, had died the previous August.

Gaiseric continued to expand the area under his control, until in 435 the Roman government accepted the inevitable and recognised his possession of the less desirable territories of Mauretania (in the far west of North Africa) in exchange for leaving the agricultural heartland of Numidia and Africa alone. The respite lasted for just four years, and in 439 Gaiseric besieged Carthage, taking it with relative ease.

It was a disaster of considerable proportions. The central government's access to grain imports from North Africa was cut off at a stroke. Considering that the grain fleets from Egypt had, since the 4th century, been supplying Constantinople rather than Rome, the ability of the Western imperial authorities to supply the urban populace with the traditional free dole of grain or bread was severely impaired.[13] In addition, the taxation revenues from North Africa dried up. By now Britain had seceded from the Empire, almost all of Gaul save the south was lost, and the imperial government's hold on Spain was precarious in the extreme. With its financial base so weak, Rome was left struggling to marshal the resources necessary to take back the one province that might have saved it.

Understandably, the feeble emperors who oversaw the final collapse of imperial administration in the West looked to their Eastern colleagues for assistance. The prestige of the Constantinople government had itself been dented by Gaiseric's progressive seizure of control over the western Mediterranean – he took Corsica and the Balearic Islands in 456, followed by Sardinia in 468[14] – but the Vandal sack of Rome in 455 was an affront that they could not long leave unavenged. A fleet that was sent in 442 to attempt a reconquest had proceeded no further than Sicily, but another more serious effort was made by Leo I in 468.[15] This was the Empire's largest military effort for decades, comprising more than a thousand vessels, but the Vandals trapped and sank the majority in Carthage harbour by sending fire-ships against them. It was a naval catastrophe on a par with the debacle on land ninety years earlier against the Goths at Adrianople.

In 474, Zeno accepted reality and recognised Vandal control over North Africa. An agreement in 442 had sanctioned the occupation of Carthage in exchange for renewed Roman control over Mauretania,[16] but the imperial government had never reasserted itself in these poorer, western regions of North Africa. Zeno's move to embrace the Vandals as allies therefore made some strategic sense in heading them off from further moves north into the Italian peninsula or eastwards towards Cyrenaica or even Egypt.

The Vandal period of rule in Africa, which extended for almost a century, did not mark, at least on the surface, a dramatic break with the preceding administration. Social ranks such as *illustres* and *clarissimi* continue to be mentioned in Vandal legislation, while in the 480s a *proconsul Carthaginis*, a certain Victorianus of Hadrumentum, is recorded, and the poet Dracontius composed verses very much in the spirit of those that had praised the last emperors.[17]

The Vandal kings set to enjoying the luxuries that a well-developed and rich province could provide. Indeed, Procopius relates that they became so corrupted by luxury (and, in particular, by baths) that their martial spirit was diminished, a key factor in their feeble defence of the province once a Byzantine counter-stroke finally came.[18] At a more humble level, the nature of rural settlements during Vandal times has been revealed by the Albertini tablets, a collection of some forty-five wooden tablets discovered in 1928 in an earthenware pot around 60 kilometres west of Gafsa, near the border between modern Algeria and Tunisia. They date from 493–6 and deal principally with land ownership and the sales of fields. Critically the tablets, which are all written in Latin, make no mention of Vandal names and seem to indicate a thriving agricultural settlement in which there is no obvious evidence of rural decline. They also demonstrate at least a reasonable persistence of literacy into the period of Vandal rule.[19]

In religious policy there was a more definite change, for the Vandals were Arians, espousing a heterodox view of the nature of Christ's humanity[20] that was particularly prevalent amongst those of Rome's barbarian neighbours who had been converted to Christianity. Catholics suffered at best discrimination, with the Catholic see of Carthage being left vacant from 440 to 454 and 457 to 481,[21] and at worst persecution, as when Gaiseric's son Huneric issued edicts against Catholics in 483 and 484. Huneric, however, was married to Eudocia, the daughter of Valentinian III, so that subsequent Vandal kings had a family link to the house of Theodosius, and blood ties to the wider Roman Christian world.

It was this marriage alliance that was to be the Vandals' undoing. For after more than half a century of peace with the Eastern Empire, the deposition by Gelimer in 533 of Huneric's son, Hilderic – who was seen by the Vandal elite as favouring the Catholic, 'Roman' variant of Christianity as opposed to their own Arian creed – provided Justinian with a pretext to intervene.[22] A force of more than 15,000 infantry and cavalry (very large by 6th-century standards) was sent to Africa, under the command of Belisarius.

By ill-chance, Gelimer had sent most of his own fleet and best men to Sardinia to put down a revolt there, and, after the defeat of his army ten Roman miles from Carthage, at a place named Ad Decimum,[23] Vandal resistance folded. Following a further defeat in December at Tricamarum (around 25 kilometres west of Carthage), Gelimer fled to a mountainous refuge even further to the west, but was starved into submission in spring 534 after a three-month siege. He was carted off to Constantinople to grace Justinian's triumph there, and on prostrating himself before the Emperor, exhibited his biblical knowledge and his own take on the transience of earthly power by quoting the Book of Ecclesiastes: 'Vanity of Vanities, all is vanity'.[24]

Hilderic's children received pensions and were sidelined; the victorious Belisarius got a consulship, but was replaced in his command by Solomon; and newly reconquered North Africa settled into prolonged and debilitating border skirmishing with confederations of Moorish tribes that had emerged during the time of Vandal rule. The Byzantine position was hardly strengthened by a law of 534, which permitted those who had had their estates confiscated by the Vandals to regain their property, thus at a stroke alienating the many soldiers who had taken Vandal wives and who had hoped to acquire the land themselves.[25] Although Solomon inflicted a pair of stinging defeats on the Moors in 535, much of Mauretania, save Iol Caesarea, remained wholly outside the control of the Byzantine government.

Over time, the administration of North Africa seemed to have no other purpose than raising the requisite taxation revenues to pay for its own prolongation, and came to take on more the aspect of a military occupation than a civilian government. The Moorish tribes (on fighting whom the Byzantine authorities expended much of their diminished resources) had had centuries to establish themselves. In many areas they had taken responsibility for defending the frontier in the 4th century and, as the Romans evacuated territory or were forced out of it, they occupied the land and saw no good reason to cede it either to the Vandals or to the newly arrived 'lawful' Byzantine conquerors. By the 530s, under such chieftains as Antalas in Byzacena,[26] they posed a well-organised and formidable challenge to the Byzantine authorities. Despite ephemeral successes and intermittent challenges, they were never really overcome, and it is telling that what resistance there was to the Arab invaders in the 7th century came from Moorish or Berber confederacies.

This powerful Moorish presence, coupled with the resumption of war with Persia in the 540s and the consequent division of resources, meant that any further attempt to recapture more of the lost western provinces would be impossible. A devastating outbreak of plague further sapped the vitality of the Eastern Empire (nearly killing Justinian himself), while much of the latter part of his reign was mired in religious controversies and a last-ditch attempt to impose the orthodoxy of the Council of Chalcedon on an increasingly unwilling Monophysite population of Syria and Egypt.[27]

In Africa, as further east in Egypt, there was a very limited store of support for the central government and its representative, the exarch, who, combining civil and military authority, ruled over his precarious realm from the coastal safety of Carthage.[28] After the Arab invasion of Cyrenaica and Tripolitania in 642, it was clear that Zeugitana, Byzacena and Numidia (the provinces into which Diocletian had divided the old Africa Proconsularis) would be next. The exarch Gregory, appealing to sentiments of local self-help, declared himself Emperor in 646 and moved his capital inland to Sufutela (Sbeitla), near the probable line that any invasion would take. It was a purely African usurpation, as Gregory made no attempt to move against Constans II in Constantinople. It was also futile, because the very next year Abdallah ibn Saad's Muslim army swept west, annihilating Gregory's forces. The exarch himself died in a desperate defence of Sufutela, while his daughter, Yasmina, captured by the victorious Arabs, is said to have committed suicide by hurling herself from the camel on which she was being carried back to Arab-held Egypt.[29]

By the 660s, the Byzantine authorities had re-established control over the north-western tip of their former territory, although the rest was largely abandoned to Berber tribal chieftains. The attempt by Constans II (641–68) to reassert religious orthodoxy by the issuing of the *Typos*[30] – which sought to avoid theological controversies associated with Monothelitism[31] by forbidding the open discussion of quite how many wills Christ might have had – did little to win the loyalty of local Christian tribes, who were more confused or outraged than reassured by the changes. In the 660s, the Arab raids were renewed on a larger scale, and in 669 a great army under Uqba took most of Tripolitania and Byzacena,[32] founding a new city at Kairouan (south-west of modern Tunis) to secure Muslim control over the new lands and ensure that the Byzantines could not use Carthage as a bridgehead to take it back.

The final years of Byzantine control over Africa are a story of successive local revolts against the Arab advance; the exarchs themselves did
almost nothing to salvage the remains of the province. In 683, Uqba
undertook a dramatic and risky expedition westwards into Mauretania
and as far as the Atlantic. On his way back he was ambushed and killed
at Thabudeos by a Berber army under Kusayla, who had emerged as the
leader of a powerful tribal confederacy, and whom Uqba had previously
had imprisoned.[33] Kusayla's army then pressed their advantage and drove
the Arabs out of Kairouan.

For three years the Berbers dominated the region until Kusayla's death
in 687, when an even more dramatic figurehead of Berber independence
took up the struggle. Kahina (or 'the Kahina', for it is unclear whether
the term is a personal name or the title of her office)[34] – who is described,
with the full force of romantic and hopeless nationalist rhetoric, as
possessing streaming hair and second sight – is North Africa's answer to
Zenobia or Boudicca. After Hasan ibn al-Nu'man had eventually captured
the provincial capital of Carthage for the Arabs in 695, she defeated him
and drove the Arab armies back towards Egypt. Ultimately, however,
Kahina could not resist a renewed campaign by al-Num'an, and she was
driven into the desert and finally defeated in 701 or 703 at a place somewhere west of the Aurès mountains of Algeria, which thereafter took
the name of 'Kahina's Well'. With no local forces left to save it, Carthage
finally and definitively fell to the Arabs in 698, leaving a shadowy hold
on several cities in Mauretania Tingitana in the far west as the only
Byzantine presence in the whole of North Africa.[35]

Tripolitania

Tripolitania was so named for the three original Phoenician settlements
at Leptis Magna, Oea (Tripoli) and Sabratha,[36] which fell to the
Carthaginians as their empire expanded in the 4th and 3rd centuries BC.
Our first ancient account of it comes from Herodotus, who conjures up
a land half-bound in myth, half-emergent into the light of historical
scrutiny. Many of the tribes he mentions, such as the Nasamones and
Garamantes, still inhabited the region in Roman times, although his
description of the Garamantes as a tribe unversed in the arts of war
hardly chimes with their bellicose reputation amongst later historians.
The most populated area has always been the coastal strip, especially
near Sabratha. Between Cyrenaica and Leptis Magna, however, the terrain
is extremely harsh and dry. Indeed, Lucan remarked that 'all the expanse

of dry sand that divides burning Berenicis from the lesser heat of Leptis knows nothing of leaves'.[37]

The first stage of the occupation by the Romans in Tripolitania was probably limited to Leptis Magna and a few other defensible sites, such as Tacapae (modern Gabes). As more forces were devoted to the region, so the frontier advanced steadily south, despite the setbacks of a war against the Garamantes in 69–70 and a revolt by the Nasamones in 85–6. During the 2nd century, earthworks known as *clausurae* were constructed, to block access north to the better grazing lands closer to the coast and probably to funnel seasonally migrating nomads along routes where they could more easily be controlled and taxed.[38] At the end of the 2nd century, Quintus Anicius Faustus, the legate of the III Augusta legion, projected a new line of defence further into the desert with the construction of forts at Gheria el-Garbia in the east, at Gholaia (Bu Ngem) in the central sector and at Cidamus (Ghadames) in the far west.[39] Gholaia, in partic-ular, has yielded a precious hoard of ostraka, inscriptions on broken pottery, which give details of its military organisation, including daily rosters of the men and their duties and reports on activities and patrols in the vicinity of the fort.

The Romans, however, persistently failed to subdue the Garamantes, who defended with great vigour their capital of Garama, which may equate to the modern village of Germa, north-east of Sabha, deep in the Libyan desert. Herodotus's account of them reveals that they had four-horse chariots with which they chased the hapless Ethiopian cave-dwellers;[40] and, more intriguingly that they possessed 'backward-grazing' cattle, which on account of their great curving horns could not move forwards, for if they did, their horns would get stuck in the ground![41]

The Garamantes first came into real contact with the Romans in the time of Augustus, not long after the unsuccessful expeditions to Arabia Felix and Ethiopia. An expedition in 20 BC led by the proconsul of Africa, Lucius Cornelius Balbus, met with more success. He penetrated some 800 kilometres into the Sahara and reached Garama, teaching the Garamantes a sharp lesson about the reach of Roman power, but not annexing their lands.[42] For his achievements, Balbus was granted a triumph in 19 BC, the last private citizen to be granted this accolade.[43]

The tribe later became involved in the revolt of Tacfarinas from AD 17 to 24, and then sent ambassadors to Rome begging for forgiveness for their transgression, afraid that they would share the fate of their erst-while allies. But their mischief-making did not cease. In AD 68–9 Leptis Magna and Oea (Tripoli) virtually came to blows over a quarrel concerning the boundaries between the two cities.[44] The citizens of Oea called in the Garamantes to help them, and the tribe proceeded with great enthusiasm to ravage the land around Leptis and do untold damage to the precious olive harvest. In retribution, the legate of Numidia, Valerius Festus,[45] was despatched south, discovering a quick route into the Garamantian lands that took only four days and that laid them open to much quicker Roman retaliatory action than hitherto.

Thereafter the Garamantes tended to be more cooperative. In around AD 100, Septimius Flaccus led an expedition, possibly from Leptis Magna, which passed through Garama and then continued three months' march further south to the land of the 'Ethiopians'. Better documented is the expedition of Julius Maternus (which was probably not military in nature), who also journeyed via Garama and was actually escorted for part of his journey by the King of the Garamantes. He then travelled for four months towards the Ethiopians, ending at a place called 'Agysimba' where he observed rhinoceroses.[46] One possibility is that he had reached as far as Darfur or Kordofan in modern Sudan. The extension of the Roman frontier under Septimius Severus by the construction of forts at Bu Ngem, Ghadames and Gheriat el-Garbia may have had an adverse effect on Garamantian power, and thereafter little is heard of them, save as a poetic synonym for the furthest-flung dwellers of the desert.

Around 575 kilometres west along the coast from the provincial border at the Arae Philaenorum, the first of the three cities of Tripolitania, Leptis Magna – it was so called to differentiate it from Leptis Minor near Hadrumetum – sits just over 100 kilometres east of modern Tripoli in Libya.[47] It seems the imperial city par excellence, its extravagant four-way Severan arch and a clutch of other grand monuments sealing its place as the stereotypical 'Roman city'. Leptis is forever associated with Septimius Severus, the local boy made good, whose ascent to the im-perial throne in 193 ensured its position as one of the smartest cities in the Empire. Yet the truth is more complex. The city as tourists see it is as much a monument to 'imperialist' archaeology as it is to the Roman Empire. The original excavations, carried out by the Italians during the 1930s, clearly did have scientific aims, but were equally tasked with resur-recting the glory of Rome at its height thus reinforcing Mussolini's plan to use Libya as a springboard for a new 'Roman' Empire of his own. The unfortunate result was that the site was cleared very quickly, and the latest levels of its settlement (particularly the Byzantine) were simply swept away, while the pre-Roman city was neglected entirely.

Founded as a Phoenician trading post no later than 500 BC, Leptis fell firmly under the shadow of Carthage, where for three centuries it remained. With the defeat of its Carthaginian patrons in the second

Punic War, Leptis was absorbed into the Numidian kingdom of Massinissa in 202 BC, becoming a free state in alliance with Rome after the Jugurthine War in 105 BC.[48] The city's production and export of olives was the source of the wealth that permitted the construction of the lavish civic buildings that so impress today. Indeed, so wealthy was Leptis that in 46 BC Julius Caesar imposed an annual tax of three million pounds of oil on it, probably in revenge for the support it had given to his senatorial opponents.[49] It took until AD 203 for Leptis to get a rebate, when Septimius Severus[50] granted it complete exemption from property and land taxes. The Emperor also funded an ambitious building programme in his native city, including the magnificent forum, the mainstay of Libya's postcard industry. Even before him, however, Leptis was a regional centre of some importance and was honoured with a promotion to *municipium* around 75 and to *colonia* in 109.[51]

Leptis never had another imperial patron, and never succeeded in really rivalling its more influential neighbour, Carthage, to the west. It did, however, reach the dizzy heights of provincial capital, when the reorganisation of the imperial administration begun by Diocletian at the end of the 3rd century led to the creation of the province of Tripolitania.[52] But by 363, Leptis was suffering the unwelcome attentions of the Austuriani, a tribe from the local desert fringes. In a massive raid, the surrounding area was laid waste, and only the city's walls preserved it from utter disaster. In desperation, the citizens of Leptis appealed to Romanus, the *comes Africae*, based in Carthage, to come to their rescue. He testily replied that he would provide no aid until they had sent him a huge list of supplies, including 4,000 camels.

After the depredations of the Austuriani, Leptis faced being fleeced by the very authorities meant to protect them, and it simply could not come up with the protection money Romanus demanded. Outraged, the citizens of Leptis sent a delegation to the court of Valentinian I at Trier, only to find that Romanus had higher-placed friends than they. Romanus managed to corrupt Palladius, the envoy sent to Tripolitania to investigate him, and as a result Leptis's own ambassador, Jovinus, was blamed for concocting the whole story and was put to death. The unsavoury tale of corruption reflects badly on Leptis, too, as the city council, also suborned by Romanus, refused to back Jovinus's story. It did them no good, for Leptis never really recovered from the Austuriani raid. Although the story did finally come out a decade later, and Palladius committed suicide, Count Romanus, tellingly, was never punished for either his original dereliction of duty or his subsequent corrupt concealment of the affair.

An earthquake in 365 was followed by the depredations of the Vandals in 455, and topped by the razing of the city by marauding tribesmen in 523. By the time Justinian's forces recaptured Leptis in 533 they must really have wondered whether it was really so 'Magna' after all. Procopius, indeed, relates that Leptis had been so badly damaged by the raids of local tribes that it was abandoned. Yet consider for a moment that, in the aftermath of all these destructions, the magnificence of what remains is astonishing, a mute testament by inference to the even greater glory of those centres such as Carthage, which have been almost totally erased by natural disasters, neglect and wilful destruction.

The Severan arch, at the western edge of the city centre, forms the junction of the *cardo* and *decumanus maximus*. Now largely restored, its four faces all decorated in marble reliefs, it stood as a grandiose statement of Leptis's relationship with the imperial house, the bulk of its great Corinthian columns and the broken pediment style of its façade neatly combining local and more traditional architectural styles. Built in 203 to commemorate a visit by Septimius to his native city, its decoration ironically included a figure of the Emperor holding the hand of his elder son Caracalla, with his younger, Geta, standing beside him – a public display of family unity that was to survive just months after the old Emperor's death.[53] The panel (the original now in the museum in Tripoli) that portrays a grave Septimius riding in a triumphal chariot, face turned to the front despite the horizontal movement of the scene, is a much more appropriate reminder of North Africa's greatest Roman.

It is easy to be deceived into thinking that before the Severans there was nothing at Leptis, and that after them it instantly collapsed into a small hamlet rattling around in the shell of a grand classical city. Just a hundred metres away from the Severan arch is unambiguous proof of the falsity of this impression. The Hadrianic Baths, built in 126–7, almost seventy years before Septimius Severus's accession, were once a grand symmetrical complex – one of the first of the great imperial baths – the roof of whose *frigidarium* soared to more than 15 metres, decorated with glass mosaics. Amid the scatter of still-upstanding and reconstructed *cipollino* columns, it is hard to gain a sense of the establishment in full swing, although near the entrance the library and the conveniently situated latrine, with at least thirty seating places in an open court, showed that none of the visitors' needs, physical or intellectual, went unprovided for.

Just beyond the baths, lying beside the Wadi Lebda, the gully that strikes inland from the harbour and severs Leptis into two quarters, is a *nymphaeum*, built as part of the Severan reconstruction of the city. Its semicircular basin would have been backed by an impressive array of Corinthian columns in *cipollino* and red granite, mimicking the stage-back of a Roman theatre, but it has now collapsed into the wadi, great blocks cascading down the slope as though shoved with enormous force. Just a few columns with beautiful vine-leaf detailing remain of a monument both intricate and extravagant. From here a colonnaded street leads on to the Severan forum, Leptis's glory. It is a vast space, imitating the imperial fora of Rome, and was originally surrounded by an immense colonnaded portico. Now the pattern of Medusa heads alternating with busts of victory lies broken, just a few still in place, most scattered in the middle of the forum. Columns lie everywhere, and pieces of capital, fragments of marble, from tiny to huge, mingle with the gorgon's head as though their stony stare had been the cause of all this chaos. The mixture of total devastation and patches of surviving (or reconstructed) decorative masterpieces has caused it to be one of Leptis's most-photographed spots.

Next door is another grandiose Severan construction, this time the basilica, a massive area more than 90 metres long, dominated by the remains of a two-storey colonnade and a huge inscription of Caracalla celebrating the completion of the building in 216, which lies in broken, undulating sections in the centre of the structure. Unlike the basilica at Trier,[54] only a section of this grand civic space was converted for Christian use (under Justinian in the 6th century). The new occupants seem to have been cheerfully undisturbed by the extensive pagan carvings on the pilasters attached to the basilica's end walls, showing the Labours of Hercules at one end and scenes from the life of Dionysus at the other.

Closer to the sea, and to Leptis's old heart, lies the original forum, flanked by the ruins of all the normal municipal buildings, the *curia*, old basilica and temples to Liber Pater, and to Rome and Augustus. An inscription of AD 53–4, in Latin and Punic (for the latter was still very much a living language here), marks improvements made at the expense of one Caius, son of Hanno, who in his name neatly reflects the mixed heritage of the city. Small marks on it indicate where bronze lettering would have been set, giving the original a splendour (and, in the noonday sun, a dazzling quality) that the simple, mute stone now lacks.

Leptis long retained many elements of its pre-Roman Punic culture; those of its citizens named on inscriptions have local, Libyan names, until, in the 2nd century, they lapse into the undifferentiated cultural anonymity of the Roman *praenomen*, *nomen* and *cognomen*.[55] Similarly, inscriptions in neo-Punic, often bilingual with Latin, persist for the first few centuries, with the last of them being found under Domitian towards the end of the 1st century.[56]

Leptis's horizons closed in on it during the late-Roman period, and old taboos about the burial of corpses within the city limits faded away.

A church was built in the forum, and a series of grave-markers associated with it are still in place, their script uncertain and wavering in comparison to the grand dedications of the high classical period. One commemorates the children of a man named Stephanos, who all died young – including Demetria, and a son, Longinus, who lived for just seven months and six days. Many of them exhibit local traits in the spelling of Latin, the stonemasons characteristically confusing b for v and hence writing Berena for the child Verena, and substituting for *vixit* ('he lived') the mistaken form of *bixit*.

Across the *decumanus* from the Old Forum lie the markets, constructed during Leptis's first period of real prosperity under Augustus. Around 8 BC a local notable, bearing the suitably Punic-Latin hybrid name of Annobal (or Hannibal) Tapapius Rufus, paid for the construction of the market. Now, just two octagonal kiosks in sandstone and green *cipollino* marble survive from it, one largely intact, the other a mere shell, inside which the market stalls would have been set up. Outside the northern one is a copy of a stone table, which bears lines marking lengths in Punic feet, Roman feet and Greek feet, for the benefit of the market's multicultural clientele.[57] Sadly for Roman chauvinists, the Roman foot at around 296 millimetres came in much shorter then the Greek-Ptolemaic cubit at 533 millimetres and the Punic cubit at around 515 millimetres, meaning that the Roman legionaries gave their Carthaginian counterparts a 219-millimetre head-start. Tables bearing sculpted indentations served similarly for the verification of different liquid measures; the oil, wine or other commodity could be poured into the basin, which would be stopped at the bottom and, once checked, could be allowed to run through and refill a container placed on the ground beneath it.

To the west of the site lies a less intensively excavated area. The *cardo* leads on to the arch of Antoninus Pius, a relatively simple affair compared to the showy grandeur of the Severan arch, though its remains indicate a quadriform shape. Nearby, the large blocks of the late-Roman wall snake downwards towards the sea, enclosing a much larger area than would its successor, Byzantine perimeter. The imperious stone gateways and procession of massive civic set-pieces give way to low sandy dunes dotted with scrubby bushes. The hurried groups on two-hour tours of Leptis rarely venture here, and in places piles of water bottles moulder, missed (or dumped) by the incongruous yellow truck that screeches around the ruins, oblivious to visitors' photos or shins. In a low hollow 100 metres or so from the shore, the reconstructed concrete domes of its roof making it look like some kind of desert scientific station, are the Hunting Baths, one of Leptis's hidden (and neglected) glories.

Through a splintered wooden door, a small polychrome mosaic of a floral design gives no sense of what is to come. Around a plunge-pool next to the former *frigidarium*, delicate wall paintings depict scenes from rural life: here two men in a boat fishing, their bronze-yellow caps with jutting brims making them look like a pair of aquatic jockeys; there a mother in a blue cloak and a small child walking back from the fields. Next door, however, the scene that gives the whole complex its name springs to life. A series of hunters, their faces vividly drawn and tense, face wild beasts – panthers and leopards. One beast has brought down his attacker and mauls his neck, the wounded hunter desperately seeking to regain his feet and escape. Another animal seems to run straight up the spear that his assailant has run into him, thus seeking in death to despatch his enemy. The hunters have their names painted beside them, Rapidus and Pictor, as though famous athletes or gladiators.

North-west along the seashore, Leptis really does seem to earn its oft-quoted nickname of 'City in the Sand', for from the side of the dunes sprout column capitals, and along the beach worn stones from the city lie alongside more modern rubbish and detritus washed up by the tide. The shoreline leads along past the Byzantine wall into the Wadi Lebda, thick with vegetation at this point, and then past a watchtower to the remains of a Roman lighthouse, surprisingly intact save for a square hole that gives stunning and precarious views over the sea's alluring blue. Beyond the old (and largely dried-up) harbour sit the shattered remains of a Doric temple and beyond that a fort in the Byzantine wall, its staircase choked with the discarded shells of nuts from impromptu picnics.

Leptis, as befitted a city of its size, did not lack in facilities for public entertainment, and it acquired a theatre comparatively early in its history. A little to the west of the old market, this was dedicated around AD 1 or 2 by the very same Annobal Tapapius Rufus responsible for its neighbour. At the top of the auditorium another inscription was found to the goddess Ceres-Augusta, dedicated by Suphunibal, daughter of Annobal Ruso, showing another local family keen to gain public recognition by embellishing the city. Closer to the shore lies the amphitheatre, half of its circle of seats providing a stunning view of the sea. It was probably the largest in Africa, with a capacity of up to 30,000, some two-thirds that of the Coliseum in Rome itself. The holding areas for animals and gladiators can still be seen, and to stand in the centre of the arena and imagine the mixture of adrenalin, sweat and terror as the men awaited their next opponent – beast or human – is to experience a real sense of menace.

Nearby is the circus, the horse-racing track, the arches of whose starting cages or *carceres* were still intact in the 19th century, but of which almost nothing now remains except the stump of its central spine. The circuses or hippodromes came to occupy a curiously central role in Roman life, acting, like the amphitheatres, as a place where high officials, and most notably the emperors, might come into regular contact with their subjects. Dangerous undercurrents and opposition to unpopular policies might surface there in the chants of the spectators or, in the most extreme examples, in political rioting. From as early as the Republic, the circus crowds differentiated themselves into four factions, named for the colours favoured by their supporters: the Reds, Whites, Blues and Greens. The latter two seem to have been by far the strongest, and wherever political activism or patronage of the powerful is documented, it is in association with them, and not the Reds or Whites. Many of the emperors are recorded as supporting one or other faction: Caligula, Nero, Domitian, Lucius Verus, Commodus and Elagabalus for the Greens; Vitellius and Caracalla and, most famously, Justinian for the Blues.[58]

At first the factions were most prominent in the West, for chariot-racing was not particularly common in the Eastern Empire, and except at Constantinople really only took place in the context of religious festivals. The few exceptions, such as Gerasa and Bostra (in Arabia),[59] were insufficient to give rise to widespread Blue and Green factions in the cities there.[60] All this changed after the early 5th century, possibly as a result of the eclipse of gladiatorial games and blood-sports in the arena, which left a gap in the provision of public spectacles that successive emperors filled through sponsorship of horse-races.

As the military resources of the Empire became stretched, the Blues and Greens began to take on something of the nature of unofficial militias, with their highly motivated partisans called upon by the authorities in cases of dire emergency. The most popular charioteer of all, Porphyrius, who is memorialised in countless monuments throughout the Eastern Empire,[61] is recorded on one monument as having taken part (together with the Green faction) in the suppression of a 'tyrant' around 500, an event that may refer to the failed usurpation of Vitalian against Anastasius in 515.[62] Further examples include the participation of the factions in the defence of Constantinople against the Kutrigurs in 559, and their manning of the Long Walls in Thrace against the Avars in 583.[63]

The role of the circus factions in crystallising opposition to politicians (under the Republic) and, later, to the Emperor was much more troublesome for the authorities. As early as 44 BC there were, according to Cicero, loud acclamations in favour of Brutus, the murderer of Caesar, during the performance of a play.[64] The most notable example of all, however, came under Justinian, when the factions came perilously close to unseating the Emperor. It all came about as two circus partisans, one from each faction, were due to be executed. On the day appointed for their hanging (12 January), the ropes snapped and both men escaped alive. The Blues and Greens then combined to petition Justinian to allow the pair to live. When the Emperor ignored their pleas, the factions in concert set to pillaging and burning the centre of the city. Their demands grew political, with shouts for the deposition of the widely despised praetorian prefect, John the Cappadocian, and the urban prefect, Eudaemon.

Finally, three days after the riots had broken out, the mob tried to elevate Probus, a nephew of the late Emperor Anastasius, to the throne and when he could not be found, they rousted out Hypatius, another nephew of the dead Emperor and proclaimed him instead. For much of this time, Justinian vacillated and seems to have been on the point of fleeing. It was only the resolve of his wife, Theodora – who flatly insisted that whilst Justinian might try to escape, she was staying firmly put to face her fate – that stiffened the Emperor's resolve. Troops were sent in to quell the riots, and in the end some 30,000 are said to have perished.

The end of the Severan dynasty, with the murder of Severus Alexander in 235, marked the start of Leptis's long decline. The building of the late-Roman wall between 250 and 350 shows an increased concern for the security of the city, and the raiding of the nomadic Austurians in 363–7 badly damaged the city's hinterland. The sand-dunes started to encroach on the city, and a series of floods, as the Wadi Lebda broke its banks, did further damage.

By the end of the 4th century, Tripolitania seems to have had its own duke (*dux*) in charge of the garrison[65] and it resisted absorption by the Vandals longer than any other part of the former Africa Proconsularis. It was only in 455 that it was ceded to Gaiseric's Vandals, who demolished the wall, but they do not seem to have settled at Leptis in any great numbers, since the solitary trace of them is a hoard of coins found in the area of the market. Leptis was reoccupied after Justinian's reconquest, but the much smaller area enclosed within the Byzantine walls indicates that life here was on a much more modest scale than before.

In 544, Leptis played host to a massacre that irrevocably soured Byzantine relations with the local tribes, and greatly hindered the government's attempts at re-establishing financial and military security in the province. A large horde of Leuathae (or Lagutans), a group apparently originating in the Western Desert oases of Egypt,[66] approached the city, promising loyalty to the new rulers in exchange for gifts, particularly the traditional insignia of office (such as a white cloak and gold boots) for their leaders. Sergius, commander of the Byzantine army, invited eighty Leuathae chieftains to a banquet, but an argument over the alleged theft of crops by his soldiers led to a fight, and all but one of the Leuathae were killed.[67] In response, rebellion swept through North Africa, and it took three years and four Byzantine commanders before John Troglita finally put down the uprising in 547.[68] Tripolitania was then largely quiet until the Arab conquest in 643, after which Leptis seems to have continued its inexorable decline. Slowly the dunes and the sea finished their silent work of concealment, leaving the city to await a new wave of incomers from Italy to unearth and reconstruct its past glory.

Oea, 125 kilometres west of Leptis along the coast, has grown subsequently to become Tripoli, the capital of modern Libya, and amid its bustling old town and newer quarter of Italian-era buildings, little remains of the antique past. Almost the sole survivor of the Roman city is a triumphal arch built around 163 during the reign of Marcus Aurelius, surrounded by the fragments of a temple to the Genius of Oea, which was dedicated in 183-5. The layout of the main streets of the bazaar are, however, believed to follow the orientation of part of the Roman grid,[69] a sense of order that it is hard to credit amidst the chaotic crowds of pre-Ramadan shoppers.

A further 75 kilometres west of Tripoli, the coastal route to Sabratha yields little save a scrubby desert, the roadsides carpeted with heaps of discarded rubbish and the wind-swept huddles of black plastic bags that blight the Libyan countryside. It all summons up a profound yearning to dip into the deep blue of the Mediterranean. Sabratha may well have been founded as far back as the 8th century BC, and although it was strongly influenced by Punic culture, it was not actually occupied by the Carthaginians.[70] Evidence of its earliest phase comes from the Mausoleum of Bes, recently reconstructed by Italian archaeologists. Reminiscent of the neo-Punic monument at Dougga,[71] with a needle shape and pointed conical top, it has lions or sphinxes arrayed on each of its four sides, together with an image of Bes, the deformed Egyptian dwarf god, who was seen as the protector of women during childbirth.

Absorbed by Rome near the end of the 1st century BC, the city lived a life of relatively quiet prosperity until the 4th century. Sabratha never produced a claimant, successful or otherwise, to the imperial throne, and so missed out on the type of lavish patronage that Septimius Severus bestowed upon Leptis Magna, though it was elevated to the rank of *colonia* no later than the 180s.[72] In the 360s, the twin disasters of a sack by the Austuriani and the massive earthquake of 363 that devastated the whole of the eastern Mediterranean ruined the city, while the latter flooded much of its shoreline. The 6th-century Byzantine wall here, as in so many other places, excluded much of what had been the civic heart of the city, and by the time the Arabs arrived at Sabratha in 643 (with such suddenness that the inhabitants did not even have time to shut the city gates),[73] the area of the forum had been converted into a cemetery.[74]

Sabratha's gem is without doubt its theatre, whose *scaenae frons* is one of the most complete in the Roman world. Begun around 190, with a capacity for some 5,000 spectators, its 95-metre-diameter auditorium makes it one of the largest in Roman Africa. The concave marble panels in front of the stage, beautifully preserved, represent a variety of scenes appropriate to the dramatic setting, including the three muses, a school-teacher rubbing his beard in meditative contemplation, a personification of Rome and Sabratha with hands joined, comic masks, the judgement of Paris and dancers.[75] Behind them more than 100 Corinthian columns tower, stacked up on a three-tiered colonnade whose grace and beauty must have been in severe danger of distracting spectators from the more mundane performances below.

Although Sabratha's mosaics lie largely entombed in the site museum, some still survive *in situ*. In the Oceanus Baths, so named for a depiction of the sea-deity (now removed), a mosaic of a strigil is still visible at the lintel of the *frigidarium*. At the Theatre Baths, a mosaic inscription originally exhorted those who were a little tentative in their ablutions to '*Bene Lava*' ('Wash Well').

On the south side of the forum stood the basilica, probably originally erected in the mid-1st century BC. The remains are those of a fairly standard civic building of the early Empire, a rectangular hall with an internal colonnade, and at one end an apse-shaped area that acted as the judge's tribunal. A section of it also served as the shrine for the imperial cult. Later on it was extensively remodelled, and around 450 part of it was converted into a Christian church. The building's resonance lies, however, in its being very probably the site of the trial, about 157, of the novelist Apuleius.

Born in Madauros, in the west of Africa Proconsularis, probably in the 120s, Apuleius (though he quite possibly had Punic as his mother tongue) received an elite education and established a flourishing career as a sophist. Having been left, together with his brother, the enormous sum of two million sesterces by their father, Apuleius was in a position to indulge in a life of letters and rhetoric, and served as a magistrate at Madauros some time before 157. He is best known for his novelistic masterpiece – known as *Metamorphoses* in ancient times, but more commonly referred to since as *The Golden Ass* – in which the protagonist is transformed into the eponymous animal and undergoes a series of fabulous adventures, culminating in a life-transforming procession at a Temple of Isis, during which he is mutated back into the form of a man.

Late in 156, Apuleius arrived in Oea (Tripoli) on his way to Alexandria and, while staying there, was joined by Sicinius Pontianus, a friend from his student days in Athens. Pontianus was looking for a husband for his recently widowed mother Pudentilla, in order to prevent her substantial fortune falling into the hands of another family. Pontianus invited Apuleius to stay at his mother's house and encouraged a bond of affection to form between them. The marriage eventually went ahead, but by then Pontianus had begun to accuse Apuleius of using magic to persuade Pudentilla to marry him.

The case was heard at Sabratha before the proconsul Claudius Maximus, and in his speech of defence (the *Apologia*) Apuleius employed the full armoury of a trained rhetor, heaping ridicule on his opponents. Throughout his defence, he persistently implied that his accusers were ignorant, ill-educated folk and that accusations that he used fish to concoct aphrodisiacs or employed a statuette of Mercury to bewitch Pudentilla were simply absurd. Even bearing in mind the inevitable editing of the text for a wider public, the image of the professional sophist defending himself on a plane that the prosecution could simply not counter, or perhaps even comprehend, is a powerful one.[76] Apuleius was probably assisted by the fact that Claudius Maximus may well have been one of the teachers who had instructed Marcus Aurelius in Stoic philosophy, and was therefore quite likely to be favourably disposed towards him. The final verdict is not recorded, but the very fact that Apuleius later published his defence speech is strong evidence for his having won the case.

It could be that Apuleius drew inspiration from Sabratha's own Temple of Isis. With a breathtaking location overlooking the sea, the shrine was originally built in the early 1st century. Eight Corinthian columns still stand guard at the water's edge, a relic of the shrine's colonnaded court-yard. It was damaged both by the encroaching of the sea, after the 4th-century earthquake, and by the late-Roman defensive wall that cut off part of its north-eastern corner.

It is a world away from the rigours of the desert, and as the fron-tier moved ever further southwards under the Severans, the *limes* and the residual threat from nomadic tribes must have seemed to recede almost to nothingness. One of the forts providing this protection was situated at Cidamus (Ghadames), a baking hot 500-kilometre journey south from Sabratha, a trip that in ancient times must have taken several days of discomfort, hopping between precious water sources in the desert. Here, the landscape is punctuated by fortified Berber granaries – pragmatic mixtures of storage and refuge, and perhaps the lineal descendants of the Roman-era *gsur*, or fortified farms, which acted as fortified posts in the more thinly populated areas. Mostly two-storey square or rectangular constructions, they offered greater security than open farms, with space for tethering animals as well as accommodation for the local population.

While Gholaia, in the eastern desert reaches of Tripolitania, was abandoned around 263, the military occupation of Cidamus may have lasted only until 238. The short-lived Roman fort is as yet unlocated, but must have been at the edge of the 'Old Town' of Ghadames, a medieval mud-brick warren whose permanent occupation was ended several decades ago as part of the Libyan government's programme to move people out of what it saw as unsightly reminders of a past unvarnished by modernity. The lure of traditional oasis life is still a strong one, though, so the narrow claustrophobic streets are not entirely deserted, and the houses are not, as elsewhere in the country, crumbling back into their constituent salt, straw and mud. The small local museum contains what little has been unearthed of Cidamus: a room of column pieces, one heavily carved with palm dates, another with a capital in the shape of a bulbous striated onion. The gravestone of Marcus Varivara, who died aged thirty-five, has very definite straight lines marked upon it to guide the stonemason's uncertain hand in chiselling the inscription.

The Old Town itself is a confusing and delightful labyrinth, composed of twists and turns, shadows and light, squares and tunnels. Running on top of the main alleyways are enclosed passages, used by the women to pass through the town without venturing onto the public street. The walls of the houses, whitewashed with white gypsum interspersed with red gypsum employed as cement, give some brightness to the gloom, reinforced by shafts of sunlight that penetrate weakly into the tunnels. Each quarter of the town has several small squares, traditionally controlled by sub-groups of the two major tribes, the Bani Walid and the Bani Wazid. On one of these, near the town's main entrance, stand four Roman pillars set into the corner of the square, a faint survival of Cidamus, yet somehow contriving to seem more modern than the Old Town itself. At the Yunis mosque, one of the oldest in the city, a few more columns stand in the main prayer hall, though from where they came seems unknown.

Nearby, on the main, neatly whitewashed square, stands the Al-Kadus, the water-clock, where a customary official, the *naib*, would regulate the supply of water to the various gardens in the oasis, counting off time for the running-out of water from four containers, and adding a knot to a tally for each container emptied. At each eighty-eighth knot counted, a waiting farmer could then run to his garden and turn off the sluice from the neighbouring plot to allow the water to irrigate his own. Tight control of the water supply was what enabled efficient exploitation of the oases' exiguous resources, even in Roman times, and evidence of settlement in areas that are not farmed or even inhabited today are explained more by the Romans' (and their predecessors') greater skill at marshalling water supplies than by any significant change in climate or rainfall.

Less tangibly, the *insulae* of the Roman settlement are supposed to have reached the wall of the Old Town, with some names of old Roman structures surviving in terms such as 'Inagdu', though whether this is a corruption of the Latin *'In Augusto'* or a mangling of some other phrase is unclear. Ghadames was reoccupied by the Byzantines in the 6th century, for there is evidence of an episcopal see there, and a basilica may have been built in the town at about this time.[77]

However, like the rest of Tripolitania, Cidamus succumbed to the advance of the Muslim armies in the mid-7th century. A short way out of Ghadames, across rough desert tracks, lies the ruined desert fort of Ras al-Ghoul ('Lord of the Ghosts'), a late-Roman fortification set atop a rocky outcrop. Isolated, but defended by a double-circuit of masonry walls, it commands a wide area, ringed in the distance by the first dunes of the deep desert. It is a place more of desperate defence than of prolonged resistance, but local tradition has it that the last Byzantine garrison of Tripolitania retreated here around 668, and held out for some time. The soldiers were assisted by the presence of a well inside the fort, but in the end made a deal with their attackers to be allowed to leave in peace.

It is a short scramble up the slope to the fort, and determined attackers would surely soon have overrun it, but the well is still there, just inside the inner keep, uncovered, and a hazardous fall for the unwary. Inside the fort are the remains of several structures, one surviving to almost half a metre high, presumably representing the accommodation blocks for the soldiers. The garrison cannot have been large, because the whole area of the upper fort is only about 12 metres in diameter. All around lies a scatter of pottery of indeterminate age, and one stone fragment has a carving roughly incised on it, an eagle, or perhaps a pelican. From here, as the setting sun casts a golden-pinkish shadow over the dune fields, it seems a fitting place for a province to have died.

Africa Proconsularis

Back on the coast, the province of Tripolitania petered out around Gigthis, about 100 kilometres to the west of Sabratha. From here westwards, the bulk of modern Tunisia (apart from the sterile areas to the south of the dried-up salt lakes of the Chott El Jerid) constituted the original core of Africa Proconsularis. The coastline and interior lowlands are dotted with ancient settlements, forming one of the economic powerhouses of the ancient world, and home also to Carthage, one of its most important cities.

Roughly midway between the modern cities of Sfax and Sousse, some 275 kilometres north-west of Gigthis along Tunisia's main arterial route, lies the great amphitheatre at Thysdrus (El Djem). It is one of the most complete in the Roman world, only really rivalled today by the Coliseum and the arena at Arelatum (Arles) in southern Gaul. It was probably the twelfth-largest in the whole Empire.[78] From afar it dominates the skyline, while from nearby it is engulfed by bazaars and shops and all the life and noise of a modern North African town. From outside its arches and engaged columns march in an almost continuous line around the building; from inside, though the seats are largely gone, the arches that supported at least four tiers of them survive intact. The building, the third of its type constructed in Thysdrus, would have been even more complete, had it not been for its bombardment by the Ottoman governor of the region in the 19th century during the suppression of a tax-revolt, a strange irony in view of the amphitheatre's earlier history.

That Thysdrus could have supported such a structure is evidence of its great prosperity during the Severan period. Yet the local landowners were not so rich that the central government could milk them indefinitely without provoking a reaction. The demands of the imperial procurator grew too exacting, and his habit of prosecuting local notables on trumped-up charges so that he could confiscate their properties once they were found guilty further inflamed feelings. By March 238 the local population had had enough, and the procurator was murdered by an angry mob. Realising that they had overstepped a dangerous mark, the rioters then sought out the eighty-year-old governor of the province, Marcus Aurelius Gordianus Sempronianus, at his headquarters in Thysdrus and proclaimed him Emperor – probably much against his better judgement.[79]

Yet the elderly Gordian I, as he is known to history, probably had some reason to hope. Although he had no access to the resources of the army, and could only muster a ragtag assortment of local militias, the 'official'

Emperor, Maximinus Thrax, was not popular, as his role in the murder of Alexander Severus in 235[80] had angered the Senate, whose support could thus be expected for the rebellion. Gordian elevated his son, also called Gordian, to be his co-Emperor (known as Gordian II), and sent an embassy to Rome. The Senate granted its recognition of his position, but the governor of Numidia, Capellianus, who was also the legate of the III Augusta legion, remained loyal to Maximinus. The two Gordians were defeated by Capellianus outside Carthage, the younger perishing in battle, while his father fled into the city and then, in total despair, committed suicide. Until his unwanted proclamation, he had lived a long and blameless life, but he survived his elevation to the imperial office by just twenty-two days.

If Maximinus and Capellianus thought their position was now secure, they were hopelessly wrong. The Senate had declared Maximinus an enemy of the Roman people and elected two new emperors, Pupienus (a former governor of Germania Superior) and Balbinus, in opposition to their 'official' sovereign. Popular opinion, which had favoured the Gordians, did not look favourably on this senatorial carve-up of power, but neither did it relish restoration of the brutal Maximinus to power. The only solution was another Gordian, and there happened to be one available: the young nephew of Gordian II, who was just thirteen years old. Pupienus and Balbinus, not keen on sharing power with this young upstart, compromised by granting him the lesser title of Caesar. Maximinus's attempt to march on Rome then collapsed when he was murdered by his own legionaries, the men of II Parthica, near Aquileia.[81]

Yet the victorious Pupienus and Balbinus fared scarcely better. Once back at Rome, they soon fell to quarrelling and mutual suspicions of the most sanguinary nature. Each feared the other was about to assassinate him. The praetorian guard, not keen on either emperor, then tried to storm the Palatine, where the imperial palaces were sited, and capture both of them. Pupienus's German bodyguard attempted to rescue him, and in the fracas both he and Balbinus were murdered. While the first two Gordians had lasted twenty-two days, Pupienus and Balbinus had survived just a hundred, meaning that, when Gordian III was proclaimed sole Emperor by the soldiers, he became the sixth sovereign in the space of four months. It was the start of the almost comic-opera period of Roman history known as the 'military anarchy' during which emperors came and went so fast that the mint-masters were hard put to keep up with the latest imperial image, and which saw no fewer than fifty emperors (or usurpers) in fifty years,[82] almost none of whom died of natural causes.

Gordian III, barely an adolescent, was hardly in a position to make policy, but his advisors went about vigorously blackening the reputation of the previous regimes. Both Pupienus and Balbinus suffered *damnatio memoriae*,[83] as did, uniquely, the III Augusta legion for its role in the death of Gordian's uncle and grandfather, its name being erased from public monuments as though a corporate public enemy. Africa was not granted another legion and was left to be defended by auxiliary troops, until the III Augusta was reconstituted by Valerian in 253. This meant that the province was dangerously exposed when the Proconsul of Africa, Sabinianus, revolted in 240,[84] but he was defeated, and for a few short years the rot in the body politic of Rome was halted.

As well as its role as a catalyst in the unseating of Maximus Thrax and the 'military anarchy' that followed, Thysdrus also played host to an important moment during the final years of the Roman presence in North Africa. It was in the Thysdrus amphitheatre, around 698, that the Berber Queen Kahina barricaded herself against the Arab army of Hasan ibn al-Nu'man.[85] Her followers mounted a spirited defence, but there was some kind of betrayal or deal done, and, whilst the Queen herself broke out with a small band of followers, her sons were appointed as commanders in the Arab army. Kahina, who had a reputation as a prophetess, was said to have 'foreseen' and approved their seditious behaviour, but it cannot have been an easy pill to swallow. Local tradition tells that the treasure of the Queen is still buried somewhere nearby, but her hidden gold and jewels have remained as elusive as the truth behind her own story.

Perched on Tunisia's north-eastern shore – some 200 kilometres north of Thysdrus – facing equally along the North African shoreline and outwards towards the islands of the Mediterranean, Carthage was Rome's hereditary enemy. The city's foundation is lost in mystery, mirroring nicely the historical haze that obscures the truth behind Rome's own earliest years. The traditional date is 814 BC, thus giving the city sixty years' seniority over its Italian rival. The legend relates that King Pygmalion of Tyre (in the Phoenician homeland of modern Lebanon) murdered the husband of his sister Elissa, who, after her own odyssey around the Mediterranean, landed in Libya. The tale was later taken up by Virgil, who makes Dido (Elissa's nickname, acquired on her voyages) the tragic heroine of his *Aeneid*. He also relates the story that the local king agreed to sell the newcomers as much land as they could cover in the hide of an ox – in other words, very little. The cunning Phoenicians cut the ox hide into very thin strips, thus enabling them to encircle an area 22 stades (around 4 kilometres) in circumference. In honour of this ruse they named their settlement Byrsa (for *bursa* or ox-hide).[86] It later became better known as Kart-asht ('New City') or Carthage.

After the last Punic War in 149–146 BC, more a vengeful campaign to extirpate the Carthaginian identity than a truly equal military struggle, Carthage itself was destroyed, although the legend that its agricultural lands were sowed with salt to render them forever infertile owes more to a Victorian sense of theatricality than to the historical record.[87] '*Carthago delenda est*' – 'Carthage must be destroyed' – intoned Cato the Elder at the close of each of his speeches in the run-up to that war, and so it was. Yet from the rubble emerged eventually, in the time of Augustus, a new Roman city built atop its wholly destroyed Punic predecessor.

Although neighbouring Utica was made the capital of the new province of Africa following the Third Punic War, Carthage, retaining the advantage offered by its unique double-harbour, soon surpassed it once more, first in prosperity and then in political importance. Julius Caesar took the decision to refound it, but his murder in 44 BC meant that it was Augustus who sent the first significant draft of colonists in 29 BC, naming it in honour of his dead adoptive father as Colonia Iulia Concordia Carthago. It became the *de facto* capital of the Latin-speaking portions of Roman North Africa (as Alexandria was for the Eastern Greek-speaking area).

For Carthage, the first three centuries of Roman rule were unremarkable, but in 308, it briefly became the capital of its very own breakaway empire when the Vicar of Africa, Domitius Alexander, briefly threw off the dominion of Maxentius, himself regarded as a usurper by the legitimate Tetrarchs, Galerius, Licinius, Maximin Daia and Constantine.[88] After a period of consolidation later in the 4th century in which it also became a leading centre of learning – attracting the young Saint Augustine, who briefly taught rhetoric there in the 380s – Carthage developed into one of the principal strongholds of Christianity in the West. As the portion of the Empire centred on Rome (and then Milan or Ravenna) weakened in the early 5th century, it grew more and more to depend on the huge grain shipments sent from the rich agricultural lands of Africa via the port of Carthage.

From 423 to 429 Carthage (and Africa) once more became semi-detached from the Empire, ruled as the fiefdom of Count Boniface. After his departure to Italy, and death in 432, no further warlords came to the city's rescue. In 439, when Gaiseric's Vandals swept eastwards from the toehold they had established in Mauretania and besieged Carthage, the frantic population did what little it could to resist and invoke whatever divine aid it could think of. One night, the whole population (Christians included) is reported to have made a sacrifice to Nocturnus, the god of night.[89] Eventually, on 19 October, the city fell, and over the next half-century, the Vandals used the naval resources and maritime knowledge they acquired to terrorise the western Mediterranean and beat back any Roman attempt to send a fleet to recapture North Africa.

Only in 533, with the defeat of the Vandals by the Byzantine general Belisarius, did Carthage re-enter the Roman fold. On the night before he entered the city, the Carthaginians lit lamps throughout the town to welcome him, as the panic-stricken Vandals took refuge in churches and sanctuaries.[90] Yet, as elsewhere in North Africa, it was a very exiguous hold, and the exarch who now administered it was more in the nature of a military governor than an official tasked to restore the province to its former prosperity.

As North Africa succumbed to the westward sweep of the Arab armies from the 640s, Carthage became an island, too strong to be taken, too weak to reclaim lost territory. Many of the suburbs, which had been occupied in the 5th and 6th centuries, were now abandoned. In 669, the foundation of Kairouan, just 150 kilometres to the south-west,[91] virtually sealed its fate. After falling in 695 and being recaptured by the Byzantine authorities two years later, Carthage finally succumbed to the army of Hasan ibn al-Numan in 698.[92] The city was razed and the conquerors chose not to settle there, instead building a new town on the site of modern Tunis.

Carthage continued to exercise a fascination for Western visitors, long after its political eclipse, though its inaccessibility in territory occupied first by the Ottomans, and then by the Barbary Corsairs, made visits rare. The poet François-René de Chateaubriand came to Tunis in 1807 on his way back from Palestine, but found little at Carthage,[93] for it had been used as a stone quarry for the expansion of Kairouan, and then by the Genoese who had occupied nearby La Goulette in 1535. Half a century later, Gustave Flaubert, in the throes of writing *Salammbô*, came to see for himself.[94] The first line of the novel, 'It was in Megara, a suburb of Carthage, in the gardens of Hamilcar',[95] evokes a city and an atmosphere forever lost. Now the buried skeleton of the ancient city sits below the charming leaf-shaded villas built in the French colonial period (and afterwards) for high officials – which line the lanes that lead to what has been unearthed, above all in UNESCO-sponsored excavations since the mid-1970s.

Remains of the late-Punic city have been excavated on the Byrsa hill. Originally, it was a cemetery in the 7th century BC, and then an industrial area. Towards the end, as Roman conquest threatened, housing was constructed here for the richer inhabitants, each dwelling with its own water cistern, the outside originally faced with red stucco. They cling to the slope of the hillside in a surprisingly dense quarter, as if the last generations of independent Carthage clustered here to await their fate. From the hill can also be glimpsed the double-harbours that gifted the city its great commercial wealth and military power, and which in times of trouble could be closed off with iron chains. In the centre of the Military Harbour sits the circle of Admiral's Island, upon which the Carthaginian naval commander had a house, and on which the Romans later built a military base.

The Roman town had the Byrsa hill as its central focus. Below the hill are the Antonine Baths, built in the 2nd century AD, and once one of the largest such complexes in the Empire, now retaining mostly just the substructures that lay beneath the main bath buildings. They are massive enough for all that, and the two huge columns restored from the above-ground complex give some sense of the gigantism of the project.

The most haunting remains of Punic Carthage lie 2 kilometres south-west of the Byrsa hill. Dating from the 8th century BC, the *tophet*, or necropolis, contains a whole field of stelae, disturbed when a Roman-era graveyard was built over the old Phoenician cemetery. Many are carved with stylised fingers or even simple grooves, a sign that they are dedicated to Baal Hammon, while those inscribed with a bottle shape, a female figure or a crescent are for the moon goddess Tanit. Moving down the slope to the left is the original Phoenician level, again filled with an array of grave-markers; along the edge of the cut that the archae-ologists made to reach this level, even more stelae are visible, entombed in the soil, one forever entangled in the roots of a palm tree.

Through a small tunnel in an area over which a Roman house and cistern were later constructed, lie several funerary urns and stelae in the darkness, a haunted place, where the ancient Carthaginians feel just a finger's touch away. A disturbing quantity of the graves in the *tophet* contained the remains of very young children, most of them aged just one to three at the time of death.[96] The allegation of infanticidal sacri-fices has long dogged the Carthaginians' historical reputation. Tradition claims that at a time of great political uncertainty in 309–308 BC, when Bomilcar overthrew the traditional political order, the city turned to this ancient rite of propitiation. Diodorus Siculus[97] paints a picture of a holo-caust in which aristocratic families sacrificed hundreds of children, placing them in the arms of a great statue of Baal Hammon, which then tipped the babies into a flame-filled pit. Yet even Diodorus makes it quite clear that he is referring to an exceptional moment in Carthaginian history, and it may be, with the undoubtedly high level of child mortality, that these were simply infants who died naturally and whose remains were then consecrated to the gods.

Despite the Romanisation of Africa, Punic culture was no more extinguished than the Hellenised Greek civilisation of the Near East. As well as the survival of the Punic language – at least in the countryside, where Saint Augustine commented on the need for clerics to preach in it to their rural flocks as late as the 5th century[98] – Semitic religious beliefs persisted for many years, albeit transmuted into a more acceptably Roman form. The fertility goddess Astarte was often equated with Venus, while Tanit became Juno Caelestis, and, most widespread of all, Baal Hammon transformed into Saturn. A huge number of finds of Tanit stelae have been uncovered in Tunisia, each bearing the stylised symbol of a crescent moon, while from the 3rd century stones bearing the inscription *Saturno sacrum* ('sacred to Saturn') are still widespread.

Just as the history of Carthage was written – with little sympathy – by the Roman victors, so Punic literature was almost entirely suppressed. The only major work that was preserved, the work of Mago, reflected the Romans' long-standing interest in agronomy and, given the agricultural lushness of North Africa at the time, is as fitting a monument as any to the achievement of Carthage. Mago advised that vineyards should be planted on hill slopes facing north, to catch the breeze in such a hot country, and counselled the digging of trenches to let air get at the roots. From Carthage came, in Roman times, not only wine, but vast quantities of olive oil, though it faced stiff competition from Spain, and patriotic writers such as Varro continued to prefer oil produced in Italy. Pomegranates, too, or 'Punic apples' (*Mala Punica*), were a renowned Carthaginian export, as were, above all, African figs. Part of Cato's theatrics in turning the Roman aristocracy in favour of renewed war against the rump of Carthage's North African territory involved bringing a plump, juicy fig into the Senate house and announcing that it had been picked in Carthage just three days before. Not a weapon of mass destruction, perhaps, but it convinced just as well.

From the traffic jams and urban fuss of Tunis, the road leads southwest through increasingly scrub-like territory, lined with olive trees to either side, and begins to climb up into the Tunisian spine of the Atlas mountains. Finally, after around 100 kilometres, on a plateau and steep hillside on the valley of the Wadi Khaled, the city of Thugga (modern Dougga) comes into view, spread out unevenly across a wide area, more like a straggling stone orchard than a meticulously regimented Roman grid. An ancient settlement established well before the Roman province, it fell at first into the territory of the Numidian kings, for whom it served as one of their chief residences, and was not finally annexed by the Romans until 46 BC. At first, the city remained largely self-governing, continuing its traditional ways, and did not reach the status of *municipium* until the start of the 3rd century as Municipium Thuggense.[99] In 261, under Galerius, it finally received the ultimate accolade as a *colonia*, its name transmuting into the hardly laconic Colonia Licinia Septima Alexandriana Thuggenses.

Thugga sits in a rich agricultural area midway between the coast and the great plains of the interior. Though never on the main routes, it is typical of the towns that dotted the province away from the great metropolis of Carthage and provided it with the crops that made Africa the great provider for the hungry mouths of Italy. Sited on a defensible hill, the streets of Thugga wind around uneasily, trying to make the best of the troublesome topography. A number of urban villas give evidence of the unassuming prosperity that must have characterised it for much of the Roman period. From the House of Ulysses came an exquisite mosaic, showing the Trojan hero straining at the mast, muscles taut, eyes alight, desperate to break his bonds and draw closer to the fatally beckoning song of the Sirens. Somewhat lower down the hill the Trifolium House boasts a highly unusual design; the western rooms have a vaulted trefoil shape, with three shell-shaped apses. It is widely pointed out by locals as the site of Thugga's brothel, for no better reason than the number of identical rectangular rooms that run off the central courtyard.

Less puzzling in terms of purpose, and more obviously magnificent, are the forum buildings of Thugga. The entrance to the square is partially blocked off by a massive masonry wall, marking the 6th-century Byzantine perimeter, a sign of the troubled times that followed the Justinianic reconquest, when the government's hold over North Africa was uncertain and very much at the mercy of Berber tribal confeder-acies that had grown up to the south (and whose descendants are the Berber population of the Maghreb today).

Along the forum's edge, the Capitolium is Dougga's most spectacular building, its four monumental Corinthian columns and the great rect-angular block of its sanctuary visible from almost all over the city. Constructed in 166–7 at a time of almost unchallenged prosperity for North Africa, its frieze contains a dedication to Jupiter, Juno and Minerva, the Capitoline Triad, for the salvation of the co-Emperors Marcus Aurelius and Lucius Verus.[100] Above it is a badly damaged carving of an eagle making off with the figure of a man. It almost certainly depicts the apotheosis of Antoninus Pius, the immediate predecessor of the emperors under whom the temple was constructed.[101]

Next to the Capitolium lies the Piazza of the 'Wind-Rose', so named from an unusual wind-compass inscribed into its paving stones, including Auster, the south wind, and Africus, the wind of the south-west. Amongst Dougga's other well-preserved remains are temples to Fortuna, to Liber Pater, to the Piety of Augustus – another example of the worship of emperors, or at least of aspects of their personality or office – to Saturn and, far to the west of the main site, to Juno Caelestis. The last two, the Romanised versions of Baal and Tanit, were perhaps the places of worship closest to the heart of the native population, and today the Caelestis temple still receives surreptitious offerings and the occasional sacrifice of a chicken by locals praying for rain.

Dougga's most venerable relic, however, is the Libyco-Punic mausoleum, a tower-grave down at the edge of the site, standing at the borders of an olive grove. Three storeys high, it is topped with a pyramid on which equestrian statues were carved. Dedicated to an unknown 3rd-century BC Numidian prince, it is a rare survival of such Carthaginian-style tombs. Local guides adamantly insist, particularly to British visitors, that it would have survived even better yet, had the British Consul in Tunis, Thomas Reade, not taken a fancy to the tomb's inscription in 1842 and demolished the edifice in his eagerness to remove it. Consul Reade has been unfairly impugned, however, for visitors in the 18th century already found the tomb in ruins, and when the Frenchman Camille Borgia came in 1840, he discovered the inscription lying on the ground. Reade's sole act of vandalism was to break it in two for easier transportation back to Britain. The inscription itself was bilingual in Punic and Numidian, and acted as a kind of 'Rosetta Stone' for the Numidian language, as Punic was already understood and the parallel texts thus enabled the decipherment of the Numidian alphabet.[102]

Seventy kilometres south of Thugga, along twisting mountain roads, Mactaris's fame rests, rather unfairly, on the testament of a single one of its antique inhabitants. But perhaps, without the inscription of the 'Reaper of Mactar', this medium-sized town of the Numidian hinterland, which lies on a plateau some 900 metres high in the Wadi Saboun valley, might have remained utterly obscure. The Mactar Reaper's inscription, now in the Louvre, relates the story of a poor peasant in the 2nd century – his name is not preserved – who rose from an impoverished start (his father did not own a house) and was forced to work as a farm labourer. After twelve years as an itinerant harvester, he then became a foreman, and finally a landowner, serving on the *curia* of the city; he was even honoured by his appointment as *censor*, the official tasked with the periodic enumeration of the citizenry. It is a rare and explicit example of social mobility and an indication that the lot of the peasant *coloni* labouring on the farm of a rich patron was not completely without hope.

The town, as many others in the region, became a haven for Carthaginians fleeing their final defeat in the Third Punic War in 146 BC, and these incomers constructed a temple and a *tophet* necropolis. Exactly a century later, it fell into Roman hands and was finally made a *colonia* by Marcus Aurelius around AD 180.[103] The place had been ringed with an old Numidian defensive wall, but the Romans demolished this circuit around AD 30.[104] The defensive deficit was made good in Byzantine times when the amphitheatre, built under the Severans, was converted into a fortress. A masonry wall and rather neat archway give, therefore, rather surprisingly onto the former oval of the arena. For those not wishing to be caught unawares, the building obligingly bears the modern label 'Amphitheatre. *Gladiateurs chasse d'animaux sauvages.*'

Mactaris's forum, built in 116, preserves the scattered remnants of its portico, and a fine triumphal arch at its southern end, commemorating the victories of Trajan against the Germans, Armenians and Parthians. Just beyond this stand the 'Great South Baths', built in 199 and remarkably well preserved, although sections of white and green geometric mosaic exposed to the air are gradually crumbling away to nothingness.

The town's other unique monument is the *Schola Iuvenum* ('School of Youths'), built around AD 88 as a kind of aristocratic youth association, whose patron was Mars.[105] It therefore had a military character, although it was not directly linked with the army, and may have provided some militia or police functions to Mactaris. The 'club-house' had a large vestibule and courtyard surrounded by the remains of Corinthian columns. There is also a basilica-shaped hall with an apse, which could have been the main meeting place. Curiously, the tomb of one Julia Bennata stands to the south – as a woman, she would have been excluded from membership. Later, the whole thing was converted into a church.

Very little is known, however, of Mactaris's late-Roman existence, save for a reference to a bishop, Victor, in the mid-6th century. Clearly it was occupied in Byzantine times, but thereafter, unmentioned in the sources, it vanishes from sight. It was the fate of many settlements in Africa Proconsularis; once the economic network that had characterised the Roman province collapsed, many of the regional centres simply lost their reason to exist.

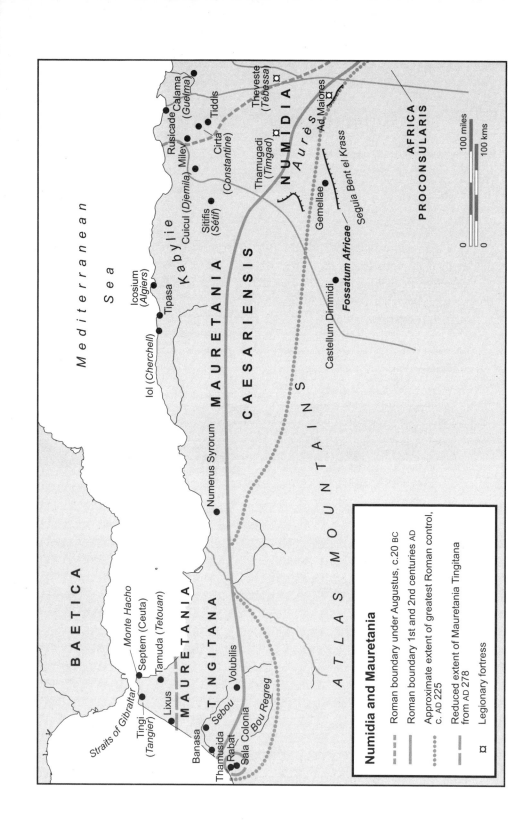

Numidia and Mauretania

- – – – Roman boundary under Augustus, c.20 BC
- ——— Roman boundary 1st and 2nd centuries AD
- ········· Approximate extent of greatest Roman control, c. AD 225
- – – – Reduced extent of Mauretania Tingitana from AD 278
- ¤ Legionary fortress

Mediterranean Sea

BAETICA

Monte Hacho
Septem (Ceuta)
Tamuda (Tetouan)
Straits of Gibraltar
Tingi (Tangier)
Lixus
Banasa
Thamusida
Rabat
Sala Colonia
Bou Regreg
Sebou
MAURETANIA TINGITANA
Volubilis

Numerus Syrorum

ATLAS MOUNTAINS

Iol (Cherchell)
Icosium (Algiers)
Tipasa
Kabylie
MAURETANIA CAESARIENSIS

Rusicade
Calama (Guelma)
Milev
Cuicul (Djemila)
Cirta (Constantine)
Tiddis
Sitifis (Sétif)
Theveste (Tébessa) ¤
NUMIDIA ¤
Aurés
Thamugadi (Timgad)
Ad Maiores ¤
Seguia Bent el Krass
Gemellae
Fossatum Africae
Castellum Dimmidi

AFRICA PROCONSULARIS

0   100 miles
0   100 kms

CHAPTER II

Numidia and Mauretania

If a man will wander in Timgad long enough of a spring morning, especially if he comes late in the season, when the rare visitors no longer reach the place, he will feel arising in himself two lives, the life of his own time which he knows and which has made him, and the life of that immemorial past. It is a terrible, a dangerous, but a fascinating experience.

Hilaire Belloc, *Many Cities*[1]

That part of North Africa to the west of the areas acquired by Rome from Carthage in 146 BC was divided into two broad zones, Numidia (the eastern portion) and Mauretania (further west), occupied by a succession of native kingdoms (but whose area was somewhat different from the later Roman provinces bearing the same names). It was a war involving Jugurtha, the ruler of Numidia, that ultimately led to the end of his kingdom's independence and a further extension of Roman power in North Africa. Having murdered one of his brothers and seized the throne, Jugurtha made the mistake, in 112 BC, of sacking Cirta (in modern Algeria), which had been sheltering his surviving sibling and rival Adherbal, and failing to prevent his victorious troops from murdering the colony of Roman merchants that had been settled there. The subsequent war ended in Jugurtha's defeat and a new carve-up of Africa, which still preserved a Numidian kingdom (under Jugurtha's half-brother Gauda), but left it reduced in extent. It was only after the end of the Roman civil war in 46 BC that the rump kingdom of Numidia, which ran roughly from the borders of modern Tunisia to a point east of Sitifis (Sétif) in modern Algeria, was abolished and joined to the Roman province of Africa Nova.[2]

To the west of Jugurtha's former kingdom, the pre-eminent tribe were the Mauri, who from around 200 BC had taken control of most of the area of modern Morocco and western Algeria, pushing the Phoenicians out of their footholds in towns such as Lixus (close to Larache) and Tingi (Tangier).[3] By 105 the Mauri were ruled by Bocchus, who married

Jugurtha's daughter, but ultimately betrayed the Numidian king and was rewarded with a slice of the monarch's territory and continued independence under the watchful eye of Rome. By the 40s BC the kingdom of Mauretania was split into two, ruled by Bocchus II and Bogud, the former of whom initially supported Pompey in the civil war, but later made up for this indiscretion by adhering to the party of Octavian. As a result, he was allowed to maintain his throne and was rewarded with the territory of his rival, Bogud, who had unwisely supported Mark Antony against Octavian. Bocchus died, childless, in 33 BC and it then looked as though the whole of Mauretania would be annexed as Roman territory. That was until, after a brief period of direct rule, Augustus chose to give the kingdom of Mauretania back its independence.

The family of Juba II, who then became King of Mauretania, boasted a breathtaking and rather dangerous pedigree. His father, Juba I, as King of Numidia, had sided with Pompey against Julius Caesar in 46 BC and had lost his life for it. The young Juba, however, was spared and brought up in Rome in the household of Octavia, Augustus's sister. In 25 BC, the Emperor then presented him with the throne of the newly minted client kingdom of Mauretania. Juba II's wife, who had also been an orphan ward of Augustus, was Cleopatra Selene. Her mother was Cleopatra VII of Egypt, and her father Mark Antony. Juba II's son Ptolemy would, then, count a king of Numidia, a queen of Egypt and a triumvir among his grandparents, a heritage that would later prove his undoing.

Juba presided over a glittering court, although, as a Roman client, his freedom of action outside his own domain was strictly confined. His realm ran from the east of present-day Algeria right to the Atlantic coast of modern Morocco. Volubilis, which lay in the far west of his kingdom, had been the traditional Mauretanian capital, but Juba based his court at Iol (modern Cherchell), which he renamed Caesarea after the patriarch of his foster family. Juba's reputation in the ancient world relied as much on his literary endeavours and his tastes as an artistic patron as on his skills as a ruler. Among his works were *On Arabia*, which he wrote as a result of the experiences he gained in Gaius Caesar's expedition of AD I,[4] as well as a history of Rome, a *Libyka*, which dealt with subjects closer to home, and works on painting, the history of the theatre and a variety of other topics.

Inevitably he became entangled with Rome's affairs in North Africa. In about AD 3, the proconsul Cornelius Lentulus was killed while on an expedition deep in the desert. The guilty party were the Nasamones, a tribe with a particular reputation for barbaric ferocity, and the incident precipitated a general uprising that brought in the Gaetulians, another of the pastoral tribes of the desert fringes.[5] Juba joined his Roman patrons in suppressing the revolt – his territory, too, had been invaded by the marauding tribesmen. On his coins for AD 6 Juba had triumphal regalia shown, but there is no evidence that he was awarded the honour by the Senate.[6] He assisted the Romans once more, during the revolt of Tacfarinas (AD 17–24), though he died just before the revolt was finally put down.[7]

After its cultural and political renaissance under Juba II and Cleopatra Selene, Mauretania retained its independence for just a few years. Their son Ptolemy angered Gaius Caligula, who was his cousin through their mutual descent from Mark Antony, and the Emperor had him executed in 40 or 41. Suetonius relates that Ptolemy had worn a purple robe in public, a prerogative by now reserved for the Emperor alone, but it is possible that he was simply sporting the garb of a high priest of the Isis cult at the dedication of a new temple at Campestris. Ptolemy's death sparked a revolt in Mauretania under Aedemon, who was said to have been a freedman of the murdered king. By 42, though, the war was over, brought to a successful conclusion by Hosidius Geta, who campaigned as far as the Atlas mountains. Mauretania was now incorporated as a province, completing Roman control of the whole of the North African coast.

The administrative organisation of the region was not quite complete, however, for it took until the late 190s, under Septimius Severus, for Numidia – which had been attached to Africa Nova since 46 BC, but had long been regarded as its own region, and had for more than a century been governed separately from Africa by the legionary legates at its principal centre at Lambaesis – to be made officially a distinct province.

Numidia

In its geography, the province of Numidia mirrored much of the rest of Roman North Africa, with a fertile coastal plain including such thriving cities as Hippo Regius, backed by the high plateau of the Tell, and then the descent into near-desert and total desert conditions in the south. The most far-flung outpost in this region was Ad Maiores, a station established under Trajan in 105,[8] in an isolated oasis some 140 kilometres to the south of Theveste (Tébessa). Occupied at least until its destruction by an earthquake in 267, it guarded the junction of a north–south road from Theveste with an east–west one that led from Capsa in Africa Proconsularis all the way to Gemellae, another desert fort in the south-east of Numidia.

This fort, just like Ad Maiores, was guarded by a series of defensive works, which have become known as the *Fossatum Africae*.[9] Composed of a network of earthworks and ditches, and largely built under Hadrian,[10] this does not run in a continuous line across the Algerian desert and so cannot be compared to the fixed defensive positions in northern Britain or, indeed, the *limes* in Germania and Raetia. The defences were probably sited both to provide some kind of shield for the forts slightly to the north and to channel the movements of desert nomads by dominating the routes along which they would have to travel when moving their flocks in search of pasture.[11] Nonetheless, those stretches that still survive, such as a 50-kilometre section south of Gemellae (known as the Seguia bent el-Krass), show that an enormous investment in time and labour would still have been required to construct this system of desert barriers.

The III Augusta legion, North Africa's only legionary garrison west of Egypt, led a fairly peripatetic existence under the early Empire. Despatched to the region in 30 BC, it was at first based at Ammaedara in Tunisia, before a westward move to Thevestis (Tebessa) in the AD 70s, finally coming to rest at Lambaesis (near Batna, 200 kilometres further to the west), probably around AD 81.[12] Around 100 kilometres south of Constantine in Algeria, this lies on a high plain at the edge of the Aurès mountains. There, in compensation for its earlier wanderings, the legion stayed for more than three centuries, until at least the early 5th century, when it was still listed as the garrison in the *Notitia Dignitatum*. From the reign of Diocletian it was also the capital of Numidia Militiana, when the old province was split into two (the northern half becoming Numidia Cirtensis).

Much of the earliest Flavian camp here has now disappeared under the civilian town that grew up on it after the military base was moved a couple of kilometres to its present site. The remains that can be seen date largely from the time of Hadrian, around 129.[13] It seems very austere, set – as befits a military camp – on a rigid grid, but the survival of most of the buildings to just a few courses gives it a stylised chequerboard feel, just a skeleton, with the life of the place long gone. However, it preserves the ideal ground plan of a Roman fort better than almost anywhere else in the Empire. Or at least it did, until the French colonial authorities thoughtfully constructed a prison across the south-western corner of the camp, destroying a part of the fortress. Those areas of the monument that were not obliterated were rendered totally inaccessible for many years, because the Algerian government still maintains the place as a high-security prison; even the pointing of cameras in the direction of the gaol is strictly forbidden. As we inspect the ruins we are accompanied, naturally at a discreet distance, by a squad of local policemen who squawk on walkie-talkies and seek to feign just the slightest pretence of interest in the Roman remains.

Looking down the camp's *via principalis*, the bulky structure of Lambaesis's most famous monument is clearly visible. The 'basilica' is a grand, showy, covered four-way arch at the intersection of the camp's main roads. A winged Victory decorates the central vault, and all around are niches, presumably for the exposition of imperial statues. The specific purpose of the basilica is not clear, but it certainly makes a statement of the legion's power and its permanence. The III Augusta legion's sojourn of more than 300 years at Lambaesis was also surely long enough to permit the construction of buildings whose utilitarian function was outweighed by their grandeur. Beyond the basilica, the camp commander's headquarters, the *praetorium*, lies in a very fragmented state, but the plan of the barrack blocks that take up much of the site is so well preserved that the larger rooms for centurions can be made out at the end of each row. The serried ranks of stones are at once both compelling and monotonous – much as, indeed, the life of the legionaries was, alternating long months of drill and construction work with only occasional bouts of campaigning.

To the west of the site lies a large military amphitheatre, used for both entertainment and military exercise. All the seats have gone, but the banked edges are largely intact, and to one side a fine double-arch survives. The central part of the arena has collapsed, exposing the pillars of the substructure, where stores were kept and prisoners who were to fight or be executed in the arena were held.

A couple of kilometres north-west lies another camp, sometimes known as 'the camp of the auxiliaries' (as distinct from the legionary camp, with its basilica). Little is visible, save from the air, but it was here that Hadrian delivered a famous address to the III Augusta legion in 128 on the occasion of a visit he made to Lambaesis while on his way to Mauretania. He praised the soldiers for their skill in javelin-throwing and for how well they had constructed a camp in a single day, when it would have taken other soldiers twice the time.[14] So pleased was the legion at these imperial plaudits that the whole speech was set down in stone, to be discovered by archaeologists in the civilian town, the *canabae*.

More than one-third of soldiers whose place of birth is listed on funerary monuments at Lambaesis or other inscriptions have it given as *castris*, or 'in the camps', an indication that their father had been a legionary, and it was here that they would have spent their early years.

Many of the tombstones sit in a garden outside the Lambaesis museum, a garden of stelae and eternal hopes. The guardian of the site and the guardian of the museum, however, seem to have a difference of opinion on the day of our visit, and the latter, who has possession of the key – a very important matter in Algeria – declares, in a funk, that not only is the key 'lost', for the moment, but that photography of the gravestones is not permitted without special permission from the ministry. Charon could not have been more strict with those lacking a coin to secure his services.

A large part of the civilian town, which grew up close to the legionary camp, is taken up by a temple to the healing god Asclepios, which, with its five standing pillars, catches the eye far more than the shattered remains of the *capitolium* or the two bathhouses. Just on the border of this site, a small portion of the wall and part of the tower of the earliest, Flavian-era camp from the 80s has been excavated, the earliest stage of the 300-year Roman military occupation here. On the Asclepios temple itself an inscription in which the name of the III Augusta legion has been scratched out and then restored shows that even here, in its base, it was not immune to its memory being erased from the official epigraphic record. Even when the III Augusta had become but a distant memory, there was still clearly a settled population here as late as 683, for in that year the Arab forces of 'Uqba fought a battle near Lambaesis, and the local peoples, defeated, shut themselves into the fortress.

Forty kilometres east of Lambaesis, the town of Thamugadi (modern Timgad) – which lay at the junction of the north–south road with the west–east highway that ran through Lambaesis and its predecessor legionary camp at Tebessa, and ultimately on to Carthage – was the furthest south of the principal Roman settlements in Numidia. It is set on a high fertile plain, at the edge of the Aurès mountains, a range that the Romans never subdued, but instead elected to ring with fortified posts and settlements in an effort to contain what they could not conquer. There were army bases far off in the desert, the most remote being Castellum Dimmidi, isolated and baking in the Algerian desert; but, as Hilaire Belloc remarked of Timgad '. . . the Romans rightly thought that upon placing their town here, they had an outpost and would go no further, for the life lived further south is not natural to our race'.[15]

Thamugadi was founded around 100 by Minucius Gallus, legate of the III Augusta, as a *colonia* in the true spirit of the word, to house veterans of the legion after their retirement. Rejoicing in the full name of Colonia Marciana Traiana Thamugadi, it was planned on a precise grid, some 1,200 Roman feet square, and in its design it replicated rather rigidly, although on a grander scale, the design of a legionary fortress, making it the Milton Keynes or Chandigarh of Roman Africa. Indeed, its forum is pretty much where a legionary camp's *principium* might be expected to lie, and the other buildings are similarly deployed. The population has been estimated at some 15,000, which, given that a legionary served twenty-five years and so a maximum of 200 were discharged each year, represented many years of time-served veterans, even when their families were taken into account. The population must, therefore, have included a significant non-military element from the start.

Looking at the city from outside the remains of the wall – which was largely demolished as the population outgrew its bounds – the uprights of the buildings (the architectural feature that has survived best) create the image of a particularly orderly cemetery interspersed with the odd more grandiose funerary monument. Serving the citizenry were no fewer than fourteen baths; one of them by the *cardo* on the north side of town was bordered by a library donated, according to an inscription, by Marcus Flavius Rogatianus, at a cost of some 400,000 sesterces. More evidence of the municipal prosperity of Thamugadi came from the forum, which was ringed with monuments. A variety of graffiti survives etched into its blue limestone, including the digits of a sundial and the inscription *Venari, Lavari, Ludere Ridere, Hoc est Vivere* (which translates as 'Hunting, bathing, gambling and laughing, now *that* is living'). The forum was bordered by the only temple built at the time of the original foundation, which was dedicated to Trajan and had in its basement a vaulted room that acted as the city treasury, much as the Temple of the Standards in a legionary camp would have housed the unit's strongroom.

It was here that the *album* of Thamugadi was found, dating from 363–4.[16] It was intended as a list of all the town's dignitaries, including the decurions (the members of the curial order). In effect, it listed all those men who were liable to compulsory service – which mainly involved the expenditure of money on a variety of public projects and duties. It is a constant complaint in the sources, and one that much late-Roman imperial legislation sought to correct, that the decurions were seeking to evade their civic obligation by any means open to them. This included outright flight from the cities, the acquisition of titles or offices locally that might exempt them, and the payment of fines which, though burdensome in themselves, were far less so than actually taking up the onerous magistracies that they were seeking at all costs to avoid.[17] After the bureaucratic reforms of Diocletian and his successors, and the establishment of something resembling a centralised civil service, not to mention the multiplication of offices when the number of provinces was greatly increased, and an extra layer of governance added at the level of the vicariate, the opportunities for central service, and thus exemption – temporary or permanent – from town duties dramatically increased.

The distress of the decurial class is often cited as evidence for the decline of towns, but, as the nature of the Empire's government changed, so too did the relationship between the traditional urban ruling classes and the centre. Officials such as *correctores* appeared[18] charged with the reform of the administration of this or that town, and cities increasingly looked to a patron (*patronus*) to protect their interests, as the base of those willing or able to devote their own personal financial resources to power on a purely local scale diminished. Finally, those families who had traditionally been eager to memorialise themselves by donating public buildings, or services such as the provision of free oil at the baths, found, after the advent of Christianity in the 4th century, a much better spiritual bargain. In giving money for the foundation of churches, and in having this liberality commemorated in stone or mosaic inscriptions, they gained immortality both for their memory amongst the living and for their souls in the next life.

The first ten on the Thamugadi list are given the title *illustrissimi*, which in the inflationary world of late-Roman honorifics gave them exemption from civic service. The next rank includes *perfectissimi*, who were exempt until 354 and may have tried to cling on to this privilege even after that date.[19] There then follows a list of various priests, including thirty-two *flamines perpetui*, four *pontifices* and three *augures*, for service in a municipal priesthood or as part of the imperial cult was one of the more prestigious ways to serve one's city. A number of the men listed who did not have a specific title are given as *excusati*, and it is probable that they had paid some kind of fine to avoid the exacting financial toll of municipal office.

At the bottom of the heap are those fifty unfortunates who are *non excusati* and therefore liable to serve as magistrates, and to pay the hefty price involved. Interestingly, the Thamugadi album lists eleven Christian clergy (*clerici*). Christian priests had been exempted by Constantine in 319 from compulsory civic duties, but the acquisition of clerical status had become such a popular way of evading public service that subsequent emperors chafed at their predecessor's liberality, and as part of the pagan reaction under Julian the priests were restored to their place in the curial order and the concomitant obligation to carry out municipal duties.

Beyond the forum of Thamugadi lies the Arch of Trajan, a curiously muted affair compared to the triumphal arches in other North African towns. It was, despite its name, actually built around 166. Its large main entrance flanked by two smaller openings and the rounded attics of the arch's architrave are said to be typical of Eastern influence, which could say something about the origins of the legionary architects responsible for its construction. On the outer side, an inscription of Severan date originally had the word 'Auggg' with the three 'g's representing the three emperors (Septimius Severus, Geta and Caracalla). But here, as elsewhere, the agents of Caracalla were ruthless in erasing one 'g' after their master's murder of his brother Geta.

To the south of the forum, with a capacity for some 3,500 spectators, lies the city's theatre, its seating largely intact, but with the stage backdrop missing to permit spectacular views over the city from the auditorium's rearmost rows. If the theatre seems out of proportion to Thamugadi's orderly layout, the *capitolium*, in the south-west of the original town, is even more so. On a 53-metre-wide podium, only four of its original six columns now standing, it is erected on an axis at variance with the main grid pattern of the city, and so was clearly not part of the original plan. Whatever the motives for its addition, it was obviously being maintained comparatively late in Thamugadi's history, for an inscription dedicated to Valens and Valentinian (and hence between 364 and 378) commemorates the restoration of the building's portico.

Around the end of the 2nd century, the city burst its bounds, much of the wall was demolished and new suburbs built, particularly to the west of the original settlement. Amongst these are two entirely separate Christian complexes, one Catholic and one Donatist, mirroring the religious strife that divided North Africa throughout the 4th and most of 5th centuries.[20] The Donatist quarter lies to the southwest, and was the powerbase of one of the most notorious of the sect's leaders, Bishop Optatus of Thamugadi.[21] His cathedral church, originally a huge construction preceded by an atrium, survives only in ruins, though it was identified by a mosaic inscription that named Optatus and then, modestly, added: 'how great the praise to his name'.[22] The whole complex also included a further chapel, the bishop's house and, a few metres away, a baptistery with a hexagonal font decorated by a fine zigzag-patterned mosaic.

The Catholic area, situated well away in the south-west suburbs, is of poorer construction reflecting, presumably, its lower status at Thamugadi. In the end, Catholicism won, a pyrrhic victory that would be entirely undone by the advent of Islam just two centuries later. Between those events, however, came the Byzantine reoccupation of Thamugadi, represented by the fort to the south of the city.

Thamugadi seems to have been destroyed by tribes from the Aurès, who razed it at the time of the Justinianic invasion 'so that the Romans would have no excuse to come near us again'.[23] But the imperial general Solomon reused some of the ruins to construct new defences, using as his base the site of a Severan temple. It stands block-like some 110 metres long and 65 metres wide, its walls still standing in places to more than 15 metres in height. A simple gateway gives access to the interior beside a building inscription commemorating Solomon's work that lies in the undergrowth. Inside, the former barracks are a jumble of stones and a Byzantine chapel, all arranged around the original *piscina* (pool) of the Severan temple.

The fact that settlement at Thamugadi continued to the very end is shown by an inscription found in a Christian cemetery near the fort, which commemorates the building of a chapel by the patrician Gregory, whose term of office ran from 641 to 647, expiring after an ill-fated attempt to establish an independent Empire in the African provinces. Thereafter Thamugadi lost its *raison d'être*. No longer an outpost against the desert tribes, who were themselves largely incorporated into the Islamic empire, and with its role as an administrative and market centre disappeared, it soon withered away, decaying into the faded skeleton of today's site.

The Donatists, who had taken such a hold in Thamugadi, were a peculiarly African breakaway group. In the way of all good sectaries, they regarded themselves as the members of the true Catholic Church, and all the rest as excommunicants – not strictly heretics, for they differed from the official Church principally in whose authority they recognised, rather than in matters of dogma. The schism had its origins in the Great Persecution of Diocletian in 303–5. The initial edict, which reached Africa in mid-May 303,[24] ordered the handing over of Christian Scriptures and the destruction of some church buildings, but it was not reinforced by a general order to make a sacrifice to the gods until the following year. The initial reaction of some bishops, such as Paulus of Cirta, was to hand over some Scriptures, while others such as the Primate of Africa Proconsularis, Mensurius of Carthage – a nice piece of casuistry this – gave up heretical writings, which surely could not count as a sinful act.[25] By the end of 304, the persecution was beginning to wane in its intensity, and those who had refused to hand over Scriptures and had been imprisoned – though many had been martyred – for their obduracy, began to turn on those who had been weaker, labelling them as *traditores*, or traitors to the Christian faith.

In 311 or 312, Mensurius died, leaving the see of Carthage empty. The senior clergy, anxious for a quick succession, chose Mensurius's archdeacon, Caecilian, to replace him. Unfortunately, Caecilian had offended a leading member of the congregation, a Spaniard named Lucilla, by scolding her for kissing the bone of a martyr before communion. In revenge, she encouraged the populace of Carthage to name one of her servants, Majorinus, as the rightful bishop. At a council held in Carthage, the African bishops sought to mend the rift.[26] Yet feelings were running too high, and once Caecilian was accused of having been consecrated by a *traditor* and thus not really, in the eyes of the extremists, a priest at all, the council fell apart and the rival factions could not be reconciled.

By 313, Majorinus had died and the anti-Caecilianist faction came to be led by Donatus of Casae Nigrae, whose acuteness and able leadership over forty years meant that the schismatics grew in strength and could not simply be bullied back into the fold. He also gave his name to the movement, which was thenceforth known as Donatism. The 'official' Catholic Church remained strong in the large cities, in the smaller towns and particularly in the villages of the hinterland – and most especially in Mauretania – but Donatism took root and thrived, though the Catholics were to take great delight over subsequent years in accusing the Donatists of being bishops of mere estates (*fundi*) or manors (*villae*) and not of real towns at all.

It had been just a few short years since Constantine I's conversion to Christianity, and the Edict of Milan that put an end to the persecutions throughout the Empire, was issued, the same year that Donatus rose to prominence. The Emperor had heard murmurs of the troubled state of the Church in Africa, and was not best pleased, for he did not wish to have subscribed to the Christian religion only to find his new faith beset by squabbling and disharmonious factions that would undermine, rather than bolster, the unity of the Empire. Constantine gave his support to Caecilian without hesitation or, it seems, much thought, authorising the imperial procurator in Africa to restore to the Catholic faction any estates that had been confiscated during the persecutions.[27]

The howls of Donatist protest were heard all the way to Rome, and a petition was sent to Constantine demanding justice. It was a pivotal moment, not only in the schism, but for Christian history in general, because now, for the first time, Christians were appealing to a Christian emperor, the supreme secular authority, to make a ruling on Church discipline.[28] Constantine, infuriated that his initial decision had been questioned, nonetheless ordered the summoning of a council at the Lateran Palace in September 313.[29] At this Pope Miltiades condemned Donatus for his schismatic ways, and in particular for insisting on the rebaptism of clergy who had originally been baptised by *traditores*. The Donatists responded by accusing Miltiades himself of being a *traditor* and demanding another judgement. Constantine, showing admirable restraint, summoned a new council at Arles for August 314, at which the Donatists were condemned once more.[30]

In 317, persecution of the Donatists began with orders that their churches were to be confiscated. In a spasm of violence unleashed by the *dux* Leontius, a crowd of Donatists was massacred in Carthage,[31] while the bishops of Advocata and Sicilabba were murdered. This served only to provide the anti-Catholic cause with a rich crop of martyrs, and in 321 Constantine granted the Donatists toleration, hoping that by ignoring them their self-righteous sense of persecution might wither away and cause them to regret their error. Far from begging for re-admission, however, Donatus used the new latitude granted by the removal of the threat of official intervention to consolidate the African Church, so that by the 340s it was the Catholics who were on the defensive, under pressure from Donatist congregations almost everywhere.[32]

In 346, so confident was Donatus that he asked the Emperor Constans for official recognition of his position as Bishop of Carthage. Constans sent two imperial notaries, Paul and Macarius, to investigate, but rumours swirled around the African provinces that they had come to condemn Donatism afresh.[33] Riots broke out in Carthage, and the more extreme elements among the Donatists played into their opponents' hands. Known as the circumcellions – possibly from their habit of hanging around country shrines (*circum cellas*) – they acted as the muscle of Donatism, actively seeking martyrdom by attacking those who opposed them (including officials) swinging clubs and crying '*Laus Deo*' ('Praise to God'). In extreme cases, when they could find a martyr's death in no more satisfactory fashion, they threw themselves, lemming-like, off the edge of cliffs. In some mountainous areas, heaps of stones lying at the foot of such precipices, each carved with the word *reditum* ('ransom' or 'offering'), are believed to represent a commemoration of such mass suicides.[34]

The result, predictably, was that Donatism was outlawed once more. The decision was reversed in 361 when the Emperor Julian, mischievously seeking to sow dissent amongst his Christian opponents, permitted the return of all those who had been exiled on account of their religious beliefs, the Donatists included.[35]

The pendulum swung yet again in 364 with the accession of Valentinian and Valens, whose restoration of Christianity as the official creed carried implicit in that decision the need to crack down once more on schismatics

and heretics. In the end it was the involvement, or at least the percep-
tion of involvement, in the revolts of Firmus in 372 and Gildas in 397[36]
that fatally undermined support for Donatism in Africa. The tireless
campaigning of Saint Augustine against the Donatists in the early 5th
century also drew supporters away from them. Although ably defended
by their very own theologian, Petilian[37] – who accused Augustine of bad
faith, and implied (as it happens correctly) that the Bishop of Hippo had
been at one point a Manichaean (and thus not a Christian at all) or was
at least sympathetic to them – Donatist congregations continued to be
pressurised. But the anti-Donatist coalition was too strong by now, and
in a dramatic denouement at the Council of Carthage in 411, Donatism
was condemned, its clergy exiled and adherence to their cause made a
crime. Although the Donatists had mustered 279 bishops at Carthage
(against the Catholics' 286, which included the rousing of a number of
invalids from their sick-beds), their threat faded away in the last twenty
years of Roman rule in Africa, but they had represented a very real local
challenge to the hegemony of a Church centralising in the West around
the see of Rome.

For the Donatists, Africa was the 'Bride of Christ' and, as they made
no headway in persuading others outside their provinces of the justice
of their cause, they came simply to ignore them. They were nourished
in their belief in a salvation reserved only to Donatist true believers by
a martyrology of their own. They prayed to saints such as Maxima,
Secunda and Donatilla, who around 304 were tortured by being made to
lie on a bed of crushed shells, then thrown into the amphitheatre, where
a savage bear piously declined to devour them, and were finally beheaded.[38]
Dedications to such martyrs, whose names are rarely found elsewhere,
are a crucial indicator for archaeologists that a North African Church was
occupied by a Donatist, rather than a Catholic, congregation.

Once the Vandals had captured North Africa in 429, however, the very
notion of a separatist Church opposed to Rome came to have no sense,
for Africa itself was now in opposition to the Roman Empire. The Vandals'
Arianism, moreover, which led them intermittently to persecute those of
a more orthodox bent, drove former Donatists and Catholics together.
Separated from the political control of Rome and persecuted by their
barbarian overlords in Carthage, the former foes were left more united
in their common adversity than at any time since the Great Persecution.

Constantine (Cirta to the Romans) lay 105 kilometres north of Timgad,
through intractable mountainous terrain. The city has antecedents
stretching even further back. Now Algeria's second city, a bustling,

crowded, traffic-choked metropolis, it is recorded as early as the 3rd century BC, when it was the capital of the Numidian King Syphax. Later it became the chief centre of Massinissa, the base from which he encroached steadily into the former territory of Carthage. In the confused period after Julius Caesar's victory against the Pompeian forces at Thapsus in 46 BC, Cirta and its territory were handed over to Publius Sittius, a mercenary adventurer and favourite of Caesar, who, with his band of followers, occupied a territory between the new province of Africa Nova and the lands of King Bocchus of Mauretania.[39]

Although Sittius himself was killed around 44–43 BC, the land around Cirta managed, together with nearby Rusicade, Chullu and Milev, to retain a separate identity for nearly a century and a half, as the confederation of 'Four Colonies', until the abolition of their privileges by Trajan and the elevation of Cirta to the rank of a more standard *colonia*. Although it was an important town in Roman times (and became the seat of the *dux Numidiae* in 534),[40] its very success in surviving into the Arab period and then beyond to become a thriving modern city has meant that almost nothing remains from the Roman era. Somewhere in the deep gorge that dramatically slashes through Constantine – dividing it into two parts connected by a precariously wobbling bridge built by the French in 1912 – lie two arches of a Roman bridge. More tangible are the five arches of an aqueduct, which lie largely forgotten in an open area above the city, part of the system that provided water to it.

Only 15 kilometres or so north-west of Cirta, but already mired deep in hill country, lies Tiddis or, to give the settlement its full name, Castellum Tidditanorum. The term *castellum* was generally applied in the North African provinces to those indigenous settlements that already acted as a focal point for their vicinities, but which were not formally organised as a *municipium* (or *colonia*) with a Roman constitution. The town lies precariously attached to a crag overlooking the gorge of the Rhumel river, as if waiting for some seismic wobble to send it tumbling into the valley below. Even relatively recently it was no easy matter to find the site, and it long remained remote from the attentions either of archaeologists or of stone-robbers. In 1893, the French historian Alfred Baraudon, hearing of some worthwhile Roman ruins there, spent a torrid day scouring the hills around in search of it, but finally gave up, declaring Tiddis to be *'vraiment introuvable'* and signing off with a bitter warning against having too much confidence in the veracity of local guides or foreign guidebooks.[41]

Had Baraudon persisted, he would have seen a town that mimicked the classical ideal in spirit, while varying from it as much in form as the vertiginous topography of the place dictated. The rosy-red barrenness of the surrounding hills makes the town's grey stones stand out more starkly as its roads and alleyways turn and switch sharply back in twists and hairpins to reach, after a half-hour's breathless climb, Tiddis's highest point. In places the slope is just too much and the walkways are replaced by flights of stairs to encourage tired travellers upwards. It has something of the character of the modern Berber villages that dot the Kabylie mountains, but actually to term it a 'Berber town' is to telescope history unduly.[42]

The site has no natural spring and is generally not well provided with water, so its innate defensibility must have outweighed this otherwise severe disadvantage. The deficit was made up by a large number of cisterns that dot the town, thristily capturing whatever rainwater the gods might provide. Tiddis's north gate has its very own monumental arch, dedicated by Quintus Memmius Rogatus, which imitates in miniature the grander affairs to be found at Timgad, Leptis or Dougga. On the arch's keystone is carved the image of a sword, as if an indication of the military purpose of the town, from the Romans' point of view – intended to defend and supervise the only partly Romanised inhabitants of the interior. Roman ways did, however, penetrate Tiddis; only a short way from the north gate lies a *mithraeum*, its shallow grotto excavated into the hillside, and with a few broken altars now lying about, some with the unmistakable image of a bull's head incised into them. The door jambs of the shrine bear a good-luck symbol of a double-winged phallus.

The city was defended in those areas accessible to intruders by a pre-Roman wall built of large cyclopean blocs, which was retained in Roman times and, much later, during the Arab period, repaired and reinforced, using demolished buildings and cutting across existing paths and edifices (including the immurement of a baptistery at the foot of the forum's retaining wall).[43]

A few bends further on lies Tiddis's tiny forum, at just 30 metres long and 10 metres wide the smallest in North Africa, and hardly the place for any but the most self-conscious mingling. Its purpose, then, was purely ceremonial. As Tiddis took on the aspect of a Roman town, so a Roman forum it had, perforce, to have. Among the altars and memorials erected in this tiny space was one to *Fortuna Augustae*, the Fortune of the Emperor, and a number to individual emperors, particularly the Severans from Septimius Severus to Alexander Severus. The last emperor honoured by name was Gordian III in 239, while the rulers of the mid-3rd-century are remembered only in a plaque attached to the baths constructed further uphill by Marcus Cocceius Anicius Faustus in 251, which states that he employed 'ruined buildings' to construct the cisterns and baths,[44] implying that the town, exposed in the hills, had suffered difficult times after the dissolution of the III Augusta legion in 238.

Here also stands a memorial to Quintus Lollius Urbicus, a local man whose family probably originated from Cirta, and whose career shows the astonishing heights to which someone from even a small hill settlement such as this could reach. Born around 100, he reached the praetorship in 129, commanded a legion in Noricum on the Danube, and was then instrumental in the suppression of the Bar Kochba revolt in Palestine in 132–5, was awarded a consulship between 136 and 138, and was then despatched to be governor of Britain in the early 140s, where he oversaw the initial construction of the Antonine Wall in 142–3.[45] Short of becoming Emperor, he had achieved everything an ambitious aristocrat could dream of. The inscription commemorates the consulate, the high-point of his career, and names him as the town's 'patron': Urbicus clearly was (or his home town hoped him to be) in a good position to swing favours on its behalf. That he did continue links with his native land is indicated by the well-appointed mausoleum that he erected for his parents at El Heri, 4 kilometres to the north of Tiddis.[46]

Christianity seems to have come late to Tiddis. There is no evidence of a bishop before the 5th century, and there is only one small Christian basilica. Indeed, the governor of Numidia at the end of the 4th century, Publius Ceionius Caecina Albinus, seems to have been responsible for the installation of a cult shrine to Vesta at Tiddis, which implies at least some residual pagan resistance to Christianisation even at that late stage. Apart from the *mithraeum*, the Christian baptistery and a small ruined Christian chapel near the north gate, the religious life of Tiddis was very varied. A substantial shrine to the harvest goddess Ceres clings halfway up the city slopes, keeping company with a nearby Temple to Asclepios, the healing god, while right at the top among a jumble of ruins and dry, parched vegetation lie the scattered remains of a shrine to that perennial North African favourite god, Saturn.[47]

From here the view down into the valley is spectacular. A series of blue ant-like figures gradually wend their way towards the summit, not taking the 'easy' way up the twisting decumanus, but cutting straight up the hillside. It is a platoon of the village militia, for Tiddis, or at least those few who visit it, still need defending from local insurgents. With their ages spanning the full range of active life and their vintage rifles glinting dully in the midday sun, they seem the rightful heirs of the last Roman defenders of the place, whose best hope of survival was probably to avoid being attacked in the first place.

The last coins found in Tiddis date from 406, during the reign of Arcadius. It seems, therefore, that regular economic activity and trade had ceased even before the Vandal invasion and normal life was not restored under Byzantine rule. In this latest period of Tiddis, a pottery kiln was installed on the site of a former villa and another in the *caldarium* of the baths. If not abandoned, the town was certainly transformed. There is evidence, indeed, from pottery found here of some sort of settlement as late as the 11th century, making it one of the most long-lived of the native towns of the region. Perhaps the mountain air encourages longevity, for one of Tiddis's monuments records thirty-one Tidditan citizens who lived to be centenarians, one of whom, Cutruvia Urbana, is said to have survived a very creditable, if scarcely believable, 130 years.[48]

The last resting place for the Roman Tidditans was a series of necropolises to the north, south and east of the town. The eastern cemetery lies close to the road, an exposed and abandoned jumble of sarcophagi, many of them commemorating deceased with the family name of the mercenary Sittius, for the Campanian *condottiere* was remembered in the region of Cirta long after his demise. Here – honour satisfied that no one has come to grief while inspecting the ruins – our guards thirstily accept a gift of water, for Tiddis's cisterns are long fallen into disrepair, and then wave us on through the 'safety' of the mountain road.

This route leads some 60 kilometres to the west, through the *bled*, the high plain ringed by mountains (here the Lesser Kabylie) that produces a surprisingly great yield in crops. Finally, nestling in a valley surrounded by almost lunar-like hills, lies Cuicul. Its Arabic name Djemila, 'the fair', accurately reflects the stern beauty of its setting. Although comparatively near to the coast, there was little ease of north–south communications, and so Cuicul's connections were largely to the east and west. Founded under Nerva as a veteran colony,[49] the town lay on a rocky outcrop between two wadis and began as a classic planned settlement on a grid pattern. Thereafter, as the population expanded, new districts had to be constructed further down, and so the lower levels seem as if they have been poured out of the original city bounds and then congealed in ten thousand dragon's teeth strewn about the hillside. Down past the remains of Cuicul's colonnaded *cardo*, an archway leads into the North Forum, the city's original civic centre, which preserves an enormous number of statue bases and inscriptions intact, giving a real sense of its role as the focus of local government, trade and self-publicity for the ruling clans. One of them preserves the tongue-twisting original name of Djemila, 'Colonia Cuiculitanorum', which must have given even native Italians pause for thought.

A series of steps run behind the forum, leading up to the raised podium on which sits the Temple of Venus Genetrix, the goddess of mother-hood, only three of its columns still standing, giving it a curiously fractured feeling. This version of Venus was traditionally seen by the Romans as the mother of Aeneas, who fled the burning ruins of Troy and, after many travails, ended up in Italy, where his descendant, Romulus, would found their city. Aeneas, crucially, was also viewed as the ancestor (through his son, Iulus) of the Julian *gens*, of which Julius Caesar was a member, and to which Augustus became attached by virtue of adop-tion. The worship of Venus Genetrix, although not particularly widespread,[50] thus became almost an adjunct to the imperial cult, and for a city to have such a splendid temple to her – mirroring that estab-lished by Caesar himself at Rome – was a formidable statement of loyalty.

Also bounding the North Forum is the market of Cosinius, dedicated in the 2nd century by two brothers, Lucius Cosinius Primus and Caius Cosinius Maximus. They were of Carthaginian origin, for Cosinius Primus had held various magistracies at that city before in turn becoming a *duumvir* at Cuicul. Still standing beside the twenty or so shops are the stone basins (one with a stone plug still intact) in which liquid measures were assayed, and an inscription showing that the construction of the complex cost the Cosinii brothers the princely sum of 30,000 sesterces.[51]

Nearby is situated a series of rich urban villas – the House of the Ass, the House of Europa and the House of Amphitrite – each named for the most splendid of the mosaics found there. The last-named was the site of one of the most spectacular of all, now in the site museum. It shows a brilliant array of Nereids depicted by the artist around a triumphant figure of Amphitrite, the consort of Poseidon, who is surrounded by dolphins and seals, the sea-creatures seen as her children, together with a very spider-like octopus. Nearby, a curious mosaic (from the House of the Ass) portrays a donkey looking rather pleased with itself, together with a variety of animals and naked figures clutching grapes; it bears the inscription *Asinus nika* ('The Ass conquers'), a mixture of Greek and Latin, which might refer to a victory of some sort by the owner of the place (who may therefore have been named Asinius).[52] Many of the mosaics were comparatively late additions, from the 4th or even 5th centuries, showing that the villas were occupied for more than 200 years after their establishment in the 2nd century.

To the south of Cuicul lies the principal area of the city's develop-ment in its middle phase. The Severan Forum, a huge irregular space, has a certain overpowering monumentality to it, just as the Empire itself was displaying a certain self-conscious effort by the late 2nd century, far removed from the easy-going expansiveness of the late Republic and the early emperors. Along one side stands a temple dedicated to the Severan family, constructed in 229, at almost the end of their rule, with two podiums stacked one atop the other, the central sanctuary being reached by a double flight of steps. Even in its partially ruined state it is the city's most imposing edifice, a statement of might by a dynasty whose rule would crumble within a decade.

Here, too, lies Cuicul's theatre, again part of the Severan reconstruction, partly scooped out of the hillside, which meant that elaborate substructures to support it were not necessary. Three curved stone sections of the backdrop survive, remnants of the three stage entrances that would have conventionally represented buildings or locations away from the main scene of the action, and through which the actors would have come onto the stage, depending on their supposed point of departure.[53] The topmost of the twenty-four rows of seats provides a wonderful vantage point to the hills beyond, the nearer ones partly wooded, then the higher peaks beyond brown and arid-looking, folded in and back over themselves in a confused muddle of slopes and wadis.

At the exit from the forum, at the start of the road that led west towards Sitifis (modern Sétif), a monumental arch (of Caracalla) built in 216 completes the collection of Severan buildings. Its single span towers high above the roadway, flanked by niches set in double-columns for the exposition of the imperial images. It was only mere chance that Cuicul preserved this magnificent arch, for in 1839 the Duc d'Orléans passed this way during an expedition against the desert tribes. So impressed was he with the monument that he decided to have it dismantled and removed to Paris. Fortunately (for Cuicul, at least), he died at the critical moment, so the structure was left in place.[54]

As in the majority of North African towns, the most visible buildings of the city's later phase are Christian in purpose. Two main basilicas, one of the 4th and one of the 5th century, together with a circular baptistery, mark the centre of the Christian quarter set on a hillside at a discreet distance from the original urban heart. The confused skeletons of the buildings are less interesting than the mosaic placed in one of them by Bishop Cresconius, which, if it was the same man as the one who attended the Council of Constantinople in 553, represents the last visible evidence for the occupation of the city.

The Council itself was called by Justinian as a means of settling the 'Three Chapters Controversy', which the Emperor himself had caused by having the works of three theologians (Theodoret of Cyrrhus, Theodoret of Mopsuestia and Ibas of Edessa) anathematised in an effort to reconcile Monophysites to the official Chalcedonian position on the nature of Christ's humanity.[55] This set off a storm of controversy, particularly in the Western Church, where many of the protagonists could neither read Greek (and so were at rather a loss as to what Justinian was trying to achieve), nor particularly welcomed continued imperial meddling in what they thought was the done deal of Chalcedon. A series of petty schisms broke out, with some bishops (such as Elias of Aquileia) point-blank refusing to have anything do with the condemnation of the Three Chapters.[56]

Ecclesiastical politics was not a pretty thing in late-Roman or Byzantine times, and Pope Vigilius, who travelled to Constantinople on an imperial summons in 546, was held a virtual hostage there for eight years, whilst the Emperor alternately tried cajoling and threats in order to get him to condemn the anathematised Chapters. Vigilius was even forced at times to take sanctuary in one or other of Constantinople's basilicas, issuing an anguished encyclical letter protesting at the outrageous treatment to which he had been subjected. Finally, after a cat-and-mouse game of acceptance, retraction and counter-retraction of the Three Chapters, Vigilius was allowed home in 555, only to die at Syracuse in Sicily before he reached Rome.[57]

Bishop Cresconius of Cuicul seems to have suffered no such indignities, but his home town had less than a century left of rule by Christian sovereigns. Here, unlike other places such as Timgad, the Byzantines did not build a fortress, but whether this was because the region was, for some reason, felt to be more secure or, just the opposite – that it could not easily be held and was not therefore worth defending – is unclear. The final fate of the city, too, is obscure. It is no longer mentioned in the sources, and presumably its population drifted away, leaving its colonnaded avenues, its arches and its splendid hilltop site untenanted and unregarded.

Mauretania

Just to the west of Cuicul, the province of Mauretania began. After the Romans acquired it in AD 40–2, it was initially governed as a single unit, but, during the reign of Claudius, around 60, this was divided into two, with the eastern part becoming Mauretania Caesariensis (whose western border was around Numerus Syrorum, modern Maghnia, 50 kilometres west of Tlemcen in Algeria), and the western portion – which covered roughly the north-west of modern Morocco – being organised as Mauretania Tingitana. Much as its Numidian neighbour to the east,

Mauretania had a comparatively densely populated coastal zone, a hilly, but still-fertile hinterland in which prosperous agricultural settlements clustered, and an arid southern portion, home to few save the odd patrol of Roman auxiliaries.

From Cuicul in Numidia, the road leads south-westwards to Sétif (ancient Sitifis), a town that lay inside the boundaries of Mauretania Caesariensis (with its capital at Iol Caesarea, modern Cherchell), but which from the 290s was the chief centre of its own miniature province of Mauretania Sitifensis.[58] The city that in fact became the capital of modern Algeria lies 225 kilometres to the north-west, on the coast. Of ancient Iconium, Algiers (its modern descendant) preserves almost nothing. The warren-like kasbah, clinging to the hill that leads down into the city's port, is crumbling through a mixture of studied neglect and programmed demolition to cleanse its teeming streets of the taint of Islamic radicalism that touched it during Algeria's vicious civil war in the 1990s. The pacification campaign that brought an end to this conflict, in which thousands died, has left an uneasy calm in places such as this, and in the regional towns to the south-east of Algiers intermittent bomb blasts are a sign that, as far as tourism and archaeological investigation go, this is a country that very much still lies on the frontier.

The kasbah sits on the site of the original Punic settlement, and its Roman successor stretched also along the coast, leaving only the traces of three bathhouses and parts of a necropolis. According to the 3rd-century Latin grammarian Solinus, the city derives its name from the Greek 'Eikosi' (meaning 'twenty', a reference to the legendary travels of Heracles in the area, during which he is said to have founded Icosium with the help of twenty companions).[59] Solinus's *Polyhistor*, however, is so stuffed with tall stories – such as the grasshoppers of Rhegium who emit no sound because Heracles was so irritated by their clicking and whirring that he told them to be silent – that the tale of the twenty founders of Icosium is probably equally fantastic.

Around 50 kilometres west along the coastal road from Icosium lies Tipasa. Its spectacular seaside setting and sheltered harbour attracted the attention of the Phoenicians as early as the 6th century BC, and there was already a thriving Punic community here by the time Mauretania became a Roman province. It was made a *municipium* under Claudius, and in the mid-1st century, Tipasa received a new circuit of city walls, some 2 kilometres in circumference, intended to guard against a Moorish attack that never came. It was made a colony under Hadrian or Antoninus Pius,[60] but never achieved outstanding pre-eminence.

It is the beauty of Tipasa's location, more than its historical standing,

that makes it unique, and its remaining buildings acquire their grandeur
more from its topography than their undoubted architectural virtuosity.[61]
The place has inspired many to raptures, including Albert Camus in his
Noces à Tipasa.[62] With its shaded pathways drawing the traveller's eyes
into a pleasing struggle between the closed green world of the trees and
the open blue expanse of the sea, the monuments seem but a series of
fleeting stone-grey impressions. Close to the site entrance, the colonnaded *cardo* leads down first to a set of baths, where two fractured lines
of brickwork standing to 14 metres indicate the remains of the *caldarium*.
Beyond, the road, with many of its cobblestones still surviving, smoothed
with age, gives on to the 'New Temple', a shrine to an unknown god,
whose cult is now commemorated only by a few orphaned columns.
Then it passes by the amphitheatre, some 80 metres long, where clear
evidence of the concrete tapering vaults to support the now-disappeared
upper levels show that the capacity of the place must have been large.
Now, in the grassy oval, where formerly blood, fear and violence ruled,
a clump of sheep tranquilly graze.

The city's forum lies on a peninsula about a kilometre from its port,
complete with civic basilica and Capitoline temple. However, its most
significant find was the House of the Mosaics, a rich private villa, whose
floors were lavishly decorated with mosaics and its walls with sumptuous
frescoes. Built on a pre-Roman cemetery, it was occupied from the reign
of Antoninus Pius until the Byzantine era. One set of rooms was converted
in the late 2nd or early 3rd century into private baths, with a summer
dining room that gave a spectacular view over the bay. Later on, the north
of the villa was converted for the manufacture of *garum*, the fish paste
so beloved of the Romans.[63] In one room, three large storage jars can
still be seen, the upper portions broken away, but the cracked bases still
set into the concrete floor. The smell of the fish as they decayed and
putrefied to just the right consistency must have tempered somewhat the
later inhabitants' enjoyment of their idyllic surroundings.

Unlike many Mauretanian and Numidian towns, Tipasa does not seem
to have been a bastion of Donatism – in fact quite possibly the opposite. After the relaxation of strictures on the sect by Constans in 347,
Tipasa suffered the wrath of the Donatists and was sacked by a mob
that included two of their bishops.[64] In 372, a revolt led by Firmus, a
local aristocrat who was alleged to have received succour from the
Donatists, suffered its fatal defeat outside the walls of the city. The inhabitants attributed their salvation to the miraculous intervention of Saint
Salsa, a thirteen-year-old Christian girl who had angered the local pagans
by stealing the most venerated of their idols, a bronze serpent with a

gilded head, and casting it into the sea. Infuriated, they beat Salsa, stoned her to death and then flung her corpse to lie with their lost snake statue at the bottom of the bay. However, a miraculous storm, blew up and the waves deposited her body on the shore, where a sea-captain from Gaul rescued it and buried the saint on the eastern promontory of the bay, at a spot where in later years a basilica was constructed and a great pilgrimage shrine sprang up.

The church lies there still, beyond the settlement walls, for the practice of not burying the dead within the city boundaries continued to be adhered to. Within the burial ground's circular enclosure, its walls embedded with decorative columns, dozens of lidless sarcopaghi cluster, as though all jostling to reach as close as possible to the city's patron saint, hoping that her sanctity would aid their own pleading on the Day of Judgement. Beyond, a thick copse of sturdy trees girdles the necropolis in soothing green. The tomb of Salsa itself borrowed a pagan sarcophagus, on which scenes were carved from the legend of Endymion, a shepherd with whom Selene the moon goddess became so enamoured that she entreated Zeus to preserve his beauty by granting him everlasting sleep – all hardly fitting for a Christian saint. In her own eternal slumber, Saint Salsa seems nonetheless to have aged, for when the sarcophagus was opened, it was found to contain the bones, not of a teenage girl, but of a middle-aged woman.

Christianity clearly took a very firm hold here. The city boasts a number of other early Christian basilicas, most notably the 'Great Basilica', also by the sea, with no fewer than seven naves (later extended to nine) and more than 50 metres long, with a series of reconstructed arches on the side facing the sea, which make the church look as if it has subsumed a miniature aqueduct within its precinct.[65]

A few kilometres west of Tipasa, the town is most dramatically highlighted against the surrounding massif of the Chenoua, whose form is imaginatively compared – as so many such low hills are – to the form of a sleeping giant. Here a road leads off towards an extraordinary funerary monument, known most widely as Le Tombeau de la Chrétienne (the tomb of the Christian woman). The huge beehive-shaped structure, visible across the plain for many kilometres, is clearly no such thing, and dates from the 2nd or 3rd century BC. Its soaring steps of brick, shorn of their covering, sit on a base more than 50 metres in diameter composed of some sixty engaged Ionic columns, making it look a little as if a Mesopotamian ziggurat had merged with the Parthenon. False double-doors set a few metres up the edifice, with stone beads and scrollwork, give a cross-like effect, which is how the popular name of the building arose.

Another, even more fanciful legend is that this was the tomb of
'Florinda La Cava', said to have been the daughter of Count Julian, the
Byzantine governor of Ceuta (in the far northern tip of Mauretania
Tingitana, opposite Gibraltar) at the beginning of the 8th century. When
the Visigothic King Roderick caught sight of her bathing naked, he was
so inflamed with lust that he raped her, leading her irate father to take
revenge by allowing the Muslim army of Tariq free passage over the
Straits of Gibraltar to destroy the Visigothic kingdom.[66] Other legends
held that the mound was the repository of a great treasure, guarded by
a fiercesome djinn. So convinced of this were the Turkish rulers of
Algiers in the 19th century that they had the mound bombarded in an
effort to outflank the djinn's sorcery and secure the gold, but, when the
French effected a more scientific excavation, they found the central burial
chamber deep inside the mound empty of valuables or, for that matter,
of bones. The high grade of the masonry, however, and the immense
effort required to bring such a mass of stone up the mountainside suggest
that it was probably a royal burial. Precisely who was interred here is
unknown, but favoured candidates are one of Mauretania's glittering
royal couple, Juba II or Cleopatra Selene.[67]

It is hard now to recapture the glory of Iol Caesarea, their capital, for
time has not been kind to the ruins, which have been engulfed by the
modern city of Cherchell, 25 kilometres to the west of Tipasa. The annexation of Juba's former kingdom in AD 40 did not mean the immediate
eclipse of Iol, for it became the capital of the new province of Mauretania
Caesariensis, and was promoted to the rank of *colonia* under Claudius. The
remains of all this glory now require the modern visitor to hunt around
the busy, crowded streets of Cherchell. The first relic, at least, is clear, for
outside the city museum an array of orphaned columns stand in a piazza
shaded by the umbrella-like foliage of delicious shade-providing trees.

The rest of the Roman city lies stranded amidst the traffic-choked
narrow streets. The theatre, which has had most of the stone from its
seats robbed, lies, rather forlorn, in the centre of a scruffy square. Most
probably completed in about 13 BC,[68] it was at a late stage in its antique
career converted into an oval shape and the stage façade removed, as
civic taste came to prefer the bloody spectacle to the refined literary set-
piece. The forum, which originally stretched almost as far as the theatre,
now lies truncated in another down-at-heel little square. The remains of
a flight of steps on which rested marble capitals can be seen turning a
corner and then disappearing beneath a modern building. As late, though,
as the 6th century economic life still sputtered on in Iol and a large
bazaar of shoddily built stalls was excavated here.[69]

Further to the west lies a two-way arch, forming the centrepiece of a dusty traffic island, rubbish-strewn and now host mainly to some focused milling-around by underemployed Cherchellites and to the screeching of motorcycle tyres. It would have formed one of the main axes of the city, but now, shorn of any decorative motifs, it seems a rather desolate relic. The city baths, a few hundred metres away, were originally more splendid, modelled self-consciously on the Baths of Agrippa in Rome. They were constructed on a monumental scale, with soaring brick vaults, but today piles of marble columns lie in the undergrowth, and the gate to the little park in which they reside is firmly locked.

Mauretania Caesariensis petered out around Numerus Syrorum, near Maghnia in the far north-west of Algeria; and beyond, stretching to the Atlantic coast of modern Morocco, lay Mauretania Tingitana. It is by no means clear that land communication between the two provinces was possible (or at least regular),[70] and travel by sea may have been necessary between them. Indeed, for much of its career as a Roman province, Mauretania Tingitana was attached administratively to Spain rather than North Africa, from the time of Diocletian forming part of the Diocese of Hispania rather than that of Africa.

On the province's far western coast, Rabat, the capital of modern Morocco, has ancient antecedents indeed. Behind the façade of the 17th-century royal capital, all gorgeously tiled doorways and stately palace gardens, lies a Punic foundation from around the 7th century BC. At 4 kilometres from the sea, on the Oued Bou-Regreg, it was not typical of the earliest Punic settlements, which tended to be trading posts clustered for safety on the shore. In the area of the city now known as Chellah, which became the royal centre of the Merinids dynasty in the 14th century, a Roman-style city was constructed under Juba II, which, in about AD 50, was remodelled with the building of a forum, basilica and baths. About this time, most of the monuments of the previous town were razed and covered in earth banks, although whether during the revolt of Aedemon or as a deliberate act on the part of the rebuilders is unclear.

The site, known as Sala Colonia, lies on a slope above the Bou-Regreg river, its buildings sitting on a series of terraces set into the slope. Dry, parched and neglected, there is no delicacy in its state of preservation; a mass of stones and a couple of columns here; a hint of geometric mosaic peeking out from underneath a dusty tarpaulin there. Amidst the jumble of ruins the easiest area to read, the forum, is a large rectangular space, off which the little cubicle-like shops can still be discerned, a single headless statue in a toga welcoming any 21st-century visitors.

The *colonia's capitolium* sat nearby, identified by a monumental statue of Jupiter excavated there. The mid-2nd-century garrison of this outpost, the *Ala II Syrorum*, was memorialised in an inscription of 144 in honour of its prefect, Sulpicius Felix.[71] In it, thirty-eight of the members of the city council thank him for his work in bringing peace and security to the town and rescuing them from the 'normal lawlessness' (*solitis iniuriis*) that had afflicted the town. That both provinces of Mauretania were under one governor at this time has been adduced as a sign that there were particularly severe security problems, but the evidence is by no means conclusive.[72]

In 288, the Bavares, Quinquigentanaei and other Mauretanian tribes rose up in revolt and were beaten back by the governor Aurelius Litua, but they continued to cause trouble and in 297 Maximian had to come in person to finish the suppression of the rebellion.[73] The Emperor stayed in Africa for eighteen months putting the provinces in order. He then decided that Mauretania Tingitana was simply not worth the expense of defending, and withdrew to an enclave around Tingis (Tangier) in the north. Almost all of the rest of Tingitana was left to the indigenous tribes, who had contested it for so long with the Romans.

Uniquely in the southern area of Mauretania Tingitana, Sala Colonia was not abandoned by the Romans at the time of the Tetrarchy. A mini *limes* of ditch and wall was erected some 10 kilometres east of the town and a Roman garrison retained there, which is mentioned in the *Notitia Dignitatum*.[74] Yet remains from this later era are sparse; an inscription of Constantine I, a Christian mosaic and a few tombs. Sometime in the 4th century, the forum was abandoned and turned into a rubbish dump; thereafter Sala was in effect an impoverished village, and its adherence to the Empire purely nominal. However, the ruins were still sufficiently impressive to be commented on by the Arab geographer El Bekri in the 11th century.[75] In the 13th century, the Merinids erected an encircling wall around the remains of the site, whose crenellated outline, pockmarked with square indentations, its mud-brick facing partly peeled off, still girdles Sala Colonia. The Merinids made use of what little remained of the Roman town, too, for in the mosque that they constructed to act as guardian to their royal tombs they employed several thin, delicately refined Roman columns. Now abandoned for a second time, they are a fitting symbol of one of Rome's most far-flung and forgotten outposts.

Northwards from Sala Colonia, the road leads towards the heart of Mauretania Tingitana. Here, on the banks of the Sebou river, lies Thamusida, 10 kilometres upstream from the modern city of Kenitra (and 50 kilometres north-east of Rabat). Although a reasonably prosperous place, it was never one of any great political importance. Its main source of visitors now are pilgrims to the shrine of the Muslim saint Sidi Ali ben Ahmed, a white domed square on the site's most prominent mound. Amidst the remains of the Roman *decumanus*, baths and temples, their children run and play, while the women in gaily coloured headscarves enjoy a picnic beneath one of the few shade-giving trees.

The city seems to have undergone its most significant growth from the time of the Flavians, when it became the location of a garrison, and had several temples, only the barest of whose outlines can be determined amongst the low grass, scrubby bushes and thistles. A larger camp was constructed under Marcus Aurelius to the south-west of the town,[76] this time big enough to hold a whole cohort or cavalry *ala*. Very eroded steps lead up to a podium, upon which most probably lay the *praetorium*, which was adapted by the addition of a large basilical hall under the Severans.

Further towards the river a series of rectangular pits arrayed in orderly rows represent vats for the production of *garum*, the fish paste that was a mainstay of Roman gourmands, and whose export was a significant source of revenue for the towns of North Africa. The defensive circuit that encloses Thamusida is a melancholy reminder that, for all the bourgeois prosperity, the garrison and the walls with their semicircular towers, it suffered the same fate as the rest of the southern part of the province, being abandoned in the 280s. Thereafter, there seems evidence only of 'squatter' occupation and a few huts, huddled together in the shell of their ancestors' much grander past.

Around 100 kilometres south-east of Thamusida, Volubilis is Morocco's most spectacular site, and the fine state of preservation of its Roman ruins creates the enticing impression that it must have been a centre of the greatest importance. For, compared to Carthage, Antioch or Alexandria – and even, at a pinch, to Constantinople itself – the remains are more splendid. Yet for all its baths, basilica and grand urban villas, for all the magnificence of its surviving mosaics, Volubilis was a place of strictly local importance, and one that the Romans abandoned relatively early.

The site lies at the foot of the Jebel Zarhoun, and it is a slight climb uphill before Volubilis really reveals itself, the remaining standing columns of the basilica gradually coming into view in a tantalising archaeological tease. The first traces of settlement on the site come from around the middle of the 3rd century BC, and the Punic influence here was strong; for the city long retained the title *suffete* for its magistrates, along the Carthaginian model.

Long before the Roman annexation and eventual division of the province, Volubilis was the western capital of the kingdom of Mauretania under Juba II. An untidy mound at the centre of the site represents the acropolis, the strong- (though not particularly high-) point around which pre-Roman Volubilis clustered. Some other elements of this stage of the city's development still survive, including a monumental altar near to the Capitoline Temple, and a shrine (often wrongly attributed to Saturn) which lies to the east of the city.

After Caligula had the Mauretanians' last king, Ptolemy, murdered in AD 40, Volubilis seems to have taken the side of Rome in the subsequent rebellion, and its reward was to be incorporated into the Empire as a *municipium*, with rights of citizenship and a ten-year tax exemption. The city, as a consequence of Juba's rule, was already partly Romanised, and under Nero and his successors development was rapid. The whole centre of the city is a grid of rich houses, many of them incorporating olive presses, evidence that even the grandest of families derived their wealth from the rural hinterland, the agro-barons of antiquity. Many of the villas, which otherwise survive in the barest outline, their walls standing to 50 centimetres or so and retaining only the odd pillar, do come to life because here, unlike so many other sites in North Africa, a large proportion of the mosaics have been left *in situ*. Dusty and fading from the effect of the summer's intense sunlight, they nonetheless give a focus and intensity to the houses, which would otherwise be bare and sterile skeletons.

An exception, however, is the House of the Voyage of Venus, whose main mosaic has been transported to Tangier. It was one of the largest of the villas, and originally had mosaics in at least eight of the rooms. The principal one, from which the house gains its modern name, showed the goddess of love, with heavily kohled eyes, impossibly perched on the prow of the boat, a series of bare-chested Graces in attendance tugging at the oars. But they are not propelling the boat, which is in fact carried along by a troupe of sea nymphs and tritons, whose strands of straggly seaweed hair stand out in contrast to the blue of the water.

Up from here runs the *decumanus*, alongside which another impressive range of houses is arrayed, leading eventually to the simple arch of the Tangier gate at the city's north-eastern end. The House of the Wild Beasts is named for the striking mosaic of wild animals on its floor, including a snarling tiger, a leopard and a somewhat damaged lion, while other villas cover the whole gamut of the classical visual repertoire, including the Four Seasons, bathing nymphs, Bacchus and the Labours of Heracles.

At the southern end of the *decumanus* lies Volubilis's most famous monument, the Arch of Caracalla, dating from around 216–17. At about 20 metres high, with a 9-metre opening, it overpowers almost everything else around it. Originally the arch would also have had an image of the Emperor riding a four-horse chariot, or *quadriga*. It may lack the grandeur of the arch at Leptis Magna, or the delight of that at Palmyra, but it is nonetheless hugely impressive.

Nearby lies the forum, which was completely renewed during the Severan era. Its squat basilica rises up dramatically beside it, double-apsed, but now lacking the two rows of columns that once ran down the middle. In the central area a semicircular depression has been cut into the floor. It is possible that this represents a baptistery and that it is evidence that this basilica – in origin a purely civil affair – was later adapted to Christian use. To the south, a small open area and steps lead up to a podium with a few columns still standing, and in front of it the bulky block of an altar. This is the *capitolium*, and the porticoed colonnade that stands beside it was dedicated under Macrinus, for even in the briefest of reigns time was found for imperial self-promotion, and it would not do for him to leave the field in North Africa entirely to the monuments of the Severan dynasty which he had supplanted.

Back on the *decumanus*, amongst the mosaic villas, lies a complex that has been dubbed 'The Palace of the Gordians'. It is in fact a collection of buildings, which was most likely the residence of the imperial procurator Ulpius Victor.[77] A unique series of inscriptions was found here on a set of altars, apparently giving details of negotiations between the Roman authorities and the local tribes, the Bavares and Baquates. Known as *colloquia*, and dated in a series that begins in 140 and ends in 280, it is difficult to determine whether they represent troubled relations with the neighbouring group, which necessitated a quick succession of peace treaties, or whether quite the contrary: that the tribes were accustomed to settle their differences with (or to seek favours from) the Romans through diplomatic means rather than warfare. The intervals between the *colloquia* grow shorter in the 3rd century, when there are eight within eighty years, as compared to the three in sixty years of the 2nd century, so whatever the reason for the dialogues, it seems to have grown more pressing. The chief of the Baquates, Iulius Matif, is referred to as *rex* in one of the inscriptions, dated 277, and his people are termed *gens foederata* ('federate peoples'). They were clearly thus outside the formal control of the Empire. There were no further *colloquia* after this, for the imperial government soon afterwards evacuated the southern portion of Mauretania Tingitana and such discussions were then rendered rather redundant.

Volubilis did not disappear, but among the indications of uncertainty is the superb bronze bust of Cato the Younger that was buried under the floor of the House of Venus at about this time. The city seems to have contracted to the south and east, into the quarter beyond the Arch of Caracalla, although some new buildings were erected there, including a late Christian basilica.

Of Volubilis, Hilaire Belloc mused, 'Here the impression is rather one of history and of contrast. Here you see how completely the new religion of Islam flooded and drowned the classical and Christian tradition.'[78] Volubilis was clearly still of sufficient importance in 788 that Moulay Idriss – in effect the founder of the Islamic Moroccan kingdom – used the much-diminished city as his capital for a time, before decamping to a new (and thus suitably pristine Islamic) settlement nearby,[79] which later took his name and played Tunis to the now-abandoned Volubilis's Carthage.

Around 150 kilometres' drive north-west of Volubilis, the road to Banasa seems to lead to nowhere, passing through sparsely populated rural territory south of the Sebou river and up a small side-route that cuts along the edge of fields of waving corn. For a city that became a *colonia* in the 2nd century, there is not a great deal to show. At first sight, even the grid pattern is hard to discern amongst the jumble of ruins covered with a low carpet of dry, parched grass and a species of thistle that snaps noisily when stepped upon. The only things that seem to be flourishing are a small group of palm trees, sucking water from the soil where all else finds only dust. The remaining stones of the city are lightly encrusted with spots of a rust-red algae that make them seem in the grip of some iron-based pox.

On the site of a pre-existing Mauretanian village, Augustus planted a veterans' colony – Iulia Valentia Banasa – some time before the region was briefly given back its independence under Juba II in 33 BC.[80] The settlement does not seem to have prospered and could well have been damaged or destroyed during the revolt of Aedemon, for the buildings that have been excavated date largely from the end of the 1st century AD or later. It was reorganised as Colonia Aurelia Banasa during the reign of Marcus Aurelius, but was devastated during the late 3rd century, probably during one of Mauretania's perennial tribal revolts, and was abandoned, together with the rest of the south of the province, during the reign of Diocletian.

To the left of the main site entrance, the ruins of a series of small buildings include a bakery, where a hoard of 457 coins was unearthed (the latest of them dating from around 259), buried in the panic before the final destruction. Further down a slight slope are the well-preserved and partly reconstructed remains of a bath with the dome of one room still half in place and a curious tower-like structure in the middle.

To the north, more substantial walls stand, though the general standard of construction is not good, for the nearest quarries are quite some distance away, and even then the quality of the stone found there is inferior. In the centre of town, the indistinct remains of the forum are situated. At its edge lies the 'Arch of the Basilica', which seems very precarious indeed, the keystone of its thin span nudged slightly out of position, fit to tumble down at the slightest tremor. Looking back into the forum from the arch, a few broken columns mark its portico, while at the south end stone steps lead up to a platform on which stand three altars, one of which has a dedication to Juno, another to Minerva, so that, although far less grand than its counterparts elsewhere in North Africa, it is clearly the Capitoline temple of the colony.[81]

The most important find from Banasa was the so-called Tabula Banasitana, a bronze tablet which – under the authority of twelve members of the imperial council, including three former proconsuls of Africa – grants citizenship to Julianus, chieftain of the Zegrenses tribe, to his wife Ziddina and their four sons (all of whom bore Latinised names). It preserves several imperial letters, the first from 168, which notes that, while it is not customary to grant citizenship to the tribespeople, in the case of Julianus an exception will be made.[82] The second letter, from 177, bestows citizenship on another Julianus, who is presumed to be the son of the first, together with his wife and children.

The grant to the wives is of some importance, for according to Roman law the children of mixed marriages did not automatically become citizens, but rather inherited the status of their non-citizen parent. The Tabula is a sign of the efforts the authorities made, through selective use of such privileges, to involve the native tribes in the dirty business of Roman patronage, and create a delicate balance in which revolt would be followed by the instant removal of the favours granted. Within half a century, however, the award of citizenship to all by the Antonine Constitution would remove this particular tool of imperial policy; and within a century the withdrawal of the *limes* north to the enclave around Tingis would render such manipulations irrelevant.

Closing on Morocco's north-western tip, Lixus (40 kilometres northwest of Banasa, and a few kilometres north of modern Larache), where the Atlantic breezes provide a pleasing respite from thousands of kilometres of North African desert heat, has some claim, at least in fable, to be the oldest settlement in Morocco. Legend relates that it was founded around 1100 BC, although archaeology has only revealed traces as far back as the 6th or 7th century BC, and no substantial buildings earlier than the 4th century BC have come to light.[83] The place first appears in the literary sources around 500 BC in the *Periplus* of the Carthaginian navigator Hanno. His extraordinary expedition sailed far down uncharted territory on the west coast of Africa, incidentally providing the first recorded description of gorillas. Quite how far he got – whether to Senegal, Cameroon or even further – is not completely clear. He was accompanied by interpreters referred to as 'Lixitae', who probably came from what was later known as Lixus, although, most unfortunately, it turned out that they were not familiar with the languages of the people who lived along the far southern shores to which Hanno brought them.

The land of the Lixitae was closely associated with the legend of Heracles. One of the traditional sites of the Gardens of the Hesperides – a rival being Euhesperides (Benghazi) in Cyrenaica[84] – lay along the banks of the Loukkos river, whose loops were said to represent the coils of the unconquerable dragon that guarded the garden's precious golden apples.

Lixus's political history was troubled. It seems to have been first destroyed during the early 1st century BC, possibly in connection with the raid by Sertorius, a Roman renegade who chose the wrong side in a civil war and who had taken refuge in Spain.[85] He invaded North Africa in 81 BC with a small expeditionary force, wreaking havoc and eventually capturing Tingis, before his successes led the Lusitanians to invite him back to Spain.[86] It then seems to have been sacked again in the turmoil that followed Gaius Caligula's assassination of Ptolemy of Mauretania. As some compensation for its travails, Claudius granted it the title of *colonia*, and thereafter it developed all the standard appurtenances of a prosperous provincial town. It was razed yet again in the middle of the 3rd century, presumably during one of the province's native uprisings. It was then rebuilt on a smaller site to the south and garrisoned by the *Cohors I Herculea*.[87] Unlike the towns and forts further south, Lixus was retained into the 4th century, but all traces of organised activity disappear before the 7th century, so that by the time the Muslims arrived, there was no one left to oppose them.

An ancient sanctuary to Heracles-Melkart (the guise in which he was worshipped most widely in Mauretania) sat atop the acropolis mound that formed the original settlement nucleus at Lixus, but before reaching it the path through the site loops like the sinuous coils of the dragon around and around the hillside's slopes. Passing by the lounging junior *gardiens*, none of them seeming a day above sixteen years old, the path leads first to the *garum* vats, laid out in a chequerboard pattern, each separated by thin stone walls for those brave enough to walk between the pools of fermenting fish. The place is safely downhill from the main settlement, which seems to some extent to bear out the almost universally bad press that *garum* has had since ancient times.

Yet for Lixus, it was a vital source of wealth. Around a hundred sites for the production of the sauce have been identified in southern Spain and northern Mauretania, but this was one of the most important, with a complex of about ten buildings devoted to the task. The industry drew much of its raw material from the annual migration of tuna, which the currents of the Mediterranean around the Straits of Gibraltar pushed close enough to the shore for teams of fishermen to catch the enormous fish (sometimes weighing up to 300 kilograms) and then to bludgeon them to death, in a ritual repeated into modern times off the coast of Sicily.

Ancient authors differed in their view of the *garum sociorum*, the finest grade of fish sauce. Pliny the Elder noted that it was as expensive as perfume,[88] while Seneca warned that gullible purchasers were simply buying rotten fish guts at inflated prices.[89] The basic production method was to remove the intestines and other parts that could not be consumed directly, then add salt to the rest of the fish and place the resulting mush in a jar, or *garum* vat, seal it and leave it for a couple of months to ferment. The exact type of fish (sometimes a mixture of several), the amount of salt paste and whether wine was added all had an effect on the final quality. Every so often the vat would be opened for stirring by strong-nosed workers.

The liquid that resulted at the top of the vat was most prized, and was drawn off to make the *garum* itself. The residue was referred to as *allex*, while a medium-quality product gathered from the paste beneath this was termed *muria* (and recommended for the treatment of burns!). The price of the best-quality sauce was extremely high; Pliny claims that two amphoras of the stuff could sell for 4,000 sesterces, an exorbitant amount that could equally have purchased a dozen top-quality slaves. Yet he may have been exaggerating somewhat, for of around 200 fish-sauce vessels unearthed in Pompeii, nearly 60 per cent were for *garum* (as opposed to *muria* or *allex*) and so it was clearly within the budget of the average citizen.[90]

From the *garum* vats and the accompanying cisterns that provided the necessary water for the process, the path leads up to the north-west and here, around a slight curve, lies the undoubted pearl of Lixus, its amphitheatre. Set in a bowl between two shallow hills, it was originally a conventional theatre; it is clear where it has been converted by building a wall some 4 metres high to protect the lower-range seats from the dangers of escaping beasts or resentful gladiators. The stage backdrop, the three upright stumps still standing, was cut off and a crude masonry oval created. Just to the east of the amphitheatre and butting against it was a small bath-complex, in which until recently stood the remains of a mosaic of Oceanus; allegedly a local youth was caught trying to dig out the face, presumably to sell it on, an ever-present temptation in countries where cultural budgets and wages are low in comparison to the lure of the international antiquities-smuggling market.

The town's river wall is composed of absolutely monumental stone blocks, from which a spectacular view over a bend of the Loukkos river is possible, lazily wending its way across the plain. From here the rest of the city is revealed, partly overgrown with low, tough bushes: the outline of a peristyle house; an almost intact cistern, with just one end of the structure broken; a small church; and a cluster of temples largely of Severan date, with now just a few columns from the porches and colonnades surviving. It is a quiet and contemplative place, little visited and mostly abandoned to the ministrations of goats and other domestic animals.

Of Tingi, the ancient capital of Mauretania Tingitana, and from which the province took its name, only hints remain. It now lies under modern Tangier, some 80 kilometres north-east along the coast from Lixus, and almost all of it has been swallowed up by the city's kasbah, where some baths and a possible Christian basilica were excavated. Once again Heracles plays a role in the city's legendary foundation. After the hero had bested the giant Antaeus in a wrestling match before seizing the golden apples of the Hesperides, which the Titan was guarding, he is said to have settled down with his defeated opponent's mother, Tingi, and sired the race which then populated north-western Mauretania. The enormous body of Antaeus was rumoured to have been buried in a nearby mound, which Sertorius ordered dug up during his expedition in the area in 81 BC. Gigantic bones were duly unearthed, to the great wonderment of the Roman general.[91] No doubt they were the bones of a dinosaur or mammoth, but the legend of Antaeus and Tingi was greatly enhanced by the discovery, and Juba II of Mauretania would later claim descent from Heracles and Tingi. The inhabitants of Tingi then had the good sense to side with Octavian against Antony and received Roman citizenship as a reward; their city became Colonia Iulia Tingi and remained quietly loyal to the Empire until the very end of Byzantine rule in North Africa.

At the northernmost tip of Morocco, just where it touches the territory of the Spanish enclave of Ceuta, another Punic settlement turned

Roman town lies on the outskirts of modern Tetouan, some 60 kilo-metres south-east of Tangier. Tamuda is situated 4–5 kilometres out of town, along roads lined with advertising hoardings and smart new devel-opments that draw their finances from the money remitted by Moroccan migrants and businessmen operating in the much more lucrative markets of Spain. It sits in open ground on a dusty promontory ringed on one side by anonymous village houses; on the other by a water-filled wadi and groves of trees, with the foothills of the Rif mountains looming in the middle distance.

Piles of stones heaped up cairn-like at the entrance to the site promise little, but the line of a rise of ramparts soon becomes apparent, revealing the army camp that was constructed in the 2nd century AD. It seems not to be of the highest quality, but was modified in the next century with the addition of projecting semicircular towers that are still evident, broken shells rising to a metre or so. Tamuda may be identical with the Tamuco listed in the *Notitia Dignitatum*,[92] in which case its garrison was the *Ala Herculaea*, a cavalry detachment. At least four gates, at the cardinal points, survive, one a double-portal, where one of the entrances was blocked up at some point before the fort's demise.

The camp sat on part of the grid of the pre-Roman town, which had been abandoned during the mid-1st century AD, a destruction blamed, as elsewhere, on the unrest following the murder of Mauretania's last king by Caligula in AD 40. About 100–200 metres to the south a large rectangular piazza represents the heart of this pre-Roman stage, while arrayed around it are small square buildings that were probably shops. Everywhere, a covering of low, dry grass, further thinned by the atten-tions of a small herd of sheep, gives the place an abandoned feel.

It is a short forty-five-minute drive north along the coast from Tetouan to the border with the Spanish enclave of Ceuta. The coastal road seems incongruously wide, the developments of apartments and hotel complexes a long way from the chaotic hustle of Tetouan or Tangier. The status of modern Ceuta, controlled by Spain since its cession by Portugal in 1680 (before which it had been Portuguese since 1415), curi-ously mirrors that of its ancient antecedent, Roman Septem. Like Ceuta, Septem was long governed as part of North Africa (or Mauretania), but, from the late 3rd century, after the evacuation of southern Tingitana, it was attached administratively to Spain, whose fate it then shared for several centuries.

It was in fact the last fragment of the North African mainland to be held by the Byzantine Empire, and thus the last piece in the long history of Roman Africa. Its defences had been left to decay by the Vandals, but

John, one of the lieutenants of Belisarius (who had led the Byzantine reconquest of North Africa for Justinian), retook it in 533–4 and had a new city wall built, also decreeing the construction of a large basilica to the Mother of God. The Visigoths tried to retake it in 546, and managed to storm the army camp, but the Byzantines, belying their reputation for sometimes self-defeating piety, attacked the invaders whilst they were at their Sunday prayers and drove them off.

Thereafter it remained under tenuous Byzantine control until the early 8th century, the walls protecting the settlement when the rest of North Africa had succumbed to the Arabs. Its final governor was Count Julian, a shadowy figure, whose allegiances – caught between the Arabs, the Visigothic rulers in Spain and the far-away Emperor in Constantinople – are hard to pin down. In 706, Musa ibn Nusayr attacked the town, which again held out.[93] However, Julian became caught up in a power struggle between contenders for the Visigothic kingdom of Spain, taking the side of Witiza, the legitimate king, against the upstart Roderick, whom he accused of violating his daughter.[94] In revenge, he assisted the Arab commander Tariq ibn Ziyad, who was based at Tingi, to cross into Spain, and then, having disturbed the delicate balance of power by which Septem survived, finally opened the gates to the Arabs in July 711.

The gates of Ceuta are still not open to all. Just as for a time Septem formed the boundary between the empire and *barbaricum*, so today it lies along the border between the European Union and the outside world. Just as most of the cross-border moves in Roman times were by groups seeking a share in the economic resources of the Empire, sometimes to plunder, but more often simply to gain access to a more prosperous way of life, so Ceuta is beset by their modern-day counterparts, trying to enter Spanish territory by any means possible, legal or otherwise. The scene at the border is pandemonium; young men and aged market women wander up and down seemingly at random, vaulting over fences that define queues of indistinguishably separate purpose, or playing grandmother's footsteps with the border guards. Some lines breeze through the immigration checks, while others seem like holding pens for those without the agility or wit to argue their way through. At the border points of the Empire, or the gates into Hadrian's Wall, it must have been like this; not so much an invasion as an insistent throng arguing and cajoling its way to be allowed to engage in some peaceful (and lucrative) commerce. A genuine invasion must at times have seemed like an orderly relief from the daily repetition of such noisy theatre.

Beyond, all seems deceptively calm. The tranquil Ceuta coastal road gives a clear view of the bulky promontory of Monte Hacho, topped by a medieval fortress, which has a strong claim to be the southern of the mythical Pillars of Hercules (with the pillar on the northern side being universally agreed to be the Rock of Gibraltar).[95] Legend relates that Heracles, seeking a shortcut on his way to fetch the Cattle of Geryon as one of this Twelve Labours, smashed through the mountain formed by the body of the giant Atlas, and so separated Europe from Africa, with the two pillars being formed to either side. Monte Hacho was known in ancient times as Abila, and was settled by the Phoenicians as a trading post and salting factory.

The Roman name for the settlement, Septem, or Septem Fratres ('Seven brothers'), was a reference to its having, like Rome, its own seven hills. The Phoenician installations for the salting of fish carried on being used into Roman times, and a variety have been found, from the 2nd to the early 5th century. An inscription found with the word *Ordo* on it has been taken to mean that the city was at some stage elevated to the rank of *municipium*. From the 4th century, though, Septem seems to have fallen into a sharp decline, and around the time of the Vandal invasion may have been abandoned entirely. What Justinian retook and trans-formed into a strategic naval base in 534 was probably but a shell.

Nonetheless, Septem did recover and is mentioned by the 7th-century Spanish bishop and encyclopaedist Isidore of Seville in his *Etymologiae* under the name Septe.[96] The city walls that guarded Byzantine Septem lie roughly along the line of the early modern Murales Reales, which cut off the isthmus from incursions from the south and west. An impres-sive series of bastions and counter-bastions (designed to deflect artillery strikes and make undermining more difficult) harbours a minute section of the Byzantine walls, and a larger portion of those built under the rule of the caliphs.

Fifteen minutes' walk from the walls the Plaza de Africa, overlooked by the imposing baroque frontage of Ceuta's cathedral, seems to have marked the heart of old Septem. Beside it, under glass, lie sections of the walls of a 7th-century house. The most substantial remains, however, are of the palaeo-Christian basilica, a few hundred metres away. Enclosed within the shell of a modern museum, the remains are thus well protected from the ravages of sun and moisture. Around 25 metres long and 10–12 metres wide with an apse in the east, it was under construction in the late 4th century, but was never completed. By the 6th century it had been converted into a necropolis – the low level of life expectancy in Septem is indicated by the fact that more than 55 per cent of burials here were of infants, while only 2 per cent of the deceased were over fifty years old.

Within the basilica walls, the burials cluster together, some of them just interments in amphoras, others with simple brick structures as grave-markers. The nave of the basilica has been cut across with low sectioning walls, and the bare earth of the floor is pitted with holes, mostly shallow, some seemingly lined with bricks. A few of the graves sit in ordered rows, many others in disordered clusters. It seems almost as if the latter are the last survivors of some catastrophe, huddling together against a force that they could never hope to understand or overcome.

And in a way, so it was; for, if not for the contemporaries of Count Julian, these graves may have been the last resting place of their grand-parents. The place is an apt symbol of the resistance of the Empire, continuing against all the odds, holding the line in such a remote outpost, at the very end of the *limes*, when all else around them had fallen.

By the early 8th century, Maia, at the western edge of Hadrian's Wall, was well into its post-Roman phase, with the imperial troops having departed three centuries before. All of the western European provinces had been lost, while the Danube line seemed fatally breached by the Slavs and Avars. In the East, the Arabs had swept aside the *limes* in Syria and Arabia and had overwhelmed Byzantine resistance in Egypt, Africa and Numidia. Of all those countless forts, town and cities that had shared in the life of the Roman frontier, it was, unaccountably, Ceuta that was practically the last to resist. It is, therefore, a fitting place to take leave of the *limes*, or, for those travelling the other way, to begin the tracing of its course.

CONCLUSION

The long expanse of the Roman frontier was not an end in itself. Its thousands of kilometres, hundreds of forts and scores of major towns and cities did not, for all that they developed an autonomous and vibrant life of their own, exist in a political vacuum. They served – whatever the individual circumstances of their position or the history of their fall – to defend what lay within. The interior provinces of the Empire, and for that matter the frontier provinces for most of the time until the late 4th and 5th centuries, experienced centuries of peace and reached a level of economic development that they simply could not have attained in less settled regions or more troubled times.

At the heart of this *pax Romana* (spiritually if not quite geographically) was the capital, Rome itself. At the core of this lay the Forum (or rather Fora, for the original was gradually embellished and supplemented by new spaces laid out under Julius Caesar, Augustus, Nerva and Trajan), and at the centre of this was the *omphalos*,[1] a small, round brick structure marking the very centre of Rome and thus of the Empire. It is utterly drowned out by the showy marble façade of the Senate house, and the imposing bulk of the arches of Septimius Severus and Titus at opposite ends of the Forum. Yet from here[2] distances all the way to the periphery of the Empire were measured and, just a few paces away beneath the *lapis niger* (or 'black stone'), the grave of Romulus himself was believed to lie.[3] It is a curiously neglected spot, the broken black marble that marked it out cracked and surrounded by an unsteady rope barrier to prevent the tourists from trampling on one of the ancient city's most sacred spaces.

The Romans' expansion from small city-state to ancient superpower was characterised by a supreme pragmatism and an ability to muddle through and adapt. From the start, Romulus accepted slaves and runaways into his new statelet, and his successors incorporated, through citizenship or bargains with the local elites, more and more people into the Roman enterprise. First the people of Latium, the territory around Rome, and then, after the Social War in 91–88 BC, the inhabitants of the

Italian peninsula gained citizenship, while, up to the Antonine Constitution of 212, a steady creep of urban magistrates and discharged auxiliaries added to the total of those who had a personal stake in the Roman Empire. There is an instructive comparison to be made with Athens, the most successful of the Greek city-states, which denied citizenship to foreigners, even long-standing residents (or *metics*) and, while it overawed a selection of other Greek-speaking cities, never managed to establish an empire of more than limited reach, in time or territory. Roman pragmatism even extended to the watering down of the importance of the city of Rome itself, when, in the late 3rd century, the tetrarchal emperors established their fixed bases elsewhere – in Antioch, Sirmium or Thessalonica – and finally, from the 4th century, Constantinople completely eclipsed Rome as a political centre.

The study of the Roman frontier has been bedevilled by a concern for fixed and traceable lines, which is why an early concentration on phenomena such as Hadrian's Wall or the Germanic *limes* seemed to provide a set of pleasing certainties, which, on closer examination, turned into a muddle of provisos, hedges and exceptions. The obsession with fixed (and often immutable) borders probably has its origin in the European psyche with the terms of the Peace of Westphalia, which brought an end to the Thirty Years War in 1648. Before, the centre of Europe was a mess of overlapping jurisdictions and untidy conflicting sovereignties, a situation that did not seem to perturb the medieval mindset, but which played unhappily on early modern monarchs, who instead craved definites and absolutes in their quest to order and unite their countries.

The Roman *limes* was in reality a much more untidy affair, only reaching anything approximating the ideal of a fixed line on the stretch that fronted Persia. Here, there existed a power of similar status to the Romans, with whom cities could be shared out in precise measure. Yet elsewhere there was none of this neatness, and a vague mist envelops discussion about exactly where the Romans viewed their territory as ending. If anything it was a zone of influence, and the garrisons and walls marked the point from which that control was projected both inwards and outwards, largely by means of the army.

The matter of frontiers has become ever more topical in Europe at the start of the 21st century, with agonised discussions about where exactly Europe should end, what the 'purpose' of Europe is, what its constitution should be, and how the borders of the European Union should be policed and controlled. If there is anything that modern Europe (and the wider world) can learn from the Roman Empire, it is that adaptation is all. Augustus solved his dilemma by stretching the constitutional norms to their limit and establishing an imperial office, while still quite happily maintaining that the Republic survived. For all the enormous expenditure on the vast frontier armies, Rome gained centuries of peace in the interior, and the Empire spread cultural homogeneity not through force, but through the convenience of economic and social interchange. Large numbers of people were accepted into the Empire, notably through conquest, but also by means of controlled migration and through the settling of federates, so that the *limes* was never the uncrossable barrier that some might imagine it to have been.

The reign of Augustus to that of Honorius (the period within which the Roman frontier, as classically defined, existed) spans four centuries. For any political entity to survive that long – and Rome in fact in one sense did so for a millennium more – and for its frontier regions to remain largely intact throughout is an astonishing achievement. For today's political settlement in Europe to reach even a fraction of this longevity would be a triumph indeed. In the end, though, all the countless pages of speculation about why the border collapsed, particularly in the West, amount to one simple fact: the Empire grew old. Adapt though it might, its mechanisms for dealing with change gradually became set and atrophied, its military 'immune system' needed more and more help from outside, and finally – faced with new generations of more vigorous neighbours, who had borrowed from the Empire what they needed to give their political systems and their cultures strength and coherence – it died of old age.

The Roman Empire gave rise to a culture with many elements in common, but still containing an astonishing diversity among its 200 million-plus inhabitants. To travel along its frontier, through more than twenty different countries and cultures, is to gain just a dim sense of this. The *limes* crosses modern political boundaries and through regions that are judged to belong today to different and conflicting geo-strategic spheres. Yet in the past Serbia and Britain, Turkey and Libya (and even Syria and Israel) all formed part of the same political entity. As well as the pleasure of tracing the ancient connections between all these countries, and the sheer richness of the remains along the frontier, to travel along the Roman frontier is to be touched by two emotions: wonder that after close to 2,000 years so much can survive, and sadness that for all our sophistication, we are unlikely ever again to create something so enduring.

ACKNOWLEDGEMENTS

I would like to express my very great thanks to all those who have helped me with a project which has been long in the making and whose scope seemed to grow every time I examined it. In particular, the team at Jonathan Cape: Dan Franklin, who was persuaded enough of the merits of the Roman frontier to take the book on; Alex Bowler, who has been a discerning and diplomatic editor; and Mandy Greenfield, the copyeditor, for her careful scrutiny of the text. Martin Brown's wonderful and clear cartography will, I hope, help guide the reader where mere words fail. Thank you also to my wonderful agent, Gill Coleridge, for all her support in a process which took longer in time and far longer in miles covered than I had ever suspected at the outset.

Many people assisted me along the way, either in travel arrangements, as guides, or simply through their kindness. Many of them did not even know of my self-appointed task to visit the whole Roman *limes* and would surely have dissuaded me if they had. To those I have omitted, or whose names I simply do not know, my apologies. In rough provincial order, thanks to: Douglas Moody for his hospitality in Falkirk; Susanne Dambacher at the Verein Deutsche Limes Straße for her assistance in arranging my tour of the German *limes*; Michaela Köhler for a delicious Roman meal at Mainhardt; Christian Weiss for showing me Vindonissa; András Bereznay for his sterling efforts in making contacts for me in Hungary; Professor Zsolt Visy for facilitating my visit there; and Máté Varga for shepherding me around the Pannonian *limes*; Mihaela Simion at the National Museum of Romania, Bucharest, for kindly showing me the collection; Edouard Popescu for his wonderful efforts in guiding me aroud Romania; Iosif Ferencz and Vladimir Brilinski for giving me such contrasting yet complimentary views of Sarmizegetusa Regia; 'Papa Bear' and 'Mama Bear' at Oreshak in Bulgaria for the heartiest meals a weary traveller could wish for; Snezana Golubović for showing me around the site at Viminacium in Serbia; Ana Wild at the Museum of Slavonia, Osijek; Tolun Cerkes for acting as the most determined and knowledgeable guide to eastern Turkey one could wish for; Nigel Fisher and Tanya Evans at Silk Road Travel for facilitating my visit to Syria; Ma'an al-Sabagh, whose enthusiasm for Syrian history and calm and pleasant companionship made my visit to the country such a pleasure; Dougan, who guided me in Jordan; Saddam at Petra, who kept me from falling off his horse more than once; Mohammed at Dajaniyah, whose kindness meant I got to see the fort close up; Rob Hitchings at Nomadic Travel for his help in arranging my visit to Egypt; Hussein Mersel for enabling me to reach Mon Claudianus and Mons Porphyrites in the Eastern Desert; Esra for showing me Alexandria; Ghada for guiding me in Aswan; and Mohammed for his assurance and determination during a gruelling summer trip in the Western Desert; Alaeddin for guiding me in Libya; Wadia in Tunisia; Renira Rutherford at The Traveller for her help in arranging my trip to Algeria; Hussein in Morocco for stepping in when others had failed me.

It is probably iniquitous to single anyone out, but I would like to express particular thanks to Torsten Pasler, one of Germany's wonderful *Limes-Cicerones*, who in four days showed me more of the German *limes* than I thought possible, as well as being an excellent companion; and Patrick Penev in Bulgaria, whose enthusiasm for my project seemed to exceed even my own, and who, in a series of long trips through Bulgaria, Croatia and Serbia, showed himself to be a wonderful guide and a true friend.

I'd like also to thank Amanda Faber, for her encouragement over many months and for making me sit down and think about the book's title. Further in the past, I owe a debt of gratitude to those who encouraged my love of history – they are many – but in particular the late Richard Rottenbury at Dover College Junior School, Tim Connor at Eton College and Professor Rosamond McKitterick at Newnham College, Cambridge.

All of these in their own way steered me from errors I might otherwise have made, but any which remain are entirely of my own commission.

Finally, my thanks are due to my partner, Tania, who endured my long absences with boundless patience, and my daughter, Livia, who shares my love for the Romans, principally because of their penchant for purple. Without them to return home to, I might well have given up at Hadrian's Wall.

NOTES

INTRODUCTION

1 For an account of the sources for the foundation of Rome, see T.J. Cornell, *The Beginnings of Rome, Italy and Rome from the Bronze Age to the Punic Wars (c.1000–264 BC)* (London 1995), pp. 10–76

2 And a very early phase of occupation by the Etruscans, a much more developed culture, to whom the Romans probably owe many of their traditions. For a discussion of Etruscan influence on Rome, see Cornell, *The Beginnings of Rome*, pp. 156–70

3 Caesar raided Britain again the following year, see p. 16

4 L. Richardson Jr *A New Topographical Dictionary of Ancient Rome*, (Baltimore 1992), pp. 293–5

5 Tacitus, *Annals*, 12.23.2–24, and 'Tacitus on Claudius and the Pomerium, Annals 12.23.2–24' by Mary Taliaferro Boatwright in *Classical Journal*, Vol. 80, No. 1 (Oct.–Nov. 1984), pp. 36–44, for a discussion of the Claudian extension

6 Tacitus, *Annals*, 1.11; see also the discussion in 'The Nature and Function of Roman Frontiers' by W.S. Hanson in *Barbarians and Romans in North-West Europe from the later Republic to late Antiquity*, ed. John C. Barrett et al. (BAR International Series 471, Oxford), pp. 55–63

7 *imperium sine fine dedi* (Aeneid I, 279)

8 'The Meaning of the Terms Limes and Limitanei' by Benjamin Isaac in *Journal of Roman Studies* 78 (1988), pp. 125–47

9 See Peter the Patrician, fr. 14, in Michael H. Dodgeon and Samuel N.C. Lieu, *The Roman Eastern Frontier and the Persian Wars (AD 226–363)* (London 1991), p. 133

10 See, for example, the discussion in W.S. Hanson, 'Why did the Roman empire cease to expand?' in Freeman et al., *Proceedings of XVIIIIth International Congress of Roman Frontier Studies* (Sep. 2002) (Limes XVIII BAR S 1084), pp. 25–34

11 On the economic argument for the borders, see the discussion in 'Supplying the System, Frontiers and Beyond' by C.R. Whittaker in Barrett et al. (eds) (above note 6), pp. 64–75

12 Most nearly after their victory over the Caledonians at Mons Graupius, possibly in Aberdeenshire, in 83

13 See the contribution by Benjamin Isaac in *The Limits of Empire: The Roman Army in the East* (Oxford 1992)

14 A.D. Lee, *Information and Frontiers: Roman Foreign Relations in Late Antiquity* (Cambridge 1993)

15 See p. 466

16 C.R. Whittaker, *Rome and its Frontier: The Dynamics of Empire* (London 2004), p.51

17 Ammianus Marcellinus, 31, 8.5, trs C.D. Yonge (London 1911)

18 Former slaves who were still beholden to their former masters by ties of reciprocal obligations. The 'imperial freedmen', who were former slaves of the Emperor, formed a particularly powerful group under the very early Empire. See Ramsay McMullen, *Roman Social Relations 50 BC–AD 284* (New Haven 1974), pp. 100–4. The number of imperial civil servants is esti-mated to have risen from only around 200–300 under the very early Empire to possibly around 30,000 in the Later Empire. In contrast, Han China in the 1st century BC had more than 130,000 bureaucrats. See Peter Garnsey and Caroline Humfress, *The Evolution of the Late Antique World* (Cambridge 2001), p. 36

19 Although these provinces in turn were the result of a previous subdivision under Septimius Severus (193–211) or Caracalla (211–217)

20 In the very early days, each of the Tetrarchs – the college of four emperors established under Diocletian to spread the burdens of power – had their own praetorian prefect, with the division on territorial grounds only becoming established a little later. R. Malcolm Errington, *Roman Imperial Policy from Julian to Theodosius* (Chapel Hill 2006), pp. 80–1

21 See, for example, Christopher Kelly, *Ruling the Later Roman Empire* (Cambridge, MA, 2004), pp. 138–86

22 Kelly, *Ruling the Later Roman Empire*, pp. 115–16

23 O.A.W. Dilke, *Greek and Roman Maps* (London 1985), pp. 112–29

24 See, for example, the discussion in *Aspects of the Notitia Dignitatum*, ed. J.C. Mann et al. (BAR Supplementary Series 15, Oxford 1976), esp. 'What is the Notitia for?' by J.C. Mann, pp. 1–11

25 Although it was in fact a joint decree with his then co-Emperor Licinius

26 Byzantium is the term generally applied to the eastern portion of the Empire from the later 5th century. Although in many ways anachronistic, as it was not the term employed at the time, it is so universally understood that I have chosen to use it to refer to the Eastern Empire after the fall of the last Western Roman Emperor in 476. For the eastern provinces between the permanent political split with the West in 395 and the deposition of Romulus Augustulus in 476, I have used 'Eastern Empire', and similarly 'Western Empire' for the western provinces.

CHAPTER 1: BRITANNIA

1 Rudyard Kipling, *Puck of Pook's Hill* (London, 1906), Chapter 6, p. 173

2 Roger J.A. Wilson, *A Guide to the Roman Remains in Britain* (4th edition, London 2002), pp. 415–24

3 See, for example, David J. Breeze and Brian Dobson, *Hadrian's Wall* (4th edition, London 2000), pp. 39–43; Malcolm Todd (ed.), *A Companion to Roman Britain* (Oxford 2007), pp. 130–1; and J. Collingwood Bruce, *A Handbook to the Roman Wall* (14th edition, by David J. Breeze, Newcastle 2006), pp. 107–13

4 In his own account (known in modern times as the *Gallic Wars*), Caesar uses technical terms such as *deditio*, which imply the formation of a province. See Sheppard Frere, *Britannia: A History of Roman Britain* (London 1991), p. 27

5 In general throughout this book I have chosen to follow the Latin place-name forms given in the *Barrington Atlas of the Greek and Roman World*, ed J.A. Talbert (Princeton 2000)

6 The invasion force was made up of four legions: the II Augusta, IX Hispana, XIV and XX, together with a number of auxiliary units

7 During its course, both St Albans and London were burnt, the latter with the alleged loss of 70,000 lives

8 He served on the staff of Suetonius Paullinus, and may have been present at the final assault on Anglesey in AD 61, which broke the back of Druidic power in Britain

9 He probably arrived in the summer of 78, and served until his recall in 83. See Frere, *Britannia*, pp. 87–102

10 Frere, *Britannia*, p. 95

11 Tacitus, *Agricola*, 30. Calgacus also picturesquely (and, some might say, accurately) called the Romans 'the plunderers of the world'

12 Of course they did not, and could not, have actually thought of it as 'Scotland' for there was no such entity until the late Middle Ages. Indeed, tribal boundaries straddled what is now the border with England, while, later on (under Hadrian), parts of what is now England lay outside the Roman province of Britannia, and for a time (under Antoninus Pius) much of the lowlands of modern Scotland lay definitely within it

13 The date is not clear, and it may have been as late as 88. See Peter Salway, *A History of Roman Britain* (Oxford 1993), p. 112

14 Wilson, *A Guide to the Roman Remains in Britain*, p. 597

15 *Perdomita Britannia et statim missa*, Tacitus, *Histories*, I, 2. See also Frere, *Britannia*, p. 102

16 See Frere, *Britannia*, p. 107, for an outline account of the evacuation

17 At Carlisle, Brampton Old Church, Nether Denton, Carvoran, Vindolanda, Newbrough and Corbridge

18 A dynasty known collectively as the 'Flavian' Emperors

19 *Historia Augusta*, Hadrian, 11, 2. Also Birley, *Hadrian*, p. 123. The *Scriptores Historiae Augustae* (SHA), or *Augustan Histories*, is one of the few continuous sources for the period 117–284. It purports to be the work of six authors, each of whom tackled the biographies of several emperors. However, it is clear that it is almost certainly the work of a single author, who posed as multiple writers as a literary affectation or imposture, probably sometime in the last quarter of the 4th century. Whilst much of the material in the earlier biographies is probably accurate, for later emperors (and particularly those during the period of the military anarchy of the 3rd century), a great deal of it is unreliable and some outright fiction. See Sir Ronald Syme, 'Controversy Abating and Credulity Curbed' in *Historia Augusta Papers* (Oxford 1983), pp. 208–23, and for a very early contribution to the debate, Norman Baynes, *The Historia Augusta, Its Date and Purpose* (Oxford 1926)

20 Probably with him arrived a new governor, Q. Pompeius Falco, to whom would be entrusted the ambitious plan that Hadrian now conceived.

21 *Historia Augusta*, Hadrian, 11, 2 (trs David Magie, London 1922)

22 One of Hadrian's first concrete actions, however, had been to order the total evacuation of the Parthian conquests. On his way back to Italy, he also ordered that part of Trajan's Dacian conquests should be relinquished to the barbarian Roxolani. It probably made defensive sense, but to senators brought up on the diet of unrelenting success under Trajan, it may have seemed shocking.

23 See p. 78

24 See p. 140

25 Birley, *Hadrian*, pp. 78–80

26 The Roman mile is 1,618 imperial yards or 1,480 metres, around 9 per cent shorter than the modern British imperial mile. The wall is in total 70 British imperial miles, or 113 kilometres, in length. See Breeze and Dobson, *Hadrian's Wall*, p. 29

27 Breeze and Dobson, *Hadrian's Wall*, p. 40

28 Todd, *Companion to Roman Britain*, p. 120

29 Todd, *Companion to Roman Britain*, p. 120; Frere, *Britannia*, p. 117, twelve forts

30 Even where no inscription has been found, subtle differences in the construction techniques of the various structures on the Wall (such as the shape of the gateways) indicate the handiwork of the different legions. See Breeze and Dobson, *Hadrian's Wall*, p. 67, and Collingwood Bruce (ed. Breeze), *Handbook to the Roman Wall*, pp. 72–3, for more details. The milecastles in particular are susceptible to such differentiation

31 For the general order and date of the building works, see Collingwood Bruce (ed. Breeze), *Handbook to the Roman Wall*, pp. 102–4

32 See Breeze and Dobson, *Hadrian's Wall*, p. 78, for details of the chronology

33 See David Mattingley, *An Imperial Possession: Britain in the Roman Empire* (London 2006), p. 157

34 See the account in Breeze and Dobson, *Hadrian's Wall*, p. 82

35 Collingwood Bruce (ed. Breeze), *Handbook to the Roman Wall*, p. 465

36 'Hadrian's Wall: A History of the Problem' by R.G. Collingwood in *Journal of Roman Studies* 11 (1921), pp. 37–66

37 In the aftermath of the Batavian revolt. See p. 78

38 A Roman centurion, therefore, commanded not 100, but 80 men

39 There is some evidence that the first cohort was a double-strength one, at least in the 1st century, leading to a slightly higher estimate of legionary strength, at 5,500–6,000 men

40 At least until the mid-3rd century, when members of the equestrian order, the next rank down in the social hierarchy, came to command legions

41 The quingenary infantry cohort consisted of six centuries, each of 80 men, and the milliary cohort of ten centuries of 80 men. The cavalry quingenary ala of 512 men was divided into 16 troops (*turmae*), each of 32 men, while the milliary ala had 24 *turma*, making 768 men

42 For the camel units or *dromedarii*, see Karen Dixon, *The Roman Cavalry from the First to the Third Century* AD (London 1992), p. 32

43 The praetorian guard, however, amongst their other privileges, served for only sixteen years. See J.B. Campbell, *The Emperor and the Roman Army 31 BC–AD 235* (Oxford 1984), pp. 110–11

44 Paul Erdkamp (ed.), *A Companion to the Roman Army* (Oxford 2007): The Augustan Reform and the Structure of the Imperial Army', Kate Gilliver, pp. 187–200; Richard Duncan-Jones, *Money and Government in the Roman Empire* (Cambridge 1994), p. 35

45 Until 140, the children of discharged auxiliaries had their marriages to non-Roman women recognised and their children became citizens, but this privilege was then withdrawn. See 'Marriage, Families, and Survival: Demographic Aspects' by Walter Schiedel in Paul Erdkamp (ed.), *A Companion to the Roman Army* (Oxford 2007), pp. 417–34. This also had the unfortunate consequence that, technically, soldiers could not transmit property to their (illegitimate) sons, a disability that was ameliorated under Julius Caesar, who granted soldiers the same right as married citizens to make wills granting goods and property to their sons. This concession then fell into abeyance and was not revived until the time of Domitian; Campbell, *The Emperor and the Roman Army*, p. 210

46 David J. Breeze, *The Antonine Wall* (Edinburgh 2006), p. 103. The Antonine Wall would be held by around 5,000 men covering roughly half the distance of Hadrian's Wall (William S. Hanson and Gordon S. Maxwell, *Rome's North West Frontier: The Antonine Wall* (Edinburgh 1983), p. 158)

47 The normal size was 500 men. See p. 25

48 W. Hutton, *The History of the Roman Wall* (London 1802), p. 265. Hutton ascribed the Vallum to Hadrian, and believed it should be called 'Hadrian's Bank' and that the Wall itself should be attributed to Septimius Severus and

thus be named 'Severus's Wall'. He rather melodramatically said of the Wall that 'This Place has been the scene of more plunder and murders, than any part of the Island, of equal extent. During four hundred years, while the Wall continued a barrier, this was the grand theatre of war, as well as during ages after its destruction.' (p. 5). The first person to provide a decent account of the Wall, however, was John Leland, whose *Itineraries*, a record of his travels throughout England and Wales in the 1540s, include material on the Roman frontier works. William Camden's *Britannia*, published in 1600, gives a far fuller account of Hadrian's Wall, though at a time when travel was still fairly hazardous in a countryside infested by bandits and cattle-rustlers. The Reverend John Horsley's *Britannia Romana* in 1732 provided the first comprehensive account of the ruins, including descriptions of elements that have disappeared since his time

49 The numbering system was established in the early 1930s. See Collingwood Bruce (14th edition, ed. Breeze), *Handbook to the Roman Wall*, pp. 10–11

50 For the Turf Wall in general, see Collingwood Bruce (14th edition, ed. Breeze), *Handbook to the Roman Wall*, pp. 58–62. For the size of the turves, see Vegetius, *De Re Militari*, III, 8. Vegetius wrote a military manual sometime in the period 383–450 addressed to the Emperor of the time (who quite probably never read it), aimed at 'restoring' the legions to the glory days of old. Part of his solution was to reduce reliance on barbarian troops by recruiting more citizens to the armed forces. He seems to have collected together and summarised the works of earlier military writers, such as Julius Frontinus's *Strategemata*, and is an invaluable resource for all kinds of Roman military tactics, such as how to reinforce walls, how the legions were supposed to march out of camp, and even, in the case of siege, what to do if the salt ran out. See Vegetius, *Epitome of Military Science* (trs N.P. Milner, Liverpool 1996)

51 Tony Wilmott, *Birdoswald Roman Fort* (London 2005), p. 28

52 A geophysical, resistivity and partial magnetometry survey in 1997 tentatively identified several of the concealed structures in the interior of the fort. See J. Alan Biggins et al., 'A Survey of the Roman Fort and Settlement at Birdoswald, Cumbria' in *Britannia* 30 (1999), pp. 91–110

53 During the governorship of Alfenus Senecio

54 See p. 52

55 See Collingwood Bruce (14th edition, ed. Breeze), *Handbook to the Roman Wall*, p. 300

56 See p. 57

57 This was carried out by the governor Aurelius Arpagius in the time of Diocletian and Maximian, when Constantius and Maximian Daia were Caesars, and thus between 296 and 305. Flavius Martinus, the centurion in charge, supervised the works. See Collingwood Bruce (14th edition, ed. Breeze), *Handbook to the Roman Wall* pp. 298–9

58 Vegetius, *De Rei Militari*, II 23
59 Later to find fame on the eastern front, where his mistreatment of the Goths contributed to the Empire's disastrous defeat at Adrianople in 378. See p. 243
60 In the words of the historian Ammianus Marcellinus; Ammianus Marcellinus, XXVII 8, 4–9
61 Possibly the *Comes Litoris Saxonici* in charge of the 'Saxon Shore' forts in southern and eastern England. See Peter Salway, *Roman Britain* (Oxford 1981), p. 378
62 *Dux* (or 'duke') was a senior rank that became common in the Later Roman Empire, particularly referring to the commander across a stretch of the frontier
63 In passing he put down a revolt by Valentinus, the brother-in-law of the praetorian prefect Maximinus, who had been sent to Britain when his death sentence for an unspecified (but presumably very serious) crime was commuted to one of exile. Such usurpations by provincial notables – or by influential outsiders co-opted to a local cause – became increasingly common in the Later Empire; as the central authorities seemed impotent to provide for the security of the provinces, local leaders often simply raised up their own 'emperor', who would, they hoped, be much more attuned to solving problems in their own back yard.

Valentinus was not the last British usurper, and certainly not the most serious one. Around 380, Magnus Maximus, a Spaniard who had been a close companion of the Emperor Theodosius I, was appointed *comes Britanniarum* ('count of Britain'). Just three years later, his troops declared him Emperor, a role that he may have taken less than unwillingly, since Theodosius's appointment of his son Arcadius as co-Emperor in January 383 had removed any lingering hope that Maximus's distinguished career might be rewarded by the ultimate prize. Unlike Valentinus, Maximus struck outside Britain, removing part of the garrison for a campaign in Gaul against the Western Emperor Gratian (367–83). So successful was Maximus that, after capturing and executing Gratian near Lyons in August, the following year he received official recognition from Theodosius as co-Emperor. It look four more years, and a rash attack on Italy by Maximus, before he was finally captured near Aquileia and in his turn executed after a salutary lecture on his crimes by his former comrade Theodosius. The troops he had withdrawn from Britain for his continental adventure were probably not returned. The effects that this had on the local economy in the north may have been as damaging as any immediate reduction in security. The number of coin finds in Britain datable to after 378 – and thus the presumed level of supply – falls sharply. As the troops' possession of cash is what had driven the local economy, here as elsewhere on the frontier, their withdrawal probably caused a dramatic localised economic depression.

64 The situation is muddied by the existence of *ripenses*, first found sometime after 325, who seem to have been a superior grade of *limitanei* with somewhat greater privileges, but not as highly regarded as the *comitatenses*, while later-still units of *limitanei* were stripped from the frontier as the central field army weakened and were upgraded to become *pseudocomitatenses*. Southern and Dixon, *The Late Roman Army*, pp. 36–7

65 Under the early Empire, the *cursus honorum* set out a defined career path for ambitious aristocrats, beginning, for young men of the senatorial order, with minor magistracies known as the *vigintiviri* in their early twenties, and then leading on to a position as the junior tribune of a legion, followed by further political positions as quaestor, aedile and praetor, then by command of a legion and then, for the truly successful, a consulate. The equestrian class had its own *cursus*, known as the *tres militiae*, which began with a prefecture of an auxiliary cohort, then a position as legionary tribune, then the prefect of an *ala* (auxiliary cavalry regiment). After this, the top equestrians could serve in positions such as Urban Prefect of Rome or Prefect of Egypt

66 Augustus raised the qualification for senators from 800,000 sesterces. See Matthias Gelzer (trs Robin Seager), *The Roman Nobility* (Oxford 1969), p. 22. The equestrians or *equites* were originally those who were liable for draft into the Roman cavalry as opposed to the infantry. The figure of 400,000 is first recorded in AD 49 (see Seager, p. 10). The process by which equestrians gained a monopoly over military commands is slightly obscure, and it is not clear whether the change came about through a conscious decision by any one emperor or as a matter of expediency to open out a career path to a wider group of serving officers. In any case, the junior officers of the legion, the *tribuni laticlavii* (they were known as this for the *laticlavius* or broad purple stripe on their togas, as opposed to the *angusticlavius* or narrow stripe allowed to equestrian officers), were also generally equestrians from about this time. It also now became possible for senior centurions to rise to the very top of the military, and, coupled with instability at the centre, the influence of the army became ever greater

67 See the discussion in Alan K. Bowman, Peter Garnsey and Averil Cameron (eds), *Cambridge Ancient History* XII (Cambridge 2005), pp. 115–20

68 See 'Strategy and Army Structure between Septimius Severus and Constantine the Great' in Erdkamp (ed.), *A Companion to the Roman Army*, pp. 267–86

69 *Cambridge Ancient History* XII, p.123; Agathias, *The Histories*, V.13.7 (trs Joseph D. Frendo, Berlin 1975), who gives this as the level the army ought to have been at, but that by the latter part of the reign of Justinian it had fallen to around 150,000 men; John Lydus, *De Mensibus*, 1.27

70 Zosimus, II.33.3

71 When their commander Flavius Secundus set up an altar. See Collingwood Bruce (14th edition, ed. Breeze), *Handbook to the Roman Wall*, p. 280

72 Breeze and Dobson, *Hadrian's Wall*, p. 291, and Collingwood Bruce (14th edition, ed. Breeze), *Handbook to the Roman Wall*, pp. 34–5. All three objects almost certainly date to the 2nd century

73 The Staffordshire skillet, confusingly, omits Aballava. Collingwood Bruce (14th edition, ed. Breeze), *Handbook to the Roman Wall*, p. 35

74 Collingwood Bruce (14th edition, ed. Breeze), *Handbook to the Roman Wall*, p. 38

75 Breeze and Dobson, *Hadrian's Wall*, pp. 291–8, and their list of forts on p.298; also J.C. Mann, 'Birdoswald to Ravenglass' in *Britannia* 20 (1989), pp. 75–9

76 This title was commonly the last of the major honorifics that were awarded to each emperor, and tended to be taken up late in an imperial reign (in the case of Augustus only in 2 BC). The first person recorded as having received the award was in fact not an emperor at all, but Marcus Tullius Cicero, for his role in suppressing the Catiline Conspiracy in 63 BC. Tiberius is said to have been offered, but refused, the title

77 For further discussion of the date, see Alan K. Bowman, *Life and Letters on the Roman Frontier, Vindolanda and its People* (London 1998), p. 15

78 Roger J.A. Wilson, *A Guide to the Roman Remains in Britain* (4th edition, London 2002), p. 499

79 They could have been for prisoners of war or as a temporary refuge for un-Romanised local inhabitants. See Wilson, *A Guide to the Roman Remains in Britain*, p. 504

80 Bowman, *Life and Letters on the Roman Frontier*, pp. 16–17

81 Tab. Vindol. II 164, see Bowman, *Life and Letters on the Roman Frontier*, p. 106

82 Tab. Vindol. II 346, see Bowman, *Life and Letters on the Roman Frontier*, p. 139

83 Tab. Vindol. II 291, see Bowman, *Life and Letters on the Roman Frontier*, pp. 71, 127

84 J.G. Crow, *Housesteads Roman Fort* (London 1989), p. 43

85 Flavius Stilicho, who was the architect of this policy, was a typical product of the Later Roman Empire; half-Roman and half-Vandal, he was, despite his part-barbarian heritage, unswervingly loyal in his service to the Empire. For almost a decade and a half, from the death of Theodosius I in 395 to his execution on charges of treason in 408, he dominated the politics of the Western Empire, though never, despite his earnest hopes and best endeavours, managing to insinuate himself into an analogous position in the East. Part powerful warlord and part skilful politician, it was men such as he who held the West together, though his consummate skill in solving immediate problems and pressing crises may have blinded him to the danger that the compromises he was forced to make might undermine the very existence of the Empire in the longer term.

In between seeking to assert his own ambitions, and dealing with the challenge posed by Alaric and the Goths, who in the later 4th century threatened alternately to establish themselves in the Balkans or to march on the Italian peninsula, Stilicho did at least find some time to spare for Britain. The poet Claudian, who as an official panegyrist could hardly be expected to criticise his master, sang his praises: 'His was the care which ensured Britain should not fear the spears of the Scot, nor tremble at the Pict, nor watch along the shore for the arrival of the Saxon.' Stilicho clearly seems to have won some sort of victory against the tribes besetting the British frontier, and the very fact that, with all his other problems, he had chosen to deal with the crisis there in person shows that it must have been grave. Claudian, moreover, claims that Stilicho fortified Britain against her barbarian enemies, which could either be a poetic turn of phrase or refer to some actual repairs to the frontier system on Hadrian's Wall.

Whatever the truth of the matter, the respite was short-lived. In 401, desperate for troops to defend Italy against Alaric, Stilicho withdrew yet another draft of troops from Britain. By now the line must have been very thin, and it could have been at about this time that a British field army, under the *comes Britanniae*, was established. With six cavalry units and perhaps a handful of others, this miniature force was perhaps intended to make up a mobile rapid-reaction unit to compensate for the decreasing force levels along the frontier itself.

86 See Todd (ed.), *Companion to Roman Britain*, p. 309; 'Economic Structures', Michael Fulford in; Strabo, *Geographia*, IV.v.2

87 It arrived there sometime before 222, and possibly even in 213; John Spaul, *Cohors²: The Evidence for and a short history of the auxiliary infantry units of the Imperial Roman Army* (BAR International Series 841, Oxford 2000)

88 Wilson, *A Guide to the Roman Remains in Britain*, p. 485

89 See, for example, 'Mithraism and Christianity in Late Antiquity' by Engelbert Winter in *Ethnicity and Culture in Late Antiquity* (ed. Stephen Mitchell and Geoffrey Greatrex, London 2000), pp. 173–82

90 Manfred Clauss, *The Roman Cult of Mithras: The God and his Mysteries* (Edinburgh 2000), pp. 34–5

91 Clauss, *The Roman Cult of Mithras*, p. 43

92 Jerome, *Epistolae*, 107.2 (trs F. A. Wright, Loeb Classical Library, London 1933); Clauss, *The Roman Cult of Mithras*, p. 170. Gracchus, the kinsman of the letter's addressee, is said to have destroyed this *mithraeum* whilst he was Prefect of Rome

93 J.S. Johnson, *Chesters Roman Fort* (London, 1990), pp. 2–9, and Collingwood Bruce (14th edition, ed. Breeze), *Handbook to the Roman Wall*, pp. 191–4

94 Johnson, *Chesters Roman Fort*, p. 37, and Collingwood Bruce (14th edition, ed. Breeze), *Handbook to the Roman Wall*, p. 195

95 Namely Sol (the sun) for Sunday, Luna (the moon) for Monday, and Mars, Mercury, Jupiter, Venus and Saturn (for Saturday). The names for Tuesday

to Friday are better preserved in Romance languages than in English (e.g. *Martedi* in Italian for Tuesday)

96 Wilson, *A Guide to the Roman Remains in Britain*, p. 476

97 J.N. Dore, *Corbridge Roman Site* (London 1989), p. 19

98 Cassius Dio, *Roman History*, LXXII, 8 (trs Earnest Cary, London 1927)

99 Dore, *Corbridge Roman Site*, p. 6

100 Dore, *Corbridge Roman Site*, p. 10, and Wilson, *A Guide to the Roman Remains of Britain*, pp. 474–5

101 The collections of the former Museum of Antiquities were moved in spring 2009 into a new home in the Great North Museum

102 Collingwood Bruce (14th edition, ed. Breeze), *Handbook to the Roman Wall*, p. 138

103 Collingwood Bruce (14th edition, ed. Breeze), *Handbook to the Roman Wall*, p. 115

104 Wilson, *A Guide to the Roman Remains of Britain*, p. 451

105 Apart from the brief notice given by Cassius Dio of tribes crossing the frontier during the reign of Commodus. A general is said to have died, but it is not clear who he was or, indeed, even if the 'wall' that Dio mentions was the old Antonine Wall or Hadrian's Wall itself; David Mattingley, *An Imperial Possession, Britain in the Roman Empire 54 BC – AD 409* (London 2006), p. 122. Todd (ed.), *A Companion to Roman Britain*, p. 139. Also Cassius Dio, LXII.8.2

106 The division may not actually have come into effect on the ground until the reign of Caracalla, however, as late as 213. See Frere, *Britannia*, p. 164

107 See p. 174, note 36

108 Peter Salway, *A History of Roman Britain* (Oxford 1981), pp. 176–7

109 Frere, *Britannia*, p. 162

110 Cassius Dio, LXXVI, 15, 2. See also Anthony R. Birley, *Septimius Severus: The African Emperor* (London 1988), p. 257

111 Birley, *Septimius Severus*, p. 189. In the aftermath of Geta's assassination, up to 20,000 of his supporters were also murdered

112 It was all part of a complex scheme to ensure the eventual successions of Marcus Aurelius and Lucius Verus in 161. Hadrian's initially preferred heir, Lucius Ceionius Commodus, was adopted in 136 (and renamed Lucius Aelius), but he was in bad health and died early in 138, just six months before Hadrian's own demise

113 Breeze and Dobson, *Hadrian's Wall*, p. 90

114 Breeze and Dobson, p. 94, and David J. Breeze, *The Antonine Wall* (Edinburgh 2006), p. 72

115 Breeze and Dobson, *Hadrian's Wall*, p. 112

116 Breeze, *The Antonine Wall*, p. 65. In the East the ratios were 4⅔ Roman miles to 3⅔ and 3

117 Because in a sense the building campaign might be said to be a sort of

military campaign, and thus merited a *suovetaurilia*. Breeze, *The Antonine Wall*, p. 70

118 Wilson, *A Guide to the Roman Remains in Britain*, p. 582

119 For the garrisons at Bar Hill, see 'The Garrison of the Antonine Wall: Some New Evidence from Bar Hill' in *Studien zu den Militargränzen Roms* III (Stuttgart 1986), pp. 53–7

120 The *Historia Augusta* records that in 161 the Emperor sent Calpurnius Agricola to deal with an impending war against the Britons, whilst the next major literary mention of the province is the cryptic remark of Cassius Dio concerning the transgression of the northern tribes across 'the wall' around 180. By this time, however, it is fairly clear that the Antonine Wall had been evacuated

121 Breeze, *Antonine Wall*, p. 167, for example

122 Such as at Chesters, and at Corbridge a little later in 163. See Breeze and Dobson, *Hadrian's Wall*, p. 167

123 Breeze and Dobson, *Hadrian's Wall*, p. 129

124 In 175, Marcus Aurelius had more than 5,000 Sarmatians deported to Britain to form part of the provincial army, although whether this was because it was the furthest-flung place to which he could deport his former enemies, or whether Britannia was indeed so hard-pressed at the time as to be in need of such substantial reinforcements, is unknown

125 Stephen Johnson, *Roman Forts of the Saxon Shore* (2nd edition, London 1979), p. 13

126 Johnson, *Roman Forts*, p. 16

127 Johnson, *Roman Forts*, p. 18. An inscription from Arles mentioning the prefect of the *Classis Britannica Philippiana*

128 Although they both wrote in the 390s, and it is possible that they may have been influenced by subsequent insecurity in the intervening century. Eutropius, *Breviarium* X, 21, and Aurelius Victor, *Epitome De Caesaribus*, xxxix, 20, and Johnson, *Roman Forts*, p. 199

129 Andrew Pearson, *The Roman Shore Forts, Coastal Defences of Southern Britain* (Stroud 2002), pp. 55–8

130 Pearson, *The Roman Shore Forts*, p. 66

131 See, for example, E.A. Thompson, *Romans and Barbarians, The Decline of the Western Empire* (Madison 1982), pp. 31–6

132 See p. 111

133 Eutropius, *Breviarium* IX, 21 (trs H.W. Bird, Liverpool 1993)

134 A panegyric of Maximian hints that this was because of bad weather (Johnson, *Roman Forts*, p. 28, and *Panegyrici. Latini* X, 119–21), but this probably conceals a reason that could not even be hinted at in such a public forum of praise for the Emperor

135 Johnson, *Roman Forts*, p. 28

136 Pearson, *The Roman Shore Forts*, p. 46

137 Eutropius, *Breviarium* IX, 22, and Johnson, *Roman Forts*, p. 31

138 He had in the meantime dealt a series of crushing blows to the barbarian Franks on the Lower Rhine, who had been in alliance with Carausius and had in effect sheltered his northern Gaulish possessions from recapture by the central authorities. Constantius was then able to capture Bononia, leaving Allectus's weakened regime isolated on the island of Britain

139 Johnson, *Roman Forts*, p. 31; Pearson, *The Roman Shore Forts*, p. 46; and Frere, *Britannia*, p. 331

140 Frere, *Britannia*, p. 331

141 It was probably at about this time that the British provinces were again reorganised, as part of a programme of subdivisions of existing units, which Diocletian ordered implemented in almost all regions of the Empire. The existing provinces of Britannia Superior and Inferior were split into two, being replaced by Britannia Secunda (with its capital at Eboracum) and Flavia Caesariensis in the north and north-east, and by Britannia Prima and Maxima Caesariensis (with its governor based at Londinium) in the south and south-east. Another province, Valentia, is also mentioned by later writers, but, rather than being a subdivision of one of the others, it may have been a new name for Maxima Caesariensis. Roger White, *Britannia Prima, Britain's Last Roman Province* (Stroud 2007), p. 37

142 Johnson, *Roman Forts*, p. 149

143 See the discussion in Pearson, *The Roman Shore Forts*, pp. 130–8

144 Pearson, *The Roman Shore Forts*, p. 85, who calculates that, again for Pevensey, this meant seventeen ships operating over 280 days, and that it would have taken a building force of 120 men working continuously three years to complete the fort

145 See the map in Pearson, *The Roman Shore Forts*, p. 106

146 Johnson, *Roman Forts*, p. 107

147 Susan Harris, *Richborough and Reculver* (London 2001), p. 34, and Valerie Maxfield (ed.), *The Saxon Shore, A Handbook* (Exeter Studies in History No. 25, 1989), pp. 136–7

148 Frere, *Britannia*, pp. 48–9

149 Harris, *Richborough and Reculver*, p. 8

150 Maxfield, *The Saxon Shore*, p. 142

151 Maxfield, *The Saxon Shore*, p. 145

152 Maxfield, *The Saxon Shore*, p. 147

153 Maxfield, *The Saxon Shore*, p. 159. There is a *Praefectus Classis Anderetianorum* (Prefect of the Anderetian fleet) listed in *Notitia Dignitatum* XLIII

154 'In this year Aelle and Cissa besieged Andreadsceaster and slew all the inhabitants; there was not even one Briton left there.' *Anglo-Saxon Chronicle*, 491 (trs G.N. Garmonsworthy, London 1953)

155 William the Conqueror landed near Pevensey, so Anderitum was in a sense his first foothold on English soil

156 John Goodall, *Portchester* (London 2003), p. 27, but see also Maxfield, *The Saxon Shore*, p. 160

157 By 342, however, Constantine's son, Constans, was forced to make an unscheduled winter visit to Britannia to sort out an unspecified problem with the barbarians. There are indications that the *areani*, who performed something of the function of scouts far out into enemy territory, were actually colluding with the barbarians, and they had to be disbanded – thus, presumably, robbing the Roman army of a vital source of intelligence. Goodall, *Portchester*, p. 27

158 Richard Stilwell (ed.), *Princeton Encyclopedia of Classical Sites* (Princeton, NJ, 1976), p. 731

159 For the date of 31 December 405, as opposed to 406 for the crossing, see Michael Kulikowski, 'Barbarians in Gaul, Usurpers in Britain' in *Britannia* 31 (2000), pp. 325–45

160 The early parts of Zosimus's history borrow extensively from earlier writers, such as Dexippus, Eunapius and Olympiodorus, but as a consequence sometimes muddle or misunderstand the original source. Nonetheless, as one of the few pagan historians writing on the 5th century, his history is invaluable

161 See Guy de la Bédoyère, *Roman Towns in Britain* (London 1992), pp. 121–9, and John Wacher, *The Towns of Roman Britain* (London 1975), pp. 411–22

162 His *Vita*, by Constantius of Lyon, is, as most hagiographies of the time, frustratingly short of the kind of detail that would really clarify the political situation in Britain just two decades after Roman rule collapsed there (and was, moreover, written some fifty years after the events it describes). See E.A. Thompson, *Saint Germanus of Auxerre and the End of Roman Britain* (Woodbridge, Suffolk, 1984)

163 See Thompson, *Saint Germanus of Auxerre and the End of Roman Britain*, p. 11, and *Vita Sancti German*, s.15 (261,23)

164 Thompson, *Saint Germanus of Auxerre and the End of Roman Britain*, p. 19

165 Thompson, *Saint Germanus of Auxerre and the End of Roman Britain*, p. 41

166 Gallic Chronicler of 452 (442). See Maxfield, *The Saxon Shore*, p. 81

167 Gildas, *De Excidio Britanniae*, 20

168 Procopius, *History of the Wars*, 3.2.31 and 38a

CHAPTER 2: GERMANIA

1 Cassius Dio, *Roman History* (trs Earnest Cary, London 1914–27), Book LVI, 4–5

2 An alternative (and probably more likely) theory for the lighthouse's location is Boulogne. See Alan K. Bowman, Edward Chaplin and Andrew Lintott (eds), *Cambridge Ancient History* X (Cambridge 2006), p. 228

3 See p. 129

4 Julius Caesar, *Gallic Wars*, IV.2 and VI.4 (trs S.A. Handford, Harmondsworth 1963); H. Schönberger, 'The Roman Frontier in Germany: An Archaeological Survey' in *Journal of Roman Studies* 59 (1969), pp. 144–97

5 There does, though, seem to have been a deliberate Roman policy of allowing friendly tribes to settle on the right bank of the Rhine, creating a buffer between Gaul and trans-Rhenish Germany. See Bowman, Champlin and Lintott (eds), *Cambridge Ancient History* X, p. 522

6 Augustus, or Gaius Octavius as he was known in his childhood (and to historians as Octavian), had a long, though privileged, route to become the first Emperor of Rome. Julius Caesar spotted his promise early and adopted him, thus gifting him simultaneously the strong legacy of the brilliant general's military prestige and the more problematic accusations that Octavian, just as his adoptive father, was intent on undermining the very basis of the Roman Republic. This suspicion about Octavian turned out, of course, to be entirely true. Although he accepted a role as a member of the Second Triumvirate (with Mark Antony and Marcus Lepidus, the latter more financier than politician or general), Octavian clearly saw himself as pre-eminent among the three, a position that Mark Antony, fresh from his victory against the forces of the Senate at Philippi in 42 BC, was wholly unwilling to concede. The domains of Rome were not big enough to accommodate the towering ambitions of both Antony and Octavian, and a decade of bitter political struggle, failed reconciliations and outright military confrontation ended with Mark Antony's defeat at Actium in 31 BC at the side of Cleopatra, his treacherous Egyptian paramour.

The Senate at Rome clamoured to shower honours on the young 'Caesar' – as he called himself, deriving propaganda advantage from the fact that Julius had been declared a god in 42 BC – and awarded him the title *imperator*, the accolade for a victorious general, which was to become a permanent epithet of the later emperors. Octavian had also been consul every year from 31 to 28 BC, and it is quite possible that he might have chosen to occupy that position on a quasi-permanent basis or to have himself appointed dictator, as Julius Caesar had done. Instead, in 27 BC he abolished all the emergency powers he had accrued during the civil war, but then allowed the Senate to grant him a ten-year command over Spain, Gaul, Syria and Egypt, the most strategically important of Rome's provinces. He also permitted himself to be known as *princeps*, a term that carried the informal sense of the leading statesman of the Republic. Also that year he acquired the title 'Augustus', the name that historians have subsequently used to refer to him.

Gradually, over the next decade, Augustus accrued further powers, acquiring in 23 BC the right to intervene in all matters of state, even those not formally under his power (*imperium proconsulare maius*) and the right to veto all legislation (*tribunicia potestas*). Without actually declaring the

Republic abolished, Augustus therefore established a position for himself of such primacy that, in control of all the levers of power, he made it next to impossible for any ambitious general or politician to follow the same path that he had done.

7 See C.M. Wells, *The German Policy of Augustus, An Examination of the Archaeological Evidence* (Oxford 1972), pp. 149–232

8 For Augustus's rise to power, see also Werner Eck, *The Age of Augustus* (trs Deborah Lucas Schneider, Oxford 2003), esp. pp. 41–67

9 See p. 406 and p. 355

10 See Wells, *German Policy of Augustus*, pp. 35–88

11 See Cassius Dio, LVI.18–22.2 for an account of the battle and Augustus's reactions. The catastrophe was accompanied by all sorts of ill omens, such as a statue of Victory that had faced towards Germany, which then did an about-turn to look instead into Italy

12 See Adrian Murdoch, *Rome's Greatest Defeat: Massacre in the Teutoburg Forest* (Stroud 2006), pp. 99–123

13 Suetonius, *Lives of the Twelve Caesars*, Augustus 23 (trs Robert Graves, London 1962)

14 See note 23 below

15 On the developing threat in the northern Rhine area, see Alan K. Bowman, Peter Garnsey and Averil Cameron (eds), *Cambridge Ancient History* XII (Cambridge 2005), pp. 414–15

16 In connection with Caracalla's campaigns against them. See Bowman, Garnsey and Cameron (eds), *Cambridge Ancient History* XII, p. 442

17 Ammianus Marcellinus, XVI, 3–4

18 For a discussion of this, see Averil Cameron and Peter Garnsey (eds), *Cambridge Ancient History* XIII (Cambridge 1993), pp. 122–3

19 The Alan, Vandal and Sueve force broke into Spain later in 407, but this did not lead to a restoration of the situation further north, and the Roman government came to rely on the use of one barbarian group of 'federates', such as the Visigoths in Aquitaine from 418, to counterbalance the demands of others. The exact terminology used to describe Roman allies is problematic, but in general *laeti* had been the earlier term to denote barbarian allies, who were settled in a particular area (often farming it), but were obliged to provide troops for the Roman army and would serve under regular Roman officers. Normally, they are only found described as such in Gaul and Italy. See E.A. Thompson, *Romans and Barbarians*, pp. 23–7 (The Settlement of Barbarians in southern Gaul); Southern and Dixon, *The Late Roman Army*, pp. 48–50. On *laeti*, see Southern and Dixon, *The Late Roman Army*, pp. 48–9

20 See in general W. A. Goffart, *Barbarians and Romans AD 418–584: The Techniques of Accommodation* (Princeton, NJ, 1980) and the refinement of his ideas in *Barbarian Tides: The Migration Age and the Later Roman Empire* (Philadelphia 2006), esp. pp. 119–86

21 Syagrius succeeded Aegidius, who had been *magister militum* in Gaul and then in effect set himself up as a semi-independent warlord, with a domain probably centred around Soissons. See Penny MacGeorge, *Late Roman Warlords* (Oxford 2002), pp. 115–64

22 These were essentially makers marks stamped into the tiles before they dried. As a large part of tile production was controlled or supplied to the military, most of the tiles which have been discovered bear the mark of a legion (or cohort) and provide invaluable evidence as to which legions may have been involved in the construction of a particular fort

23 Tacitus, *Annals*, 4.72–4. The Frisians had been relatively content under arm's-length Roman control. The tax levied on them had been tied to the value of a certain number of ox-hides. However, Olennius, the relatively junior army officer entrusted with collecting it, decided this meant the hide of an auroch, a much larger and rarer beast, thus vastly increasing the tax due. A detachment under Lucius Apronius sent to deal with the revolt was almost wiped out, after which the Romans cut their losses and withdrew from Frisia

24 See p. 79

25 See p. 16

26 The banded leather armour typical of legionaries in the early Empire

27 See pp. 178–81 for a further discussion of the types of gladiator

28 See C.F.C. Hawkes in *Journal of Roman Studies* 22, Part 2 (1932), pp. 251–2, review of Professor F.J. de Waele, *Noviomagus Batavorum (Romeinsch Nijmegen)*, (Nijmegen-Utrecht 1931)

29 See J. Thyssen, 'The late Roman fort at the Valkhof in Nijmegen at the transition from the Roman period to the middle ages' in Philip Freeman, Julian Bennett, Zbigniew T. Fiema and Birgitta Hoffmann (eds), *Proceedings of the XVIIIth International Congress of Roman Frontier Studies* (BAR International Series 1084 (i), Oxford 2002), pp. 453–9

30 See 'The Theban Legion of St Maurice' by Donald F. O'Reilly in *Vigiliae Christianae*, Vol. 32, No. 3 (Sep. 1978), pp. 195–207 for further discussion of the legend

31 Joachim von Elbe, *Roman Germany, A Guide to Sites and Museums* (Mainz, 1975), p. 473

32 *Qualis artifex pereo.* (see Suetonius, *Lives of the Twelve Caesars*, Nero 49). His very last words were *'Haec est fides'* ('That is fidelity'), to his slave, Sero, who had obeyed his master's command and stabbed him to death

33 In 69, one of Vespasian's former legions (the III Gallica) had been trans-ferred to Moesia, where, seeing at first hand the chaos gripping the Empire after Otho (defeated in a series of battles by Vitellius) had taken his own life, its soldiers declared their old commander Emperor. Bolstered by the predictable support of his own Syrian legions and recognition from Tiberius Alexander, the governor of Egypt, Vespasian's allies in the Danube legions

then marched on Rome, where by 20 December they had secured Rome for their master. Whilst Vitellius was dragged into the Forum and beaten to death by a mob, Vespasian's son Domitian, who had escaped the Vitellian forces the day before disguised as a priest of Isis, tried to restore some order to the imperial government.

34 See Tacitus, *Histories*, 4.12–18

35 See Tacitus, *Histories*, 4.20–37, 54–79, 5.14–26

36 Municius Lupercus

37 The same Cerealis who had been so badly beaten by Boudicca's forces in Britain in 60 and later returned as governor in the early 70s, suppressing the Brigantes. See p. 16

38 The narrative in Tacitus, *Histories*, breaks off at Book 5, 16, with the final result of the rebellion (and the fate of Civilis) unclear

39 Including to Hadrian's Wall in Britannia

40 The development of Roman administrative terms for towns outside Italy was complex. In general, those native centres that continued to run their own affairs (under Roman supervision, of course) were termed *civitas*, and their inhabitants were not Roman citizens. Where a settlement had developed further, and was judged worthy of recognition, it might be promoted to a *municipium*, receiving a constitution based on a Roman model and, in general, replacing whatever form of city governance it had previously possessed with two annually elected magistrates (normally called *duumvirs*), backed up by a *curia*, an assembly of the leading local notables. Those who held the position of *duumvir* (and occasionally other, lesser positions in the city government) would be awarded Roman citizenship, together with their families. Gradually, therefore, the proportion of Roman citizens in the provincial urban elite crept up and, with it, their loyalty to the Roman cause. A *municipium* might ultimately be promoted to *colonia*, an urban status that gave all its free male inhabitants the right to Roman citizenship. Strictly speaking, a *colonia* should have been a fresh foundation composed of former legionary veterans, but quite quickly under the Empire the reserves of such men proved insufficient to stock many new cities, and the temptation to the emperors of having the gift of *colonia* status in their armoury proved difficult to resist. By the late 2nd and early 3rd centuries, under Septimius Severus and his successors, the number of these grants became very high, though by the mid-3rd century, with a more general extension of Roman citizenship throughout the Empire, the status of *colonia* became less obviously attractive and the awards much rarer

41 10,000 inhabitants in 73 hectares (or 0.73 square kilometres) is equivalent to 13,698 per square kilometre as against 6,422 for Hong Kong and 6,336 for Singapore. See *United Nations World Populations Prospects Report* (2006 revision, New York 2007). Figures are for 2005 estimated populations

42 An epidemic of an unspecified sickness in Rome in AD 65 is said to have

killed 30,000 people, while in an outbreak of plague in 189 some 2,000 people a day died in the capital. See Ralph Jackson, *Doctors and Diseases in the Roman Empire* (London 1988), p. 173

43 At the time of Diocletian, the cost of a cartload of hay was 600 denarii, and the cost to transport it a mile was 20 denarii, meaning that for distances of more than 30 miles the cost was prohibitive (though of course for higher-value goods, such as silk, this may not have been the case). See 'The Evolution of Land Transport in the Middle Ages' by R.S. Lopez in *Past and Present* 9 (Apr. 1956), pp. 17–29

44 The largest temple was the Capitoline, which has not been so extensively restored

45 Gerta Wolff, *Roman-Germanic Cologne* (Cologne 2003), p. 8

46 See p. 71

47 Wolff, *Roman-Germanic Cologne*, p. 144

48 Suetonius, *Lives of the Twelve Caesars*, Vitellius, 8

49 Led by Ingenuus

50 See p. 304

51 For Postumus's position, see *Cambridge Ancient History* XII, p. 45. He may also have been Gallienus's praetorian prefect, see J.F. Drinkwater, 'The Gallic Empire, Separatism and Continuity in the North-Western Provinces of the Roman Empire AD 260–7', *Historia* 52 (Stuttgart 1987), p. 25

52 Drinkwater, 'The Gallic Empire', p. 24

53 Alaric Watson, *Aurelian and the Third Century* (London 1999), p. 35

54 Drinkwater, 'The Gallic Empire', pp. 28–9

55 Since Alexander Severus in 232

56 Drinkwater, 'The Gallic Empire', pp. 34–5

57 After a brief reign by Marius (268). See Eutropius, *Breviarium*, 9.9–10, and Watson, *Aurelian and the Third Century*, pp. 89–90

58 See p. 234

59 Eutropius, *Breviarium*, 9.13.2, and Aurelius Victor, *Epitome de Caesaribus*, 35.4. Also Watson *Aurelian and the Third Century*, 93. He sent a verse of Virgil (*eripe me his, invicte, malis* – 'Rescue me, unconquered one, from these ills': Virgil, *Aeneid*, VI, 365)

60 Bowman, Garnsey and Cameron (eds), *Cambridge Ancient History* XII, p. 55

61 He did not live long enough, however, to enjoy the fruits of his signal achievement. After some unspecified mopping-up operations in Gaul, he was murdered in Thrace in 275, possibly whilst on his way to renew the war against the Persians; Bowman, Garnsey and Cameron (eds), *Cambridge Ancient History* XII, p. 53

62 Silvanus was in fact cornered into revolt by allegations against him that he was going to lead a rebellion. Once these were believed at court, he had little choice but to follow through with the plan that his enemies had devised for him. Ammianus Marcellinus, XV, 5.31

63 Cameron and Garnsey (eds), *Cambridge Ancient History* XIII, p. 3. Edward Gibbon called this a 'promiscuous massacre' and it involved the murder of no fewer than nine of the future Emperor Julian's male relatives

64 Shaun Tougher, *Julian the Apostate* (Edinburgh, 2007), p. 31

65 Ammianus Marcellinus, 15.8.19, and Tougher, *Julian the Apostate*, p. 32

66 Julian, *Letter to the Athenians*, 278–81 (trs in *The Works of the Emperor Julian* by Wilmer Cave Wright, London, 1913) and Tougher, *Julian the Apostate*, p. 33

67 Ammianus Marcellinus, XVI, 12.6. The Romans are said to have lost just 243 men to the Alamanns' 6,000 dead

68 He was then drafted into a Roman army unit, but died soon afterwards in Rome; Adrian Murdoch, *The Last Pagan: Julian the Apostate and the Death of the Ancient World* (Stroud 2003), p. 62

69 Ammianus Marcellinus, XVII, 3.5

70 See p. 308

71 Wolff, *Roman-Germanic Cologne*, p. 136

72 Wolff, *Roman-Germanic Cologne*, p. 23

73 Wells, *German Policy of Augustus*, p. 136, and Tacitus, *Annals*, I, 23–42, II, 5–28

74 See Chapter 4, note 35

75 Wolff, *Roman-Germanic Cologne*, p. 190

76 See p. 472

77 Wolff, *Roman-Germanic Cologne*, pp. 198–224

78 Wolff, *Roman-Germanic Cologne*, p. 144

79 Wolff, *Roman-Germanic Cologne*, p. 169

80 Wolff, *Roman-Germanic Cologne*, p. 260

81 The I Germanica was involved in a mutiny in AD 13 that demanded higher pay and a shorter term of service. It escaped serious punishment on that occasion, but Vespasian disbanded the legion in 70 for their involvement in the Batavian revolt

82 And indeed a reproduction of the monument can be seen just outside the Cathedral of Saint Victor in Xanten

83 The inscription says 'in bello Variano', which may mean just during the war. There are indications that the stone was not a cenotaph, but formed part of the outer wall of an actual burial chamber. Von Elbe, *Roman Germany*, p. 79

84 Barbara Levick, *Vespasian* (London 1999), p. 163

85 Pat Southern, *Domitian: Tragic Tyrant* (London 1997), pp. 79–80

86 Tacitus, *Germania*, 30 (trs R.B. Townshend, London 1895) and Pat Southern, *Domitian*, p. 82

87 I Adiutrix, XIV Germina, VIII Augusta, XI Claudia from Germania Superior and XXI Rapax (from Bonna in Lower Germany)

88 Levick, *Vespasian*, p. 85. See also Brian W. Jones, *The Emperor Domitian* (London 1992), p. 150

89 Domitian's character seems to have degenerated in the last years of his reign and life, for those with any level of political involvement, became dangerous in the extreme; Pliny describes him as *demens* ('mad'). Finally a plot was hatched, possibly involving the two praetorian prefects, Secundus and Norbanus, but carried out by members of the Emperor's household staff, who stabbed him to death. The Senate – once his demise was made known – lost no time in declaring a *damnatio memoriae*, and his name was carefully chiselled out of as many inscriptions as the authorities could lay their hands on. Thus, for all his achievements in stabilising the *limes*, Domitian fell firmly (as far as Roman and subsequent historians were concerned) into the camp of 'bad' emperors, and certainly suffered the most unfavourable comparisons with his immediate successors

90 Alan K. Bowman, Peter Garnsey, Dominic Rathbone (eds), *Cambridge Ancient History* XI (Cambridge 2000), p. 63

91 *Notitia Dignitatum*, occ. XLI, which lists a *praefectus militum balistarorum* at Bodobrica

92 News of the uprising reached Rome in January 89, and Domitian hurried to the scene with but a single legion, the VII Gemina from Spain, to face Saturninus's potential four: the two of the Mainz garrison and those from Vindonissa and Argentorate (Strasbourg). In the event, the XI Claudia at Vindonissa and the VIII Augusta at Argentorate did not defect. With the tide not flowing in his favour, Saturninus was defeated by Aulus Lappius Maximus, the governor of Germania Inferior, in a battle somewhere near Remagen. Lappius is said to have burnt all Saturninus's correspondence, suggesting that he himself may have been implicated in the rebellion, or that he was trying to protect others

93 The provinces may not have been formally created yet, hence the uncertainty. See Southern, *Domitian*, p. 101

94 Alexander Severus, who had been only thirteen at the time of his accession in 222, had struggled to escape the influence of his strong-minded mother, Julia Mamaea. On the influence of Julia Mamaea, see 'Studies in the Lives of Roman Empresses: Julia Mamaea' by Mary Gilmore Williams in Henry A. Sanders (ed.), *Roman Historical Sources and Institutions* (London 1904). The Emperor, moreover, never succeeded in gaining authority over the army; indeed, his praetorian prefect, the leading jurist Ulpian, was murdered in 223 and the soldiers responsible went unpunished. In 233, Alexander, who had been in the midst of prosecuting a war against the Persians, was forced to hurry west at the news of a serious Alamannic threat in the region of the Taunus. The Emperor and his mother arrived at Mogontiacum in 234, but failed to take decisive action, and resentment smouldered amongst the troops, to whom this smacked of indecision (not to mention that the Illyrian legionaries were concerned that their families might be exposed to barbarian attacks in the Balkans in their absence)

95 See Pat Southern, *The Roman Empire from Severus to Constantine* (London 2001), pp. 62–3

96 Maximinus, meanwhile, faced immediate counter-uprisings by supporters of Alexander, but, once these had been put down, he did not march (as might have been expected) straight on Rome. In fact he never made it there at all, dying in 238 during the siege of Aquileia in northern Italy, while attempting to put down the revolt that would lead to the elevation of Gordian III (238–44) to the throne

97 See Mary Beard, John North and Simon Price, *Religions of Rome: A History*, Vol 1(Cambridge 1998), pp. 146–7

98 See p. 255

99 On Isis worship in general, see Beard, *Religions of Rome*, pp. 264–6 and 308

100 Such a curse was blamed for the death of Tiberius's adoptive son, the general Germanicus, in AD 19. See Beard, *Religions of Rome*, p. 234.

101 Von Elbe, *Roman Germany*, p. 256

102 Chester G. Starr, *The Roman Imperial Navy*, (2nd edition, Cambridge 1960), pp. 38–40

103 Starr, *The Roman Imperial Navy*, p. 67

104 Starr, *The Roman Imperial Navy*, p. 70

105 For the Roman navy in general, see Starr, *The Roman Imperial Navy*

106 There were, however, fleets in the East. The *Classis Pontica* patrolled the Black Sea from its base in Trapezus, while a *Classis Syriaca* was based at Seleucia Pieria and is presumed to have existed from at least AD 93. In Egypt, the *Classis Alexandrina* patrolled the Nile and Mediterranean coast, while there is some scant evidence for an African fleet, the *Classis Nova Libyca*; Paul Erdkamp, *A Companion to the Roman Army* (Oxford 2007)

107 Starr, *The Roman Imperial Navy*, p. 142

108 Starr, *The Roman Imperial Navy*, p. 147

109 Starr, *The Roman Imperial Navy*, p. 151

110 Starr, *The Roman Imperial Navy*, p. 152

111 *Ante Roman Treviris stetit annis mille tercentis. Perstet, et aeterna pace fruatur, amen*

112 Edith Wightman, *Roman Trier and the Treveri* (London 1970), p. 16

113 Caesar, *Gallic Wars*, II.4

114 For a discussion of the date and significance of evidence, see Wightman, *Roman Trier and the Treveri*, pp. 40–1

115 The sources speak of an *obsidio*, a siege of the town or possibly just a threatened attack (Wightman, *Roman Trier and the Treveri*, p. 52)

116 A mosaic panel bearing Victorinus's name has been found (Wightman, *Roman Trier and the Treveri*, p. 52)

117 Stephen Williams, *Diocletian and the Roman Recovery* (London 1985), pp. 102–14

118 Williams, *Diocletian and the Roman Recovery*, pp. 64–5

119 Ausonius was a member of a leading family in Aquitania, who spent the

early part of his career teaching rhetoric at Bordeaux. Around 366, he was summoned by Valentinian I to Trier to act as the tutor to the young Gratian (the precise date is not clear). Whilst there, he accompanied the Emperor on an expedition against the Alamanns in 369 (the last time a Roman emperor campaigned across the Rhine), but it was at court that his influence was most keenly met. He rose to the rank of *comes*, and then praetorian prefect in 378, a giddy height indeed for a poet and rhetor. In 379, he even became consul, whilst his many relatives shared in his good fortune – an almost inevitable feature of the world of Roman patronage – with his son-in-law Thalassius becoming vicar of the diocese of Macedonia in 377 and his nephew Arborius being appointed *comes sacrarum largitionum* (the senior minister in charge of the imperial finances). See 'The Academic Career of Ausonius' by Alan D. Booth in *Phoenix* 36, No. 4 (Winter 1982), pp. 329–43; John Matthews, *Western Aristocracies and the Imperial Court, AD 364–425* (Oxford 1975), pp. 70–1

120 Wightman, *Roman Trier and the Treveri*, p. 65

121 Wightman, *Roman Trier and the Treveri*, p. 66, and Ausonius, *Mosella*, 9 (trs Hugh G. Evelyn Wright, London 1921)

122 There is a story in the *Chronicle of Fredegar* of a last stand in the amphitheatre. Wightman, *Roman Trier and the Treveri*, p. 68, and Fredegar, 2.60

123 Merobaudes (*Mon. Germ. Auct. Antiq* 14.1, pp. 11–18) in Wightman, *Roman Trier and the Treveri*, pp. 69–70

124 John Rich and Graham Shipley, *War and Society in the Roman World* (London 1993), p. 285

125 Von Elbe, *Roman Germany*, p. 396

126 Wightman, *Roman Trier and the Treveri*, p. 78. This possibly took place under Hadrian

127 This is what is implied in Martial. See Garrett G. Fagan, *Bathing in Public in the Roman World* (Ann Arbor 1999), pp. 14–20

128 Fagan, *Bathing in Public in the Roman World*, pp. 69–71

129 For example, Martial, *Epigrams*, 3.51 (to Galla). See Fagan, *Bathing in Public in the Roman World*, p. 28, for a discussion

130 Ovid, *Ars Amatoria*, 3.638–40 (trs Rolph Humphries, London 1958); Fagan, *Bathing in Public in the Roman World*, p. 40

131 Fagan, *Bathing in Public in the Roman World*, p. 38

132 *Historia Augusta*, Hadrian, 17.5–7

133 Wightman, *Roman Trier and the Treveri*, p. 114

134 See von Elbe, *Roman Germany*, p. 403

135 See Wightman, *Roman Trier and the Treveri*, p. 108

136 See, for example, Christopher Kelly, *Ruling the Later Roman Empire* (Cambridge, MA, 2004), pp. 23–4

137 Procopius, *History of the Wars*, III 2.22–5 (trs H.B. Dewing, London 1916)

138 Wightman, *Roman Trier and the Treveri*, p. 73

139 Wightman, *Roman Trier and the Treveri*, p. 239

140 Alex R. Furger, *Augusta Raurica* (trs Cathy Aitken and Christoph Maier, Augst 1995), p. 12

141 See p. 99

142 *Princeton Encyclopaedia of Classical Sites*, p. 116 (citing CIL x, 6087) and also Furger, *Augusta Raurica*, p. 12

143 Furger, *Augusta Raurica*, p. 23

144 Furger, *Augusta Raurica*, p. 4 (2nd-edition supplement)

145 Furger, *Augusta Raurica*, p. 53

146 Ammianus Marcellinus, XIV, 10.6

147 Furger, *Augusta Raurica*, p. 61

148 Furger, *Augusta Raurica*, p. 66

149 This is the characteristic fine ware of the early Roman Empire, with a typical red glaze, which is found throughout Roman territory and beyond. The main workshops were located in Gaul and in Roman Germany, and the productions of each workshop are generally distinct enough to enable the tracing of pots to particular regions of origin

150 Trajan is said to have had oysters despatched to him on his campaign in Persia, and they were so fresh they were still alive on arrival, while the usurper Clodius Albinus is said to have been so fond of them that he was capable of downing 400 at a single sitting. See 'Oysters as a Food in Greece and Rome' by Alfred C. Andrews in *Classical Journal* 43 (1948), pp. 299–303

151 'Whatever happened to the Agri Decumates' by J.G.F. Hind in *Britannia*. 15 (1984), pp. 187–92

152 *Saltus* was the normal term for an imperial estate, which was usually (at least initially) in rural areas. Only later did some of them begin to develop the characteristics of urban settlements, as in the case of Sumelocenna. Over time the emperors acquired huge estates, by inheritance from their predecessors and by confiscation

153 Von Elbe, *Roman Germany*, p. 343

154 See p. 99

155 The *antoninianus* was introduced by Caracalla in 213 as part of a currency reform. Worth twice the denarius, it was only one and a half times its weight and had just 80 per cent of the silver of two individual denarii pieces, thus providing a useful windfall for the treasury, if only a temporary one because the expedient, once detected, had the inevitable consequence of fuelling inflation. See Kenneth W. Harl, *Coinage in the Roman Economy 300 BC to AD 700* (Baltimore 1996), p. 128

156 Just three others on the German *limes* are hexagonal (Wp 1/26, Wp 1/48 and Wp 4/11), making four out of some 1,000 watchtowers along the frontier

157 Probably for Septimius Severus's campaign against the Caledonians; Spaul, *Cohors²*, pp. 72–4

158 For oak from 15 to 5 per cent, for fir from 13 to 5 per cent

159 Number 9/96 in the German numbering system

160 This is Tower Wp 9/98 a few hundred metres north of Murrhardt

161 The unit had been at Canstatt in the reign of Domitian and was then probably transferred to Welzheim. In the 3rd century, the *ala* would be stationed
at Mainz; John E.H. Spaul, *ALA²: The Auxiliary Cavalry Units of the Pre-Diocletianic
Imperial Roman Army* (Andover 1994), p. 192

CHAPTER 3: RAETIA AND NORICUM

1 Eugippius, *Vita Sancti Severini* (trs George W. Robinson, Cambridge, MA, 1914)

2 See p. 78

3 In November 2008, dendrochronological research on the wood used in
the foundations of the wall in the marsh of Ehinger–Dombach resulted
in the first clear date of the building of the Roman wall; the wood was
cut in the winter of 205–6

4 Ammianus Marcellinus, XVII, 6

5 W. Warde Fowler, *The Roman Festivals of the Period of the Republic* (London
1899), pp. 224–6. On the earliest Roman religion and festivals, see Beard,
North and Price (eds), *Religions of Rome*, Vol. 1, esp. pp. 171–80

6 A distinction it shares with Hadrian's Wall and (since July 2008) the Antonine
Wall in Scotland

7 For a list of the milliary *alae*, see P.A. Holder, 'Roman auxiliary cavalry in
the second century AD' in *Archaeology Today* 8 (June 1987), pp. 12–16. The
Ala Augusta Galliorum Petriana milliaria civium Romanorium bis torquata was
the unit at Stanwix, while the camel unit was the *Ala Ulpia dromedariorum
milliaria* raised under Trajan. See Karen Dixon and Pat Southern, *The Roman
Cavalry from the First to the Third Century AD* (London 1992), p. 32

8 Born in 1817, Mommsen's long and distinguished career was most marked
by his ground-breaking works on the Roman world, including an unfinished history of Rome and the *Corpus Inscriptionum Latinarum*, intended to
be a collection of all known Latin inscriptions (and which has been updated
periodically since his day). He also found time to serve as a member of
parliament in the German Reichstag and as the first head of the
Reichslimeskomission. He was the second recipient of the Nobel Prize for
Literature in 1902, and died the following year

9 A process known as *Flurbereinigung*

10 The class of councillors in Roman towns

11 As Rome was traditionally founded in 753 BC, AD 2008 would therefore be
AUC 2761

12 See p. 192

13 Confusingly, another unit with precisely the same name was based in Britain
at the time. It is believed, though, that they were two distinct cohorts (Spaul,
Cohors², pp. 92–5. Another unit, the *Cohors II Aquitanorum equitata*, was also

based in Raetia and may have served in or around Regensburg (Spaul, *Cohors*[2],
p. 146 and Von Elbe, *Roman Germany*, p. 322)

14 Bowman, Garnsey and Cameron (eds) *Cambridge Ancient History* XII, p. 66
15 For the career of Elagabalus, see p. 347, note 20
16 *Conversio Beatae Afrae* (Migne, *Patrologia Latina*, Vol. 142)
17 The map was in fact discovered by a Konrad Celtes, a friend of Peutinger's,
in 1507. A copy was made before Peutinger's death in 1547, and then another
one in 1598 by Marcus Velser. As most of the original has almost disappeared, modern reproductions are based on these copies. Although the exact
date of the original is disputed, and what Celtes found was in turn a medieval
copy, the route network shown is believed to date from sometime between
the mid-4th and mid-5th centuries. See 'The Peutinger Table' by R.A. Gardner
in *Geographical Journal* Vol. 136, No. 3 (Sept. 1970), pp. 489–90
18 Von Elbe, *Roman Germany*, p. 234
19 Herbert Schutz, *The Romans in Central Europe* (New Haven 1985), p. 6
20 Géza Alföldy, *Noricum* (trs Anthony Birley, London, 1974), p. 32
21 Cassius Dio, *Roman History*, LIV 20, 2 (trs Earnest Cary, London 1917)
22 Alföldy, *Noricum*, p. 80
23 Alföldy, *Noricum*, p. 135
24 Alföldy, *Noricum*, p. 96
25 Alföldy, *Noricum*, pp. 155–6
26 Alföldy, *Noricum*, p. 162
27 Alföldy, *Noricum*, p. 201–2
28 Alföldy, *Noricum*, p. 214
29 Southern, *The Roman Empire from Severus to Constantine*, p. 220
30 Bowman, Garnsey and Cameron (eds), *Cambridge Ancient History* XII, p. 445
31 See p. 243
32 See p. 244. See also Michael Kulikowski, *Rome's Gothic Wars from the Third
Century to Alaric* (Cambridge 2007), pp. 154–78, for a general discussion of
Alaric and the Goths
33 Kulikowski, *Rome's Gothic Wars*, p. 165
34 Bowman, Garnsey and Cameron (eds), *Cambridge Ancient History* XII, p. 512
35 Kulikowski, *Rome's Gothic Wars*, p. 170
36 Thomas S. Burns, *Barbarians within the Gates of Rome* (Indiana University
Press 1994), p. 227
37 See Kulikowski, *Rome's Gothic Wars*, pp. 173–4
38 Such as Orosius, *History against the Pagans*, and Saint Augustine in *The City
of God*
39 'The End of Noricum' in E.A. Thompson, *Romans and Barbarians, The Decline
of the Western Empire* (Madison 1982), pp. 113–33; 'Eugippius and the Closing
Years of Noricum Ripense' by Charles Christopher Mierow in *Classical
Philology*, Vol. 10, No. 2 (Apr. 1915), pp. 166–87

40 Alföldy, *Noricum*, p. 222. One of his men, Avitus, accompanied Mamertinus on his journey into the ecclesiastical life, becoming a priest

41 *Vita S Severini*, 20.1

42 Near Naples. Confusingly, there is another Saint Severin, who was actually a native of Naples, but who became Bishop of Septempeda in the modern Marche region of Italy

43 Alföldy, *Noricum*, p. 117

44 Alföldy, *Noricum*, p. 104

45 Alföldy, *Noricum*, pp. 160, 199

46 Alföldy, *Noricum*, p. 186

47 'Six Saints of Sweepdom' by George Lewis Phillips in *Folklore*, Vol. 74, No. 2 (Summer 1963), pp. 377–86

48 The *I Commagenorum* had previously served in Egypt; Spaul, *ALA²*, p. 95

CHAPTER 4: PANNONIA AND MOESIA

1 Edward Gibbon, *Decline and Fall of the Roman Empire* (ed. David Womersley, London 2005), Chapter XXV

2 Although Marcus Aurelius pushed Roman positions across the river into Slovakia in preparation for an expansion of Roman territory into Bohemia, this was not consolidated by his son, Commodus

3 András Mócsy (trs Sheppard Frere), *Pannonia and Upper Moesia. A History of the Middle Danube Provinces of the Roman Empire* (London 1974), pp. 10–14

4 Mócsy, *Pannonia and Upper Moesia*, p. 14, and Eutropius, *Breviarium*, vi, 2

5 Mócsy, *Pannonia and Upper Moesia*, p. 33

6 Zsolt Visy (ed.), *The Roman Army in Pannonia, An Archaeological Guide of the Ripa Pannonica* (Budapest 2003), p. 21

7 Mócsy, *Pannonia and Upper Moesia*, pp. 41–2

8 Mócsy, *Pannonia and Upper Moesia*, p. 83

9 See p. 254

10 A triumph was the parade through the streets of Rome awarded to successful generals in honour of their victory. A frequent award for generals in the late Republic, under the Empire it became rapidly confined to members of the imperial house and particularly the emperors, in many cases for campaigns in which their participation had been at best a token one

11 Visy, *The Roman Army in Pannonia*, p. 25

12 By a force under Hadrian's friend, Quintus Marcius Turbo

13 Mócsy, *Pannonia and Upper Moesia*, p. 194

14 See p. 196

15 The general term for Septimius Severus and his successors up to Alexander Severus

16 See p. 226

17 Mócsy, *Pannonia and Upper Moesia*, p. 268

18 See p. 270

19 Mócsy, *Pannonia and Upper Moesia*, p. 293, though see Lynn F. Pitts, 'Relations between Rome and the German "Kings" on the Middle Danube in the First to Fourth Centuries AD' in *Journal of Roman Studies* 79 (1989), pp. 45–58

20 Mócsy, *Pannonia and Upper Moesia*, p. 347, citing Claudian, *De Consolatu Stilichonis*, ii, 191–207

21 *Notitia Dignitatum* V

22 Mócsy, *Pannonia and Upper Moesia*, p. 350

23 Including most particularly its double-headed eagle symbol, which mirrors the eagle standards of the Roman legions

24 Visy, *The Roman Army in Pannonia*, p. 53

25 That an emperor should espouse the doctrines of Stoicism was in itself something of a paradox, for the first of the distinguished line of Roman Stoics was Cato the Younger, whose involvement with Brutus and Cassius, the murderers of Julius Caesar, might hardly have recommended him to the lineal successor of Augustus, Caesar's adoptive son. The Stoics continued to have a hard time of it, acting as a kind of principled but impotent opposition to the more extreme manifestations of imperial tyranny. Under Nero, Thrasea Paetus was executed for writing a biography that portrayed Cato in a favourable light, while Domitian had two other Stoics put to death: Arulenus Iunius Rusticus, who had in turn written a biography of Thrasea; and Herennius Senecio. By the 2nd century and the era of the adoptive emperors, rulers and philosophers were somewhat more in tune, and the Greek sophist Dio Chrysostom lavished effusive (and it seems sincere) praises on Trajan. Marcus's adoptive 'grandfather' Hadrian was well known to be interested in all things Greek, and especially philosophy, and he chose Cornelius Fronto, a well-known rhetor, to be one of his young protégé's tutors

26 Marcus Aurelius, *Meditations*, vii, 10 and vii, 19 (trs. Gregory Hays, London 2003)

27 Marcus Aurelius, *Meditations*, vi, 47

28 See Anthony Birley, *Marcus Aurelius* (London 1966), pp. 284–7. An inscription at Trenčín in Slovakia, some 125 kilometres north of the Danube, and known to the Romans as Leugaricio, records a stay there by the II Adiutrix legion

29 Although Cassius Dio says that the Emperor's doctors were responsible for his death (Cassius Dio, *Roman History*, LXII 33, 4–34). One classical authority (Tertullian) gives Marcus's place of death as Sirmium and not Vindobona. See Birley, *Marcus Aurelius*, p. 288

30 *Princeton Encyclopaedia of Classical Sites*, p. 982

31 Another type of settlement that grew out of the military camps, this one being used only in the context of a legionary fortress, while the villages that grew up next to auxiliary forts were called *vicus*; Erdkamp, *A Companion to the Roman Army*, p. 410

32 In all, there were six officers' houses on the site. *Römische Ruinen unter dem Hohen Markt* (Wien Museum, Vienna [undated]), pp. 7–8

33 Mócsy, *Pannonia and Upper Moesia*, pp. 80, 89, 92

34 Mócsy, *Pannonia and Upper Moesia*, p. 99

35 The insurrection, which in the end proved to be successful, had its origins in events in Rome the previous year. The regime of Commodus, the son of Marcus Aurelius, had grown increasingly unpopular and even those close to the Emperor had come to fear his mercurial nature and the increasingly evident instability that had led him, amongst other eccentricities, to spend most of his time in the amphitheatre. There, on one occasion, he is said to have shot the heads of ostriches and then waved the bloody trophies in the direction of those senators present, as if to imply that they would be next. He even fought as a gladiator, though needless to say his opponents never had any chance of laying a sword upon him. A conspiracy headed by the praetorian prefect, Aemilius Laetus, arranged for Commodus's mistress Marcia to have him poisoned (and then, when this did not work, strangled). The reins of power were picked up by Pertinax, a senior senator, but the murdered Commodus had been popular with the army, and within days of his accession an attempted coup by the praetorian guard had to be put down. Exactly when news of Pertinax's accession reached Pannonia is unclear, but Septimius duly swore allegiance to the new Emperor and made the customary sacrifice. Soon afterwards, on 28 March, some 200 members of the praetorian guard arrived at the palace just as Pertinax was inspecting the palace slaves. They set upon the Emperor and killed him after a reign of just eighty-seven days. There then followed one of the most inglorious (at least up to that point) episodes in the history of the imperial office. The troops, having murdered the Emperor, had no clear plan and retired to consider their positions. Pertinax's father-in-law, Sulpicianus, who had been Urban Prefect, tried to have himself proclaimed Emperor, and as he was in charge of the Urban Cohorts he possessed at least some muscle with which to enforce his will. Unfortunately, several tribunes of the praetorian guard, fearing the family link between Pertinax and Sulpicianus might lead the Urban Prefect to exact revenge for the assassination of his son-in-law, persuaded the eminent senator Didius Julianus to make his own bid for power. When he arrived at the camp of the praetorians, he found the gates barred, and that Sulpicianus had arrived there as well. The two senators then engaged in an unseemly auction as to who would award the guard the higher donative on his accession as Emperor. Sulpicianus put in a final offer of 20,000 sesterces, but Julianus trumped this by raising the odds to 25,000 sesterces, yelling out his bid and indicating the increased amount with hand-signals. It got him his day as Emperor, but it did not win him the Empire.

Julianus had the support of the governor of Pannonia Inferior,

Valerius Pudens, which gave him another legion, and he also sought the assistance of the six legions in Moesia and Dacia. In parallel, however, Clodius Albinus, the governor of Britain, who had three legions, and Pescennius Niger, governor of Syria, who had an equal number and the support of more from neighbouring provinces, declared themselves Emperor. Septimius, who soon won over the Rhine legions, could by now call on sixteen legions to Niger's probable ten and, moreover, took advantage of his comparative proximity to the centre of power by launching a rapid march on Rome. Julianus's supporters defected as rapidly as was seemly, and the lame-duck Emperor had a decree passed making Septimius his co-Emperor. On 1 June, Julianus was murdered in the palace, just two months after Pertinax had suffered a similar fate.

36 Septimius neutralised Albinus by offering him the subordinate post of Caesar, and he then defeated Pescennius Niger in a series of campaigns culminating at Issus in northern Syria in April 194, after which Niger was killed fleeing for the imagined safety of Antioch. Septimius then turned on Albinus, who, short of troops, tried to make a dash for Rome, but was finally defeated on 19 February 197 near Lugdunum (Lyons) and then committed suicide. The battle was hard fought, and at the critical moment (according to Herodian) Septimius actually threw off his purple cloak and tried to flee the battlefield, but Septimian reinforcements arriving at the last minute drove Albinus's men off the field

37 The background of the would-be Emperor is unclear; the *Historia Augusta* attributes to him descent from the great Dacian king Decebalus, but this seems a fanciful fabrication. The Emperor Gallienus had recently lost his son (Valerian II) who had been in nominal control of the Danube provinces, whilst the real power there, the governor Ingenuus, had himself revolted shortly beforehand. Matters had been made worse by a serious Gothic raid along the coasts of the Black Sea in 257, increased pressure from the Alamanns along the Rhine front, and a mounting threat from Persia in the East, which meant that reinforcements from his father, Valerian, were unlikely

38 See p. 183

39 Charles Matson Odahl, *Constantine and the Christian Empire* (London 2004), p. 87

40 Odahl, *Constantine and the Christian Empire*, pp. 90–1

41 'Diocletian's Palace at Split' by A.J. Brothers in *Greece & Rome*, Second Series 19, No. 2 (Oct. 1972), pp. 175–86

42 See p. 206

43 F. Humer, *Carnuntum, The Roman City Quarter in the Open Air Museum*, (Petronell 2004), p. 15

44 Humer, *Carnuntum*, p. 16

45 Tertullian, *De spectaculis*, 22

46 Michael Grant, *Gladiators* (London 1967), p. 10

47 Thomas Wiedemann, *Emperors and Gladiators* (London 1992), p. 2

48 Pliny the Elder, *Natural History*, VIII, 20 for the rhinoceros

49 Wiedemann, *Emperors and Gladiators*, p. 6

50 Wiedemann, *Emperors and Gladiators*, p. 7, who dismisses the story that the first were in 105 BC at the time of the consul P. Rutilius Rufus

51 Although rarer, there were amphitheatres in the eastern provinces such as at Antioch and Berytus (Beirut) in Syria and at Caesarea in Palestine

52 Grant, *Gladiators*, p. 32

53 Grant, *Gladiators*, p. 35

54 Wiedemann, *Emperors and Gladiators*, p. 11

55 Grant, *Gladiators*, pp. 122–3

56 Grant, *Gladiators*, p. 123. When Telemachus, a monk from Asia Minor, rushed into the arena to push the fighters apart and was torn to pieces by the angry crowd, leading Honorius finally to stamp out the practice

57 Salvian, *De gubernatore Dei*, 6 cited in Wiedemann, *Emperors and Gladiators*, p. 158

58 This was provided for by the Ostrogothic king Theoderic; Wiedemann, *Emperors and Gladiators*, p. 154

59 Visy, *Roman Army in Pannonia*, pp. 58–60

60 Visy, *Roman Army in Pannonia*, pp. 61–2

61 *Princeton Encyclopedia of Classical Sites*, p. 812

62 Review of Spekke (see note 64 below), by Marija Gimbutas in *American Slavic and East European Review*, Vol. 17, No. 4 (Dec. 1958), pp. 571–2

63 Pliny the Elder, *Natural History*, XXXVII, 45

64 Arnolds Spekke, *The Ancient Amber Routes and the Geographical Discovery of the Eastern Baltic*, (Stockholm 1957), p. 33

65 Visy, *Roman Army in Pannonia*, p. 69

66 Visy, *Roman Army in Pannonia*, pp. 93–4

67 Visy, *Roman Army in Pannonia*, pp. 97–9

68 *Princeton Encyclopedia of Classical Sites*, pp. 80–1

69 Mócsy, *Pannonia and Upper Moesia*, p. 273

70 Ammianus Marcellinus, 19.11.8

71 A. Lengyel and G.T.P. Radan, *The Archaeology of Roman Pannonia*, (Budapest 1900) p. 261

72 Visy, *Roman Army in Pannonia*, p. 186, though an alternative view is that the governor's headquarters were at Gorsium

73 Visy, *Roman Army in Pannonia*, p. 187

74 In 86 BC, for example, the plebs at Rome set up a statue in honour of Marius Gratidianus, a praetor responsible for a popular currency reform, and made offerings of incense and wine to it. Lily Ross Taylor, *The Divinity of the Roman Emperor* (Philadelphia 1975), pp. 48–9

75 'Apotheosis of the Roman Emperor' by Larry Kreitzer in *Biblical Archaeologist*, Vol. 53, No. 4 (Dec. 1990), pp. 211–17

76 Essentially former slaves freed by their masters, who in many cases possessed significant personal wealth, but little means of expressing it through the holding of traditional offices

77 See Beard et al., *Religions of Rome (volume I)*, p. 354

78 Suetonius, *Lives of the Twelve Caesars*, Vespasian 23 (trs Robert Graves, London 1962). According to Suetonius, Vespasian could not resist another series of death-bed jokes. On seeing a comet, a clear portent of his demise, he remarked, 'Look at that long hair! The King of Parthia must be going to die.'

79 Seneca, *Apocolocyntosis Divi Claudii*

80 For a more complete account of the excavations, see Ference Fülep, *Sopianae, The History of Pécs during the Roman era and the Problem of Continuity of the Late Roman Population* (Budapest 1984), esp. pp. 24–35

81 Visy, *Roman Army in Pannonia*, p. 160

82 Ingenuus, a senior officer in the Pannonian legions, persuaded his troops to raise him to the purple. It was a critical moment for the Empire; Gallienus had been hard-pressed to restore the Rhine frontier in the face of serious Frankish incursions, and restlessness amongst the soldiers there would lead, within a year, to the breaking away of the British and Gaulish provinces, while in the East a serious Persian invasion had been pushed back in 253 and, again within a year or so, Gallienus's father Valerian would be captured in battle against the Persians, a catastrophe that led to virtually the whole of the East breaking away. However, at Mursa, Gallienus's cavalry commander defeated Ingenuus, who died in the battle, ensuring that when the storm broke next year, the centre, at least, would hold

83 By 350, the sons of Constantine had been ruling the Empire for nearly fifteen years, exhibiting a strictly limited level of fraternal affections amongst themselves. Constans, the youngest, to whom had fallen rule of the West, created a great deal of discontent amongst both provincials and officials for the financial exactions he imposed to fund his campaigning against the German frontier tribes. Eventually, in 350, Flavius Magnus Magnentius, the commander of the elite field regiments, the Joviani and Herculiani, rose up in revolt at Autun in Gaul, securing the adherence of many of Constans's senior civil and military officers. Constans, taken by surprise at the widespread support for the rebellion, fled south and was captured and murdered at Helena in southern Gaul.

Magnentius, having first taken Rome in the face of a counter-usurpation by the luckless Nepotianus (a nephew of Constantine I who lasted just twenty-eight days), then sought to move east and expand the area under his control into the Danubian provinces. It was at Mursa that he received a double-check, the second of them fatal. First, Vetranio, who had been the *magister peditum* of Constans, was proclaimed Emperor in the city, though there is some suggestion that this was a put-up job to obtain the loyalty of the Pannonian army under a trusted general until Constantius could with fresh troops. Duly, Vetranio went over to Constantius in December 350 and the two armies united at Naissus (Niš). Second, by appointing his cousin Gallus as Caesar and sending him to Antioch to hold the line in Syria, Constantius made it clear to Magnentius that there was no hope of a rapprochement between them. Having managed to suborn one of Magnentius's leading supporters, the Frankish general Silvanus, Constantius went on the offensive and, on 28 September 351, the two armies met just outside Mursa. It was an extremely bloody clash; according to Zonaras, two-thirds of Magnentius's men perished and half of Constantius's. If there was one force that a Roman legion could not outmatch in fighting ability, it was another Roman legion, and so, whenever the opposing forces in the civil wars of the 3rd and 4th centuries chose to stand and fight, rather than broker a deal to get rid of one or other contending emperor, the losses could be truly terrible, and the damage to the Empire's longer-term ability to keep the frontiers secure might be serious indeed. Magnentius survived the battle and fled westwards, but his power was broken and he soon lost control of Italy, committing suicide near Lugdunum (Lyons) in August 353.

84 Ammianus Marcellinus, XXVI, 4

85 One of the bears rejoiced in the name of 'Innocence'. Ammianus Marcellinus, XXIX, 3.9

86 Ammianus Marcellinus, XXIX, 6.5

87 Probably in 133, under Hadrian. Visy, *Roman Army in Pannonia*, p. 161

88 Visy, *Roman Army in Pannonia*, p. 145

89 *Princeton Encyclopedia of Classical Sites* p. 831; Mócsy, *Pannonia and Upper Moesia*, pp.82–3

90 Mócsy, *Pannonia and Upper Moesia*, p. 350

91 For further discussion of the Avars, see p. 217

92 Claudius Ptolemaeus (or Ptolemy) was an Alexandrian geographer, who lived from around 86 to 161. His *Geography* included an account of the whole known world, and may originally have been illustrated with maps – those now reproduced as 'Ptolemaic maps' are reconstructions. He estimated the circumference of the world at 500 stades, around one-sixth too small. He also wrote treatises on mathematics (the *Al-Magest*) and on astrology (*Tetrabiblos*).

93 See p. 216 below

94 Pat Southern, *The Roman Empire from Severus to Constantine* (London 2001), pp. 96–7. On the history of mints in the 3rd century in general, see Harl, *Coinage in the Roman Empire*, p. 144

95 See Bowman, Garnsey and Cameron, *Cambridge Ancient History* XII, pp. 37–8

96 See p. 227

97 Some sources indicate 276 and arguments have been made for a date as late as 288. See *Cambridge Companion to the Age of Constantine*, ed. Noel Lenski (Cambridge 2006), p. 9

98 On religious practice under the Empire, see Mary Beard, John North and Simon Price, *Religions of Rome, Volume I: A History* (Cambridge 1998), pp. 313–62

99 Alaric Watson, *Aurelian and the Third Century* (London 1999), pp.188–98; Southern, *The Roman Empire from Severus to Constantine*, p. 124

100 Odahl, *Constantine and the Christian Empire*, p. 94

101 Orosius, *Seven Books of History against the Pagans*, VI, 28

102 Odahl, *Constantine and the Christian Empire*, pp. 104–6

103 For a discussion of the Constantinian conversion, see Lenski, *Cambridge Companion to the Age of Constantine*, pp. 110–14

104 The surviving copy, however, comes from the eastern provinces and is that promulgated by Licinius

105 Although Licinius paid lip service to the idea of the *summus deus* ('highest god'), the Empire was not big enough for both his and Constantine's ambitions and, once he had disposed of Maximin Daia in late 313, the inevitable frictions came to the surface. They first came to blows in 316 in a quarrel over the appointment of Bassianus, Constantine's brother-in-law, to be Caesar with authority in Italy. Licinius was defeated at Cibalae on 8 October 316, but managed to preserve part of his army intact. A new peace was patched up at Serdica in 317, by which Constantine took control of Pannonia and Moesia in addition to his original possessions. In 324, the uneasy concord broke down once more, and this time Licinius's defeat, at Chrysopolis (Scutari), was final. He surrendered to Constantine, who feigned clemency and let his former imperial colleague retire as a private citizen to Thessalonica. There, the next year, Licinius was conveniently executed on suspicion of treasonous plotting

106 Such as Symmachus, who was urban prefect in 384

107 Flavius Constantius was a career army officer, who by the 410s had risen to a high army command, and who in 414 managed to push the Visigoths out of the province into Spain, thereby raising the prospect of a Roman reoccupation of the revenue-rich southern area of Gaul. Despite the fact that by 417 the Visigoths were filtering back, Constantius was seen by many as providing the Empire's greatest hope of a military leader who might revive the glories of Constantine, Diocletian or even Trajan, and in that year he married Galla Placidia, the sister of the Western Emperor, Honorius. It was not a particularly happy marriage; Galla's previous husband had been the Visigothic king Athaulf and after his murder she had been traded by the new ruler, Wallia, in exchange for a treaty that allowed the Visigoths back into Aquitaine. It was as a very unwilling bride that she was forced by Honorius to wed Constantius. The marriage did at least produce a son, Valentinian III, who presided in total ineffectiveness over the dwindling of the empire from 425 to 455. His much more able father Constantius was proclaimed Augustus and co-Emperor by Honorius in 421, but sickened and died after enjoying the imperial office for just over six months

108 Odahl, *Constantine and the Christian Empire*, p. 114

109 When Anastasius died in 518, after a reasonably successful reign of twenty-seven years in which he had fought off the Slavs in the Balkans and kept the Persians at bay, he had failed to nominate an heir. Justin took advantage of his position at the centre of power, and his possession of the enforcement muscle of the imperial guard, to have himself declared Emperor. He advanced his nephew rapidly, giving him the title *comes* in 519 and promoting him to *magister equitum* (commander of the cavalry) the following year.

Justin's rule was largely uneventful; in 524–5 he gave support to an expedition by the (Christian) Ethiopian Axumites against the (Jewish) Himyarite kingdom of Yemen, and he dabbled in the politics of the Laz kingdom in the Caucasus by sponsoring the baptism of King Tzath, a move that sparked a small-scale war with Persia. In 525, Justin passed a curious law permitting women who had been actresses to marry lawfully if they showed repentance for their former profession – which was regarded as tantamount to prostitution. The measure was directed in favour of Theodora, a woman of doubtful background whom Justinian had met and fallen madly in love with. The daughter of a courtesan and a bear-tamer, no less, she followed in her mother's footsteps by becoming a mime in a theatre troupe. Much of the information about her comes from Procopius, who, although he wrote an ostensibly pro-regime account of Justinian's wars, also penned a vitriolic denunciation of the court and its mores in his *Secret History*, a manuscript that was never intended to see the light of day during his imperial master's lifetime. He accuses Theodora of all kinds of immorality: of night-long orgies with ten men at a time, of a long-running affair with the governor of Libya, and of already possessing an illegitimate daughter. After Justin's change to the law, and the death of the Empress Euphemia, who had bitterly opposed the match, Justinian and Theodora were married. In 527, Justin raised his nephew to be co-Augustus, and six months later he was dead, leaving Justinian as sole Emperor.

110 John Moorhead, *Justinian* (London 1994), p. 149

111 Williams, *Diocletian and the Roman Recovery*, p. 196

112 See *Gamzigrad, An Imperial Palace of Late Classical Times* (Belgrade 1983), p. 194

113 See *Gamzigrad, An Imperial Palace*, p. 195

114 Ammianus Marcellinus, XXXI, 2.1–2

115 Jerome, *Epistolae*, 60

116 For a more detailed account of the career of Aëtius, see p. 231

117 Socrates, *Historia Ecclesiastica*, VII, 43.3

118 Included in its number, by a strange historical coincidence, were Ediko, a former leader of the Scirian peoples and a vassal of Attila, and Orestes, a Roman from the lands south of the Danube now occupied by the

Huns. Their children were both to play key roles in the final disappearance of the Roman Empire in the West, for Orestes's son would become
the Emperor Romulus Augustulus, whose brief reign in 475–6 was brought
to an abrupt end by his deposition by Ediko's son, Odovacar, who then
chose not to install another puppet emperor, but to rule Italy as a king
on his own authority

119 Priscus of Panium was born sometime between 410 and 420. He was probably a professional civil servant, and in this capacity accompanied the
embassy to Attila. After the mid-450s, nothing further is known of him. See
R.C. Blockley, *The Classicising Fragmentary Historians of the Later Roman
Empire* (Liverpool 1981), pp. 48–50

120 John Man, *Attila* (London 2005), p. 178

121 *Cambridge Companion to the Age of Constantine*, p. 65, citing Eusebius, *Vita
Constanti*, 1.35.1

122 Priscus fr 11, 355–370 (trs R.C. Blockley *The Classicising Fragmentary Historians
of the Later Roman Empire* (Liverpool 1981)

123 Priscus, fr 11, 405–505 (trs Blockley, *Classicising Fragmentary Historians*). The
embassy finally ended in disaster as a plot to assassinate Attila was uncovered. Attila then held as hostage Vigilius, the Roman ambassador who had
been sent with the gold to pay Ediko (who was to arrange the killing) for
his services. In exchange for his release, Attila extorted a further 50 pounds
of gold from Theodosius. Having learnt a salutary lesson about the faith-
lessness of Romans – something he was not backward in lecturing the
Emperor about through the medium of Orestes, who appeared at the court
in Constantinople with a bag containing Ediko's gold theatrically hung
around his head – Attila now turned his attention westwards

124 See 'Résultat des fouilles de la ville antique de Ratiaria au cours des années
1976 à 1982', Jordana Atanassove-Georgieva in *Studien zu Den Militärgrenzen
Roms* III (Stuttgart 1986), pp. 437–40

125 Stephen Mitchell, *A History of the Later Roman Empire AD 284–641* (Oxford
2007), pp. 405–6

126 Mitchell, *A History of the Later Roman Empire*, p. 398

127 Marija Gimbutas, *The Slavs* (London 1971), p. 98

128 P.M. Barford, *The Early Slavs: Culture and Society in Early Medieval Eastern
Europe* (London 2001), pp. 45–66

129 Mócsy, *Pannonia and Upper Moesia*, pp. 2, 25

130 Odahl, *Constantine and the Christian Empire*, p. 226

131 About 4 kilometres east of modern Svištov in Bulgaria

132 See 'Valetudinarium at Novae' by Ludwika Press in *Studien zu den
Militargränzen Roms* III (Stuttgart 1986), pp. 529–35

133 See p. 264

134 For more on Novae's baths, see Andrezej B. Biernacki, 'The Roman legionary
bath from the C2nd AD in Novae (Moesia Inferior)' in *Proceedings of the*

XVIIIth International Congress of Roman Frontier Studies, ed. Philip Freeman, Julian Bennett, Zbigniew T. Fiema and Birgitta Hoffmann (BAR International Series 1084 (i), Oxford 2002), pp. 649–61

135 In its final form it was 46.4 metres long and 24.3 metres wide; Stefan Parnicki-Pudelko, *The Episcopal Basilica in Novae, Archeological Research 1976–1990* (Poznan 1995)

136 The lists of bishops of Novae carries on into the 10th century (Parnicki-Pudelko, *The Episcopal Basilica in Novae*, p. 55)

137 Indeed, evidence of destruction in the *principia* of the camp from around 316/17 has been interpreted as the result of some kind of mutiny or military revolt (the ceiling of the *principia* collapsed after being bombarded by stone catapult balls); T. Sarnowski, 'La Destruction des principa à Novae vers 316/317 de notre ère. Révolte militaire ou invasion gothique?' in *Archaeologia* 30 (1979), pp. 119–28

138 Peter Heather, *The Goths* (Oxford 1996), p. 158

139 Fergus Millar, *A Greek Roman Empire, Power and Belief under Theodosius II (408–450)* (Berkeley 2006), pp. 21–5

140 Andrew Poulter, *Nicopolis ad Istrum: A Roman, Late Roman and Early Byzantine City* (Society for Promotion of Roman Studies, Journal of Roman Studies Monograph 8, London 1995), p. 11

141 Poulter, *Nicopolis ad Istrum*, pp. 22–5

142 Poulter, *Nicopolis ad Istrum*, p. 12

143 R.F. Hoddinott, *Bulgaria in Antiquity, an Archaeological Introduction* (London 1975), p. 149

144 Poulter, *Nicopolis ad Istrum*, p. 16

145 Augustus was seventy-five at the time of his death and Tiberius seventy-nine. Nerva and Pertinax were older than Decius at their respective accessions, both being sixty-six years old

146 Possibly under Diocletian around 292, see Teofil Ivanov and Stojan Stojanov, *Abritus* (Razgrad, 1985), p. 13

147 There is a certain irony in Abritus, the place where Decius met his end, playing host to an important Christian complex. For Decius's greatest fame came not as a soldier or administrator, but as one of the most infamous persecutors of Christians. The new religion had come to the attention of the Roman authorities before: Nero had tried to deflect responsibility on them for the great fire in Rome in AD 69, and Pliny the Younger had tried to get instructions from Trajan as to whether it was right to take action against Galatian Christians who had committed no other crime (Pliny, *Letters*, 10.96–7). Yet it was Decius who set off the first Empire-wide and consistent attack on the Christian Church. Late in 249 or at the start of 250, new orders were issued from Rome to all provincial governors. There was to be a universal ceremony of sacrifice to the gods, in which a libation had to be poured and a tasting made of sacrificial meat.

Certificates, *libelli*, were to be issued as proof of compliance with the directive and those unable to produce them on demand were to be put on trial. (J.B. Rives, 'The Decree of Decius and the Religion of Empire' in *Journal of Roman Studies* 89 (1999), pp. 135–54). Christians could not, of course, perform the rite without being considered to have apostatised and so many refused. Some purchased false *libelli* as a way of avoiding their obligations, while a few actually did make the sacrifice. Many prominent Christians, including bishops, simply fled; others were seized by the authorities. In Alexandria, no fewer than eighteen victims are known (Bowman, Garnsey & Cameron (eds), *Cambridge Ancient History* XII, p. 633) and in Rome the most prominent victim of the persecution, Pope Fabian, was martyred (Southern, *The Roman Empire from Severus to Constantine*, p. 74). Yet in Ephesus the bishop himself apostatised, while in Alexandria many socially eminent Christians took the easier course of sacrificing and awaiting easier times. The result was a legacy of bitterness and divisions against the *lapsi* – those who had either bought their freedom through obtaining false certificates or who had actually performed the damnable pagan rituals. The competition to be among the purest and most unsullied, who had refused all engagement with Decius's project, was an ominous portent of the even worse trials that the Christian Church would face fifty years later, under Diocletian.

148 *Notitia Dignitatum*, XL

149 Erdkamp, *Companion to the Roman Army*, p. 214

150 See p. 171

151 The ceremony of presentation of the codicils, the supreme moment in a bureaucrat's career, is shown on the Missorium of Theodosius I. The emperor is depicted wearing a pearl diadem, and the official who has received the codicil is shown with his hands veiled (to avoid the offence of actually touching the imperial fingers). Kelly, *Ruling the Later Roman Empire*, p. 19

152 Kelly, *Ruling the Later Roman Empire*, pp. 20–1

153 One problem with the whole story is that the day of Dasius's martyrdom, 20 November, is actually a month *before* the date of Saturnalia ('The Testament of the Piglet', Edward Chaplin in *Phoenix*, Vol. 41, No. 2 (Summer 1987), pp. 174–83)

154 Maurice Whiles, *Archetypal Heresy, Arianism through the Centuries* (Oxford 1996), pp. 1–4

155 As defined at the Council of Nicaea

156 Whiles, *Archetypal Heresy*, pp. 43–4

157 Penny MacGeorge, *Late Roman Warlords* (Oxford 2002), p. 9

158 Ioannes had been *primicerius notariorum*, or head of the notaries' department

159 Bowman, Garnsey and Cameron (eds), *Cambridge Ancient History* XII, p. 136

160 Mitchell, *A History of the Later Roman Empire*, p. 111

161 Procopius, *History of the Wars*, III, iii, 21–2. Averil Cameron, Bryan Ward-Perkins and Michael Whitby, *Cambridge Ancient History* XIV (Cambridge 2000), p. 6

162 Cameron, Ward-Perkins and Whitby, *Cambridge Ancient History* XIV, p. 13; *Gallic Chronicler of 452*, (trs Richard Burgess, 'The Gallic Chronicle of 452: A New Critical Edition with a Brief Introduction' in Ralph W. Mathisen, Danuta Shanzer *Society and Culture in Late Antique Gaul: Revisiting the Sources*, Aldershot 2001)

163 Cameron, Ward-Perkins and Whitby, *Cambridge Ancient History* XIV, p. 15; John Man, *Attila, the Barbarian King who Challenged Rome* (London 2005), pp. 200–4

164 Man, *Attila*, pp. 250–6

165 Man, *Attila*, pp. 277–8

166 Procopius *The Secret History* III, iv.28

167 Pliny the Elder *Natural History*, VII, 24

168 Appian, *History of Rome* XII, 16.111–12 (trs Horace White, London 1899)

169 The son of the *triumvir*

170 Mócsy, *Pannonia and Upper Moesia*, p. 42

171 Mócsy, *Pannonia and Upper Moesia*, p. 41

172 See Thomas S. Burns, *Rome and the Barbarians* 100 BC–AD 400 (Baltimore 2003), pp. 172, 202, 345, 348–9

173 Ramsay McMullen, *Changes in the Roman Empire* (Princeton 1990), pp. 48–9

174 Which was replaced under Diocletian by a detachment of the II Herculea legion. See Paul MacKendrick, *The Dacian Stones Speak* (Chapel Hill 1975), p. 169

175 Augustus also built himself a 'trophy' in stone at La Turbie, near Nice, to commemorate his victory over the Alpine tribes in 7–6 BC. The origins of the 'trophy' are, however, lost in time. The historian Florus says that the first example was that dedicated by Fabius Maximus and Domitius Ahenobarbus following their victory against the Gauls in 121 BC, but alternative traditions associate the practice with Tarpeia. She was custodian of the citadel at Rome at the time of Romulus and was said to have opened the gates to a party of Sabine invaders, who promised her all the jewels they carried. But on being admitted, they threw not only the gems and gold, but all their shields on top of her, crushing her to death and creating a grizzly 'trophy'. It was the same Tarpeia for whom the Tarpeian rock was named, from which traitors to Rome were hurled. See Gilbert Charles Picard, *Les Trophées Romains, Contributions à l'histoire de la Religions et de l'Art triumphal de Rome* (Paris 1957), pp. 103–48

176 The identity of this officer is unclear. It has even been suggested that the altar was erected after Domitian's campaigns and that the officer was Cornelius Fuscus, who perished in that war. See 'The Lower Moesian Limes and the Dacian Wars of Trajan' by Andrew G. Poulter, in *Studien zu den Militargränzen Roms* III (Stuttgart 1986), pp. 519–28

177 MacKendrick, *The Dacian Stones Speak*, pp. 172–4

178 MacKendrick, *The Dacian Stones Speak*, p. 115

179 MacKendrick, *The Dacian Stones Speak*, p. 182

180 MacKendrick, *The Dacian Stones Speak*, p. 182

181 A mixed culture of Getae and Dacians

182 Ptolemy, *Geographia*, III, 8, 2. It is also mentioned in the Antonine Itinerary (225,5) as Diniguttia and in the *Notitia Dignitatum* (XXXIX 24) as Dirigothia. For a general account of the site, see 'La forteresse de Dinogetia à la lumière des dernières fouilles archéologiques' by Alexandru Barnea in *Studien zu den Militärgränzen Roms* III (Stuttgart 1986), pp. 447–50

183 MacKendrick, *The Dacian Stones Speak*, p. 169

184 MacKendrick, *The Dacian Stones Speak*, p. 149

185 There was in fact a bridgehead fort at Alobrix/Aliobrix on the Ukrainian side

186 Ammianus Marcellinus, XXVII, 5.6. C. Scorpan, *Limes Scythiae: Topographical and stratigraphical research on the late Roman fortifications on the Lower Danube* (BAR International Series 99, 1980), p. 18

187 Cameron and Garnsey (eds), *Cambridge Ancient History* XIII, pp. 507–9

188 Ammianus Marcellinus, XXXI, 4.10–11

189 Lenski, *Failure of Empire*, p. 336

190 Ammianus Marcellinus, XXXI, 10

191 Ammianus Marcellinus, XXXI, 13.1–8

192 Ammianus Marcellinus, XXXI, 13.12–19

193 See p. 36

194 See p. 156

195 MacKendrick, *The Dacian Stones Speak*, p. 146

196 MacKendrick, *The Dacian Stones Speak*, p. 23

197 MacKendrick, *The Dacian Stones Speak*, p. 184

198 Tacitus, *Annals*, I, 53

199 Hermann Fränkel, *Ovid, A Poet between Two Worlds* (Berkeley 1945), p. 113

200 Alessandro Barchiesi, *The Poet and The Prince, Ovid and Augustan Discourse* (Berkeley 1997), p. 14

201 Ovid, *Metamorphoses*, XV, 234

202 Hoddinott, *Bulgaria in Antiquity*, pp. 228–9

203 Hoddinott, *Bulgaria in Antiquity*, p. 229

204 Michael Maas (ed.), *Cambridge Companion to the Age of Justinian* (Cambridge 2005), p. 50

205 The very last ruling Emperor in Constantinople, Constantine XI, was a Palaiologos

206 Review of *The Kantakouzenoi* by Anthony Bryer in *Classical Review*, New Series, Vol. 20, No. 2 (Jun. 1970), pp. 219–22

207 Donald M. Nicol, *The Byzantine Family of Kantakouzenos ca 1100–1460, A Genealogical and Prosopographical Study* (Dumbarton Oaks 1968), p. 229

CHAPTER 5: DACIA

1 Cassius Dio, *Roman History* (trs Earnest Cary, London 1914–27), Book LXVIII, 13.1,5

2 Julian Bennett, *Trajan Optimus Princeps* (London 1997), p. 86

3 Mócsy, *Pannonia and Upper Moesia*, pp. 21, 22–4

4 MacKendrick, *The Dacian Stones Speak*, p. 149

5 MacKendrick, *The Dacian Stones Speak* p. 149

6 Bennett, *Trajan Optimus Princeps*, p. 87, and Cassius Dio 68.6.1

7 MacKendrick, *The Dacian Stones Speak*, p. 71, gives 100,000–150,000. Bennett, *Trajan Optimus Princeps*, p. 89, has 50,000

8 Lino Rossi *Trajan's Column and the Dacian Wars* (trs J.M.C. Toynbee, London 1971), p. 13

9 Lepenski Vir is also one of Europe's most important Mesolithic sites, the home of a culture that produced characteristic stone sculptures in the shape of stylised fish

10 Bennett, *Trajan Optimus Princeps*, p.93 (I Italica, I Minervia, I Adiutrix, IV Flavia Firma, V Macedonica, VII Claudia Pia Fidelis, XII Fulminata, XIII Gemina, XV Apollinaris, XX Valeria Victrix, XXI Rapax, XXX Ulpia)

11 Bennett, *Trajan Optimus Princeps*, p. 94, and Cassius Dio, *Roman History* LXVIII 9.4–7

12 Bennett *Trajan Optimus Princeps*, p. 95. See also discussion in Ioana Bogdan Cătăniciu, *Evolution of the system of defence works in Roman Dacia* (trs Etta Dumitrescu, BAR International Series 116, Oxford 1981), pp. 9–10

13 Bennett, *Trajan Optimus Princeps*, p. 97

14 Bennett, *Trajan Optimus Princeps*, p. 98

15 Cassius Dio, 69, 4

16 Trajan's Column, Panel LXXXVI–LXXXVII, Rossi, *Trajan's Column and the Dacian Wars*, p. 181

17 See Rossi, *Trajan's Column and the Dacian Wars*, pp. 202–4, vs Bennett, *Trajan Optimus Princeps*, p. 100

18 Cassius Dio, 68, 14.3–5

19 This is the same trick that is said to have been used to conceal the grave of Alaric and is a sufficiently common ruse that it may be a mere literary topos rather than a true account of the concealment of Decebalus's hoard

20 Bennett, *Trajan Optimus Princeps*, p. 101

21 'The Captor of Decebalus: A New Inscription from Philippi' by Michael Speidel in *Journal of Roman Studies* 60 (1970), pp. 142–53

22 Bennett, *Trajan Optimus Princeps*, p. 101

23 Cataniciu, *Evolution of the system of defence works in Roman Dacia*, p. 11

24 *Princeton Encyclopedia of Classical Sites*, p. 285

25 MacKendrick, *The Dacian Stones Speak*, p. 133

26 The fort at Orăştioara de Sus, however, was retained until the 3rd century; Cătăniciu, *Evolution of the system of defence works in Roman Dacia*, p. 14

27 MacKendrick, *The Dacian Stones Speak*, p. 64

28 Herodotus, *Histories*, 4, 94–6 and see the discussion in 'Zalmoxis' by Mircea

Eliade and Willard R. Trask in *History of Religions*, Vol. 11, No. 3 (Feb. 1972), pp. 257–302

29 MacKendrick, *The Dacian Stones Speak*, p. 55

30 Jordanes, *Getica* 74 (trs. Charles Christopher Microw, Princeton 1915)

31 MacKendrick, *The Dacian Stones Speak*, p. 142

32 See p. 266

33 MacKendrick, *The Dacian Stones Speak*, p. 114. It occupied this role from at least the reign of Alexander Severus (222–35)

34 MacKendrick, *The Dacian Stones Speak*, p. 112

35 MacKendrick, *The Dacian Stones Speak*, p. 123

36 'The Defensive System of Roman Dacia' by Nicolae Gudea in *Britannia* 10 (1979), pp. 63–87

37 See *Princeton Encyclopedia of Classical Sites*, p. 74

38 MacKendrick, *The Dacian Stones Speak*, p. 126

39 MacKendrick, *The Dacian Stones Speak*, p. 126

40 *Princeton Encyclopedia of Classical Sites*, p. 729. The *Torquata* refers to a torque or decoration for valour that must have been given to the unit, whilst *civium Romanorum* shows that at some time those serving in the unit had been granted citizenship, again for some act of great bravery or loyalty

41 Birley, *Septimius Severus*, p. 190. Note that a group called *dediticii* was specifically excluded; the meaning of this is never clearly defined, but equates more or less to enemy who had surrendered or been captured, and their descendants

42 Cătăniciu, *Evolution of the system of defence works in Roman Dacia*, p. 17

43 Cassius Dio, 78, 20.3–4

44 Cătăniciu, *Evolution of the system of defence works in Roman Dacia*, p. 58, although there may simply be evidence that has been missed, and it is never entirely safe to use a *terminus post quem* from coins as an absolutely final date

45 Watson, *Aurelian and the Third Century*, pp. 255–8

CHAPTER 6: CAPPADOCIA

1 See David Magie, *Roman Rule in Asia Minor to the End of the Third Century After Christ* (Princeton, NJ, 1950), pp. 3–33

2 The Roman defeat of the Seleucid Antiochus III had led to the potential acquisition of lands in Asia Minor by the Treaty of Apameia in 188 BC. But the Romans gifted their share to Eumenes of Pergamon, their ally in the war, as the Senate did not wish at that stage to become involved. It fell to them anyway in 133 BC. See Magie, *Roman Rule in Asia Minor*, p. 16

3 On the course of the war, see Magie, *Roman Rule in Asia Minor*, p. 152

4 Following the death of King Archelaus of Cappadocia, who had been summoned to Rome to face a trial on charges of treason and who, at the

age of eighty, seems simply to have expired of old age or exhaustion brought on by the long journey before the trial actually began. See Magie, *Roman Rule in Asia Minor*, p. 491

5 On the death of Antiochus, rival factions sent embassies to Rome, one arguing for the continued independence of Commagene, the other lobbying for its annexation by Rome. The pro-Roman lobby, unsurprisingly, won out. See Magie, *Roman Rule in Asia Minor*, p. 496

6 This included the restoration of Commagene independence under Antiochus III's son, Antiochus IV

7 This involved the deposition of Aristobulus, who had been given the kingdom under Nero in 54. Initially it included the whole of eastern Asia Minor. See Magie, *Roman Rule in Asia Minor*, p. 574

8 See Magie, *Roman Rule in Asia Minor*, pp. 670–82

9 On the Mithridatic Wars, see Magie, *Roman Rule in Asia Minor*, pp. 177–230, 321–50

10 For uncertainty about Strabo's date of birth, see Daniela Dueck, *Strabo of Amaseia* (London 2000), pp. 2–3

11 He was later to become involved in an abortive invasion of Yemen. See p. 355

12 Dueck, *Strabo of Amaseia*, p. 7

13 Strabo, *Geographia* (trs H.C Hamilton and W. Falconer, London 1854), 12.3.39

14 His exact dates are uncertain, but he reigned in the second quarter of the 2nd century BC

15 Appian, *History of Rome*, XII, 16.113

16 Intermittently during the early Empire and more definitively from the 6th century. Roman power did extend further east into the Caucasus, leaving such remains as the castle of Apsarus in modern Georgia. Roman diplomacy from the time of Justinian onwards centred on the struggle to influence or control minor kingdoms such as that of the Laz, which steered an awkward course between absorption by the Romans and falling under the sway of Persia. The furthest-flung evidence of Roman advances to the northeast is the inscription at Gobustan in modern Azerbaijan, left by a centurion from the XII Fulminata, probably in the reign of Domitian

17 See Magie, *Roman Rule in Asia Minor*, pp. 554–9

18 This was on the enforced 'retirement' of Polemo II. Cassius Dio, 63, 6.5; Magie, *Roman Rule in Asia Minor*, p. 561

19 William Miller, *Trebizond: The Last Greek Empire* (London 1926), p. 84

20 Miller, *Trebizond*, p. 98

21 Miller, *Trebizond*, pp. 108–9

22 Miller, *Trebizond*, p. 112

23 Ioannides, *Historia kai Statistike Trapezountos*, 59 (cf. Miller, *Trebizond*, pp. 8–13)

24 'Trebizond, A Medieval Citadel and Palace' by D. Talbot Rice in *Journal of*

Hellenic Studies, Vol. 52, Part I (1932), pp. 47–54

25 Anthony Bryer, *The Byzantine Monuments and Topography of the Pontos* (Dumbarton Oaks 1995), p. 218. The tomb of Theodora, daughter of John IV, who married Uzin Hasan, was once to be seen in Saint George's church in Diyarbarkir

26 See Roger Matthews (ed.), *Ancient Anatolia, Fifty Years of Work by the British Institute of Archaeology of Ankara* (London 1999) p. 271

27 Miller, *Trebizond*, p. 61

28 Miller, *Trebizond*, p. 62

29 Matthews (ed.), *Ancient Anatolia*, p. 268

30 Procopius, *Buildings* (trs H.B. Dewing, London 1940), III.4

31 'Biliotti's Excavation at Satala' by T.B. Mitford in *Anatolian Studies* 24 (1974), pp. 221–44

32 Replacing XVI Flavia Firma, which had been there since about 75. See C.S. Lightfoot, 'Survey Work at Satala' in Matthews (ed.), *Ancient Anatolia*, pp. 273–84

33 *Notitia Dignitatum*, XXXVIII

34 Beate Dignas and Engelbert Winter, *Rome and Persia in Late Antiquity, Neighbours and Rivals* (Cambridge 2007), p. 28

35 See Lightfoot in Matthews (ed.), *Anatolia*, p. 279

36 The modern settlement of Samsat is no longer on the site of ancient Samosata, which was indundated by the rising waters caused by the Atatürk Dam. The inhabitants of the old Samsat, which had sat on the Roman site, were moved to a newly constructed town, which was also called Samsat

37 Antiochos appears for the first time during the Third Mithridatic War. Wise to the new diplomatic realities, he offered support to Lucullus and Pompey in their campaigns in Asia Minor and adopted the unmistakably ingratiating title 'Just and manifest God, friend of the Romans and friend of the Greeks'. Even so, an accusation of complicity with the Parthians in the invasion by Pacorus in 51 BC resulted in Antiochos having to pay a massive bribe to persuade the Romans to desist from a siege of the royal capital. His successor Mithridates II then made the tactical error of supporting Mark Antony against Octavian in the civil war, but somehow managed to get away with his life and his kingdom

38 After the early Empire, the main consuls (or *ordinarii*) for the year would often resign and be replaced by additional (or suffect) consuls, who would serve the rest of the year, sometimes being themselves replaced by a new pair (or pairs) of suffects. The position was still prestigious, if not as highly regarded as the position of main consul for the year. The height of the practice was reached under Commodus in 190, when no fewer than twenty-five men served as consul, one of them being the future Emperor Septimius Severus

39 'The Excavation of the "Hierothesion" of Antiochus I of Commagene on

Nemrud Dagh (1953–1956)' by Theresa Goell in *Bulletin of the American Schools of Oriental Research* 147 (Oct. 1957), pp. 4–22

40 The second Achaemenid statue may be of Xerxes I, though this is disputed. The Seleucids include a range from Seleucus I, the founder of the dynasty. The inscriptions associated with the image of Alexander seem to indicate that he was already known as 'the Great' in the 1st century BC; Donald H. Sanders (ed.), *Nemrud Daği The Hierothesion of Antiochus I of Commagene, Volume I: Text* (Winona Lake, IN, 1996), pp. 89–90, 323–4

41 Such a scene is more prosaically known to historians and archaeologists as a *dexiosis*

42 The first, and long-accepted, calculation of the date was done by Otto Puchstein, who was part of the initial scientific expedition to Nemrud Dagh in 1882–3. He came up with a date of 17 July 98 BC, which he believed to represent the date of Antiochus's conception (even though Antiochus himself stated he was born in December, which would make him four months' premature). Hamdy Bey, who also visited in the 1880s, believed the monument to belong to Antiochus IV, and thus dated between AD 38 and 72. Otto Neugebauer recalculated the date to be 7 July 62 BC, which cannot be the date of the coronation of Antiochus I, as he is known to have been ruling in 62 BC. It seems that it may refer to the date of the settlement by which Pompey confirmed him on the throne of Commagene (see Sanders (ed.), *Nemrud*, pp. 89–90)

43 Harriet I. Flower, *The Art of Forgetting*, (Chapel Hill, NC, 2007), pp. 28–30

44 Flower, *Art of Forgetting*, p. 116

45 Flower, *Art of Forgetting*, p. 133

46 See p. 451

47 In 69 BC, Lucullus, the Roman general tasked with bringing Mithridates to heel, dealt him a stinging defeat, and the Pontic king took refuge at the Armenian capital at Tigranocerta as a rather unwelcome guest. A peremptory demand to surrender Mithridates or face Roman retribution was met with a polite refusal, and so, in summer 69, Lucullus's army crossed the border into Armenia, sparking a war against a country with which Rome really had no quarrel, and igniting a furious controversy in the Senate, which ultimately resulted in the general's replacement by his rival Pompey. Magie, *Roman Rule in Asia Minor*, pp. 346–52

48 Anthony Birley, *Marcus Aurelius* (London 1966), p. 172

49 Sohaemus had actually served as consul, and so had clearly been in exile in Rome for some years. See Birley, *Marcus Aurelius*, p. 175

50 See p. 309

51 R.C. Blockley, *East Roman Foreign Policy, Formation and Conduct from Diocletian to Anastasius* (Leeds 1992), pp. 32–7

52 Simon Payaslian, *The History of Armenia from the Origins to the Present* (London 2007), p. 54

53 Payaslian, *History of Armenia*, pp. 57–8

54 Ammianus Marcellinus, XVIII, 9.3

55 'Sapor Before the Walls of Amida' by C.S. Lightfoot in French and Lightfoot (eds), *The Eastern Frontier of the Roman Empire* (BAR International Series 553 (i), Oxford 1989), pp. 285–94

56 Ammianus Marcellinus, XIX, 1–7

57 Ammianus Marcellinus, XIX, 8.4

58 Edward Gibbon, *The History of the Decline and Fall of the Roman Empire* (ed. David Womersley, London 2005), Chapter XXVI, p. 1073

59 Bennett, *Trajan Optimus Princeps*, p. 199

60 Bennett, *Trajan Optimus Princeps*, p. 199

61 Fergus Millar, *The Roman Near East, 31 BC–AD 337* (Cambridge, MA, 1993), p. 126

62 Dignas and Winter, *Rome and Persia in Late Antiquity*, pp. 122–30

63 Dignas and Winter, *Rome and Persia in Late Antiquity*, p. 41

64 Dignas and Winter, *Rome and Persia in Late Antiquity*, pp. 37–8

65 A treaty that in turn largely restated the terms of the 421 Roman-Persian treaty. See Blockley, *East Roman Foreign Policy*, pp. 91–2

66 On Procopius and Dara in general, see Brian Croke and James Crow, 'Procopius and Dara' in *Journal of Roman Studies* 73 (1983), pp. 143–59

67 Mitchell, *A History of the Later Roman Empire*, p.396; Croke and Crow, 'Procopius and Dara', p. 150

68 For a further description of Dara, see M. Whitby, 'Procopius's Description of Dara' in Philip Freeman and David Kennedy (eds), *The Defence of the Roman and Byzantine East* (BAR International Series 297 (ii, Oxford 1986), pp. 737–83

69 T.A. Sinclair, *Eastern Turkey, an Architectural and Archaeological Survey*, Vol. III (London 1989), p. 222

70 For an account of the Tur Abdin as it was in the early 20th century, see Gertrude Bell, *Churches and Monasteries of the Tur Abdin and Neighbouring Districts* (Heidelberg 1913)

71 Sinclair, *Eastern Turkey*, Vol. III, p. 241

72 Although the patriarch of the Syrian Orthodox Church was in fact based until 1932 at Deir ez Zafferin, the 'Saffron Monastery'

73 Sinclair, *Eastern Turkey*, Vol. III, p. 252

74 Gregory of Nyssa, *Oratio de deitate Filii et Spiritus Sancti*

75 W.H.C. Frend, *The Rise of the Monophysite Movement, Chapters in the History of the Church in the Fifth and Sixth Centuries* (Cambridge 1972), pp. 12–14

76 Bowman, Garnsey and Cameron (eds), *Cambridge Ancient History* XII, pp. 98–9

77 Of course matters were considerably more complex than that. Nestorius admitted that some kind of union or joining of the two natures occurred in Christ, but avoided the Greek term *enosis* used by other theologians,

preferring *symphoneia*, which had the sense of a joining together without any sense of mingling or loss of the separate identity of the two natures. For a detailed discussion of Nestorian doctrine, see J.N.D. Kelly, *Early Christian Doctrines* (revised edition, London 1980), pp. 310–17

78 Frend, *The Rise of the Monophysite Movement*, pp. 46–9
79 Atiyah, *A History of Eastern Christianity*, p. 72
80 See p. 481
81 Maas (ed.) *The Age of Justinian*, pp. 230–34
82 Atiyah, *A History of Eastern Christianity*, pp. 180–4. Lives of Saint Jacob maintain that he may have ordained as many as eighty-nine bishops
83 Segal, *Edessa the Blessed City*, pp. 26–7
84 Steven K. Ross, *Roman Edessa, Politics and Culture on the Eastern Fringe of the Roman Empire* (London 2001), pp. 1–2
85 Segal, *Edessa*, p. 5
86 Segal, *Edessa*, pp. 73–6
87 See p. 323
88 Segal, *Edessa*, pp. 1–2
89 M.L. McClue and C.L. Feltoe, DD, *The Pilgrimage of Etheria* (New York 1919), vii–xxxii. Egeria was one of the earliest pilgrims to produce a record of his voyages, preceded only by an anonymous pilgrim from Bordeaux in 333. See John Wilkinson, *Jerusalem Pilgrims before the Crusades* (Warminster 1977), p. ix. The practice of pilgrimage was first popularised by Helena, the mother of Constantine I, who, amongst other useful items, is said to have rediscovered the True Cross as the result of a dream, and who visited the Holy Land sometime after 324. See E.D. Hunt, *Holy Land Pilgrimage in the Later Roman Empire, AD 312–460* (Oxford 1982), pp. 28–49
90 Segal, *Edessa*, pp. 73–5, and McClue and Feltoe, *The Pilgrimage of Etheria*, p. 32
91 Segal, *Edessa*, p. 9
92 Segal, *Edessa*, p. 15
93 Dignas and Winter, *Rome and Persia in Late Antiquity*, p. 22
94 Dignas and Winter, *Rome and Persia in Late Antiquity*, p. 23
95 Segal, *Edessa*, p. 19
96 Segal, *Edessa*, pp. 34–8
97 Segal, *Edessa*, pp. 114–15
98 Genesis 29, 1
99 Ramsay MacMullen, *Christianity and Paganism in the Fourth to Eighth Centuries* (Newhaven 1997), p. 28
100 'The Planet Cult of Ancient Harran' by J.B. Segal in E. Bacon (ed.), *Vanished Civilizations* (London 1963), esp. pp. 210–18
101 Dignas and Winter, *Rome and Persia in Late Antiquity*, pp. 15–16
102 Michael Grant, *The Severans, The Changed Roman Empire* (London 1996), p. 22

103 Dignas and Winter, *Rome and Persia in Late Antiquity*, p. 13

104 Although he had been given a Christian education under the tutelage of Bishop George of Cappadocia, the young prince had been drawn towards leading sophists and polytheists, and by the early 350s was studying philosophy at Pergamon, where he was drawn into the orbit of the Neoplatonist Maximus of Ephesus; Cameron and Garnsey (eds), *Cambridge Ancient History* XIII, p. 46

105 The obligation on this class was to provide civic services to the cities, often at great personal expense and from which, under normal circumstances, there was no escape

106 Cameron and Garnsey (eds), *Cambridge Ancient History* XIII, p. 67

107 Cameron and Garnsey (eds), *Cambridge Ancient History* XIII, p. 67

108 Robert Browning, *The Emperor Julian* (London 1975), p. 136

109 Cameron and Garnsey (eds), *Cambridge Ancient History* XIII, p. 68

110 Ramsay McMullen, *Christianizing the Roman Empire (AD 100–400)* (New Haven 1984), p. 178

111 Ammianus Marcellinus, XXV, 3.3

112 'The Death of Julian the Apostate in a Christian Legend' by Norman H. Baynes in *Journal of Roman Studies*, Vol. 27, Part 1: Papers Presented to Sir Henry Stuart Jones (1937), pp. 22–9

113 A senior officer of the imperial bodyguard, ranking only below the *comes domesticorum*

114 Dignas and Winter, *Rome and Persia in Late Antiquity*, pp. 131–5; Blockley, *East Roman Foreign Policy*, p. 27

115 Blockley, *East Roman Foreign Policy*, p. 30 (Zosimus 3.34.2)

116 Ammianus Marcellinus, XXV, 9.9

117 J.B. Segal, 'The Planet Cult of Ancient Harran' in Bacon (ed.), *Vanished Civilizations*, p. 212

CHAPTER 7: SYRIA

1 Geoffrey Chaucer, *The Canterbury Tales*, VII 2247–54, 2303–6

2 In the southern portion the Mediterranean sea coast fell into the territory of Judaea or Palestina, which (as not strictly speaking, border provinces) fall outside the remit of this book

3 See p. 273

4 See Maurice Sartre, *The Middle East Under Rome* (Harvard 2007), p. 26; Alan K. Bowman, *Egypt after the Pharaohs* (London 1986), p. 31

5 It only officially became a consular province in 58 BC. See Fergus Millar, *The Roman Near East*, p. 27

6 Sartre, *The Middle East under Rome*, p. 43

7 See p. 307

8 Sartre, *The Middle East under Rome*, p. 49

9 Millar, *The Roman Near East*, p. 39

10 See p. 356

11 Sartre, *The Middle East under Rome*, p. 77

12 See p. 174

13 See Millar, *The Roman Near East*, pp. 181–4. Although, strictly speaking, the road may have been called Strata Diocletiana only in certain stretches and, for example, from Khan el-Qattar to Khan el-Trab may have been called Strata Diocletiani et Maximiani. See Ariel Lewin, 'Diocletian: Politics and limites in the Near East' in *Proceedings of the XVIIIth International Congress of Roman Frontier Studies*, Philip Freeman, Julian Bennett, Zbigniew T. Fiema and Birgitta Hoffmann (eds.), (BAR International Series 1084 (i), Oxford 2002), pp. 91–102

14 Glanville Downey, *Ancient Antioch* (Oxford 1972), pp. 92–3, calculates in the region of 150,000

15 The precise legal position of the Hatay is the subject of a dispute between Syria and Turkey, the former maintaining that the French (then in control of Syria) illegally ceded the territory to Turkey, the latter that the 1939 plebiscite which confirmed the change of political allegiance was an entirely fair and free reflection of the wishes of the population of Hatay

16 Confusingly, no fewer than fifteen towns founded by Seleucus received the name Antioch. See Downey, *Ancient Antioch*, p. 31

17 In fact the port of Antioch, at Seleucia Pieria, was founded a month earlier, but the flight of a sacred eagle that made off with the sacrificial meat at the foundation celebrations for Pieria and then landed on the future site of Antioch persuaded Seleucus that, to be on the safe side, he had better establish a city there too, which then became the royal capital. See Downey, *Ancient Antioch*, p. 31

18 See 'Notes on Seleucid and Parthian Chronology' by Elias J. Bickerman in *Berytus* 8 (1943), pp. 73–84

19 See Downey, *Ancient Antioch*, p. 75

20 See Downey, *Ancient Antioch*, p. 98

21 See, in general, J.H. Liebeschuetz, Antioch, *City and Imperial Administration in the Later Roman Empire* (Oxford 1972)

22 Which were successful in 256, 260 and 540

23 See Downey, *Ancient Antioch*, p. 113

24 On deportations from Roman territory into Persia in general, see 'Captives, Refugees and Exiles: A Study of Cross-border civilian movements and contacts between Rome and Persia from Valerian to Jovian' by Samuel, N.C. Lieu in *The Defence of the Roman and Byzantine East*, Philip Freeman and David Kennedy (eds), (BAR International Series 297 (ii), Oxford 1986), pp. 475–505

25 See p. 321

26 He was caught on the outskirts of the city by Septimius's commander-in-chief

Anullinus. He had, it seems, intended to flee into the Parthian Empire. Birley, *Septimius Severus*, p. 113

27 See Downey, *Ancient Antioch*, pp. 118–19

28 See Acts of the Apostles 11,26

29 See Downey, *Ancient Antioch*, p. 126, who points out that Peter is said to have been the bishop in Rome for twenty-five years before his martyrdom in AD 65, thus making it difficult for him to have been bishop in Antioch in the AD 40s

30 See Downey, *Ancient Antioch*, p. 162

31 See Downey, *Ancient Antioch*, p. 169

32 See Downey, *Ancient Antioch*, p. 175

33 For the 'Riot of the Statues', see Potter, *The Roman Empire at Bay*, pp. 515–16; John Chrysostom, *Homily on Saint Babylas*; Socrates, *Historia Ecclesiastica* 3.18; John Matthews, *The Roman Empire of Ammianus* (London 1989), pp. 429–31. See also Stephen Williams and Gerard Friell, *Theodosius, the Empire at Bay* (London 1984), pp. 67–8

34 'The Riot of 387 in Antioch: The Role of the Theatrical Claques in the Later Empire' by Robert Browning in *Journal of Roman Studies* 42 (1952), pp. 13–20

35 Williams and Friell, *Theodosius*, p. 67. Theodosius's personality was marked, throughout his reign, by a quickness to anger, followed by bouts of guilt, which – coupled with a straightforward devotion to the orthodox Catholic position as defined by the Council of Nicaea – rendered him peculiarly intolerant of pagans and heretics. It was Theodosius who overtly established the Catholic Church as the official one, and who, in 391, forbade conversion from Christianity to paganism (Williams and Friell, *Theodosius*, p. 121). Although both praetorian prefects in that year were pagan, the active approval or tacit connivance of the Emperor led to an outburst of destruction of pagan temples, particularly in the East, from Heliopolis to Gaza and, most notably, in Alexandria. In 392, Theodosius issued an even sterner edict, criminalising any form of sacrifice or divination, on pain of death, and decreeing the confiscation of property for anyone displaying pagan symbols, whether in private or in public (Williams and Friell, *Theodosius*, pp. 122–3). Henceforth, although it was perfectly possibly to hold pagan beliefs, it was next to impossible to engage openly in pagan practices (save in exceptional cases such as Philae in Egypt) and, since paganism had always been more of a way of life and of practice than a theology, its final withering away was only a matter of time

36 Julian, *Misopogon*, 361; Downey, *Ancient Antioch*, p. 167

37 Downey, *History of Antioch in Syria*, p. 206

38 Millar, *Roman Near East*, p. 29

39 'Legions in the East from Augustus to Trajan' by Lawrence Keppie in *The Defence of the Roman and Byzantine East*, Freeman and Kennedy (eds) pp. 411–29

40 See 'Legions in the East from Augustus to Trajan' by Lawrence Keppie in *The Defence of the Roman and Byzantine East*, Freeman and Kennedy (eds) pp. 414–15

41 Ross Burns, *Monuments of Syria, An Historical Guide* (London 1999), p. 530

42 Bowman, Garnsey and Rathbone (eds), *Cambridge Ancient History XI*, p. 177

43 Birley, *Marcus Aurelius*, p. 256

44 Cassius Dio, 72, 24.1–3

45 Cassius Dio, 72, 28.1

46 The rebellion had more unfortunate consequences for some: although Marcus wrote to the Senate asking that his reign not be stained by the blood of others, one of Cassius's sons, Maecianus, had already been murdered. The Empress Faustina died near Tyana in Cappadocia, accompanying her husband en route to Syria. There were rumours that she had committed a diplomatic suicide, shamed by her complicity with Cassius. The Emperor carried on his journey, spending a year in the East before returning to Rome – the whole experience resulting in an edict that henceforth no governor should serve in the province of his birth

47 Although not supporting the position of Nestorius, who maintained that Christ had two fully independent natures (human and divine) not joined together in one person, Theodoret felt that Cyril of Alexandria's 'Twelve Chapters' anathematising the Nestorian position went too far. Christopher Baumer, *The Church of the East, an Illustrated History of Assyrian Christianity* (London 2006), pp. 42–8; István Pásztori-Kupán, *Theodoret of Cyrrus* (Oxford 2006), pp. 10–12

48 During the course of which Roman soldiers entered the council chamber, shaking manacles as a warning to any bishops considering voting the 'wrong' way. As an additional incentive the bishops were forced to sign voting forms in front of the soldiers. W.H. Frend, *The Rise of the Monophysite Movement* (Cambridge 1972), pp. 39–43

49 Pásztori-Kupán, *Theodoret of Cyrrus*, pp. 26–7

50 Warwick Ball, *Rome in the East, the Transformation of an Empire* (London 2000), pp. 229–32; Kevin Butcher, *Roman Syria and the Near East* (London 2003), pp. 145–53

51 Robert Doran, *The Lives of Simeon Stylites* (Spencer, MA, 1992), p. 16

52 Theodoret, *Historia Religiosa* 13 (in Doran, *The Lives of Simeon Stylites*, p. 77)

53 Ramsay McMullen, *Christianizing the Roman Empire* (New Haven 1984), p. 2, and Theodoret *Historia Religiosa* 14

54 The last stylite, however, was recorded as late as 1848 in Djgqondidi in Georgia by the traveller Brosset. Atiyah, *A History of Eastern Christianity*, p. 189

55 'While the servants pitched my tents, I went out and sat upon St Simon's column – there is still a little bit of it left – and considered how very different he must have been from me. And there came a big star and twinkled at me

through the soft warm night, and we agreed together that it was pleasanter to wander across the heavens and the earth than to sit on top of a pillar all one's days.' 31 March 1905, from Kalaat Simaan; Florence Bell (ed.), *The Letters of Gertrude Bell* (London 1927), Vol. 1, pp. 207–8

56 Burns, *Monuments of Syria*, p. 216

57 For the durability of the monastery, see Tchalenko, *Villages antiques de la Syrie du Nord*, p. 206

58 Ball, *Rome in the East*, pp. 229–32; Kevin Butcher, *Roman Syria and the Near East* (London 2003), pp. 145–53

59 Burns, *Monuments of Syria*, pp. 69–70

60 Tchalenko, *Villages antiques de la Syrie du nord*, pp. 320–42

61 The nearby baths are dated to 473. Burns, *Monuments of Syria*, p. 219

62 Williams, *Diocletian*, pp. 94–5; Southern and Dixon, *The Late Roman Army*; but for a contrary view, see G.W. Bowersock, 'Limes Arabicus' in *Harvard Studies in Classical Philology* 80 (1976), pp. 219–29

63 Burns, *Monuments of Syria*, p. 207

64 Burns, *Monuments of Syria*, p. 209

65 See p. 343

66 Irfan Shahid, *Byzantium and the Arabs in the Sixth Century* (Dumbarton Oaks 1995), pp. 32–6

67 Shahid, *Byzantium and the Arabs in the Sixth Century*, pp. 439–78

68 Shahid, *Byzantium and the Arabs in the Sixth Century*, pp. 266–82

69 The Romans also held the town of Kifrin and built a fort on the Euphrates island of Bijan, some 150 kilometres further downriver from Dura, which were the very furthest outposts, only around 200 kilometres from Ctesiphon, the Persian capital

70 There were walls on these sides, but the topography meant they did not need to be strong, and in places in the north-east of the city the original mud-brick was never replaced; Ann Perkins, *The Art of Dura Europos* (Oxford 1973), p. 12

71 Nicanor was a Macedonian general who governed Syria for a while, but as cities were normally referred to as being founded by a ruler, the reference to Nicanor in the chronicle of Isidore of Charax could possibly be a mistake for 'Nicator' – in other words, King Seleucus I; Perkins, *The Art of Dura Europos*, p. 4

72 Dignas and Winter, *Rome and Persia in Late Antiquity*, p. 13

73 Ammianus Marcellinus, 24, 1.5

74 Clark Hopkins, *The Discovery of Dura Europos* (New Haven, 1979), p. 242; Clark Hopkins, 'The Siege of Dura' in *Classical Journal*, Vol. 42, No. 5 (Feb 1948), pp. 251–9

75 In January 2009, Dr Simon James of Leicester University presented evidence that the dead tunnellers were Roman and that, more fascinatingly, they may well have died as a result of the earliest identified use of chemical warfare:

their Persian opponents may have lit braziers laced with bitumen and sulphur crystals which would have emitted choking fumes and rendered the Roman soldiers unconscious within minutes

76 Hopkins, *The Discovery of Dura Europos*, p. 1

77 Hopkins, *The Discovery of Dura Europos*, p. 92

78 The current version was a reconstruction of an earlier synagogue, which was originally founded sometime between 165 and 200 (Perkins, *The Art of Dura Europos*, pp. 26, 29)

79 Though not unprecedented for this era; there are figurative representations in the 6th-century synagogue of Beth Alpha in Galilee (Nicholas de Lange, 'Jews in the Age of Justinian' in Michael Maas (ed.), *The Cambridge Companion to the Age of Justinian* (Cambridge 2005), p. 416)

80 This is the date of the dedication of the *praetorium* of the new camp (Perkins, *The Art of Dura Europos*, p. 26)

81 'The Roman Military Feriale' by J.F. Gilliam in *Harvard Theological Review*, Vol. 47, No. 3 (Jul. 1954), pp. 183–96

82 This was the festival in honour of Vesta, the goddess of the hearth, during which, at Rome, the inner sanctum of her temple would be opened to Roman women, and the Vestal Virgins would bake special cakes in her honour

83 The soldiers were paid three times a year, a practice that lasted from the early Empire at least until the 3rd century

84 Unfortunately his work lasted for only five years, before another earthquake brought it down in 563

85 When Tiglath-Pileser I mentions that the people of Tadmor were amongst the many other peoples he had defeated. Iain Browning, *Palmyra* (London 1979), p. 19

86 Sartre, *The Middle East Under Rome*, pp. 51, 69

87 Browning, *Palmyra*, pp. 24–6

88 Browning, *Palmyra*, p. 53

89 James Dawkins and Robert Wood, *The Ruins of Palmyra* (London 1753), p. 35

90 Browning, *Palmyra*, p. 114

91 Dawkins and Wood, *The Ruins of Palmyra*, Plate 19. As well as the purely architectural plates, Dawkins's and Wood's book includes beautiful panoramas of the site as it appeared in the mid-18th century, unencumbered by site clearances, reconstructions or the general tidying up that has enhanced the accessibility, yet diminished the romantic appeal of many sites on the Roman frontier. Plates 35 and 42 are particularly fine examples

92 The habit of veiling women was fairly prevalent in the Near East even before the advent of Islam in the 7th century. An Assyrian law code of the 20th century BC enjoins that free women must be veiled if outside their

house (though slave girls and concubines could go uncovered). The Christian writer Tertullian in his *De Virginibus Velandis* also advised pious women to veil themselves in public. See Browning, *Palmyra*, p. 32

93 Browning, *Palmyra*, p. 15

94 The original of the tariff, which contains the longest text yet discovered in Palmyrene, now resides in the Hermitage Museum in St Petersburg

95 Browning, *Palmyra*, p. 27

96 Sartre, *The Middle East under Rome*, p. 354

97 *Corrector Totius Orientis*. See Browning, *Palmyra*, p. 45

98 Richard Stoneman, *Palmyra and its Empire, Zenobia's Revolt against Rome* (Ann Arbor 1992), pp. 78–9

99 Sartre, *The Middle East under Rome*, p. 355

100 Stoneman, *Palmyra and its Empire: Zenobia's revolt against Rome*, p. 117

101 Sartre, *The Middle East under Rome*, p. 356

102 *Historia Augusta*, Aurelian, (trs David Magie, London 1954) XXVI, 7

103 *Historia Augusta*, Aurelian, XXVII, 1

104 *Historia Augusta*, Thirty Pretenders, XXX, 7. Zosimus, however, relates the far less romantic version that Zenobia died (or committed suicide) on the way back to Rome and so never appeared in Aurelian's triumph, let alone lived out the rest of her days as a dutiful Roman wife

105 Edward Gibbon, *The History of the Decline and Fall of the Roman Empire*, (ed. David Womersely, London 2005), Vol. I, Chapter XI, p. 313

106 Letter to H.W. Wynn, 30 June 1813 (*The Life and Letters of Lady Hester Stanhope* by the Duchess of Cleveland (London 1914), p. 159)

107 Six hundred piastres was at least a lot less than the 3,000 piastres initial asking price. When they finally did arrive, Mangles and Irby were ambivalent about the place, much as they would be about Petra. Although, taken together, they deemed the ruins as 'presenting altogether the most imposing sight of the kind we have ever seen . . .', their final verdict was far less favourable: 'Take any part of the ruins separately, and they excite but little interest; and altogether, we judged the visit to Palmyra hardly worthy of the time, expense, anxiety, and fatiguing journey through the wilderness, which we had undergone to visit them . . . The sculpture, as well of the capitals of the columns, as of the other ornamental parts of the door-ways and buildings, is very coarse and bad.' (Irby and Mangles, *Travels in Egypt and Nubia, Syria and Asia Minor*, pp. 268–9)

108 See the discussion of its function in Browning, *Palmyra*, p. 188

109 Browning, *Palmyra*, p. 50

110 Malcolm A.R. Colledge, *The Art of Palmyra* (London 1976), p. 22

111 Browning, *Palmyra*, p. 196

112 Named Malé, Saadai and Naamain, with the construction being in the mid-2nd century. Browning, *Palmyra*, p. 205

113 On tomb reliefs; Colledge, *The Art of Palmyra*, pp. 68–9

114 Burns, *The Monuments of Syria*, pp. 201–2
115 Cameron and Garnsey (eds), *Cambridge Ancient History* XI, p. 659
116 Butcher, *Roman Syria and the Near East*, pp. 343–4
117 Birley, *Septimius Severus*, p. 72
118 Gibbon, *Decline and Fall of the Roman Empire*, Vol. I, Chapter XI, p. 150
119 Southern, *The Roman Empire from Severus to Constantine*, p. 58
120 The teenager took his position as priest very seriously and refused to dress in a Roman toga, continuing to affect the robes of a Syrian priest, and even going so far as to send the Senate a portrait of himself in this garb so that the august fathers could become better acquainted with their new imperial master. This disregard of traditional forms did not go down well, nor did his installation of the sacred black stone of Elagabalus in the Temple of Capitoline Jupiter, once he finally arrived in Rome in September 219. Things went from bad to worse: the young Emperor took up the title of 'most magnificent priest of the sun god Elagabalus' on coins, and relegated or dropped the revered appellation of *Pontifex Maximus*. He declared his own deity to be the supreme one of the pantheon, and even married Julia Aquila Severa, a Vestal Virgin, the normal penalty for having sexual relations with whom should have been death; Bowman, Garnsey and Cameron (eds), *Cambridge Ancient History* XII, p. 21
121 David S. Potter, *The Roman Empire at Bay* (London 2004), p. 157
122 *Historia Augusta*, Aurelian, 25.2
123 Burns, *Monuments of Syria*, p. 25
124 Jean Starcky, 'The Nabataeans: A Historical Sketch' in *Biblical Archaeologist*, Vol. 18, No. 4 (Dec. 1955), pp. 81–106
125 Burns, *Monuments of Syria*, pp. 79–80
126 From Psalm 145, 13. Burns, *Monuments of Syria*, p. 84
127 Acts of the Apostles 9, 11
128 Mark Twain, *Innocents Abroad*, Chapter 44
129 Dignas and Winter, *Rome and Persia in Late Antiquity*, pp. 47, 230
130 The peace that Khusraw II had accepted in 591 as the price for being restored to his throne had left the Sassanids smarting at the loss of Dara and other strategic positions (Dignas and Winter, *Rome and Persia in Late Antiquity*, p. 43). When Khusraw's 'benefactor' Maurice was slaughtered in the palace revolution that placed Phocas on the imperial throne in 602, the Persian found the perfect pretext to avenge his dead ally through a series of campaigns in the Byzantine borderlands. Much-contested Dara fell first in 604, and by 610 Khusraw's armies had taken Amida, Edessa and Mardin, opening the way to Syria and Palestine (Mitchell, *A History of the Later Roman Empire*, p. 412). By 609, the line had been breached in Armenia and Cappadocia too, with the loss of Satala and Theodosiopolis (modern Erzerum). Phocas's critically weak position was further undermined by the revolt of Heraclius, the exarch of Africa. Egypt was lost to the rebels in

609, and the following October Heraclius's fleet – led by his similarly named son – cruised into the Bosphorus. The citizens of Constantinople, clearly seeing which way the wind was blowing, showed their contempt for Phocas by murdering him and dragging his mutilated body through the streets. The younger Heraclius, who was now declared Emperor, was at first unable to turn the Persian tide, having to acquiesce in the loss of Damascus in 613 and Jerusalem the following year. By 620, not only had eastern Asia Minor fallen, but Khusraw's forces had captured Egypt, cutting off the supply of grain on which Constantinople depended. By 626 a Persian army was camped at Chalcedon, but the lack of an effective naval arm, and the failure of the Avar kagan to ferry them over, meant it had to withdraw. Heraclius, meanwhile, had taken the risky decision to strike at the Persian capital rather than defending his own. In December 627, he decisively defeated the Persians near Nineveh, and within three months Khusraw had been deposed by his son Kavadh, who himself died six months later. In the confusion, Heraclius opened negotiations with a Persian general, Shahbaraz, who, in return for support in gaining the throne, offered to evacuate all the recently conquered territories, return the True Cross and even allow his eldest son to be baptised. That Shahbaraz was in turn assassinated within three months only added to utter chaos engulfing the Sassanid state (Dignas and Winter, *Rome and Persia in Late Antiquity*, p. 48)

131 Mitchell, *A History of the Later Roman Empire*, p. 420

CHAPTER 8: ARABIA

1 John William Burgon, *Poems (1840 to 1878)* (London 1885), pp. 25–6
2 G.W. Bowersock, *Roman Arabia* (Cambridge, MA, 1983), p. 13
3 Bowersock, *Roman Arabia*, p. 16
4 Whilst there, unable to temper his curiosity, Pompey desecrated the Holy of Holies by entering it, but came out again declaring that it was entirely empty
5 Bowersock, *Roman Arabia*, p. 33
6 Maria Giulia Amadasi Guzzo and Eugenia Equini Schneider, *Petra* (trs Lydia G. Cochrane, Chicago 2002), p. 51. The traditional view that the monsoon was discovered by a mariner named Hippalus was rather spoilt when it was realised this was probably a corruption of Hypalos, the Greek name for the south-west monsoon wind
7 Bowersock, *Roman Arabia*, pp. 46–8
8 Strabo, *Geography*, XVI, 4.23–4
9 The Nabataeans escaped punishment, so perhaps Augustus was more exasperated with his bumbling prefect than suspicious of any connivance by the royal court in Petra. Syllaeus eventually got his come-uppance in 5 BC, when, during a possible bid to seize power, he became implicated in a nasty

series of assassinations of high-ranking opponents and was summoned to Rome, where he was decapitated on the personal orders of the Emperor; Bowersock, *Roman Arabia*, pp. 52–3

10 Bowersock, *Roman Arabia*, pp. 55–6

11 For the dates of Nabataean kings, see G.W. Bowersock, 'A Report on Arabia Provincia' in *Journal of Roman Studies* 61 (1971), pp. 219–42

12 And when he did, they bore the legend *Arabia Adquista* (the Acquisition of Arabia) rather than *Arabia Capta* (the Conquest of Arabia), again implying a more peaceful absorption. See S. Thomas Parker. 'The Roman Frontier in Jordan: an overview' in *Proceedings of the XVIIIth International Congress of Roman Frontier Studies*, Philip Freeman, Julian Bennett, Zbigniew T. Fiema and Birgitta Hoffmann (eds) (BAR International Series 1084 (i), Oxford 2002), pp. 77–84

13 S. Thomas Parker, 'History of the Late Roman Frontier East of the Dead Sea' in *The Roman Frontier in Central Jordan, Interim Report on the Limes Arabicus Project*, S. Thomas Parker (ed.) (BAR International Series 340 (ii), Oxford 1987), pp. 793–825

14 Bowersock, *Roman Arabia*, pp. 78–9

15 S. Thomas Parker, 'History of the Late Roman Frontier East of the Dead Sea' in *The Roman Frontier in Central Jordan*, pp. 793–825

16 Irfan Shahid, *Byzantium and the Arabs in the Sixth Century* (Dumbarton Oaks 1995), pp. 307–73

17 Southern, *The Roman Empire from Severus to Constantine*, p. 70

18 Southern, *The Roman Empire from Severus to Constantine*, p. 71

19 For an account of the evidence (which concludes that he might have been Christian), see Irfan Shahid, *Rome and the Arabs – A Prolegomenon to the Study of Byzantium and the Arabs* (Dumbarton Oaks, 1984), pp. 65–95

20 The area was even more built over until 1974, when the Jordanian General Directorate of Antiquities and Museums decided to clear away all the modern housing that had obscured much of the complex until then. See Hassan Hatoum, *Canatha and Philippopolis* (Damascus, 2001) p. 105; Arthur Segal, 'Roman Cities in the Province of Arabia' in *Journal of the Society of Architectural Historians*, Vol. 40, No. 2 (May 1981), pp. 108–21

21 Although opinions vary and M.G.H. Amer and M. Gawlikowski (1985) believe that it should not be classified as a *kalybe*, but as a temple of the imperial cult

22 Matthew 4, 25

23 Hatoum, *Canatha and Philippopolis*, p. 16

24 Which picturesquely translates into English as 'the torrent of the bay-tree'

25 The *odeon* cost 10,000 denarii, donated by Marcus Ulpius Lysias. See Hattoum, *Canatha and Philippopolis*, p. 19

26 Burns, *Monuments of Syria*, p. 66

27 See p. 300

28 Such as al-Tabari in his *Tarikh al-Tabari*

29 It could also have been used as the later residence of a Christian bishop. Burns, *Monuments of Syria*, p. 69

30 For a description of the archaeological soundings, see Maurice Lenoir, 'Le camp de la légion IIIa Cyrenaica à Bostra. Recherches récentes' in *Proceedings of the XVIIIth International Congress of Roman Frontier Studies* (BAR International Series 1084 (i)), pp. 175–9

31 See p. 343

32 Millar, *The Roman Near East*, pp. 433–5

33 On relations between Zenobia and the Arabs, see 'Zenobia and the Arabs' by David F. Graf in *The Eastern Frontier of the Roman Empire*, D.H. French and C.S. Lightfoot (eds) (BAR International Series 553 (i), 1989), pp. 143–67

34 See Tabari, *Tarikh al-Tabari*, 1.621–7, quoted in Graf, 'Zenobia and the Arabs' in *The Eastern Frontier*

35 Bowersock, *Roman Arabia*, p. 140

36 Irfan Shahid, *Byzantium and the Arabs in the Fourth Century* (Dumbarton Oaks 1983), pp. 33, 414–15

37 Shahid, *Byzantium and the Arabs in the Fourth Century*, pp. 31–53

38 Bowersock, *Roman Arabia*, p. 138

39 Bert de Vries, 'Umm el-Jimal in the First Three Centuries AD' in Freeman and Kennedy, *The Defence of the Roman and Byzantine East*, pp. 227–41; Bert de Vries, 'What's in a Name: The Anonymity of Ancient Umm el-Jimal' in *Biblical Archaeologist*, Vol. 57, No. 4 (Dec. 1994), pp. 215–19

40 See Bowersock, *Roman Arabia*, p. 237

41 See p. 363

42 See de Vries, 'Umm-el Jimal in the First Three Centuries AD' p. 231

43 See p. 356

44 T.E. Lawrence, *Seven Pillars of Wisdom* (London 1935), Chapter LXVV

45 Millar, *Roman Arabia*, pp. 412–13

46 Cassius Dio, 69, 12–15

47 G.W.L. Harding, *The Antiquities of Jordan* (London 1959), p. 88

48 *Princeton Encyclopedia of Classical Sites*, p. 349

49 S. Thomas Parker, 'Preliminary Report on the 1980 Season of the Central Limes Arabicus Project' in *Bulletin of the American Schools of Oriental Research* 247 (Summer 1982), pp. 1–26

50 S. Thomas Parker, 'Preliminary Report on the 1980 Season', p. 5. The building also seemed to lack a *valetudinarium* or hospital.

51 See S. Thomas Parker, 'Retrospective on the Arabian Frontier after a Decade of Research' in Freeman and Kennedy, *Defence of the Roman and Byzantine East*, p. 644

52 See p. 30

53 For a summary of the history of the site, see S. Thomas Parker, 'Research

on the Central *Limes Arabicus, 1980–1982'* in *Studien zu den Militargränzen Roms* III (Stuttgart 1986), pp. 641–8

54 S. Thomas Parker, *The Roman Frontier in Central Jordan, Interim Report on the Limes Arabicus Project, 1980–1985* (BAR International Series 340 (i), Oxford 1987), p. 258

55 Guzzo and Schneider, *Petra*, pp. 79–82

56 'Edward Lear in Petra' by G.W. Bowersock in *Proceedings of the American Philosophical Society*, Vol. 134, No. 3 (Sep. 1990), pp. 309–20

57 Guzzo and Schneider, *Petra*, p. 133

58 John Lewis Burckhardt, *Travels in Syria and the Holy Land* (London 1822), p. 424. In contrast, the next group of visitors, the British naval officers Irby and Mangles, found Nabataean architecture to be 'loaded with ornaments in the Roman manner, but in a bad taste, with an infinity of broken lines and unnecessary angles and projections, and multiplied pediments and half pediments, and pedestals set upon columns that support nothing. It has more the air of a fantastical scene in a theatre than an architectural work in stone; and for unmeaning richness and littleness of conception, Mr Bankes seemed to think, might have been the work of Boromini himself.' (Charles Leonard Irby and James Mangles, *Travels in Egypt and Nubia, Syria and Asia Minor during the years 1817 and 1818* (London 1823), Letter V, pp. 413–14). Irby and Mangles further noted the damage caused by musket shots, which was visible on the Khazneh façade even at this early date

59 Guzzo and Schneider, *Petra*, p. 33

60 Guzzo and Schneider, *Petra*, p. 178

61 Guzzo and Schneider, *Petra*, p. 75

62 Strabo, *Geography*, XVI, 4.26

63 Guzzo and Schneider, *Petra*, p. 176

64 Guzzo and Schneider, *Petra*, pp. 47–8

65 Cassius Dio, 68, 14.5

66 Bowersock, *Roman Arabia*, p. 83

67 Bowersock, *Roman Arabia*, pp. 76–82

68 John W. Eadie and John Peter Oleson, 'The Water-supply Systems of Nabataean and Roman Humayma' in *Bulletin of the American Schools of Oriental Research* 252 (May 1986), pp. 49–76

69 Eadie and Oleson, 'The Water-supply systems of Nabataean and Roman Humayma', p. 51

70 Eadie and Oleson, 'The Water-supply systems of Nabataean and Roman Humayma', p. 52

71 Philip Mayerson, 'The First Muslim Attacks on Southern Palestine' in *Transactions of the American Philological Association* 95 (1964), p. 173

72 Also known by the Arabic form of his name as Imru' al-Qays, but not to be confused with the 4th-century ruler whose inscription was found at Nemara (see p. 364)

73 See Irfan Shahid, *Byzantium and the Arabs in the Fifth Century* (Dumbarton Oaks, 1989), pp. 59–90

CHAPTER 9: AEGYPTUS AND CYRENAICA

1 William Shakespeare, *Antony and Cleopatra*, Act II, Scene 2, 200–11
2 Strabo *Geographia*, XVII, 1.12
3 'Octavian's Propaganda and Antony's *De Sua Ebrietate*' by Kenneth Scott in *Classical Philology*, Vol. 24, No. 2 (Apr. 1929), pp. 133–41
4 Cassius Dio, 51, 16.5
5 Bowman, Garnsey and Cameron (eds), *Cambridge Ancient History* XII, pp. 320–2
6 Bowman, Garnsey and Cameron (eds), *Cambridge Ancient History* XII, p. 318
7 Bowman, Garnsey and Cameron (eds), *Cambridge Ancient History* XII, pp. 175–6. In essence the combination of the *iugum* (the size of the plot of land) and the *caput* (the amount of labour to work it) would yield a value in notional units. The amount of tax per unit was then varied up and down, depending on the government's needs. This was vastly more efficient than a fixed tax on a piece of land, or per head of population, but understandably those faced with the new system may have believed that it was yet another attempt to extract extra revenue from them
8 'Lucius Domitius Domitianus Augustus' by Allan Chester Johnson in *Classical Philology*, Vol. 45, No. 1 (Jan. 1950), pp. 13–21
9 Williams, *Diocletian*, pp. 120–5. There is some evidence for the taxation cycle originating earlier than Diocletian, possibly as early as the 2nd century (Duncan-Jones, *Money and Government in the Roman Empire*, p. 59)
10 See 'L'enceinte du camp militaire romain de Louqsor' by Jean-Claude Golvin and Michel Reddé in *Studien zu den Militärgränzen Roms* III (Stuttgart 1986), pp. 594–9
11 The sequence is complex. In about 314, the new province of Egypt was split into two (Herculia and Iovia), with Herculia being further divided in 322 with the creation of a new province of Mercuriana. In 324, however, the two-province division into Egypt and Thebaid was restored, only for a tripartite division to be restored in 357. Roger S. Bagnall, *Egypt in Late Antiquity* (Princeton 1993), p. 63
12 On the Vandal Kingdom of North Africa, see p. 432
13 J.D. Fage (ed.), *Cambridge History of Africa*, Vol. 2 (Cambridge 1978), pp. 495–500; E.M. Forster, *Alexandria: A History and a Guide* (Alexandria 1938), pp. 48–9
14 On the Monophysite controversy, see p. 299–300
15 In 638 the Emperor Heraclius promulgated the *Ecthesis*, an attempt to reconcile the question of whether Christ had one or two natures, by affirming that within him there was only one will (*thelos*). Cyrus was a key figure in the failed attempt to impose this compromise on Egypt.

Frend, *The Rise of the Monophysite Movement*, p. 352. Forster, *Alexandria: A History and a Guide*, p. 49. See also Cyril Hovorun, *Will, Action and Freedom, Christological Controversies in the Seventh Century* (Leiden 2008), pp. 55–76

16 Heraclius had previously had a go with a short-lived doctrine, which became known as Monoenergism, which held that, though having two natures, Christ had only one 'energy'. Having failed with his single energy, the Emperor then moved on to Christ's single will

17 Alan K. Bowman, *Egypt after the Pharaohs* (London 1986), p. 52

18 Forster, *Alexandria: A History and a Guide*, p. 50; Theodore Vretto, *Alexandria, City of the Western Mind* (New York 2001), pp. 212–13

19 Christopher Haas, *Alexandria in Late Antiquity: Topography and Social Conflict* (Baltimore 1997), pp. 45–7

20 They had originally been erected by Thutmosis III in Heliopolis around 1450 BC, but were uprooted and moved to Alexandria when the Caesareum was built

21 Judith Mackenzie, *The Art and Architecture of Alexandria and Egypt c. 300 BC to AD 700* (New Haven 2007), p. 252

22 Arculf's account of this and the Holy Places of Palestine was written down by Adomnan, the Bishop of Iona from 679 to 704, in a compilation known as *Holy Places*. See John Wilkinson, *Jerusalem Pilgrims before the Crusades* (Warminster 1977), p. 9

23 Mackenzie, *The Art and Architecture of Alexandria and Egypt*, p. 10

24 Roy MacLeod (ed.) *The Library of Alexandria, Centre of Learning in the Ancient World* (London 2000), p. 96

25 On the name of 'Pompey's Pillar', see Forster, *Alexandria: A History and a Guide*, p. 136; Alfred Butler, *The Arab Conquest of Egypt* (2nd edition, Oxford 1978), p. 368

26 The column was dedicated by Publius, the Prefect of Egypt, on the occasion of Diocletian's recapture of the city; Jean-Yves Empereur, *Alexandria Rediscovered* (trs. Margaret Maehler, London 1998), p. 102

27 Bowman, *Egypt after the Pharaohs*, p. 44; John Malalas, *Chronographia*, 308–9

28 The original Ptolemaic temple in fact burnt down in a fire in AD 181 and was rebuilt by the Romans around 216. Thus the temple that was destroyed in 391 had been in place for only 175 years (Mackenzie, *The Architecture of Alexandria and Egypt*, p. 149)

29 Empereur, *Alexandria Rediscovered*, pp. 90–3

30 Beard, North and Price, *Religions of Rome*, Vol. 1, p. 264

31 Law of 399, in *Cambridge Ancient History XIII*, p. 553 (*Codex Theodosiana*, XVI.10.15)

32 The Temple of Philae in the south of Egypt, near Aswan, survived for more than a century these waves of anti-paganism. See p. 404

33 David Franfkurter, *Religion in Roman Egypt, Assimilation and Resistance* (Princeton, NJ, 1998), pp. 281–2; Empereur, *Alexandria Rediscovered*, pp. 94–5

34 Haas, *Alexandria in Antiquity*, pp. 162–3

35 Empereur, *Alexandria Rediscovered*, p. 206

36 Mary Beard, John North and Simon Price, *Religions of Rome* (Cambridge 1998), p. 264

37 Vretto, *Alexandria, City of the Western Mind*, pp. 204–5

38 It may first have appeared in the works of the Jacobite Syrian bishop Bar Hebraeus in the late 13th century, who relates a story that 'Amr sent a message back to the Caliph Umar asking what he should do about the library. The reply came back that if the books disagreed with the Qu'uran they should be burnt, but that if they agreed with its message, then they were not needed and should be burnt anyway.' Atiyah, *A History of Eastern Christianity*, p. 81

39 Empereur, *Alexandria Rediscovered*, p. 156

40 Vretto, *Alexandria, City of the Western Mind*, pp. 84–5

41 Or even 'The Tomb of Caracalla'. See Empereur, *Alexandria Rediscovered*, p. 170

42 See Cassius Dio, 78, I 22–3; *Historia Augusta*, Caracalla, 6

43 Mackenzie, *The Art and Architecture of Alexandria and Egypt*, p. 214

44 Roger S. Bagnall (ed.), *Egypt in the Byzantine World, 300–700* (Cambridge 2007), p. 203

45 Empereur, *Alexandria Rediscovered*, pp. 155–75

46 Founded in AD 356, just after the saint's death

47 Robert B. Jackson, *At Empire's Edge, Exploring Rome's Egyptian Frontier* (New Haven 2002), p. 4

48 See p. 211

49 On this and Mons Porphyrites and Mons Claudianus in general, see 'The Roman Remains in the Eastern Desert of Egypt' by David Meredith in *Journal of Egyptian Archaeology* 38 (1952) pp. 94–111. The large granite columns from Mons Claudianus were transported to the Nile on enormous twelve-wheeled carts for shipment to the Nile delta and thence across the Mediterranean to their ultimate destinations (including far-off Rome). See Marijke van der Veen, 'High living in Rome's distant quarries' in *British Archaeology* 28 (October 1997)

50 Jackson, *At Empire's Edge*, pp. 24–7

51 Meredith, 'Roman remains in the Eastern Desert of Egypt', pp. 94–111, plan by Leo Tregenza

52 The temple probably dates to 113. See Meredith, 'Roman Remains in the Eastern Desert of Egypt', p. 107

53 Jackson, *At Empire's Edge*, pp. 7–8

54 Jackson, *At Empire's Edge*, pp. 46–50

55 See Meredith, 'Roman Remains in the Eastern Desert of Egypt', p. 107. Pliny says that Vitrasius Pollo brought statues made of imperial porphyry to Rome from Egypt during the reign of Claudius, and so from this it was presumed that the mines were being worked then

56 Jackson, *At Empire's Edge*, p. 37

57 Although not the largest monolithic columns of ancient times, as the obelisks in the Karnak Temple at Luxor, erected by Hatshepsut, are 27.5 metres tall, while the broken unfinished obelisk at Aswan is more than 40 metres long

58 Hélène Cuvigny, 'The Amount of Wages Paid to the Quarry-Workers at Mons Claudianus' in *Journal of Roman Studies* 86 (1996), pp. 139–45

59 Kelly, *Ruling the Later Roman Empire*, p. 21, for a description of this and its significance

60 Jackson, *At Empire's Edge*, p. 112.

61 Jackson, *At Empire's Edge*, p. 114

62 See pp. 392–393

63 Pliny the Elder, *Historia Naturalis*, V.10.58; Jackson, *At Empire's Edge*, p. 119

64 J.D. Fage (ed.), *Cambridge History of Africa*, Vol. 2, p. 193

65 Jackson, *At Empire's Edge*, p. 130

66 Pliny, *Historia Naturalis*, V.8.46

67 Fage (ed.), *Cambridge History of Africa*, Vol. 2, p. 206

68 Fage (ed.), *Cambridge History of Africa*, Vol. 2, p. 424; Jackson, *At Empire's Edge*, p. 152

69 Jackson, *At Empire's Edge*, p. 146

70 'Olympiodorus of Thebes' by E.A. Thompson in *Classical Quarterly* Vol. 38, No. 1/2 (Jan.–Apr. 1944), pp. 43–52; see also R.C. Blockley, *The Fragmentary Classicising Historians of the Later Roman Empire* (Liverpool 1981), pp. 27–47

71 Jackson, *At Empire's Edge*, p. 218

72 Amelia B. Edwards, *A Thousand Miles up the Nile* (London 1877), p. 308

73 'Chronology of the Campaigns of Aelius Gallus and C. Petronius' by Shelagh Jameson in *Journal of Roman Studies*, Vol. 58, Parts 1 and 2 (1968), pp. 71–84; L.P. Kirwan, 'Rome Beyond the Southern Egyptian Frontier' in *Geographical Journal*, Vol. 123, No. 1 (Mar. 1957), pp. 13–19

74 See p. 79

75 Jackson, *At Empire's Edge*, p. 137

76 Jackson, *At Empire's Edge*, p. 145, and T.C. Skeat, 'A Letter from the King of the Blemmyes to the King of the Noubades' in *Journal of Egyptian Archaeology* 63 (1977), pp. 159–70

77 Jackson, *At Empire's Edge*, p. 137

78 On Juvenal and Nestorius's exile, see Jackson, *At Empire's Edge*, p. 164

79 'The Wells of Hibis' by Peter J. Parson in *Journal of Egyptian Archaeology* 57 (1971), pp 165–80

80 Ahmed Fakhry, *The Necropolis of El-Bagawat in Kharga Oasis* (Cairo 1951), p. 4

81 Dating from the early 4th century; see Fakhry, *Necropolis of El-Bagawat*, p. 2

82 Fage (ed.), *Cambridge History of Africa*, Vol. 2, p. 412

83 Frend, *The rise of the Monophysite Movement*, p. 279

84 See p. 472

85 Fage (ed.), *Cambridge History of Africa*, Vol. 2, p. 425

86 William Harmless, SJ, *The Desert Christians* (Oxford 2004), p. 35

87 Athanasius was sentenced in 335, 338, 339, 349 and 351 and spent the years 335–7, 339–46 and 356–63 in exile (G.W. Bowersock, Peter Brown and Oleg Grabar, *Late Antiquity, A Guide to the Postclassical World* (Cambridge, MA, 1999), p. 320)

88 Jackson, *At Empire's Edge*, pp. 190–5

89 Jackson, *At Empire's Edge*, p. 175

90 Jackson, *At Empire's Edge*, p. 167

91 I.M.F. Gardner and S.N.C. Lieu, 'From Narmouthis (Medinet Madi) to Kellis (Asmant el-Kharab): Manichaean Documents from Roman Egypt' in *Journal of Roman Studies* 86 (1996), pp. 146–69

92 A merchant named Scythianus, who travelled with his goods to Berenice on the Red Sea coast, was instrumental in the early spread of the Manichaeist sect in Egypt. See Samuel N.C. Lieu, *Manichaeism in the Later Roman Empire and Medieval China, a Historical Survey* (Manchester 1985), pp. 71–2

93 Jackson, *At Empire's Edge*, p. 209, for the slave sale

94 On the imperial cult, see pp. 190–191

95 Jackson, *At Empire's Edge*, p. 216

96 Jackson, *At Empire's Edge*, p. 220

97 G.A. Hoskins, *Visit to the Great Oasis of the Libyan Desert* (London 1837), pp. 225–6, although Hoskins is relating second-hand material from the French traveller Cailliaud. He reports that the arch then sat on a platform 128 feet long and was itself 25 feet high and equipped with a staircase to the upper levels. Only the central arch was still standing, the rest having long collapsed, a fate that much of the rest of the structure has since endured

98 Ahmed Fakhry, *Baharia Oasis*, Vol. II (Cairo 1950), pp. 41–8

99 Ahmed Fakhry, *Siwa Oasis, its History and Antiquities* (Cairo 1944), p. 29

100 Fakhry, *Siwa Oasis*, p. 41

101 For Alexander's visit, see Fakhry, *Siwa Oasis*, pp. 36–40

102 Ian Worthington (ed.), *Alexander the Great: A Reader* (London 2003), pp. 237–40

103 On oracle shrines in Roman Egypt in general, see Frankfurter, *Religion in Roman Egypt*, pp. 147–97

104 Strabo, *Geographia*, 17, 1.43

105 Caracalla had the place reopened in 215 and, instead of purloining any further treasures as his predecessor emperors had done, laid his own purple cloak and precious rings upon the body as an offering

106 Empereur, *Alexandria Rediscovered*, p. 148

107 Forster, *Alexandria: A History and a Guide*, p. 96

108 Jackson, *At Empire's Edge*, pp. 250–1

109 Jackson, *At Empire's Edge*, p. 251

110 Fage (ed.), *Cambridge History of Africa*, Vol. 2, p. 198

111 Fage (ed.), *Cambridge History of Africa*, Vol. 2, p. 198

112 See 'Africa' by Charles Daniels in John Wacher (ed.), *The Roman World*, Vol. 1 (London 1987), pp. 223–65

113 See 'Roman and Byzantine "Limes" in Cyrenaica' in *Libyan Studies: Select Papers of the late R.G. Goodchild* (ed. Joyce Reynolds, London 1976), pp. 195–209

114 Such as the use of the former forum at Cyrene as a type of citadel. See Goodchild, *Libyan Studies*, p. 204

115 He had responsibility for the Thebaid in Egypt too. His full title was *Dux Aegypti Thebaidos utrarumque Libyarum*. See Goodchild, *Libyan Studies*, p. 195

116 MacKendrick, *The North African Stones Speak*, pp. 121–3

117 MacKendrick, *The North African Stones Speak*, pp. 125, 129

118 MacKendrick, *The North African Stones Speak*, p. 129

119 See p. 393

120 The *aurum coronarium* or 'crown gold' had originally been a gift voted to victorious generals after a major victory (particularly if they had been awarded a triumph), and did actually involve the presentation of a golden crown, but by the 3rd century it had become simply another tax imposition

121 Jay Bregman, *Synesius of Cyrene, Philosopher-Bishop* (Berkeley 1982), pp. 52–3. Synesius's reference in it to the heretical Aryan religion of the Goths – who were then highly influential at court, and threatened to reduce the authority of the Eastern Emperor to the same ineffectual state as that of his brother Honorius – may have been an opportune one. Anti-Gothic sentiment was on the rise and finally erupted in 401, leading to the downfall of Gainas, the leading Gothic official, the murder of many of his countrymen and the breaking of the Gothic monopoly on power. Gainas managed to flee, but as he made his way north of the Danube, he was killed by the Hun Uldin and his head sent back to Arcadius as a little present to the Emperor

122 Bregman, *Synesius of Cyrene*, pp. 60–78

123 Bregman, *Synesius of Cyrene*, p. 155

124 Bregman, *Synesius of Cyrene*, p. 159. Synesius also refused to affirm that the world would be destroyed, since in Neoplatonic belief there is no time when the cosmos will not be, whilst similarly the soul is regarded as an immortal entity divorced from time, and so not created by God

125 Claudia Rapp, *Holy Bishops in Late Antiquity: The Nature of Christian Leadership in an Age of Transition* (Berkeley 2005), pp. 158–9

126 Williams, *Diocletian*, p. 129

127 See Williams, *Diocletian*, pp. 128–32

128 Simon Corcoran, *The Empire of the Tetrarchs: Imperial Pronouncements and Government AD 284–324* (revised edition, Oxford 2000), pp. 205–33

129 Graeme Barker, John Lloyd and Joyce Reynolds, *Cyrenaica in Antiquity* (BAR International Series 236, Oxford 1985), pp. 36–8

130 Barker, Lloyd and Reynolds, *Cyrenaica in Antiquity*, pp. 30–2

131 Robert Wheeler, *Roman Africa in Colour* (London 1966), p. 14

132 Though the best candidate is Ras el Aali, 6 kilometres inland, where there are the remains of a boundary monument set up under Diocletian. See 'Boreum of Cyrenaica', RG. Goodchild, *Journal of Roman Studies*, Vol. 41, Parts 1 and 2 (1951), pp. 11–16

133 'Una tappa di nostra cammina a marciare nella pace per [. . .] domani'

CHAPTER 10: AFRICA

1 Gustave Flaubert, *Salammbô* (trs J.C. Chartres, London 1956)

2 See Chapter 11

3 This is in stark contrast to Britain with two legions, Germania Inferior alone with four legions at the peak of its garrison, and little Noricum, which still had one

4 It may have been along the line of, or in part based on, an earlier ditch, which been dug in 202 BC on the orders of Scipio Africanus following the defeat of Hannibal in the Second Punic War, and which had been intended to mark out the borders of the territory to which Carthage was then reduced; Dexter Hoyos, *Hannibal's Dynasty: Power and Politics in the western Mediterranean* (London 2003), pp. 180–1

5 See Fage (ed.), *Cambridge History of Africa*, Vol. 2, p. 192

6 See p. 465

7 Its Roman name is unknown

8 See p. 74

9 Cameron, Ward-Perkins and Whitby (eds), *Cambridge Ancient History* XIV, p. 121

10 See p. 232

11 *Historia persecutionis africanae provinciae*, 1.2 (trs John Moorhead, Liverpool 1992). The figure of 80,000 is one often used in the ancient sources simply to mean 'a huge number' and may not be intended to represent anything like a precise figure (see Whittaker, *Rome and its Frontiers*, p. 54)

12 Augustine, *The City of God*, Book I, 1 (trs Marcus Dods, London 2000), p. 3

13 Already there had been portents of what this might mean; the attempted usurpation of Heraclian, the *comes Africae*, in 413 had been accompanied by the blocking of the grain fleets bound for Italy

14 Cameron, Ward-Perkins and Whitby (eds), *Cambridge Ancient History* XIV, p. 125

15 Cameron, Ward-Perkins and Whitby (eds), *Cambridge Ancient History* XIV, p. 125

16 Fage (ed.) *Cambridge History of Africa*, Vol. 2, p. 479

17 His *Laudes Dei* were particularly admired. See Susan Raven, *Rome in Africa*, p. 197

18 Raven, *Rome in Africa*, pp. 196–200

19 Peter Pentz, *From Roman Proconsularis to Islamic Ifriqiyah* (Göteborg 2002), p. 89. See also Raven, *Rome in Africa*, pp. 200–4; A.H. Merrills (ed.), *Vandals, Romans and Berbers: New Perspectives on Late Antique North Africa* (Ashgate 2004), pp. 200–14. Around 68 per cent of the male sellers of land are recorded as illiterate, with only 16 per cent signing with an autograph, leading to a literacy rate of somewhere between one-third and one-sixth

20 See p. 231

21 Fage (ed.), *Cambridge History of Africa*, Vol. 2, p. 480

22 Justinian, the man who had conceived and directed the reconquest of North Africa, was one of the Empire's most extraordinary rulers and perhaps its greatest law-giver. The first decade of his reign saw a string of astonishing achievements and successes. As well as recapturing North Africa from the Vandals, in 535 Justinian sent Belisarius to Italy, where with astonishing rapidity he overthrew Ostrogothic control in the south of the peninsula, capturing Naples and Rome itself the following year. Visigothic Spain in turn followed in 551 or 552, but this time Justinian's armies contented themselves with taking a broad band of territory in the south-west centred on Cartagena. The following decades brought little but disappointment; the last stages of the war in Italy were mishandled, and it took until 554 to suppress the last Ostrogothic resistance, leaving a country ravaged and to which the war of reconquest had done far more damage to the Romanised institutions of the peninsula than had eighty years of 'barbarian rule'. Yet despite the troubles there, at the time of his death in 565, it seemed that Justinian had at least restored the Empire's partial control over North Africa and Italy. Justinian's other and much more enduring legacy was his reform of the Roman legal system, an achievement that Edward Gibbon could still refer to more than 1,200 years later as 'a fair and everlasting monument'. Under the Empire, Roman law had been essentially reactive, with the emperors issuing responses to problems that were placed before them, which then achieved the force of law (as 'rescripts' or 'constitutions'). A very limited legislative role had originally been assigned to the Senate, but this was, by the Later Empire, all but redundant as a law-making body. The result was that, although the laws provide an interesting insight into the kinds of challenges that faced the imperial administration, there was a chaotic assemblage of legislation, often contradictory and, crucially, with no central archive that held all of the rulings. Lawyers, unsurprisingly, made hay out of the confusion, and legal cases could often turn on which of two contradictory (but apparently equally valid) laws was accepted by the judge to be the relevant one. The situation was aggravated even further after 395, when the Eastern and Western parts of the Empire were finally separated politically, and so it was unclear whether a law passed by the Eastern Emperor had validity in the West or vice versa; and the absence of any central archive meant that lawyers in each half did not necessarily

have access to copies of laws passed in the other half, even when they were supposedly binding in all parts of the Empire. An attempt to clear up the muddle was made by Theodosius II, who appointed a commission in 429 to collect all laws made since the reign of Constantine I and codify them. The resulting Theodosian Code was published in 438 in the East, and a copy that was sent to the Western Emperor, Valentinian III, was promulgated in his domains the following year, restoring a semblance of harmony between the legal systems in the two parts of the Empire.

In 528, a century after Theodosius II had begun his project, Justinian tried again. He appointed a commission led by the praetorian prefect John of Cappadocia to collect all the imperial constitutions from the reign of Hadrian to that of Justinian himself. The sources for this included a wide range of legislative texts, from private letters of the emperors to officials to more public pronouncements and decisions. The Code of Theodosius and a yet earlier set of rationalised laws from the reign of Diocletian (the Codex Gregorianus and Codex Hermogenianus) provided a principal quarry for the work of Justinian's legal team. It took just a year for the resulting Codex of Justinian to be promulgated (in April 529), although such was the pace of legislation and the need to refine the original that it was replaced within five years by a second edition. Yet this and the succeeding Digest – which was intended to collect together, sift and simplify the mass of decisions and commentaries by five centuries of Roman jurists – finally created a solid benchmark for Roman law and established the Emperor once and for all as the sole fount of valid legislation.

23 Meaning 'at the tenth milestone'
24 Ecclesiastes 1, 2
25 Raven, *Rome in Africa*, p. 213; R. Denys Pringle, *The Defence of Byzantine Africa from Justinian to the Arab Conquest* (BAR International Series 99 (i), Oxford 1990) pp. 23–4
26 Pringle, *Defence of Byzantine Africa*, pp. 28–9
27 See p. 299
28 Raven, *Rome in Africa*, pp. 218–22
29 Raven, *Rome in Africa*, p. 225; Fage (ed.), *Cambridge History of Africa*, Vol. 2, p. 505; Charles-André Julien, *A History of North Africa – Tunisia, Algeria, Morocco* (trs John Petrie, London 1970), p. 3
30 Cyril Hovorun, *Will, Action and Freedom* (Leiden 2008), p. 82
31 See p. 388
32 Raven, *Rome in Africa*, p. 226
33 Brett and Fentress, *The Berbers*, pp. 84–5; 'Historiography, Mythology and Memory in Modern North Africa: The Story of the Kahina' by Abdelmajid Hannoum in *Studia Islamica* 85 (1997), pp. 85–130
34 'Historiography, Mythology and Memory in Modern North Africa', pp. 85–130

35 Fage (ed.), *Cambridge History of Africa*, Vol. 2, p. 505

36 See David Mattingly, *Tripolitania* (London 1995), p. xiii

37 Lucan, *The Civil Wars* (trs J.D. Duff, London 1928), IX, 524

38 See MacKendrick, *The North African Stones Speak*, pp. 240–41

39 Elizabeth W.B. Fentress, *Social, Military and Economic Aspects of the Frontier Zone* (BAR International Series 53, Oxford 1979), pp. 82–119

40 Herodotus *Histories* (trs George Rawlinson, London 1927) IV, 183, 4

41 Charles Daniels, *The Garamantes of Southern Libya* (Stoughton, WI, 1970); Herodotus, *Histories*, IV, 183; Pliny the Elder, *Natural History*, VIII, 178

42 Balbus's route, as related by Pliny the Elder (Pliny, *Natural History*, V, v.34) led through Phazania (the Fezzan) and the cities of Alele, Cillaba, towards Sabratha and Cidamus (Ghadames), before crossing the Black Mountains and the desert to Garama. It is not totally clear which of the towns that his army passed through were actually controlled by the Garamantes, but, as well as Garama itself, they seem to have dominated Bu Ngem

43 Although Aulus Plautius did receive an ovation (a lesser form of triumph) in AD 47 for his part in the Claudian conquest of Britain. See Mary Beard, *The Roman Triumph* (Cambridge,MA, 2007), pp. 290–1, 296–7

44 Fage (ed.), *Cambridge History of Africa*, Vol. 2, p. 200

45 Daniels, *The Garamantes of Southern Libya*, p. 22

46 'The Garamantes and Trans-Saharan Enterprise in Classical Times' by R.C.C. Law in *Journal of African History*, Vol. 8, No. 2 (1967), pp. 181–200; Fage (ed.), *Cambridge History of Africa*, Vol. 2, p. 285

47 It is often spelled Lepcis, which may in fact be a better transliteration of the original Phoenician name LPQY. See Mattingley, *Tripolitania*, p. xiii

48 Fage (ed.), *Cambridge History of Africa*, Vol. 2, p. 186

49 'The Oil of Leptis' by Richard Haywood in *Classical Philology* (1941), pp. 65–76

50 Septimius Severus is regarded as one of Rome's great military emperors. He was born in Leptis in 146, and though his uncles Publius Septimius Aper and Caius Septimius had become senators and held consulates in the 150s, he himself was brought up in Africa. The *Historia Augusta* claims that he spoke with an African accent even in his old age, and he is certainly recorded as having been embarrassed that his first wife Paccia Marciana, a local woman, could scarcely speak Latin, and that his sister, Octavilla, had an even worse grasp of the language (Anthony R. Birley, *Septimius Severus* (London 1999), p. 35). By 164, Septimius was in Rome, seeking the first steps on the *cursus honorum* that would lead to his advancement as commander of the IV Scythica legion in Antioch in 182. After a brief fall from grace, when his patron Pertinax fell out of favour with Commodus, Septimius was successively governor of Gallia Lugdunensis, proconsul of Sicily and governor of Upper Pannonia. Here he had command of three legions and, with his brother Geta occupying the governorship of neighbouring Lower

Moesia with its complement of two legions, this left the family well placed when Commodus was assassinated in 192 to make a bid for the imperial throne itself. The Emperor's pathological tendency to kill those nearest him, and his disturbing propensity for appearing in the gladiatorial arena where he fancied himself a new Heracles, led his closest advisors to murder him. But the new Emperor, Pertinax, angered the praetorian guard (who had rather liked Commodus and the favours he showered on them) by his meanness with the level of the donative he bestowed upon them to mark his accession. After Pertinax's murder in the imperial palace, and the undignified bidding war for the throne that led to the accession of Didius Julianus, the prestige of the Emperor sank to a new low. With the office so demeaned, the various large concentrations of troops in the Empire had no compunction in declaring emperors of their own. After his successful execution of the civil war, Septimius would rule largely unchallenged and, for the most part, respected, apart from the embarrassing affair of his over-reliance on the long-serving prefect of the praetorian guard, Fulvius Plautianus, which ended in the latter's murder in 205

51 See Mattingly, *Tripolitania*, p. 116

52 D.E.L. Haynes, *The Antiquities of Tripolitania* (Tripoli 1955) mentions that it was only under Maxentius that the province was first actually recorded

53 See p. 52

54 See p. 117

55 These were the *tria nomina* that marked out the full Roman citizen in Republican and early imperial times. The *nomen* usually indicated the clan to which the person belonged, such as the Julii or Claudii

56 Fergus Millar, 'Local Cultures in the Roman Empire: Libya, Punic and Latin in Roman Africa' in *Journal of Roman Studies* 58, Parts 1 and 2 (1968), pp. 126–34

57 'Doric Measure and Architectural Design 1: The Evidence of the Relief from Salamis' by Mark Wilson Jones in *American Journal of Archaeology*, Vol. 104, No. 1 (Jan. 2000), pp. 73–93

58 Alan Cameron, *Circus Factions: Blues and Greens at Rome and Byzantium* (Oxford 1976), p. 62; J.H.W. Liebeschuetz, *The Decline and Fall of the Roman City* (Oxford 2001), pp. 210–18

59 See Chapter 8

60 Cameron, *Circus Factions*, pp. 203–4

61 Alan Cameron, *Porphyrius the Charioteer* (Oxford 1973)

62 Cameron, *Circus Factions*, p. 107

63 Cameron, *Circus Factions*, p. 108

64 The circus factions also came to be represented at the theatre, so that there, too, there were Blue and Green cliques. See Cameron, *Circus Factions*, pp. 195–229

65 Mattingly, *Tripolitania*, p. 173

66 Mattingly, *Tripolitania*, p. 175

67 Procopius, *History of the Wars*, IV, 21.4–10

68 Denys Pringle, *The Defence of Byzantine Africa from Justinian to the Arab Conquest* (BAR International Series 99 (i), Oxford 1981), pp. 33–9

69 Mattingly, *Tripolitania*, pp. 123–4

70 MacKendrick, *The North African Stones Speak*, p. 165

71 See p. 459

72 Mattingly, *Tripolitania*, p. 125

73 Pringle, *Defence of Byzantine Africa*, p. 223

74 Pentz, *From Roman Proconsularis to Arab Ifriqiyah*, p. 39

75 Haynes, *The Antiquities of Tripolitania*, p. 131

76 S.J. Harrison, *Apuleius, A Latin Sophist* (Oxford 2000), pp. 38–86

77 Isabella Sjöström, *Tripolitania in Transition, Late Roman to Early Islamic Settlement* (Aldershot 1993), pp. 203–4

78 'Amphitheatres of the Roman World' by Herbert W. Benario in *Classical Journal* (1981), pp. 255–9

79 Raven, *Rome in Africa*, p. 142

80 See p. 103

81 Bowman, Garnsey and Cameron (eds), *Cambridge Ancient History* XII, p. 33

82 Bowman, Garnsey and Cameron (eds), *Cambridge Ancient History* XII, p. 28

83 See p. 285

84 Bowman, Garnsey and Cameron (eds), *Cambridge Ancient History* XII, p. 34

85 See p. 436

86 Virgil, *Aeneid* (trs Frederick Ahl, Oxford 2007) I, 360–70

87 See Lance Sergel, *Carthage, A History* (trs Antonia Nevill, Oxford 1995), p. 428. The story may initially have appeared in the very first edition of the *Cambridge Ancient History*

88 In the confused power-politics of the time, Domitius seems to have gained some support from Constantine, who saw him as a means to weaken Maxentius and lever him out of Italy. Around 311, however, Maxentius sent an expeditionary force to Carthage under the command of his praetorian prefect Volusianus, and Domitius, who had managed to expand his diminutive domain only as far as Sardinia, was captured and executed

89 Frank M. Clover, *The Late Roman West and the Vandals* (Aldershot 1993), p. 14

90 Procopius, *History of the Wars*, III, 21.25

91 Raven, *Rome in Africa*, p. 226

92 Raven, *Rome in Africa*, p. 228

93 See Sergel, *Carthage*, p. 439

94 See Sergel, *Carthage*, p. 441

95 See Sergel, *Carthage*, p. 442

96 See Sergel, *Carthage*, p. 249

97 Diodorus Siculus, *Library of History* (trs Russell Geer, London 1954), XX, 14, 4–7

98 Raven, *Rome in Africa*, p. 146

99 *Princeton Encyclopedia of Classical Sites*, p. 918

100 *Princeton Encyclopedia of Classical Sites*, p. 918

101 For more on the imperial cult and the deification of dead emperors, see pp. 190–191

102 The site was also visited in 1765 by James Bruce and Luigi Balugani, who already found the monument in ruins. When Camille Borgia visited in 1840, the top three levels of the monument had gone and the inscription was lying on the ground. There were originally two inscriptions, which were clearly mounted on the outside (they were too big to go on the inside). In 1842 Thomas Reade simply removed them from where they lay

103 MacKendrick, *The North African Stones Speak*, p. 76

104 MacKendrick, *The North African Stones Speak*, p. 75

105 MacKendrick, *The North African Stones Speak*, pp. 76–7; *Princeton Encyclopedia of Classical Sites*, pp. 540–1

CHAPTER 11: NUMIDIA AND MAURETANIA

1 Chapter XVI, p. 128

2 See Chapter 10. An area around Cirta (Constantine in Algeria) was given to the independent Roman general Sittius, which he ruled until his assassination by the Libyan prince Arabion in 44 BC. Arabion was in turn chased out by Octavian's general T. Sextius and the area returned to the control of the central Roman government

3 Fage (ed.), *Cambridge History of Africa*, Vol. 2, pp. 188–90

4 G.W. Bowersock, *Roman Arabia*, p. 56

5 Mattingly, *Tripolitania*, pp. 29–30, 33, 52

6 Duane W. Roller, *The World of Juba II and Kleopatra Selene* (London 2003), p. 111

7 Mattingly, *Tripolitania*, p. 71

8 See *Princeton Encyclopedia of Classical Sites*, p. 9

9 Jean Baradez, *Fossatum Africae* (Paris 1949); Mattingly, *Tripolitania*, pp. 79, 106–7, 114; Raven, *Rome in Africa*, pp. 76–8

10 David Cherry, *Frontier and Society in Roman North Africa* (Oxford 1998), pp. 45–7

11 See MacKendrick. *The North African Stones Speak*, p. 241; Cherry, *Frontier and Society in Roman North Africa*, p. 63

12 See MacKendrick, *The North African Stones Speak*, p. 221

13 See MacKendrick, *The North African Stones Speak*, p. 222

14 ILS 2487, reproduced in Brian Campbell, *The Roman Army 31 BC–AD 337: A Sourcebook* (London 1994), p. 18

15 Hilaire Belloc, *Many Cities* (London 1928), pp. 126–7

16 'Decurions and Priests' by Michael G. Jarrett in *American Journal of Philology* (1971), pp. 513–38

17 Peter Garnsey, *Social Status and Legal Privilege in the Roman Empire* (Oxford 1970), pp. 274–6

18 J.H.W Liebeschuetz, *The Decline and Fall of the Roman City* (Oxford 2001), pp. 111–23

19 Jarrett, 'Decurions and Priests', pp. 521–2

20 See p. 472

21 He engaged in a prolonged polemic with Saint Augustine, the champion of the orthodox cause. Optatus's attempt to secure his and the Donatists' power base ended when he was executed – or, as the Donatists would have it, 'martyred' – for alleged involvement in the rebellion of Gildo

22 MacKendrick, *The North African Stones Speak*, p. 236

23 Procopius, *History of the Wars*, IV xiii 26; Michael Brett and Elizabeth Fentress, *The Berbers* (Oxford 1997) p. 79

24 W.H.C. Frend, *The Donatist Church, A Movement of Protest in North Africa* (Oxford 1952), pp. 8–9

25 Frend, *The Donatist Church*, p. 6

26 Frend, *The Donatist Church*, p. 18

27 Frend, *The Donatist Church*, pp. 145–46

28 It was not the very first appeal to an emperor, as Aurelian (albeit not a Christian) had been sent a petition in 271 regarding the activities of the heretical bishop Paul of Samosata; Philip Hughes, *A History of the Church* (London 1979), p. 168

29 Frend, *The Donatist Church*, p. 149

30 Frend, *The Donatist Church*, pp. 150–51

31 Frend, *The Donatist Church*, p. 159

32 Frend, *The Donatist Church*, pp. 168–74

33 Frend, *The Donatist Church*, p. 178

34 Frend, *The Donatist Church*, pp. 175–76; Fage (ed.), *Cambridge History of Africa*, Vol. 2, p. 472

35 Frend, *The Donatist Church*, pp. 187–91

36 The political eclipse of Donatism began in 397, when Gildo, the *comes Africae*, made the seemingly extraordinary move of offering to transfer the allegiance of Africa from the Western Emperor in Italy, in whose territory it had traditionally sat, into the domain of the Eastern Emperor at Constantinople. In doing so, he was trying to exploit a tricky piece of dynastic rivalry. For on the death of Theodosius, the Empire had fallen to his two young sons, with Honorius inheriting the West and Arcadius the East. The ten-year-old Honorius was firmly under the thumb of Theodosius's overmighty *magister militum*, the half-Vandal Stilicho, who was married to the late Emperor's niece Serena. Stilicho maintained that Theodosius had appointed him guardian to both his sons, a claim that Arcadius's advisors in Constantinople vigorously opposed

(Cameron and Garnsey (eds), *Cambridge Ancient History*, p. 113). In the West, however, Stilicho was without serious rivals, cementing his position by marrying his own daughter Maria to Honorius. Gildo's offer, therefore, was a cunning one, enabling him to dissemble loyalty to the Empire at least on the surface, while using Arcadius's antipathy to Stilicho as a shield to protect him from the consequences of his previous involvement with the supporters of the usurper Eugenius in 392–4. He withheld the grain supplies from Rome, threatening to topple Stilicho by starving Italy. Had he succeeded, his reward from a suitably grateful Eastern government might have been immense. It all turned out, however, to be too clever by half. Just as Gildo had exploited a family quarrel, so too did Stilicho, and he sent Gildo's brother Mascezel with a modest force from Italy. No assistance arrived from the East for Gildo, and when the two sides met near Theveste in 398, his troops melted away, and he fled, dying a hunted fugitive. (Raven, *Rome in Africa*, p. 184). The principal result of the revolt was that the Donatists became tarred with the taint of treason. The leading, and extremist, Donatist bishop Optatus of Thamugadi (Timgad) was on friendly terms with Gildo, and his own private army of circumcellions in turn offered pious and thuggish support for the Count of Africa. Once Gildo was defeated, the tendency that had become established over the past half-century just to leave the Donatists well alone was replaced by more deliberate action to uproot them and favour more strongly their Catholic opponents.

37 Frend, *The Donatist Church*, pp. 253–57. Petilian had in fact originally been an orthodox Catholic, but around 395 was kidnapped by Donatists who rebaptised him in their creed. Petilian became convinced this was the will of God and ever after served the Donatist cause faithfully and effectively.

38 *Donatist Martyr Stories: The Church in Conflict in North Africa* (trs Maureen A. Tilley, Liverpool 1996)

39 Raven, *Rome in Africa*, pp. 53–4

40 Pringle, *Defence of Byzantine Africa*, p. 194

41 André Berthier, *Tiddis, Antique Castellum Tidditanorum* (1952, reissued Algiers 1991) p. 18

42 Pentz, *From Roman Proconsularis to Islamic Ifriqiyah*, p. 48

43 Berthier, *Tiddis*, p. 52

44 Jean Marie Blas de Roblès and Claude Sintes, *Sites et monuments antiques de L'Algérie*, (Aix-en-Province 2003), p. 131

45 See p. 52

46 Berthier, *Tiddis*, p. 263

47 Blas de Roblès and Sintes, *Sites et monuments antiques de L'Algérie*, p. 134

48 Berthier, *Tiddis*, p. 276

49 MacKendrick, *The North African Stones Speak*, p. 221

50 'Venus Genetrix outside Rome' by James Rives in *Phoenix*, Vol. 48, No. 4 (Winter 1994), pp. 294–306

51 Blas de Roblès and Sintes, *Sites et monuments antiques de l'Algérie*, p. 109

52 MacKendrick, *The North African Stones Speak*, p. 229

53 Richard C. Beacham, *The Roman Theatre and its Audience* (London 1991), pp. 60–2

54 Blas de Roblès and Sintes, *Sites en monuments antiques de l'Algérie*, p. 110; Wood, *Roman Africa in Colour*, p. 128

55 See p. 300

56 The resulting schism in which the northern Italian Church broke from Rome lasted for more than a century. See John Moorhead, *Justinian* (London 1994), p. 137

57 Frend, *The Rise of the Monophysite Movement*, pp. 281–2

58 B.H. Warmington, *The North African Provinces from Diocletian to the Vandal Conquest* (Cambridge 1954), p. 1

59 'The Myth of Numidian Origins in Sallust's African Excursus (Iugurtha 17.7–18.12)' by Robert Morstein-Marx in *American Journal of Philology* (2001), p. 188

60 *Princeton Encyclopedia of Classical Sites*, p. 925

61 Tipasa is, however, a UNESCO World Heritage site and of undoubted architectural and cultural importance

62 Camus began, '*Au printemps, Tipasa est habitée par les dieux et les dieux parlent dans le soleil et l'odeur des absinthes, la mer cuirassée d'argent, le ciel bleu écru, les ruines couvertes de fleurs et la lumière à gros bouillons dans les amas de pierres*'. Albert Camus, *Noces à Tipasa* (Paris 1976), p. 9

63 See p. 495

64 Raven, *Rome in Africa* p. 180

65 Blas de Roblès and Sines, *Sites et monuments antiques de L'Algérie*, p. 59

66 See p. 498

67 See Brett and Fentress, *The Berbers*, p. 43. Alternative theories are that the tomb was built for Bocchus of Mauretania or even for an unknown potentate as late as the 5th or 6th century AD. Blas de Roblès and Sintes, *Sites et monuments antiques de L'Algérie*, pp. 74–6

68 Roller, *The World of Juba II* and Kleopatra Selene, p. 123

69 T.W. Potter, *Towns in Late Antiquity: Iol Caesarea and its Context* (Oxford 1995), pp. 48–61

70 MacKendrick, *The North African Stones Speak*, p. 224

71 MacKendrick, *The North African Stones Speak*, p. 299

72 MacKendrick, *The North African Stones Speak*, p. 299

73 Raven, *Rome in Africa*, p. 162

74 *Notitia Dignitatum*, XXVI

75 *Princeton Encyclopedia of Classical Sites*, p. 714

76 See 'La fortification des villes de Tingitane au second siècle' by Gilbert Hallier, in *Studien zu den Militargränzen Roms* III (Stuttgart 1986), pp. 605–24

77 Raymond Thouvenot, *Maisons de Volubilis: Le Palais dit de Gordien et la Maison a la Mosaïque de Vénus* (Rabat 1958)

78 Hilaire Belloc, *Many Cities*, p. 129. However, Belloc made the contrast between the two towns as 'that between a Poussin or a David and an arabesque of Toledo. It is the contrast between the superbly simple replica of Inigo Jones which forms the façade of the English School at Rome and the Mosque of Cordova – two worlds wholly distinct; the one that pagan and late Christian world of which we are the children; we live by our return to its noble classic lines; the other, the fantasy which the Mohammedan developed from the Byzantine.'

79 *Princeton Encyclopedia of Classical Sites*, p. 989

80 *Princeton Encyclopedia of Classical Sites*, p. 140

81 Although this is not universally accepted. *Princeton Encyclopedia of Classical Sites*, p. 140

82 A.N. Sherwin-White, 'The Tabula of Banasa and the Constitutio Antoniniana' in *Journal of Roman Studies* 63 (1973), pp. 86–98; MacKendrick, *The North African Stones Speak*, pp. 294–5

83 MacKendrick, *The North African Stones Speak*, pp. 287–9

84 See p. 425

85 Sertorius was a partisan of Marius, who fought a bitter civil war against Sulla in the 80s BC, which prefigured the later wars between Julius Caesar and Pompey, and Mark Antony and Octavian (Augustus), but which did not have such immediately catastrophic consequences for the institutions of the Roman Republic.

86 Sertorious then fought a long campaign against Pompey and conspired with Mithridates of Pontus, before finally being assassinated at a banquet in 72 BC.

87 *Princeton Encyclopedia of Classical Sites*, p. 521

88 Pliny the Elder, *Natural History*, XXXI, 42, 93–4

89 Seneca, *Letters to Lucilius* (trs E. Phillips Barker, Oxford 1932), 95.25

90 Pliny, *Natural History*, XIII 42, 94, and Robert I. Curtis, 'In Defense of Garum' in *Classical Journal*, Vol. 78, No. 3 (Feb.–Mar. 1983), pp. 232–40; Thomas H. Corcoran, 'Roman Fish Sauces' in *Classical Journal*, Vol. 58, No. 5 (Feb. 1963), pp. 204–10

91 Robin Lane Fox, *Travelling Heroes* (London 2008), p. 193

92 *Notitia Dignitatum*, XXVI; *Princeton Encyclopedia of Classical Sites*, p. 876

93 Pringle, *The Defence of Byzantine Africa*, p. 50

94 Whom one legend related was buried in the 'Tombeau de la Chrétienne' (see p. 485)

95 The other candidate in Morocco is Jebel Musa

96 Isidore of Seville, *Etymologiae*, XV, 1.73

CONCLUSION

1 This is the Greek form of the name. In Latin, it was also known as the *Umbilicus Urbis* (or 'navel of the city'), and it seems it was also known in the earliest times as the *Mundus*. Here, according to Plutarch, the inhabitants of the new cities threw sods of earth from their original homes in a symbolic abjuration of their places of origin; Filippo Coarelli, *Il Foro Romano* (Rome 1983), pp. 214–16

2 Or, more precisely, from the *Miliarium Aureum*, the golden milestone, a bronze column set at the opposite end of the stairs beside which both it and the *omphalos* stood

3 Alternative theories are that it was the tomb of Hostus, father of Rome's third king, Tullus Hostilius, or of a shepherd who was said to have brought up Romulus and Remus. Found beneath it was the oldest-known inscription in Latin, dated to about 525 BC, which contains a curse against anyone who defiled this most sacred of spots; Michael Grant, *The Roman Forum* (London 1970), pp. 49–53

APPENDIX A

Roman Emperors, 27 BC–AD 711

Dates are of reign as Augustus (dates of joint rule or, under the Tetrarchy, rule as Caesar are shown in brackets). Usurpers are shown in italics. Note that not all usurpers are indicated, particularly during the 'Military Anarchy' of the 3rd century.

27 BC–AD 14	Augustus
AD 14–37	Tiberius
37–41	Gaius Caligula
41–54	Claudius
54–68	Nero
68–69	Galba
69	Otho
69	Vitellius
69–79	Vespasian
79–81	Titus
81–96	Domitian
96–98	Nerva
98–117	Trajan
117–138	Hadrian
138–161	Antoninus Pius
161–180	Marcus Aurelius
161–169	Lucius Verus (co-Emperor)
180–192	Commodus
193	Pertinax
193	Didius Julianus
193–194	*Pescennius Niger*
195–197	*Clodius Albinus (officially recognised as Caesar 193–195)*
193–211	Septimius Severus
198–217	Caracalla (co-Augustus with Septimius Severus 198–211)
209–211	Geta (co-Augustus with Septimius Severus 209–211)
217–218	Macrinus
218	Diadumenianus (co-Augustus)
218–222	Elagabalus
222–235	Alexander Severus

235–238	Maximinus Thrax
238	Gordian I and Gordian II
238	Pupienus and Balbinus
238–244	Gordian III
244–249	Philip I
247–249	Philip II (co-Augustus)
249–251	Decius
251	Herennius Etruscus (co-Augustus)
251–253	Trebonianus Gallus
251	Hostilianus (co-Augustus)
251–253	Volusianus (co-Augustus)
253	*Uranius Antoninus*
253	Aemilianus
253–260	Valerian
253–268	Gallienus
	(co-Augustus 253–260)

		Gallic Empire		Empire of Palmyra	
258–259	*Ingenuus*				
260	*Regalianus*	259–269	Postumus	267–272	Zenobia and Vaballathus
260–262	*Macrianus*				
260–262	*Quietus*				
268	*Aureolus*				
268–270	Claudius Gothicus				
270	Quintillus				
270–275	Aurelian	268	*Laelianus*		
275–276	Tacitus	268	*Marius*		
276	Florian	269–271	Victorinus		
276–282	Probus				
282–283	Carus	271–274	Tetricus		
283–284	Numerian				

283–285	Carinus (co-Augustus 283–284)
284–305	Diocletian[*]
297	*Domitius Domitianus*
297–298	*Aurelius Achilleus*
286–305	Maximian (Caesar 285–286, co-Augustus 286–305)[*]
286–293	*Carausius (British Emperor)*
293–296	*Allectus (British Emperor)*
305–306	Constantius I Chlorus (Caesar 293–305, co-Augustus 305–306)[*]
305–311	Galerius (Caesar 293–305, co-Augustus 305–311)[*]
306–307	Severus (Caesar 305–306, co-Augustus 306–307)[†]
306–308	*Maximian (reinstated)*
306–312	*Maxentius*
	L. Domitius Alexander (usurper against Maxentius in Africa)

308–324	Licinius[†]
310–313	Maximin Daia (Caesar 305–310, co-Augustus 310–313)[†]
306–337	Constantine I (Augustus 306, Caesar 306–307, co-Augustus 307–324)[†]
337–340	Constantine II (Caesar 317–337, co-Augustus 337–340)
337–361	Constantius II (Caesar, 324–337, co-Augustus 337–350)
337–350	Constans (Caesar 333–337, co-Augustus 337–350)
350	*Vetranio*
350–353	*Magnentius*
355	*Silvanus*
360–363	Julian (Caesar 355–360)
363–364	Jovian
364–375	Valentinian I
372–375	*Firmus*
364–378	Valens
365–366	*Procopius*
367–383	Gratian (co-Augustus 367–383)
383–388	*Magnus Maximus*
375–392	Valentinian II (co-Augustus 375–392)
392–394	*Eugenius*
379–395	Theodosius I (co-Augustus 379–392)

Western Empire

395–423	Honorius (co-Augustus 393–395)		
		Eastern Empire	
		395–408	Arcadius (co-Augustus 383–395)
408–411	*Constantine III*		
409–410/		408–450	Theodosius II (co-Augustus 405–408)
414–415	*Priscus Attalus*		
411–413	*Jovinus*		
421	Constantius III (co-Augustus)		
423–425	*Johannes*		
425–455	Valentinian III		
455	Petronius Maximus	450–457	Marcian
455–456	Avitus		
457–461	Majorian		
461–465	Libius Severus	457–474	Leo I
467–472	Anthemius		
472	Olybrius		
473–474	Glycerius		
474–475	Julius Nepos (reigned in Illyricum to 480)	474–475	Zeno (deposed)
		475–477	Basiliscus
475–476	Romulus Augustulus		

Eastern/Byzantine Empire

477–491	Zeno (restored)
488–494	*Leontius*
491–518	Anastasius
518–527	Justin I
527–565	Justinian
565–578	Justin II
578–582	Tiberius II
582–602	Maurice
602–610	Phocas
610–641	Heraclius
641	Heraclonas
641	Constantine III
641–668	Constans II
646–647	*Gregory*
668–685	Constantine IV
685–695	Justinian II (deposed)
695–698	Leontius
698–705	Tiberius III
705–711	Justinian II (restored)

* First Tetrarchy
† Second Tetrarchy

APPENDIX B

Chronology

BC

814	Traditional date of foundation of Carthage
753	Traditional date of foundation of Rome
509	Roman Republic established
390	Gaulish victory at Allia; Gauls capture Rome
331	Alexander the Great visits oracle of Ammon at Siwa
323	Alexander the Great dies at Babylon
264–241	1st Punic War, after which Romans gain Sicily
221	Philip V becomes king of Macedonia
218	2nd Punic War begins; Hannibal invades Italy
216	Disastrous Roman defeat at Battle of Cannae
210	Massinissa of Numidia allies with Carthage
206	Massinissa defects to Rome
203	Scipio Africanus lands in Africa at Utica
202	Battle of Zama ends 2nd Punic War
190	Battle of Magnesia (Romans defeat Seleucid Antiochus III)
168	Roman ultimatum forces Antiochus IV to evacuate Egypt; Romans defeat Perseus of Macedonia at Pydna
149	Rome declares war on Carthage, beginning 3rd Punic War
148	Death of Massinissa of Numidia
146	Carthage captured by Romans after a seige and destroyed; province of Africa formed; Romans sack Corinth
133	Attalus III of Pergamum dies and bequeaths his kingdom to Rome
120	Province of Transalpine Gaul created
c.113	Mithridates VI comes to power in Pontus
111–105	Jugurthine War
105	Jugurtha captured, ending war
101	Battle of Vercellae, Roman victory over the Cimbri
96	Tigranes I becomes king of Armenia; Ptolemy Apion bequeaths Cyrene to Rome; Sulla is proconsul of Cilicia
91	Tigranes I occupies Cappadocia; Mithridates VI seizes Bithynia; beginning of Social War in Italy (to 88 BC)

89	1st Mithridatic War begins
88	Massacre of Roman citizens in Asia
83	2nd Mithridatic War begins
74	Nicomedes of Bithynia wills his kingdom to Rome
73	3rd Mithridatic War begins; Slave Revolt of Spartacus (to 72 BC)
72	C. Scribonius Curio celebrates Triumph over Dardanians
71	Mithridates flees to court of Tigranes of Armenia
69	Lucullus invades Armenia; Battle of Tigranocerta
68	Lucullus campaigns in northern Armenia; Nisibis captured; Mithridates returns to Pontus
67	Romans defeated by Mithridates at Zela; Tigranes retakes Cappadocia
66	Pompey given command against Mithridates
65	Mithridates flees to Crimea
64	Pompey annexes Syria; birth of geographer Strabo at Amaseia
63	Death of Mithridates; Pompey captures Jerusalem; Aemilius Scaurus makes unsuccessful attack on Petra; Julius Caesar becomes *pontifex maximus*
61	Pompey's Triumph over Mithridates and Tigranes celebrated
60	First Triumvirate of Caesar, Pompey and Crassus established
57	Gallic Wars begin; campaigns of Caesar against Helvetii, Belgae and Nervii
55	Campaigns of Caesar against Veneti; Caesar crosses the Rhine; Caesar's first expedition to Britain
54	Caesar's second expedition to Britain
53	Crassus defeated and killed by Parthians at Carrhae; Gallic rebellion under Vercingetorix; Caesar's second Rhine crossing
52	Siege and capture of Alesia, defeat of Vercingetorix
51	Cleopatra VII (and Ptolemy XIII) succeed to Egyptian throne; Parthians invade Syria
49	Julius Caesar leads army across Rubicon into Italy; Caesar appointed Dictator
48	Caesar defeats Pompey at Pharsalus; Pompey flees to Egypt and is assassinated
47	Caesar defeats Pharnaces of the Crimea at Zela
45	Caesar defeats Pompeian army at Munda; Parthians invade Syria
44	Caesar assassinated (15 March); Brutus and Cassius flee to the East; Lucius Munatius Planus founds Augusta Rauricorum; death of Burebista of Dacia
43	Octavian appointed consul; Second Triumvirate established (Octavian, Mark Antony and Lepidus)
42	Deification of Julius Caesar; Battle of Philippi (Brutus and Cassius defeated and commit suicide)
41	Antony meets Cleopatra in Alexandria; Antony fails to capture Palmyra

40	Parthians under Pacorus invade Syria
38	Second Triumvirate renewed for five years; Agrippa resettles the Ubii on the Roman side of the Rhine
37	Appointment of client kings in Cappadocia, Galatia and Pontus
36	Antony's failed campaign against the Parthians
35–33	Octavian's campaigns in Balkans (captures Siscia in 35)
34	Antony invades Armenia; the 'Donations of Alexandria'
33	Bocchus of Mauretania dies
32	Antony divorces Octavian's sister, Octavia
31	Battle of Actium (2 September)
30	Octavian captures Alexandria; suicide of Antony and Cleopatra
29–28	Campaigns of Licinius Crassus in Thrace
28	Campaign of Cornelius Gallus beyond First Cataract of the Nile
27	Octavian receives name Augustus and grant of a *provincia* for ten years
26–25	Campaign of Aelius Gallus in Arabia Felix
25	Juba II becomes king of Mauretania; Galatia annexed; Meroites invade Egypt
23	Augustus receives tribunician power for life
21	Treaty with Meroites
20	Recovery from Parthia of Roman standards seized after Battle of Carrhae; expedition of Lucius Balbus reaches Garma
19	Campaign of Cornelius Balbus against Garamantes
15	Tiberius and Drusus campaign in Raetia, reach Danube; Regnum Noricum annexed
13	Campaign of Agrippa in Pannonia; Augustus awarded *imperium proconsulare maius*
12–9	Campaigns of Tiberius in Balkans and of Drusus in Germany
12	First legionary camp built at Vetera (Xanten); Rhine fleet circumnavigates Denmark
11	Official annexation of Pannonia
9	Drusus reaches Elbe in Germany, dies after accident; altar to Augustus and Rome set up at Ara Ubiorum (Cologne)
2	Augustus given title *pater patriae*
AD	
4	Tiberius campaigns in Germany
5	Tiberius reaches Elbe
6	Outbreak of revolt in Pannonia and Illyricum
8	Ovid banished to Pontus
9	Pannonian revolt suppressed; Varus defeated at Teutoberger Wald with loss of three legions

14	Mutinies in Rhine and Danube armies; death of Augustus, succeeded by Tiberius
15	Cappadocia made a province, Moesia organised as a province
15–16	Germanicus's campaigns in Germany
17	War against Tacfarinas begins in Numidia; death of Ovid
c.18	Establishment of quarries at Mons Porphyrogenitus
19	Death of Germanicus
21	Revolt of Sacrovir in Gaul
24	Final defeat of Tacfarinas
28	Revolt of the Frisians
31	Tiberius's praetorian prefect Sejanus dies
37	Tiberius dies; accession of Caligula
40	Caligula's abortive invasion of Britain; murder of Ptolemy of Mauretania, Mauretania revolts
40–43	Mauretania reconquered by Hosidius Geta and annexed as a province
41	Caligula murdered, succeeded by Claudius
43	Invasion of Britain
46	Thrace annexed
47	Corbulo orders construction of *Fosso Corbulonis*
c.50	Raetia constituted as a province
53	Parthians seize Armenia
58	Corbulo invades Armenia
59	Capture of Armenian capital Tigranocerta by Corbulo
60	Romans appoint Tigranes king of Armenia; Corbulo governor of Syria; revolt of Iceni in Britain
62	Caesennius Paetus surrenders to Parthian king Vologaeses
66	Outbreak of Jewish revolt
67	Vespasian appointed legate in Judaea
68	Revolt of Vindex in Gaul; Galba proclaimed Emperor by army in Spain (April); suicide of Nero (June)
69	Year of the four Emperors: Otho proclaimed Emperor by praetorian guard (January); Galba murdered; Vitellius proclaimed Emperor (April); Otho commits suicide; Vespasian proclaimed Emperor (July); Vespasian's forces defeat Vitellius at Cremona; Vitellius murdered (December); Vespasian sole Emperor
69–70	Batavian revolt
69–70	War against the Garamantes
70	Capture of Jerusalem, end of Jewish revolt
71	Accession of Rabbel II, last Nabataean king
72–73	Commagene annexed; Armenia Minor joined with Cappadocia
73–74	Campaign of Pinarius Clemens in Agri Decumates
c.75	Emesa annexed

77–84	Agricola's governorship of Britannia
81	Domitian becomes Emperor
82–83	Domitian's war against the Chatti
83	Caledonians defeated at Battle of Mons Graupius
85–88	War against the Dacians
85–90	Organisation of provinces of Germania Inferior and Germania Superior
85–96	War against Nasamones in North Africa
86	Legionary fortress at Inchtuthill in Scotland evacuated
89	Revolt of Antonius Saturninus in Germania Superior
98	Trajan becomes Emperor
100	Thamugadi founded
101–102	Trajan's 1st Dacian War
c.104	Withdrawal from advanced positions in Scotland
105–106	Trajan's 2nd Dacian War
106	Annexation of Nabataean kingdom and establishment of province of Arabia
107/108	Tropaeum Traiani set up at Adamklissi
114–116	Trajan's Parthian War; Armenia, Mesopotamia and Assyria annexed
115	Serious earthquake strikes Antioch; Jewish uprising in Cyrene
116–118	Revolt in the East; Mesopotamia and Assyria break away from Empire
117	Hadrian becomes Emperor
122	Hadrian visits Britannia; beginning of work on the Wall
132–135	Bar Kochba revolt
c.136–137	Last fort on Hadrian's Wall (Carvoran) built
138	Antoninus Pius becomes Emperor
139–142	Construction of Antonine Wall
c.150	Antoninus Pius advances the *limes* in Germany
159	Dacia divided into three provinces
161	Marcus Aurelius and Lucius Verus become co-Emperors
c.161	Evacuation of Antonine Wall frontier
162–166	Lucius Verus's Parthian War
163	Statius Priscus captures Artaxata
166–170	Plague strikes the Empire
166–180	Marcommanic Wars
175	Revolt of Avidius Cassius
180	Commodus becomes Emperor
192	Murder of Commodus; Pertinax becomes Emperor
193	Pertinax murdered; Didius Julianus becomes Emperor (murdered in June); Pescennius Niger declared Emperor by troops in Antioch; Septimius Severus declared Emperor by Danube armies, takes Rome; Clodius Albinus, governor of Britannia, made Caesar by Septimius

194	Niger defeated at Issus
195	Clodius Albinus declares himself Emperor
197	Clodius Albinus defeated and killed near Lyons
197–202	Septimius Severus's eastern campaigns
198	Caracalla made Augustus; Severus takes Ctesiphon
199–201	Septimius Severus visits Egypt
208	Septimius Severus, Caracalla and Geta arrive in Britain
211	Septimius Severus dies at York; Caracalla and Geta return to Rome, where Geta is murdered
212	*Consitutio Antoniniana* grants near-universal citizenship
213	Caracalla's campaigns against Alamanns; Caracalla annexes Edessa
215	Caracalla invades Parthia; massacre in Alexandria ordered by Caracalla
217	Caracalla assassinated near Carrhae; Macrinus appointed Emperor
218	Elagabalus declared Emperor; Macrinus makes peace with Parthia, then is defeated and killed near Antioch
221	Elagabalus adopts cousin Alexianus
222	Elagabalus murdered; succeeded by Alexianus (as Alexander Severus)
226	Ardashir, first Sassanid ruler, becomes shah of Persia
230	Persians invade Mesopotamia and besiege Nisibis
234	Maximinus Thrax declared Emperor by Pannonian army
235	Murder of Alexander Severus; Maximinus campaigns against Alamanns; Persians again invade Mesopotamia
238	Gordian I and Gordian II declared Emperor; they are defeated and killed near Carthage. Senate elects Balbinus and Pupienus Emperors; after their murder Gordian III appointed Emperor; Maximinus murdered during siege of Aquileia (June)
241	Shapur I becomes shah of Persia; invades Mesopotamia
239–242	Edessa again independent under Abgar X
242	Gordian III and praetorian prefect Timesitheus begin campaign to counter Persian invasion
244	Shapur defeats Romans, death of Gordian III; Philip 'the Arab' becomes Emperor, makes peace with Shapur
244–246/ 248–253	Goths and Carpi invade Balkans
248	Philip organises celebrations for Rome's 1000th birthday; Decius campaigns successfully in Balkans
249	Philip dies in battle against Decius near Verona; Decius becomes Emperor; Decian persecution of Christians
251	Decius dies in battle against Goths at Abritus; Trebonianus Gallus Emperor

253	Valerian becomes Emperor; Gothic seaborne attacks in Asia Minor; Shapur invades Syria and takes Dura Europos; usurpation of Uranius Antoninus
254	Marcomanni attack Pannonia; Alamanni ravage Raetia; Shapur takes Nisibis; Valerian retakes Dura
255	Renewed Gothic seaborne attacks on Asia Minor
256	Shapur again takes (and destroys) Dura Europos
257	First Frankish raids recorded; Gallienus campaigns against Alamanns from base at Trier
258/259	Usurpation of Ingenuus in Pannonia put down by Gallienus
259	Alamanns invade Illyricum; Iuthungi attack Italy
260	Valerian defeated and captured by Shapur at Edessa; Macrianus and Quietus declared emperors in East; Persians capture parts of eastern provinces; usurpation of Postumus in Gaul and establishment of Gallic Empire; Augsburg Victory Altar dedicated
c.260	Evacuation of Agri Decumates
261	Macrianus killed in Illyricum; execution of Quietus; Odaenathus of Palmyra given title of *corrector totius Orientis*
262	Successful campaign of Odaenathus against Persians
266	Death of Odaenathus; his wife Zenobia takes power at Palmyra
267	Goths invade Greece and Balkans; revolt of Gallienus's cavalry commander Aureolus
268	Gallienus murdered; succeeded by Claudius II (Gothicus)
269	Claudius II defeats Goths at Naissus; assassination of Postumus in Gaul; succeeded by Victorinus; Zenobia extends Palmyrene territory
270	Claudius II dies of plague at Sirmium; Aurelian proclaimed Emperor; Zenobia annexes Egypt, Syria and much of Asia Minor
271	Tetricus becomes Emperor in Gaul; evacuation of Dacia; Vaballathus (son of Zenobia) declared Augustus
272	Defeat and capture of Zenobia
273	New revolt in Palmyra suppressed
274	Defeat of Tetricus and reabsorption of Gallic Empire
275	Alamanns invade Gaul; murder of Aurelian
276	Probus declared Emperor by army in the East
278	Probus campaigns against Vandals and Burgundians in Raetia
282	Probus murdered; Carus declared Emperor; campaigns against Sarmatians and Quadi
283	Carus dies near Ctesiphon; succeeded by Carinus and Numerian; Carinus campaigns against Germans in Gaul
284	Diocletian becomes Emperor after murder of Numerian
285	Battle of Margus; Diocletian defeats Carinus
286	Maximian declared Augustus; revolt of Carausius in Britain

293	Constantius I and Galerius declared Caesars, establishment of the Tetrarchy; Carausius killed by Allectus
296	Constantius I recaptures Britain; Diocletian defeats Quadi
297	Maximian in Africa to suppress revolt; Narses of Persia defeats Galerius near Carrhae; revolt of Domitius Domitianus in Egypt
298	Galerius takes Ctesiphon; end of Egyptian revolt; Diocletian pulls back border in Egypt to Syene
298	Treaty with Persia
301	Edict of Maximum Prices
303	Start of Great Persecution of Christians
305	Diocletian and Maximian abdicate; Constantius I and Galerius replace them as Augusti, with Severus and Maximin Daia as Caesars
306	Constantius I dies at York; Constantine I declared Emperor by soldiers; usurpation of Maxentius (son of Maximian) at Rome
307	Constantine recognised as Augustus by Maximian; Severus attacks Rome, forced to retreat and abdicates
308	Carnuntum Conference; Maximian retires again, Licinius appointed Augustus; revolt of Domitius Alexander in Africa
310	Death of Maximian
311	Galerius issues Edict tolerating Christians; death of Galerius
c.312	Death of Diocletian
312	Constantine defeats Maxentius at Battle of Milvian Bridge (28 October)
313	Licinius defeats Maximin Daia at Adrianople; Edict of Milan recognises freedom of religious belief; Council at Rome on Donatist problem
314	Council of Arles condemns Donatists; Constantine campaigns in Germany
315	Arch of Constantine constructed at Rome
316	Constantine defeats Licinius at Cibalae
324	Constantine defeats Licinius at Chrysopolis; foundation of Constantinople
325	Council of Nicaea
326	Execution of Constantine's eldest son Crispus
328	Death of Imru' al-Qays at Nemara
332	Constantine campaigns against Goths
334	Constantine campaigns against Sarmatians
336	1st Council of Constantinople
337	Death of Constantine I; Constans, Constantine II and Constantius II co-Emperors
337–350	Wars of Constantius II against Persia
340	Death of Constantius II
343/344	Battle of Singara
343	Council of Serdica

350	Persian siege of Nisibis; Magnentius proclaimed Emperor in Gaul; death of Constans
353	Death of Magnentius
355	Silvanus declared Emperor in Gaul (and assassinated)
357	Battle of Strasbourg, Julian defeats Alamanns; raids by Iuthungi in Raetia
359	Persians capture Amida after siege
360	Julian declared Caesar in Gaul
361	Death of Constantius II
362–363	Julian resident at Antioch
363	Julian dies on campaign against Persia; Jovian declared Emperor, makes treaty with Persia, ceding several districts across Euphrates and Nisibis
363–364	Album of Thamugadi inscribed
364	Death of Jovian; Valentinian I declared Emperor, with Valens as co-Emperor
365–366	Revolt of Procopius
367	'Barbarian Conspiracy' in Britannia
367–369	Valens's campaigns across the Danube
369	Valens makes peace with Gothic chieftain Athanaric
372	Revolt of Firmus in Africa
375	Valentinian I dies of apoplexy after campaign against Quadi and Sarmatians
376	Tervingi Goths cross Danube in great numbers
378	Battle of Adrianople; Valens defeated and killed by Goths
379	Theodosius I declared Emperor
381	2nd Council of Constantinople
382	Peace treaty with Goths
383	Revolt of Magnus Maximums; Gratian killed by his army
387	Riot of the Statues at Antioch; Persian-Roman treaty partitions Armenia
388	Revolt of Magnus Maximus suppressed
391–392	Anti-pagan edicts of Theodosius I
391	Temple of Serapis at Alexandria destroyed
392	Suicide of Valentinian II; usurpation of Eugenius
394	Battle of Frigidus River, Eugenius killed
395	Death of Theodosius I; Honorius and Arcadius Emperors in West and East (effective political separation of two parts of Empire)
395	Augustine becomes bishop of Hippo; first major Hunnish incursions
396	Armies of Alaric ravaging Balkans
397	Alaric recognised as *magister militum* by Eastern Empire
397–398	Revolt of Gildo in Africa
397–398	Visit of Synesius to Constantinople

400	Gainas killed by Hun Uldin
404	Last recorded gladiatorial games at Rome
405–406	Vandals, Alans and Sueves cross Rhine
407	Alaric and Goths invade Italy; death of Stilicho
410	Alaric sacks Rome
410	Britannia secedes from Empire after usurpation of Constantine III; Synesius becomes bishop of Ptolemais
411	Council of Carthage condemns Donatism
412	Simeon Stylites joins community at Telanissos
415	Murder of philosopher Hypatia in Alexandria
421	Olympiodorus of Thebes visits the Blemmyes
423	Death of Honorius
427	Eastern Empire regains control of Pannonia
429	Vandals cross over into Africa under Gaiseric; first visit of Bishop Germanus of Auxerre to Britain
430	Death of Saint Augustine
431	Vandals capture Hippo Regius; 1st Council of Ephesus deposes Nestorius
433	Pannonia lost to the Huns
438	Theodosian code issued
439	Vandals capture Carthage
440	Persians under Yezdegird attack Mesopotamia
441	Attila ravages Balkans
443	Aëtius settles Burgundians in Savoy
446	'Groans of the Britons', appeal for aid by British notables to patrician Aëtius
449	2nd Council of Ephesus ('the Robber Council'); Embassy to Attila and failed assassination attempt
451	Attila defeated at Catalaunian Fields by Aëtius; Council of Chalcedon
452	Attila invades Italy, turns back without attacking Rome
453	Death of Attila
454	Murder of Aëtius
455	Vandals sack Rome
456	Vandals capture Corsica and Balearics
460–482	Saint Severinus active in Noricum
468	Eastern fleet fails to defeat Vandals
475	Orestes revolts and appoints his son Romulus (Augustulus) as Western Emperor
476	Odovacer deposes Romulus Augustulus; end of Western Roman Empire
476–483	Theoderic the Amal based at Novae
482	Acacian schism breaks out; Zeno's *Henotikon*

486	Syagrius defeated by Frankish king Clovis in Soissons, collapse of 'Roman' enclave in Gaul
488	Theoderic the Amal invades Italy
491	Anglo-Saxons capture Anderitum, last 'Saxon Shore' fort
493	Theoderic takes Ravenna and kills Odovacer
502	Persians under Kavadh invade
505	Truce with Persians; Dara constructed
518	Acacian schism ends
527	Justinian becomes Emperor
528	Justinian appoints commission to codify laws
529	First edition of Justinian's Code
530	Persians defeated at Satala
532	Nika Riot; 'Endless Peace' signed with Persia
533	Hilderic deposed by Gelimer as Vandal king, gives pretext for Byzantine intervention; Vandals defeated by Belisarius in battles at Ad Decimum and Tricamarum; *Digest* of Justinian completed
534	Gelimer surrenders; end of Vandal War
536	Belisarius invades Italy, captures Rome
540	Khusraw I of Persia invades and sacks Antioch; Jacob Baradaeus becomes bishop of Edessa
544	Massacre of Leuthae chiefs at Leptis Magna
546	Gothic king Totila recaptures Rome
552	Totila defeated at Busta Gallorum
553	Council of Constantinople, condemnation of 'Three Chapters'
562	Fifty-Year Peace with Persia
568	Lombards invade Italy
572	War with Persia begins
573	Persians capture Dara; Justin II becomes insane
574	Truce with Persia
581	Ghassanid sheikh al-Mundhir arrested
582	Avars capture Sirmium
602	Emperor Maurice murdered; Phocas becomes Emperor
609	Revolt of Heraclius in Africa
610	Heraclius captures Constantinople, becomes Emperor
613	Persians capture Damascus
614	Persians capture Jerusalem
616	Persians take Egypt
622	The Hegira (flight of Prophet Muhammad from Mecca)
623	Persians and Avars fail to take Constantinople
627	Heraclius defeats Persians at Nineveh
636	Arab Muslims defeat Byzantine army at Yarmuk
638	Jerusalem captured by Arabs
640	Arab Muslims conquer Armenia

640–641	Arab Muslims conquer Egypt
642	Final Byzantine evacuation of Alexandria; Arabs invade Cyrenaica and Tripolitania
646	Usurpation of Gregory, the exarch of Africa
648	Constans issues *Typos* in attempt to restore unity to Christian Church
669	Arabs under Uqba take most of Tripolitania and Byzacena
674–678	First Arab siege of Constantinople
683	Uqba killed by Berber chieftain Kusayla
695	First Arab capture of Carthage; the Arabs are driven out by Kahina
698	Final Arab capture of Carthage
717–718	Second Arab siege of Constantinople
701/703	Death of Kahina
711	Arabs take Septem (last Byzantine possession in North Africa)
726	Beginning of Iconoclast controversy
750	Beginning of Abbasid caliphate
751	Ravenna falls to Lombards; effective end of Byzantine presence in northern Italy
787	2nd Council of Nicaea restores icons
800	Charlemagne crowned Emperor at Rome (first 'Holy Roman Emperor')
863	Mission of Constantine and Methodios to the Slavs
864	Khan Boris of Bulgaria baptised
913	Khan Symeon of Bulgaria reaches walls of Constantinople; crowned 'Emperor' by the patriarch
944	John Kourkouas takes Amida, Dara and Nisibis for Byzantine Empire; besieges Edessa
968	Nikephoros Phocas retakes Antioch and Aleppo, annexing northern Syria
970s	John Tzimiskes captures Damascus, Tiberias and Caesarea
976	Basil II becomes Emperor
995	Basil II's victorious campaign in the East
1014	Basil II defeats Bulgarians at Kleidion
1045	Byzantines conquer Armenia
1064	Seljuk Turks take Armenian capital Ani
1071	Battle of Manzikert; disastrous defeat of Romanos IV by Seljuk Turks under Alp Arslan
1096	First Crusaders reach Constantinople
1098	Crusaders take Antioch
1099	Crusaders take Jerusalem
1147	Second Crusaders reach Constantinople
1176	Battle of Myriokephalon; Manuel I Komenos defeated by Seljuk Turks
1189	Third Crusade begins

1204	Fourth Crusaders take Constantinople (12 April); beginning of Latin Empire
1214	Treaty between Latin Empire and Greek Empire of Nicaea
1261	Michael VIII captures Constantinople; end of Latin Empire
1389	Battle of Kosovo Polje; Serbs defeated by Ottoman Turks, opening Balkans to Turkish domination
1402	Battle of Ankara; Timur's Mongols destroy Ottoman army, temporarily reprieving Byzantine Empire
1453	Ottoman sultan Mehmed II captures Constantinople (29 May)
1460	Ottomans occupy Despotate of Morea (Peloponnese)
1461	Emperor David surrenders the city of Trebizond to Ottomans (15 August), thus ending last Byzantine (and Roman) state

BIBLIOGRAPHY

ANCIENT SOURCES

Ammianus Marcellinus *Res Gestae* (trs C.D. Yonge, London 1911)

The Anglo-Saxon Chronicle (trs G.N. Garmonsworthy, London 1953)

Appian, *History of Rome* (trs Horace White, London 1899)

Augustine, *The City of God* (trs Marcus Dods, London 2000)

Aurelius Victor, *Epitome De Caesaribus* (trs H.W. Bird, Liverpool 1994)

Ausonius, *Mosella* (trs Hugh G. Evelyn Wright, London 1921)

Cassius Dio, *Roman History* (trs Earnest Cary, London 1914–27)

Claudian, *De Consolatu Stilichonis* (trs Maurice Platnauer, London 1922)

Diodorus Siculus, *Library of History* (trs Russell Geer, London 1954)

Eutropius, *Breviarium* (trs H.W. Bird, Liverpool 1993)

Gildas, *De Excidio Britanniae* (trs Michael Winterbottom, London 1978)

Herodotus, *Histories* (trs George Rawlinson, London 1927)

Historia Augusta (trs David Magie, London 1954)

Isidore of Seville, *Etymologiae* (trs Stephen A. Barney, Cambridge 2006)

Jerome, *Epistolae* (trs C.C. Mierow, Westminster, MD, 1963)

John Malalas, *Chronographia* (trs Elizabeth Jeffreys, Michael Jeffreys and Roger
    Scott, Melbourne 1986)

Jordanes, *Getica* (trs Charles Christopher Mierow, Princeton, NJ, 1915)

Julian, *Misopogon* (trs Wilmer Cave Wright, London 1913)

Julius Caesar, *Gallic Wars* (trs S.A. Handford, Harmondsworth 1963)

Lucan, *The Civil Wars* (trs J.D. Duff, London 1928)

Marcus Aurelius, *Meditations* (trs Gregory Hays, London 2003)

Martial, *Epigrams* (trs Walter C.A. Kerr, London 1919–20)

Orosius, *History against the Pagans* (trs Irving Woodworth Raymond, New York 1936)

Ovid, *Ars Amatoria* (trs Rolph Humphries, London 1958)

Pliny the Younger, *Letters and Panegyricus* (trs Betty Radice, London 1969)

Pliny the Elder, *Natural History* (trs H. Rackham, W.H.S. Jones, D.E. Eichholz,
    London 1949–67)

In Praise of Later Roman Emperors: The Panegyrici Latini (trs R.A.B. Mynors, C.E.V.
    Nixon and Barbara Saylor Rodgers, London 1994)

Procopius, *History of the Wars* (trs H.B. Dewing, London 1914–35)

Procopius, *Buildings* (trs H.B. Dewing, London 1940)

Procopius, *Secret History* (trs Richard Atwater, Ann Arbor 1961)

Seneca, *Letters to Lucillus* (trs E. Phillips Barker, Oxford 1932)

Strabo, *Geographia* (trs H.C Hamilton and W. Falconer, London 1854)

Suetonius, *Lives of the Twelve Caesars* (trs Robert Graves, London 1962)

Tacitus, *Germania* (trs R.B. Townshend, London 1895)

Tacitus, *Annals* (trs A.J. Woodman, Indianapolis 2004)

Vegetius, *De Re Militari* (trs N.P. Milner, Liverpool 1996)

Victor of Vita, *Historia persecutionis africanae provinciae* (trs John Moorhead, Liverpool 1992)

Virgil, *Aeneid* (trs Federick Ahl, Oxford 2007)

Zosimus, *Historia Nova* (trs James J. Buchanan and Harold T. Davies, San Antonio, Texas 1967)

GENERAL WORKS

Andrews, Alfred C., 'Oysters as a Food in Greece and Rome' in *Classical Journal* 43 (1948), pp. 299–303

Antaya, Roger, 'The Etymology of Pomerium' in *The American Journal of Philology*, Vol. 101, No. 2 (Summer 1980), pp. 184–9

Atiyah, A.S., *A History of Eastern Christianity* (London 1968)

Austin, N.J.E. and Rankov, N.B., *Exploratio: Military and Political Intelligence in the Roman world from the Second Punic War to the Battle of Adrianople* (London 1995)

Ball, Warwick, *Rome in the East, the Transformation of an Empire* (London 2000)

Barchiesi, Alessandro, *The Poet and The Prince, Ovid and Augustan Discourse* (Berkeley 1997)

Barnes, Timothy D., *The New Empire of Diocletian and Constantine* (Harvard 1982)

Barnwell, P.S., *Emperors, Prefects & Kings: The Roman West, 395–564* (London 1992)

Beacham, Richard C., *The Roman Theatre and its Audience* (London 1991)

Beard, Mary, *The Roman Triumph* (Cambridge, MA, 2007)

Beard, Mary, North, John and Price, Simon, *Religions of Rome: A History*, Vol. 1, (Cambridge 1998)

Benario, Herbert W., 'Amphitheatres of the Roman World' in *Classical Journal* (1981), pp. 255–9

Bennett, Julian, *Trajan Optimus Princeps* (London 1997)

Biggins, J. Alan et al., 'A Survey of the Roman Fort and Settlement at Birdoswald, Cumbria' in *Britannia* 30 (1999)

Birley, Anthony R., *Marcus Aurelius* (London 1966)

Birley, Anthony R., *Septimius Severus: The African Emperor* (London 1988)

Birley, Anthony R., *Hadrian, The Restless Emperor* (London 1997)

Blockley, R.C., *The Classicising Fragmentary Historians of the Later Roman Empire* (Liverpool 1981)

Blockley, R.C., *East Roman Foreign Policy: Formation and Conduct from Diocletian to Anastasius* (Leeds 1992)

Boatwright, Mary Taliaferro, 'Tacitus on Claudius and the Pomerium, Annals 12.23.2–24' in *Classical Journal*, Vol. 80, No. 1 (Oct–Nov. 1984), pp. 36–44

Bowersock, G.W., Brown, Peter and Grabar, Oleg, *Late Antiquity, A Guide to the Postclassical World* (Cambridge, MA, 1999)

Bowman, Alan K., Garnsey, Peter and Rathbone, Dominic (eds), *The Cambridge Ancient History, Volume XI, The High Empire, AD 70–192* (Cambridge 2000)

Bowman, Alan K., Garnsey, Peter and Cameron, Averil (eds), *The Cambridge Ancient History, Volume XII, The Crisis of Empire, AD 193–337* (Cambridge 2005)

Brauer, George C. Jr, *The Age of the Soldier Emperors AD 244–284* (Park Ridge, NJ, 1974)

Braund, David, *Rome and the Friendly King: The Character of Client Kingship* (London 1984)

Brown, Peter, *The World of Late Antiquity* (London 1971)

Brown, Peter, *Society and the Holy in Late Antiquity* (London 1982)

Brown, Peter, *Authority and the Sacred: Aspects of the Christianization of the Roman World* (Cambridge 1995)

Burns, Thomas S., *Barbarians within the Gates of Rome: A Study of Roman Military Policy and the Barbarians, ca. 375–425 AD* (Bloomington 1994)

Burns, Thomas S., *Rome and the Barbarians 100 BC–AD 400* (Baltimore 2003)

Cameron, Alan, *Porphyrius the Charioteer* (Oxford 1973)

Cameron, Alan, *Circus Factions: Blues and Greens at Rome and Byzantium* (Oxford 1976)

Cameron, Averil, *The Mediterranean World in Late Antiquity, AD 395–600* (London 1993)

Cameron, Averil and Garnsey, Peter (eds), *The Cambridge Ancient History, Volume XIII, The Late Empire, AD 337–425* (Cambridge 1993)

Cameron, Averil, Ward-Perkins, Brian and Whitby, Michael (eds), *The Cambridge Ancient History, Volume XIV, Late Antiquity: Empire and Successors, AD 425–600* (Cambridge 2000)

Campbell, Brian, *The Roman Army 31 BC–AD 337: A Sourcebook* (London 1994)

Campbell, J.B., *The Emperor and the Roman Army 31 BC–AD 235* (Oxford 1984)

Casson, Lionel, *Travel in the Ancient World* (Baltimore 1974)

Clauss, Manfred, *The Roman Cult of Mithras: The God and his Mysteries* (Edinburgh 2000)

Coarelli, Filippo, *Il Foro Romano* (Rome 1983)

Collins, Roger, *Visigothic Spain 409–711* (Oxford 2004)

Corcoran, Simon, *The Empire of the Tetrarchs: Imperial Pronouncements and Government AD 284–324* (revised edition, Oxford 2000)

Cornell, T.J., *The Beginnings of Rome, Italy and Rome from the Bronze Age to the Punic Wars (c. 1000–264 BC)* (London 1995)

Cornell, Tim and Matthews, John, *Atlas of the Roman World* (Oxford 1982)

De Serviez, J.R., *The Roman Empresses* (Vol. 2, London 1899)

Dignas, Beate and Winter, Engelbert, *Rome and Persia in Late Antiquity, Neighbours and Rivals* (Cambridge 2007)

Dilke O.A.W., *Greek and Roman Maps* (London 1985)

Dixon, Karen, *The Roman Cavalry from the First to the Third Century* AD (London 1992)

Dodgeon, Michael H. and Lieu, Samuel N.C., *The Roman Eastern Frontier and the Persian Wars (AD 226–363)* (London 1991)

Drummond, Steven K. and Nelson, Lynn H., *The Western Frontiers of Imperial Rome* (New York 1994)

Dunbabin, Katherine M.D., *Mosaics of the Greek and Roman World* (Cambridge 1999)

Duncan-Jones, Richard, *Money and Government in the Roman Empire* (Cambridge 1994)

Dyson, Stephen L., *The Creation of the Roman Frontier* (Princeton 1985)

Eck, Werner (trs Deborah Lucas Schneider), *The Age of Augustus* (Oxford 2003)

Elton, Hugh, *Warfare in Roman Europe 350–425* (Oxford 1996)

Erdkamp, Paul (ed.), *A Companion to the Roman Army* (Oxford 2007)

Errington, R. Malcolm, *Roman Imperial Policy from Julian to Theodosius* (Chapel Hill 2006)

Evans, J.A.S., *The Age of Justinian: The circumstances of imperial power* (London 1996)

Everitt, Anthony, *The First Emperor: Caesar Augustus and the Triumph of Rome* (London 2006)

Fagan, Garrett G., *Bathing in Public in the Roman World* (Ann Arbor 1999)

Ferrill, Arthur, *The Fall of the Roman Empire: The Military Explanation* (London 1986)

Finley, M.I., *Atlas of Classical Archaeology* (London 1977)

Flower, Harriet I., *The Art of Forgetting* (Chapel Hill 2007)

Fränkel, Hermann, *Ovid, A Poet between Two Worlds* (Berkeley 1945)

Freeman et al. (eds), *Proceedings of XVIIIIth International Congress of Roman frontier studies (Sep. 2002)* (BAR International Series 1084 (i), Oxford 2002)

Frend, W.H.C., *The Rise of the Monophysite Movement, Chapters in the History of the Church in the Fifth and Sixth Centuries* (Cambridge 1972)

Gardner, R.A, 'The Peutinger Table' in *The Geographical Journal*, Vol. 136, No. 3 (Sept. 1970), pp. 489–90

Garnsey, Peter, *Social Status and Legal Privilege in the Roman Empire* (Oxford 1970)

Garnsey, Peter and Humress, Caroline, *The Evolution of the Late Antique World* (Cambridge 2001)

Geffcken, Johannes (trs Sabine MacCormack), *The Last Days of Greco-Roman Paganism* (Oxford 1978)

Gelzer, Matthias (trs Robin Seager), *The Roman Nobility* (Oxford 1969)

Gibbon, Edward, *The History of the Decline and Fall of the Roman Empire* (ed. David Womersley, London 2005)

Goffart, W.A., *Barbarians and Romans AD 418–584: The Techniques of Accommodation* (Princeton, NJ, 1980)

Goffart, W.A., *Barbarian Tides: The Migration Age and the Later Roman Empire* (Philadelphia 2006)

Goldsworthy, Adrian, *Roman Warfare* (London 2000)

Goldsworthy, Adrian, *The Complete Roman Army* (London 2003)

Goodman, Martin, *The Roman World 44 BC–AD 180* (Oxford 1997)

Grant, Michael, *Gladiators* (London 1967)

Grant, Michael, *The Roman Forum* (London 1970)

Grant, Michael, *The Severans, The Changed Roman Empire* (London 1996)

Harl, Kenneth W., *Coinage in the Roman Economy 300 BC to AD 700* (Baltimore 1996)

Holder, P.A., 'Roman auxiliary cavalry in the second century AD' in *Archaeology Today* 8 (June 1987), pp. 12–16.

Honoré, Tony, *Emperors and Lawyers* (London 1981)

Hovorun, Cyril, *Will, Action and Freedom, Christological Controversies in the Seventh Century* (Leiden 2008)

Hughes, Philip, *A History of the Church* (London 1979)

Isaac, Benjamin, 'The Meaning of the Terms Limes and Limitanei' in *Journal of Roman Studies* 78 (1988), pp. 125–47

Jones, A.H.M., *The Later Roman Empire* (Oxford 1964)

Jones, Brian W., *The Emperor Domitian* (London 1992)

Kean, Roger Michael and Frey, Oliver, *The Complete Chronicles of the Emperors of Rome* (Ludlow 2005)

Kelly, Christopher, *Ruling the Later Roman Empire* (Cambridge, MA, 2004)

Kelly, J.N.D., *Early Christian Doctrines* (revised edition, London 1980)

Kennedy, David and Riley, Derrick, *Rome's Desert Frontier from the Air* (Austin, TX, 1990)

Kreitzer, Larry, 'Apotheosis of the Roman Emperor' in *The Biblical Archaeologist*, Vol. 53, No. 4 (Dec. 1990), pp. 211–17

Kulikowski, Michael, *Rome's Gothic Wars from the Third Century to Alaric* (Cambridge 2007)

Lane Fox, Robin, *Pagans and Christians* (London 1986)

Lane Fox, Robin, *Travelling Heroes* (London 2008)

Lee, A.D, *Information and Frontiers: Roman Foreign Relations in Late Antiquity* (Cambridge 1993)

Lenski, Noel, *Failure of Empire, Valens and the Roman State in the Fourth Century AD* (Berkeley 2002)

Lenski, Noel (ed.), *Cambridge Companion to the Age of Constantine* (Cambridge 2006)

Levick, Barbara, *Vespasian* (London 1999)

Liebeschuetz, J.H.W., *The Decline and Fall of the Roman City* (Oxford 2001)

Lieu, Samuel N.C., *Manichaeism in the Later Roman Empire and Medieval China, a Historical Survey* (Manchester 1985)

Lopez, R.S., 'The Evolution of Land Transport in the Middle Ages' in *Past and Present*, No. 9 (Apr. 1956), pp. 17–29

Luttwak, Edward N., *The Grand Strategy of the Roman Empire from the First Century AD to the Third* (Baltimore 1976)

McClue, M.L. and Feltoe, C.L., *The Pilgrimage of Etheria* (New York 1919)

MacGeorge, Penny, *Late Roman Warlords* (Oxford 2002)

MacMullen, Ramsay, *Roman Social Relations 50 BC–AD 284* (New Haven 1974)

MacMullen, Ramsay, *Roman Government's Response to Crisis AD 235–337* (New Haven 1976)

MacMullen, Ramsay, *Christianizing the Roman Empire (AD 100–400)* (New Haven 1984)

MacMullen, Ramsay, *Corruption and the Decline of Rome* (New Haven 1988)

MacMullen, Ramsay, *Changes in the Roman Empire* (Princeton 1990)

MacMullen, Ramsay, *Christianity and Paganism in the Fourth to Eighth Centuries* (New Haven 1997)

Mann, J.C. et al. (eds), *Aspects of the Notitia Dignitatum* (BAR Supplementary Series 15, Oxford 1976)

Mann, J.C., 'The Notitia Dignitatum – Dating and Survival' in *Britannia* 22 (1991), pp. 215–19

Mathisen, Ralph W. and Sivan, Hagith S., *Shifting Frontiers in Late Antiquity* (Aldershot 1996)

Matthews, J.M., *Western Aristocracies and the Imperial Court AD 364–425* (Oxford 1975)

Matyszak, Philip, *The Enemies of Rome* (London 2004)

Millar, Fergus, *The Roman Empire and its Neighbours* (London 1967)

Millar, Fergus, *The Emperor in the Roman World (31BC–AD 337)* (London 1977)

Millar, Fergus, *A Greek Roman Empire, Power and Belief under Theodosius II (408–50)* (Berkeley, 2006)

Millar, Fergus, 'Emperors, Frontiers and Foreign Relations, 31 B.C. to A.D. 378' in *Britannia* 13 (1982), pp. 1–23

Mitchell, Stephen, *A History of the Later Roman Empire AD 284–641* (Oxford 2007)

Mitchell, Stephen and Greatrex, Gregory (eds), *Ethnicity and Culture in Late Antiquity* (London 2000)

Momigliano, Arnold (ed.), *The Conflict between Paganism and Christianity in the Fourth Century* (Oxford 1970)

Moorhead, John, *Justinian* (London 1994)

Murdoch, Adrian, *The Last Pagan: Julian the Apostate and the Death of the Ancient World* (Stroud 2003)

Nicasie, M.J., 'The Borders of the Roman Empire in the Fourth Century' in *Roman Frontier Studies 1995* (ed. W. Groenman-van Waateringe, B.I. van Beek, W.J.H. Willems, S.L. Wynia, Oxford 1997)

Odahl, Charles Matson, *Constantine and the Christian Empire* (London 2004)

Pohl, Walter, Wood, Ian and Reimitz, Helmut, *The Transformation of Frontiers from Late Antiquity to the Carolingians* (Leiden 2001)

Potter, David S., *The Roman Empire at Bay* AD 180–395 (London 2004)

Rapp, Claudia, *Holy Bishops in Late Antiquity: The Nature of Christian Leadership in an Age of Transition* (Berkeley 2005)

Rees, Roger, *Diocletian and the Tetrarchy* (Edinburgh 2004)

Rich, John (ed.), *The City in Late Antiquity* (London 1992)

Rich, John and Shipley, Graham, *War and Society in the Roman World* (London 1993)

Richardson, L. Jr, *A New Topographical Dictionary of Ancient Rome* (Baltimore 1992)

Rutherford, R.B., *The Meditations of Marcus Aurelius: A Study* (Oxford 1989)

Sanders, Henry A. (ed.), *Roman Historical Sources and Institutions* (London 1904)

Sanford, Eva Matthews, 'Nero and the East' in Harvard Studies in Classical Philology 48 (1937), pp. 75–103

Saradi-Mendelovic, Helen, 'Christian Attitudes toward Pagan Monuments in Late Antiquity and Their Legacy in Later Byzantine Centuries' in Dumbarton Oaks Papers 44 (1990), pp. 44–61

Southern, Pat, *Domitian: Tragic Tyrant* (London 1997)

Southern, Pat, *The Roman Empire from Severus to Constantine* (London 2001)

Southern, Pat and Dixon, Karen Ramsay, *The Late Roman Army* (London 1996)

Spaul, John E.H., *ALA²: The Auxiliary Cavalry Units of the Pre-Diocletianic Imperial Roman Army* (Andover 1994)

Starr, Chester G., *The Roman Imperial Navy* (2nd edition, Cambridge 1960)

Stilwell, Richard (ed.), *Princeton Encyclopedia of Classical Sites* (Princeton, NJ, 1976)

Swain, Simon and Edwards, Mark, *Approaching Late Antiquity* (Oxford 2004)

Talbert, J.A., *Barrington Atlas of the Greek and Roman World* (Princeton 2000)

Taylor, Lily Ross, *The Divinity of the Roman Emperor* (Philadelphia 1975)

Thompson, E.A., *Romans and Barbarians: The Decline of the Western Empire* (Madison 1982)

Todd, Malcolm, *The Northern Barbarians* 100 BC–AD 300 (London 1975)

Tougher, Shaun, *Julian the Apostate* (Edinburgh 2007)

Wacher, John (ed.), *The Roman World* (London 1987)

Ward-Perkins, Brian, *The Fall of Rome and the End of Civilization* (Oxford 2005)

Ward-Perkins, John B., *Roman Imperial Architecture* (London 1981)

Ward-Perkins, John B., *Roman Architecture* (London 1988)

Warde Folwer, W., *The Roman Festivals of the Period of the Republic* (London 1899)

Watson, Alaric, *Aurelian and the Third Century* (London 1999)

Whiles, Maurice, *Archetypal Heresy, Arianism through the Centuries* (Oxford 1996)

Whitby, Michael, *Rome at War* AD 293–696 (Oxford 2002)

Whittaker, C.R., *Rome and its Frontier: The Dynamics of Empire* (London 2004)

Whittow, Mark, *The Making of Orthodox Byzantium, 600–1025* (Basingstoke 1996)

Wiedemann, Thomas, *Emperors and Gladiators* (London, 1992)

Wilkinson, John, *Jerusalem Pilgrims before the Crusades* (Warminster 1977)

Williams, Derek, *Romans and Barbarians: Four Views from the Empire's Edge* (London 1998)

Williams, Stephen, *Diocletian and the Roman Recovery* (London 1985)

Williams, Stephen and Friell, Gerard. *Theodosius: The Empire at Bay* (London 1998)

Wilson Jones, Mark, 'Doric Measure and Architectural Design 1: The Evidence of the Relief from Salamis' in *American Journal of Archaeology*, Vol. 104, No. 1. (Jan. 2000), pp. 73–93

Witt, R.E., *Isis in the Ancient World*, Baltimore 1997

Yarshater, Ehsan (ed.), *The Cambridge History of Iran, Volume 3, The Seleucid, Parthian and Sasanian periods* (Cambridge 1983)

Yegül, Fikret, *Baths and Bathing in Classical Antiquity* (Cambridge, MA, 1992)

CHAPTER 1: BRITANNIA

Alcock, Leslie, *Arthur's Britain* (London 1989)

Bidwell, Paul (ed.), *Hadrian's Wall 1989–1999: A Summary of Recent Excavations and Research* (Newcastle upon Tyne 1999)

Biggins, J. Alan et al., 'A Survey of the Roman Fort and Settlement at Birdoswald, Cumbria' in *Britannia* 30 (1999), pp. 91–110

Birley, Anthony, *Garrison Life at Vindolanda* (Stroud 2002)

Birley, Robin, *Magna and Carvoran – The Fort at the Rock* (Carlisle 1998)

Bowman, Alan K., *Life and Letters on the Roman Frontier, Vindolanda and its People* (London 1998)

Breeze, David, *The Northern Frontiers of Roman Britain* (London 1982)

Breeze, David J., *Roman Forts in Britain* (Princes Risborough 2002)

Breeze, David J., *The Antonine Wall* (Edinburgh 2006)

Breeze, David J. and Dobson, Brian, *Hadrian's Wall*, (4th edition, London 2000)

Collingwood Bruce, J., *A Handbook to the Roman Wall* (14th edition, by David J. Breeze, Newcastle 2006)

Collingwood, R.G., 'Hadrian's Wall: A History of the Problem' in *Journal of Roman Studies* 11 (1921)

Carroll, Kevin K., 'The Date of Boudicca's Revolt' in *Britannia*, Vol. 10 (1979), pp. 197–202

Cleary, A.S. Esmonde, *The Ending of Roman Britain* (London 1989)

Crow, J.G., *Housesteads Roman Fort* (London 1989)

Dark, Ken, *Britain and the End of the Roman Empire* (Stroud 2000)

Dark, K.R., 'A Sub-Roman Re-Defence of Hadrian's Wall?' in *Britannia* 23, (1992), pp. 111–20

De la Bédoyère, Guy, *Roman Towns in Britain* (London 1992)

De la Bédoyère, Guy, *Eagles over Britannia* (London 2001)

Dore, J.N., *Corbridge Roman Site* (London 1989)

Faulkner, Neil, *The Decline and Fall of Roman Britain* (Stroud 2000)

Fields, Nic, *Rome's Saxon Shore: Coastal Defences of Roman Britain* (Oxford 2006)

Frere, Sheppard, *Britannia: A History of Roman Britain* (London 1991)

Goodall, John, *Portchester* (London 2003)

Green, Miranda J., *The Gods of Roman Britain* (Princes Risborough, 2003)

Hanson, William S. and Maxwell, Gordon S., *Rome's North West Frontier: The Antonine Wall* (Edinburgh 1983)

Harris, Susan, *Richborough and Reculver* (London 2001)

Heurgon, Jacques, 'The Amiens Patera' in *Journal of Roman Studies* 41, Parts 1 and 2 (1951), pp. 22–4

Hill, Peter, *The Construction of Hadrian's Wall* (Stroud 2006)

Ireland, S., *Roman Britian, A Sourcebook* (London 1986)

Johnson, J.S., *Chesters Roman Fort* (London, 1990)

Johnson, Stephen, *Roman Forts of the Saxon Shore* (London 1979)

Jones, Michael E., *The End of Roman Britain* (Ithaca 1986)

Mann, J.C., 'The Northern Frontier after AD 368' in *Glasgow Archaeological Journal* 3 (1974), pp. 34–42

Mann, J.C., 'Birdoswald to Ravenglass' in *Britannia* 20 (1989), pp. 75–9

Mattingly, David, *An Imperial Possession: Britain in the Roman Empire* (London 2006)

Maxfield, Valerie (ed.), *The Saxon Shore, A Handbook* (Exeter Studies in History No. 25, 1989)

Maxwell, Gordon S., *The Romans in Scotland* (Edinburgh 1989)

Miller, M., 'Stilicho's Pictish War' in *Britannia* 6 (1975), pp. 141–5

Pearson, Andrew, *The Roman Shore Forts, Coastal Defences of Southern Britain* (Stroud 2002)

Philip, Brian, *The Roman Fort at Reculver* (Dover 1970)

Robertson, Anne S., *The Antonine Wall: A Handbook to the Surviving Remains* (3rd edition, Glasgow 1990)

Salway, Peter, *A History of Roman Britain* (Oxford, 1993)

Shotter, David, *The Roman Frontier in Britain* (Preston 1996)

Thompson, E.A., *Saint Germanus of Auxerre and the End of Roman Britain* (Woodbridge, Suffolk, 1984)

Todd, Malcolm (ed.), *A Companion to Roman Britain* (Oxford 2007)

Wacher, John, *The Towns of Roman Britain* (London 1975)

Wacher, John, *Roman Britain* (London 1978)

Wilmott, Tony, *Birdoswald Roman Fort* (London 2005)

Wilson, Roger J.A., *A Guide to the Roman Remains in Britain*, (4th edition London 2002)

CHAPTER 2: GERMANIA

Alföldi, Andreas, 'The moral barrier on Rhine and Danube' in *The Congress of Roman Frontier Studies 1949* (ed. Eric Birley, Durham 1952), pp. 1–16

Barrett, John C., Fitzpatrick, Andrew P., Macinnes, Lesley, *Barbarians and Romans in North-West Europe from the later Republic to late Antiquity* (BAR International Series 471, Oxford 1989)

Blandt, Roel and Slofstra, Jan, *Roman and Native in the Low Countries, Spheres of Interaction* (BAR International Series 184, Oxford 1983)

Booth, Alan D., 'The Academic Career of Ausonius' in *Phoenix*, Vol. 36, No. 4 (Winter 1982), pp. 329–43

Carroll, Maureen, *Romans, Germans and Celts* (Stroud 2001)

Drinkwater, J.F., 'The Gallic Empire, Separatism and Continuity in the North-Western Provinces of the Roman Empire AD 260–7' in *Historia* 52 (Stuttgart 1987)

Furger, Alex R., *Augusta Raurica* (trs Cathy Aitken and Christoph Maier, Augst 1995)

Hawkes, Christopher and Hawkes, Sonia (eds), *Greeks, Celts and Romans: Studies in Venture and Resistance* (London 1973)

Hind, J.G.F., 'Whatever happened to the *Agri Decumates*' in *Britannia* 15 (1984), pp. 187–92

Johnson, Anne, *Roman Forts of the 1st and 2nd Centuries AD in Britain and the German Provinces* (London 1983)

King, Anthony, *Roman Gaul and Germany* (London 1990)

Kulikowski, Michael, 'Barbarians in Gaul, Usurpers in Britain' in *Britannia* 31 (2000), pp. 325–45

MacKendrick, Paul, *Roman France* (London 1971)

Murdoch, Adrian, *Rome's Greatest Defeat: Massacre in the Teutoburg Forest* (Stroud 2006)

O'Reilly, Donald F., 'The Theban Legion of St Maurice' in *Vigiliae Christianae*, Vol. 32, No. 3 (Sep. 1978), pp. 195–207

Rieche, Anita, *Guide through the Archaeological Park Xanten* (Xanten 1994)

Roymans, Nico, *Ethnic Identity and Imperial Power: The Batavians in the Early Roman Empire* (Amsterdam 2004)

Schönberger, H., 'The Roman Frontier in Germany: An Archaeological Survey' in *Journal of Roman Studies* 59 (1969), pp. 144–97

Springer, Lawrence A., 'Rome's Contact with the Frisians' in *Classical Journal*, Vol. 48, No. 4 (Jan. 1953), pp. 109–11

Verwers, W.J.H., *North Brabant in Roman and Early Medieval Times* (Amersfoort 1998)

Von Elbe, Joachim, *Roman Germany, A Guide to Sites and Museums* (Mainz 1975)

Von Petrikovits, Harold, 'Fortifications in the North-Western Roman Empire from the Third to the Fifth Centuries AD' in *Journal of Roman Studies* 61 (1971), pp. 178–218

Wells, C.M., *The German Policy of Augustus, An Examination of the Archaeological Evidence* (Oxford 1972)

Wightman, Edith Mary, *Roman Trier and the Treveri* (London 1970)

Wightman, Edith Mary, *Gallia Belgica* (London 1985)

Wolff, Gerta, *Roman-Germanic Cologne* (Cologne 2003)

CHAPTER 3: RAETIA AND NORICUM

Alföldy, Géza (trs Anthony Birley), *Noricum* (London 1974)

Mierow, Charles Christopher, 'Eugippius and the Closing Years of Noricum Ripense' in *Classical Philology*, Vol. 10, No. 2 (Apr. 1915), pp. 166–87

Phillips, George Lewis, 'Six Saints of Sweepdom' in *Folklore*, Vol. 74, No. 2 (Summer 1963), pp. 377–86

Pitts, Lynn F., 'Relations between Rome and the German Kings on the Middle Danube in the First to Fourth Centuries A.D.' in *Journal of Roman Studies* 79 (1989), pp. 45–58

Schutz, Herbert, *The Romans in Central Europe* (New Haven 1985)

CHAPTER 4: MOESIA AND PANNONIA

Aricescu, Andrei, *The Army in Roman Dobrudja* (BAR International Series 86, Oxford 1980)

Atanassove-Georgieva, Jordana, 'Résultat des fouilles de la ville antique de Ratiaria au cours des années 1976 à 1982' in *Studien zu Den Militargränzen Roms III* (Stuttgart 1986), pp. 437–40

Barford, P.M., *The Early Slavs: Culture and Society in Early Medieval Eastern Europe* (London 2001)

Brothers, A.J., 'Diocletian's Palace at Split' in *Greece & Rome*, Second Series, Vol. 19, No. 2 (Oct. 1972), pp. 175–86

Carter, Francis W. (ed.), *An Historical Geography of the Balkans* (London 1977)

Champlin, Edward, 'The Testament of the Piglet' in Phoenix, Vol. 41, No. 2, (Summer 1987), pp. 174–83

Gamzigrad, An Imperial Palace of Late Classical Times (Belgrade 1983)

Gimbutas, Marija, *The Slavs* (London 1971)

Heather, Peter, *The Goths* (Oxford 1996)

Hind, J.G.F., 'Greek and Barbarian Peoples on the Shores of the Black Sea' in *Archaeological Reports*, No. 30 (1983), pp. 71–97

Hoddinott, R.F., *Bulgaria in Antiquity, an archaeological introduction* (London 1975)

Humer, F., *Carnuntum, The Roman City Quarter in the Open Air Museum* (Petronell 2004)

Ivanov, Teofil and Stojanov, Stojan, *Abritus* (Razgrad, 1985)

Lengyel, A. and Radan, G.T.P., *The Archaeology of Roman Pannonia* (Budapest 1980)

Man, John, *Attila the Barbarian King who Challenged Rome* (London 2005)

Mócsy, András (trs Sheppard Frere), *Pannonia and Upper Moesia. A History of the Middle Danube Provinces of the Roman Empire* (London 1974)

Nicol, Donald M., *The Byzantine Family of Kantakouzenos ca 1100–1460, A Genealogical and Prosopographical Study* (Dumbarton Oaks 1968)

Oliva, P., *Pannonia and the Onset of Crisis in the Roman Empire* (Prague 1962)

Parnicki-Pudelko, Stefan, *The Episcopal Basilica in Novae, Archeological Research 1976–1990* (Poznan 1995)

Petulescu, Liviu, 'The Roman Army as a Factor of Romanisation in the North-Eastern Part of Moesia Inferior' in *The Roman and Late Roman City* (International Conference, Veliko Turnovo 26–30 July 2000) (Sofia 2002), pp. 31–42

Pitts, Lynn F., 'Relations between Rome and the German Kings on the Middle Danube in the First to Fourth Centuries AD' in *Journal of Roman Studies* 79 (1989), pp. 45–58

Popović, Vladislav (ed.), *Sirmium – Archaeological Investigations in Sirmian Pannonia* (Belgrade 1971)

Poulter, A.G. (ed.), *Ancient Bulgaria: Papers presented to the International Symposium on the Ancient History and Archaeology of Bulgari* (Nottingham 1981, 1983)

Poulter, Andrew, *Nicopolis ad Istrum: A Roman, Late Roman and Early Byzantine City* (Society for Promotion of Roman Studies, Journal of Roman Studies Monograph 8, London 1995)

Press, Ludwika, 'Valetudinarium at Novae', in *Studien zu den Militargränzen Roms* (III Stuttgart 1986), pp. 529–35

Rives, J.B., 'The Decree of Decius and the Religion of Empire' in *Journal of Roman Studies* 89 (1999), pp. 135–54

Schutz, Herbert, *The Romans in Central Europe* (New Haven 1985)

Spekke, Arnolds, *The Ancient Amber Routes and the Geographical Discovery of the Eastern Baltic* (Stockholm 1957)

Syme, Ronald, 'Lentulus and the Origin of Moesia' in *Journal of Roman Studies* 24 (1934), pp. 113–37

Visy, Zsolt (ed.), *The Roman Army in Pannonia, An Archaeological Guide of the Ripa Pannonica* (Budapest 2003)

CHAPTER 5: DACIA

Cătăniciu, Ioana Bogdan, *Evolution of the system of defence works in Roman Dacia* (trs Etta Dumitrescu, BAR International Series 116, Oxford 1981)

Bichir, Gh. (trs Nubar Hampartumian), *The Archaeology and History of the Carpi from the Second to the Fourth Century AD* (BAR Supplementary Series 16 (i), Oxford 1976)

Eliade, Mircea and Trask, Willard R., 'Zalmoxis' in *History of Religions*, Vol. 11, No. 3 (Feb. 1972), pp. 257–302

Gudea, Nicolae, 'The Defensive System of Roman Dacia' in *Britannia* 10, (1979), pp. 63–87

MacKendrick, Paul, *The Dacian Stones Speak* (Chapel Hill 1975)

Picard, Gilbert Charles, *Les Trophées Romains, Contributions à l'histoire de la Religions et de l'Art triumphal de Rome* (Paris 1957)

Poulter, Andrew G., 'The Lower Moesian Limes and the Dacian Wars of

Trajan' in *Studien zu den Militargränzen Roms* III (Stuttgart 1986), pp. 519–28

Rossi, Lino (trs J.M.C. Toynbee), *Trajan's Column and the Dacian Wars* (London 1971)

Scorpan, C., *Limes Scythiae: Topographical and Stratigraphical Research on the late Roman fortifications on the Lower Danube* (BAR International Series 99, Oxford 1980)

Speidel, Michael, 'The Captor of Decebalus: a New Inscription from Philippi' in *Journal of Roman Studies* 60 (1970), pp. 142–53

CHAPTER 6: CAPPADOCIA

Akurgal, Ekrem, *Ancient Civilizations and Ruins of Turkey* (London 2002)

Barnard, L. W. 'The Origins and Emergence of the Church in Edessa during the First Two Centuries AD' in *Vigiliae Christiane* Vol. 22 No. 3 (Sept. 1986), pp. 161–175

Baumer, Christopher, *The Church of the East, an Illustrated History of Assyrian Christianity* (London 2006)

Baynes, Norman H., 'The Death of Julian the Apostate in a Christian Legend' in *Journal of Roman Studies* 27, Part 1, pp. 22–9

Bell, Gertrude, *Churches and Monasteries of the Tur Abdin and Neighbouring Districts* (Heidelberg 1913)

Bryer, Anthony, *The Empire of Trebizond and the Pontus* (London 1980)

Bryer, Anthony and Winfield, David, *The Byzantine Monuments and Topography of the Pontos*, Vols 1–2 (Washington 1985)

Croke, Brian and Crow, James, 'Procopius and Dara' in *Journal of Roman Studies* 73 (1983), pp. 143–59

Dueck, Daniela, *Strabo of Amaseia* (London 2000)

Freeman, Philip and Kennedy, David, *The Defence of the Roman and Byzantine East* (BAR International Series 297 (ii), Oxford 1986), pp. 737–83

French, D.H. and Lightfoot, C.S. (eds), *The Eastern Frontier of the Roman Empire* (BAR International Series 533 (i), Oxford 1989)

Goell, Theresa B., 'The Excavation of the "Hierothesion" of Antiochus I of Commagene on Nemrud Dagh (1953–1956)' in *Bulletin of the American Schools of Oriental Research*, No. 147 (Oct. 1957)

Jones, A.H.M., *Cities of the Eastern Roman Provinces* (Oxford 1937)

Magie, David, *Roman Rule in Asia Minor* (Princeton 1950)

Matthews, Roger (ed.), *Ancient Anatolia, Fifty Years of Work by the British Institute of Archaeology of Ankara* (London 1999)

Miller, William, 'The Chronology of Trebizond' in *English Historical Review*, Vol. 38, No. 151 (July 1923), pp. 408–10

Miller, William, *Trebizond: The Last Greek Empire* (London 1926)

Mitford, T.B., 'The Euphrates Frontier in Cappadocia' in *Studien zu den Militargränzen Roms* II (Bonn 1977), pp. 502–10

Mitford, T.B., 'Biliotti's Excavations at Satala' in *Anatolian Studies* 24 (1984), pp. 221–44

Payaslian, Simon, *The History of Armenia from the Origins to the Present* (London 2007)

Ross, Steven K., *Roman Edessa, Politics and Culture on the Eastern Fringe of the Roman Empire 114–242 CE* (London 2001)

Sanders, Donald H. (ed.), *Nemrud Daği, The Hierothesion of Antiochus I of Commagene*, Vol. 1: Text (Winona Lake, IN, 1996)

Segal, J.B., *Edessa: The Blessed City* (Oxford 1970)

Segal, J.B., 'The Planet Cult of Ancient Harran' in E. Bacon (ed.), *Vanished Civilizations* (London 1963)

Sinclair, T.A., *Eastern Turkey, an Architectural and Archaeological Survey*, Vols I–IV (London 1989)

Stark, Freya, *Rome on the Euphrates* (London 1966)

Talbot Rice, D., 'Trebizond, a Medieval Citadel and Palace' in *Journal of Hellenic Studies*, Vol. 52, Part 1 (1932), pp. 47–54

Wheeler, R.E.M., 'The Roman Frontier in Mesopotamia' in *The Congress of Roman Frontier Studies 1949* (ed. Eric Birley, Durham 1952), pp. 112–29

CHAPTER 7: SYRIA

Balty, Jean, 'Apamea in Syria in the Second and Third Centuries AD' in *Journal of Roman Studies* 78 (1988), pp. 91–104

Bell, Florence (ed.), *The Letters of Gertrude Bell*, Vol. 1 (London 1927)

Bickerman, Elias J., 'Notes on Seleucid and Parthian Chronology' in *Berytus* 8 1943 pp. 73–84

Browning, Iain, *Palmyra* (London 1979)

Browning, Iain, *Jerash and the Decapolis* (London 1982)

Browning, Robert, 'The Riot of AD 387 in Antioch: The Role of the Theatrical Claques in the Later Empire' in *Journal of Roman Studies*, Vol. 42, Parts 1 and 2 (1952), pp. 13–20

Burns, Ross, *Monuments of Syria, An Historical Guide* (London 1999)

Butcher, Kevin, *Roman Syria and the Near East* (London 2003)

Colledge, Malcolm A.R., *The Art of Palmyra* (London 1976)

Dawkins, James and Wood, Robert, *The Ruins of Palmyra* (London 1753)

De Vries, Bert, 'What's in a Name: The Anonymity of Ancient Umm el-Jimal' in *Biblical Archaeologist*, Vol. 57, No. 4 (Dec. 1994), pp. 215–19

Doran, Robert, *The Lives of Simeon Stylites* (Spencer, MA, 1992)

Downey, G., 'Aurelian's Victory over Zenobia at Immae, AD 272' in *Transactions and Proceedings of the American Philological Association* 81 (1950), pp. 57–68

Downey, Glanville, *A History of Antioch in Syria from Seleucus to the Arab Conquest* (Princeton, NJ, 1961)

Downey, Glanville, *Ancient Antioch* (Oxford 1972)

Frankfurter, T.M., 'Stylites and Phallobates: Pillar Religions in Late Antique Syria' in *Vigiliae Christianae*, Vol. 44, No. 2 (June 1990), pp. 168–98

Gilliam, J.F., 'The Roman Military Feriale' in *Harvard Theological Review*, Vol. 47, No. 3 (Jul. 1954), pp. 183–96

Hopkins, Clark, *The Discovery of Dura Europos* (New Haven 1979)

Hopkins, Clark, 'The Siege of Dura' in *Classical Journal*, Vol. 42, No. 5 (Feb. 1948), pp. 251–9

Isaac, Benjamin, *The Limits of Empire: The Roman Army in the East* (revised edition Oxford 1992)

Kennedy, David, *The Roman Army in Jordan* (revised edition, London 2004)

Liebeschuetz, J.H., *Antioch, City and Imperial Administration in the Later Roman Empire* (Oxford 1972)

Matthews, J.F., 'The Tax Law of Palmyra: Evidence for Economic History in a City of the Roman East' in *Journal of Roman Studies* 74 (1984), pp. 157–80

Millar, Fergus, *The Roman Near East, 31 BC–AD 337* (Cambridge, MA, 1993)

Nicasie, M.J., *Twilight of Empire: The Roman Army from the Reign of Diocletian until the Battle of Adrianople* (Amsterdam 1998)

Nicolle, David, *Yarmuk AD 636* (Westport 1994)

Pasztori-Kupán, István, *Theodoret of Cyrrus* (Oxford 2006)

Perkins, A., *The Art of Dura-Europus* (Oxford 1973)

Pollard, Nigel, *Soldiers, Cities and Civilians in Roman Syria* (Ann Arbor 2000)

Richmond, I.A., 'Palmyra under the Aegis of Rome' in *Journal of Roman Studies*, Vol. 53, Parts 1 & 2 (1963), pp. 43–54

Rostovtzeff, M., *Caravan Cities* (Oxford 1932)

Rostovtzeff, M., *Dura-Europos and its Art* (Oxford 1938)

Sartre, Maurice, *The Middle East Under Rome* (Harvard 2007)

Segal, Arthur, *From Function to Monument: Urban Landscapes of Roman Palestine, Syria and Provincia Arabia* (Oxford 1997)

Sha'ath, Shawqi (trs Dorothy Stele, Yahya Abu Risha), *Qal'at Sim'an (and other sites): An Archaeological and Historical Guide* (Aleppo)

Stanhope, Lady Hester (ed. The Duchess of Cleveland), *The Life and Letters of Lady Hester Stanhope* (London 1914)

Stoneman, Richard, *Palmyra and its Empire – Zenobia's revolt against Rome* (Ann Arbor 1992)

Tchalenko, Georges, *Villages antiques de la Syrie du Nord* (Paris 1953)

Vasiliev, Alexander A., 'Notes on some Episodes concerning the Relations between the Arabs and the Byzantine Empire from the Fourth to the Sixth Century' in *Dumbarton Oaks Papers* 9 (1956), pp 306–16

Zahran, Yasmine, *Zenobia between Reality and Legend* (BAR International Series 11669, Oxford 2003)

CHAPTER 8: ARABIA

Bowersock, G. W., 'A Report on Arabia Provincia' in *Journal of Roman Studies* 61 (1971), pp. 219–42

Bowersock, G.W., 'Limes Arabicus' in *Harvard Studies in Classical Philology* 80 (1976), pp. 219–29

Bowersock, G.W., *Roman Arabia* (Cambridge, MA, 1983)

Bowersock, G.W., 'Edward Lear in Petra' in *Proceedings of the American Philosophical Society*, Vol. 134, No. 3 (Sep. 1990), pp. 309–20

Browning, Iain, *Jerash and the Decapolis* (London 1982)

Burckhardt, Johann Ludwig, *Travels in Syria and the Holy Land* (1822, reprinted London 1992)

Damiani, Anita, *Enlightened Observers: British Travellers to the Near East* (Beirut 1979)

Eadie, John W. and Oleson, John Peter, 'The Water-supply Systems of Nabataean and Roman Humayma' in *Bulletin of the American Schools of Oriental Research* 252 (May 1986), pp. 49–76

Guzzo, Maria Guilia Amadasi and Schneider, Eugenia Equini (trs Lydia G. Cochrane), *Petra* (Chicago 2002)

Harding, G.W.L., *The Antiquities of Jordan* (London 1959)

Hatoum, Hassan, *Canatha and Philippopolis* (Damascus 2001)

Jameson, Shelagh, 'Chronology of the Campaigns of Aelius Gallus and C. Petronius' in *Journal of Roman Studies*, Vol. 58 Parts 1 and 2 (1968), pp. 71–84

Lander, James and Parker, S. Thomas, 'Legio IV Martia and the Legionary Camp at El-Lejjun' in *Byzantinische Forschungen, Internationale Zeitschrift für Byzantinistik* 8 (1982), pp. 185–211

Khouri, Rami G., *Jerash: A frontier city of the Roman East* (London 1986)

Khouri, Rami G. and Whitcomb, Donald, *Aqaba* (Amman 1986)

Lawrence, T. E., *Seven Pillars of Wisdom* (London 1935)

MacAdam, Henry Innes, *Studies in the History of the Roman Province of Arabia* (BAR International Series 295, Oxford 1986)

Mayerson, Philip, 'The First Muslim Attacks on Southern Palestine', *Transactions of the American Philological Association* 95 (1964), p. 173

Nicholson, Oliver, 'Two Notes on Dara' in *American Journal of Archaeology*, Vol. 89, No. 4 (Oct. 1985), pp. 663–71

Parker, S. Thomas 'Preliminary Report on the 1980 Season of the Central *Limes Arabicus* Project' in *Bulletin of the American Schools of Oriental Research* 247 (Summer 1982), pp. 1–26

Parker, S. Thomas, *The Roman Frontier in Central Jordan, Interim Report on the Limes Arabicus Project* (BAR International Series 340 (i & ii), Oxford 1987)

Segal, Arthur, 'Roman Cities in the Province of Arabia' in *Journal of the Society of Architectural Historians*, Vol. 40, No. 2 (May 1981), pp. 108–21

Shahid, Irfan, *Rome and the Arabs – A Prolegomenon to the Study of Byzantium and the Arabs* (Dumbarton Oaks 1984)

Shahid, Irfan, *Byzantium and the Arabs in the Fourth Century* (Dumbarton Oaks 1989)

Shahid, Irfan, *Byzantium and the Arabs in the Fifth Century* (Dumbarton Oaks 1989)

Shahid, Irfan, *Byzantium and the Arabs in the Sixth Century* (Dumbarton Oaks 1995)

Starcky, Jean, 'The Nabataeans: A Historical Sketch' in *Biblical Archaeologist*, Vol. 18, No. 4 (Dec. 1955), pp. 81–106

Stoneman, Richard, *Palmyra and its Empire, Zenobia's Revolt against Rome* (Ann Arbor 1992)

Welsby, Derek A., 'Qasr al-Uwainid and Da'ajaniya: Two Roman Military Sites in Jordan' in *Levan* 30 (1998), pp. 195–8

CHAPTER 9: AEGYPTUS

Alston, Richard *Soldier and Society in Roman Egypt: A Social History* (London 1995)

Bagnall, Roger S., *Egypt in Late Antiquity* (Princeton 1993)

Bagnall, Roger S., 'Archaeological Work on Hellenistic and Roman Egypt, 1995–2000' in *American Journal of Archaeology*, Vol. 105, No. 2 (Apr. 2001), pp. 227–43

Bagnall, Roger S. (ed.), *Egypt in the Byzantine World, 300–700* (Cambridge 2007)

Barnard, L.W., 'Athanasius and the Meletian Schism in Egypt' in *Journal of Egyptian Archaeology* 59 (1975), pp. 181–9

Barnes, T.D., 'The Career of Abinnaeus' in *Phoenix*, Vol. 39, No. 4 (Winter 1985), pp. 368–74

Bowman, Alan K., *Egypt after the Pharaohs* (London 1986)

Butler, Alfred, *The Arab Conquest of Egypt and the last thirty years of the Roman Dominion* (2nd edition, Oxford 1978)

Cuvigny, Hélène, 'The Amount of Wages paid to the Quarry-Workers at Mons Claudianus' in *Journal of Roman Studies* 86 (1996), pp. 139–45

Edwards, Amelia B., *A Thousand Miles up the Nile* (London 1877)

Empereur, Jean-Yves (trs Margaret Maehler), *Alexandria Rediscovered* (London 1998)

Fakhry, Ahmed, *Siwa Oasis, its History and Antiquities* (Cairo 1944)

Fakhry, Ahmed, *Baharia Oasis* Vol. II (Cairo 1950)

Fakhry, Ahmed, *The Necropolis of El-Bagawat in Kharga Oasis* (Cairo 1951)

Forster, E.M., *Alexandria: A History and a Guide* (Alexandria 1938)

Franfkurter, David, *Religion in Roman Egypt, Assimilation and Resistance* (Princeton, NJ, 1998)

Gardner, I.M.F. and Lieu, S.N.C., 'From Narmouthis (Medinet Madi) to Kellis (Asmant El-Kharab): Manichaean Documents from Roman Egypt' in *Journal of Roman Studies* 86 (1986), pp. 146–9

Golvin, Jean-Claude and Reddé, Michel 'L'enceinte du camp militaire romain de Louqsor' in *Studien zu den Militärgränzen Roms* III Stuttgart 1986, pp 594–9

Haas, Christopher, *Alexandria in Late Antiquity: Topography and Social Conflict* (Baltimore 1997)

Harmless, William, *The Desert Christians* (Oxford 2004)

Jackson, Robert B., *At Empire's Edge, Exploring Rome's Egyptian Frontier* (New Haven 2002)

Jameson, Shelagh, 'Chronology of the Campaigns of Aelius Gallus and C. Petronius' in *Journal of Roman Studies*, Vol 58, Parts 1 and 2 (1968), pp. 71–84

Johnson, Allan Chester, 'Lucius Domitius Domitianus Augustus' in *Classical Philology*, Vol. 45, No. 1 (Jan. 1950), pp. 13–21

Kirwan, L.P., 'Rome Beyond the Southern Egyptian Frontier' in *Geographical Journal*, Vol. 123, No. 1 (Mar. 1957), pp. 13–19

Mackenzie, Judith, *The Architecture of Alexandria and Egypt c. 300 BC to AD 700* (New Haven 2007)

Mackenzie, Judith S., Gibson, Sheila Reyes, A.T., 'Reconstructing the Serapeum in Alexandria from the Archaeological Evidence' in *Journal of Roman Studies* 94 (2004), pp. 73–121

MacLeod, Roy (ed.), *The Library of Alexandria, Centre of Learning in the Ancient World* (London 2000)

MacQuitty, William, *Island of Isis: Philae, Temple of the Nile* (London 1976)

Meredith, David, 'The Roman Remains in the Eastern Desert of Egypt I' in *Journal of Egyptian Archaeology* 38 (Dec. 1952), pp. 94–111

Parson, Peter J., 'The Wells of Hibis' in *Journal of Egyptian Archaeology* 57 (1971), pp. 165–80

Peacock, D.P.S., *Rome in the Desert: A Symbol of Power* (Southampton 1993)

Peacock, David and Maxfield, Valerie, 'On the Trail of Imperial Porphyry' in *Egyptian Archaeology* 5 (1994), pp. 24–226

Scott, Kenneth, 'Octavian's Propaganda and Antony's De Sua Ebrietate' in *Classical Philology*, Vol. 24, No. 2 (Apr. 1929), pp. 133–41

Sidebottom, S.E., 'The Roman Frontier in the Eastern Desert of Egypt' in *Roman Frontier Studies 1995* (ed. W. Groenman-van Waateringe, B.L. van Beek, W.J.H. Willems, S.L. Wynia, Oxford 1997), pp. 503–9

Skeat, T.C., 'A Letter from the King of the Blemmyes to the King of the Noubades' in *Journal of Egyptian Archaeology* 63 (1977), pp. 159–70

Thompson, E.A., 'Olympiodorus of Thebes' in *Classical Quarterly*, Vol. 38, No. 1/2 (Jan.–Apr. 1944) pp. 43–52

Van der Veen, Marijke, 'High living in Rome's distant quarries' in *British Archaeology* 28 (October 1997)

Vivian, Cassandra, *The Western Desert of Egypt* (Cairo 2000)

Vretto, Theodore, *Alexandria, City of the Western Mind* (New York 2001)

CHAPTER 10: AFRICA

Barker, Graeme, Lloyd John and Reynolds, Joyce, *Cyrenaica in Antiquity* (BAR International Series 236, Oxford 1985)

Barton, I.M., *Africa in the Roman Empire* (Accra 1972)

Bregman, Jay, *Synesius of Cyrene, Philosopher-Bishop* (Berkeley 1982)

Broughton, T.R.S., *The Romanization of Africa Proconsularis* (New York 1968)

Buck, D.J. and Mattingly, D.J., *Town and Country in Roman Tripolitania – Papers in Honour of Olwen Hackett* (BAR International Series 174, Oxford 1985)

Caffarelli, Ernesto Vergara and Giacomo, *The Buried City: Excavations at Leptis Magna* (London 1966)

Cherry, David, *Frontier and Society in Roman North Africa* (Oxford 1998)

Clover, Frank M., *The Late Roman West and the Vandals* (Aldershot 1993)

Daniels, Charles, *The Garamantes of Southern Libya* (Stoughton, WI, 1970)

Fage, J.D., *Cambridge History of Africa* Vol. 2 (Cambridge 1978)

Fentress, Elizabeth W.B., *Social, Military and Economic Aspects of the Frontier Zone* (BAR International Series 53, Oxford 1979)

Goodchild, R.G., 'The Roman and Byzantine Limes in Cyrenaica' in *Journal of Roman Studies* 43 (1953), pp. 65–76

Goodchild, R.G., 'Boreum of Cyrenaica' in *Journal of Roman Studies*, Vol. 41, Parts 1 and 2 (1951), pp. 11–16

Hannoum, Abdelmajid, 'Historiography, Mythology and Memory in Modern North Africa: The Story of the Kahina' in *Studia Islamica*, No. 85 (1997), pp. 85–130

Harrison, S.J., *Apuleius, A Latin Sophist* (Oxford 2000)

Haynes, D.E.L., *The Antiquities of Tripolitania* (Tripoli 1955)

Haywood, Richard, 'The Oil of Leptis' in *Classical Philology* (1941), pp. 65–76

Hoyos, Dexter, *Hannibal's Dynasty: Power and Politics in the western Mediterranean* (London 2003)

Hurst, H.R. and Roskams, S.P., *Excavations at Carthage: The British Mission. Volume 1, The Site and Finds other than Pottery* (Sheffield 1984)

Julien, Charles-André (trs John Petrie), *A History of North Africa – Tunisia, Algeria, Morocco* (London 1970)

Law, R.C.C., 'The Garamantes and Trans-Saharan Enterprise in Classical Times' in *Journal of African History*, Vol. 8, No. 2 (1967), pp. 181–200

MacKendrick, *The North African Stones Speak* (London 1980)

Manton, E. Lennox, *Roman North Africa* (London 1988)

Mattingly, David J., 'A Tribal Confederation in the Late Roman Empire' in *Libyan Studies* 14 (1983), pp. 6–108

Mattingly, D.J., *Tripolitania* (London 1995)

Mattingly, David J. and Hitchener, Bruce, 'Roman Africa: An Archaeological Survey' in Journal of Roman Studies 85 (1995), pp. 165–213

Merrills, A.H. (ed.), *Vandals, Romans, Berbers: New Perspectives on Late Antique North Africa* (Ashgate 1994)

Millar, Fergus, 'Local Cultures in the Roman Empire: Libya, Punic and Latin in Roman Africa' in *Journal of Roman Studies*, Vol. 58, Parts 1 & 2 (1968), pp. 126–34

Oost, Stewart Irvin, 'Count Gildo and Theodosius the Great' in *Classical Philology*, Vol. 57, No. 1 (Jan. 1962), pp. 27–30

Pentz, Peter, *From Roman Proconsularis to Islamic Ifriqiyah* (Göteborg 2002)

Pringle, R. Denys, *The Defence of Byzantine Africa from Justinian to the Arab Conquest* (BAR International Series 99 (i), Oxford 1990)

Raven, Susan, *Rome in Africa* (3rd edition, London 1993)

Reynolds, J. (ed.), *Libyan Studies: Selected Papers of R.G. Goodchild* (London 1976)

Rives, J.B., 'Imperial Cult and Native Tradition in North Africa' in *Classical Journal*, Vol. 96, No. 4 (Apr.–May 2001), pp. 424–36

Scott, Kenneth, 'Mussolini and the Roman Empire' in *Classical Journal*, Vol. 27, No. 9 (Jun. 1932), pp. 645–57

Sergel, Lance (trs Antonia Nevill), *Carthage, A History* (London 1997)

Shaw, Brent D., *Rulers, Nomads and Christians in Roman North Africa* (Aldershot 1995)

Sjöström, Isabella, *Tripolitania in Transition, Late Roman to Early Islamic Settlement* (Aldershot 1993)

Warmington, B.H., *The North African Provinces from Diocletian to the Vandal Conquest* (Cambridge 1954)

Wheeler, Robert, and Wood, Roger, *Roman Africa in Colour* (London 1986)

CHAPTER II: NUMIDIA AND MAURETANIA

Baradez, Jean, *Fossatum Africae* (Paris 1949)

Belloc, Hilaire, *Many Cities* (London 1928)

Berthier, André, *Tiddis, Antique Castellum Tidditanorum* (1952, reissued, Algiers 1991)

Blas de Roblès, Jean Marie and Sintes, Claude, *Sites et monuments antiques de l'Algérie* (Aix-en-Provence 2003)

Brett, Michael and Fentress, Elizabeth, *The Berbers* (Oxford 1997)

Camus, Albert, *Noces à Tipasa* (Paris 1976)

Corcoran, Thomas H. 'Roman Fish Sauces' in *Classical Journal*, Vol. 58, No. 5 (Feb. 1963), pp. 204–10

Curtis, Robert I., 'In Defense of Garum' in *Classical Journal*, Vol. 78, No. 3 (Feb.–Mar. 1983), pp. 232–40

Euzennat, Maurice, 'Le Limes de Volubilis' in *Studien zu den Militargränzen Roms, Vortrage des 6 Internationalen Limeskongresses in Süddeutschland* (Cologne 1967), pp. 194–9

Fentress, Elizabeth W. B., *Numidia and the Roman Army; Social, Military and Economic Aspects of the Frontier Zone* (BAR International Series 53, Oxford 1979)

Ferguson, John, 'Roman Algeria' in *Greece & Rome*, 2nd Ser, Vol. 13, No. 2. (Oct. 1966), pp. 169–87

Fishwick, Duncan, 'The Annexation of Mauritania' in *Historia* 20 (1971), pp. 467–87

Fred, W.H.C, *The Donatist Church: A Movement of Protest in North Africa* (Oxford 1952)

Hallier, Gilbert, 'La Fortification des villes de Tingitane au second siècle' in *Studien zu den Militargränzen Roms* III (Stuttgart 1986), pp. 605–24

Jarrett, Michael G., 'Decurions and Priests' in *American Journal of Philology*, Vol. 92, No. 4 (Oct. 1971), pp. 513–38.

Lixus – Actes du colloque organisé par l'Institut des sciences de l'archéologie et du patrimoine du Rabat avec le concours de l'École française de Rome, Larache, 8–11 novembre 1989 (Rome 1992)

Lugan, Bernard, *Histoire du Maroc, des origines à nos jours* (Paris 1992)

Morstein-Marx, Robert, 'The Myth of Numidian Origins in Sallust's African Excursus (Iugurtha 17.7–18.12)' in *American Journal of Philology* (2001), p. 188

Potter, T.W., *Towns in Late Antiquity: Iol Caesarea and its Context* (Oxford 1995)

Pringle, R.D., *The Defence of Byzantine Africa* (BAR International Series 99, Oxford 1989)

Rives, James, 'Venus Genetrix outside Rome' in *Phoenix*, Vol. 48, No. 4 (Winter 1994), pp. 294–306

Roller, Duane W., *The World of Juba II and Kleopatra Selene* (London 2003)

Sherwin-White, A.N., 'The Tabula of Banasa and the Constitutio Antoniniana' in *Journal of Roman Studies* 63 (1973), pp. 86–98

Sigman, Marlene C., 'The Romans and the Indigenous Tribes of Mauritania Tingitana' in *Historia* 26 (1977), pp. 415–39

Spaul, John, 'Across the Frontier in Tingitana' in *Roman Frontier Studies 1995* (ed. W. Groenman-van, Waateringe, B.l. van Beek, W.J.H. Willems, S.L Wynia, Oxford 1997), pp. 253–58

Thouvenot, Raymond, *Maisons de Volubilis: Le Palais dit de Gordien et la Maison à la Mosaïque de Vénus* (Rabat 1958)

Tilley, Maureen A., *Donatist Martyr Stories: The Church in Conflict in North Africa* (Liverpool 1996)

Watkins, Thomas H., 'Colonia Marciana Traiana Thamugadi: Dynasticism in Numidia' in *Phoenix*, Vol. 56, No. 1/2 (Spring–Summer 2002), pp. 84–108

Weech, W.N., 'Rambles in Mauretania Caesariensis' in *Greece & Rome*, Vol. 1, No. 1 (Oct. 1931), pp. 3–12

INDEX